W9-ACC-264

UNIVERSITY OF CONNECTICUT — GROTON, CONN. — SOUTHEASTERN BRANCH LIBRARY — UNIVERSITY OF CONNECTICUT

AUG 18 68

Japanese Court Poetry

STANFORD STUDIES IN THE CIVILIZATIONS
OF EASTERN ASIA

ARTHUR F. WRIGHT   GEORGE SANSOM   JOHN D. GOHEEN
THOMAS C. SMITH   ROBERT H. BROWER   MARY CLABAUGH WRIGHT

THE FRONTISPIECE portrays Lady Nakatsukasa (fl. ca. 970). It is from a famous thirteenth-century scroll depicting the "Thirty-six Poetic Geniuses" (Sanjūrokkasen), and was formerly in the possession of the family of Marquis Satake. The painting is attributed to Fujiwara Nobuzane (1175–ca. 1265), the calligraphy to Fujiwara (Gokyōgoku) Yoshitsune (1169–1206). The two lines of heavy script at the extreme right identify Nakatsukasa as the daughter of Prince Atsuyoshi and of the famous poet Lady Ise, adding that she lived during the time of Emperor Enyū (959–91). The two lines of lighter, cursive script immediately to the right of the figure are the text of one of her poems (*SIS*, I: 10):

Uguisu no	But for its song—
Koe nakariseba	The warbler that now first is heard
Yuki kienu	In my mountain village—
Yamazato ikade	How could I tell amid the still unmelted snow
Haru o shiramashi.	That the longed-for spring has come?

The lady is depicted in the act of listening to the song of the bird. The Satake Scroll is considered the finest surviving example of the popular genre of representing six or thirty-six famous poets by poems in a scroll. Such series became popular in the tenth century, and in the thirteenth century the vogue of portraiture led to the addition of imaginary "portraits" of the poems' authors.

Japanese Court Poetry

BY

Robert H. Brower

AND

Earl Miner

*

STANFORD UNIVERSITY PRESS
STANFORD, CALIFORNIA
1961

STANFORD UNIVERSITY PRESS
STANFORD, CALIFORNIA

© 1961 BY THE BOARD OF TRUSTEES OF THE LELAND STANFORD JUNIOR UNIVERSITY
ALL RIGHTS RESERVED

LIBRARY OF CONGRESS CATALOG NUMBER: 61-10925
PRINTED IN THE UNITED STATES OF AMERICA

Published with the Assistance of the Ford Foundation

FOR

Jinichi Konishi

Preface

JAPANESE Court poetry possesses at once an intrinsic attraction, a special role in defining the nature of Japanese literary experience, and a character that both enhances and challenges the poetic achievements of other nations. Our aim in this volume is to present Court poetry by using a critical method adapted from modern Western literary studies. We have emphasized description, analysis, and evaluation as the proper functions of a critical study, although since this is the first extended treatment in a Western language of Court poetry, we have found it necessary to provide both historical information and translations of almost three hundred poems. We have in mind three kinds of readers—those seriously interested in literature of the major traditions, students of Japanese literature, and specialists. We must inevitably at times dwell upon concerns not shared equally by all three groups, but it is our hope that in some measure each will find our study useful.

The intrinsic importance of Japanese Court poetry can be more readily felt than explained. To the extent that we can demonstrate its interest and describe the nature of its appeal, we have done so chiefly in the chapters of Part Two ("The Ideals, Development, and Practice of Court Poetry"), especially in the sections discussing the poetic practice of each period. The poems selected for analysis and illustration in these sections vary in quality, but the reader will find at least a representative selection of the finest poems in Japanese. Each poem is presented in transliteration and in English translation. Although we have sought in our translations to do justice to the effects of the poems in Japanese, we have surely on occasion made poor verses seem better than they are, and more often we have failed to render great poems in their true beauty. We have sometimes given close, word-for-word versions for analytical purposes, but in general we have not hesitated to attempt to convey the important unspoken implications of poems along with their more immediate meanings. We must emphasize that in any case our translations into the English of our day inevitably distort the Japanese of centuries ago; and that our analyses refer to the Japanese originals rather than to our English renderings.

Although the special role of Court poetry in defining the nature of literary experience for the Japanese is a subject that in many respects lies outside the scope of this book, it is treated implicitly in Part One ("The Nature of Japanese Court Poetry") and in the sections on the ideals of poets in each of the period chapters in Part Two. In addition, Part Two concludes with an explicit discussion of the role of Court poetry in defining the nature and practice of the *renga,* or linked verse. It is also a special feature of our procedure to employ comparisons between Japanese and Western literatures, chiefly English, a feature most extensively developed in Part Three ("The Tradition of Japanese Court Poetry").

Such comparisons may help to show what is particularly Japanese about the experience conveyed by the literature of the Court poets. At the same time, the comparisons, as well as other aspects of the long essay that makes up Part Three, are meant to show the ways in which Court poetry at once affirms and calls into question the literary achievements of other nations. One can hardly fail to be struck by the way in which certain common Western expectations about literature are not fulfilled, or by how, on the other hand, Court poetry provides literary experiences of a nature not to be found in the poetry of other countries.

A poetic tradition like that of Japanese Court poetry, extending as it does over some eight centuries (from about A.D. 550 to 1350), can only be discussed if it is divided into manageable parts. The relative simplicity of a chronological organization seemed to us essential. In general, we have followed traditional Japanese practice in designating periods, but have departed from the usual Japanese names (with their untranslatable associations) in an effort to give some suggestion of the continuity or discontinuity between different periods. For these reasons, our term "classical" is neither specific nor strictly accurate. We employ it for its usefulness in relating three successive periods (our early, mid-, and late classical periods) that share many important assumptions and practices, and in differentiating these periods from the two that precede them (the period of primitive poetry and song and the early literary period). Hopefully such terms will mean, or seem to mean, more to many readers—and in some cases they are more accurate—than "The Late Kamakura–Early Muromachi Period" or "The Period of the *Shinkokinshū.*" Having so divided eight centuries of poetry for convenience in discussion, we have found it equally important to emphasize survivals, anticipations, cross-currents, and changes in the pace of development. Such emphasis is to be found in the period chapters of Part Two, but Parts One and Three also have their place in showing what remains constant amid change and, indeed, what is characteristic of the changes themselves.

Finally, it should be emphasized that this book is primarily a critical study, rather than a literary history, and that our critical method is essentially West-

ern rather than Japanese. For whereas modern Western critical method is
well known and often brilliantly practiced by Japanese students of Western
literatures, only a very few scholars of Japanese literature have come to be
acquainted with its assumptions, terminology, and techniques. Consequently,
although we could not have engaged in any but the most superficial discussion of Court poetry without drawing upon the work of Japanese scholars,
our approach, and occasionally our conclusions, have differed from theirs.

The nature of our attempt makes it clear why we must express our appreciation of Japanese scholarship. It also explains in part why this is a collaborative study, in which every page has been written or rewritten by its
two authors, each of whom has some command of the language and history
of Japanese literature as well as of Western literature and modern criticism.
It need scarcely be added that neither the resources of Japanese scholarship
nor collaborative authorship would have brought this book to completion in
its present state without the material assistance that is set forth in the Ac-
knowledgments.

R. H. B.
E. M.

Acknowledgments

O UR WORK has had the active support of numerous individuals and corporate groups. The Rockefeller Foundation generously aided us with two grants extending over eighteen months. The Research Committee of the University of California, Los Angeles, and the Committee on the Graduate Division of Stanford University have supplied funds for assistance of various kinds. The Stanford-Tokyo Collaborative Studies Program together with the Stanford Committee on East Asian Studies have put at our disposal funds granted to Stanford University by the Rockefeller Foundation and the Ford Foundation. A favorable environment for our work and continuous encouragement have been given us particularly by John D. Goheen of Stanford University and also by Arthur F. Wright of Yale University and Thomas C. Smith of Stanford University. The editors of *The Journal of Asian Studies, The Hudson Review, Orient/West,* and *Japan Quarterly* have generously allowed us to use materials previously published in their pages.

Our colleagues in two universities who have read all or parts of our work while it was in various stages of preparation have been helpful in innumerable matters. We wish to express our gratitude especially to Frank W. Wadsworth, Lowry Nelson, Jr., and Robert P. Stockwell of the University of California, Los Angeles. Howard S. Hibbett of Harvard University, Hans H. Frankel of Yale University, and David S. Nivison of Stanford University have also contributed valuable help. And we feel unusually fortunate to have been able to draw upon the wisdom and taste of Sir George Sansom in discussions ranging from minute particulars to matters of far-reaching importance.

We have contracted other debts of benefit to this book. Officers of the Tokyo National Museum assisted us in acquiring both the facsimile that appears as a frontispiece and the permission to use it. The East Asiatic Library of the University of California, Berkeley, aided us in finding suitable material for some of the illustrations in the text. The Director and the Editor of the Stanford University Press have been of great assistance in seeking ways to publish in the most satisfactory way a book with many unusual problems. Mrs. Linda L. Brownrigg has been the devoted and discerning editor of our work. Mrs. Laura Ley Gray and Mrs. Jeanne D. Kennedy have lent welcome assistance in reading proof and preparing the Index.

The opportunity to discuss the subject of a book affords a major pleasure in writing it. In this we have been singularly fortunate. We wish most particularly to acknowledge the pleasure and aid we have had in working closely for two summers and more with the distinguished scholar and friend to whom this book is dedicated, Jinichi Konishi, Professor of Japanese Literature at the Tokyo University of Education. Professor Konishi's understanding of the great range of Japanese and Chinese poetry has been of incalculable value to us, and we are grateful to the Stanford-Tokyo Collaborative Studies Program for making our meetings with him possible. In the many hours spent freely exchanging ideas and discussing both Japanese and Western literature with him, we have enjoyed an experience that we feel to be unique.

Contents

PART THREE

The Tradition of Japanese Court Poetry

List of Illustrations

Note on Pronunciation, Scansion, and Names

THE TRANSLITERATION of poems, proper names, and Japanese terms in this volume follows the standard Hepburn system. But since the period covered represents some eight centuries of linguistic as well as poetic development, our use of this system throughout involves a certain compromise with the purity of linguistic fact. In general, we have not attempted to be linguistic purists in transcribing pronunciations that have not survived into modern Japanese, to insist upon *ɸoko* for *hoko* or to designate vowels such as *ö,* when not even Japanese scholars know what their pronunciation was. Fortunately, the failure to reproduce these sounds does not, like the disregard of the final *e* in Chaucer, destroy the prosody of the language, so that we have felt justified in normalizing our texts. It has often been a far greater and more important problem to decide just what constitutes a word in Japanese. In the absence of any linguistic evidence—usage in other poems, voicing of the initial consonant of the second element, or parallelism with other words in the poem—we have been forced to make arbitrary decisions based upon little more than our sense of the language.

Despite these difficulties, the phonological structure of Japanese, classical and modern alike, is quite simple. In the Hepburn system, vowels are pronounced more or less as in Italian, consonants as in English. The consonant clusters *ch, sh,* and *ts* are pronounced as follows: *ch* as in *church, sh* as in *she,* and *ts* as in *its.* In classical Japanese, a syllable may consist of: a single vowel; a consonant or consonant cluster plus a vowel; *m* or *n* preceding a consonant (except *y*) within a word; *n'* before a vowel or *y* within a word; or a final *n.* Vowels marked by macrons are long and count as two syllables. Thus the line *kinō kyō to wa* contains seven syllables, the word *Man'yōshū* six syllables. There are no "silent" letters; such a proper name as Samine therefore consists of three syllables, Sa-mi-ne, pronounced "Sah-mee-nay." Double consonants occur only in Sinico-Japanese compounds; the first consonant of such a double consonant cluster counts as a separate syllable. Thus *hokku* contains three syllables, *ho-k-ku.*

In scanning poetry, the final vowel of a word is sometimes elided with an initial vowel in the following word. In early song and poetry a great deal of prosodic irregularity is found; after about the mid-eighth century a given line may contain one more syllable than the normal five or seven, but never more than one and never fewer than either five or seven.

We have given names in the Japanese fashion when they are used in full—the surname is followed by the given name. But Japanese practice varies greatly on other matters, and we have tried to follow what seems to be simplest and most pleasing to the ear. We have used the mediary *no* only when the surname is short: "Ono no Komachi" but "Kakinomoto Hitomaro." Well-known poets are referred to usually by their given names or styles (whichever seems more common Japanese practice) rather than by their full names or surnames: thus, Hitomaro for Kakinomoto Hitomaro and Shunzei for Fujiwara Toshinari. Sometimes partial translation and sometimes simplification have seemed most suitable for rendering titles of rank. "Lady Kōgi Mon'in" seemed better than "The Lady-in-Waiting in the Service of ex-Empress Kōgi," and "Shunzei" more natural than "Chamberlain of the Empress Dowager, Shunzei." In general, and apart from royalty, we have used proper names where they are known and have omitted titles of rank.

PART ONE

The Nature of Japanese Court Poetry

1

The Distinctive Common Elements of Japanese Court Poetry

I N THE FIRST and most famous statement of the nature of Japanese Court poetry, Ki no Tsurayuki (884–946) declared what he believed to be the most important characteristics of Japanese poetry in particular and the *raison d'être* of poetry in human life. His remarks, in the Preface to the first of the imperial anthologies, the *Kokinshū,* provide the most appropriate introduction to any discussion of our subject. They emphasize certain concerns common to the entire tradition of Japanese Court poetry—concern with lyricism, with the social contexts of poetry rather than social subjects, with nature, and with qualities of experience rather than with moral or other absolutes.

The poetry of Japan has its roots in the human heart and flourishes in the countless leaves of words. Because human beings possess interests of so many kinds, it is in poetry that they give expression to the meditations of their hearts in terms of the sights appearing before their eyes and the sounds coming to their ears. Hearing the warbler sing among the blossoms and the frog in his fresh waters—is there any living being not given to song? It is poetry which, without exertion, moves heaven and earth, stirs the feelings of gods and spirits invisible to the eye, softens the relations between men and women, calms the hearts of fierce warriors.

Centuries after Tsurayuki wrote these words, English poets and critics were to speak of the ends of poetry as being pleasure and profit, terms that Tsurayuki and his contemporaries would not have used. Poetry to them was a rather different creation of the human sensibility, and if Tsurayuki's predecessors and successors wrote poetry that differed in major respects from his own, they would surely have agreed nonetheless with his general conception of poetry in all its particulars. We who approach Japanese Court poetry from a distance of several centuries and from another culture must, therefore, attempt to understand the character of the Japanese tradition as it differs from our own before we find in it the deeper artistic values common to all civilized men.

We must begin by assuming certain principles: that the poetry of every nation is a complex expression of the history, character, and individual genius of a people; and that as each successive generation evaluates a native or an alien poetic tradition from its own historical standpoint, it discovers values as well as limitations in the poetry it reads. Each generation must make such a reassessment for itself, but the attempt to describe the elements that underlie Japanese poetic expression nevertheless seems particularly necessary today, when we can no longer be satisfied with the older extremes of Victorian condescension toward "Japanese epigrams"; with the exclusively historical or biographical treatment that evades direct analysis of the poetry; or with that too easy exoticism which prefers ignorant rapture to the disciplined effort of literary criticism. Our experience of Japanese poetry today must reflect contemporary critical standards and techniques, the means of understanding given to us by our age.

Such limitations and principles are basic; but the scope of our study is further limited chronologically to a single continuous segment of the total Japanese poetic tradition—to what may be called the primitive, the early literary, and the classical periods, from approximately the sixth century A.D. to the middle of the fourteenth century. We shall consider the secular poetry of the period, leaving aside such exclusively religious literature as Shinto or Buddhist liturgies and hymns. Further, except for the primitive age (extending to the mid-seventh century), we shall be concerned with the literary poetry, or *waka*, the product of the Court society. Our materials are therefore derived in the main from the early chronicles, of which the *Kojiki* (712) and the *Nihongi* (720) contain most of the extant primitive verse; from the *Man'yōshū* (ca. 759), the first anthology of Japanese poetry, the bulk of whose 4,500-odd poems belong to the seventh century and the first half of the eighth; and from the first seventeen of the twenty-one imperial anthologies, beginning with the *Kokinshū* (ca. 905) and continuing through the *Fūgashū* (ca. 1345), which are the most important collections of Court poetry written from the late eighth century to the mid-fourteenth. These major collections will be supplemented by numerous private collections and other sources, which become increasingly available from about the tenth century.

The poems we study illustrate the two major poetic forms developed and practiced during these eight centuries. The first is the *chōka* (also called *nagauta*) or "long poem," which came to comprise an indefinite number of pairs of 5-syllable and 7-syllable lines, with an additional 7-syllable line at the end, and to which might be added one or more "envoys" (*hanka* or *kaeshiuta*). The second form, more important to the development of the poetic tradition, is the *tanka* or "short poem," which consists of 31 syllables grouped in five lines, in which the first and third lines contain 5 syllables, and the others 7 syllables.

Two other forms, which are much less significant for the tradition, deserve some mention here. The *sedōka* or "head-repeated poem" derives its strange name from its form of two stanzas, each with three lines of 5, 7, and 7 syllables respectively. Few distinguished examples of the sedōka exist—the form seems never to have been very successful and gradually died out. Perhaps the finest example of a sedōka is a poem from "The Hitomaro Collection" (*Hitomaro Kashū* in *MYS*, VII: 1294).*

Asazukuhi	The new moon rises
Mukai no yama ni	Above the mountains ranged beyond
Tsuki tateru miyu	Where the sun will strike at dawn;
Tōzuma o	There must be another
Mochitaru hito shi	In whom its brightness raises thoughts
Mitsutsu shinuban.	Of yearning for his distant wife.

The second form—the *renga* or linked verse—during most of the period we shall study is merely a tanka in which two people participate, one composing three lines of 5, 7, and 5 syllables, and the other a couplet of 7-syllable lines. The *Kin'yōshū* (ca. 1125) is the first imperial anthology to include examples of this form. Although the renga eventually developed into a serious poetic form of impressive length, the short linked poems, or *tanrenga*, were almost always of a humorous, playful nature, and their frivolous character precludes them from serious consideration in the poetic tradition.

The poetry of the period and types with which we are concerned has three characteristics that deserve to be called basic formative elements in the development of an integral poetic tradition. These characteristics are not confined to the waka, and are not unique to Japanese poetry, but they are the ultimate sources of its special character. The first characteristic is constancy; there are certain constants—the language itself, prosody, rhetorical techniques, imagery, and a social concept of poetry—that distinguish Japanese poetry from the poetry of other nations. The second is the recurrence of certain patterns of change in poetic concerns and motives, patterns that are repeated over the centuries with striking regularity. The third is the cumulative effect of the poetic tradition, the temporal sequence of development which makes every poet mindful of his place in the history of the tradition. These three formative elements operate in complex interrelationships at all times, but for the purposes of an introductory analysis it is useful to discuss them sepa-

* Abbreviations of the principal imperial anthologies and the *Man'yōshū* are based on the chief elements of the name (thus *MYS* for *Man'YōShū*). Roman numerals following these abbreviations in the text indicate the book or scroll number of the collection in which the poem will be found. Arabic numerals indicate the number of the poem as indexed in *Kokka Taikan* (which assigns separate numbers to the envoys that appear with a chōka). Collections other than the *Man'yōshū* and the imperial anthologies are indicated in the following manner: *K. Taikei* for *Kōchū Kokka Taikei*. In such references Roman numerals indicate the volume, Arabic numerals the page number or numbers. Further notes on our method of citation and a list of all abbreviations used in the text will be found on pp. 493–94. The principal collections referred to in this study are discussed in greater detail in the Appendix (pp. 481–88) and the Bibliographical Note (pp. 489–502).

rately. Constancy is the subject of this chapter; recurrence, of the next chapter. The cumulative development of the poetic tradition is, of course, the subject of the book as a whole.

One of the most important as well as the most ineffable of the constant elements in any poetry is the medium itself, the language. Classical Japanese shares with classical Chinese a concrete particularity different from Western poetic language. Although we may find in the older Japanese poetic vocabulary terms for such physical and emotional abstractions as "whiteness," "sadness," and "love," and although the language is capable of making formal as well as metaphorical abstractions, the language nevertheless does not include words for such abstractions as "truth" or "honor": there is no Holiness to ride into a Spenserian allegorical field, nor a Pity to shed a baroque tear. The personified abstraction, or the abstraction of a moral or ethical quality, which we owe to Hebrew, late Latin, and medieval literature, simply is not a part of Japanese poetry. It is alien to the Japanese tradition, which expresses in other ways the part of human experience conveyed in our poetry by such abstractions. This emphasis upon the particular, the concrete, helps explain why many Westerners, especially the moral Victorians, have been inclined to emphasize what is "lacking" in Japanese poetry, treating it therefore with thinly veiled condescension. The problem, then, is really a dual one: to explain why Japanese poetry is concrete in its functioning, and to suggest how larger, more general meanings are conveyed. The first part of the problem may be dealt with now, and the second deferred to a discussion of imagery and other matters.

A central feature of the Japanese language, one which has led to such subtle particularities, is the nature of its nouns, verbs, adjectives, and particles. (Syntax is also of crucial significance, although in somewhat different ways. Since it is too complex a subject to be treated without an analysis of particular poems, we shall defer discussion to later chapters, apart from a few general remarks here.) The nouns employed in almost all Court poetry name objects apprehensible by the senses; therefore almost every noun is psychologically an image and incipiently a literary image. Japanese nouns have thus a greater potential for connotation than do the nouns of our more generalized vocabulary, a fact which can be demonstrated in two very different ways: intrinsically, because Japanese is one of the world's few poetic traditions in which even nouns of place have connotative, semi-metaphorical significance; and historically, because the imagistic potential of Japanese is precisely what attracted recent Western poets who were wearied by the abstract moralizing of a diluted nineteenth-century tradition.

While Japanese poetry shares a concrete noun-vocabulary with Chinese, its verbs and adjectives (as well as its syntax) make it an entirely different poetic medium. Few modern languages have such a range of possible inflections for adjectives, few are capable of such subtle verbal distinctions. Japanese verbs of the classical language employed in the Court period do not have our seven so-called tenses, but as many as seven morphemes expressing various kinds of aspect combined with as many as fourteen morphemes expressing mood. The result of the highly complex system of inflections is a particularly fine adjustment of tone (ultimately beyond the reach of translation) and an instrument especially well suited to exploring states of feeling, mind, and being.

The functions of Japanese verbs are indicated by such inflections in agglutinative terminations; the functions (or "cases") of nouns are indicated by postpositive particles, which are often omitted in poetic syntax. There are neither definite nor indefinite articles nor any formal distinctions of number or person. Verbs and verbals made from adjectives or nouns conclude their clauses; and since Japanese employs attributive rather than relative constructions, such subordinate clauses normally precede the nouns they modify. Thus, instead of saying, in effect, "The temple which I visited is old," Japanese syntax would follow the order "I visited temple old-is." In this awkward "translation," the fact that the verb, "visited," would in Japanese end with an attributive inflection is of course not indicated, nor is the fact that "is" would normally be conveyed by a finite, indicative inflection of the adjective "old."

Two other matters call for special attention. Japanese grammar employs topics as well as subjects. The difference between the two is primarily one of relative emphasis: topics are usually less explicit than subjects; they indicate involvement, but not necessarily participation, in an action or state. What would be a subject, an object, or even an adverbial phrase in English might be a topic in Japanese. Personal pronouns are very apt to be treated as topics rather than subjects, although most often they are omitted altogether, so that our hypothetical sentence would more likely read: "Visited temple old-is." In classical prose, the concept of the person speaking (the identity of the topic) is often conveyed by the degree of formality of prefixed or suffixed honorifics, by the level of diction, by conventions of esthetic distance, and by other means sanctioned by tradition. Two sentences such as "I admire these mountains" and "The emperor admires these mountains" would therefore be expressed somewhat differently. The first would run, in effect: "As for me [topic], these mountains [subject] admired"; or more likely, "These mountains admired." If the topic were the emperor or if the statement were a generalized one, the fact would be indicated by the choice of verb, its inflections, and the kind of accompanying honorifics. In poetry, such honorific verbs or inflected suffixes are usually replaced by neutral forms which provide in themselves no clue to the speaker's sex or social position. It must also be said that the omission of topics and subjects often has the effect of making translation nearly impossible: the stress is taken from the participants in an action and placed upon the action itself in a way impossible in English.

The other special characteristic of classical Japanese grammar is the use of the possessive particles—*no, ga, tsu*—which not only appear more often than English possessives but also function somewhat differently. In English we may say either "England's Queen" or "The Queen of England." Japanese employs the order of the first in that the chief noun, "Queen," is so to speak possessed by its qualifier (in the usual Japanese manner of preceding attribution). In English we feel a certain reluctance in joining more than a couple of possessives. "The future of the son of the Queen of England" seems awkward, and "England's Queen's son's future" is completely out of the question. But in Japanese such a sequence, or one even longer, can be made to seem quite natural.

A review of classical Japanese must include one other feature—the methods of indicating coordination and subordination. The principal method is that of verbal and adjectival terminations, rather than the conjunctions, adverbs, prepositions, and relative pronouns of English. If the terminal inflection of a Japanese verb or adjective is a participle, or sometimes simply an infinitive, then the syntax is coordinate; if the verb ends with an attributive, concessive, or provisional inflection, then the clause is subordinate to what follows. Some attributive inflections are, however, identical in sound with certain clause-final indicative forms, and a poet may often arrange matters so that he achieves the benefits of a syntactical ambiguity in which, for example, he may convey at once the sense of the end of a period and also the feeling that the clause in question functions attributively to what follows.

A few illustrations will show the delicacy of distinctions obtained by the inflections of verbs—the same point might be made with adjectives. To take a fairly simple example, *nureken* (linguistically, *nure-ke-m-u*) can be rendered in English as "had probably become wet." The base form of the intransitive verb, "wets," has been successively inflected with perfective, presumptive, and attributive or indicative (the forms are the same here) inflections. Or, *kazashitarikeri* (*kazas-it-ar-ik-er-i*) can be rendered "has been adorning." But how far such a rendering is from the true sense of the Japanese can be realized by the fact that the verbal base (*kazas-*) is followed by four pre-modal inflections (active, durative, perfective, durative) and an indicative modal inflection. Just how one is to translate into English in any natural way the sense of a verb expressing action, perfection, and duration (twice) with any hope of preserving the literary quality of the original seems to us an insoluble problem, and one, moreover, which makes it manifestly clear that there is no such thing as a literal translation of Japanese poetry. Some avowedly literal translations have been made, with more brackets and footnotes than success; but to render *nakenaku*, with an attempt at that linguistic precision which alone is literalness, as "the fact being not that there is not" is absurd. Such efforts stifle the poem and confuse the reader, because they violate the canons of one language in trying to reproduce those of another.

Two kinds of particles increase the resources of the Japanese poet, although the distinction between them is more one of poetic than true grammatical function. Those particles may be called grammatical which follow nouns to indicate their functions ("cases"), and those rhetorical which are related to the syntax and meaning as a whole, and provide varieties of exclamation, questioning, and stress. The rich texture these particles give to the verse can be appreciated by comparing their verbal grace to punctuation marks or their variety to the monotonous "Oh's" and "Ah's" of translators. The following tanka (*SKKS*, I: 59) by Fujiwara Shunzei (1114-1204) may be taken as an example:

Kiku hito zo	He who hears them:
Namida wa otsuru	His tears break at their cries—
Kaeru kari	The wild geese wing
Nakite yuku naru	In sad departure from the beauty
Akebono no sora.	Of springtime dawn spread through the sky.

In this poem the particles *zo* and *wa* emphasize *kiku hito* ("he who hears them") and *namida* ("tears"), and at the same time establish a relationship of implicit contrast between these words and the words *kari* ("wild geese") and *nakite* ("crying") in the lines that follow. Largely by the use and placement of these particles, Shunzei brings man and nature into close relationship. The geese "cry," but it is the man who weeps; the man is sad at the poignant beauty of dawn, but it is the geese who are made to feel reluctant to leave the scene. Without the *wa* after *namida*, the poem would not convey this reciprocal symbolism. Viewed in the light of the aims the poetic medium sets for itself, such particles and other poetic-linguistic constituents give it at once an economy and a subtlety which are the despair of the translator.

These aspects of linguistic structure are fundamental, but they cannot be evaluated in isolation any more than a stream can be measured by cupfuls. And Japanese poetry does have an almost stream-like, flowing cadence that reminds one of Sir John Denham's image (in "Cooper's Hill") of the Thames as his poetic ideal:

Though deep, yet clear, though gentle yet not dull,
Strong without rage, without o'er-flowing full.

The qualities in Japanese poetry of depth (or sonority), gentleness, strength (or firm consonance), and fullness (or assonance in harmony with movement) grow from two familiar features of the language. Japanese has an unusually high proportion of vowels in regular alternation with consonants, and it is a language of little accent. Perhaps only Virgil or Ben Jonson could write verse with such melodious assonance and strong consonance as the famous tanka (*KKS*, XVI: 861) by Ariwara Narihira (825–80).

Tsui ni yuku	Though formerly I heard
Michi to wa kanete	About the road that all must travel
Kikishikado	At the inevitable end,
Kinō kyō to wa	I never thought, or felt, today
Omowazarishi o.	Would bring that far tomorrow.

But it is more than sound which lends Japanese poetry its cadence. The highly inflected nature of the language gives it a freedom, even a looseness, and a startling variety of syntax in extended writing that lends a sinuous forward pressure to the verse. At the same time, the syntax is more fixed within the clause than, say, in Latin, with the result that the general effect of the movement of verse, especially in the chōka, is something between the Latin and the English. It is a style of great fluidity between closely ordered syntactical units, which are characteristically strengthened by parallelism between the constituent clauses and by harmony within them. The cadences of Japanese poetry are indeed so gracefully smooth that some poets seem guilty of the folly often imputed to Tennyson and Swinburne—that of playing too good a tune with the language to pay much attention to the libretto. Although it is not really true of the Japanese poets any more than of Tennyson, the greatest of them are aware of this pleasant folly, and roughen their verse texture with elisions, irregular lines, abrupt sounds, perturbations of syntax, and changes in pace. But to speak of these matters is to raise a second topic, namely, the constant element that we find in Japanese prosody and style.

Prosody is of course closely related to language, and little need be said here about the syllabic fives and sevens of Japanese poetry. The problem of where these syllabic lengths came from, like the problem of the origins of blank verse, will probably never be solved satisfactorily. Whether they come from an analogy with Chinese verse patterns, or from rhythms suited to an ancient musical form, or from some wholly different source, the fact remains that the alternation of shorter and longer lines is a part of the genius of the language, just as accented and alliterative verse was the best medium for the strongly stressed, prevailingly short words of the old Germanic languages.

There seems to be an artistic equivalent for Newton's third law of motion, however—that in order to receive an advantage from a literary convention, one must also accept the equal and opposite disadvantage. The fluid smoothness of Japanese prosody is not always any more suitable for sustained poetic forms than the involuted conceits of the English Metaphysical poets. The great poets of the chōka, principally Kakinomoto Hitomaro (fl. ca. 680–700) and Yamanoe Okura (?660–?733), not only deliberately roughen the texture of their verse, but also stiffen it by means of rhetorical techniques—parallelism of thought and sound, single and double parallelism, antithesis, the echoing and re-echoing of idea and sound in different parts of the poem, closely worked out formal structure, ironies, and various other sophisticated techniques also found in Western poetry. With these techniques to give the chōka strength and to slow down the cadence or, what is the same thing, to slow down our response to the cadence, the poets could also reap the advantages of the onward-pressing melodic sweetness of the Japanese prosodic style. But it took a great poet to merge these contradictory elements into a single effect. Indeed, it seems likely that one of the many reasons for the much-lamented decline of the chōka in the eighth century is that the tanka length was such a ready compromise; it offered a form in which not only the greatest poets but those of lesser genius as well could write without lapsing into that gravest of literary sins, monotony. The tanka was found to be an ideal unit of cadence and thought for the uses to which Japanese poetry typically came to be put, especially as successive generations of poets sought greater depths and refinement within a narrowed poetic range. How melodic and yet how strong the tanka form is can be understood by comparing a favorite example—the poem by Narihira already quoted—with such a famous haiku as the following one by Matsuo Bashō (1644–94):

Kareeda ni	A crow is perched
Karasu no tomarikeri	Upon a leafless withered bough—
Aki no kure.	The autumn dusk.

The haiku has rhythm, but it is not protracted enough to give a sense of melodic movement; it consists almost entirely of images related by juxtaposition rather than by a coherent placement in a syntactical, rhythmic flow.

The evidence of history bears out the tanka's claim to be the norm of Japanese poetry. For whereas chōka were seldom written after the end of the eighth century, and the serious renga and the haiku did not come into prominence until the feudal period, the tanka has endured throughout the history of the literary tradition. To say this is not to make a moral or esthetic judgment, but merely to observe that soon after the age of the first primitive songs and the emergence of a literary sense, the tanka form was realized, and that although it was to undergo many vicissitudes, and other forms were to have their hour, the formal constant of the Japanese prosodic tradition is this verse of 31 syllables.

The unique persistence through nearly a millennium and a half of this brief, deceptively simple tanka form is a literary marvel which often evokes in Western amateurs two equally fanciful reactions. Some are led to think of Japanese poetry as the essence of pure poetry so quintessentially distilled that the Western poet need only dilute it with Parnassian waters and serve the mixture to the enraptured reader. Others are led to dismiss Japanese poetry as being too slight, or (what amounts to the same thing) to think they can, as Westerners, compose a real tanka. Such popular misconceptions derive from a foolish exoticism and from an ignorance of the useful techniques and often unique conventions by which Japanese poets, over the years and centuries, have transcended the limitations of their form—techniques which demand our attention and a respect that should freeze the anxious poetaster's hand. Some of the transcending rhetorical techniques have already been mentioned— parallelism, irony, and the like—and are for the most part shared with Western poetry. Others, characteristically and in some cases uniquely Japanese, fall between the constants of language and prosodic style. Such devices are the *makurakotoba* or "pillow-word," the *kakekotoba* or "pivot-word," the *jo* or semi-metaphorical "preface," the *engo* or "word association," and the *honkadori* or "allusive variation." A few illustrations will make clear the nature of these techniques.

Perhaps few techniques in the history of poetry have been as impatiently criticized or as plaintively defended as the *makurakotoba,* a stylized semi-imagistic epithet, normally of five syllables, used to modify certain fixed words. Its defenders proclaim its daring freedom and its superiority to the Homeric epithets. Its detractors allow that it may be decorative, but with the glow of dead wood in poems that can ill afford such a rhetorical luxuriancy. We must seek to avoid either of these extremes by remembering the literary principle that no technique used by good poets and poor poets alike is either good or bad in itself. The question is rather one of what is made of a technique in relation to other techniques, ideas, and poetic needs, and our approach must be historical as well as critical.

The earliest glimpse we get of the makurakotoba is in the poems of the primitive period, first committed to writing in the eighth-century chronicles, the *Kojiki* and the *Nihongi*. From the beginning it is used partly for sound, partly for rhetorical amplification, and partly for imagery. But we really begin to understand the potentialities of makurakotoba in the poetry of Hitomaro. As nearly as we can tell, he created for himself about half of his pillow-words, and he uses them for the mingled purpose of amplifying or heightening his style, as well as for sound and for metaphor half-submerged in formality. Hitomaro wrote for his court as Pindar, Spenser, and Dryden did for theirs, and, like them, he appears not to have been a part of the highest levels of society. The makurakotoba was perhaps chiefly a technique for poems addressed to an audience of social peers or superiors on occasions with elevated subjects—in short, it was used to elevate Hitomaro's style as surely as Pindar's theogenies, Spenser's allegories, or Dryden's metaphors of Augustan Rome. In Hitomaro's hands, the technique created an effect at once ritualistic and fresh; in feebler hands, the technique often did become dead wood. But we must realize that even poets of much later periods, when the audience had changed, could use the technique meaningfully, now by creating new makurakotoba, now by using old ones to recall the glories of the tradition's earlier days in ways like T. S. Eliot's echoings, or to give the technique a new meaning in a fresh context—say, by integrating its effect of public grandeur into a poetry of private lyricism, as in this poem (*SCSS*, XVII: 1170) by Fujiwara Teika (1162–1241). (The makurakotoba is italicized.)

Momoshiki no	Night after night
Tonoe o izuru	When I leave the guardsmen's hall
Yoiyoi wa	Of the Palace, *fortress-strong,*
Matanu ni mukau	I alone of all men find you waiting,
Yama no ha no tsuki.	O gracious moon upon the mountain's rim.

The technique of the pivot-word (*kakekotoba*) is essentially one of using a particular series of sounds in two overlapping syntactical and semantic patterns, as in this poem (*KKS*, I: 9) by Ki no Tsurayuki.

Kasumi tachi	With the spreading mists
Ko no me mo *haru* no	The treebuds *swell* in early *spring*
Yuki fureba	And wet snow petals fall—
Hana naki sato mo	So even my flowerless country village
Hana zo chirikeru.	Already lies beneath its fallen flowers.

The word *haru* means both "swell" (as buds) and the season, "spring." It seems significant that this technique, which may be called a syntactical conceit, came to its fullest development only with the emergence in the ninth century of the tanka as the pre-eminent form. The tanka needed, far more than the chōka, to transcend its limits by such techniques, and one seriously doubts whether the kakekotoba is any more suited for long poems than the analogous forms of wit in our Metaphysical poetry. In large measure, however, such a technique represents a constant element in Japanese poetry of all forms—a strong emphasis upon a rich poetic texture, whether the result of such verbal dexterities or of vividly presented images.

Another technique employed to give a rich verbal texture is the *jo,* or "preface." The significance of this technique and its complexities are the subject for another chapter, but an example here will show its basic nature. The preface has been likened by the Japanese to the pillow-word, since it usually precedes the basic "statement" of the poem. It is, however, of unspecified length and is joined to the statement by various techniques of juncture—by word play, by similarity of sound, or by an implied metaphorical relationship. The preface in the following anonymous poem (*MYS*, XI: 2440) extends through the word *kakurete* in the fourth line, which must also be taken as the first word of the statement. What we have translated as a simile is really a juxtaposition of the images in the preface (ll. 1–3) with a statement (ll. 4–5), the two joined by a pivot-word.

Ōmi no umi	A lonely ship rows *out*
Okikogu fune ni	*Of sight* upon the sea of Ōmi, where its
Ikari oroshi	anchor
Kakurete kimi ga	*Drops* into the depths:
Koto matsu ware zo.	So I *drop from the sight* of curious eyes
	As I await your sending me some word.

Engo is the use of a word that has or creates an "association" with a preceding word or situation, often bringing out an additional dimension of meaning. A poem by Taira Motonori (d. 908) on the departure of Fujiwara Nochikage as ambassador to China illustrates the technique to an unusual degree, since three words—*tachi* ("rise" or "leave"), *harenu* ("does not clear"), and *wataran* ("will cross" or "spread")—are associations for *akigiri* ("autumn mists") (*KKS*, VIII: 386).

Akigiri no	If we must part,
Tomo ni *tachi*idete	And you *leave* together with the autumn *mists*
Wakarenaba	tumn *mists*
Harenu omoi ni	That *rise* and *cover all*,
Koi ya *wataran*.	Then through the thickening days my feelings
	Will last *unclearing* in sad thoughts of you.

The last and most complex of these rhetorical techniques is "allusive variation" (*honkadori*). This is primarily an echoing of an older poem or poems, not just to borrow material or phrasing, but to raise the atmosphere—something of the situation, the tone, and the meaning—of the original. The result is a complex neoclassicism whose implications are beyond definition here (see Chap. 6, below), but the verbal aspects of the technique can be illustrated by Fujiwara Teika's reshaping (*Shūi Gusō* in *K. Taikei*, XI, 335) of Ki no Tomonori's (fl. ca. 890) poem of some three centuries before (*KKS*, II: 84):

Hisakata no
Hikari *nodokeki*
  Haru no hi ni
Shizugokoro naku
Hana no chiru ran.
  (TOMONORI)

On this day in spring
When the lambent air suffuses
  Soft tranquility,
Why should the cherry petals flutter
With unsettled heart to earth?

Ika ni shite
Shizugokoro naku
  Chiru hana no
Nodokeki haru no
Iro to miyu *ran.*
  (TEIKA)

What reason is there
That these cherry petals fluttering
  With such unsettled heart
Should symbolize the essential color
Of the soft tranquility of spring?

Allusive variation, like all these rhetorical techniques, is more character-istic of one period than another, but they all represent a constant element in Japanese poetry—techniques giving the verse a texture rich enough to tran-scend the brevity of the poetic forms. It is significant, moreover, that each technique impinges upon, even conveys, important aspects of imagery, our next constant element. Imagery is of course a technique of all poets, but our concern is with the characteristic use and nature of imagery that contributes to the unique quality of Japanese poetry.

It is well known that Japanese poetry has an unusually high proportion of images drawn from nature, and there are probably several important reasons for this fact. We have noticed the sensory nature of Japanese nouns and the characteristic particularity of Japanese thought and expression. In addition, an altered or redefined animistic impulse from the Shinto religion has con-tinued to survive in Japanese culture, giving nature an attraction and an emotional value reflected in everyday life as much as in poetry. Another factor is a more sophisticated and philosophical concept, coming from a mingled Buddhism and Taoism, of the oneness of all natural life, which gives what we call external nature a closeness and relevance to human nature that is not found in Western cultures, shaped as they are by various dualisms between spirit and matter, man and nature, and the like. Finally, there is the example and prestige of Chinese poetry, whose use of natural images has at times played an important role in shaping the Japanese tradition. Natural imagery is so much a part of the thought and practice of Japanese Court poetry that Tsurayuki finds its use inevitable as he begins his Preface to the *Kokin-shū*: "The poetry of Japan has its roots in the human heart and flourishes in the countless leaves of words."

Japanese Court poetry often gives natural images another dimension, that of personification, and it is instructive to compare Japanese personification with our own. Fujiwara Shunzei's reflection on the poignancy of present beauty in the beautiful song of a bird when one's mind is filled with thoughts of the past gives us a Japanese example (*SKKS*, III: 201). (The *hototogisu* is in appearance like the cuckoo, in song and legend like the nightingale.)

Mukashi omou	I recollect the past
Kusa no iori no	While the summer rain falls through
Yoru no ame ni	the dark
Namida na soe so	About my grass-thatched hut,
Yamahototogisu.	But, *hototogisu,* singing at last among
	the hills,
	Do not call out a freshening of my tears.

Shunzei's personification is typically Japanese in that it involves an emotional bond between nature and the speaker, and in its use of apostrophe. Shakespeare's "morn, in russet mantle clad" is a personified natural image, but its function is not so much to humanize the image as to decorate it and to give a sense of action; and of course there is no address to the personification. There is apostrophe in the lovely opening line of Samuel Daniel's sonnet, "Carecharmer Sleep, son of the sable night," but here there is very little imagery; moreover, the personification is of an abstraction, which, as we have seen, is alien to Japanese poetry. Keats's address to the nightingale comes closer to the Japanese, but his anguished sense of the gulf between the immortal bird and the mortal poet is too sharp a dualism to be accepted in most Japanese poetry.

Although very few Western personifications have the quality of the Japanese, it is interesting to note that not only do both traditions employ allegory, but both tend to employ it for the same purposes—to express the themes of love and religious morality. As we would expect, however, in Japanese allegory we do not find such abstractions as Guillaume de Lorris's Esperance or Spenser's Justice. Moreover, Japanese allegory is less "transparent," more "closed" than Western. It is not announced by type-names—the Western hallmark of abstraction—or by the poet's declaration that a Beatrice stands for Love and Revelation. Japanese allegory is often hinted at, if not announced, by diction or images which alert the reader; such expressions as "person" (*hito*) often prepare us for a love allegory, and such an image as the dew is frequently a sign of religious allegory. But these hints are only hints: the words and images may be used in nonallegorical poems, and there may be allegory without them. As a matter of fact, there is often nothing in the verses (as the reader of the poetic messages in the *Tale of Genji* will recall) to show that the poem is allegorical in mode; and sometimes only a prose context, tradition, or critical supposition gives any inkling that a poem carries a "darke conceit." This suggests an important distinction between the allegorical modes of our two cultures: Japanese allegorical poems are often descriptive lyrics or other single expression and can exist as independent artistic wholes without the necessity for the private meaning conveyed, say, as a message of love. Western allegory is usually monolithic—without the meaning conveyed by the metaphor, the poem has little significance. Japanese allegory, on the other hand, is often Janus-headed, with one preoccupied face turned toward the images of the natural scene and with the other giving a knowing wink to some dear girl or fellow priest.

The lines between image, metaphor, allegory, and symbol are not always easy to draw in Western poetry, and the distinctions are even more difficult to make in Japanese, where the image of quails crying in the autumn dusk may be not only an image but also an affective metaphor for a sad loneliness and a symbol of the experience of the poet, as in the poem which Shunzei is said to have preferred among his own work (*SZS*, IV: 258).

Yū sareba	As evening falls,
Nobe no akikaze	From along the moors the autumn wind
Mi ni shimite	Blows chill into the heart,
Uzura naku nari	And the quails raise their plaintive cry
Fukakusa no sato.	In the deep grass of secluded Fukakusa.

Insofar as this poem describes a scene, the dusk, the autumn wind, the quails, and the village of Fukakusa (literally, "deep grass") are images. Insofar as these images are vehicles of a melancholy tenor, they are metaphors. But the images also function as symbols of states of mind and represent a truth, because centuries of Buddhist monism and poetic practice had invested these natural images with overtones which made clear their relationship to man.

We are left, then, with something of a paradox. The private or individual response of the poet is expressed in terms of images and symbols which arise from a cultural convention or religious belief. This paradox of original conventionality, as it might be called, is at once the resource and the bane of Japanese poetry, since it enables the poet to say in few words either a great deal or, indeed, very little at all. Unfortunately, the Western reader is not always able to distinguish mere convention from subtle originality. And the paradox leads us to another constant in Japanese poetry: not only the imagery but also the mode or function of a poem is more social and conventional than in Western poetry. In the West, this social concept of poetry was perhaps most closely approached in the Roman and English Augustan ages.

The social quality takes many forms. Japanese poetry is often used where we would use prose—as a mode of discourse. Letters, congratulations, and addresses or declarations of many kinds are occasions for poetry from the time of the *Kojiki* on. Lucretius did indeed express his Epicurean philosophy in the poetry of *De rerum natura* and Pope his Deism in his *Essay on Man,* but these are poems of philosophical or moral ratiocination, types of generalization uncongenial to the Japanese, who find social poetry better suited to the particularities of discourse. Japanese poetry is far more occasional than ours; it tends to arise from clearly defined situations, to deal with topics which are socially accepted and considered proper to poetry, and to convey these in ways suggested by tradition. Departures from accepted norms often have aroused debate, at least among Japanese critics. In one poem, for example (*MYS,* I: 30), Hitomaro seems to personify the Cape of Kara. Since capes are usually not personified (while a bird or a tree might be), some commentators have argued that Hitomaro is using a synecdoche, that it was not the cape which was waiting but some unspecified people standing on it. Modern opinion holds for personification, but the critical fuss shows how strong a pressure tradition can exert. It is true that some kinds of later classical poetry become more reflective and less overtly occasional, but the occasional modes survive, and the reflective modes employ a symbolism that tends to be the public kind of Buddhism rather than the homespun variety of Yeats's cycles of the moon.

We must pick our way carefully, however, since some important distinctions in Japanese poetry tend to be blurred by the English terms "public" and "social." We must recognize two kinds of distinctions: between *public* and *private,* and *formal* and *informal* poetry. In public poetry, as we know it in the West, the poet appears before his audience in a social role as a member of a group with whom he shares hope, grief, or some common experience. In private poetry, the poet chooses—for the purposes of the poetic act—to address himself to a personal audience, to himself, or to something near to him. In these terms, Wordsworth's expression of grief on the death of "Lucy" is a private poem, whereas Shelley's mourning of Keats's death in *Adonais* is public. The matter is not quite so simple in Japanese poetry, partly because Japanese Court poets have made a somewhat different distinction between public and private poetry. To them, poetry is public if it is composed for a wide audience, and private if it is addressed to an individual, as, say, a love poem urging a tryst. The Japanese distinction is important because it differentiates critically between the different styles that were employed: much more attention and care were lavished on poems meant for the public eye. We feel that this difference is best expressed by the terms "formal" and "informal," and wish to reserve "public" and "private" for their Western meanings, which are just as applicable to Japanese poetry as to ours. As a matter of fact, the Japanese formal-informal distinction is a useful one for Western poetry, since Dryden's verse letter to Etherege and some of Swift's "bagatelles" are informal, while Dryden's *MacFlecknoe* and Swift's "Verses on the Death of Dr. Swift" are formal. The areas of agreement and conflict between the terms as we apply them to Japanese poetry can be illustrated by something of a parody of a textbook example of logic: all informal poems are private, but not all private poems are informal; all public poems are formal, but not all formal poems are public.

Such considerations of the public-private nature of Japanese poetry also involve the meanings conveyed by metaphor and the great constant, if not invariable, subjects and themes of Japanese poetry. They need only be named to be understood, but they may be grouped somewhat differently from the usual Japanese patterns (poems of the seasons, of love, of religious subjects, of lament, and so on). It seems more meaningful to say that nature, love, and human affairs apart from love provide what may be called the basic poetic staples. Then there is time, which threatens these basic values and which has been a preoccupation of Japanese poets for centuries. And finally there are concerns that transcend the conflict with time—matters of public significance, religion, secular mysticism, cosmic irony, and a broad sense of human identity.

In the context of Japanese imagery and social modes, the concerns are handled in a more direct fashion than in most Western poetry. The lack of abstraction, for example, makes the poet's response to his subject more immediate and therefore importantly affects the two kinds of esthetic distance. On the one hand, there is usually less apparent distance between the poet and his subject or materials, whether the subject is nature or the woman loved; on the other, there is often less of a distinction to be drawn between the individual poet and the speaker of his poems. This lesser esthetic distance was approximated in Western Romantic poetry, and it may be significant that the Romantics, like the Japanese, were deeply interested in writing about nature. Japanese poetry cannot be called Romantic, however, because its highly social nature, so much like our Augustan poetry, cancels out, or rather harmonizes with, the expression of individual personality. We can only say that Japanese poetry is at once lyrical and social. Indeed, so many of the qualities already discussed are related to this central fact that it does not seem too superficial to conclude a discussion of the constant qualities of Japanese poetry by characterizing the tradition as one employing a personal lyricism in a public and conventional context. With this basic quality and the constant elements of technique in mind, it is possible to raise questions involving historical problems.

2

Recurring Formative Elements
in the Court Tradition

THE ELEMENT of time must be taken into account in a study of Japanese Court poetry, not only as an important theme, but also with respect to the growth of the tradition. Such a consideration reveals elements underlying recurrent patterns over the centuries—a recurrence of certain ideals, relationships, influences, qualities, and movements.

One of the most important of the recurring patterns is that which underlies the attempt made by poets in age after age to achieve a meaningful balance between what, for lack of more graceful terms, must be called the personal and the impersonal. In each period, the poet needed to bring his personal lyricism into balance with such impersonal, social concerns as relations between classes, relations between men and women, and relations between the poet and public affairs, and also into balance with the larger concerns of a broad humanity, the world of nature, and religion. These polar opposites of the personal and the impersonal were essential to each other, and everything was to be gained by their proper harmony. Too much personalism repeatedly led not to obscurity, as in our fragmented world, but to sentimentality; and too much impersonalism led, not as in the West to over-generalization and didacticism, but to excessive artificiality, monotony, cliché, and formalism. Either extreme might become flaccidly conventional.

In age after age, we see the poet struggle to achieve a meaningful balance peculiar to his age, usually by harmonizing a new concept of his relation to the external world with a growing sophistication of technique. A harmony between poet, subject, and audience is achieved again and again through a fineness of tone, an importance of theme, a propriety of esthetic distance, and a response to the needs of the age. More than that, it is possible to map the course of such a period as the early classical by its progress from a new search for a more vital personalism of a highly subjective nature to a balance and then to a decadent and impersonal conventionality, a pattern characteristic of earlier and later periods as well.

The sequence from a meaningful personalism to conventionality outlined above leads to more specific cyclic elements of poetic practice by which poets attempted to achieve their harmony. Very early (perhaps much earlier than is usually recognized, since it begins with the generation of Hitomaro in the seventh century), there is a tendency, impulse, or practice which may be called primitivism. In Western taste, we normally identify two kinds of primitivism, chronological and cultural. Chronological primitivism turns to an older age for its values; cultural primitivism turns to a contemporary but alien culture. Both kinds of primitivism may be recognized in Japanese poetry, but in highly modified form. Something like chronological primitivism has repeatedly occurred, especially in transitional times when, tiring of an over-sophistication, poets admire and emulate older poetry for both its presumed simplicity and its fancied superiority over the sophisticated complexity of a later age. A conscious and artful simplicity or naïveté of manner is often adopted by the poets, sometimes simply as a fresh alternative to a more complex style, sometimes in an attempt to find an antidote to conventionality and to establish the proper balance between the personal motives of the age. Such primitivism occasionally borrowed fresh language from the spoken tongue, but more typically it led poets to older, simpler diction and images and to a treatment of their subjects with simple declaration of the speaker's feelings.

A second form of Japanese primitivism, its motivation the same as that of the first, is the turning to a less sophisticated, contemporaneous people for directness of response and simplicity. But in Japan, as perhaps in China, the practice ought really to be called social rather than cultural primitivism, since the poets turned not to the Noble Savage of Africa, America, or the South Seas, but to their own countrymen of lower station—to the lives and, to a lesser extent, the songs, of workers, peasants, or beggars—for renewed poetic inspiration. Moreover, given the human probabilities, the social and historical situation, Japanese social primitivism may be more accurately described as a kind of pastoralism. In other words, we usually see the sophisticated poet reaching down to the commoner for local color and simpler views adaptable to contemporary modes, rather than the commoner reaching up to save the nation from the poetic disaster of conventionality. No doubt Court poetry filtered down to the people just as themes of the Western courtly romances entered into ballads during the Middle Ages, but this process is that of the sophistication of the unlettered, not the expression of the *vox populi*. Hito-maro is thought to have had his skilled hand in the so-called "songs of the palace-workmen" in the *Man'yōshū*, and Ōtomo Yakamochi (718–85) tried his hand at the "song of the frontier guard." There may indeed have been one or two "mute inglorious Miltons" in Japanese country churchyards, but the point is that the poetry we know and talk about was the possession of the Court class and those who came under its influence. Sone no Yoshitada (fl. ca. 985) wrote with a truly primitive realism and was laughed at by his contemporaries, who would not tolerate such unprecedented and low images as "my lover's hair soaked with sweat." All this has been said in part to adjust the impression most of us have been given by the stock comments on the *Man'yōshū*—that it represents poetry by a cross-section of all the people from the emperor to the lowliest beggar—but more fundamentally to point out that sophisticated Japanese poets had simpler modes to draw upon in order to bring a new freshness or personalism to their poetry. This act is a very sophisticated one, as we can see from Western pastoralism—a poetic mode which is the product of such refined periods as Virgil's, the Renaissance, and Augustan England. There is no pastoralism in the Greek or Germanic epics or in the *Kojiki*.

We must also distinguish this social primitivism, or pastoralism, from that commonness and simplicity in poetry which is the product of perfected art, whether in the breath-taking final speeches of Shakespeare's *King Lear*, or in Hitomaro's grand vision of human identity in his poem on a dead body on the island of Samine, or in Saigyō's (1118–90) poems of retirement. The Japanese did indeed turn to the past and to simpler people or to unsophisticated materials that might bring less refined emotions into poetry, but the example of Saigyō's withdrawal to a life of refined simplicity amid rustic surroundings reminds us that there is a Buddhist-Taoist tradition of retirement which is anything but primitive.

In fact, almost everywhere one looks in Japanese Court poetry, what first seem to the Western eye to be primitivistic elements or an impulse toward naïve simplicity turn out to be, if not pastoralism, the expression of a literary or cultural ideal that is not essentially primitivistic. One such ideal is merely that of an alternative style of greater simplicity and directness, a style which a sophisticated poet might find appropriate for some occasions and out of place for others. Again, what appears to be a simple turning to an idealized past may in fact be the expression of a conservative ideal or an adherence to fashion: it may be motivated not so much by a fresh naïveté or simplicity as by a mere reverence for the past or for some newly popular Chinese poet.

One does not get far in one's study of the older Japanese—or Chinese—poetry unless one realizes that the works of the past hold all but complete sway over the minds of later poets. The Western cult of novelty and the faith that change means progress must be opposed to the traditional East Asian veneration of the past and fear of sudden or startling breaks with it. To some readers, such reverence for tradition will no doubt present a considerable cultural barrier, and to answer them one can only ask for exercise of the historical imagination. It should be remembered that our own medieval poets believed that what was written by "olde clerkes" was true because it was written, and that our Renaissance writers were as excited by the discovery of the Graeco-Roman past as the Japanese by their readings in Chinese. Moreover, Japanese poets no more than European poets had printed books in A.D. 1000. Indeed, even at the Japanese Court paper was almost prohibitively expensive, and the few manuscripts which existed were treasured almost as scriptures of civilization. The culture of eleventh-century Japan, and of subsequent centuries, was at once extraordinarily sophisticated and completely dependent upon those few collections of the writings of the past preserved by an aristocracy whose sense of identity as cultivated men depended on their preserving their past.

This discussion may perhaps make it clear why the primitivistic impulse is often swallowed up by another, more powerful, recurrent motive—also an act of borrowing from the past—which is best called neoclassicism. The neoclassical urge is strongest in the mid- and late classical periods (1100–1350), when society seemed to be in chaos. Fujiwara Teika, for example, could look upon poetry as a means of achieving immortality in an age of chaotic strife between the Minamoto and the Taira clans. "My ears are full of tales about the current uprisings and the campaigns to quell them," he wrote in his diary, the *Meigetsuki* (9th moon, 1180), "but I pay no attention to them. 'The chastisement of the red banner of the insurgents is no affair of mine.'" This withdrawal, with its accompanying reflection on old poetic traditions and its echoing of the poetic past, is typical of the late Heian and early medieval period, when men might make a religious commitment to poetry as "a way of life." But even Hitomaro, Yamanoe Okura, and Ōtomo Tabito (665–731) are neoclassicists to a considerable degree. Hitomaro's "public" chōka usually begin with a kind of overture in celebration of the glories of the human, imperial, or divine past. Tabito in his poems on *sake* (*MYS*, III: 338–50) and Okura in his "Dialogue on Poverty" (*MYS*, V: 892–93) are neoclassical in their borrowings of themes from Chinese poetry to give meaning to their world. This turning to the literature of China is not subservience, but the age-old view of art as tradition.

At the same time it must be said that some periods are more tradition-minded than others, and the examples of Tabito and Okura bring us to our final recurrent pattern, that of the repeated importance of China to the Japanese esthetic and to poetic practice. The importance of Chinese thought is obvious in Tabito's Taoistic epicureanism and in Okura's partially Confucian social consciousness. But a poetic sensibility resembling the Chinese had been awakened before their time; it may be seen in Princess Nukada's famous poem from the late seventh century on the rival beauty of the hills of spring and autumn, a sophisticated poetic theme which shows the dawn of a Japanese poetry with literary as well as immediate human concerns (*MYS*, I: 16; for a translation, see below, p. 85). But although in this early period writers appear to have given close attention to Chinese poetry, especially of the period of the Six Dynasties (222–589), the first cycle of Chinese influence involved for the most part a borrowing of themes and images, and of course did not end with a final commitment by Japanese poets to a view of poetry and poetic technique specifically "Chinese." Tabito, Okura, and their contemporaries could and usually did write in many styles often having no connection with China. Even when the techniques employed are most Chinese, they are given a "local habitation," if not invariably a Japanese name. This broader and more striking versatility, proper to an age of bold experimentation, gives to the poetry of the seventh and eighth centuries its variety of forms, themes, and materials so much admired by modern Japanese, who point to the *Man'yōshū* as the glory of their poetic literature. However, the prestige of Chinese poetry—and the vogue for imitations—continued to increase from the eighth century to the beginning of the tenth. In the face of this competition from a vastly older tradition with a complicated and articulate poetic, Japanese poetry continued to lose ground. By the beginning of the ninth century it was in danger of becoming permanently relegated to the undignified function of a plaything in the half-serious business of gallantry. In this first period, then, Chinese poetry increasingly threatened to replace rather than enrich the native tradition.

The beginnings of the second period of Chinese influence can be seen in the seemingly sudden appearance, in the first half of the ninth century, of the so-called Six Poetic Geniuses, with their new and more vital subjectivity. These poets—most notably Ariwara Narihira (825–80) and Ono no Komachi (fl. ca. 850)—created a new and meaningful Japanese poetry with techniques borrowed and adapted from Chinese poetry of the late Six Dynasties. But it was more particularly due to the conscious efforts of the compilers of the *Kokinshū*, Ki no Tsurayuki and others, that the Chinese poetic tradition took on a new relevance for Japanese poetry, and that the native poetry was in turn accorded a renewed, permanent status as the highest art in Japan. It would be a mistake to see in what we may call Tsurayuki's "Defense of Japanese Poetry"—the Preface to the *Kokinshū*—an expression of cultural xenophobia, or even the complacent belief that the Japanese Muse is every bit as good as the Chinese, if not better. Rather, the Preface reveals the emergence of a critical consciousness, as distinguished from the earlier birth of literary awareness; it is an attempt to create a theory and prescribe a practice for Japanese poetry that would entitle it once again to social acceptance, this time as an art on a level with Chinese poetry. The effort appears to have entailed an insistence upon an established poetic language with the prestige of tradition, and a channeling of individual expression to important but subtle adjustments of the relation between the originality of the individual poet and the conventionality of his prescribed materials.

It is one of the commonplaces of Japanese literary history that the *Kokinshū* shows a marked concern with poetic technique; and it is also true that the poetic vocabulary of the *Kokinshū*—a vocabulary which significantly excludes all words of identifiably Chinese origin—became standard for the poetry written during the rest of the Court period. In spite of this development of

Drawing of Ki no Tsurayuki by Reizei Tamechika (1823–64) from a set of illustrations for the famous HYAKUNIN ISSHU (SINGLE POEMS BY ONE HUNDRED POETS), *a very popular anthology of Court poetry attributed to Fujiwara Teika*

native poetic resources, it seems possible, at least in the case of Tsurayuki and his contemporaries, for us to trace many specific aspects of their theory and practice to the so-called "oblique" (*i-p'ang*) style of late Six Dynasties (ca. 420–589) and early T'ang (618–ca. 705) poetry, and to account in part for the appearance of a new stylized subjectivity in the *Kokinshū* by recognizing it as an attempt to adapt this strictly controlled technique to the Japanese tradition. Once again China had provided Japanese poets with a useful example, meaningful ideals, and usable techniques.

This was not the last period in which Japanese poets looked admiringly toward China, nor does so brief a description adequately present the complexities of Sino-Japanese literary relationships. But in this period, as in others, a certain consistency in the method of borrowing is worthy of note. Educated Japanese men (and some women) read Chinese poetry, usually of a century or more before their time. Then they imitated these poems in Chinese compositions of their own. And finally some Chinese poetic techniques and materials were transferred into Japanese poetry, almost always with such alteration that no Chinese would recognize them. This process has two significant aspects, both of which go far toward relieving the Japanese poets of the stigma of being mere borrowers. In the first place, they knew Chinese well enough not to require translations. It was their "classical" language, as much a part of a man's education as Latin once was in the West. When so high a value is put upon an activity, the proper word is not borrowing but participation. Second, except for short-lived periods of faddism, the Japanese selected from the Chinese with such care and adapted what they chose with such thoroughness that it became their own. Japanese poetry is not marked by half-digested characteristics of Chinese, as English is often scarred by Latinisms. Indeed, it might be argued that the Japanese ought really to be blamed for not adopting more from China, and the Chinese for borrowing from Japan only such unpoetic products as gold, mercury, fans, swords, and timber.

The story of subsequent periods of interest in Chinese poetry is more properly the subject of later chapters, when we will take up the relationship between lesser cyclical changes in Japanese poetry within the classical periods (784–1350) and the successive influences of mid- and late T'ang and Sung poetry (ca. 705–1279). It may be said, however, that in the early classical period the Japanese tradition was fundamentally and permanently affected: the esthetic ideal of *miyabi,* "courtliness" or "elegance," which certain poets of the *Kokinshū* derived from the Chinese, gave to the tanka an aristocratic character and the enduring strength of a literary tradition which could last for centuries.

The recurring elements which helped form the poetic tradition of the Court take on greater meaning if they are briefly related to the historical development of the tradition. Such a description, intended primarily for those to whom Japanese literary history is somewhat unfamiliar, must combine a discussion of changes in response to recurrent forces with one of a steady, secular development; and this raises the problem of periodization. Leaving aside for the moment the questions of survivals, cross-currents, and pre-figurings, five periods may be briefly outlined: the primitive, from ca. A.D. 550 to 686; the early literary, 686–784; the early classical, 784–1100; the mid-classical, 1100–1241; and the late classical, 1241–1350. To simplify further the account of what will later be analyzed in detail, we shall consider only two subjects—nature and time—and two esthetic relationships—that of the poet to his materials and that of the poet to his audience.

The primitive period is obscured, to a large extent, in the darkness of prehistory, and we have small hope of knowing to what degree the surviving poems were reshaped by later poets or whether their attributed dates are at all accurate. But the extant poems do suggest that one of their most important characteristics is the relationship between poet and audience. These old poems, or more properly songs, deal primarily with personal subjects and are almost always declarations, whether to a lover, to one's self and the world before committing suicide, or to an emperor on such occasions as his impending death. Nature is almost always employed for direct comparison, and time is only part of the situation of the poem and not properly a subject at all.

We can see this overriding importance of declaration in such a charming piece of poetic address as that of the coy Princess Nunakawa to the Deity Eight Thousand Spears (*Kojiki,* No. 3).

Yachihoko no	Divine august one,
Kami no mikoto	Deity Eight Thousand Spears,
Nuekusa no	Since I am only
Me ni shi areba	A maiden wavering as the grass
Wa ga kokoro	And my heart
Urasu no tori zo	A bird scampering on the shore,
Ima koso wa	I am right now
Wadori ni arame	A bird you cannot tame,
Nochi wa	But before long
Nadori ni aramu o	A bird completely yours;
Inochi wa	So do not destroy
Na shisetamai so.	Your life with overhasty love.

Such poems as this are not only declarative but also almost completely occasional, whether the occasion is one from recognizable human experience or one got up in the trappings of myth and legend. The naïve delight of this poem, the princess's clever femininity, is expressed with such wholehearted directness that it would be romantic and almost shameful to credit it with a literary awareness, much less a conscious primitivism or traditionally-minded neoclassicism.

The mode of declarative poetry in which nature and time are only the vehicles of the declaration and in which the relation of the poet to his materials is unreflecting survives in the tanka to the end of this early period. The Consort of the Emperor Tenchi (626–71) addresses his spirit on the occasion of his impending death (*MYS*, II: 148).

Aohata no	Over your mountain home,
Kohata no ue o	Kohata whose green forests wave
Kayou to wa	Like hempen flags,
Me ni wa miredo mo	Your spirit hovers before my eyes
Tada ni awanu ka mo.	While I grieve that we can never meet again.

This is more sophisticated than Princess Nunakawa's sweet reluctant amorous delay in its gentle assonance and vivid imagery, but the two poems are founded upon the same technique.

The remarkable poetic achievements of the century spanned by the early literary period (686–784) were founded upon elements which the primitive age so notably lacked: a literary consciousness, the example of Chinese literature, a sophisticated primitivism which led poets to collect the works of such less cultivated men as frontier guards, and a neoclassical respect for what was meaningful in Chinese poetry and in the native primitive period. In this way, while such a poet as Kakinomoto Hitomaro might employ a declarative mode, he redefines it in terms of public themes or in terms of a broad humanity, as can be seen in the poem "On Seeing the Body of a Man Lying Among the Stones on the Island of Samine" (*MYS*, II: 220–22; for a full translation, see below, pp. 97–98). The chōka ends:

Nami no to no	And then we saw you:
Shigeki hamabe o	Pillowed upon your shaking beach,
Shikitae no	Using those wave-beaten rocks
Makura ni nashite	As if the coast were spread out for your
Aradoko ni	bedding;
Yorifusu kimi ga	On such a rugged place
	You have laid yourself to rest.
Ie shiraba	If I but knew your home,
Yukite mo tsugen	I would go tell them where you sleep;
Tsuma shiraba	If your wife but knew this home,
Ki mo towamashi o	She would come here searching for you,
Tamahoko no	But knowing nothing of the way—
Michi dani shirazu	The way straight as a courtier's spear—
Oboboshiku	How must she be waiting,
Machi ka kou ran	How anxiously now longing for you,
Hashiki tsumara wa.	She the dear one you called wife.

The author of the poem has become at once a public figure, a self-conscious poet, and a man; and the relation of the poet to his audience has become formalized to the extent that the most renowned poet at the somewhat decadent end of the period, Yakamochi, sometimes seems almost to be all poet and no man.

In the early literary period, time becomes an important theme, although one treated in direct response, as Okura's "Lament on the Instability of Human Life" so eloquently proclaims. After telling what time does to carefree girls and bold lads, Okura concludes in his envoy (*MYS*, V: 805):

Tokiwa nasu	How I yearn to be
Kaku shi mo ga mo to	Unalterably what once I was,
Omoedo mo	Immovable as a rock,
Yo no koto nareba	But because I belong to this world,
Todomikanetsu mo.	There is no stop to time.

Nature—its beauties and its perils—is an even more common subject than time, but, like time, it is treated directly; the response is one of objective presentation, as in the passage quoted from Hitomaro's poem. Nature is part of the scene upon which man finds himself, and is no more or less real than human suffering, a palace, or a sea voyage. We find a balanced relationship between the subjective spectator poet and his object. The result is a tone of repose, of balance which is pre-eminent in the work of Hitomaro and Tabito, and common even to the more eccentric Okura, the softer Yakamochi, and the other poets of the period.

At the end of the early literary period and throughout the early classical period, contemporary experience and poetic experimentation led to two important developments: the definition of the poetic tradition in terms of the tanka and the emergence of a new subjectivity. The new poetic importance of the poet himself as subject was built upon the formalizing and socializing of the poet's role in the preceding period, and upon the concept borrowed from Chinese poetry (along with the techniques to convey the concept) that art may distort the details of sensory experience into patterns of subjective, even seemingly irrational truth. Ono no Komachi explores the relative merits of states of subjective experience, in what we would call the realms of fantasy and real life (*KKS*, XIII: 658).

Yumeji ni wa	Although my feet
Ashi mo yasumezu	Never cease in running to you
Kayoedo mo	On the path of dreams,
Utsutsu ni hitome	Such nights of love are never worth
Mishi goto wa arazu.	One glimpse of you in your reality.

So intense is this expression of Komachi's subjective experience that the chimerical world of her desires is converted by the imagination into an objective realm of running feet and a seemingly real path—and yet the wished-for and impossible "reality" has an even greater reality, as it were, than the passionate conjurings of her imagination. A Hitomaro might write about time-honored traditions or the glories of the past, and an Okura about the ruinous effects of time on golden lads and girls, but to a great poet of the ninth or tenth century, time and nature—reality perhaps—have little existence apart from himself. This subjectivity led to poetic topics that were more metaphysical than the prevailingly ethical ones of the preceding age. Such themes as the meaning of love and the difference between appearance and reality are constant concerns, as a reader of that great *speculum amantis,* the *Tale of Genji,* will recall. And as we can see in the poem of Ki no Tomonori (fl. ca. 890) cited earlier, a vision of nature may become so subjective that like a person it may grow out of tune with its own laws (*KKS*, II: 84).

Hisakata no   On this day in spring
Hikari nodokeki   When the lambent air suffuses
Haru no hi ni   Soft tranquility,
Shizugokoro naku   Why should the cherry petals flutter
Hana no chiru ran.   With unsettled heart to earth?

As we might expect of such an age, the most subjective of all normal human experience, love, is the great theme to which time and nature are subordinated, and the poet's usual audience is the lady or lover to whom the poem is addressed. But love poetry and subjectivity can degenerate into mere convention as easily as anything else, and toward the end of the tenth century the subjective mode did decline, although not without leaving its permanent mark on the tradition. Poets became the victims of their own techniques, and what had been brilliant wit with deep penetration into human awareness came to be little more than the display by virtuosi of the techniques earlier adapted from the Chinese poetry of the Six Dynasties and thereafter all too often heard in Japanese modifications. Not only technique, but diction, imagery, treatment, and styles as well were deadened by all but meaningless convention. What had been the vehicle of a subjectivity in which personal states of mind and larger metaphysical concerns were attuned to each other became largely stereotyped techniques with little personal significance.

Toward the end of the early classical period and at the beginning of the mid-classical period (1100–1241), there are signs of change which gradually led to the formation of a new style. It is largely descriptive, and often the poet seems to be writing to no audience at all—a kind of esthetic distance bequeathed later to the haiku. The objective outer world takes on a poetic existence which the poet does not seem to be sharing with another human being. For that matter, it often seems as if the poet himself has retired from the scene and the objective world exists as a thing in itself. But it is necessary to insist upon the obvious fact that the loss of audience and poet is only apparent, in part for reasons too complex to enter into here, and in part because the style is one best characterized as descriptive symbolism. That is to say, the personal concerns of the poet on the one hand (the details of nature he finds moving), and his relations with men, and the poet's personal aims on the other hand (the truths and attitudes he attempts to convey) are symbolically fused with the natural scene into a new whole. For the natural scene, which is presented as if for itself alone, is really symbolic in emotional, intellectual, and religious ways of the poet and other men bound up in a Buddhist world in which the laws of nature governing withered leaves are representative of the laws governing men's lives.

This is a very complex poetry, and the complications are only hinted at here. The style may be best illustrated at this point with a work by a poet of the mid-classical period who aimed at simplicity, the priest Saigyō (*SKKS*, VI: 625).

Tsu no kuni no	Only a dream!
Naniwa no haru wa	The bygone glories of the spring
Yume nare ya	At Naniwa in Tsu—
Ashi no kareba ni	Everywhere the rough wind rustles over
Kaze wataru nari.	The frost-withered leaves of reeds.

Saigyō has taken advantage not only of the liquid sounds of his language, but also of the Buddhist symbolism in which the fates of all living things are representative of each other. Men as well as reeds grow old, and dreams imply a human dreamer.

The seemingly objective description is highly subjective after all, and it is easy to see that the accomplishments of the style of descriptive symbolism built upon the highly subjective manipulation of poetic materials in the preceding age. The external world is granted a disparate existence only long enough to set it down and reshape it symbolically into materials relevant to the poet. Saigyō's poem shows another transcendent quality of this descriptive symbolism. He mentions spring and implies winter. Time and, *ipso facto* to this Buddhist thought, change are as it were the enemies whose hostility to the natural scenery and to men brings sadness. But what is true of the glories of spring become withered wintry reeds is also true of the course of human life: the identity gives man's existence a meaning, shows that it is based upon natural laws. The sadness remains, but it may be accepted and affirmed when man can see an eternal, transcendent significance in it.

The difficulty in creating poems of such rich dimensions is apparent. The practice of the new style had its result in effecting techniques of descriptive imagery which could blend with other styles available to poets in the age. Such skill can best be appreciated in the poetry of Saigyō and of the circle of poets about his two greater contemporaries, Fujiwara Shunzei and Shunzei's son Teika. A poem by such a lesser light as Fujiwara Sueyoshi (1152–1211) shows both the new skill in description gained from the great poets of his age and the old habit of searching for reasons inherited from the preceding age (*SKKS*, VI: 648).

Sayo chidori	Toward Narumi Beach
Koe koso chikaku	The cries afar of plovers in the dark
Narumigata	Wing nearer through the night—
Katabuku tsuki ni	Perhaps because the moon now sinks beyond
Shio ya mitsu ran.	And swelling tides roll in upon the shore?

Although one would not wish to deny the charm of this poem, the reason given in the last two lines is more purely esthetic and pretty than significant, and the description has little more than an effect of pleasing virtuosity.

The last great age of Japanese Court poetry, the late classical period (1241–1350), developed from the age of Shunzei, Saigyō, and Teika by building upon it in new, in some respects in startlingly new, ways. One of the novelties of this period is the acrimony of literary disputes, whose bitterness was intensified by the political and social implications, not of the poetry itself, but of the prestige of carrying on the true poetic tradition. More important, it is difficult to imagine a greater novelty in the tradition than the consistent composition of poems with no imagery; and poems which consist entirely of images are only scarcely less surprising. But in this period many of the seasonal poems are indeed completely imagistic, and many of the love poems completely devoid of imagery.

Such extremes can best be identified by example and reconciled by reference to our two subjects, time and nature, and our two kinds of esthetic distance. The imagistic style of the seasonal poetry may be typified by Kyō-goku Tamekane's (1273–1332) poem on a spring scene (*FGS*, I: 41).

Uguisu no	The warbler's voice
Koe mo nodoka ni	Rises in its song but also deepens
Nakinashite	The spring's serenity,
Kasumu hikage wa	And in the dusk the hazy sunlight
Kuren to mo sezu.	Fades toward the dark but does not die.

Similarly, a poem by ex-Empress Eifuku (1271–1342) shows the nonimagistic style characteristic of the love poetry (*GYS*, XII: 1707).

Yowarihatsuru	In my heart,
Ima wa no kiwa no	Weakened now by your betrayal
Omoi ni wa	To the point of death,
Usa mo aware ni	Even misery takes on pathetic beauty
Naru ni zo arikeru.	And my bitterness is gone.

Both poems reveal a new treatment of time and nature. The timelessness —that is, the deep sense of time found in the universally true—which characterizes the poetry of the preceding period is here altered to an emphasis upon that which is particularly true of a specific experience at a specific moment of time. Of course, the dusk of every spring day will presumably share certain qualities with the dusk of Tamekane's poem, and the misery of the betrayed woman in ex-Empress Eifuku's poem would be shared by every woman in her plight. But these common elements are not at the center of the poems. The poets have gone beyond the universals to create experiences that are primarily true only in terms of the specific situation. Not every spring day lasts forever, and not every unhappy woman has the experience of suffering so deeply that her wretchedness at the moment of deepest suffering turns into a kind of beauty. The truth of the particular moment is what these poets have chosen to explore, and their aim often leads them to violate the canons of traditional diction or ways of treating a given subject: in this poetry a woman may become resigned to her lover's indifference, or an eternity may be symbolized by the sunlight that lingers briefly at the end of a spring day. The same quality of the special, of the particular, of the finely distinguished, is therefore true of the handling of nature, although in view of the absence of imagery from the love poems we must broaden our definition of nature to include human nature and psychological realities. Nature so defined is less the timeless reality transcending change found in earlier poetry than the timeless reality wedded to the particulars of a specific occasion. In other words, these poets attempted to give, through the aptness of their observation and the intensity of their style, a conviction that the particularities they discriminate have a truth as weighty as the universal elements also expressed in their poems.

This balance between what is universally true and what is intensely true of the moment suggests a new solution to the problems of esthetic distance. The personal response of the poet and his originality lie in the exploration of the moment, while the traditional materials and the conventions of technique which he reshapes are assumed to represent the universal. The tradition had become so awesomely impersonal by this time, so much greater than the individual poet, that in order to arrive at truth the poets sought to lessen the esthetic distance between themselves and their materials. Consequently, their poetry, whether on love or other subjects, treats the moment and the details which make it up, presenting the artistic whole as if the moment were one that interrupted the forward thrust of time. Along with this lessening of the esthetic distance between the poet and his materials, there is an increase in the distance between the poet and his audience. If the moment is something so important, it is exceptional as well as true. Both a day that will not close and a misery that turns to beauty represent special experiences of a highly individual speaker in a very particular situation. The audience is given the pleasure of the special, the rich, the strange, as in Western Metaphysical or Romantic poetry, and its response must be one more of appreciation than of shared experience.

In this respect, the poets of the age can be said to have turned back to the age of Narihira, Komachi, and Tsurayuki (when, significantly, a few poems may be found without imagery) for a kind of subjectivity of the special moment. But they also inherited from the age of Shunzei and Teika the idea that poetry is a serious, even grave, search for truth. In such poetry there is little room for the wit of a Komachi, and at its worst the poetry suffers from solemnity: some poems seem to fall between poetry and prose, lacking the virtues of either. But at its best the poetry is new with the originality—not of inevitable truth—but of that which is freshly observed. This freshness of observation, which sometimes imparts a quality like that to be found in Impressionist painting, is all the more remarkable in that it comes at the end of a long literary tradition.

For this age does mark the end of greatness in the tradition of Japanese Court poetry. The political power of the Court had long since been seized by less polite hands, and the courtiers had little to retain except their traditions and a nominal rule. The earlier poets had built well, and so the tradition was strong enough and varied enough to outlast for a time the decline of the particular society that had created it. But the inexorable effects of time and change meant that the decline of the society must sooner or later be reflected in its culture.

As the old order weakened before the new, darkness descended upon the Court. The tanka survived, more in numbers than in quality, after the middle of the fourteenth century, and re-emerged in modern times as a form expressive of interests and subjects often far different from those of the Court six centuries and more ago. But its survival is probably less significant for the history and the continuity of the Japanese poetic tradition than for the reshaping of the techniques and the aims of Court poetry by the poets of the renga, or linked verses, and the further alteration of techniques and interests by the haiku poets. It is these forms of feudal Japan, with certain aspects of the drama, which are the true heirs of the Court poetry, since the continuation of a living poetic tradition is far more significant than the survival of any single literary form. To choose a specific example, the haiku of Bashō (1644–94) are far more like the tanka of a Saigyō or a Tamekane—in vitality and even in technique—than are the tanka which in modern times are submitted to the emperor on New Year's Day. These later developments lie outside the scope of this book, and are mentioned only to suggest that wide as the chronological limits of this study are, they by no means either cover the whole range of Japanese poetry or even encompass the tradition of the Court poetry in all its importance.

Before beginning the second and main part of this study—the analysis of the poetry of the five important periods of Japanese Court literature—we feel it important to raise and make explicit two questions that will doubtless occur to some readers: are the Japanese poetic forms long enough to be considered poems; and, if they are poems, how significant are they for Western readers? The chronological sequence of the chapters which follow may well heighten such questions, since although many of the primitive songs and the chōka of the early literary period are of familiar poetic length, the tanka—the form which is predominant in later periods—is apt to seem, by contrast, almost fragmentary.

No doubt to answer properly the question of whether the tanka is long enough to be considered an adequate poetic form, we should have to begin with an acceptable definition of poetry and then test the tanka by such a standard. Unfortunately, or perhaps fortunately, we are not estheticians and do not see the merit, much less the possibility, of our philosophizing on this subject. Ben Jonson's statement that a poem may consist of a single line—he quotes the verse hung up by Aeneas with his armor—or Jeremy Bentham's well-known description of poetry as that species of writing in which all the lines do not go to the end of the page—such statements and more philosophical ones as well seem to us evasions of the problem that may trouble even the best-disposed Western reader.

Perhaps the most useful way to approach both problems is to rephrase them into three different questions: What have the Court poets made or accomplished in a form as short as the tanka? Are there any ways in which Japanese poets can be said to have transcended the limits of their form—ways other than the usual vague claims to concision and suggestiveness? And what is to be our final judgment of the place of Japanese Court poetry in world literature?

The first question is one that is discussed throughout the next five chapters in an analysis of the poetry itself. The second question can be answered both succinctly and affirmatively. For the fragmentation, as it may be called, of larger lyric forms into shorter forms (whose logical end is perhaps the seventeen-syllable haiku) that marks Japanese literary history has as its counterpart a force best named integration. By this term we do not mean such things as concision and suggestiveness, for while these do mark Japanese poetry, they are characteristics of a great many kinds of poetry the world around; rather, the term denotes those specific techniques by which Japanese poets have enlarged the scope of an individual poem—some techniques have been mentioned and others will be later—and which have brought together individual tanka into unified sequences. These latter techniques of integration are discussed under the head of poetic sequences in Chapters 6 and 7, although the same premises about poetry and similar techniques mark Japanese poetry from beginning to end.

The question of the place of Japanese Court poetry in world literature is one of those problems for final or personal judgment and is comparable to such issues as the ultimate superiority of the lyric, the drama, or the epic, or to the issue of the possibility of poetry in the modern world. We have said already, and shall have occasion to observe more than once again, that Japanese Court poetry characteristically appeals to an aspect of our poetic sensibilities different from that taken by Western poetry as its special literary province.

This difference is also one which we hope to establish in the next five chapters, and we feel entitled to pass our final judgment on Japanese Court poetry only after close scrutiny of poems written over the eight centuries or so we have chosen to discuss. This final judgment and our reasons for it must again be deferred to the summary essay with which the book concludes.

We are conscious of having raised some questions here that we have not answered. But we hope that by posing them we have shown our awareness of such problems, and that by deferring our answers we have, instead of begging the issues, put them into the proper terms. In the main, the best and perhaps the only answer most of us will find to such questions as what poetry is, what use it has, and whether a given poem or form is truly classifiable as poetry is the experience of pleasure we get from reading. This answer carries a conviction that no amount of theory can gainsay; and to discover that Japanese Court poetry gives pleasure and helps, like all literature, to form and enlarge our experience of ourselves in our world is no doubt answer enough. We would have given such an answer to begin with, except that it is of a kind that each reader must discover for himself and the one which we hope the succeeding chapters will bring to him with conviction and pleasure. Pious and evasive as such conclusions must seem, they are the only answers possible at this point. The questions are too basic and sweeping in their implications to be answered in any terms other than those of the poetry itself —poetry composed over a period of eight centuries, beginning about the time of the fall of Rome and ending before Chaucer had attained manhood.

PART TWO

The Ideals, Practice, and Development
of Japanese Court Poetry

3

Primitive Song and Poetry

Ca. 550–686

SCHOLARS AND CRITICS differ widely in their attitudes toward the earliest
Japanese song literature. Some hold that it exhibits the pristine loveliness of Japanese lyricism—a lyricism unmannered, sincere, and direct in
expression. Others, including the redoubtable Arthur Waley, are so far from
seeing "any value as literature" in the productions of this early period that
they can conclude: "A chronological study of Japanese poetry would certainly
cause the student to abandon the subject in despair." We have not become
enthusiasts for early Japanese song, and we have not despaired, because we
find that it holds an intrinsic historical interest: for it shows in more detail
than most early literatures the origins of the literate civilization to follow and
it clarifies the nature of the poetic assumptions and techniques of later
poetry.

Moreover, it has a genuine if limited artistic appeal. Some of the songs
are of abiding intrinsic interest, although we feel that their quality springs
from rather different virtues than those so esteemed by the enthusiasts. Since,
however, the earliest Japanese poetic achievement raises so many questions of
a historical and literary nature that cannot be answered with satisfaction to
all, this chapter is one which must be founded upon an unusual degree of
caution and candor. Our candor will begin with the confession that, historical
considerations aside, we have no sympathy for the folksiness of "folk poetry."
Poetry is, we think, good or bad in itself, whether written by a Cuddy or a
Queen Caroline. As Bernard Berenson said so well in his *Aesthetics and Art
History* (New York, 1954; Anchor Books ed., p. 247):

Folk, as folk, has never originated, never created anything. Folk is at best a term
for an abstraction subsuming a number of individuals belonging to what is supposed to be the basic layer of society. When something is created by it then it is
the gifted individual sprung from that mass, in other words, a sport, who invents
it, not some mystic body uttering the messages of the Earth Mothers.

We share this attitude wholeheartedly.

Before we turn to the specific characteristics of the primitive songs, it
should be made clear in what sense they may be called poems, and what may
be said about them in terms of their history. The poetry dealt with under
this title is really a tradition of oral song preserved in written records that
often demonstrably distort the original meaning of a given composition. It is

not possible to fix with any certainty the dates when these songs were originally created or when others of a similar nature ceased to be composed. The queried date for the beginning of this primitive period, A.D. 550, is nothing more than the approximate time at which the Japanese chronicles begin to become accurate, and is not a proper *terminus a quo* of these songs. Most of the songs were taken down from reciters in the early eighth century or preserved in religious ceremonies; but although there is both linguistic and literary evidence and the conservative Japanese traditionalism to suggest that the songs might have been handed down for centuries very much as the reciters had received them, and although there had been in the more powerful clans a special class of memorizers and reciters (*kataribe*), it would be rash to assign to the very earliest songs a date earlier than the fifth century, and surely few if any were recited in their present form before 550. Songs like the ones preserved may indeed have been composed many centuries earlier, but it is hazardous to infer details about ancestors by looking at descendants. The terminal date for this period, 686, is also approximate, because songs such as these continued to be sung and composed well into the age of literacy and the development of true poetry at a literary-minded Court. However, the farther one moves into the Court tradition, the more one finds the song literature to show influences derived from the Court; and what is more important, after about 686 there are such striking new poetic developments that a new period in the history of Japanese poetry can easily be said to have begun.

Certain characteristics of primitive Japanese song seem clear enough. Those songs which have survived in writing come—directly or in modified form—from an oral tradition in which they seem to have been preserved more carefully—with less revision—than comparable early European poetry. Most of them are mannered as well as simple, and are limited in conception, range, techniques, and conventions. Many of the mannerisms seem appropriate to the reciters' trade, or at least designed to facilitate the memorizing and reciting of oral poetry. The form of these songs is often more traditional and conventional than vital to the individual poetic structure. The earliest songs—or what are generally agreed to be the earliest—are also not fixed in prosody. They have no fixed number of syllables and no regular alternation of long and short lines. Consistency in the use of syllabic fives and sevens usually combines with other evidence to show that a song is of later composition or has been revised. These early songs are marked by an overriding emphasis upon ritual or social occasion; far from being lyric cries of the *Volksstimme*, they are tied to presentation at a social gathering or social ritual. A peasant lad may well have composed a personal lyric about his girl or the beauty of the morn—but in order for him to make the distinction in his mind between speaking to himself and singing he would need to have been aware of the conventions of song: of the required diction, of the appropriate occasion, and of the rudimentary prosodic fact of lines. And if such private, personal songs were indeed composed, they survive only in writing and in a greatly altered context, for they were long since adapted to public social occasions such as entertainments, even for pantomiming before groups. The best word we know for such an emergent artistic milieu is "primitive."

The conventions in the primitive song—and no art, no literature, no originality, is possible without conventions—are both few and obtrusive, so that they give an effect of constraint in comparison with the more numerous, more supple conventions of later poetry. The materials are similarly meager, confined as they are to simple human affairs, the simplest emotions, and the simplest observations of fact. These materials are usually presented in an equally restricted manner. There are some poems with dramatic elements and some that are meant to be narrative, and surely pantomime or recitation emphasized these modes. But the basic mode of these songs is declaration, and we search almost in vain—if we expect such art from primitive poetry—for true drama or true narration, not to speak of reflection or description.

Still, there is always room in the great canon of a nation's poetry for simple poems, and these are always the more acceptable when they have the integrity of having been composed by an unsophisticated age. It is historically important that the simplicity of primitive songs is founded upon the technique of declaration, since this mode has had its enthusiasts in Japan ever since. The reasons for the enthusiasm are not altogether clear, but perhaps it grows from a desire to find a directness of expression in poetry that is not to be discovered in the oblique social forms and civilities of well-mannered Japanese life. Even such unquestionably sophisticated poets as Ki no Tsurayuki and Fujiwara Teika turned late in life to simpler, more declarative poetic modes in order to achieve a simple integrity (*makoto*) that seemed to them lacking in their earlier poetry. For such reasons, the Japanese have often prized the simple earlier poetry with a fervor particularly their own.

Among these earlier songs and poems, however, there are some of a descriptive nature and others that for other reasons seem to be exceptions to the above generalizations about primitive song. These are the products of a later age, one approaching or following the date of literacy and Court influence. To explain this situation and to clarify some earlier remarks, we must look briefly at the wells from which primitive Japanese songs are drawn.

SOURCES OF EARLY JAPANESE SONG

In a recent and authoritative edition, *Anthology of Ancient Song* (*Kodai Kayōshū*), Professors Tsuchihashi and Konishi have garnered almost 500 primitive songs. Like others before them, they took as their principal sources two early-eighth-century chronicles, the *Kojiki,* "Records of Ancient Matters," (712) and the *Nihongi* (or *Nihonshoki*), "Chronicles of Japan," (720); certain additional continuations and collections of the late eighth and early ninth centuries; some later heterogeneous collections of songs whose occasion of performance led to their names, *kagura* or "sacred music," *saibara* or "horse-readying music" (the horses apparently were to take offerings from the provinces); and songs from other late collections. Subtracting duplications and adding the primitive poems in the *Man'yōshū,* we have a collection that varies from brief fragments to long sequences dealing with a single figure, such as the Deity Eight Thousand Spears.

Matters would be considerably simpler if the chronology of the pseudo-history in the *Kojiki* and the earlier sections of the *Nihongi* were accurate, and if the poems related to the most primitive myths and stories were themselves the most primitive. As it is, the stories are fabulous, the dates before about 550 are invented, and there is no relation between the pseudo-historical dates of the mythical events and the age of the songs that are fitted, often with literary violence, into the "history."

The date of the composition of any of these songs can be surmised only on the basis of language, form, technique, and some historical evidence—and then only tentatively. Moreover, some of the songs were transferred whole into the later prose contexts, whereas others seem to have been altered by later reciters or the compilers of the *Kojiki* and *Nihongi*; and within a given episode many of the primitive poems rest uneasily side by side with songs that date from a generation as late as that of the compilers. It is as if some of the Psalms had been placed into prose contexts in Genesis or Kings along with a larger number of such primitive compositions as the Song of Deborah and Samson's riddles. Such complexities make accurate dating impossible and raise many insoluble problems. But perhaps the surprising and noteworthy fact that arises from all the uncertainty is that a relatively large number of songs have actually survived from a prehistoric, oral tradition. The fortunate corollary to this fact is that we have a large enough body of this early literature, with enough recurrence of similar forms and expressions, to analyze with reasonable confidence the techniques and accomplishments of primitive Japanese song.

Our emphasis is primarily critical rather than historical, but these few paragraphs of introduction will serve to explain what facts and truths we have, and to distinguish these from speculations. The difficulty in sorting out songs, in determining their age, and in deciding whether or how much they have been altered in transmission or recording should now be apparent. And the paradox of all primitive literatures surviving from the remote past is again illustrated: we must study oral poetry on the basis of what has survived in writing. The natural comparison for primitive Japanese song is with the poetry of the Germanic tribes. But one further distinction must be made before it is possible to talk about the place of song in the lives of the early Japanese or about their literary techniques and accomplishments. We must distinguish between the songs themselves and the contexts into which they have been thrust by the later compilers and revisers, often in such a way that their meanings are drastically changed.

PRIMITIVE SONGS AND LATER CONTEXTS

There are two ways of studying the songs in Sir Philip Sidney's *Arcadia* —as separate and isolated lyrics or as poems related to a prose narrative context of character, action, and ideas. Now if we were to suppose that the *Arcadia* was in part fable and in part history; that it had been written down by compilers who had had the prose and songs recited to them; that few if any of the songs were by the compilers, although they may have been altered in the compiling; that some of the songs were, though anonymous, by Elizabethan poets and others by contemporaries of Lydgate, of Chaucer, and so on back to a misty anonymity like Cynewulf; and if the songs were presented as utterances by the characters in the *Arcadia*—then we would have a literary product something like the *Kojiki* or the *Nihongi*. And our study of the poems in this hypothetical *Arcadia* would have to proceed along two different lines. If we wished to understand them as their anonymous authors had meant them to be understood, we would need to take them from their prose contexts and study them apart. If we chose to study them as part of a new, unified literary work, we would need to study them in their relations to the fictional context. Earlier Japanese scholars failed to make such distinctions in studying the songs embedded in the prose of later contexts, and so led themselves and their readers into many confusing paths. Recent Japanese scholarship has made these distinctions; and for our purposes, we find it useful to differentiate by speaking of "contextual songs" when we talk of the meaning the songs acquire within the *Kojiki* or *Nihongi* or in the artificial sequences of the *kagura*; and of "poems of single expression" when we talk of the poems apart from their contexts.

As poems of single expression, the 500 or so extant primitive songs can be distinguished in the usual literary fashion on the basis of their subjects, their types (to call them genres would perhaps be misleading), and their modes. The subjects are limited in that they relate closely to the lives of the early Japanese. There are work songs, love songs, travel songs; songs of children at play, of victory, and of praise. The songs of praise may deal with such objects as swords; with such mitigations of the human condition as the strange mash liquor of the early Japanese (perhaps it was eaten, perhaps drunk, but the poetic praise shows that it had in any case the usual effect); with such superior beings as heroes, clan leaders, and divinities; and with such less immediate subjects as one's native land. A representative song of praise is this charmingly plaintive one from the "Songs for the Eastern Dances" (*Azumaasobiuta,* No. 8).*

Ōhire ya	O Great Hire
Ohire no yama wa	And Little Hire Mountain, too!
Ya	*Ya!*
Yorite koso	When you come close by,
Yorite koso	When you come close by,
Yama wa yora nare	How splendid are these mountains—
Ya	*Ya!*
Tōme wa aredo.	Though not much to look at from afar.

We like our hills, even if nobody else does—so goes the burden of this song of the land-praising variety. It also illustrates some of the qualities of early song with its repetitions and use of interjections by the performers. To render such exclamatory "ya's" and "hare's" and "aiso's" as "hey's" and "ding-a-ding's" or "nonny's" would hardly suggest their timbre or fit with twentieth-century styles of translation.

This song, probably a provincial song brought up to the capital, seems always to have existed as a single expression, but another song of praise, this time of the mash liquor, will show how such a song might with a little alteration become a contextual song (*Kojiki,* No. 49).

Susukori ga	Susukori brewed
Kamishi miki ni	This august heavy liquor,
Ware einikeri	And oh, how drunk I am!
Kotonagushi	On the evil-chasing,
Egushi ni	Laugh-giving liquor—
Ware einikeri.	And oh, how drunk I am!

It was not difficult to adapt such a song, composed as it were in some clan mead-hall, without alteration into the *Kojiki* Section CXI, although since it is there the Emperor Ōjin who imbibes, in context our rendering probably ought to follow older styles of translation and so read that he was augustly intoxicated rather than drunk. The flavor of the poem in context can be gained from Basil Hall Chamberlain's translation of the paragraph that follows. "On his walking out singing thus, he hit with his august staff a large stone in the middle of the Ōsaka road, upon which the stone ran away. So the proverb says: 'Hard stones get out of the drunkard's way.'"

Since, as Dr. Johnson said, kings and commoners feel the effects of wine

---

* Citations of songs in this chapter specify the work or group in which the song has been preserved and the number assigned it in Tsuchihashi and Konishi, *Kodai Kayōshū.*

alike, a drinking song might be taken into the manifold augustness of the *Kojiki* without doing serious violence to its original meaning. The problem of the original conception of the poem becomes more acute, however, when the poem and its new context are not naturally related, and when the songs are so short or so neutral in subject that the original meaning can only be surmised. Such a situation arises in Section XC of the *Kojiki* in which, after the death of Prince Yamatotakeru, his wives and children create a terrible stir in their mourning. He turns into a bird, and they endure great pain as they chase him, or it, through the fields and along the seashore, although not so much pain that they are unable to sing several songs that thereafter became, we are told, traditional at imperial funerals. On other occasions in the *Kojiki* and *Nihongi,* doughty heroes facing each other at swordpoint sing similarly improbable songs that would surely have been mortal to the singer had his foe's hand not been restrained by the operatic desire to retaliate with a song of his own. If the poems sung at Prince Yamatotakeru's demise were really laments or dirges, we might feel that they had been composed along with the prose narrative or had been all along identified with the unhappy prince, but as matters stand the songs were obviously composed at some prior date for other purposes. What those other purposes were is not easy to say, but some idea of the complications one faces in dealing with the *Kojiki* can be gained by comparing different interpretations of this song (No. 34).

The poem may be translated in this fashion as a contextual poem.

Nazuki no	Among the rice stalks,
Ta no inagara ni	Among the rice stalks of the fields
Inagara ni	Lying side by side,
Haimotōrō	They twine and crawl about—
Tokorozura.	The creeping vines.

The compilers treated this poem allegorically: the vines are the mourners who are distractedly crawling about the fields near Prince Yamatotakeru's barrow. It was clearly necessary to put some sort of construction upon the poem, since there is no very convincing relation between the poem as single expression and its context.

The problem of what the poem really means is another matter. No reputable Japanese scholar has considered this to be a piece of pure description by an observing poet, for the very good reason that as such it would have no tone and nothing approaching theme. One interpretation argues that the tonelessness and meaninglessness of the poem, read much as we have translated it for the context of the *Kojiki*, show that it was a children's play song. Certainly it is possible to imagine the song as accompaniment for some game involving action or a kind of hide-and-seek.

But since, as usual, there are no pronouns in the Japanese text, it is quite easy to read the song differently. It has been argued that it is a love song allegorizing the exertions the man must go through in order to visit secretly the girl he loves.

> Through the rice stalks,
> Through the rice stalks of the fields
> Lying side by side,
> I twine and crawl to you
> Like the creeping vine.

Still another interpretation holds that the poem makes best sense when read as a song of field laborers who must weed out vines from the rice before harvesting. This reading is based in part upon dissatisfaction with other interpretations and in part upon different readings of some of the words in the text.

> Through the rice stalks,
> Through the rice stalks of the field
> In which we slave,
> They twine and crawl about,
> The hateful vines.

The differing interpretations show how the fictional context of a later age might distort the nature and meaning of the primitive originals introduced into the prose text; and also, even though we know of the distortion, how difficult it is to decide what the primitive original really meant. The difficulty is not primarily a linguistic one, despite the alternative readings, but rather one that arises from the very nature of primitive Japanese song. Song after song seems simply to declare such a fact as that the vines grow among the rice stalks. The tonal and thematic values are therefore less inherent in the songs themselves than in the situation or occasion of recitation—children at play, men at work, or people in love. Only by discovering—or postulating— the occasion and the speaker of such songs can we gain any notion of the underlying attitude and idea which must shape our reading of them.

Having dwelt this long on what cannot be known, we must add what can be said with confidence and what may be conservatively surmised about the poems. To begin with, it is clear that the prose contexts may distort the meaning of the song or at least give it a new, fictional occasion and a new speaker. One can also proceed comparatively and rule out certain interpretations by modern scholars when they seem to conflict with what can be learned of poetic practice from reading other less quizzical poems. So for example, we would tend to reject the interpretation of the poem about the vines as a love song on nearly the same grounds that the contextual reading must be rejected. This interpretation proceeds, as it were, from without, by pressing upon the song a love allegory that seems to us to require the sophistication of a later period. Surely it is a counsel of desperation to classify as love allegories those poems that cannot be interpreted otherwise. To read the song as a children's or a laborer's song is at least to accept the images for what they are, without suggesting such later allegorical treatments that are the product of a more sophisticated mind. We cannot choose with certainty between the other two alternatives, and they must remain only more likely hypotheses. Unsatisfactory as such an ambiguous solution must be, it has the comfort of a certain degree of historical sobriety. And there is also some comfort in the fact that not only primitive and not only Japanese poems admit of more than one reading. Moreover, short songs such as this one are the hardest to understand, since they are the most closely tied to a situation outside the poem, the most a part of the occasion of their singing. A reader of the Greek Anthology often encounters the same difficulty, for to take away the context of such a famous poem as "Stranger, go tell the Lacedaemonians that we lie here obedient to their commands" is to shear away its meaning. And so with the shorter primitive Japanese songs.

Longer songs not only reveal an internal context and hint the identity of the speaker, but also are often extended enough to let us judge something of their relative age from the context in which they appear. In the case of any surviving poem, the date of its being written down is of course the latest possible date of composition, but it is often possible to push back the dating of the primitive songs, if never to arrive at a specific date. Songs in such definite forms as tanka, sedōka, *bussokusekika* (5, 7, 5, 7, 7, 7), or regular chōka are clearly of later date and are better called poems than songs (although they may be revisions of earlier songs), if by poems we may mean products of the conventions of a literate and literary-minded age, whether or not they were written to be sung. Songs in consistent fives and sevens but in no regular form may be regarded as slightly earlier in date; and perhaps songs that are irregular in both form and prosody date from an even earlier age. The general rule is that irregularity denotes antiquity, and regularity either revision or later composition. But the general rule should not be rigorously applied to the specific case, since primitive songs may still be composed after more sophisticated poems have appeared, and since the process of development could only have been intermittent as far as particular composers are concerned, even while it was steady in the tradition as a whole.

Subject matter, sophistication of attitude, and complexity of literary treatment would be better criteria for judging the relative age of a song if they were not so open to freewheeling impressionism. However, there does seem to be one sophisticated literary technique that tells us something about the age of the song as it survives. (It may of course have existed in earlier versions.) This technique is one of increasingly complex forms of parallelism. The simplest form of parallelism is repetition (A-A). True parallelism in contiguous lines (A-A′) is more complex. And interweavings of alternating parallelism (A-B, A′-B′, etc.) are so much more complex that they suggest a great advance in literary technique. Repetition and contiguous parallelism are features of early Chinese as well as early Japanese literature, but it is difficult to imagine that alternating parallelism, which took about ten centuries to develop in China, could have been devised in a period only a fraction of that time in Japan. In short, it seems most likely that when we find alternating parallelism in an early song, it is a symptom of borrowing from Chinese poetry. But the borrowing may be at different removes—either direct by a Japanese who read Chinese, imitative by a person who did not read but had heard Japanese songs and poems recited which used the technique, or revisional by a person who chose to bring up to date the techniques of the song as he inherited it.

The advance in technique can be illustrated by three poems taken from three different kinds of contexts, the *kagura*, the *Man'yōshū*, and the *Nihongi*. (As it happens the three songs are progressively more advanced in technique, and later in age, whereas the dates of the collections in which they are found are progressively older—a fact that shows the care necessary in dealing with this earliest Japanese literature.) The first is part of *kosaibari*, one of the units of a *kagura*, and the unit that is generally agreed by scholars to preserve the oldest poems in the *kagura*. Its technique is that of simple repetition with incrementation (*Kagura*, No. 47).

Ame naru *hibari*	*You skylark* in the heavens,
Yoriko ya *hibari*	*O skylark*, fly down here;
Tomikusa	*Rich grasses*,
Tomikusa mochite.	*Rich grasses* bear to me.

The context of the *kagura* shows this to be a plea for blessings from above, although it may originally have been a children's song or at any rate one of some other kind not connected with religious ceremonial.

The second song is the famous first poem in the *Man'yōshū*, one which the Emperor Yūryaku (?418–?479) is said to have addressed to a young maid he chanced upon, was attracted by, and wished to take as a wife. Since neither emperor nor maid would have remembered seventeen lines of oral address, this context is obviously as fictional as the others we have discussed. The song is really one in which a chief or lord of the Yamato clan is imagined to be addressing a girl he finds particularly attractive.

Ko mo yo	With a basket,
Miko mochi	A pretty basket,

Fugushi mo yo	With a trowel,
Mifugushi mochi	A pretty trowel in your hand,
Kono oka ni	O young maid gathering
Na tsumasu ko	Greens on this hill,
Ie kikana	Tell me your home,
Na norasane	Please give me your name.
Sora mitsu	With power over
Yamato no kuni wa	This country of Yamato, a land
Oshinabete	Broad as heaven,
Ware koso ore	I am a chief known to all;
Shikinabete	Famous everywhere,
Ware koso mase	My power is known to all.
Ware ni koso wa	And so to no one else,
Norame	Yes, to me alone,
Ie o mo na o mo.	Tell of your home and your name.

This justly admired poem is not unlike many of the primitive songs in its combination of certain earlier elements with certain later ones. By themselves, the lack of a fixed syllabic prosody and the absence of a regular form would suggest an early date. But the alternating parallelism shows that the song cannot be very early, at least in its present form. Some resolution of this dilemma can be gained by a look at the first four lines of the Japanese. We do find alternating parallelism, but of the simplest kind—it closely resembles alternating repetition with slight incrementation. The song is clearly later than the preceding one from the *kagura*, but the new technique is used with something less than consummate ease.

A still later song is another one fictionally attributed to Emperor Yūryaku. In Section XIV of the *Nihongi* (No. 77), he is said to have had "an outburst of feeling" about the beauty of the scenery of Hatsuse; whereupon he "made a song." What we really have is a work of the type of the land-praising poem, and its form is that of a little chōka, with the last line repeated as something of a refrain.

Komoriku no	O the mountains
Hatsuse no yama wa	Of Hatsuse the hidden land,
Idetachi no	The lovely mountains
Yoroshiki yama	That face me when I leave my house,
Washiride no	The lovely mountains
Yoroshiki yama no	That face me when I hasten forth—
Komoriku no	O the mountains
Hatsuse no yama wa	Of Hatsuse the hidden land,
Aya ni uraguwashi	How beautiful they are!
Aya ni uraguwashi.	How beautiful they are!

The parallelism here seems at first glance to show little advance over that in the preceding poem, since much of it involves repetition; but the skillful return in the last four lines, making them quietly parallel to the opening lines, shows that the author of this song felt more at ease in using the technique. The almost perfectly realized chōka form is another sign of the song's later date. It is of course impossible to say whether the present text represents an original composition or a revision of an older song, but this is a question we need not bother to answer. The important thing is that new techniques are being used more and more skillfully as the New Learning from China, to borrow a phrase from historians of the European Renaissance, is gradually spread through the Court and across the land. It would not be long after such a poem as this appears that a poem would be composed by an identifiable poet under his own name; and it would not be long before the imaginary emperors with imaginary motives would no longer be said, in fictional contexts, to compose songs. Each of the three songs we have examined is given such a context, and in each case the context is misleading. The age had not yet arrived when literary merit would be the chief basis for a poem's survival. A primitive song gained its "immortality" by being attributed to an exalted person like an emperor or by being taken over into legend.

Such primarily literary contexts were not the only kind to determine the practice of primitive Japanese song. The melodies to which the songs were sung no doubt affected the author's attitude toward his art, his practice of composition, and most certainly the way in which his song was presented. Little is known about the melodies themselves or even the instruments that produced them, but the names of some of the later tunes at least survive. The *Kojiki* frequently comments after it has quoted a song: "This is a floating song" or "This is a rustic lifting song." Scholars are agreed that some of these comments refer to types of melodies or ways of singing, and evidently there were a number of such recognized types for which words might be composed. (Other designations referred to the subjects of the songs or particular groups of people with whom they were associated.) Apparently a given song would be identified with a specific melody of a given type only if the identification had been made because of repeated recitation on such an occasion as performance of the Shinto liturgy. The tendency to identify a certain set of words with one melody seems to have been progressive, and for the older songs that survived popularly, to have been complete by the end of the eighth century. By that time some songs, like the *saibara,* were looked upon as one type because they were sung to Chinese melodies, and others, like the *ōuta,* were another type sung at court to Japanese tunes.

In earlier times, the melodies no doubt had the effect, discernible in our popular songs today, of giving an appearance of regularity to irregular verses whose sounds might be lengthened or run together in singing. The increasing regularity of Japanese verse is therefore probably not due to the fitting of words to a given melody, but to a more properly literary sensibility that makes increasing headway after the introduction of reading and writing. This fact in no way denies the considerable influence the melodic contexts would have upon composition. For although new melodies were no doubt sometimes composed for new words, or old melodies adapted, it seems more likely that a new song would be composed on the analogy of an old one, and would often be sung to the same tune. The closer the analogy was, the more similar in length and verse form the new song would be to the old. In an atmosphere of imitation and performance, originality and complexity were hardly the effects sought—no doubt then even as now many a voice was heard proclaiming the virtues of "the good old songs."

Apparently not all the songs were fitted to melodies. Some seem to have been recited rhythmically in a chanting delivery, perhaps to the accompaniment of a beat and to those exclamatory interjections like *ya, aiso,* and *hare,* which still mark recitation and song in the Japanese theater or private recitation. Such rhythmical chanting doubtless followed certain patterns which, like the melodic contexts, must have made memorizing and performing an easier task for the reciter or chorus, especially in the case of irregular songs. The early rhythmic and melodic contexts have of course disappeared, a fact which points to one of the significant differences between them and the fictional prose contexts into which songs were put in the *Kojiki* and *Nihongi.* These chronicles belong to the later age of writing, whereas in earlier times "publication" took the form of singing or chanting before an audience—the true ambience of primitive Japanese song, although one that in any given instance cannot be rediscovered in exact detail. Song was clearly a part of the lives of the early Japanese in a rather different way than written poetry was in later ages. The difference involves the relations between the singer or reciter and his audience; it is basically a matter of esthetic distance.

THE PLACE OF SONG IN EARLY JAPANESE LIFE

Only in the film, in the opera, and in such other conventional contexts as the Japanese chronicles, does one burst into song instead of saying what is on one's mind. And as Molière's bourgeois gentleman testifies, it requires a certain degree of sophistication even to know that one speaks in prose. Without such contexts for song, one does not sing before others—no matter how good the tune or how stirring the words—unless there is a socially sanctioned occasion, a social convention, as opposed to an artistic one. Such an occasion may of course vary widely in formality—from the precariously uncertain singing after rounds of drinks to the sober rendition of a national anthem. On such occasions, the role played by the song depends upon who is singing to whom. Or to speak in artistic terms, we must distinguish between the singer or reciter and his audience. By making such distinctions, it is possible to discuss the social occasions of song, differing kinds of esthetic distance, and the purposes of song—and so prepare the way for analysis of the literary techniques employed.

It is not difficult to see four relationships between the reciter (or singer) and his audience in primitive Japanese society. The first of these embraces those songs which were sung together by groups of people. On such occasions, the reciter and the audience were the same, as on such occasions today when alumni gather to sing the old college songs, or when the spectators rise to their feet before a football game to sing the national anthem. There is relatively little esthetic distance on such occasions, and the effect of this kind of singing is to assert the fellowship of the group, to affirm its social identity and common interests. In a second kind of singing in groups, one still very dear to the Japanese, members of the audience become the reciter in turn, and, when finished, become once again a part of the audience, allowing someone else to take his turn. This kind of recitation has a somewhat greater esthetic distance than group singing, because the reciter of the moment is identifiably separate from the group, his audience. At the same time, singing by turns retains much of the social character of group singing, and its purpose is similar. By taking his turn, each member makes his contribution to the group, which may in turn show its recognition or affirmation of his contribution by beating time or applauding. Even if he has sung lamely, forgetting words or losing pitch, he has done his part and proved his right to belong to the group.

The third kind of reciter-audience relationship is one in which the reciter addresses an individual, and this type is capable of widely varying esthetic distances depending upon the identity of the audience and the nature of the occasion. We doubt that the primitive Japanese love songs which survive were often sung outside the door of the beloved or in face-to-face wooing. But there do appear to have been social formulas in lieu of betrothal or marriage ceremonies at which a kind of dialogue was recited. The burden of such an exchange would perhaps be a woman's asking, "Why are you here?" The man would reply, in effect, "Because I wish to make you mine." So the ritual would have been performed and, the parents or society willing, the couple would be man and wife. It is difficult to judge the esthetic distance of such an exchange without knowing whether the pair were alone or observed by witnesses. Songs might also be addressed by an individual to someone of importance, such as the clan leader. These songs were no doubt performed by a reciter who in effect represented the other followers, standing by more as witnesses than as an audience in the strict sense. The purpose of such a song would be to affirm the fact of leadership and fealty. And finally, songs that were essentially prayers might be addressed by a speaker to an individual deity. (The Shinto deities were thought to "come down" to favorite places if satisfactorily invoked.) The esthetic distance of such performances might also vary between the private prayer of an individual and the representational function of the shaman or priest. In each of these instances, the seemingly close esthetic distance of an individual's address to another individual is greatly increased or conventionalized by the fact that the performance itself is a ritual act.

The fourth, and in many ways the most interesting, relation between reciter and audience is the one that existed when a professional performer or reciter entertained a group audience separate from him in social rank or function. Here the separation between reciter and audience is complete and the esthetic distance is at its greatest. This relationship has great importance for later literary developments and could lead to a higher degree of artistic competence in the creation of songs.

There seem to have been at least two kinds of such professional performers in early Japan: the *kataribe* or reciters, who were organized into guilds and were charged with the duty of memorizing the genealogies, accomplishments, and stories of the clan; and the *wazaogi*, mummers or performers, whose chief function was entertainment pure and simple. (There were also specialists in Shinto ritual, such as the Nakatomi and Imibe sacerdotalists, who recited at religious ceremonies.) The *kataribe* inherited their clan office by birth, and in a real sense were the historians of the tribe. With the introduction of writing, their *raison d'être* was gone, and they gradually disappeared as a class, although not until after they had created and transmitted a body of clan legends and techniques for recitation. They lasted for some time into the age of literacy, and tradition holds that the *Kojiki* was taken down from the recitations of one of the survivors of such a guild. Given the synthetic form of the *Kojiki*, we can see that the *kataribe* probably felt as free to adapt songs to old stories as the compilers did. It would therefore require considerable temerity to guess how long a process lies behind one of the episodes or how many layers of accretion it represents. The fact that within an episode there may be songs of various ages shows how gradual the process most likely was.

The *wazaogi*, or mummers as we shall refer to them, take us from clan history, albeit often mythical history embellished with fiction and song, to artistic performance with the esthetic end of entertainment. It appears that the mummers were often called upon to perform songs like those of the *kataribe*, but the effect would be different, since their primary aim seems not to have been recording or repetition but entertainment. Their performances made up a kind of quasi-drama involving miming, dancing, and dialogue or narration. Some of their songs were complex enough to require two or more roles and sometimes to require an actor to shift his role in acting, now to play the part of a crab, perhaps, and now a human being.

Since the primitive songs were so closely related to social occasions, another important factor in establishing differing degrees of esthetic distance was the relation of a particular song to the occasion of its performance. On the one hand, an effort seems to have been made by the *kataribe* to set their songs off from the specific occasion, both by formulas at the end of a passage— sometimes a few verses testifying to the traditional nature of the materials —and by a refusal to refer to anything happening at a given gathering. The reciters might revise their materials ahead of time to improve them, but they would not alter them to fit the occasion of the performance. The mummers, on the other hand, seem to have delighted themselves and their audiences by beginning their acts with lines that were patterned but impromptu refer- ences to people present, the location of the performance, or even the food that had been eaten. This practice is far from dead, even in the West, as visitors to country fairs or ex-soldiers formerly entertained by traveling performers will recall. Almost invariably, such performances begin with local references and then proceed to the usual rehearsed entertainment. This kind of relation to the occasion of performance is perhaps more native to Japanese poetic practice, however, than to most Western traditions. The informality, the partial break- ing of the esthetic illusion is an intimate part of the practice of informal love poetry and similar exchanges in later periods.

Such different methods of recitation, such differing esthetic distances, lend a certain primitive variety of a quasi-literary nature to primitive Japanese song. For one thing, a given social gathering might progress through different stages of recitation. We might imagine, for example, a clan gathering begin- ning in the daytime, when the *kataribe* would recite the wonders of the clan and its leader. Then food and mash liquor would be passed around, and with the general relaxation there would be group singing, different members of the audience would take part in song, and finally the professional enter- tainers would enter and put on their act. There is no reason to suppose that such an order should be inviolable, but the analogy of the *kagura* ritual to some such pattern makes the secular pattern completely credible. The *kagura* began with a series of songs of a rather elevated nature to bring down the god (*torimono*). This section was followed by songs to put the deity into a happy mood (*ōsaibari*), and then in turn by songs in which god and man alike could have their fun (*kosaibari*).

Such variety is almost wholly the result of tone and esthetic distance, both tied to the occasion of performance. The structures and subjects are limited— the same materials, even the same song might be used for such different pur- poses, often suffering little revision or none at all. A particular song might be sung by a group or by a member of a group to his fellows; it might be incorporated contextually by the *kataribe* into clan legends; it might be pan- tomimed by performers; it might be treated metaphorically as a part of a *kagura*. No one song would go through so many transmigrations, perhaps, and different techniques were felt to be more or less suitable for different types of song or different occasions; but one would be hard pressed to discover materials that belong to only one type of song. With primitive Japanese song, as with much of the poetry of later ages, no small part of the interest of a song was felt to lie in its particular connection with the occasion of its performance. Perhaps this may be considered a kind of decorum of performance, to distinguish it from Western notions of the propriety of subject matter. But such a decorum did not prevent the early Japanese from appreciating, for example, a very private-seeming love song from the lips of a man who was known by his group to be happily married to two women. The performance had its decorum, but it did not destroy esthetic illusion of this kind; and all in all, the occasions of performance often seem to have more variety than the songs themselves and their materials.

The literary techniques of the songs seem to have become progressively more complex as the early Japanese matured esthetically and as the New Learning from China was gradually adapted to native verse. This is to say, the songs became more interesting, although they still retained their oral nature, their relation to social occasion, and their circumscribed materials. Lacking any real historical information, we cannot follow the process of growth in any detail; but the songs that are the most primitive in technique are also known to be the oldest on other grounds, and the latest songs are often almost indistinguishable from the contemporary poetry being composed at court. Such development does not mean that once new techniques were introduced the old ones ceased to be used: we know that some of the primitive songs were composed at a very late date, presumably in the provinces, and serve almost as atavistic reminders of what once had been.

The lack of detailed, reliable historical information rules out all but a few assured conclusions, although these are of considerable importance. Most of the songs that survive come to us anonymously or with an attributed authorship that may be rejected. Although there are some songs that are identified with a clan hero or with a specific clan, the majority cannot be attributed to a special social group or to a specific region of the country. This is a generalization; it is open to amplification and exception. Early Japan was made up of a number of ethnically related clans or peoples (in addition to certain others that had been on the islands when these tribes arrived, probably from the Korean peninsula), among which there was a struggle for power. The Yamato people, originally from Kyushu but identified in name with the area in which it settled in central Japan, gradually overcame the others, including their most powerful rivals, the Izumo people in northwestern Honshu. This political development has as its cultural parallel the literary absorption by the Yamato people of the myths of the other tribes, myths which were either incorporated into its own mythology, or were rejected and so passed into oblivion, or were absorbed into other contexts. The process of absorption was nearly complete: only a few of the Izumo myths and some songs like those of the Kume clan stand out separately from the others. Along with such exceptions there are also some eastern songs, the "Songs for the Eastern Dances" (*Azumaasobiuta*), that a later, more sophisticated Court enjoyed preserving with something of the zeal of the antiquarian, the anthropologist, and the primitivist. But only thirteen of these have survived, and they affect our conception of primitive Japanese song but little. On the whole, the anonymous and unlocalized character of this early oral literature remains inviolate. Perhaps this character alone goes far toward justifying our calling the songs primitive.

There are other reasons. The limited technical range of this literature and its limited artistic outlook are the truly deciding factors. As we have seen, because the creations of this tribal world were oral, and because they were for the most part short lyrics, they could be easily passed about and adapted to many different purposes and sung on various occasions calling for song. The borderline between social and religious occasions appears to have been as shifting as the lyric materials were neutral in use, so that what began as ritual might soon end as entertainment. Once songs had been made for mumming and similar performances, the conception had emerged of song and other arts as arts capable of appealing to a desire for entertainment, and the Japanese had become sufficiently sophisticated to treat their songs as a separate esthetic phenomenon. No one can say how or when this important step toward civilization was made, but it is in a way reflected by the contextual use of earlier songs, since this practice shows how earlier songs used for ritual occasions were remade fictionally into new entities. The change in attitude and practice is basically one from song to poetry. It was hastened, completed, and given new direction when literacy made the act of composition a literary one and when the discovery of Chinese poetry gradually unfolded a new world to the Japanese. The space between the beginnings and the end of this development is *terra incognita,* but if it is a world we cannot revisit, it is one from which these 500 or so songs survive. They survive to tell us a good deal more than such other mysterious monuments of the past as Stonehenge, although a good deal less than the Acropolis. And in what survives we have a body of songs which—having now been distinguished from historical, contextual, and social complications—may be studied in a literary fashion for their techniques and their accomplishment.

COMPOSITION AND TECHNIQUE

As a new generation of Japanese scholars has been freed from a nationalistic pressure to treat the chronicles as sacred books and to accept their contexts literally, the poems and songs embedded in these narratives have, for the most part, been shown to be older works of single expression. Not infrequently the old confusion has yielded to new problems. The song is a song, but its words seem to mean, as Humpty-Dumpty said to Alice, what one chooses them to mean, neither more nor less. That is, all the songs are, or seem to be, social in nature and tied to a particular occasion; and yet we are frequently unable to say what the particular occasion may have been. The songs themselves often have nothing in them to tell us whether they are happy or sad, simple statements or metaphorical comparisons. We may know the words and recognize individual poetic techniques and yet have no idea of the tone and meaning intended by the unknown authors.

While such difficulties stem basically from insufficient information about a remote, prehistoric past, they are also the result of the methods of composition and the techniques of primitive Japanese song. The rather limited materials of these early songs are combined in many ways for widely varying social and occasional contexts, and can convey any tone or meaning within the range of a particular song. Perhaps this is true because the poetic materials are drawn from the external world in which the composers of the early songs found themselves; for given a mountain or a river as an objective rather than a subjective or symbolic thing, it may provoke happiness or sadness in the speaker, depending upon the occasion of the song. Like the materials employed, the subjects treated are those of the lives, one might say the external lives, of the early Japanese—war, drinking, food, objects, scenery, work, play, and love. The relation between the singer and his materials remains direct and unreflecting, regardless of the simplicity or complexity of the techniques, in which alone some kind of historical development is discernible. Perhaps the clearest way of stating these matters is to say that the early songs show a simple, naïve, and unreflecting attitude toward the world of experience which was made into song. Any extended discussion of these songs must, therefore, concern itself more with the techniques they employ than with the relatively unvaried materials from which they are made.

The songs that we take to be the most primitive are so irregular in form that they defy classification, and we can only generalize to the extent of characterizing them as short exclamations or, sometimes, incantations and statements; the irregular length of these songs and the lack of fixed prosody are symptoms either of an absence of a prosodic sense or of a close tie to certain melodies in which they might acquire regularity through extension or elision of sounds. Such amorphousness often makes division into verse or line units a difficult matter, but there appear to have been from earliest times two possible groupings of lines: an even number of lines of nearly equal length, or alternations of an odd number of longer and shorter lines. The shorter lines might be made up of as few as three syllables and the longer of as many as ten. Japanese scholars conventionally say that the corpus of early song also includes such regular forms as the tanka, the sedōka, the *ḳatauta* (or "half poem," three lines of 5, 7, and 7 syllables), and the chōka; and they often treat the irregular songs as variants of these. But this seems unhistorical. The regular forms do appear in the chronicles, but they either are of later composition or are revisions of earlier songs: they represent a transition from song to poetry. Thus, for example, the first poem in both the *Kojiḳi* and the *Nihongi*:

Yakumo tatsu	I build a covering fence
Izumo yaegaki	Around my home in Izumo,
Tsumagomi ni	Land of covering clouds,
Yaegaki tsukuru	A covering fence around my wife,
Sono yaegaki o.	And, oh, that covering fence!

The song is certainly primitive enough in mode and content, but its prosodic regularity and form betray the hand of a later writer reshaping older materials and working within an established tradition of poetic form—as even the older Japanese commentators suspected.

The professional reciters gradually developed a useful native prosody, partly from practice and partly from what they learned at the Japanese court. The Court was increasingly embellished by the New Learning from China, which taught the Japanese important rhetorical techniques and methods for organizing poems into structures that could express the kinds of experience the reciters knew. But the development was gradual, so that many, perhaps most, of the songs fall between the complete formlessness of the earliest works and the realized forms of a literary-minded Court. As a result, it seems wisest to us to ignore the patently later poems, to treat the songs as single expression outside their fabricated contexts, and to group them by type rather than to attempt to impose upon them forms that had never occurred to their original composers. One such type is the monologue, the statement of a single speaker or of a single group of speakers. Another is the dialogue, in which two speakers are represented in some kind of verbal exchange. There are also narrative songs in which the monologuist develops a sequence, and some quasi-dramatic songs in which narrative passages may be added to dialogue or monologue, sometimes employing a kind of choral address to the speaker or speakers of the dialogue. These more complex types may perhaps be better called sequences rather than truly narrative or dramatic units, although the different parts of the song make up one whole.

The monologue varies considerably in length and complexity, as poems already quoted have shown. The same variety is true of the dialogues, which at their simplest may consist of such a brief question and answer as this exchange (*Kojiḳi,* Nos. 17–18):

THE GIRL

Ametsutsu	Why stare at me
Chidori mashitoto	With your bright, wide-open eyes
Nado sakeru tome.	Like a swallow, a plover, a finch?

THE MAN

Otome ni	I stare at you
Tada ni awan to	With bright, wide-open eyes
Wa ga sakeru tome.	To show how much I want you, girl.

It appears that this particular exchange is a form of dialogue belonging to a courtship ritual in early Japan. Either the man or the woman might initiate such a ceremony, no doubt after some preliminary understanding had been reached, and in cases like this one the girl's final acceptance of the suit would depend in part upon the wit of the reply. In the context of the *Kojiki*, the reply is spoken by the legendary first Emperor Jimmu to a woman he finds particularly attractive, and a sentence in prose comes between the question and the answer. In this context, then, there are really two poems, each a variant on the *katauta* (here 4, 7, 7). But the two halves are obviously part of one whole—in form, in meaning, and in the repeated "sakeru tome," "bright, wide-open eyes." Moreover, they make up the sedōka form imposed on these earlier materials by some later revisionist. *Katauta,* "half poems," were thought to be incomplete, and we can see from such a famous exchange as that assigned to Prince Yamatotakeru and the old fire-lighter in the *Kojiki* (Section LXXXVI) that the two halves of a sedōka were often used for dialogue.

The dialogue form was capable of very much more interesting developments. One of the most pleasing of all the early songs develops dialogue with other elements in a complex way (*Kojiki*, No. 42).

The Maid on the Road to Kohata
THE MAN

| Kono kani ya | Say, you crab, |
| Izuku no kani | What land is it that you come from? |

THE CRAB

| Momozutau | A crab from Tsunuga, |
| Tsunuga no kani | Many a day's journey away. |

THE MAN

| Yoko sarau | Scuttling along, |
| Izuku ni itaru | What land are you bound for? |

THE CRAB

Ichijishima	Reaching Ichiji Isle,
Mishima ni toki	Making my way to the Isle of Mi,
Miodori no	Plunging and rising
Kazuki ikizuki	Like a waterfowl gasping for breath,
Shinadayū	I struggled along
Sasanamiji o	Up the steep Sasanami Road—

THE MAN

Sukusuku to	Well, as for me,
Wa ga imaseba ya	I shot up that slope with ease;
Kohata no	And on the road
Michi ni	To Kohata,
Awashishi otome	The lovely maid I came upon—
Ushirode wa	Oh, her back rose
Odate ro ka mo	Straight as a well-made shield,
Hanami wa	And her teeth shone
Shii hishi nasu	White as meat of acorns, chestnuts.
Ichihii no	In Ichihii,
Wanisa no ni o	Taking the earth of Wani Hill,
Hatsuni wa	Since she found
Hada akarakemi	The upper earth too red
Shiwani wa	And because
Niguroki yue	The lower earth was far too black,
Mitsuguri no	Of the three layers
Sono naka tsu ni o	She baked the middle earth,
Kabu tsuku	Not with a head-searing
Mahi ni wa atezu	But with a careful flame she fired
Mayogaki	The paint for her brows
Ko ni kakitare	And painted them thick and curving,
Awashishi omina	The lovely maid I came upon.
Ka mo ga to	How I wanted her,
Wa ga mishi kora	The beautiful maid I saw—
Kaku mo ga to	Oh, I wanted her,
A ga mishi ko ni	The lovely maid I saw.
Utatake dani	But I had never dreamed
Mukaioru ka mo	We would now be face to face
Isoioru ka mo.	And together side by side.

In its humorous contrast between the struggles of the awkward crab to make his way and the rapid strides of the young man, the song represents an advance in skill with dialogue that is reflected otherwise in the rhetorical complexity of the song. This song was no doubt performed by mummers who pantomimed or danced in imitation of the scuttling of the crab and the rapid, easy steps of the young man. The crab disappears shortly and is replaced, we may imagine, by another performer playing the part of the woman and pantomiming her actions as the young man narrates them. In stage terms, we have here three roles and two parts.

The fourth song type is the quasi-dramatic sequence, a type which raises the most formidable problems of interpretation and division. The sequences deal with the activities of various deities and clan heroes and seem to have been developed for performance by the reciters—probably for such occasions as clan ceremonies. In essence, the sequences are not unlike the combinations of prose and verse which make up the texts of the *Kojiki* and the *Nihongi*. The difference is that the prose passages are contexts that artistically and historically distort the songs, while the narrative passages of the sequences make up an integral part of the artistic whole. Within the song sequences we find a kind of observer-narrator who sketches in events or addresses the main characters, who speak to each other in passages of dialogue. The problems begin when one tries to distinguish between the lines spoken by the narrator—almost a chorus—and those uttered by the main characters.

One variety of problem arises from the nature and the traditions of the language. In ancient Japanese, as in modern, the verbs are "impersonal"— they do not indicate the person or the number of the speaker, as those of the Indo-European languages usually do. And the verbs in primitive song are often not finite; infinitives and participles, or their Japanese equivalents, abound. The verbs would be less of a problem if the Japanese used the many pronouns with which their language is endowed, but the authors of the songs are very miserly with their linguistic riches. In later Japanese, honorific elements and skillfully used diction sometimes show that the speaker is addressing someone of great importance or else is himself an emperor or deity. For many centuries emperors have had their special honorific terms to refer to themselves, and we might use such a tradition to determine the speakers of these older songs, were it not for the fact that the use of special terms grew from misreading these very same old songs. The reciters used the special honorifics because they were talking about exalted beings, but later readers took the language to be that of the emperors themselves, and so as the cult of the emperor grew, the language of rulers and deities was shaped by what was wrongly imagined to be the practice of the past. In short, the confusion between narration and dialogue grew in large part out of the misapprehension of honorifics.

Another variety of problem in distinguishing between dialogue and narration grows, like many other problems, out of the confusion of the compilers of the chronicles as they attempted to combine the prose contexts and the earlier songs. Where today the logic and sense of a given series of lines seem to demand division into narrative and dialogue, the compilers attribute the whole to one of the speakers in the context or make divisions which seem to have little propriety. What is narrative usually becomes unlikely dialogue attributed to one of the characters in the prose narrative.

A final problem in making these divisions is presented by the reciters' formulas attesting to the authoritative nature of what they have recited. The usual form is:

Koto no	These are the words,
Katarigoto mo	The words forever sung,
Ko oba.	Yes, these.

Sometimes the reciter adds to this an identification of his clan and occupation. These formulas were certainly recited at performances, and up to a point they help to distinguish between the divisions of a sequence, to set off narration from dialogue. But they are not used with any consistency, and their presence or absence cannot be taken as infallible guides for divisions unless internal evidence supports them. Perhaps our concern with such matters is excessive and should not be allowed to clutter a discussion of literary techniques. But it is just such problems as these that lie in the path of a person who wishes to understand the workings of this early song; and comparison with the later aristocratic Nō, with the popular theater, and even with fictional dialogue shows that narrative elements persist through all Japanese drama, and that the line between narrative and dialogue is a shadowy one in prose as well. These are the problems, at any rate, and anyone who wishes to talk critically about the more complex songs must recognize them.

One of the most interesting of these quasi-dramatic sequences deals with the courtship of the coy Princess Nunakawa by the impulsive Deity Eight Thousand Spears (*Kojiki*, Nos. 2–3). We will here defy tradition and give what we believe to be the most coherent reading of the sequence.

The Wooing of Princess Nunakawa by the Deity Eight Thousand Spears

RECITER

Yachihoko no	The Divine August One,
Kami no mikoto wa	The Deity Eight Thousand Spears,
Yashimakuni	Through the Eight Isles
Tsuma makikanete	Could find no wife as pillow for his bed;
Tōdōshi	Yet having heard
Koshi no kuni ni	That in the distant land,
Sakashime o	In far-off Koshi

Ari to kikashite
  Kuwashime o
Ari to kikoshite
  Sayobai ni
Aritatashi
  Yobai ni
Arikayowase
  Tachi ga o mo
Imada tokazute
  Osui o mo
Imada tokaneba
  Otome no
Nasu ya itato o
  Osoburai
Wa ga tatasereba
  Hikozurai
Wa ga tatasereba—

There lives a clever girl,
  Yet having heard
There lives a lovely girl—
  To court her
He sets forth,
  To court her well.
He travels on, arriving at her house,
  And not even
Pausing to take off his sword,
  Nor even
Pausing to take off his head-scarf,
  He shoves, he tugs
Upon the sturdy wood-plank door
  To where she sleeps;
And as he stands and waits impatiently
  He pulls upon her door,
And as he stands and waits impatiently—

THE DEITY EIGHT THOUSAND SPEARS

  Aoyama ni
Nue wa nakinu
  Sano tsu tori
Kigishi wa toyomu
  Niwa tsu tori
  Kake wa naku
  Uretaku mo
Naku naru tori ka
  Kono tori mo
Uchiyamekosene.

"In the green hills
The midnight finches have begun to
  sing;
  The bird of the moor,
The pheasant now screams its cry;
  The bird of the yard,
  The cock now crows—
  What torment!
These cursed birds that call the dawn,
  These wretched birds—
Come, make them stop their noise!"

PRINCESS NUNAKAWA

  Yachihoko no
Kami no mikoto
  Nuekusa no
Me ni shi areba
  Wa ga kokoro
Urasu no tori zo
  Ima koso wa
Wadori ni arame

"Divine August One,
Deity Eight Thousand Spears,
  Since I am only
A maiden wavering as the grass
  And my heart
A bird scampering on the shore,
  I am right now
A bird you cannot tame,

Nochi wa	But before long
Nadori ni aran o	A bird completely yours—
Inochi wa	So do not destroy
Na shisetamai so.	Your life with overhasty love."

RECITER—TO THE DEITY EIGHT THOUSAND SPEARS

Aoyama ni	When in the green hills
Hi ga kakuraba	The sun has hidden itself away,
Nubatama no	Then with the night
Yo wa idenan	Black as beads of jet, come forth,
Asahi no	Come forth radiant,
Emisakaekite	Smiling like the morning sun,
Takuzuno no	To her whose arms
Shiroki tadamuki	Are white as a bleached fiber cord,
Awayuki no	Whose skin is soft
Wakayaru mune o	As flakes of newly fallen snow;
Sodataki	Then you may clasp,
Tadakimanagari	May clasp each other in your arms
Matamade	And pillow yourselves
Tamade sashimaki	Upon your precious, jewel-like arms,
Momonaga ni	And you may sleep
I wa nasan o	Your sleep with legs outstretched.
Aya ni	So do not be
Na koikikoshi	Too urgent with your love—
Yachihoko no	O Divine August One,
Kami no mikoto.	Deity Eight Thousand Spears!

As an integrated whole (from which we have dropped the reciters' formulas), the sequence holds together very well, although there are gaps that would horrify or bewilder a nineteenth-century English novelist. We are not told where the princess stands when she speaks, nor how she came to know the name of her suitor. But much of the quality of the whole comes from its typically Japanese economy and implication. The princess must be speaking through her door, since she has heard what the deity says and yet does not yield to him—till the next night. She cleverly picks up his imagery of birds, just as the concluding narrative sequence begins by referring to the green hills the deity has mentioned.

Some Japanese writers have speculated that this sequence is part of a larger body of stories about the Deity Eight Thousand Spears, since the *Kojiki* contains several other longish songs of this type dealing with his exploits and troubles. (His first wife did not like his carryings-on with Princess Nunakawa.) It would be very satisfying to critics and literary historians if these songs made up a kind of Japanese Ring-Cycle, and perhaps once they did, but too few have survived to give us any real basis for supposing what the cycle might have been like in its totality or whether it was at all integrated. Moreover, other, simpler sequences have survived, and it would be a mistake to assume that this song type is invariably the most complex. Some dialogue poems, like "The Maid on the Road to Kohata," are more highly developed and more interesting than many of the sequences. But rather than illustrate the types with more examples, we must examine the particular elements and techniques of which these types are composed.

Imagery is in its way as basic to most primitive Japanese songs as it is to the literary poetry of later ages. All the songs contain concrete images from nature or from the activities and objects of daily life. Many poems are composed entirely of such images and, as a glance at the poems already quoted shows, the images tend to be simple and homely in nature. Insofar as it is possible to judge today, there seem to have been few areas of the experience of the early Japanese that might not be drawn upon for imagery. The major exceptions are images of death, of sickness, and of other "unclean" things held in abhorrence by a people whose religious beliefs stressed ritual purity and freedom from various "pollutions." The *Iliad* might describe the agonies of a warrior whose blood and entrails fell from his wounds, but the early Japanese war songs contain only threats of future mayhem or harmless images of nature used metaphorically to represent acts of bloodshed and violence, as in the "War Song of the Men of Kume" (*Kojiki*, No. 11; *Nihongi*, No. 13—this text from the *Kojiki*).

Mitsumitsushi	In the millet field
Kume no kora ga	Of the augustly powerful
Awafu ni wa	Children of Kume,
Kamira hitomoto	Grows a single onion stalk—
Sone ga moto	That very stalk,
Sone me tsunagite	Roots and leaves together,
Uchite shi yaman.	We will destroy once and for all.

Even so shadowed a threat appears to have been popular enough for some later revisionist to give the song the regular form of a short chōka. (The version in the *Nihongi* has an extra short line but is otherwise regular.)

Apart from such few taboos, however, the range of imagery in the songs of the early Japanese appears to have been limited only to the extent that their experience—that is to say, their understanding of the world—was limited; and in many of these songs there are images that would have appalled later generations of more sensitive poets and readers. Along with such inelegant images as onions, radishes, and scuttling crabs, the authors of primitive songs had various devices for beautifying or heightening images. These are chiefly such decorative or intensifying prefixes as *ma* ("true"), *mi* ("beautiful"), and *tama* ("jeweled"). The decorative prefixes typically appear in the songs that are most complex in other technical ways and that treat more or less elevated subjects. Perhaps they were devised by the professional singers as a means of raising the tone of their songs above the level of common, popular songs. They pose a serious problem to the translator, because the modern Western tradition lacks any real equivalents in poetic style. Moreover, like some later techniques, they raise the question of whether or not they should be treated as images in their own right. Their use and something of their effect can be seen in such a poem as "In Longing for His Wife" (*Kojiki*, No. 90); we have rendered the prefix *ma* as "true" and *i* as "sacred."

Komoriku no	In the river
Hatsuse no kawa no	Of Hatsuse the hidden land
Kami tsu se ni	They tamp the sacred poles
Ikui o uchi	Within the upper shallow reaches;
Shimo tsu se ni	They tamp the true poles
Makui o uchi	Within the lower shallow reaches;
Ikui ni wa	They hang the mirror
Kagami o kake	Upon a pounded sacred pole;
Makui ni wa	They hang true jewels
Matama o kake	Upon a pounded true pole—
Matama nasu	Like the true jewels,
A ga mou imo	Is the girl I deeply love;
Kagami nasu	And like the mirror,
A ga mou tsuma	Is the wife I deeply love—
Ari to	If only someone
Iwaba koso yo	Could assure me she is there,
Ie ni mo yukame	I would leave for my home,
Kuni o mo shinohame.	I would long for that land!

Given such usage, it seems likely that however richly these prefixes may once have glowed as images, they must have soon deteriorated into vaguer signs of amplification that served two functions. The first was to heighten the tone in a way that is difficult to illustrate in modern English, except in colloquial corruptions of such adjectives-become-adverbs as "real." But these elements functioned more importantly by acting as controls over the neutral poetic materials used in the songs. There is nothing about the image of a pole to make us feel that it is especially good or bad, but with such an intensifying sign, the singer could make it seem as if the pole were something important and praiseworthy.

This same song of lament is useful for what it shows about imagistic practice, since it is fairly representative of the techniques of the large body of songs composed by the reciters. A more literal translation will follow the imagistic order with greater fidelity:

> Hidden land
> Hatsuse River's
> Upper shallow reaches in
> Sacred poles tamp
> Lower shallow reaches in
> True poles tamp
> Sacred pole on
> Mirror hang
> True poles on
> True jewels hang
> True jewel making
> I love sweetheart
> Mirror making
> I love wife
> "Is there"
> If say indeed
> To home even go
> Land also long for.

Such a rendition—in addition to showing the impossibility of "literal" translation from the Japanese—demonstrates that up to the end of the poem there is practically nothing but a succession of images ordered into patterns. Since the last eight lines exploit the first ten, we may leave them aside for the moment.

The progression of imagery in the long opening passage follows a standard formula. The poem begins with a pillow-word for a certain area, and the second line names the area, Hatsuse, and localizes it to the river. The next four lines develop action in different parts of the specified area in the usual pattern of upper and lower, a pattern sometimes varied with a middle, and there seems to be no reason why the sacred and the true poles might not have been reversed in position. The imagery of the next four-line section continues the action but particularizes it in terms of objects mentioned in the preceding passage, again following a rigidly schematic pattern that seems to have no really necessary order. In effect, the images seem almost to have lost their force by the very pattern which insists upon their iteration—incantation has very nearly swallowed up song.

Fortunately, the detailed pattern is part of a larger whole, which is integrated, if rather stiffly. The images move from the large to the small, from the whole to the part. We feel a certain sense of rising climax in following this process, and our feeling is in some measure justified by the relation of the mirror and jewels—very rare and precious imports in ancient Japan—to the wife. The imagistic technique is not unlike the cinematic device of beginning a motion picture or episode with a broad panning that is gradually narrowed to the real object of attention.

Many songs are more schematic, and some are even more prodigal with their imagery to even less effect. "Princess Kage's Lament" (*Nihongi,* No. 94) is an almost exasperating example of what might be called a lavish niggardliness with imagery.

Isu no Kami	Passing Furu
Furu o sugite	"Which is in Isu no Kami,"
Komomakura	Passing Takahashi,
Takahashi sugi	"High like a mat-covered pillow,"
Monosawa ni	Passing Ōyake
Ōyake sugi	"Where things are bountiful,"
Haruhi	Passing Kasuga,
Kasuga o sugi	"Hazy as a day in springtime,"
Tsumagomoru	Passing Osao
Osao o sugi	"Where men retire with their wives";
Tamake ni wa	Even putting rice
Ii sae mori	Into a precious vessel,
Tamamoi ni	Even putting water
Mizu sae mori	Into a jeweled bowl—
Nakisobochiyuku mo	And shedding tears with every step,
Kagehime aware.	Oh, the grief of Princess Kage!

The first ten lines march like soldiers in a regular succession of pillow-words and place names, and to stress the artificiality of the technique we have placed quotation marks around the pillow-words, most of which have no specific tonal effect in this song. The next four lines specify certain womanly actions with enough in the way of decorative prefixes to make them regal, and the last two declare the princess's sorrows.

The "Lament" is a contextual poem of a special kind, the *monogatariuta,* in which the song is set against a prose background. Princess Kage is to be imagined on a trip requiring her to pass by the places mentioned in the song as she bears for her funeral offering the containers mentioned toward the end of the song. In context the images of the song therefore take on a significance which is absent when the context is removed. Out of context the poem is not very impressive. It is built upon a structural technique of preparation (passing many places, doing certain actions) and conclusion (the exclamation of Princess Kage's grief) that provides the form for many of the longer primitive songs. And yet it offers little more than a monotonous naming of places, rather like announcements in railway stations or air terminals with an advertisement for each stop. As the song stands by itself, its imagery has little poetic function. It is rather part of an incantation—even more than in "Longing for His Wife"—and so is employed as a technique of vague amplification. We are evidently meant to say, open-eyed, "If she has passed all those places and done all those things—why, there are so many that she must certainly be very unhappy." Even within its context the song seems at once stiff and thin, qualities which may show off those of other songs to advantage.

Such imagistic sequences sometimes serve purposes other than mere amplification, as we can see from another and much better timetable poem (*Kojiki*, No. 58; *Nihongi*, No. 54).

A Lament for the Land of Takamiya

Tsuginefu ya	Going up
Yamashirogawa o	The river of Yamashiro
Miya nobori	Of the rolling hills,
Wa ga noboreba	As I go upstream to Miya,
Aoni yoshi	Passing Nara,
Nara o sugi	Rich in colored earth,
Odate	Passing Yamato
Yamato o sugi	Where mountains rise like shields—
Wa ga	Oh, the land,
Migashoshikuni wa	The country that I long to see again,
Kazuraki Takamiya	Takamiya in Kazuraki,
Wagie no atari.	The country of my home!

In this poem, every place passed by the speaker seems to take him yet one station farther from his native land, and the beauties of the trip only serve to remind him of his own home, Takamiya. In such songs as this, the imagery serves a discernible narrative function that is artistically superior to the vague amplification of the peregrinations of Princess Kage. But one must not stretch the merits of this poem too far. Narrative technique is but a slightly glimpsed possibility here, more a way of handling imagery, that puts the song in quality and unity somewhere between "Princess Kage's Lament" and "The Maid on the Road to Kohata," which is perhaps the finest extant example of narrative song in this early period.

Some of the songs just quoted show that similes and metaphors were techniques known to the authors of primitive song, but the problem of distinguishing simple imagery from imagery metaphorically employed is by no means as simple as the translations have suggested. We rendered two lines of "Longing for His Wife" as a simile:

Kagami nasu	And like the mirror
A ga mou tsuma	Is the wife I deeply love

The sense of the Japanese is "mirror make / I love wife," or, more idiomatically, "the wife I love / makes a mirror." The verb "makes" (*nasu*) is used transitively, but the effect is intransitive—as if the word meant "resembles." The force of a simile is conveyed, even if the rhetorical apparatus we expect in English is missing.

Metaphors are even more difficult to isolate, although there are a few indisputable examples like the hateful onion by which the "War Song of the Men of Kume" exemplifies the enemy shortly to be annihilated. Normally, however, the image does not convey a meaning so wholly different from itself—or, to speak more technically, the metaphorical vehicle usually expresses a tenor of feeling related to the vehicle, rather than a highly different idea or object. As a result, the metaphorical images are almost indistinguishable from images rich in connotation. For example, the Deity Eight Thousand Spears begins his song to Princess Nunakawa:

> In the green hills
> The midnight finches have begun to sing;
> The bird of the moor,
> The pheasant now screams its cry;
> The bird of the yard,
> The cock now crows . . .

There is a splendid dual progression of imagery in this passage: a spatial-visual progression from the far hills, to the nearer moor, to the yard; and a temporal-aural progression in the cries of the finches, pheasant, and cock, since they convey the passage of time from midnight to dawn. But it is extremely difficult to say whether the three birds function metaphorically to represent these three advancing periods, or whether the images work simply by connotation in a rhetorically ordered pattern. A similar analytical problem arises at the end of the song when Eight Thousand Spears curses the birds and asks the princess to come out and hush them. Since what he really wants is not peace and quiet so much as a night of love with the princess, the effect seems metaphorical; but, as the princess's response implies, the birds indicate that the day is too brightly at hand to make his wishes acceptable, although if he will only come back the next night . . . And yet, about the time we have decided that these are images, after all, her song picks up the imagery of birds and uses them metaphorically, coyly. She says, in effect, you do not like birds, but I am one, and hard to catch, too.

Let us agree that these images function metaphorically. There is a significant if slight difference between their function and that of the image of the crab struggling along the road to Kohata. But there is also a difference between the metaphorical functioning of this imagery and most Western metaphor. To take an extreme Western example, Donne's famous conceit of the draftsman's compass is an image, but there is little or no necessary connection between the image and what it represents—the separated but united lovers. There is no such wit or intellectual play in primitive Japanese poetry, in which an image is so much a part of the situation that it is difficult to say whether it "stands for" something else or whether it merely has a wide range of connotation. So the noisy birds are unwanted by a would-be lover on a secret nocturnal visit, and as such, the birds are imagistically employed; but to the extent that they also convey the passage of time and stand for a passion felt for the princess, they are metaphorical. This matter is important because it illustrates what we postulated in the first chapter—that Japanese poetry characteristically explores emotional rather than intellectual experience. Even so familiar a poetic element as metaphor often functions quite differently, at least in emphasis, in Japanese poetry, and this difference is nowhere more clearly seen than in the primitive song.

However, as "Princess Kage's Lament" shows, there are other elements in primitive song besides the Japanese sensibility to explain why there is often so little disparity between the image and what it metaphorically conveys. The fact that the images in that poem are so tenuously related to any sort of statement, whether of idea or feeling, means that the images of places can hardly be said to "stand for" anything other than places. In addition, the highly declarative, even incantatory nature of the verse takes attention away from the concrete images. The effect is one of blurring or confusion. This blurring often precludes what seems to be incipient allegory. In allegory, we expect the image and what it stands for to be separate (a fictional dragon stands for Sin); and further we expect other imagistic vehicles to be equally separate from what they convey (the knight who stands for Holiness is as fictional as the dragon). Now there are some poems in the chronicles that are treated as allegories by the compilers, but as we have said before, these are really instances in which more sophisticated readers have foisted new meanings on earlier songs. Treated as songs rather than poems in contexts, there are a few pieces that suggest allegory. One of them is the "War Song of the Men of Kume," which is worth looking at again.

> In the millet field
> Of the augustly powerful
> Children of Kume,
> Grows a single onion stalk—
> That very stalk,
> Root and leaves together,
> We will destroy once and for all.

If this is allegory, it is broken in half. The enemy may be an onion in our field, but we remain the Children of Kume. It is as though Spenser's dragon

of Sin were being chased through an allegorical field, not by the Redcrosse
Knight, but by Sir Philip Sidney. This poem undoubtedly employs metaphor,
and metaphor in which the image and its meaning are unusually discrete
for primitive Japanese song; but at most we can call the poem only half
allegorical, as though the reviser who fashioned the early materials into a
short chōka tried, only half successfully, to make the poem allegorical, after
the tastes of his own age.

Besides the major rhetorical techniques of early song—parallelism, pillow-
words, and the preface or *jo*—there is another technique which resembles the
pivot-word (kakekotoba) that becomes so much a feature of the tanka in
later centuries. Significantly, the songs employing these word-plays are usually
tanka, and therefore of suspicious age. The following love song from the
Kojiki (No. 79), for example, is a tanka whose third line contains elements
that require its being read differently with both the preceding and the following lines.

Sasaba ni	Upon the leaves
Utsu ya arare no	Of the bamboo grass the hail
Tashidashi ni	Beats straight—
Ineten nochi wa	Straight off I'll lead her to my bed,
Hito wa kayu to mo.	And if she leaves me afterwards, who
	cares?

Our suspicions about the age of this piece are considerably strengthened by
the fact that the technique is not common. It has all the marks of the new
and the unusual.

Another reading of any of the longer poems we have quoted will show
the two principal rhetorical techniques used in the songs—pillow-words and
varieties of parallelism. Each of these represents a stylistic heightening and
ordering scarcely to be found in the less formal early songs. The reciters
found in them techniques for elevating their subjects in ways analogous to
the effect of such decorative prefixes as "jewel-like" and "true." The analogy
is especially close for the pillow-words, which in the Japanese always precede
the words they qualify. Parallelism in its various forms is another, more
complex matter involving the historical problems dealt with earlier in this
chapter. But the simplest form of parallelism—repetition—no doubt grew
out of the practice observable in the songs of all countries of using refrain-
like clauses. Contiguous parallelism represents a technical advance, because
it is a device for introducing something new and yet retaining resemblances;
it adds, but it also helps create form from point to point.

The more complex varieties of parallelism learned from Chinese poetic practice are of course a still greater technical advance marking the later songs of the primitive period, or the songs that were revised toward the end of the period. The striking thing about the use of these techniques in early song is that in comparison with the poems of the later Court poets, the songs are so obsessed with the technique that they often contain little else. It is not the free expression of the folk spirit that sets these songs apart, but all too often a monotonous mannerism of technique. "Princess Kage's Lament" is an extreme but by no means unique example; it alternates pillow-words with place names for ten parallel lines, tells us about two of the princess's actions in more parallel lines, and until we come to the concluding two lines we have no idea what the subject of the poem could possibly be, who is going where, or whether the tone is cheerful or what.

A more pleasing example of what might be done with parallelism, even in this early period, is the "Praise of the Clan Lord and His Palace at Hishiro" (*Kojiki,* No. 100). So complex, even obtrusive, is the parallelism of the middle section that we can only conclude that some time near the end of the primitive period the Chinese techniques of parallelism became almost a fetish with reciters, who then revised the old songs to suit a new fad. The song is basically one of praise and in particular deals with an auspicious omen; a leaf has fallen in a cup of wine offered by a serving maid to the clan lord. The event is auspicious, because the sound made by the leaf recalls the one made by the god Izanagi when he swirled his spear in the waters and then created the isles of Japan.

Makimuku no	Oh, the palace
Hishiro no miya wa	In Hishiro of Makimuku
Asahi no	Is a palace
Hideru miya	Shone on by the morning sun,
Yūhi no	A palace
Higakeru miya	Colored by the evening sun,
Take no ne no	A palace where bamboo
Nedaru miya	Roots deep and firm,
Ko no ne no	A palace where tree roots
Nebau miya	Grow gnarled and strong,
Yaoni yoshi	A palace raised
Ikizuki no miya	On a great earth-pounded base.
Maki saku	By the halls
Hi no mikado	Made of towering cypress,
Niinaeya ni	By the Hall of the Solemn Tasting,
Oidateru	Stands the great elm,
Momodaru	Rooted fast
Tsuki ga e wa	And richly leaved.

Ho tsu e wa	Its upper branches
Ame o oeri	Spread wide across the heavens,
Naka tsu e wa	Its middle branches
Azuma o oeri	Spread across the distant lands,
Shi zu e wa	Its lower branches
Hina o oeri	Spread across the nearby lands.
Ho tsu e no	From the upper branches,
E no uraba wa	From these branches the leaves
Naka tsu e ni	To the middle branches
Ochifurabae	Bend down and touch their tips;
Naka tsu e no	From the middle branches,
E no uraba wa	From these branches the leaves
Shimo tsu e ni	To the lower branches
Ochifurabae	Bend down and touch their tips;
Shi zu e no	From the lower branches,
E no uraba wa	From these branches now a leaf
Arikinu no	Has fallen and floats—
Mie no ko ga	Like oil on water—
Sasagaseru	In the great wine cup
Mizutamauki ni	Which the serving maid from Mie,
Ukishi abura	Land of three-fold silken robes,
Ochinazusai	Holds up to the noble lord;
Mina kōro	And the liquid
Kōro ni	Gurgle-gurgles.
Ko shi mo	How auspicious,
Aya ni kashikoshi	Like the waters swirled by the parent gods,
Takahikaru	O august child
Hi no miko.	Of the high-shining sun!

Like so many of the more highly wrought songs (or poems), this one has as its basic structure a development from large to small, from the general to the immediate. The song holds together very well as a song of praise, but in terms of the action, the elaborate parallelism of the first thirty-four lines is only prefatory to the short statement about a leaf dropping into a cup. The effect in this song and in others (like "Princess Kage's Lament") in which the technique is used is one of a gigantically tall hat on a tiny head.

But the technique of preparation-conclusion could be put to better use as a rhetorical technique, since it offered a scheme to give structure to a lengthy song. It is possible to go further and say that the technique of preparation-conclusion is the major recurrent structural principle of the longer works of the period; even the best poems employ it, as one can see by looking at a narrative poem such as "The Maid on the Road to Kohata" or a quasi-dramatic sequence such as "The Wooing of Princess Nunakawa." Or rather, one might say that such songs as these, and to a somewhat lesser degree songs like the one just quoted, show how the technique might be adapted to make a unified, balanced poem—how the preparation might be made to serve as an integral part of the song or its performance. It is necessary to add "performance" because in the strictest technical sense the songs are often not unified internally. The opening exchange between the crab and the young man in "The Road to Kohata" has little to do with the maid discovered along the way. It seems rather to be a witty reference to the food eaten by the audience before the performance began, the mummers beginning their show with what amounts to a topical allusion in the opening section, and then going on to the traditional part of the performance. Even so, this particular song flows naturally from the dialogue to the narrative, and is not like some of the other songs, which have a long-winded, uninterestingly monotonous preparation or an absurdly anti-climactic conclusion.

In addition to the technique of preparation-conclusion there are two other principal structural patterns in the songs, although they are often made parts of the more prevailing pattern. The first of these is sequential statement, by which a song says that this event followed that, and another followed this, and so on; or that this cause produced that effect, and that effect in turn produced another. Many, almost all, of the preparatory passages in the lengthier songs either are made up of such sequential statements or else frustrate us when they seem to pretend to it without really employing it. A simpler alternative to this technique is pure statement or expostulation, without a discernible sequence. Most of the shorter songs are of this kind, and in a few somewhat longer works it becomes miniature narrative. One of the longest of these is "The Zithern" (*Kojiki*, No. 74; *Nihongi*, No. 41), a contextual song telling how a zithern was made from the wood of the ship Karano.

Karano o	Burning Karano's wood
Shio ni yaki	To yield up salt
Shi ga amari	From its sea soaking,
Koto ni tsukuri	From what was left I made a zithern;
Kakihiku ya	And when I pluck it,
Yura no to no	It makes a sound
Tonaka no ikuri ni	Like the swaying kelp that grows
Furetatsu	Upon the rocky piles
Nazu no ki no	Of the Yura Straits,
Saya saya.	Echoing *saya, saya*.

The other common structural principle is dialogue. Sometimes, as in the case of betrothal songs, the form is one of a question and a reply. In more complex songs like "The Maid on the Road to Kohata" or "The Wooing of Princess Nunakawa," the dialogue is developed in longer and more or less unequal passages that are more truly dramatic.

These three main techniques, dialogue, statement, and preparation-conclusion, are the chief structural patterns of early Japanese song, but there are some works with a structural development too much their own to be typified. One of the most interesting of these is a monologue, "On the Man with Two Wives" (*Kojiki,* No. 9; *Nihongi,* No. 7). His neighbors, the collective speaker of the song, observe that he has attempted to inveigle an assignation with the younger, more desirable wife, only to catch, or be caught by, the elder. Such a situation was made possible by the free and easy marriage customs of the day, but the bantering humor and ironic metaphors of the neighbors are what really give the poem its saltiness.

ON THE HUSBAND

Uda no	In a flat place
Takaki ni	On a high hill in Uda
Shigiwana haru	He hung a net to catch a snipe.
Wa ga matsu ya	Instead of catching
Shigi wa sayarazu	The snipe he lay in wait for,
Isukuwashi	What he caught
Kujira sayaru	Was a great whale of a beast.

TO THE HUSBAND

Konami ga	If your elder wife
Na kowasaba	Asks for some food,
Tachisoba no	Slice off for her
Mi no nakeku o	A piece as stingy as the fruit
Kokishi hiene	Of the small-berried hawthorn;
Uwanari ga	If your younger wife
Na kowasaba	Asks for some food,
Ichisakaki	Cut off for her
Mi no ōkeku o	Great pieces ample as the fruit
Kokida hiene	Of the full-berried evergreen.

ON THE HUSBAND AND THE WIVES

Ee	Oh—
Shi ya koshi ya	The stupid fools!
Ko wa inogou so	The fools now scream abuse!
Aa	Ah—
Shi ya koshi ya	The stupid fools!
Ko wa azawarau so.	The fools now laugh in scorn.

The structural techniques of the primitive songs are basically inseparable from their modes of expression. Almost all of the verse is declarative in mode, with interrogation the most common alternative and exclamation the usual method of heightening. Declaration and exclamation easily become statement or narrative, and interrogation becomes dialogue; but even a monologue like "The Man with Two Wives," a narrative like "The Maid on the Road to Kohata," or a quasi-dramatic sequence like "The Wooing of Princess Nunakawa" is basically declarative in mode. These three are among the most appealing of the songs—in the larger body of usually less attractive works the declarative element is much more obtrusive, and there are times when one almost cries aloud for an occasional descriptive or reflective song. The monotony of declaration is occasionally relieved, but it is never broken. We search in vain for a song that takes us away from a specific speaker declaring his feelings on a specific occasion. It was to take a longer acquaintance with the New Learning before poets could express in other modes than bald declaration what it was they saw when they looked upon their world. And many years were required to develop a more civilized attitude toward art, an attitude that would encourage poets to see more in their world than objects, or to probe and understand their own feelings more deeply. They needed both a new attitude and new techniques to perceive and express more complex notions than those conveyed by such statements as "And oh, how drunk I am!" or "Those wretched birds!"

Similarly, the range of subjects and themes of the primitive songs needed to be enlarged before Japan could claim to have a real literature. In a sense, the materials of the songs are the limits of the subjects; and their subjects set the limits of their themes. If theme is the predication a poet makes about his subject, then we must say that the themes are usually so simple as almost to defy separation from the subject. And if the subject is what the materials show that it is about, then we must say that it is usually about one thing whose parts or location are developed by piling up rather than by exploration. A song on the subject of mash liquor has as its materials a declaration of the name of the brewer and the fact that the speaker has partaken of it; and the theme is that the liquor is good and the speaker is drunk. A song whose materials are images of the splendors of a palace has as its subject the splendors of a palace and its ruler, and as its theme the predication that all the splendors are truly splendid. There is in this primitive song no deep searching of the heart, no elevated thought, not even a simple but searching and moving generalization like that of the anonymous Anglo-Saxon poet: "Those sufferings passed—these may also."

Such a comprehensive statement of what primitive Japanese song lacks may seem to deny any kind of literary interest. Such is not the case. The songs have at their best a vividness, a convincing re-creation of the here and now, that can appeal to the most sophisticated reader. The images are all the more vivid because there is never a question about the reality they represent—what is seen or heard exists and is true because it was seen or heard. Moreover, although time or the distortions of the compilers have often obscured the speaker and the occasion of a song, the songs that remain intelligible take on an additional clarity by virtue of the specific nature of the occasion and the way the speaker stands out in it. In lieu of the Anglo-Saxon poet's moving generalization, these songs take us up to the very brink of the world from which they grew. Even the long introductions with their back-and-forth parallelisms, their frequent disassociation from what they are supposed to introduce, even these are so vivid that we are caught in the spell of the reality of a way of life.

There is also a basic psychological truth in the very pattern of so many of these songs. The progression in most of the lengthier songs from the wide or general to the small and particular draws us further and further toward this world and a sense of the reality of the things in it. Although the technique itself is monotonously repeated, it accords with our experience of more complex realities: we often learn first through general impression and then gradually as we apprehend detail. This gradual process in the songs is ordered so as to take us to what is important at the end of the song; and often even though we sense the artificiality of divisions of parallel passages, the skill with which a passage is made to seem a part or division or outgrowth of what precedes takes us smoothly and without protest from beginning to end.

Perhaps what has been said can be reduced to the statement that this primitive song gives a sense of conviction, of truth, that what the poems declare is what the world—the external world—of their authors was like. No doubt the objective world is realized so completely because the subjective world has been all but ignored, or more accurately, because it has not yet been clearly glimpsed. In later Japanese poetry, the subjective world will come to dominate; and subtlety, refinement, and awareness will replace the direct vividness of this primitive world. When we come upon a later poem that is only third- or fourth-rate, whose awareness is more conventional than real, we may recall these early songs with something of a nostalgia for a simpler world. And at the same time, these songs are historically interesting for the light they shed on the superiority of later poetry: this is how Japanese poetry begins, and the primitive songs help us appreciate the rich changes wrought in later centuries. But the great corollary of the law of change is constancy, and for all of the developments of later periods, we can observe in the primitive song many of the characteristic norms of Japanese poetry, just as a zoologist may observe characteristics of advanced life in the simpler forms from which they have evolved. However great the changes were to be in the poetry of the Japanese Court, they were to take place, to large degree, in the terms established by primitive song.

4

The Early Literary Period

686–784

T HE MOST remarkable developments in the whole tradition of Japanese poetry occurred between the period of simple, primitive song and the extraordinary flowering of poetic genius in the eighth century. The primitive verse
usually exhibited something of the quality of Samson's riddles or the Song of
Deborah; the new poetry burst forth with the lyric beauty and intensity of
the Psalms and Job. So great are the accomplishments of the early literary
period, especially in comparison with the primitive age, that one can understand and in part forgive the modern Japanese for treating the poetry of this
age as if it were something sacred, beyond the touch of time or human hands.
But striking as the changes were, they occurred within a continuing tradition.
The native genius was not in some sense superseded; it was transformed into
lasting literary art.

The changes that led to this new wealth of poetry can be partially understood in terms of the Japanese use of the New Learning from China and the
development of a concept of poetry as a literary art. The interrelation between
these two phenomena is at once obvious in general terms and obscure in detail.
To state it simply, however, the Japanese would never have achieved their
great literary flowering without the example of China; and yet their language
and traditions were such that the poetry they created is in almost every important respect un-Chinese in its cast. Another important determinant of
poetry in the early literary period is the changed relation between the poet and
his audience. Several matters are involved—changes in the concept of the role
and prominence of the poet and of his audience; the creation of new modes,
genres, and guises in which the poet might appear before his audience and
the consequent variation in esthetic distance; and changes in the concept of
the poetic act itself.

We shall discuss the questions of an esthetic of poetry and the critical ideals
that these changes imply; we shall examine in detail the subject of the practice
of poetry (its techniques and meanings), which involves the more certain
results of such ideals; and since a rise to greatness implies a subsequent falling-
off, we must also concern ourselves with the events and forces that led the
age to decline. But before approaching these topics, some things may be said
by way of introduction to show the general tenor and character of poetry in
this period.

Chronologically, this is the time of the so-called Dark Ages in Europe, and in some historical respects the period is not a little shadowy in Japan. We know of the existence of several anthologies that have been lost; but the poetry that survives does so almost entirely in one anthology, the *Man'yōshū*, or "Collection for Ten Thousand Generations." This collection comprises some 4,500 poems, chiefly chōka and tanka but with a sprinkling of such other forms as the sedōka and short renga. Who the compilers of the *Man'yōshū* were and when they did their work have long been matters of energetic study and conjecture among Japanese scholars. The earliest poet named in the anthology is Empress Iwa, who died ca. 347, and the last datable poem is one from the year 759, but neither date can be accepted with complete confidence as defining the historical range of the anthology. This much may be said, however: the period most richly represented is the century and a half between 600 and 750, and one of the several compilers was Ōtomo Yakamochi (718–85), who is also one of the most important poets of the age.

Essentially, then, the *Man'yōshū* is an anthology devoted to the period dealt with in this chapter, with a fairly small body of poems from the primitive period and a large body of anonymous "folk" poems—of uncertain date—that often retain primitive characteristics. The fact that notes within the twenty books of the *Man'yōshū* tell us that a group of poems is from such a nonextant anthology as "The Collection of Ancient Poems" (*Kokashū*) or from "The Classified Forest of Poems" (*Ruijū Karin*), and the fact that different books follow different methods of organization—whether chronological, topical, or otherwise—make it clear that the *Man'yōshū* is essentially an anthology of anthologies. This point is significant, if only as a reminder to historian and critic alike that a far wider body of poetry was probably omitted and has therefore been lost. We can only hope that what has survived is a representative selection of the poetry of the age, a hope that falters when we consider that perhaps twelve of the twenty books in the *Man'yōshū* were compiled by Yakamochi, and might be expected to reflect his personal tastes and include only the work of a limited circle of acquaintances. But happily for the student of Japanese poetry, Yakamochi's tastes seem to have been as various as he was versatile (judging from the wide range of poems he selected), and our hope that the poems which survive truly represent the achievement of the age is stronger for this period than for such a later imperial anthology as the *Shingosenshū* (1303), compiled as it was by a poet strongly committed to one school of poetry.

The body of poetry that we have lost from the four centuries or so covered by the *Man'yōshū* represents a serious deprivation; but curiously enough the poets at the end of this early literary period suffered an even greater one. By the early ninth century the Japanese could no longer read, at least not with confidence, most of the poetry that had been collected for the *Man'yōshū*.

It is almost as though Wyatt and Surrey had made a collection of Anglo-Saxon poetry, of poetry by Chaucer, the Scots poets, and Lydgate, and of their own poems, and then found themselves unable to read the earliest poems. The comparison is not wholly just, however, because whereas Wyatt's and Surrey's difficulties would have been linguistic, Japanese poets were unable to read the earlier poetry largely because of changes in the method of writing down the language. Poems in the *Man'yōshū* are transcribed in Chinese characters according to several methods—sometimes phonetically according to the Japanese version of the Chinese pronunciation, sometimes in "Chinese composition" (*kambun*), with the characters used for their semantic value and in Chinese syntax, and sometimes in a combination of these two systems. Such complexities are involved in these various methods that many centuries of cumulative work by scholars and poets were required to complete the explication of the tangled schemes of transcription. Even today linguistic and textual problems remain, and the Japanese have made in recent times such striking discoveries as that the older language contained eight vowels instead of the five of modern Japanese.

Since the revival of native scholarship in the seventeenth and eighteenth centuries, many scholars and critics have taken pride in an elusive quality in the *Man'yōshū* which may be called the "Man'yō Spirit"—the temper and character of the poetry of this early period—and something perhaps ought to be said of this "spirit" here. A careful reader of literary histories knows that the Zeitgeist is an elusive creature not to be caught in the trap of critical terminology; and while he may be surprised to hear of a "Sammlungsgeist," we may at least spare him the pains of hearing once again that such an age as the one we are discussing was an age of transition or paradox. Transitions of course there were; but what the Japanese themselves have admired in the poetry of the early literary period is its "pure simplicity," its democratic representation of poets from all walks of life, its "sincerity," its variety, and its "individualism." Only the last two attributes seem to us to be valid. The variety is reflected in the many styles and modes of poetry, but more important, in the manifold subjects, tones, and themes. We would prefer to qualify "individualism" as "direct personalism," a kind of poetic response to the world which later ages left behind. The world, gods, men, magic, love, death, nature, and other aspects of human awareness seem to have been felt as a whole in which the poet participates directly and which, with the tradition at a certain stage of development, he therefore expresses directly. The lesser poets of the age write not so much with Wordsworth's "emotion recollected in tranquility" as with the contrary "spontaneous overflow of powerful feelings"; the greater poets maintain the illusion of direct response in a complex art. Despite all of the wonder, the mystery, and even the precariousness of life, the poets show no hesitation in expression. In the best poetry of the age there is that repose which we call classic—in which noumenon and phenomenon seem to be one, and in which the perceiving sensibility seems wholly harmonious with the perceived object. This direct relation between the poet and his materials represents not so much an optimism—since death and suffering are realities—as a confidence that what one has experienced is true in a world of variety, liveliness, and interest.

Such vagaries of impression characterize the elusive "Man'yō Spirit" but poorly, and the accomplishments of the age are best imaged in the genius of a man known to us in little more than name, Kakinomoto Hitomaro (fl. ca. 680–700). There were of course other great poets, but Hitomaro's brilliant sense of poetic structure, his skill with imagery, his fertile creation of new forms and modes, his kind ironies, his response to public occasions, and his deep human sympathy emerge in a consummate art with such suddenness that one is almost convinced that history has lost a host of transitional poets. He and the other outstanding poets of the period give the developing tradition the status of real literature, for in them the poet appears, in full maturity, as at once a real person and an artist.

Although it is the poetry itself that concerns us, it is significant that this period saw important developments in other broad cultural areas as well. The swift poetic maturation is paralleled in the political developments following the Taika Reform (645), in the remarkable achievements in sculpture and architecture, in the establishment of the first "permanent" capital at Nara (710), and indeed in almost all phases of life. If the early literary period was not in fact one of the best times in history to be alive and conscious of one's place in the world, the poetry almost makes it seem so. How the literature developed to the point that we can gain this impression, developed from the great example of Chinese literature and the more essential stream of native inheritance is the story of the first great age of Japanese literature.

POETRY AS A LITERARY ART AND THE CHINESE EXAMPLE

A few of the latest poems in the chronicles and the earliest poems in the *Man'yōshū* are attributed to individuals who are known to have actually lived, and for this reason the historical atmosphere that surrounds them seems more "authentic" than the context of myth and legend that provides the setting for most primitive poetry. However, the attribution of poems to persons who are said to have lived in the fourth or fifth century is altogether suspect, and one can hardly take seriously the claim that such figures as Emperor Yūryaku or Empress Iwa actually composed the poems that are ascribed to them. The poetry attributed to such persons is probably still the work of the "anonymous bard," and the substitution of the exalted human "poet"—Emperor or Empress,

Prince or Princess—for the god or culture hero was no doubt largely an accepted convention. In any case, down to the mid-seventh century primitive Japanese poetry continues to be the direct and unreflecting response of the individual to an emotional stimulus in an occasional—mythical, legendary, or social—context. The principal texts which preserve this early poetry are, as we have seen, the chronicles of the early eighth century and the *Man'yōshū*, compiled during the last half of the eighth century. It is important that we bear in mind, therefore, that these sources, especially the chronicles, contain poetry of a period much earlier than the time of compilation.

In discussing primitive song, we observed that many of the compositions are accompanied by notations. Annotations such as "This is a quiet song" or "This is a floating song" appear merely to designate the kind of melody to which the poem was sung. But others—"This is a drinking song" or "This is a song of longing for home"—indicate a certain awareness of poetic themes, a rudimentary literary consciousness. The notations, however, probably reflect traditional, indigenous ways of classifying poetic materials, and we may attribute to the compilers a greater degree of literary sophistication than these terms alone seem to represent. The very existence of the chronicles presupposes a considerable familiarity with certain types of Chinese literature and belle-tristic chronicles. The *Nihongi*, the Chinese preface to the *Kojiki*, and some prose sections of the *Man'yōshū* demonstrate the ability of the Japanese of the first half of the eighth century to write elegant Chinese with the parallel syntax of the Six Dynasties style; and the *Kojiki* reflects the Japanese familiarity with Chinese translations of Indian Buddhist scriptures in which the Chinese had adapted their written characters to phonetic transliteration. Many of the Chinese works that the Japanese élite of the seventh and eighth centuries appear to have found most useful in their effort to assimilate the Chinese literary heritage were anthologies, whose contents were arranged under various headings that rendered them particularly convenient as handbooks.

There are still many gaps in our knowledge of just what Chinese books were studied by the Japanese in the early literary period. But the fact of a time lag between the dates of composition or compilation of the Chinese anthologies and their introduction, or at least wide circulation, in Japan, is a consideration that is already important in the seventh and eighth centuries, and that remains more or less constant throughout the history of the poetic tradition of the Court. One of the collections best known to the literate group in Japan in the early literary period was probably the *Wen Hsüan*, or "Anthology of Literature," compiled by Hsiao T'ung (501–31), and made up of selections of Han and Six Dynasties poetry and prose. The great prestige enjoyed by this anthology in its homeland was reflected by the importance attached to it by the Japanese, but at the same time it led the Japanese to the study of poetic forms and styles that were already passing out of fashion in

China. In spite of such time lags, Chinese precedents for classified anthologies of literature as well as for chronicles and other writings were known to the Japanese at least by the seventh century, and the very compilation of the *Man'yōshū*, the *Kojiki*, and the *Nihongi* reflects the desire of the Japanese to possess their own equivalents of the Chinese books that were known to them.

The example of China, then, is patent in the compilation, arrangement, and classification of the *Man'yōshū*; but more important than this, over the hundred years from, say, 650 to 750, Japanese poetry itself gives evidence of striking changes that must be attributed to the sophisticating influence of the self-conscious Chinese poetic tradition. These changes involve the concept of the relation of the poet to his materials; the appearance of new, "literary" occasions for poetry; the consciousness of the growth of a poetic tradition over time; the emergence of a critical spirit; the deliberate experiment with modes, themes, and techniques unknown to primitive poetry; and the apparent effort to establish genres comparable to at least some kinds of Chinese verse. With China for an example, Japanese poetry became literary and self-conscious during the hundred-odd years from the Taika Reform to the date of the last poem in the *Man'yōshū* (759); it developed from an orally transmitted folk tradition into a written art that might endure for "ten thousand generations."

The individual historical developments are complexly interrelated, and they are obscured by our ignorance of the degree of critical awareness achieved by the poets in the early part of this first literary period. The attitude shown by the compilers of the *Man'yōshū* toward their materials—the classification of poems into formal and modal categories, the consciousness of good and bad poetry, and the like—indicates the degree to which literary ideas of Chinese origin had been assimilated by the Japanese literati by the middle of the eighth century rather than the growth of these ideas among the original composers of these poems. Fortunately, poetic practice after the middle of the seventh century indicates the gradual development of a sophisticated tradition, and it is the poetry itself, rather than the mechanics of the arrangement and classification of the twenty books of the *Man'yōshū*, which will primarily concern us here.

Among the earliest surviving poems that hint at the appearance of a new poetic sensibility based upon literary rather than immediate human concerns are some which were composed by Emperor Tenchi (626–71) and high-ranking members of his court during the latter part of the seventh century. The inclusion of poems in Chinese by Tenchi and his circle in the *Kaifūsō* (751), the first collection of Chinese verse by Japanese poets, indicates the degree to which the aristocracy was emulating many Chinese literary practices. It is therefore no surprise to find that the Japanese poems composed by these literate aristocrats are much in advance of most of the other poetry of the same period.

A poem attributed to Tenchi (*MYS*, I: 15) gives evidence of a Chinese-inspired interest in nature for its esthetic value.

Watatsumi no	We have seen the sun
Toyohatakumo ni	Make colored banners of the clouds
Irihi mishi	As it set in the sea—
Koyoi no tsukuyo	If only now that darkness falls
Saya ni teri koso.	The radiant moon will fill the night.

A more striking example from the late seventh century is provided by the famous poem of Princess Nukada, "In Preference of the Autumn Hills" (*MYS*, I: 16); her sophisticated preference of autumn over spring expresses an elegant, literary concern.

Fuyugomori	When spring at last
Haru sarikureba	Is freed from winter's bonds,
Nakazarishi	The silent birds
Tori mo kinakinu	Arrive in their full song,
Sakazarishi	And lifeless flowers
Hana mo sakeredo	Burst forth in brilliant bloom;
Yama o shigemi	Yet I cannot find
Irite mo torazu	The flowers on the too luxuriant slopes
Kusa fukami	Or appreciate the blossoms
Torite mo mizu.	Hopelessly entangled in the grass.
Akiyama no	However, when I see
Ko no ha o mite wa	The leaves upon the autumn hills,
Momiji o ba	My eager hands
Torite zo shinobu	Tremble with their load of crimson
Aoki o ba	leaves
Okite zo nageku	And with reluctance
Soko shi urameshi	Leave the green ones on their boughs—
Akiyama ware wa.	Yes, the green ones are the pity,
	And the autumn hills for me.

As these examples show, some of the poets of the late seventh century begin to emerge as conscious creative artists and individuals, who express in their poetry attitudes that are pre-eminently sophisticated; in this their debt to the Chinese example is obvious. Moreover, even among the more traditional poems of the age certain important changes can be observed. Thus, the custom of adding one or more hanka or "envoys" to the chōka is already becoming established, and this practice probably can be attributed to the influence of the Chinese *fu,* a long and highly ornate composition that was sometimes followed by a short concluding poem called a *tz'u* or *fan tz'u*, "repeating words." This borrowing from Chinese practice (if it was the borrowing it seems) was accompanied by a definition of the different forms in Japanese poetry—chōka, tanka, sedōka—and the regularizing of the number of syllables in each line to five or seven. The process of regularization, which was part of the transition from folk-song to literary poetry, had been accomplished by the end of the seventh century. Finally, during this same period the chōka underwent a rapid development, expanding from the short, incantatory song characteristic of primitive verse to a long, sustained, complex form.

It is difficult to point to the direct influence of Chinese poetry in these developments, since the capabilities of the Japanese poetic medium—the language—are so very different from the Chinese. The definition of the chōka and its expansion into a highly complex form appear to have been almost entirely the work of a single genius, Hitomaro, whose poetry grows, paradoxically, much more directly out of the ancient Japanese tradition of the bards than from the Chinese literary heritage. Nonetheless, although Hitomaro is one of the most pre-eminently "Japanese" of poets, his chōka show a sophisticated technique and a complexity of structure that appear so suddenly in the Japanese tradition as to be inexplicable unless we take into account the stimulus of Chinese poetry. The highly elaborate technique of noncontiguous parallelism, which Hitomaro employs with dazzling effect in his long poems, demands a literary skill that took perhaps a millennium or more to develop in China. It is difficult to believe that a Japanese poet—even a poetic genius like Hitomaro—could have invented the technique unaided.

How complex the question of Chinese influence is can be seen in a problem of literary history that has troubled Japanese scholars. The similarity between passages in Hitomaro's chōka and certain of the Shinto *norito*, or liturgies, has been pointed out by numerous writers, and it has been suggested that Hitomaro may have borrowed much of his technique and elevated subject matter from these religious texts. But the explanation seems unsatisfactory. In the first place, the *norito* were not recorded in written form until the ninth century, more than a hundred years after the death of Hitomaro, and although many of them are undoubtedly older than the period in which they were written down, we have no way of knowing how much literary revision they underwent, or indeed, whether in fact the influence might not have gone in the opposite direction, from Hitomaro to the *norito*. Secondly, we are still left to account for the elaborate structure of the *norito* themselves, if we assume that Hitomaro borrowed from them, and in this case the same question repeats itself—how could such an elaborate technique have been invented with such astonishing suddenness? Whichever side one takes, the conclusion seems inescapable that the highly sophisticated technique of noncontiguous parallelism found in both Hitomaro and in the *norito* was inspired, however gener-

ally or remotely, by the example of Chinese poetry, and more particularly perhaps, by the *fu,* which employs this technique most conspicuously.

Hitomaro's contribution to the chōka was not confined to the elaboration
of technique, for we must attribute to this extraordinary poet numerous
genres of public and private poetry which became the norms for the later poets
of the period. The elegy and the lament, for example, although not wholly
absent from primitive poetry, were developed by Hitomaro into solemn and
lofty public forms, in which the position of the poet is like that of a laureate
whose poetry expresses an awareness of national tradition, public loss, and
various social concerns. His poems on these subjects tend to have a certain consistency of structure, and it does not seem too extreme to suggest that Hitomaro was attempting thereby to establish a poetic genre suitable to great public
occasions and solemn subjects, a genre for which counterparts existed in Chinese poetry, again particularly in the *fu.*

This is not to say that Hitomaro slavishly imitated the techniques, themes,
and imagery of the Han or the Six Dynasties *fu*—to do so would have been
impossible even had it been his intention. Much of the effect of the Chinese
genre lay in a dazzling array of synonyms that exploited to the full the resources of the huge Chinese vocabulary, and the lexicon of seventh-century
Japanese would have been quite inadequate for this purpose. What Hitomaro
succeeded in doing was to elevate, refine, and enlarge the scope of the chōka
to the point that it expressed something akin to the atmosphere of some of
the public modes of Chinese poetry, even while he kept his poetry firmly
grounded in his own linguistic and cultural tradition. Thus, the "overtures"
in Hitomaro's public elegies and laments, which trace the human present to
its origins in the divine national past, have no counterpart in Chinese poetry,
in which there is little or no attempt to deal with "genealogy." It is hard not
to feel that the overtures lend Hitomaro's poems a quality of solemn dignity
that is in its own way equivalent to the atmosphere of some of the Chinese
fu, reproducing their grandeur in purely Japanese terms.

The appearance of new subjects for poetry is in many ways intimately
related to developments in the wider cultural scene. Hitomaro's celebrations
of imperial visits to pleasure palaces in the countryside, for example, would
never have been written had not his imperial patron been inspired to make
these journeys, and Hitomaro inspired by the Chinese example to celebrate
them. At the same time, in the poetry of Hitomaro and other outstanding
poets of his generation like Takechi Kurohito (fl. ca. 690–710), there is a
satisfying harmony between the originality of the subject suggested by the
sophisticated new concerns of the Court society and the folk tradition of myth,
legend, and poetic craft inherited by the poets from their own culture.

Certain subjects and occasions for poetry are more clearly Chinese in inspiration than others. The treatment of these materials by Japanese poets from

the mid-seventh century on frequently reflects characteristically Chinese ways of looking at things and dealing with them in poetry. We might consider the following poem from the "Hitomaro Collection" (*MYS*, VII: 1068).

Ame no umi ni	In the ocean of the sky
Kumo no nami tachi	Course the undulating waves of cloud,
Tsuki no fune	Rising by the moon-boat
Hoshi no hayashi ni	As it seems to disappear in rowing
Kogikakuru miyu.	Through the forest of the stars.

This poem is one of many that the compilers of the *Man'yōshū* classified as "Poems on Things." The critical term is Chinese, and such poems—in which the subject is an objective thing, whether the "sky," as in this case, or the moon, clouds, rain, mountains, or rivers—reflect a new importance of the poetic "subject" that derives from Chinese habits of composition. Many Chinese poets from the middle of the Six Dynasties period to the early T'ang period essayed such poems on things, and the range of subjects was broadened to include even man-made objects like desks and ink-slabs. Very few of the poems were purely descriptive, since the usual intent to praise the beauty or utility of the object involved the use of various attributes and metaphors subjectively employed. The corresponding Japanese poems in the *Man'yōshū* make up a rather heterogeneous group, but the very strong personal quality of most of them—a number of which are love poems—contrasts with the Chinese practice. The above poem from the "Hitomaro Collection," however, with its subjective use of natural images as metaphors for other natural images, is unusually close in tone and technique to the Chinese descriptive lyric.

The growing sophistication of Japanese aristocratic society, as it prospered and came under the influence of Chinese civilization, was paralleled by an increase in the range of specifically literary occasions for poetry and by references to certain Chinese myths, practices, ideas, and popular beliefs. The poem by Princess Nukada on the relative merits of the spring and autumn hills has already been mentioned as one of the earliest examples of a Japanese poem on a quasi-Chinese literary occasion, but in the age of Hitomaro the variety of such occasions suddenly increased. Although some of these Chinese borrowings were not permanently assimilated, others were rapidly domesticated to native Japanese beliefs and customs, becoming an inseparable part of the Japanese poetic tradition over the centuries. The most tenacious of these Chinese elements were the ones that were connected in some way or other with seasonal observances—the New Year, the flowering of the plum trees in spring, and the like. One Chinese myth in particular that was associated with a literary festival was the myth of the Celestial Lovers, the Herd Boy and the Weaver Maiden (represented by the stars Altair and Vega), who are separated by the River of Heaven (the Milky Way) and are able to meet only once each year, on the seventh night of the seventh moon of the lunar calendar. The festival, known in Japan as Tanabata or Seventh Night, was celebrated by Chinese poets, and emerges with apparent suddenness in Hitomaro's poetry as one of the accepted literary occasions. Indeed, more than 120 poems in the *Man'yōshū* treat this romantic tale in various ways. Hitomaro expresses the envy of the frustrated lovers for the freedom enjoyed by the other gods in the following tanka (*MYS*, X: 2033), one of his few datable poems (680).

Ama no gawa	How happy are those gods
Yasu no kawara no	Who need not suffer the constraints
Todomarite	Of time in separation,
Kamu tsu tsudoi wa	But can assemble freely on the shores
Toki matanaku ni.	Of the Tranquil Stream of Heaven.

It is significant that Hitomaro has given his Chinese motif a uniquely Japanese setting by placing it in the context of Shinto belief: his image of the gods assembling in Heaven to take counsel stems from native mythology rather than Chinese, in which no such belief existed. What is Chinese is the placing of the meeting of the gods in the bed of the River of Heaven, an image for the Milky Way that not only is Chinese, but must have been very new in the generation of Hitomaro's youth, when the poem was written. Such fresh juxtapositions of native and foreign elements are most conspicuous in the poetry of Hitomaro, who stood in a much closer relationship to the native tradition of Shinto belief and primitive poetry than later poets, and who, unlike his successors, did not hesitate to use Chinese motifs in "unnatural" contexts. Like the Elizabethan poets, Hitomaro and others of his generation were less troubled by a sense of decorum that might forbid the combining of classical and modern elements. The rapid assimilation of foreign elements in the Japanese early literary period, as in Elizabethan times, sometimes led to curious poems, but in the best poetry of both periods (which are comparable on other grounds as well), there is often an excitement lacking in the moderation of succeeding generations of poets.

The growth of a new urban culture after the establishment of Japan's first "permanent" capital at Nara (710) was accompanied by a conspicuous widening of the gap between popular modes and styles and the new, elegant poetry created by the urban society. Popular, folk poetry continued to be composed, but the fact that most folk poetry of the Nara period (710–84) preserved in the *Man'yōshū* is in the tanka form, which was defined by the educated court class, indicates that this poetry was considerably influenced by the urban example. The city dwellers for their part could now turn with a kind of sophisticated primitivism to the poems and songs of the common people, collecting them in anthologies or even themselves composing poems that express the feelings, say, of a provincial youth about to set out for hazardous military duty in a remote part of the country, or the sorrows of his wife and parents who were left behind. Yakamochi's poem "On the Parting Sorrows of a Frontier Guard" (*MYS*, XX: 4408-12) and the poems of his contemporary Takahashi Mushimaro (fl. ca. 730), who is noted for his narrative poems on local legend, may or may not have been written in conscious imitation of Chinese practice; but it is certainly true that there was an established Chinese precedent for such poetry. And the poems of these men show that there was by now a marked disparity between the cultural level of the educated class and that of the common people.

Most of the best-known poets of the early literary period—Ōtomo Tabito (665-731) and his son Yakamochi, Yamanoe Okura (?660-?733), and Takahashi Mushimaro—were members of a group of civil servants of lesser rank. Regardless of the former glories of their ancient, aristocratic clans, they served as officials and governors of provinces under the growing dominance of powerful clans struggling to control the imperial family. These men were far more thoroughly grounded in Chinese literature and culture than their predecessors of the seventh century (Okura, for example, spent twenty years studying in China), and their poetry reflects their varied interests in Chinese philosophy as well as a new sense of literary discrimination. Around Tabito, who was Viceroy of Tsukushi (modern Kyushu) from 728 to 730, a group of officials with Chinese tastes formed a kind of literary coterie whose elegant gatherings and poetic exchanges were the last word in fashionable behavior *à la chinoise*. Some of these poets played a major role in the compilation of the *Man'yōshū* from pre-existing anthologies and private collections of verse, exhibiting high literary standards and an ability to distinguish clearly between the crude and the elegant, the old and the new in poetic composition.

The height of fashionable elegance was reached at the famous party held by Tabito at his Viceroy's mansion on the thirteenth day of the first month of 730. The season was early spring, the occasion the flowering of the plum trees, and officials under Tabito's command gathered from all over the island to feast and drink sake, hold literary converse, and compose graceful tanka in praise of the beauty of the blossoms and the generosity of the host. As Lady Murasaki observed some centuries later, the quality of the verse produced on such occasions is not likely to be very high, and the group of thirty-two poems in the *Man'yōshū* (V: 815-46) that were inspired by Tabito's generous table and flagons bear her out. The significance of poems written on such occasions lies in the evidence they provide of the degree of sophistication of the Nara poets, and the existence of what might be called a society of esthetically-minded poets with fashionable literary tastes.

Although the prestige of Chinese poetry was to prove harmful to native poetry some decades later, the Chinese example inspired the generation of Tabito, Okura, and Yakamochi to experiment, to attempt, sometimes with conspicuous success, to use Japanese poetry as a vehicle for the expression of new concerns, often learned from China. Each of the educated poets of the age emerges as a distinct individual, whose poems are immediately recognizable for their possessing a Confucian or a Taoist spirit, or for their exploitation of the possibilities offered by didactic, descriptive, and narrative modes as well as lyrical. Okura's Confucian-inspired "Dialogue on Poverty" (*MYS*, V: 892–93) opens up an entirely new field in Japanese poetry, as do Tabito's poems on sake (*MYS*, III: 338–50), with their spirit of Taoistic epicureanism. From the point of view of the total range of themes and subjects treated in the poetry of the *Man'yōshū*, these poems contribute markedly to its often praised variety. Yet from the perspective of literary history, they remain only curiosities, evidence of experimentation briefly attempted by single poets in one generation and then abandoned forever. Like the abortive Elizabethan attempts to write quantitative verse in English, these experiments with Chinese subjects could hardly be adapted to the language and tastes of the Japanese in any direct way. Only when tempered, basically altered, and subordinated to native concerns— just as quantity was subordinated to stress in Ben Jonson's lyrics—did Chinese subjects drawn from Taoism or Confucianism find their place in Japanese poetry.

Perhaps one reason for the gradual contraction of the range of Japanese poetry in the mid-eighth century is the emergence of a growing sense of decorum among Japanese poets—in particular a feeling that the Japanese language was better suited to personal lyricism than to didactic or philosophical modes. At the same time, there seems to have been a certain lack of harmony between the equable Japanese temperament in the early literary age and what might be called the extremes of Confucian didacticism and Taoist irresponsibility. Of all the foreign ideas taken up by Japanese poets, it was the Buddhist awareness of the transience of worldly things, so close to the Japanese awareness of time, which remained throughout the tradition as a major theme. The resignation that Okura expresses in the envoy to his "Dialogue on Poverty" is Buddhist rather than Confucian, and in the following generation Yakamochi, whose clan had continued to fall in status and power, advocates not the Taoist virtues of wine, but the Way of the Buddha (*MYS*, XX: 4468–69).

The growing interest of Japanese poets in the Chinese literary medium during this period is illustrated by the appearance of hybrid forms in the work of Tabito, Okura, Yakamochi, and other literati. These forms, which usually consist of a story or other explanatory matter in Chinese prose, accompanied by one or more Japanese poems ostensibly composed on the occasion described, were inspired by Chinese prototypes. The "Exchange of Poems on the Occasion of an Outing to the Matsura River" (*MYS*, V: 853–63) is a group of tanka with an introduction in elegant Chinese that describes a romantic encounter between the poet and a bevy of beautiful maidens. The poems are to be viewed as exchanges between them. This bit of pleasantry, which has been attributed both to Tabito and to Okura, owes something in subject and in details of phrasing to a Chinese tale called the "Visit to the House of Beauties" (*Yu Hsien K'u*), a "mildly improper little romance" which was extremely popular among the fashionable set. Such a blend of early T'ang dynasty parallel prose with Japanese tanka may seem bizarre to us, but far from sensing any disharmony in such hybrid forms, the Japanese literati (like Western macaronic poets) took a delight in juxtaposing the two languages they knew. In the Nara period we find both chōka and tanka in such contexts; but in general there was a trend in the direction of substituting Chinese prose for the chōka in narrative and philosophical modes, and it is significant that the prose form developed apace as the tanka usurped the pre-eminence of the chōka. The trend may be seen in a comparison of the treatment of the same legendary motif by Takahashi Mushimaro (*MYS*, IX: 1809–11) of the early Nara period and by an anonymous later poet (*MYS*, XVI: 3786–87). Mushimaro tells the story of a maiden and her lovers (she committed suicide because of her distress at the hostility between her two suitors) in a long chōka, which he follows by two tanka expressing his own feelings on visiting the maiden's tomb. The anonymous poet tells the story in Chinese prose, adding two tanka which he attributes to the bereaved suitors.

The picture that has been drawn thus far of some of the ways in which the Chinese example affected Japanese poets in the early literary period is only an outline. Innumerable details could be added to show how phrases from Chinese poetry and prose were translated into Japanese by Nara poets and used for imagistic effect, and comparisons could be made between the arrangement of Japanese poetry by form, subject, and chronological sequence in the *Man'yōshū* and the classifications in the Chinese anthologies that were known to the compilers of the Japanese collection. These details are interesting and important in themselves because they show differences as well as similarities, but they would add little to the general outlines of the sketch which has been given.

The increasing self-confidence of the Japanese literati in using the Chinese language, and the growing prestige of Chinese literature among the now sophisticated intelligentsia, led, as we have suggested, to a narrowing of the range of Japanese poetry, which tended to become more private, more personal, and even more frivolous as it continued to give ground before the pressure of a vastly older and more sophisticated tradition. The *Kaifūsō*, the first collection of poems in Chinese by Japanese poets, was compiled in 751, shortly before the *Man'yōshū*, and it was followed in the early decades of the ninth century by three imperial anthologies of poetry in Chinese. We may conjecture that good Japanese poetry continued to be composed even during the height of passion for Chinese verse, but it was not taken very seriously nor considered fit for solemn occasions—and its restriction to private modes and informal uses meant that very little of it was regarded as worthy of preservation. The *Kakyō Hyōshiki* of 772, which is the earliest attempt to forge a systematic poetic for Japanese poetry, is a ludicrous example of the incongruous application of Chinese rules of metric and other formal standards to a medium that remains obstinately Japanese, an attempt very much like the ill-advised efforts of some Renaissance English poets systematically to impose classical rhetorical theory upon English poetry. The attempt could only fail, and we may be amused by its extremes today, but it presages things to come in the ninth and tenth centuries. When the prestige of the native tradition was restored, it was done by a more knowing and at the same time more fundamental application of Chinese techniques to Japanese poetry.

Much of what has been said may give the impression that the effect of the Chinese example on Japanese poetry in the early literary period was merely to enervate or divert the native tradition. This may indeed be said with some justice of the poetry written toward the end of the period. At the same time, Japanese poetry throughout this age shows an independence from Chinese influence—one might almost say a resistance to such influence—which is remarkable. Nowhere is the stubborn persistence of the native tradition more apparent than in the poetic vocabulary. If we think of comparable ages of intercultural influence in the West—the age of Chaucer in England, or of the Renaissance in France—we might reasonably expect the Japanese poetic vocabulary to have been flooded with Chinese loan-words, just as Chaucer's was enriched with borrowings from the French, and the Renaissance poets' with new words coined from the Latin. But no such thing happened in Japan. In the late poetry of the *Man'yōshū*, one can find after diligent searching a scant handful of Chinese Buddhist and Taoist religious terms, one or two Chinese place names, and a few miscellaneous words of Chinese or Sanskrit origin, but these are used more often than not for the comic effect created by the very fact of their strangeness. The overwhelming majority of Chinese expressions, images, and ideas that we have discussed were assimilated into the Japanese poetic vocabulary only by translation: the Chinese *T'ien ho* or "River of Heaven" became *Ama no gawa*; *Fo tao* or the "Way of the Buddha" simply *Michi*, "path" or "way," and so on.

The differences between the phonological structure of Chinese and Japanese are indeed much greater than between English and French or French and Latin, and poets in this period seem to have sensed an inevitable disharmony between the two languages. Moreover, foreign words were probably still too unfamiliar to be understood by audiences to whom the native poetry was still communicated largely by way of oral recitation. In any case, one of the most important reasons for the fundamentally "Japanese" quality of the poetry of the early literary period is the persistence of native usage in the poetic language. This consciousness of the irreconcilable differences between the poetic media of China and Japan led in the following age to strict taboos against the use of any words of recognizably Chinese origin in serious Japanese poetry. The language itself gave protection to the native tradition in an age of bold experimentation and a manifold, if not unquestioning, indebtedness to China. In the final analysis, the remarkable thing about the poetry of the early literary period is not its Chinese cast, but its greatness as the first flowering of a native tradition. The great poetry of the age remains Japanese in essence; it is directed, not dominated, by the Chinese example.

THE POET AND HIS AUDIENCE

The importance of China to the development of a Japanese literary tradition should not be underestimated; without such help the Japanese would have had no method of writing, no real concept of style, a far smaller body of poetic genres and materials—in short, almost no literary sense at all. Yet the Japanese poet who was awakened by China to a sense of his identity as a poet looked upon himself as a Japanese poet, and pursued his craft along native lines in a language very different from the Chinese. To him China was more important in creating a literary consciousness than in stipulating the terms in which this new awareness was to be expressed. Even while China was assisting Japanese poets in such an important way, it was playing a similar role in helping to create the complement to literary poets—a literary audience. To say that the new audience was literary means both that its members could appreciate a more complex art, and that they responded in a literary fashion as readers or listeners who could take esthetic pleasure in the distinction between art and reality, rather than as ritual participants awed by mythic fable. Like the poets, however, the audience remained Japanese. Native experience, native customs, and native needs were the determinants of the relationship between the poet and his audience.

The new culture was civilized most essentially in its ability to read, to write, and to preserve its products in writing. Although the great fact of literacy represented the crucial difference between primitive and civilized Japan, this development and the growth of a literary consciousness did not mean that the poetry of the period was restricted to the literati. Japanese poetic forms were then as now relatively short and easily memorized, poems were still recited, the civilized portion of the country was still very small, and as the central government spread its political and cultural influence over the areas of the islands it ruled, it was easy for commoners to receive many of the poetic benefits of the new tide of culture. Educated priests, and more especially the growing class of government officials whose duties took them to the provinces, carried with them the new poetry, re-creating, however sketchily, the audience at Court. Shortly thereafter, the cultural tide ebbed back to the capital, carrying a few new modes and an increased poetic stock. The Chinese genres of poems of parting and travel were given vital meaning by the experience of travel to and from the provinces; places of natural beauty at distant points were celebrated until they became familiar to the ears even of men who did not venture from the capital; and such genres as "Poems of the East" (*Azumauta*), having been wrought into new, acceptable forms, added in fresh ways to the range of sophisticated Japanese poetry. The development of a true literary atmosphere now made it possible to absorb the increasingly complex variety of experience of this expanding society into a rapidly developing native tradition.

Much of the poetry of the age has come down to us shadowed in anonymity, but this is more the result of the vagaries of history than a literary fact, since almost all the poems in the *Man'yōshū,* whatever their literary quality, smack of individuality and particular human experience. Of course, it is easy to exaggerate this element of direct personalism, as some patriotic Japanese critics have done, into the legend that the *Man'yōshū* is a collection with a poem, as it were, by every member of the eighty clans. But the real direction of the early literary period, as well as its greatest accomplishments, is to be found in the work of poets who are identifiable, if only as names, artists who were sensitive courtiers of lesser or greater rank.

The best known of these names is Hitomaro, and the "Hitomaro Collection" (*Hitomaro Kashū*) is perhaps the best guide not only to his greatness but to the nature of the new culture as well. Like almost all great poets, he established a tradition that attracted writers of inferior stature, and that led later writers to attribute to him a miscellany of poems good and bad which were written in his styles or which could acquire luster by being associated with his bright name. In earlier times, a poem and a poet could survive only indirectly, as it were, by attribution to an emperor, a divine or mythological personage, or an important occasion. Such attribution was now made to a historical individual, a person of no exalted social rank (Hitomaro held only inconspicuous posts at Court and in the provinces), simply because he was a famous poet. Other groups of poets made up the literary scene and are represented by the poems that survive in the *Man'yōshū.* The two groups that we can most clearly determine are members either of the royal household, who tended to retain certain qualities from earlier poetry in their work, or of the Ōtomo clan and its associates. Ōtomo Yakamochi, one of the compilers of the *Man'yōshū,* chose copiously from among the poems of such writers as his father Ōtomo Tabito; his aunt Lady Ōtomo of Sakanoe (fl. ca. 750) and her elder daughter Yamanoe Okura, who was associated with Tabito and admired by Yakamochi; as well as from his own works. This was not merely a preference dictated by clan loyalty or a prejudice in favor of the styles of his own group; it was also the readiest and even the only possible way to gather together a collection in days before printing had spread manuscripts into readily available books. Yakamochi's role in preserving the poetry of his group tells us even more about the practice of poetry in this age. It suggests by example that other powerful literary groups, now only imperfectly represented in the *Man'yōshū*, and often anonymously, were prolific in poetry of a high order. But perhaps Yakamochi's accomplishment as an editor and compiler is most significant for what it shows of the general advancement in literary civilization. There were other groups like his own with their shared books, poems, traditions, styles, genres, materials, and discoveries; and there was also intercourse between such groups, as the spread of Hitomaro's influence shows. We may now speak with confidence of a literary scene, literary movements, and a conscious literary tradition.

A series of ten poems and their headnote (*MYS,* XVII: 3890–99) gives us a revealing insight into the identity of poets and audiences of this age, with a fine glimpse besides of the sophistication of the poetic act. The poems are written by retainers of Ōtomo Tabito, who took a different route from their master's when he was called back to the capital to receive a promotion. The headnote adds that the retainers composed their poems on "The Sorrows of the Journey." If such a fact does not seem to argue an unusual refinement, an esteem of poetic composition, we have only to ask ourselves when a governor of one of our states encouraged his subordinates to write poetry. It is still more important for our understanding of the developing Japanese tradition that we can see several implications in this situation: a respect for poetry; an assumption that these men could perform as poets; the selection of a relatively fixed topic of an occasional nature; and the emulation of Chinese practice in choosing such a topic. Tabito's men could expect to hear their leader's poem when they arrived in the capital, from which we can infer that the poetic audience was very largely an audience of men who were themselves poets.

The burgeoning new literary culture enabled poets to write meaningfully of themselves and their world, but in addition to the means of poetry, poets of every age and place require some sort of formal relationship between themselves and their world. It was no longer possible in the early literary period to treat poetry merely as a ritual or as the purely social act of the minstrel. The poets were faced with the problem of adjusting their own personalities to the literary situation. This meant that they needed to create in their imaginations both a view of themselves (or someone else) as the speaker of the poem and a view of their audience as tutored people who could respond to the poetic speaker as well as to the poetic materials. In this sense, the poet and his audience were brought together by the work of art itself to participate in the poetic act. The act of poetic composition involves the important distinctions between public and private, as well as formal and informal, poetry that we have treated among other constant elements of the tradition. One of the glories of the poetry of Hitomaro and Okura is their splendid public and formal conception of the relation between poet and audience—without losing the direct personalism which is characteristic of their age. This can best be shown by such a poem as Hitomaro's "On Seeing the Body of a Man Lying Among the Stones on the Island of Samine in Sanuki Province" (*MYS*, II: 220–22).

Tamamo yoshi	O the precious land of Sanuki,
Sanuki no kuni wa	Resting where the seaweed glows like
Kunikara ka	polished gems!
Miredo mo akanu	Perhaps for its precious nature
Kamukara ka	I never tire in my gazing on it,
Kokoda tōtoki	Perhaps for its holy name
Ametsuchi	It is the most divine of sights.
Hitsuki to tomo ni	It will flourish and endure
Tariyukan	Together with the heavens and earth,
Kami no miomo to	With the shining sun and moon,
Tsugite kuru	For through successive ages it has come down
	That the landface is the face of a god.

Naka no minato yu	Having rushed our ship upon the breakers
Fune ukete	From the busy port of Naka,
Wa ga kogikureba	We came rowing steadily till the wind
Toki tsu kaze	That rises with the tides
Kumoi ni fuku ni	Stormed down from the dwelling of the
Oki mireba	clouds—
Toinami tachi	Looking back upon the open sea,
He mireba	I saw waves gather in their mounting
Shiranami sawaku	surges,
	And looking off beyond the prow
	I saw the white waves dashing on the surf.

Isanatori	In awe of the terrible sea,
Umi o kashikomi	Where whales are hunted down as prey,
Yuku fune no	We clutched the steering oar,
Kaji hikiorite	Straining the plunging ship upon its
Ochikochi no	course;
Shima wa ōkedo	And though here and there
Nakuwashi	We saw the scattered island coasts
	To dash upon for safety,

Samine no shima no	We sought haven on rugged Samine,
Arisomo ni	The isle so beautiful in name.
Iorite mireba	Erecting a little shelter, we looked about,
Nami no to no	And then we saw you:
Shigeki hamabe o	Pillowed upon your shaking beach,
Shikitae no	Using those wave-beaten rocks
Makura ni nashite	As if the coast were spread out for your
Aradoko ni	bedding;
Korofusu kimi ga	On such a rugged place
	You have laid yourself to rest.
Ie shiraba	If I but knew your home,
Yukite mo tsugen	I would go tell them where you sleep;
Tsuma shiraba	If your wife but knew this home,
Ki mo towamashi o	She would come here searching for you,
Tamahoko no	But knowing nothing of the way—
Michi dani shirazu	The way straight as a courtier's spear—
Oboboshiku	How must she be waiting,
Machi ka kou ran	How anxiously now longing for you,
Hashiki tsumara wa.	She the dear one you called wife.

Envoys

Tsuma mo araba	If your wife were here,
Tsumite tagemashi	She would be out gathering your food,
Sami no yama	She would pick the greens
No no e no uhagi	From the hillslopes of Samine—
Suginikerazu ya.	But is their season not now past?
Oki tsu nami	So you rest your head,
Kiyoru ariso o	Pillowed on the rocky spread-out bedding
Shikitae no	Of this rugged shore,
Makura to makite	While the furious, wind-driven surf
Naseru kimi ka mo.	Pounds ever in from off the sea.

The complex skill of the poem makes clear its formal nature, but perhaps it is not immediately evident why such a subject as finding an unnamed body should be called public. The answer is of course that Hitomaro's treatment of his subject renders it public. Only the last third or so of the chōka and the two envoys deal directly with the dead man. These are moving enough in themselves, but by themselves would constitute a far less significant poem. The middle section of the chōka enlarges the meaning of the pathos in the last section, since Hitomaro (or his poetic speaker) has himself made a trip to the island of Samine through a storm that nearly cost him and his fellow voyagers their lives. This connection between the speaker and the poetic situation charges the poem with a personal integrity that is all the more effective for Hitomaro's avoidance of any overt, moralizing connection between the dead man's experience and his own. The fact that the speaker barely escaped with his life raises the tone of the last section from one of pathos to one of broad human sympathy. Like the dead man, he too has had to leave his wife and home behind. At first glance, Hitomaro's overture in the first section of the chōka may seem to have little more than a geographical connection with the rest of the poem, but such an opening is of prime importance to the poem's tone and meaning. In most general terms, it elevates the subject to a realm of universal significance by relating the death of an unnamed man to a divinely ordered scheme. Moreover, the very nature of the overture is such that it appeals to a profound instinct in man, or at least to the sensibility of man in many civilizations: the need to know the origin of man, a civilized impulse which is closely related at once to a religious and a historical sense. Not all civilizations feel, or in any event give poetic expression to, such a need; but the account of origins is a conspicuous feature in Japanese poetry of the early literary period, and appears in altered forms in later periods. An overture such as Hitomaro's is indeed rhetorically little more than the "preparation" so much in evidence in primitive song, and its theme is not new, for the Japanese had long been interested in their mythical past. Yet few passages would show so well as this one, with its stylistic elevation and poetic relevance, how far Japanese poetry had advanced since the days of a song like "Princess Kage's Lament."

The interest of the Japanese in their origins bears a close relation to their veneration of the past and their deep response to time, and these three concerns may be regarded as crucial elements in their sensibility. Often these concerns heighten the tone and meaning in poems dealing with other, more particular subjects; and often they are only implicit. Whatever form they may take, these concerns are an indigenous element in the poetic sensibility and cannot be accounted for by reference to contact with Chinese poetry. The Chinese did indeed venerate the past, but they systematized it into recurring cycles that tended to break the sense of continuity so crucial to the Japanese concept. Comparable passages in Chinese poetry are, therefore, more ethical in tone— as one dynasty is like another, so this ruler is like that just king or tyrant— and the emotional tenor produces a far different view of the world. Japanese concern with time and origins (though not perhaps the veneration of the past) is best compared with certain Western interests and their expression in poetry. In pagan and Judaeo-Christian writings alike we find similar interests. In

On the Sublime, the pseudo-Longinus declares in a famous passage that the most sublime expression ever written was the *In principio* with which the Old Testament begins. The same appreciation and prizing of the past can be found stated in terms remarkably like Hitomaro's in the opening passages of many of Pindar's odes. The *Tenth Pythian* (Richmond Lattimore's translation) begins:

> Blessed is Lakedaimon,
> happy Thessaly. Both have kings of one line
> from Herakles, best in battle.
> Is this boasting to no point? But Pytho and Pelinna lead me
> on, and Aleuas' sons, to bring to Hippokleas
> ringing praise of a chorus of men.

The technique of the two poems, the value placed on divine origins, and the effect are very much the same. The satisfaction of possessing such origins elevates Pindar's ode tonally, and enriches the significance of its subject by illuminating the present with a valued past. There are of course important differences, too, but these are secondary ones determined by the individual cultures and need not concern us here. The technique of the overture, as we have called it, is common to both cultures and can be found in modern times in certain English odes. Dryden's *Song for St. Cecilia's Day,* for example, opens with the same sweep of background, here the creation of the world through divine music: "From harmony, from heav'nly harmony / This universal frame began." In all three poems, great beginnings establish the tone for poets dealing with public poetry, helping to raise the significance of such subjects as music or a dead man to sublime concern. With his overture, then, Hitomaro both touches upon profound elements in the Japanese sensibility—depths it shares with ours—and lends a dignified beauty to his subject.

The overture has another, more specific function in the poem; it casts a tragic, if kind, irony over the rest of the poem and makes the poem public in scope as well as sympathetically personal in tone. The irony stems from the fact that the province of Sanuki is such a beautiful place and, more than beautiful, auspicious and divine. Its lovely island of Samine is the last place where one would expect to be killed in shipwreck. Yet this is where the man died, leaving behind a wife who does not even know that she must grieve. The ironic discrepancy between what is and what ought to be is a tragic one echoed in many passages in the poem—for example, in the first envoy. It would do the wife no good to gather food for her shipwrecked husband—he is dead, after all—and ironically it is not the season for greens that has passed, but the season of a man's life.

The tragic irony is kind, however, because of Hitomaro's gentle sympathy and the involvement of his speaker in the same experience of the storm at sea.

Moreover, beyond this tempering of the irony, the fact remains that Sanuki is a beautiful place and the land is divine. It is not the worst place to die, and the eternal if inscrutable decree of the god of the land assures us of divine control and meaning, even when they are tragically difficult for men to find.

The role of the overture is equally crucial in lending the tragedy a public significance. The poet suggests that all men know these things, and that he need only reaffirm them in terms relevant to the particular situation of the poem. Because of the overture, the dead man serves as a symbol of all human beings, and the poet wisely does not touch on particular details of the dead man's appearance, but rather treats his position on the beach and his private-social relationship with a wife. Between the beginning and the end, the divine overture and the dead body, stands Hitomaro—a man, a voyager, and a poet. Because of his testimony of experience and his art, his audience finds it possible to participate in the poetic materials. A perfect relation between the poet and his audience has been achieved.

The poets and cultured readers among Hitomaro's audience shared even more with him. In this poem, as in others, they would recognize his use of familiar traditions and materials in new ways. We have discussed the complex question of the relation between his overtures, the *norito* (Shinto liturgy), and the Chinese *fu*. Other poems by Hitomaro lead us to believe that he probably borrowed ideas and phrasing from earlier poets whose work is now lost. Whether there is such borrowing in "On Seeing the Body of a Man" we cannot say, but his first envoy to "On Passing the Ruined Capital of Ōmi" (*MYS*, I: 30) has the same general conception as that of an earlier tanka by one Lady Toneri Kine (*MYS*, II: 152). Kine's poem reads:

Yasumishishi	The Cape of Kara
Wa go ōkimi no	In the land of Shiga must be waiting,
Ōmifune	Even longing,
Machi ka kou ran	For the great ship of my Lord,
Shiga no Karasaki.	Who ruled the land in peace.

And Hitomaro's envoy:

Sasanami no	The Cape of Kara
Shiga no Karasaki	At Shiga in Sasanami still remains
Sakiku aredo	As it ever was,
Ōmiyabito no	But though it wait throughout the ages,
Fune machikanetsu.	The courtiers' pleasure boats will not return.

Borrowings and redefinitions are characteristics of the age in that they involve open use of older materials and forms, not because of a neoclassical desire to call to mind the atmosphere and meaning of the original, but for the material or form itself, in the manner of Chaucer and Shakespeare in a later age and in another country.

Not all the poems of the period are public and formal in nature, and yet even in some of the most informal verses we frequently find surprising resemblances to Hitomaro's public treatment of his materials. A curious poem by Lady Ōtomo of Sakanoe survives with a title sounding at once public and primitive, "At a Religious Service for Her Ancestral God" (*MYS*, III: 379–80). Lady Ōtomo's prayer, however, is not the kind of poem to be chanted in public, and the poem is completely informal. The first sixteen lines constitute a preparation; the section addresses the god of the Ōtomo clan and describes her imagined posture of prayer—"Bending my legs like a deer." The ritual is one of a familiar, public Shinto rite, and the opening of the poem is not unlike one of Hitomaro's overtures in tone. The startling thing about the service is that it is all imaginary, and that the chōka and the envoy both end with an extraordinary plaint:

> Kaku dani mo   In spite of prayer,
> Ware wa koinan   Shall I never find a chance
> Kimi ni awaji ka mo.   To meet the man I love?

Such a strange mélange was probably written half as a prayer and half as a novel appeal to a lover, to whom it might be sent in a letter. It is not a blasphemous poem, since the god properly watched over the interests of the clan, but still it is not the sort of thing Lady Ōtomo would wish to have spread abroad. She has used public materials for a private response, Hitomaro private materials with a public treatment. Both poems, however, have a complete tonality, and both presume an audience awake to the varieties of esthetic distance.

Obviously Lady Ōtomo's poem is greatly inferior to Hitomaro's, but the inferiority is significant in more than one respect. In the first place, Lady Ōtomo meant this as an informal poem and therefore felt no necessity to do her very best or to appeal to a wide audience. Then, too, the use of the informal mode for private discourse is typical of a large portion of Japanese poetry from its beginnings to the present day; the novel thing about the poem lies in its strange use of public materials. And finally, Lady Ōtomo lived toward the end of the period, and her poem shows the increasing tendency to use native poetic forms for informal verse. The public splendors of Hitomaro and the other great poets of the age were fast fading.

The early literary period also produced a very substantial amount of private but formal poems, those meant for wide scrutiny but on topics of private interest. Ōtomo Yakamochi excelled brilliantly in this mode, and his work lends a real beauty to the twilight of the period. One of his tanka "On seeing the

Blossoms of the Peach and Damson Trees" (*MYS*, XIX: 4139), is a single melodious syntactical flow which is given an imagistic development of increasingly narrow focus from the season, to the garden, to the trees, to the path, and to the woman—although in translation English syntax demands the reversal of this order.

Haru no sono	A woman appears
Kurenai niou	And gazes from the little path
Momo no hana	That reflects the radiance
Shitateru michi ni	Of the peach trees flowering crimson
Idetatsu otome.	In the garden warm with spring.

The care Yakamochi has lavished on this poem shows how much he felt it worthy of a wide audience. He has a series of three similarly lovely poems on spring which are also formal if private compositions, for all his notes claiming that they were composed on the spot (*MYS*, XIX: 4290–92 with accompanying headnotes).

Haru no no ni	Now it is spring—
Kasumi tanabiki	And across the moors the haze
Uraganashi	Stretches heavily—
Kono yūkage ni	And within these rays at sunset,
Uguisu naku mo.	A warbler fills the radiant mist with song.

Wa ga yado no	From my garden
Isasa muratake	Where bamboo stands in little clusters,
Fuku kaze no	Faintly comes the sound
Oto no kasokeki	Of the leaves that rustle darkly
Kono yūbe ka mo.	In the breeze of this spring night.

Uraura ni	The lark soars
Tereru harubi ni	Into the spring air that shines
Hibari agari	So gloriously—
Kokoro kanashi mo	But I am left behind alone,
Hitori shi omoeba.	And burdened with my thoughts.

Such carefully wrought poems as these by Yakamochi are private, and like many English lyrics by the Metaphysical and Romantic poets, pretend to have no audience except the poet's own musing sensibility. This is only a convention of course, and the wider audience of readers is meant to appreciate the poems at an esthetic remove.

There are, however, some private poems in the *Man'yōshū* that have no counterpart in serious Western poetry, poems composed in a manner which was to have increasing importance for later poetic ages. This is the practice of what might be called composing private poetry on social occasions. When Ōtomo Tabito's men wrote their poems on "The Sorrows of Travel," some of them wrote about such highly personal subjects as their regrets in leaving behind the girls to whom they had formed attachments. (See *MYS*, XVII: 3897.) The practice of writing personal poems on a fixed topic (*dai*) was to become an increasingly important convention of Japanese poetry, and when it did not degenerate into mere virtuosity, it helped to give a public status to the poetic act, if not to the poem itself. This is an entirely different concept of the poetic act from that of Western poets, even from the practice in Leigh Hunt's circle of composing poems on such subjects as "The Grasshopper and the Cricket," since a poem like the one by Keats on this subject was written privately among friends rather than in the public atmosphere of imperial poetry parties or the departure of the Viceroy of Tsukushi for the capital. Such an essentially different approach to the poetic act helps explain why the Japanese distinguish more readily between formal and informal than public and private poetry: their distinction is clear for the act of composition, while ours is often blurred.

The sophistication implied by such methods of composition did not, however, prevent the cultured poets of the period from taking a lively interest in what, for lack of any satisfactory term, must be loosely called folk poetry. The fact that the folk poetry of the *Man'yōshū* involves the relation between poet and audience will be evident once certain unusual aspects of these genres are explained. It must be said at the outset that from the time the *Man'yōshū* was compiled there have been strong suspicions about the folk authorship of many poems. Our suspicions are even stronger than those of the compilers. The so-called "Poems of the Fisher-Folk of Shiga" (*MYS*, XVI: 3860–69), for example, contain primitive sentiments and materials, but the original note attributes them to Yamanoe Okura, an attribution that we can the more readily believe in view of his sympathy for the lower classes expressed in such a poem as his "Dialogue on Poverty." In this instance, and we may believe the same of many other poems, a sophisticated poet has embodied folk materials into the sophisticated form of the tanka.

The complexity of the problem increases when we consider the "Poems of the Frontier Guards" (*Sakimori no uta*). These are poems with two or three main themes, most typically an expression of the guardsman's willingness to obey the imperial call or else a lament at leaving his home for hazardous duty from which he may not return. Some poems express the sadness of the wife who is left behind. A note to a group of these poems (see *MYS*, XX: 4432) tells us that they had been copied down by a certain Iware Morogimi and sent to Yakamochi. Mixed in with these poems are others in the same genre, some definitely and some very likely by Yakamochi himself (e.g., *MYS*,

XX: 4434-35), and there is no way of telling how much Yakamochi may have touched up the poems sent him, or how many of the "Poems of the Frontier Guards" were written by men as sophisticated as Yakamochi. There is, moreover, the additionally complicating fact that a similar genre had long existed in China, where the literati often composed poems expressing the feelings of men of low station on being conscripted into military service.

Few assured conclusions can be drawn from such a tangled heap of evidence. Most Japanese commentators have had their suspicions, but have maintained that many of the poems express a true folk spirit. Perhaps so, but the folk spirit is a vague thing. We note that all of these poems are tanka, none are of the various forms of even-numbered lines that characterize most Japanese folk songs. This fact suggests that even when the poems are composed by frontier guards, the folk spirit has found expression in an artistic form which the cultural influence of the capital has spread through the provinces. Some of these poems may indeed have been composed by simple people putting simple materials into more or less sophisticated styles developed at the capital; but it would have been far easier for sophisticated poets to embody the simple materials in forms long since familar to them. Some of the folk poets were sophisticated men, and the largest audience for their poems was to be found at the capital, the only place with a large body of literate people for whom an anthology might be compiled.

Poems written in another genre, the "Poems of the East" (*Azumauta*) were grouped in the fourteenth of the twenty books of the *Man'yōshū* under rubrics indicating the eastern provinces from which they were collected. They are of uncertain date, but there is one convincing argument in favor of their having been composed by the people of the provinces rather than by Court poets. This is the proven fact that the poems are in a different dialect from the one spoken at the capital—a dialect whose different phonological system as well as vocabulary is clearly reflected in the manner in which the "Poems of the East" are recorded. It is, therefore, practically certain that they are of provincial authorship, even though they were doubtless written down by a literate official from the capital.

The form of these poems is not, however, of provincial origin; like the other so-called folk poems, they are tanka. Like the "Poems of the Frontier Guards," the "Poems of the East" represent the spread of Court influence into the provinces, where folk themes were rendered into the now dominant tanka form. It might be observed that a little more help from Court poets would have been welcome, since the poems are far from being the most interesting in the collection for their artistic merit. The virtue they possess is usually a kind of naïveté that more sophisticated poets, especially in China and Japan, have ever found appealing, as the fact that these poems were collected into the *Man'yōshū* shows. One of the most attractive of the poems is one that is of value if only for the way it shows that the course of true love occasionally does run smoothly in Japanese poetry (*MYS*, XIV: 3373).

Tamagawa ni	Is it not wonderful
Sarasu tezukuri	That like the homespun brightly bleached
Sarasara ni	In the Tama River,
Nani zo kono ko no	This girl somehow, more and more,
Kokoda kanashiki.	Grows ever dearer to my eyes?

This and similar poems show another quality that is of great importance to our understanding of the identity of poets and audiences. Most of the "Poems of the East" seem to grow from what might be called a town culture, little societies in contact with the Court, however distantly or belatedly. The poem just quoted suggests communal bleaching, and there are other poems about men conscripted (*MYS*, XIV: 3480), or post-couriers (*MYS*, XIV: 3439), or of a young girl who anticipates the night when the son of the district lord will hold her work-roughened hands (*MYS*, XIV: 3459). These are clearly provincial poems, but not folk poems in the Western sense. It appears that the culture of the provinces was being shaped by the gradual influence of the Court, which brought a new literary consciousness to outlying settlements, not that the folk had long been singing poems which now suddenly caught the attention of the capital. The political and cultural consolidation of the country seems to have extended the number of both poets and audiences.

One question about the "Poems of the Frontier Guards" and the "Poems of the East" remains unanswered. Why did such a poet as Yakamochi go to the trouble of collecting and including them among the works of such sophisticated poets as himself? A partial explanation may be that the Court was interested in finding native poems comparable to similar Chinese genres, to show that the Japanese poets were every bit as versatile as the Chinese. But this does not show why poets like Okura and Yakamochi should themselves write poems in these genres. Perhaps there are other explanations—apart from the Chinese example—for their interest. The example of Yakamochi's imitations suggests a primitivistic impulse among sophisticated poets toward the end of the early literary period, an impulse that led them to search for naïve poetic staples that could bring a new freshness into their poetic experience. When the poets of Hitomaro's generation used older materials, they did so with the very different aim of reconstituting the simple into forms of complex art. In addition, although these poems did not alter other, more sophisticated modes in any appreciable way, they offered poets alternative styles and modes in which to express a wider range of feeling. Closely related to the opportunity to employ alternative styles is another attraction—the possibility of finding in these simpler poems subjects that would be considered out of place, even indecorous, in the usual poetry of the Court. And finally, the composition of poems in the folk genres enabled poets to conceive of themselves in new roles as the poetic speakers of their poems. The problem of how to pose before one's audience is central to the poetic act, and a Yakamochi could find a certain novelty in posing as someone simpler than himself.

Yakamochi's and Okura's technique of posing as someone other than themselves suggests a final aspect of the relation between the poets and audiences of the period. In one sense, the use of assumed roles was no new thing to Japanese poetry. As we have seen, primitive poems are mostly attributed to gods, legendary members of the imperial family, or real historical figures who could not have written them. Real poets had composed real, if primitive, poems in the guise of unreal or socially exalted figures. When later, more sophisticated writers posed as other people, they chose to represent themselves as more-or-less ordinary human beings with whom all men could share, by virtue of their art, the experience dealt with by the poem. The motives that appear to lie behind the use of assumed roles seem to be a mingled primitivism and consciousness of Chinese practice, a sympathy for other human beings, and a purely literary desire to bring a dramatic intensity into poetry. Yakamochi's composition of poems in the genre of "Poems of the Frontier Guards" seems to show a mingled Chinese and primitivistic impulse, but such a motive cannot be attributed to him alone, and we cannot at this distance feel certain that his motives were purely esthetic, that he lacked sympathy for men of lower classes.

There are many poems in the *Man'yōshū* that express a strong human sympathy for other human beings who suffered every bit as deeply as courtiers. Poems like Hitomaro's "On Seeing the Body of a Man" or "On the Death of a Woman of the Court" (*MYS*, II: 217–19) show such sympathy without the creation of a fictional speaker greatly different from himself. Poems like Okura's in the pose of "The Fisher-Folk of Shiga," however, or the "Twenty-Three Laments for the Crown Prince by the Palace Guards" (*MYS*, II: 171–93), in which Hitomaro is thought to have had a hand, show the technique fully realized. Once developed, the technique of assumed roles was of great use in gaining a dramatic intensity for poems that otherwise would have to be purely lyric or narrative in nature.

The presentation of the "voice" or thoughts of a fictional speaker varies widely in use in the *Man'yōshū* and accounts for some of its most interesting poems. There are some beggar-songs (e.g., *MYS*, XVI: 3885–86), which present animals telling the story of their sufferings. Of the more than sixscore "Seventh Night Poems" (*Tanabata no Uta*) in the *Man'yōshū*, one of the most attractive is by an unknown author who presents the emotions of the Weaver Maid by making her the speaker of the poem (*MYS*, IX: 1764–65).

Another chōka and envoy (*MYS*, XIII: 3295–96) have been rendered doubly dramatic by combining the genre of the dialogue poem with assumed roles. The chōka represents an exchange between a mother and her son about his beloved, and the envoy the lad's soliloquy as he later hastens off to meet his girl. An amusing note to a lament (*MYS*, XIX: 4236–37) shows how highly developed the dramatic consciousness of poets and audiences in the age had become. In this lament, a man mourns the death of a wife who had been very dear to him. But a postscript tells us that the poem was recited by a certain Gamō, a courtesan!

Although these examples might be multiplied by many other anonymous poems that use the technique of assumed roles, the best illustration of what might be accomplished in a literary way with the poet posing as someone else is probably Yamanoe Okura's vivid "Dialogue on Poverty" (*MYS*, V: 892–93). The poem is a dramatic creation of a fictional situation. There are three speakers—a Poor Man and a Destitute Man in the chōka, and the Poet in the envoy—with Okura's art and sympathy fusing in the sharply etched imagery. (For a translation, see below, pp. 121–23). His dramatic bent and fervent moral sympathy led him to compose other poems in assumed roles representing people of many ranks. "Six Poems Representing the Feelings of Ōtomo Kumagori" (*MYS*, V: 886–91), for example, present the feelings and words of Kumagori as he lay dying on the road to the capital. Unfortunately, Okura's strain of moral generalization prevents these poems from achieving the vivid character of his "Dialogue on Poverty."

Yakamochi's style sometimes has a preciosity which makes one reluctant to grant him Okura's vitality. When he adopts the pose of his wife and pretends to yearn for his mother-in-law because her voice is as sweet as orange blossoms in summer when the *hototogisu* sings, one feels some hesitation in believing that his feelings were deeply stirred on the occasion—specified by the headnote of the poem as "Being Asked by His Wife for a Poem Which She Could Send to Her Mother in the Capital" (*MYS*, XIX: 4169–70). And yet he could adopt a pose with great feeling, as his poems conveying "The Parting Sorrows of a Frontier Guard" show (*MYS*, XX: 4398–4400 and 4408–12).

Such poems as these with their assumed roles are striking proof of the advances of literary technique during the early literary period. More specifically, they show a greater sophistication in the concept of the artistic identity of the poet, in the imaginative agility of audiences, and in the complex possibilities of the relation between poets and their audiences. Perhaps we would not be surprised to find the technique of assumed roles employed by the great poets of the age, but the fact that many other poets also adopted complex poses shows that the advances made over primitive modes were the possession of most poets of the age. A wide variety of subjects and tones were conveyed with

the assurance of poets who know their art and who could expect an apprecia-
tive response from their readers. The two poetic acts of composition and re-
ception (by either reading or listening) could now take place in poems complicated by artistic removals. This is to say that simple declaration has given way
to a complex poetic relationship in which there may be two poetic speakers
and two audiences—on the one hand the poet and his fictional speaker, and
on the other the person the fictional speaker addresses and the audience of
real people reading or hearing the poem. In artistic terms, a greater esthetic
distance and a more complex presentation of materials characterize the poetry
of this age. Such a development shows that the early literary period was an
age of self-conscious literary artists and alert audiences. Once a nation's poetry
has reached this stage, there is no turning back to naïveté except self-con-
sciously. At this point, every aspect of poetry is reflected in the techniques
employed.

POETIC PRACTICE

THE VARIETY OF GENRES, MODES, AND TONES

From time to time we have stressed the variety of forms, genres, modes,
and tones in the poetry of the early literary period. It is now necessary to
explain why this variety is important, how it came into being, and what its
literary effect was upon the poetry of the age. A multiplicity of forms is not,
in itself, a determinant of great art, but the strong Japanese esteem for tradition has often led to more and more limited forms in which a correspondingly
increased complexity of technique might choke the talents of all but the most
gifted poets. Such a situation, as twentieth-century poets and readers in the
West know all too well, can break down what might be called the atmosphere
of creative rapport between a poet and his audience.

On the other hand, the wide realm of experience that Japanese poets and
audiences shared in the generation of Hitomaro meant that many aspects of
their lives could also be shared in art. The development of a complex relationship between poet and audience and the wide realm of shared experience
alike were expressed in a heterogeneous poetry which the Japanese tradition
was not to know again until modern times. Viewed in one way, there are few
poetic forms in the *Man'yōshū*—in fact, for all real purposes only two, the
chōka and the tanka. However, if we view the poetry of the time in terms of
the genres and modes employed, or of the range of tone, we find a very rich
variety. The paucity of poetic form on the one hand and the profusion of
modes on the other are typical of Japanese poetry of most periods after the
primitive; and although it would be an oversimplification, it would hardly be
wrong to epitomize the history of the Court tradition as the development of
a growing complexity within narrowing boundaries of poetic forms.

Drawing of Kakinomoto Hitomaro by Reizei Tamechika

To simplify the history of the development of poetic modes in the early literary period, it might be said that the age inherited a basic declarative mode from the primitive past. There were, however, a few quasi-narrative primitive poems that seem to anticipate the development of what a Westerner might call lyrical narration in the chōka of Hitomaro, Okura, Kasa Kanamura, Yakamochi, and others. These later narratives were usually lyrical because of the strong personal and descriptive elements they contained, as one may recall from Hitomaro's "On Seeing the Body of a Man." But lyricism took many forms in Japanese poetry. It harmonized with description as well as narration; it colored public as well as private poetry; it made possible the combination of prose with poetry; and it even was to help determine the cast of Japanese dramatic forms. In other words, for us to say, as we must, that the chōka and tanka are almost the only forms in the classical tradition, and that the Japanese poetic genius is predominantly lyrical, is not to say very much about the true variety of Japanese poetry. It tells us little more than would the statement that Shakespeare wrote nothing of worth except in iambic pentameter, because where the Japanese achieve a true variety beyond the reach of Western poetry is in the realm of tone, for which their lyric genius is eminently suited.

Poetic tone is usually defined by Western critics as the attitude, often only implied, of the poet toward his materials and his audience. Our experience in reading Japanese poetry and criticism has led us to extend this definition to include the attitude of the poet toward himself and the poetic tradition. Perhaps a study of Japanese poetry would be useful to students of comparative literature if only to show how right the Japanese have been in emphasizing these additional attitudes, although we believe the standard Western conception must also be used for fullest understanding of the tonal range of Japanese poetry.

There is, then, a very subtle variety in the tone of Japanese Court poetry, but also, in the early literary period, a wide range of a clearly defined nature. As we have seen from a detailed study of Hitomaro's "On Seeing the Body of a Man," there is a sublimity in Hitomaro's poetry that includes a tone akin to tragic elevation and an affirmation of man's relation to a divinely ordered world. The vehicle of this mingling of tragedy and affirmation is a kind of irony that simultaneously absorbs and expresses a wide human experience. The ironic tone is by no means confined to poems by Hitomaro, although no other poet uses it quite as universally or as warmly. Okura's "Lament on the Instability of Human Life" (*MYS*, V: 804–5; for a translation see below, pp. 133–35) develops an irony of girls and boys who engage in youthful pleasure unaware that age will make them miserable, and concludes with an irony finer —although less richly conveyed—in which the adult poet, who is conscious of the irony of time, finds he too can do nothing about it. The ironic tone may vary widely, from the open sarcasm of Yakamochi's telling a certain Yoshida Iwamaro to eat eels if he is suffering from summer-thinness in the heat (*MYS*, XVI: 3853–54) to the same poet's subtle self-irony in another poem of joy "Composed When He Dreamed of His Stray Hawk" (XVII, 4011–15)—the joy lasts only as long as the dream.

Loosely allied to irony in some ways is the vein of criticism and moral exhortation that is best characterized in the writings of this period by the poetry of Okura—probably because he was most congenially interested in similar tones and genres in Chinese poetry. His "Admonition to a Straying Mind" (*MYS*, V: 800–801) at one point addresses the reprobate thus:

Ame e yukaba	Please yourself at will
Na ga manimani	When you arrive in Paradise,
Tsuchi naraba	But while here on earth
Ōkimi imasu . . .	Remember that our Emperor rules!

The ironic tone is not, of course, a necessary condition of such exhortation, as we can see from Yakamochi's strongly worded "Rebuke to the Scribe, Owari Okuhi" (*MYS*, XVIII: 4106–9), who was unfaithful to his wife, or from the "Exhortation to His Clansmen" (*MYS*, XX: 4465–67), when one of them was dismissed from office and brought discredit on the Ōtomo family.

We find many forms of humor in the *Man'yōshū*, sometimes ironic, sometimes of mere good spirits, sometimes in *jeux d'esprit,* and sometimes with serious intent. Once, during a merry party, the men heard a fox bark. The nimble-witted Naga Okimaro was asked to compose a poem referring to a utensil at the party, to the fox, and to a bridge. He promptly replied with a tanka (*MYS*, XVI: 3824).

| Sashinabe ni | Hurry up, lads, |
| Yu wakase kodomo | Heat some water in a kettle— |

Ichihizu no	We'll dash it on the fox
Hibashi yori kon	When he comes over the cypress planks
Kitsu ni amusan.	Of the bridge at the Ichihi Ford.

Tabito's poems in praise of sake include one (*MYS*, III: 348) in which he laughs at the Buddhist teaching that men who waste their lives will be reincarnated as lower forms of life by saying that he is willing to be reborn a bird or an insect in his next life if he can be happy with wine in this one. Okura has a pervasive if somewhat bitter wit that is directed at almost everything. As the Poor Man in the "Dialogue on Poverty" says in part,

Hige kakinadete	I stroke the straggly hairs of my beard,
Are o okite	Declaring to myself:
Hito wa araji to	"There is no one worth thinking about
Hokoroedo . . .	—Apart, of course, from me."

Besides these more complex tones, the poetry naturally touches such simpler tones as the pathetic, the sentimental, and the melancholy. Such tonal attitudes are found more characteristically in the private and informal poetry than in the public and formal poetry, for the good reason that a lover or one's parent is happy to be told he is loved and does not require more than the tinkle of verse to carry the message. For a poet to say in public poetry that he loves his wife requires more considerable pains. The increasingly private nature of poetry toward the end of the early literary period brought a danger that poets would drift off into sentimentality. To avoid such soft attitudes, they experimented with a variety of complex and largely private attitudes that were to become extremely important in the following, more subjective period of the tradition. One of the more complex tonal attitudes is, paradoxically, naïveté—the conscious simplicity of a sophisticated poet like Yakamochi as he wrote in the genre of the "Poems of the Frontier Guards." Even before Yakamochi, Yamabe Akahito (d. ?736) had achieved another, more complex attitude—that of esthetic sensuousness. Japanese poets characteristically are sensuous in their particularity, but Akahito created a style that sometimes aimed only to convey a tonal aura of beauty. In other words, the details were not affective or intellectual vehicles for any readily definable metaphorical tenor. The only connotations were those of beauty, as in this lovely scene of contrast (*MYS*, VI: 1001):

Masurao wa	The noble warriors
Mikari ni tatashi	Set forth upon the royal hunt,
Otomera wa	While the ladies
Akamo susobiku	Trail their scarlet skirts
Kiyoki hamabi o.	Along the clean-swept beach.

How lovely, how simple, we say. But the art and the attitude of mind are highly complex. Akahito grounded his poem on several contrasts: men and women for one, of course, but also the shouting and the bustle of the hunt as opposed to the delicate promenade of the ladies; the strength of the armed men as opposed to the elegant postures of the women; the inland disappearance of the nobles as opposed to the nearly static, colorful movement of the ladies toward the shore; and the bright red of the women's skirts as opposed to the white stretch of sand. Behind this art of beautiful detail, much of it wholly implicit, lies an attitude whose complexity can be understood if we think for how many centuries English poetry was written before it was written for the sake of esthetic sensuousness alone. What we were not to achieve until the nineteenth century, Japanese poetry had accomplished, partly by study of Chinese descriptive poetry, partly on its own, within a century of its growth into a literary art.

A final complex attitude that appears late in this period is what might be called elegant personalism. In part it involves a certain "indoors" spirit, a tone of privacy, of remoteness from the outer world which is gazed at from afar, as we can see in these lines from Yakamochi's "Expressing My Own Thoughts" (*MYS,* XX: 4360–62):

Unabara mireba	When I look upon the great sea plain,
Shiranami no	Where the whitecaps
Yae oru ga ue ni	Splash about upon each other,
Ama obune	I see the fishing boats
Harara ni ukite	Bobbing here and there afar
Ōmike ni	As they gather in
Tsukaematsuru to	Food for the imperial table—
Ochikochi ni	Yes, widely scattered,
Izaritsurikeri.	The boats are fishing on the sea!

No longer does the poet seem to be caught up as a participant in the activities of men in the world, as the speakers of Hitomaro's and Okura's poems are. Instead, he seems almost visibly to retire to his study to compose poems about what the outside world must be like, or he walks alone in his garden and there contemplates a humanly ordered nature. Yakamochi writes of his garden in tones of elegant bewilderment (*MYS,* XIX: 4140):

Wa ga sono no	Fallen in my garden,
Sumomo no hana ka	But lying in the courtyard there,
Niwa ni chiru	Are they damson blossoms,
Hadare no imada	Or patches of lately fallen snow
Nokoritaru ka mo.	Lingering whitely on the ground?

The elegant personalism that we find at the end of the period represents only one style available to the poets of the day. Yakamochi essayed almost every style and attempted to express almost every poetic attitude his generation had inherited—adding some new ones of his own. And the true poetic range of his generation may have been even wider, since the poetry that survives comes to us largely through his hands. The note of personalism is perhaps the dominant undertone of the poetry of the Ōtomo family, probably for the reason given by some Japanese scholars: now in decline, and sometimes in disgrace, the Ōtomo family was forced into a kind of retirement. However, strong as it is, this tone of personalism did not prevent Yakamochi from essaying other attitudes or keep him from developing old attitudes in new ways; and the poetry of the next age seems to develop its poetic attitudes along lines explored by Yakamochi. His lyric poetry has a tonal variety that can be found in the work of very few poets, whether early or late, Japanese or Western.

POETIC LANGUAGE

The great variety of tone in the poetry of the early literary period has its counterpart in the poetic language. This does not mean that the vocabulary of this poetry is a far-ranging one—it is surprisingly small and almost purely Japanese. There are a few words of ultimate Sanskrit or Chinese origin in some of the poems of the *Man'yōshū* (see, for example, XVI: 3846, 3849, 3851, and 3856)—rare exceptions that serve to prove the rule. But although Chinese loan-words are all but excluded from the poetic language, it must also be remembered that the poets from the late seventh century on composed purely Chinese poetry with a certain technical skill. The practice may be compared loosely to that in eighth-century England, when native Anglo-Saxon and Latin writing were two separate media: the Japanese were proficient in both their vernacular and, to a lesser degree, in their "classical" language. The diction of the *Man'yōshū* is further limited in its lack of technical terms, whether of the professions or of religion. What is left is a language chiefly made up of particular nouns, verbs, and adjectives. For example, analysis shows that, apart from particles, the fifty-five lines of Hitomaro's poem "On Seeing the Body of a Man" is made up of fifty-seven nouns, thirty-five verbs, and six adjectives. When it is remembered that the nouns are all particular, and the verbs and adjectives highly inflected, it will be realized what concreteness, economy, movement, and subtlety of a particular kind the language possesses. It is not so much the variety of a poetic medium as the flexibility that is important, and this flexibility for lyric and narrative modes is precisely what the language of the period possesses.

But it is also important to compare the diction of this period with that of later periods if we wish to know something of its special character within the Japanese tradition. Viewed from this standpoint, its most important aspect is that it is not yet established by conscious usage and precedent. To use a convenient Western term, the poetic diction is not yet fixed by decorum. When words are borrowed from earlier poems, they are taken not for their decorous qualities but for what they say; the emphasis is upon the borrowing of material rather than material in a certain phrasing. In the *Man'yōshū* as a whole, there are also many examples of dialect words, words used humorously, and colloquial speech, any one of which would have led Ki no Tsurayuki and his fellow compilers of the *Kokinshū* in the tenth century to categorize the poems separately under the rubric of "unconventional poems" (*haikaiuta*). Indeed, it may have been this growing suspicion of indecorous language that led the fastidious Yakamochi to assign to one special section of the *Man'yōshū* the humorous poems or the rare verses in which non-Japanese words appear.

IMAGERY

The fact that almost all nouns in the poetry of this period are names for particular things, places, or people suggests that in speaking of Japanese poetry, language is closely related to imagery. Perhaps Okura alone wrote poems marked by generalization, but even in his work the short, generalizing conclusions follow long passages of vivid imagery. One cannot escape the truth that Japanese poetry is more richly imagistic than our own. But the comparison between Japanese and Western poetry on the basis of imagery is again only a small part of the story. The more important questions concern the kinds of imagery employed, the uses to which they are put, the changes in imagistic technique during the period, and comparisons with later periods.

The most fruitful way to discuss the kinds and uses of imagery in the poetry of the early literary period is by an analysis of the poets' handling of imagery in whole poems. We might look, for example, at a poem by Hitomaro—"On Parting from His Wife as He Set Out from Iwami for the Capital" (*MYS*, II: 135–37).

Tsuno sahau	It was by the Sea of Iwami
Iwami no umi no	Where the clinging ivy creeps across the
Koto saeku	rocks,
Kara no saki naru	By the waters off Cape Kara,
Ikuri ni zo	A land remote as the speech of far
Fukamiru ouru	Cathay—
Ariso ni zo	Yes, there where the seaweed grows,
Tamamo wa ouru	Clinging to rocks fathoms beneath the
Tamamo nasu	waves,
Nabikineshi ko o	And where on the stony strand
	The seaweed glows like polished gems.
	My young wife dwells there,
	Who like seaweed bent to the current of
	love,

Fukamiru no
Fukamete moedo
Saneshi yo wa
Ikuda mo arazu

The girl who slept beside me
Soft and lithesome as the gem-like water
     plants.
Now those nights seem few
When we held each other close in sleep.

Hau tsuta no
Wakare shi kureba
Kimo mukau
Kokoro o itami
Omoitsutsu
Kaerimi suredo
Ōfune no
Watari no yama no
Momijiba no
Chiri no magai ni
Imo ga sode
Saya ni mo miezu

We parted unwillingly,
Clinging to each other like ivy creepers;
My heart ached and swelled
Against the ribs that would hold it,
And when my yearning drew me
To pause, look back, and see her once again
Waving her sleeves in farewell,
They were already taken from my sight,
Hidden by the leaves
Falling like a curtain in their yellow whirl
At the crest of Mount Watari,
A crest like a wave's that bears a ship away.

Tsumagomoru
Yakami no yama no
Kumoma yori
Watarau tsuki no
Oshikedo mo
Kakuroikureba
Amatsutau
Irihi sashinure

Although I longed for her—
As for the voyaging moon when it glides
Into a rift of clouds
That swallow it up on Mount Yakami,
     where,
They say, men retire with their wives—
I took my lonely way, watching the sun
Coursing through the sky
Till it sank behind the mountains.

Masurao to
Omoeru ware mo
Shikitae no
Koromo no sode wa
Tōrite nurenu.

Though I always thought
Myself a man with a warrior's heart,
I found that my sleeves—
Wide as they were, like our bed clothes—
Were all soaked through with tears.

Envoys

Aogoma no
Agaki o hayami
Kumoi ni zo
Imo ga atari o
Sugite kinikeru.

My gray-white horse
Has carried me at so swift a pace
That I have left behind
The place where my beloved dwells
Beneath the cloudland of the distant sky.

Akiyama ni	O you yellow leaves
Otsuru momijiba	That whirl upon the autumn slopes—
Shimashiku wa	If only for a moment,
Na chirimagai so	Lift the fluttering curtain of your fall
Imo ga atari min.	That I may see where my beloved dwells.

The imagery of the poem consists of details of nature that are employed to convey a concatenation of events and human emotions, and therefore offers a lyric equivalent of narration; but the imagery also gives the poem much of its structural richness and tonal development. The first section of the chōka is dominated and therefore unified by imagery of the sea; the second by imagery of the land; and the third by imagery of the heavens. The chōka concludes with a short, generalizing section in which the speaker describes his reaction to what has gone before. The ease with which one section merges into the next can be seen by the way in which the seaweed imagery of the first section is developed into the very similar imagery of vines in the second. Or in more complex fashion, within the second section, the images are ordered in terms of their suggestion of increasing height. Vines yield to leaves and leaves to mountains, so preparing the way for the celestial imagery of the third section, even as the development grows from the imagery of ocean depths in the first section. The two envoys redefine the earlier imagery by casting it with new images that draw the poem to its conclusion. The imagistic details of the first two sections of the chōka can be further characterized by the connotations they bear—the homely, familiar associations of things intimately known in one's daily life. Seaweed and ocean—seaweed employed both for its wifelike lithe and graceful clinging and its familiarity in the daily diet, and the ocean for its unknown depths. These images, which are treated with a homely delicacy, might have been treated by folk poets with primitive naïveté; and later courtiers, with a highly developed sense of decorum, would have used them only for a sophisticated primitivistic effect. Here they are doubly appropriate, because they are images of place that fix the point of the poet's departure from his wife, and because they convey the familiar intimacy of husband and wife. The images of the rocky shore and the vastness of the sea that holds the seaweed also suggest tonally the dangers of travel and the unknown depths that encompass human life.

In the second section of the chōka the vine image half-submerged in the pillow-word that begins the poem reappears as a transition. It is like the seaweed in its involutions, but it parts to pursue separate ways, even as Hitomaro and his wife must part. It also provides a transition to natural imagery of the land, rather than the sea, and this change both prepares us for the land journey by horse we read about in the first envoy, and makes a sea-land distinction metaphorically comparable to Hitomaro's being with and being parted from his wife. The simile of parting vines is made to convey the actual parting, since the poet tells us no more about the leave-taking, except that he turns back to return his wife's farewell wave.

Now the pathos of separating vines is transformed into the deeper sadness of the shower of leaves in autumn. This leaf image in itself appropriately conveys pathos, since its autumnal associations are sad; but in context it is even sadder—these falling leaves will not part or interrupt their cascade from the trees so that he can fully see his wife. Moreover, the leaves fall in a particularly appropriate place—on Mount Watari, which means "crossing" and so represents the last possible chance for him to see his wife. The next images, those of the moon and clouds, have a double appropriateness. Even as the sight of his wife had earlier been hindered by the falling leaves, so the brief glimpse of the moon will soon yield to its being obscured by clouds. And the fact that the imagery of night (the moon) follows earlier images of day suggests that time is passing, that the journey is taking the speaker ever farther from his wife. The place name and its pillow-word are again significant. At the end of the second section, Hitomaro had employed a similar device of using a named mountain with a pillow-word before it:

> Ōfune no   At the crest of Mount Watari,
> Watari no yama no   A crest like a wave's that bears a ship away.

Although we have taken some liberties with the Japanese to convey an approximate imagistic effect, in the original as in our translation, the pillow-word serves to remind us of the sea imagery in the first section. The new sequence—*Tsumagomoru* / *Yakami no yama no* (". . . on Mount Yakami, where, / They say, men retire with their wives")—of course suggests the disappearance of his wife behind the leaves and is related to the images of clouds and moon above the mountain, but it also conveys a poignant irony: the pillow-word indeed suggests withdrawal and retirement, but of a very different kind from the deprivation suffered by the poet.

The place names have another function: they imply two geographical points and so suggest that the journey is continuing, a suggestion strengthened by the succession of images of night after those of day. If the imagery of the third section had been of dawn, the implication would be that the poem represented two days of travel. As it is, the imagery is of sunset, and so suggests not the next day but the passage of an indeterminate amount of time. The effect is very subtle—images are so ordered that the sequence itself functions as a metaphor for narration—and may be compared with the balder effects of Yeats, who has his speaker say in "Sailing to Byzantium,"

> And therefore I have sailed the seas and come
> To the holy city of Byzantium.

The narrative effect of the imagery is not unlike its effect in other respects, for even as the images represent particular details of a wholly realized scene and situation, they imply other meanings: vines recall the image of seaweed representing the wife and suggest the moment of departure. The technique is clearly metaphorical in nature, although unlike comparable Western figures of language, Hitomaro's metaphors are equally true in terms of the vehicle (the image of vines) and the tenor (the meaning of departure). They are used primarily to express tone, and do not so much represent or stand for something as suggest it by virtue of their relation with each other.

In another sense, the imagery of the first two sections is of two kinds—that which is held or hidden, implying the wife, and that which holds or hides, especially through movement, implying either the husband or his departing on his journey. With the introduction of the sun, matters become rather more complex. The sun sets in the west of course, and therefore in the direction of Iwami (on the western, Japan Sea side of the main island of Honshu), which he has left for his journey to the capital. In view of the significance attached earlier to imagery of movement, we would think that the setting sun might need to be taken as a metaphor for his trip. This clearly is not possible, since it moves in the opposite direction. Rather the image introduces a kind of counter-movement that suggests the way in which the husband's feelings and thoughts go back toward Iwami and his wife (even as his vision from Mount Watari had been back toward his home) as he continues on his way eastward. This ironic turn to the imagery is made clear by the first envoy, in which the horse almost appears not to have done its master's will in taking him so rapidly to the east. Hitomaro brings his chōka to a characteristically quiet close after the grand imagery of the heavens by the confession that he is not the man he thought he was.

Both envoys echo in part the earlier images of the poem, adding to them certain fresh ones. The first envoy treats the celestial imagery of the third section of the chōka, now in the more general terms of the sky, absorbing the moon metaphor for the wife and the complex sun metaphor for his yearning. The second envoy takes us back further toward the beginning of the chōka, for once again the falling leaves obscure his sight of his wife. Now, however, the image of the falling leaves, which he sees only in his imagination, becomes a breathtaking conceit for the separating distance he would like to abolish in order to be once more with his wife. Even the leaves, since they are closer to his home, take on the fluttering quality of his wife's sleeves as she waved goodbye. The two envoys are related by virtue of the fact that their last noun series (*imo ga atari*) is identical—"the place where my beloved dwells" is the last substantive he mentions in each case. Throughout the poem, the experience of parting is conveyed in a dazzling combination of apposite images— some homely, some grand—into a convincing artistic re-creation of the event,

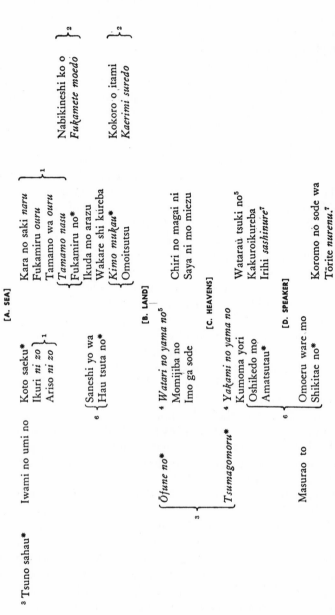

CHART I. THE STRUCTURE OF HITOMARO'S "ON PARTING FROM HIS WIFE"

(Read along a single line from left to right)

[A. SEA]

[3] Tsuno sahau*   Iwami no umi no   Koto saeku*   Kara no saki *naru*
                                     Ikuri *ni zo* ⎱[1]   Fukamiru *ouru*
                                     Ariso *ni zo* ⎰   Tamamo wa *ouru*
                                                       ⎰*Tamamo nasu*   Nabikineshi ko o ⎱[2]
                                                       ⎱Fukamiru no*   *Fukamete moedo* ⎰
                                     [6]⎰Saneshi yo wa   Ikuda mo arazu
                                        ⎱Hau tsuta no*   Wakare shi kureba   Kokoro o itami ⎱[2]
                                                         ⎰*Kimo mukau**   *Kaerimi suredo* ⎰
                                                         ⎱Omoitsutsu

[B. LAND]

[4] *Watari no yama no*[5]   Chiri no magai ni
    Ōfune no*   Momijiba no   Saya ni mo miezu
    [3]   Imo ga sode

[C. HEAVENS]

    Tsumagomoru*   [4] *Yakami no yama no*   Watarau tsuki no*[5]
                       Kumoma yori   Kakuroikureba
                   [6]⎰Oshikedo mo   Irihi *sashinure*[7]
                      ⎱Amatsutau*

[D. SPEAKER]

    Masurao to   Omoeru ware mo   Koromo nō sode wa
                   [6]⎰Shikitae no* Tōrite *nurenu*.[7]

* Makurakotoba.   1. Parallel and identical verb or particle terminations.
2. Two sets of four clauses parallel in grammatical structure.   3. Parallel introductory makurakotoba.
4. Parallel images of mountains.   5. Contrast of mountain and moon through similar prefixed words.
6. Similarly ordered clauses—similarly assonant lines and makurakotoba.   7. Similar grammatical constructions and sounds.
Italics call attention to important similarities in sound and grammatical construction.

an integrated whole exhibiting the broad sensibility of Hitomaro. Most later poets would seek a different imagistic coherence—probably, considering the subject, a train of imagery less homely than Hitomaro's seaweed and less exalted than his sun and moon.

Other poems by Hitomaro reveal equally complex subtleties and astonishing richness under close analysis. It is certainly of more than casual interest that—when properly adjusted to the history, conventions, and suppositions of the Japanese poetic tradition—modern Western methods of critical analysis are as applicable to all periods of Japanese Court poetry as to our own; or that, to put it differently, such an adjustment of analytical technique should make so abundantly clear that Japanese poetry possesses artistic riches comparable to our own. We have spoken of modern Western critical analysis, but the Japanese have a tradition of rhetorical analysis of their own inherited (if too seldom employed) from the learned scholars of the Edo period. Saitō Mokichi (1882–1953), a poet in his own right and the author of an exhaustive five-volume study, *Kakinomoto Hitomaro* (Tokyo, 1934–40), has given a brilliant graphic analysis of the structure of the poem. We have adapted the analysis in Chart I (see Saitō, II, 562–63), using symbols that are explained on the chart. (The envoys are not included.)

Okura's "Dialogue on Poverty" (*MYS,* V: 892–93) is another poem expressing suffering, but with suffering conceived in terms of imagery of contrasts, of the constitution of society, and of man's place in the world.

THE POOR MAN

Kaze majiri	On those dreary nights
Ame furu yo no	When rain falls freezing in the wind,
Ame majiri	On such bitter nights
Yuki furu yo wa	When snow falls mixed with freezing
Sube mo naku	drizzle,
Samuku shi areba	I have no better comfort
Katashio o	In the onslaught of the numbing cold
Toritsuzushiroi	Than to sit and nibble
Kasuyuzake	On this poor lump of blackened salt
Uchisusuroite	And sip from time to time
Shiwabukai	Upon this wretched brew of sake lees.
Hana bishibishi ni	Then as my body warms
Shika to aranu	I clear my throat and sniffle,
Hige kakinadete	As I glow with drink
Are o okite	I stroke the straggly hairs of my beard,
Hito wa araji to	Declaring to myself:
Hokoroedo	"There is no one worth thinking about

Samuku shi areba	—Apart, of course, from me."
Asabusuma	But in the face of the numbing cold
Hikikagafuri	I still draw up about me
Nuno kataginu	My thin bedding of paltry hemp,
Ari no kotogoto	And pile on in layers
Kisoedo mo	Every thin fiber vest I own—
Samuki yo sura o	And still I freeze,
Are yori mo	So bitter is the freezing night;
Mazushiki hito no	So what of you,
Chichi haha wa	Whose wretchedness is worse than mine?
Ue samukaran	Your father and your mother
Me kodomo wa	Must be famished in the bitter cold,
Sakurinaku ran	Your wife and children
Kono toki wa	Can only whine and sob in pain.
Ika ni shitsutsu ka	In times as hard as these
Na ga yo wa wataru.	By what devices do such as you
	Make shift to endure your lives?

THE DESTITUTE MAN

Ame tsuchi wa	Though the saying goes
Hiroshi to iedo	That the heavens and earth are vast,
A ga tame wa	My experience is
Saku ya narinuru	That they have shrunk upon me;
Hi tsuki wa	And though the saying is
Akashi to iedo	That the sun and moon are radiant,
A ga tame wa	My experience is
Teri ya tamawanu	That they have failed to shine on me.
Hito mina ka	Do all men suffer so,
Are nomi ya shikaru	Or is this the case with me alone?
Wakuraba ni	With blessed fortune
Hito to wa aru o	I was born in this world as a man,
Hitonami ni	And in the fields
Are mo tsukuru o	I have toiled as hard as any.
Wata mo naki	And yet my clothes
Nuno kataginu no	Consist of this one unpadded vest
Miru no goto	Of coarse hempen fiber
Wawakesagareru	Hanging across and down my shoulders,
Kakafu nomi	Dangling all in tatters
Kata ni uchikake	No better than ragged strips of kelp.
Fuseio no	My house is a hovel,
Mageio no uchi ni	Low-roofed and half fallen in,
Hitatsuchi ni	With cold bare earth

Wara tokishikite	Beneath the scattered straw.
Chichi haha wa	In the seat above
Makura no kata ni	My father and mother crouch,
Me kodomo wa	While down below
Ato no kata ni	My wife and children lie
Kakumiite	And press about me,
Ureisamayoi	Groaning in their wretchedness.
Kamado ni wa	Upon the hearth
Hoke fukitatezu	No fire sends up its smoke,
Koshiki ni wa	And in the pot
Kumo no su kakite	Only a spider drapes its web—
Ii kashigu	We have forgotten
Koto mo wasurete	Even the manner of cooking food,
Nuedori no	And like the night finch
Nodo yobioru ni	We raise weak-throated cries.
Ito nokite	Yet this is not all.
Mijikaki mono o	For to cap our misery, to cut—
Hashi kiru to	As the saying goes—
Ieru ga gotoku	What was already short still shorter,
Shimoto toru	The growling voice
Satoosa ga koe wa	Of the tax collector with his stick
Neyado made	Even disrupts our sleep,
Kitachiyobainu	And he stands threatening at the door.
Kaku bakari	Must life be only this,
Sube naki mono ka	So hopelessly beyond our powers?
Yo no naka no michi.	Is this the only way of the world?

Envoy

THE POET

Yo no naka o	One of us may feel
Ushi to yasashi to	That life holds only pain, and another
Omoedo mo	That our lot is shameful,
Tobitachikanetsu	Yet since we are not birds, but men,
Tori ni shi araneba.	We cannot find escape in flight.

Okura has developed his imagery in part upon a contrast between indoors and out-of-doors. But his drama involves more than mere contrast, for each of his sections moves indoors to the speaker—from the general setting to the immediate stage. Both the Poor Man and the Destitute Man are proud, and they are conscious of a larger world than themselves. The Poor Man glances at the cold outside, his poor food and drink, himself, his clothing, and his surroundings in the house. The imagery of this section is extremely vivid (even his beard is thin and straggly); but brilliantly conceived as it is, it is surpassed by that of the next section. Up to the appearance of the village headman, the tax collector, there is a wonderful imagistic showpiece, beginning with the wide sweep of heaven and earth, sun and moon, moving indoors to the man himself, his straw bed, his pillow, and the pot with its spider web, and ending by transference to human psychology with the fine hyperbole, "We have forgotten / Even the manner of cooking food."

The social concern of the Poor Man for those worse off than himself is translated into the arrival of the headman to collect taxes from the Destitute Man at the end. The proverb (how fond the Destitute Man is of proverbs, although they are grimly inapplicable to his case!), the rod, the threatening voice of the tax collector, all are images that particularize the suffering. The envoy, spoken by the Poet, is in the tone of generalization that characterizes many of Okura's envoys. There is only one image, because Okura wishes to strengthen the universality of suffering.

The poems of the "Tanabe Sakimaro Collection" (*Tanabe Sakimaro no Kashū*), found in the seventh and ninth books of the *Man'yōshū*, show some of the changes in imagistic technique that took place after the generation of Hitomaro. Comparison is all the easier since Sakimaro (fl. ca. 750) leans so heavily upon Hitomaro's genres and poems, as we can see from the poem, "On Seeing a Dead Man When Crossing the Pass of Ashigara" (*MYS*, IX: 1800).

Okakitsu no	Your loving wife
Asa o hikihoshi	No doubt spread and bleached the threads
Imonane ga	For your white hempen robe
Tsukurikiseken	Upon the brushwood fence that stood
Shirotae no	about
Himo o mo tokazu	Your modest eastern home.
Hitoe yuu	Perhaps she wove that robe for you to wear
Obi o mie yui	In your labors for the Court.
Kurushiki ni	You must have toiled long, not stopping
Tsukaematsurite	to untie
Ima dani mo	Your hempen belt for sleep,
Kuni ni makarite	But winding it more tightly round your
Chichi haha mo	waist
Tsuma o mo min to	Girded yourself not once, but thrice.
	And then at last you earned a few brief days
	Of rest and set out for your home,
	Thinking to see your parents and your wife.

Omoitsutsu	At last you reached the east—
Yukiken kimi wa	Land of crowing cocks—you reached this
Tori ga naku	pass,
	Awesome abode of gods.
Azuma no kuni no	But in such rugged mountains
Kashikoki ya	Your softly woven robe
Kami no misaka ni	Could not have kept your wasted body
Nikihada no	warm;
Koromo samura ni	For you look cold,
Nubatama no	With your long hair as lustrous black
Kami wa midarete	As jewels of jet
Kuni toedo	Lying loose and tangled round about you.
Kuni o mo norazu	Though I speak to you
Ie toedo	To ask about your native land,
Ie o mo iwazu	You do not reply;
Masurao no	And though I ask you of your home,
Yuki no manimani	You do not speak:
Koko ni koyaseru.	But lie outstretched, courageous man,
	Asleep forever on your journey home.

Sakimaro's chōka (no envoys appear with the poem) corresponds to only the last third of Hitomaro's "On Seeing the Body of a Man." He chooses images that convey the appearance of the man, his home, and the road with vivid particularity. The effect is one of great pathos, but little more, and compared with Hitomaro's poem, this is a less impressive work. Sakimaro sends us, as it were, a pathetically moving verse report of an incident on a journey. Hitomaro participates in his dead man's fate by means of the long second section in which his speaker's own brush with death is related. In addition, Hitomaro chooses images that are particular enough to convey the sense of loss (the rocks are the pillow, the wife would gather herbs from the hillside, if she only could), but not in such profuse detail that the man is only one particular man, that he may not also function as a symbol of universal human suffering.

Sakimaro also chooses to drop the overture at the beginning of Hitomaro's poem, the passage concerning the beauty and divinity of Sanuki. The absence of such an emphasis in Sakimaro's poem means that the irony, tragedy, and affirmation of Hitomaro's have disappeared. Death is now a localized event, not a universal phenomenon in a world charged with tragedy, mystery, and divinity. In other chōka of Sakimaro in which the patriotic and divine material of Hitomaro's overtures is used, it is often used more as a convention than anything else. The poem on Futagi Palace, for example (MYS, VI: 1053–

58), breaks up the initial overture into several parts, perhaps because Sakimaro wished to escape the convention of Hitomaro's form. But the result is that the solemn lines in which the hope is expressed that the palace will endure as long as the unbroken succession of emperors seem almost sententious after the imagery of deer crying and bright leaves falling, and the image of the palace is compared in a forced conceit to the spinning of "Reel Mountain" into an imperial dwelling place. The awkwardness suggests that poets were having to force the gods and emperors into imagistic conceits that lacked the universal significance of former days.

Such changes in belief call for changes in poetic technique. Kasa Kanamura's (fl. 715–33) answer to the problem was to intrude his own personality into the poem. (See, for example, the poems on imperial journeys in *MYS*, VI: 907–9; 920–22; 928–30; and 935–37.) The general effect of the changed imagistic technique is not, however, a drawing of Kanamura and the reader into participation in a larger world, but a description of what the poet sees nearby. The world is brought closer to us; we see more details, but find less significance in them.

The shift from the narrative or dramatic to the descriptive that we observe in some poets of the generation after Hitomaro has not yet broken the relationship between chōka and envoy in Kanamura's poetry. However, in the poetry of Yamabe Akahito (d. ?736), we find that the real vitality of the poet's art lies in the tanka form of the envoy, not in the chōka. One of Akahito's poems on the Yoshino Palace (*MYS*, VI: 923–25) shows the tendency toward shorter chōka as well as other developments more closely related to imagery.

Yasumishishi	To our great Sovereign
Wa go Ōkimi no	Who rules over all the land in peace
Taka shirasu	Belongs this lofty palace,
Yoshino no miya wa	Majestic Yoshino, divinely built.
Tatanazuku	Range high on range,
Aokakigomori	Green mountain walls enshrine it,
Kawanami no	While pure and clear
Kiyoki kōchi zo	Flow the blessed waters of the stream.
Harube wa	In the springtime
Hana sakiōri	Bright flowers blossom on the mountain
Aki sareba	walls,
Kiri tachiwataru	And in the autumn
Sono yama no	Soft mists rise gently from the stream.
Iya masumasu ni	Again and yet again
Kono kawa no	Like the mountains range on range,
Tayuru koto naku	And never ceasing
	Like the stream that ever flows,

Momoshiki no	The courtiers will come
Ōmiyabito wa	In reverent corps to these imperial halls
Tsune ni kayowan.	Erected on foundations multi-walled.

Envoys

Mi-Yoshino no	From among the branches
Kisayama no ma no	Of the trees upon Mount Kisa's slopes,
Konure ni wa	The flocks of birds
Kokoda mo sawaku	Fill the lovely vale of Yoshino
Tori no koe ka mo.	With their free and joyous songs.

Nubatama no	The jet-black night
Yo no fukeyukeba	Deepens to a hush among the birches
Hisagi ouru	In the stream's pure bed,
Kiyoki kawara ni	Where the plovers softly raise their call
Chidori shiba naku.	Above the gentle murmur of the stream.

The imagistic technique of the chōka is not without distinction. The implied comparison of the palace to a great Shinto shrine, the paired semi-contrasts of spring and autumn, of rugged mountains and the gentle stream, are very effective. But the imagery is effective only as description that conveys beauty. Everything is part of a pattern, a wholly visual pattern. The chōka here has no function beyond what might be accomplished by a series of tanka. The really vital part of the poem are the two envoys. For all real purposes, they are two poems separate from the chōka and each other, but at the same time, as separate poems, they are two of the loveliest tanka in the *Man'yōshū*.

Like the chōka, the envoys are completely impersonal, but there is little other connection between the two groups. The presence of imagery of mountains in both the chōka and the first envoy does not obscure the fact that in the chōka the mountain imagery is related by metaphor to the palace, and by parallelism to the river, while in the first envoy the mountain is a backdrop for the crying of the birds. The second envoy has imagery of birds and is equally beautiful, but these are birds by a darkened river, now utterly changed from the daytime. Although the river image connects this envoy with the conclusion of the chōka, and although the adjective "lovely" or "pure" (*kiyoki*) is repeated from the beginning of the chōka, the imagery of the second envoy is really related only to the senses of the poetic speaker. Unlike the visual imagery of the chōka, the imagery of the envoys is almost entirely aural. Akahito enjoys, as it were, dividing his senses in the second envoy by writing of what he might see if it were light, and what he does hear now that it is dark. The imagistic technique is eminently sophisticated and successful, but there is no reason why it should be used in a chōka when it is more suited to the lyricism of the tanka. The chōka is dying as a form expressive of the interests and needs of the age.

The 479 poems of Ōtomo Yakamochi make up somewhat over one-tenth of the *Man'yōshū*. But number alone does not make him a remarkable poet: his reputation is also due to the variety of his modes, forms, and techniques. This wide representation and great variety means that no one poem is completely characteristic, so that an illustrative selection is very difficult. Yakamochi wrote many public chōka on such subjects as the discovery of gold in Michinoku province (*MYS*, XVIII: 4094–97), as well as an Okura-like "Admonition to Owari Okuhi" (*MYS*, XVIII: 4106–9), Hitomaro-like elegies for Prince Asaka (*MYS*, III: 475–77; 478–80), and poems on such private concerns as illness and separation from the capital (*MYS*, XVIII: 3962–64).

The imagery of one of the elegies on the death of Prince Asaka (*MYS*, III: 475–77) shows the changes Yakamochi had wrought in the public mode of Hitomaro. The first section of the chōka of this poem gives us a Hitomaro-like overture that ends with imagery of a lovely springtime in the capital. The imagery of the next section continues the imperial motif—Prince Asaka seems to have made a progress to Mount Wazuka—but the imagery of his courtiers, dressed in white as they follow the palanquin, shows that the trip is to the mausoleum. In other words, what looks so beautiful is really tragic. The imagery of the second envoy continues this idea of a topsy-turvy world; the flowers described as just now blossoming have really fallen, at least for the speaker, whose every joy is dead with the Prince.

The imagistic technique is one of an elegant bewilderment, which we have already seen in Yakamochi's pleasant confusion over the white patches in his garden—are they the fallen blossoms of the damson or some remaining snow? This elegant bewilderment—an attitude no doubt suggested to Yakamochi by the example of Chinese poetry—can be made the vehicle of very moving private poetry dealing with subjective states of mind, as we see in similar poetic turnings of the poet upon himself in the next period of Japanese poetry or again in the poetry of a Donne. But such conceits are not suited to public poetry. In the second envoy the denial of the value of the imagery conveying the beauty of spring is also a denial of the imperial theme and spring imagery of the first half of the chōka. The poet and the public theme are separated here—the prince's death has little more literary significance than the cavorting trout, and both are objective pawns to be moved by the impulses of Yakamochi's subjective states of mind.

Such commentary on the imagery of the elegy is not meant to deny the poem's beauty, but rather to show, by means of the imagery, the essential discord between the public subject and the private poet toward the end of the early literary period, a discord we can see developing in the chōka of Kanamura and Akahito. On the other hand, Yakamochi's private and informal love poems (for example, *MYS*, VIII: 1462–63) show more ingenuity than feeling. It is as though his civilized sensibility made informality and passion difficult. The true vehicle of his poetic powers is the private but formal poem. Such poems need not express the depths of the heart, but they require feeling, a refined sensibility, assurance in tone, and great skill. These are powers that Yakamochi possessed to perfection. Such a poem as the one "Sent with Orange Blossoms to the Elder Daughter of Lady Ōtomo of Sakanoe" (*MYS*, VIII: 1507–9) shows the fineness if not the range or greatness of his style. We may object to the over-prettiness of detail, but the work has a real artistic integrity.

A still better example of Yakamochi's particular genius is the "Lament" he sent to his son-in-law, Fujiwara Toyonari, who had just lost his mother (*MYS*, XIX: 4214–16).

Ame tsuchi no	Since that ancient time
Hajime no toki yu	When the heavens and earth began,
Utsusomi no	It has been decreed
Yasotomo no o wa	That of the eighty noble clans
Ōkimi ni	Each living man
Matsurou mono to	Shall follow obediently the commands
Sadamareru	Of our great Sovereign.
Tsukasa ni shi areba	So I, an official of the Court,
Ōkimi no	Heard with veneration
Mikoto kashikomi	The sacred words of our great Sovereign;
Hinazakaru	And now I live,
Kuni o osamu to	Governing this distant province
Ashihiki no	Here in the wilds,
Yama kawa henari	Cut off from home by hills and streams.
Kaze kumo ni	Since my coming here
Koto wa kayoedo	You and I have had but winds and clouds
Tada ni awanu	To bear our messages;
Hi no kasanareba	And as days have piled on days and still
Omoikoi	We have not met again,
Ikizukioru ni	I have longed to see you more and more,
Tamahoko no	And sighed with yearning.
Michi kuru hito no	Straight as a courtier's spear
Tsutegoto ni	Was the road he came on,
Ware ni kataraku	The traveler who has brought these
Hashiki yoshi	tidings:
Kimi wa kono goro	He reports that you,
Urasabite	My amiable and noble friend,
Nagekaiimasu	Are struck in grief
	And lately spend your days in mourning.

Yo no naka no	Truly the span of life
Ukeku tsurakeku	Is filled with sorrow and suffering:
Saku hana mo	The very flowers open
Toki ni utsurou	Only to wither and fall with time,
Utsusemi mo	And we living men
Tsune naku arikeri	Are creatures of like impermanence.
Tarachine no	Even that noble lady,
Miomo no mikoto	Your gracious and beloved mother,
Nani shi ka mo	Shares the human lot,
Toki shi wa aran o	And with it a fate for a certain hour.
Masokagami	And now this news:
Miredo mo akazu	That in the full bloom of her womanhood,
Tama no o no	When one might still gaze
Oshiki sakari ni	Upon her beauty with such rare delight
Tatsu kiri no	As on a polished mirror,
Usenuru gotoku	Cherishing her like a string of precious
Oku tsuyu no	jewels,
Kenuru ga goto	Even she has faded away,
Tamamo nasu	Vanished like the rising mists,
Nabikikoifushi	Like dew on the grass;
Yuku mizu no	That she lay listless as the gem-like
Todomikanetsu to	seaweed
Tawagoto ya	Bending to the tide;
Hito no iitsuru	That like a running stream she ebbed away
Oyozure o	And could not be held back.
Hito no tsugetsuru	Can this be some fantastic tale I hear?
	Is not the message false,
	Merely a rumor of a passing traveler?
Azusayumi	Though from afar—
Tsuma hiku yo to no	Like the warning sound of bowstrings
Tōto ni mo	twanged
Kikeba kanashimi	By palace guards at night—
Niwatazumi	I hear this news, my grief is freshened,
Nagaruru namida	And I cannot withhold
Todomikanetsu mo.	The tears from flowing down my cheeks
	Like rivulets from a sudden shower.

Envoys

Tōto ni mo	This news I hear,
Kimi ga nageku to	That you, my friend, are plunged in grief,
Kikitsureba	Comes from afar,

Ne nomi shi nakayu	But still I must raise my voice in weeping:
Aimou ware wa.	Your distant sorrow weighs closely on my heart.

Yo no naka no	You know as I
Tsune naki koto wa	The nature of this illusory world,
Shiru ran o	How nothing stays—
Kokoro tsukusu na	Endeavor to be brave and stalwart,
Masurao ni shite.	Do not wear out that heart in grief.

The overture is related in a personal way to Yakamochi's own immediate experience: men have ever had imperial appointments; I hold one now. This provides a lofty and formal introduction of a causal nature, showing why he left home, and offering an exposition that explains his sense of separation. The imagery of hills, rivers, wind, and clouds is very aptly employed to convey the sense of separation, once the reason for it has been given. But the most effective, even startling, imagery is the brilliant combination of the woman, her mirror, the mist, and the dew; the seaweed, which relates alogically to the stream; and finally the distant, sad twanging of the bowstring. The mirror metaphor is very effective, the more so since the woman's spirit was once reflected in it, since it is priceless, and since it is a remembrance of the woman who owned it. It is not apparent to us Westerners that the images of the mirror and the mist are related by a buried image of something covered and then opened to sight. The costly mirrors imported from China were kept in boxes from which they were taken for use. The mirror may now be taken from its box, but it will not reflect the woman's face; and similarly, the mist may now fade, but it will not reveal what once stood behind—metaphorically, the woman. Dew is of course a symbol for evanescence, and the undulations of seaweed for the lithe and loving bending of a woman to a man's heart. The bowstring is heard from afar, like the news of Toyonari's cause for grief, and is all the more apt a symbol for Toyonari, since the second envoy urges him to be brave and stalwart as befits a warrior.

It would be difficult to overpraise the skill with which Yakamochi has merged his images in a fluent, limpid style; in this poem narration, description, and above all a beautiful lyricism are combined into a new whole, a private or personal and yet formal style which, however much it lacks the grandeur of Hitomaro or the vividness of Okura, constitutes a style of great beauty and integrity. Yakamochi may have written to his secretary and friend, Ōtomo Ikenushi, that he could not "find the way through the gates of Yamanoe Okura and Kakinomoto Hitomaro" (MYS, XVII: 3969, headnote), but with their example and his own genius, he was able to fashion his own "gate" on the poetic downslope of the age.

The images, metaphors, and symbols of the time offer us widely varying pleasures and frequent insights into the differing poetic modes of this century of poetry, and it will be useful to inquire about one more facet of the imagery, allegory. Allegory is not the vehicle of the best poetry of this age, and, unfortunately, most of the poems in this mode are "anonymous," with the result that we are often unable to say with confidence what the allegory was meant to convey. But in any case, allegory was a technique sufficiently developed to lead the compilers of the *Man'yōshū* to recognize it as a distinct genre and to provide a tradition useful to the poets of later ages. There are perhaps three distinct, though not wholly unrelated, kinds of allegory. We find in different volumes of the *Man'yōshū* groups of poems called "comparison poems" (*hi-yuka*) and "poems that express thoughts by referring to things" (*kibutsu chinshika*), which are often allegorical and, when so, are almost always love allegories, so far as we can determine today. (See *MYS*, VII: 1296–1402; XI: 2415–2507, 2619–2807, 2828–40; XII: 2851–63, 2964–3100.) There are also love allegories that do not involve a deliberate intent to compare things, as we see in a poem in which Yakamochi challenges Lady Ki's charge to him to observe the silk tree (popularly called the "sleeping-shrub") and conduct himself like it (her poem: *MYS*, VIII: 1461). He replies, using the silk tree allegorically to describe her reluctance to grant him his wishes (*MYS*, VIII: 1463):

Wagimoko ga
Katami no nebu wa
  Hana nomi ni
Sakite kedashiku
Mi ni naraji ka mo.

My dearest lady,
You send me blossoms of the sleeping-
  shrub
As a reminder of yourself,
But is it not true that these lavish sprays
Are flowers only and will never bear me
  fruit?

We have been able to find in the *Man'yōshū* almost no poems that indisputably employ public allegory. One of the rare examples of the technique is the second envoy to Hitomaro's poem "On the Lying-in-State of the Crown Prince Hinamishi" (*MYS*, II: 169):

Akane sasu
Hi wa teraseredo
  Nubatama no
Yo wataru tsuki no
Kakuraku oshi mo.

Although the sun
Still brightens the heavens with scarlet dye,
  Our dear moon is lost
In darkness heavy as a jewel of jet,
The bright moon that used to ford the
  night.

Earlier imagery in the chōka and the first envoy makes it clear that the still-shining sun is the reigning emperor, the vanished moon a symbol of the dead prince. There may be other examples of public allegory that are lost on us today as we stand twelve centuries distant from the age of Hitomaro, but as far as we can determine, the allegorical technique is chiefly important in the *Man'yōshū* as an indication of the experimenting temper of the poets, and at this point in the tradition as an alternative technique which later poets were to develop in greater variety.

POETIC RHETORIC AND SYNTAX

The subject of imagery of course raises questions of rhetoric, some of which we have already touched on (parallelism, the structure and development of poems, the disposition of imagery). By rhetoric we mean both fixed techniques by which to achieve desired ends and those techniques for the disposition of materials that may vary from poem to poem. The parallelism in such primitive poems as "Princess Kage's Lament" (see above, p. 68) is obtrusive because there is practically nothing else to the poem. To later, more sophisticated poets, however, parallelism was a useful technique that might add firmness to a tanka and that was well-nigh indispensable to stiffen and direct the fluid Japanese syntax in the chōka. Although almost any poet from Hitomaro to Yakamochi might serve as an example, Okura in his "Lament on the Instability of Human Life" (*MYS*, V: 804–5) shows especially clearly the way in which parallelism may give structure to a line, a group of lines, and the poem as a whole.

Yo no naka no	Life is such in this world
Sube naki mono wa	That our struggles are all in vain:
Toshi tsuki wa	Years rise on months
Nagaruru gotoshi	And time flows ever onward,
Toritsuzuki	Flooding us away;
Oikuru mono wa	A hundred trivial concerns
Momokusa ni	Oppress us in succession
Semeyorikitaru	And stifle us under their weight.
Otomera ga	So women bent with age
Otomesabisu to	Once rejoiced in being young—
Karatama o	Carefree girls binding,
Tamoto ni makashi	As girls are ever known to do,
Shirotae no	Binding foreign jewels
Sode furikawashi	About their gaily draped arms—
Kurenai no	They waved white linen sleeves,
Akamo susobiki	Trailing the hems of their scarlet skirts
Yochikora to	As hand in hand they went,
Te tazusawarite	Spending their time in happy play,
Asobiken	And all were girls together.

Toki no sakari o
Todomikane
Sugushiyaritsure
Mina no wata
Kaguroki kami ni
Itsu no ma ka
Shimo no furiken
Kurenai no
Omote no ue ni
Izuku yu ka
Shiwa kakitarishi

Masurao no
Otokosabisu to
Tsurugi tachi
Koshi ni torihaki
Satsuyumi o
Tanigirimochite
Akagoma ni
Shizukura uchioki
Hainorite
Asobiarukishi

Yo no naka ya
Tsune ni arikeru
Otomera ga
Sanasu itado o
Oshihiraki
Itadoriyorite
Matamade no
Tamade sashikae

Saneshi yo no
Ikuda mo araneba
Tazukazue
Koshi ni taganete
Ka yukeba
Hito ni itowae
Kaku yukeba
Hito ni nikumae

But time has the power of seasons,
And irresistibly
Summer has given way to winter,
As at an unremembered hour
Those glistening tresses as black
As the mud-snail's innards
Were whitened with a silent frost;
As from some source unmarked,
Those cheeks that glowed so bright,
Those scarlet cheeks,
Were wrinkle-scratched by time.

So the bold young men
Rejoiced to prove their manliness:
Like warriors girded their hips
With their straight or curving swords,
Clutched tightly in their hands
Their deadly, beast-destroying bows,
Threw upon their roans
Saddles of woven workmanship,
Climbed upon their mounts,
And eagerly galloped away to the hunt.

But is the way of the world
Such that these moments could long
      endure?
The girls with eager hands
Slide ajar the creaking door to love,
Clasp the groping hands
The precious, jewel-like outstretched
      hands—
And then they fall asleep,
Asleep with dear arms intertwined.

But youth knows few such nights
And soon must lean upon the staff
Bound henceforth to the side,
And then go stumbling ever onward,
Scorned by the passer-by;
He must go stumbling endlessly,
Despised by passing crowds.
For such is the common course of life,

Oyoshio wa	That this should be,
Kaku nomi narashi	Not more or less, so pitiable is life,
Tamakiwaru	No greater in its span
Inochi oshikedo	Than the length of hand to grip the wrist,
Sen sube mo nashi.	And our struggles are all in vain.

Envoy

Tokiwa nasu	How I yearn to be
Kaku shi mo ga mo to	Unalterably what once I was,
Omoedo mo	Immovable as a rock,
Yo no koto nareba	But because I belong to this world,
Todomikanetsu mo.	There is no stop to time.

The chōka begins with words of generalization repeated at the end. In between, we have two parallel passages followed by a third passage that combines the subjects of the first two. The two passages parallel the ignorance of time, first on the part of girls, then of young men. The third section develops out of these two by bringing the two sexes together, and is tied closely with the fourth by parallel imagery of hands, wrists, and arms (which may be designated, as Okura does, by the same Japanese word), an imagistic pattern that recalls, for example, the bracelets of the first section. In addition to these large parallels of imagery and sense, there is an almost unbelievable amount of complex verbal and syntactical parallelism, often at the most distant removes.

Along with parallelism, two of the most common and important rhetorical techniques of the poetry in this period are the makurakotoba (pillow-word) and the jo (preface), encountered already in primitive song. Japanese scholars have usually considered the two together, since the syntactical function of the two is nearly the same—both precede a word, a phrase, or a section of the poem to which they are attached by varying kinds of connections or juncture. However, we find it useful to consider them separately and to treat them, at least as they are used in the poetry of the early literary period, in a rather different fashion from the Japanese critics.

We find it impossible to call the makurakotoba "fixed epithets" as some Westerners have, when such a poet as Hitomaro created about half the makurakotoba he employed. In fact, the term and the notion of epithets seem beside the point, and we feel it necessary to borrow another concept from Western criticism to explain the function of this technique. In traditional rhetoric, "amplification" signifies the expansion of a statement for a desired effect, usually to "raise" or "lower" a subject in our estimation. Since such a raising is precisely the point of the makurakotoba, the Japanese pillow-word may be translated rhetorically to mean a word, a phrase, or an image used for amplification. "Amplification" is employed for decoration, or to create an effect of beauty, dignity, or even joyousness. Moreover, we believe that the pillow-words have an imagistic potential that Japanese critics have been at some pains to deny. If Hitomaro and other poets could create their own pillow-words, it is hard to see how these can be treated as epithets or expressions whose latent images must be avoided or discarded. Perhaps something of the effect of amplification and stylized imagery conveyed by the makurakotoba can best be expressed by italicizing some of the imagistic attributives (for that is the grammatical function of the Japanese and English words) or adjectives in Pope's description of various rivers in *Windsor Forest* (ll. 343–48).

> Cole, whose *dark* streams his *flowery* islands lave;
> And *chalky* Wey, that rolls a *milky* wave:
> The *blue, transparent* Vandalis appears;
> The *gulfy* Lee his *sedgy* tresses rears;
> And *sullen* Mole, that hides his *diving* flood;
> And *silent* Darent, stained with Danish blood.

The makurakotoba differ from Pope's attributives in their length, in their tendency to become fixed to a specific place or thing (as if, for example, the Wey were almost always termed chalky, the Vandalis blue), and in their contrast to the greater vividness of other images in the poem.

In his chōka, Hitomaro often uses makurakotoba to add sublimity of a quasi-hieratic nature to public subjects or to add a heightened value—to the Japanese sensibility, a radiant tone—to such a private subject as his loneliness in separation from his wife. *Mutatis mutandis,* the effect of this technique for Japanese lyrical handling is not unlike the longer, narrative epic similes of Western poetry. In each case the "action" of the narration or statement is briefly halted so that it may be stressed by means of amplification. Such rhetorical effects are often very subtle, or at least so indigenous to the culture that the translation of words is not a translation of poetic technique and effect. For this reason, rather than attempting to convey the effect of the makurakotoba in a lengthy commentary on a long poem, we think it best to illustrate Hitomaro's use of the technique in one of his "Poems of Travel," written in the tanka form. The second of a series of eight of these poems (*MYS,* III: 249–56) has been acclaimed as one of his masterpieces, although it might be reduced to the simple statement, "Passing Minume, our boat has arrived at the Cape of Noshima."

> *Tamamo karu*   Passing Minume,
> Minume o sugite   *Where they cut the gem-like seaweed,*
> *Natsukusa no*   Our boat has touched

Noshima ga saki ni   The landpoint of the Isle of No,
Fune chikazukinu.   *Luxuriant in its summer plants.*

The italicized phrases are makurakotoba whose effect is to make a statement of safe arrival into a rich poetic experience. Since Hitomaro has apparently created the two makurakotoba in this poem, the effect is one of freshness as well as beauty and, in context, happiness at again touching land. The contrast between the simplicity of the statement and the richness of the amplification constitutes the basic technique of the poem, but so appropriate is the amplification to the statement that the poet has fused both into a complete poetic whole.

Hitomaro's seeming freedom and creativity in inventing makurakotoba, which were to become part of the "word hoard" of later poets, are signs not only of his most remarkable genius, but also of the lasting effect his poems have had on the tradition. Like many of his other "Poems of Travel," the one quoted above seems to have been transmitted orally and re-shaped by later traveling poets who passed shores other than Minume and who arrived safely by land as well as by sea. For such poets, it was enough to raise the spell of Hitomaro's poem; but for Hitomaro himself, the makurakotoba was but one of many techniques which formed the basis of a highly individual and complex style.

The jo or semi-metaphorical preface is basically a technique of anticipation of something later in the poem, and it may be joined to the later element in various ways. The juncture is often made by means of illustrative example, verbal resemblance, or metaphor. Sometimes the relevance of the preface is so weak that the poem is divided into two parts with no satisfactory relation between them. In other poems, the connection is a richly complex verbal or metaphorical technique.

A few examples will make clear the various kinds of prefaces employed and the kinds of juncture that relate the preface to the statement. Many of the poems employing prefaces are grouped together in the *Man'yōshū* under the rubric "poems that express thoughts by referring to things," and many of these become metaphorical or allegorical in the act of assimilating into one poetic whole both some concrete thing and a feeling or idea stemming from it. Sometimes, however, there is no relation of any kind between a preface and a statement. The following poem, for example, has as its "thing" a straw bed-mat and as its "thought" the hope of the lover to see the girl more often. What connects the two halves of the poem is a pun on *shikite*: "spreading" and "more and more." But there seems to be no more connection between preface and statement in the Japanese than in our translation, in which the English syntax has been distorted to show the technique (*MYS,* XI: 2643).

Tamahoko no	Tired from the road
Michi yukitsukare	As straight as a courtier's spear,
Inamushiro	My rice-straw mat I *spread*
Shikite mo kimi o	*Again and again* to meet you
Min yoshi mo ga mo.	Would be exactly what I wish.

Although the two halves of this poem seem to lack any real connection, it is possible that the central images have a metaphorical, erotic tenor that unifies the poem. If so, this poem, one of the most extreme examples of division we can find, more than confirms our suspicion that, like the makurakotoba, the technique of the preface is more imagistically alive than modern Japanese critics allow.

It might be argued, as some Japanese commentators implicitly do, that in such poems as this a kind of emotional logic is employed, whereby an image has a lyrical status that brings the speaker of the poem to make a seemingly unrelated statement. But such a construction is clearly the work of critics in despair who wish to find some connection other than word play at the juncture of preface and statement. It is not tonal sincerity or presumed autobiographical appropriateness that makes the jo poem meaningful, but a developed semantic or metaphorical relationship. The technique in itself is rhetoric devoid of meaning.

The most clearly satisfactory of these poems are those in which the relationship between preface and statement is openly metaphorical, as it is in Hitomaro's second envoy to "On the Lying-in-State of Prince Takechi" (*MYS*, II: 201).

Haniyasu no	Just as the waters
Ike no tsutsumi no	Pent-up by walls in Haniyasu Pool
Komorinu no	Do not know where to flow,
Yukue o shirani	So now the courtiers of the Prince
Toneri wa madou.	Are trapped with no direction to their lives.

The juncture here, *yukue o shirani* ("not knowing where to go") applies to both the metaphorical vehicle (the enclosed waters) and the metaphorical tenor (the bewildered courtiers). The original does not make the comparison as explicit as our translation, but the metaphorical nature of the relationship is clear because of the juxtaposition and the technique of juncture in which one phrase is used to join two different thought sequences in a manner something like the technique of the pivot-word (kakekotoba). In a poem like this one, the preface provides images metaphorically germane to the statement: just as the water is bound motionless within the stone walls and is unable to fulfill its function of water flowing for irrigation, so the courtiers, now that their Prince is dead, are walled in by their grief, are unable to fulfill their function in wait-ing upon him; their lives have become meaningless. The fact that the meta-phor is conveyed by a juncture that involves a verbal telescoping of the fourth line, rather than by overt comparison, means that the poet has managed both to gain, as it were, an extra line for his poem and to make known, by a meta-phor understandable to all the citizens of the capital, the loss all must feel at the death of Prince Takechi.

At its best the technique of the preface is a splendid vehicle for compressed metaphor; at its worst merely a piece of ingenuity. Most of the poems using the technique fall somewhere between, in that they are metaphorical, but not always with the appropriateness of Hitomaro's envoy. As far as we can tell, the technique of the jo is unique to Japanese poetry. It illustrates the way in which the Japanese, for all their consciousness of the riches of Chinese poetry, took their own way in transforming what they borrowed, and in creating tech-niques that accorded with their language, syntax, and native tradition. In the early literary period, moreover, the use of the jo illustrates the typical cyclic pattern of Japanese poetry: it was borrowed from primitive poetry, made into a splendid technique, and fell into decline as it became merely conventional.

Among the broader rhetorical elements of poetry, syntax is one of the most significant for rhythm and even for meaning, as the example of Milton's prac-tice so clearly shows in English; and structure is essential if mere writing is to take on the status of art. Rhetorical techniques, structure, and syntax are so closely related that their embodiment in poetry is correlative: a change in the meanings poets sought to express in successive ages is sure to lead to closely related changes in all three. Within a given period of poetry, the lesser em-phases within the three mark the style of a given poet, setting it apart as his own vehicle, while within the tradition as a whole, a certain range of practice in rhetoric, syntax, and structure distinguishes the Japanese tradition from the traditions of other languages.

We may explore each of these generalizations in the poetry of the early literary period, choosing syntax as a special concern. (See also the more gen-eral remarks on syntax in Chapters 1 and 8 as well as the sections treating specific syntactical issues in the other period chapters.) In the early literary period parallelisms, apostrophes, unusual syntax, and varieties of artifice in construction are everywhere to be found. Such techniques are at times varia-tions from, at times complications of, normal Japanese syntax. Their particu-lar importance to the poets of the period is to be found in the fact that the chōka is meaningfully practiced only in the early literary period. The chōka required such perturbations to direct the natural onward-pressing flow of Japa-nese into meaningful channels and to assure that the vocalic softness of the language would not become monotonously sweet. Significantly, the tanka of the period, whether employed as envoys or used as separate poems, are far simpler in construction; the problem of syntactic monotony does not arise in five lines.

The characteristic use of given syntactical patterns is as much a stylistic mark of the poets of the *Man'yōshū* as of a Milton or a Pope. Okura's study of Chinese poetry reinforced the strong moral concern that led him to employ short, assertive paratactic units. Like the early English satirists, he employs a deliberate crabbedness, seemingly disjunct clauses, and harsh clusters of sounds to convey the fervor of his concerns. He seems ill at ease with the looser style of his generalizations, which often are rather flat; and his most moving lines— those in the first envoy to the poem on the death of his son (*MYS*, V: 905; see below, p. 151)—employ a typically broken syntax to convey the surges of emotion that he feels. Hitomaro, on the other hand, typically begins with a few rather short clauses in his overture, and then launches into lengthier passages which, in their rise to a climax, display that fine adjustment of sweet assonance and complex richness of which he is such a master. His endings usually return to shorter clauses as the tone falls toward a resolution. Akahito is often rather mannered in his chōka—the parallelism is particularly obtrusive—but he skillfully manages to prepare the imagistic ground for his envoys, which issue forth in a freely flowing lyric beauty unmatched in the period. It is more difficult to describe the syntax of Yakamochi's characteristic style, since he experimented with so many, but he is at his best when absorbed in poetic reflection. The reflection is expressed in passages, often sentences, of musing that merge thought and lyricism in a delicate balance. Often the effect given by the style and the syntax of which it is made is one of variations on a theme, a motif which on other occasions he treats with notable success in series of tanka.

The differences in kinds of meaning that may be conveyed by the range of syntax in Japanese as opposed to that in English can best be shown by a comparison between two masters. The epic proposition with which *Paradise Lost* begins is both familiar and sufficiently reflective to serve as an English example which, in its emphasis upon the experience itself rather than the actors, is as close as one may come to the normal interest of Japanese poetry. We have discussed Hitomaro's "On Seeing the Body of a Man" at enough length to make preliminary explication unnecessary; and it is an especially suitable example because its treatment of an active, even violent, event renders it comparable in subject with the most robust English poems. Since the texts of both are readily accessible, we shall diagram them syntactically in such a way as to bring out their likenesses and differences, if not to attempt a rigorous linguistic description. The matters for attention are syntactic divisions and stops, paratactic or coordinate units, hypotactic or subordinate units, subjects, and topics. Milton's first sixteen lines make up one grand sentence and so offer as close a comparison as may readily be found with the fluid Japanese syntax of Hito-maro's chōka (see Charts II and III).

Milton's magnificent sentence falls naturally into three parts dealing with the subject of the poem, the Heavenly Muse, and the stylistic aim of elevation. Such extended syntax is possible—that is, pleasurable and meaningful—in English poetry only if it achieves its larger rhythms by a suitable adjustment of paratactic and hypotactic syntax. Milton's device is to introduce what is in effect the grammatical object of his sentence first, to divide it by coordination into its constituents, to introduce sufficient subordination for variety, and to give enough of a sense of series that he can express both a sense of descent in the short concluding clauses to prepare for the beginning of the next section and yet sufficiently elevated thought ("one greater Man") to provide a first climax. The second unit begins with the principal verb and "subject," so charged with feeling by the inversion of the long object clause. The syntax of this section is by far the most complex, beginning as it does with the sub-ordinate relative clause ("That . . . didst inspire"), a clause itself interrupted with hypotaxis and parataxis ("on . . . or"). This leads to further and yet further hypotaxis ("who . . . in") that stops for breath only after the lengthy clause on creation rising from chaos. This in turn yields to a parallel and therefore paratactic sub-section on other possible locations for inspiration, but the coordination is immediately followed by subordination, before the effect of coordination has begun to be felt ("or, if . . .") and continues on to suc-ceeding clauses that end much as those in the first section. The third section begins with the introduction of the poet-narrator and six hypotactic clauses that add or accumulate, but whose rhythm provides a gradual slackening of the energy of the passage in order to prepare for the rise of the next sentence. In terms of prose and literary history, Milton has constructed a periodic sen-tence modeled on Latin syntax, which permits such an inversion as his and which taught him how to preserve order in so long a period with carefully modulated rhythms.

Clear as it is that Milton's periodic syntax expresses a humanistic debt to the Ciceronian tradition, and his inversions to an adapted Virgilian flexibility, it is even more apparent that Milton is conscious of the potentialities as well as the limitations of his own language. He has used suspension, parallelism of syntax and idea, and inversion to create a sentence far longer and more complex than normal poetic periods; and yet, he has wisely stopped short of mannerism by calculating the degree of extension and especially of inversion that English may be made to employ. Had he been content with parataxis alone, he might have joined together more coordinate units, but the complex nature of his thought demands the greater degree of subordination he has employed. This is a remarkable poetic sentence—one exceptional rather than exemplary in its procedure.

CHART II

SYNTACTICAL DIAGRAM OF "PARADISE LOST" (I, 1–16)

Of man's first disobedience,
+ and the fruit of that forbidden tree
  − whose mortal (taste) brought death
  − into the world,
+ and all our woe
+ with loss of Eden,
    − till one greater (Man) restore us,
    + and regain the blissful seat,

Sing (Heavenly Muse),
  − that
    − on the secret top of Oreb,
    + or of Sinai,
  − didst inspire that (shepherd),
    − who first taught the chosen seed,
    − in the beginning
      − how the (heavens and earth) rose
      − out of chaos
  + or
    − if (Sion hill) delight thee more,
    + and (Siloa's brook)
      − that flowed fast
      − by the oracle of God;

(I) thence invoke thy aid
  − to my adventurous (song),
  − that
  − with no middle flight
  − intends to soar
    − above the Aonian mount,
    − while (it) pursues things
      − unattempted yet
      − in prose
      + or rhyme.

( )   subjects or substantives referred to by relative pronouns that are subjects
+   parataxis: coordination and coupling
−   hypotaxis: subordination and attribution

If we feel that only Milton could sustain such periods without lapsing into obscurity, we must also grant that he has done so by realizing to the utmost certain capabilities of his language. And this is as true in detail as it is in general. In each section of his period he has properly assigned an initial position for his most important ideas in that section. It is possible to imagine his ending the first section after "into the world," his omitting from the second section the material between "that shepherd" and "out of chaos" and the part after "Siloa's brook," and from the third section all that follows after "my adventurous song." Had he done so, the effect of the period would have been different, for on the whole the sections thereby omitted would have taken from the sentence much of the sense of action embodied in what is primarily a reflective passage. The verbs of the first section are perhaps not highly active in any case, but such an omission would leave only "brought"; it would lose "restore" and "regain." Roughly the same thing would happen to the second unit, for although "inspire" would be retained, the even more active verbs, "rose" and "flowed," would be lost. And from the third section he would lose both "soar" and "pursues." For the most part these more active verbs are to be found in hypotactic clauses, and they function to amplify and strengthen the style—or more specifically, to give a sense of latent heroic action to the reflective statement of his subject. To give this sense of action is clearly desirable for Milton's purpose, and the high degree of hypotaxis and periodic structure makes it possible for him to introduce such verbs. We should not have criticized him if his opening statement lacked such a sense of activity with its promise of more to come, but the passage as he wrote it is clearly more effective for an epic poem than a simple announcement of his subject.

The extent to which Milton has given activity to a basically inactive subject can be judged by comparing his syntax with Hitomaro's. Hitomaro's subject is inherently more active, even violent, than Milton's statement that he wishes to write in an elevated fashion about the fall and salvation of man. Appropriately, therefore, the second and third sections of Hitomaro's poem—describing his voyage through the storm to Samine—are full of active verbs. And yet, curiously, the effect is not nearly as active as one would expect, or as our translation has suggested. To say why this is so, we must refer to our diagram of the syntax of the chōka. The most remarkable thing about this syntax is the way in which it plays upon certain inflectional endings of verbs and adjectives in an ambiguous fashion. In eleven instances there are constructions that may be taken as finite and so conclusive, but at the same time as attributives to what follows. The effect is a masterpiece of syntactic fluidity that contrasts startlingly with Milton's comparatively rigid syntax.

In short, what Hitomaro has really done is to present us with a poem that consists of a single sentence in which every successive syntactic element is governed by what precedes, all the way back to the beginning of the poem. More than this, the last word and the particle, *tsumara wa* (topic: "as for

CHART III

SYNTACTICAL DIAGRAM OF HITOMARO'S "ON SEEING THE BODY OF A MAN"

(Every line except the first is modified by earlier attribution or is an incomplete sentence. Verbs and adjectives that function both as finite forms in their clauses and as attributives for what immediately follows are repeated.)

Tamamo yoshi — Sanuki no [kuni wa] —
kunikara ka miredo mo —
akanu ·
akanu — kamukara ka kokoda tōtoki ·
tōtoki — ametsuchi hitsuki to tomo ni —
tariyukan ·
tariyukan — kami no miomo to
tsugite + kuru ·
    kuru — Naka no minato yu —
    fune ukete +
    (wa ga) kogikureba —
    (toki tsu kaze) kumoi ni fuku ·
    fuku — ni — oki mireba —
    (toinami) tachi +
he mireba —
(shiranami) sawaku ·
    sawaku — isanatori — umi o kashikomi +
    yuku ·
    yuku — fune no kaji hikiorite +
ochikochi no [shima wa] ōkedo —
nakuwashi — Samine no shima no arisomo ni — iorite +
mireba —
shigeki hamabe o makura ni — nashite +
aradoko ni korofusu ·
korofusu — kimi ga ie shiraba —
ki mo towamashi o ·
    towamashi o — tamahoko no michi dani shirazu ·
    shirazu + oboboshiku machi ka kou ·
kou + ran ·
kou + ran — hashiki ·
hashiki — [tsumara wa].

[   ]   topics
(   )   subjects
+   parataxis: coordination and coupling
—   hypotaxis: subordination and attribution
·   attributive/finite verbs or adjectives

[your] wife," with the suggestion in the endearment plural *ra* of family, homeland, and all associated with her), are not only governed by everything that precedes but also are the beginning of the "main" sentence of the poem, a sentence that stops with no more than this topic. Such syntax is unimaginable in English, but something of its effect can be gained by beginning with the last word of the Japanese and working back in translation, without a break, to the initial line of the poem. This backwards movement, however, destroys the succession of images and the very order of the experience. So the point remains that Japanese syntax, which employs prepositive attribution, can do things that our prevailingly postpositive attribution (in relative clauses, for example) cannot do—just as English is capable of effects denied to Japanese.

Hitomaro's poem ends, as we would say, inconclusively, with much being suggested about the agony of the wife but nothing being said syntactically, at least not in such a way as to conclude the sentence. And yet, much has been said by what precedes and, it may be noted, the first envoy begins with the same word, "wife" (*tsuma*), and proceeds to a complete sentence. Such planning reflects as clearly as Milton's the most consummate art. In each case we have poets who have realized to an extraordinary degree the potentialities of their language for extended writing. But his genius apart, Hitomaro is working with a language that has a different poetic process. To follow this process further is to lead us toward our question of why the poem seems less active than we might expect from its subject.

It is a matter of linguistic fact that Japanese is well endowed with nouns and personal pronouns, either of which may serve as topics or subjects; but when we look at Hitomaro's poem, we find that he has avoided them. There are three topics—one at the beginning of the poem (*kuni wa*), one in the middle (*shima wa*), and one at the very end (*tsumara wa*). We do not expect of topics that they should typically govern verbs, much less active verbs, but the fact that there are so few topics shows that there are very few people specified who might be considered part of the *dramatis personae* of the poem. Indeed, the three topics mean successively, "country," "islands," and "wife"; and as we have seen, there is no verb in the one clause that includes a human being as a topic. Further, there are only four subjects, and they all appear in the second section of the poem. These are, with their verbs: "as I came rowing" (*wa ga kogikureba*), "the tidal breeze . . . blows" (*toki tsu kaze . . . fuku*), "surging waves rise" (*toinami tachi*), and "white waves dash" (*shira-nami sawaku*). Again, only in one instance is a human being mentioned, and this the narrator rather than the dead man whose violent death is the subject of the poem. He is never named, and only once is there a pronoun that refers to him—the honorific "you" (*kimi*)—toward the end of the third section. So that although there is action aplenty in the second and third sections of the poem, it does not syntactically involve the chief human actors of the poem, except in the one case in which the narrator is said to be rowing in his boat.

It may of course be argued that subjects are implied earlier in the poem, that human agency may be inferred, and this is true to a point. But if one were to ask how many people are in the narrator's boat, who it is that builds the hut, and so on, there is no answer in the Japanese. In translating the poem, we have taken our chances and specified such subjects as "I" or "we," or added subjects, precisely because we readers of English poetry—indeed, like English syntax itself—require just such information. For Hitomaro, the actors are less important than other matters, and therefore, in spite of the active verbs, the result—the linguistic process of the poem—conveys less of what we imply in English by action: actors, actions, responsibility, and results. For like Milton, who has realized the utmost limit of elasticity in English syntax, partly to give the sense of action in a reflective passage, so Hitomaro has employed some of the resources of his language to an unusual degree and has managed in doing so to draw our attention to that which interests him.

Primarily what interests him is not so much the actors as the actions, not so much the issue of responsibility as the integrated nature of the process of a complex experience. Consequently, there are verbs in abundance and noun images to create the scene vividly. And the syntax is so organized that in spite of the numerous semi-stops, the stops are transformed into attributives for the nouns and clauses that follow. The skill involved is prodigious, as one can see from the transition between the first and second section. The first section ends with the two verbs *tsugite kuru* forming an idiom something like "transmitted." The effect is to say that it has been transmitted that the land of Sanuki is divine. But *kuru* is also used separately, apart from the idiom and attributively, for the next clause. Here *kuru* achieves more of its usual sense as an active verb in a clause something like, "coming to the harbor of Naka," as if one could take in English the "-mit" from "transmit" and use it in its root Latin sense of "send" as part of a relative clause. There are, as we have said, eleven such double-functioning verbs or adjectives in the poem, and the result is that by such hypotaxis Hitomaro manages to integrate all the elements of the poem into one continuous poetic and linguistic process, into one experience. This technique is clearly related to the meaning of the poem as we have analyzed it (pp. 98–101), pointing out that the divinity of Sanuki, the narrator's hazardous voyage, the death of the man, and the sufferings of the wife are rendered thematically into one whole. The poem presents all these elements as happenings that show the complex variety in human experience, a variety held together technically by the syntax, structure, and imagery, and tonally by the kind irony that is so typical of Hitomaro.

Hitomaro's mastery of the syntax of his language is but one aspect of his remarkable genius. Yet this aspect is crucially symptomatic of the others, as we can readily understand by comparing him with later poets of the chōka. Akahito and Yakamochi are great poets, but in their poetry the syntax has been smoothed, regularized, and, to a considerable degree, denied a total purpose. By concentrating on the aural beauty of single lines and passages, they forfeit the greater beauty of larger patterns of syntactical richness in the poem as a whole. It is no accident that they came to find a better medium for short lyrics than the chōka, or blends of lyricism with narration and description different from the complex style of Hitomaro. Yakamochi turned to reflection in musing passages of variations; Akahito and others shortened the chōka considerably. Both also practiced the tanka in ways that were by no means inferior to Hitomaro's. And there was another medium at hand for longer poems—the Chinese poetry which was practiced by many of the poets represented in the *Man'yōshū*.

POETIC THEMES AND SUBJECTS

Since the major purpose of literary techniques is to enable writers to treat certain subjects, to provide them with a means of expressing their thematic concerns, some general remarks about the kinds and range of meaning of poetry in the early literary period (apart from the poems already discussed) will convey the major interests of the poets, the meanings which the techniques were designed to express. One of the distinctions that can be made, although not so cleanly that there is no overlapping, is the distinction between public and private subjects. One of the most important groups of public subjects is that of religion and morality. The poetry of this period reveals the continuing influence of Shinto, notably in the divine nature ascribed to places and mountains, and, more important, in the concept that the imperial succession is a divinely ordained polity. This is of course the theme of many of Hitomaro's overtures—that the gods grant divinity to the life of men by sustaining an imperial order originated in heaven.

The Chinese, and somewhat alien, ideas of Confucianism, Taoism, and Buddhism appear in the works of only a few poets of the period, although these poets—Okura, Tabito, and Yakamochi—are among the most important figures of the age. Only Okura, perhaps because he alone of the great poets of this century had intimate, first-hand experience of Chinese life, appears to have absorbed to any degree the Chinese idea of the didactic, political function of poetry. His Confucian moral emphasis can be seen in such poems as his "Admonition to a Straying Mind" (*MYS*, V: 800–801), a mind that strays too far from the Confucian filial and familial codes. Perhaps an inference can be drawn from his "Dialogue on Poverty" that such wretched conditions would not exist if all were well with the government. However, both Okura's implied criticism of the state and Tabito's anti-social Taoism were points of view not rigorously held. The poets seem to have experimented with Chinese ideas as with Chinese techniques, rejecting after a time those they found incompatible. Tabito's poems on sake (*MYS*, III: 338–50) represent what may be called Taoistic epicureanism, but it is difficult to say how seriously these poems were meant to be taken: they are not Tabito's most carefully written poems.

Except for such historically noteworthy and unusual poems, there is little out-and-out Taoism in the poetry of the period. Indeed, except for Yakamochi, who deeply admired Okura, very few poets at the end of the period show any inclination to deal with these alien ideas. The notions that a divinely instituted order might be criticized, and that alcohol is the best answer to the problems of the world, appear to have been too alien to Japanese custom and social practice to gain a permanent place in the poetic tradition.

Drawing of Ōtomo Tabito from the ZENKEN KOJITSU, *a book on ancient customs and practices by Kikuchi Takeyasu (Tokyo, 1903)*

Okura also shows the effect of Buddhist thought—it would be too much to say he expresses it thematically—in his "Lament on the Instability of Human Life." The idea that this is an unstable world of change is Buddhistic; his attachment to the world in spite of its instability is not. But the conflict between life as we would have it—beautiful, unchanging, full of youth and love—and the inexorable effect of time becomes one of the major concerns of Japanese poetry in later ages. This and other subjects of Buddhist inspiration are incipient rather than developed in the poetry of this early period; but by the middle of the eighth century, Yakamochi expresses his desire to pursue the Way of the Buddha (*MYS*, XX: 4468–69), and we may recognize in the increasing emphasis upon the fragility, transience, and ultimate sadness of life a native sensitivity shaped and developed by Buddhist teaching. Even in the poetry of this early period, the typical Japanese reaction to grief, loss, old age, and the other tragic realities of life is one of regret tinged with a Buddhist-inspired resignation and a consciousness that man is helpless to change his fate.

The early literary period may be readily distinguished from the primitive age in the kind of mythical and legendary materials used. The myths of primitive poetry are passed off as true history or religion, but the myths used by poets in the early literary period are, apart from the theme of divine polity, specifically literary myths. The Seventh Night or Tanabata theme has already been mentioned. There is also the legend of Urashima, of uncertain origin and in plot rather like the story of Rip Van Winkle (*MYS, IX*: 1740–41). However legendary or mythical the poems which treat these subjects are, their emphasis is wholly literary. Unlike the use of myth in primitive poetry, the treatment of legend in the early literary period is no more religious in emphasis than Ovid's in his *Metamorphoses*, since however magical the situation, the element of fiction is uppermost.

Nature is of course one of the most important poetic subjects. Between Princess Nukada's comparison of the spring and autumn hills, an early example of sophistication, and Yakamochi's careful observation of his garden, we find several different attitudes toward nature. Hitomaro treats nature as one part of life, as real as human actions, buildings, and all else. It is this sense of both the reality and the significance of things, with Hitomaro participating in them, which lends such conviction to his poetry. Without being naïve, his attitude toward himself and his world seems simple—but simple with the same wonder that Chaucer expresses upon going out of doors on a May morning. Hitomaro's is an attitude of awareness, with a keen sense of such contingencies as sorrow and death. A poet of moral emphasis like Okura naturally focuses on man and uses nature for little more than comparison. With the increasingly descriptive lyricism of such poets as Akahito and Yakamochi, we find that not only is nature taken for her beauty, but also the poet knows that by selecting and arranging he can improve upon what the natural scene presents. He is closer to his materials, yet less involved in them. Like Okura's didactic interests, the possibility of descriptive lyricism was suggested to the Japanese by the Chinese example, but we have only to contrast the supreme importance of this mode to the growing tradition with the brief duration of moral themes to see that the lyrical description was far more congenial to the inclinations of the Japanese.

The poets of the age seem to have felt there were four thematic concerns that best represented their understanding of life and that cut across the subjects and themes mentioned thus far. These basic themes were beauty, "tragedy" (perhaps better, irony), cause and effect, and time. It is remarkable that hazardous as journeys were, the poets warmly described what they saw on their trips. In modern European literature, such great natural objects as seas and mountains are unsympathetically treated until the eighteenth century. Only then did poets feel safe enough in nature to write familiarly, as one may say, of what before had seemed to be too forbidding and unpleasant. The Japanese, whose Shinto religion emphasized awe and veneration rather than fear of nature, have been able to find beauty even where there are forces that might mean their death. The poem which would probably come to the mind of every Japanese in this connection is the envoy to Akahito's "On a Distant View of Mount Fuji" (*MYS*, III: 318).

Tago no ura yu	Emerging from behind
Uchiidete mireba	The barrier shadow cast by Tago's shore,
Mashiro ni zo	I am startled by
Fuji no takane ni	The lofty cone of Fuji whitely dazzling
Yuki wa furikeru.	Underneath its newly fallen snow.

In addition to this esthetic mode of viewing the world, the Japanese of this period also saw life with an ironic feeling akin to tragedy. Death and (what was very nearly the same thing) partings cast portentous shadows across the age. One of Hitomaro's poems is "On the Death of a Court Lady from Tsu" (*MYS*, II: 217–19), a member of the petty aristocracy and a woman whom he had seen casually only a time or two. And yet this very fact of slight acquaintance fills the poet with a sense of human loss—his life would have been fuller if he could really have known her. In the words of the second envoy (*MYS*, II: 219),

Sora kazou	On the day I met her,
Ōshitsu no ko ga	This lady of the Court from Ōtsu,
Aishi hi ni	I casually looked
Obo ni mishikaba	With an indifferent glance that now
Ima zo kuyashiki.	Reminds me of the grievous waste of death.

Although anonymous, much of the best poetry in the *Man'yōshū* deals with such subjects as partings and separations. One of the finest examples of a poem of parting (*MYS*, XIV: 3570) is ascribed to a Frontier Guard, but the sophisticated skill of its imagery and its haunting cadences reveal a poet of long training and cultured sensibility.

Ashi no ha ni	I shall miss you most
Yūgiri tachite	When twilight brings the rising mists
Kamo ga ne no	To hang upon the reeds
Samuki yūbe shi	And as the evening darkens cold
Na oba shinuban.	With mallards' cries across the marsh.

The poetry of the *Man'yōshū* reveals not only a high sense that human failure consists in not getting the very most from life, but also the more pathetic, the softer but touching emotion that befits the grief parents feel for children. Even the moral toughness of Okura softened at the death of his child, Furuhi, as we see in the lovely first envoy to his "Elegy on the Death of Furuhi" (*MYS*, V: 905):

Wakakereba	Since he is so young,
Michiyuki shiraji	He will not know the road to take:
Mai wa sen	I will pay your fee—
Shitabe no tsukai	O courier from the realms below,
Oite tōrase.	Bear him there upon your back!

While life was full of beauty, wonder, irony, and anguished surprise to these poets, they also expressed an implicit awareness of cause and effect, although this causal sense is no highly developed, explicit logical postulate. The overtures expressing divine polity in the chōka have no counterpart in Chinese poetry, historically minded as the Chinese were. The overtures assume not only that there is an unbroken succession of rule, but also that the divinely ordained causes have had their effects in shaping Japan's destiny. In their middle sections, the numerous elegies very often show a sophisticated bewilderment: how could the cause-and-effect chain of life be broken so that a Prince Takechi dies when it was he who gave meaning to our lives? The later sections of the elegies usually accept the fact of death and show its effects on the living. The most pathetic state of all is that of people like the wife of the dead man Hitomaro found on Samine. She is not aware of the cause which will have such effects of deprivation on her life. Her awareness of the grim irony of cause and effect in human life can develop only over a very grievous period of time.

Time itself is one of the chief subjects of this, as of all, periods of Japanese Court poetry. The envoy to Okura's "Lament on the Instability of Human Life" may be repeated here, since it expresses one thematic aspect of this subject most openly.

> How I yearn to be
> Unalterably what once I was,
> Immovable as a rock,
> But because I belong to this world,
> There is no stop to time.

The pressure of time here explains why life is transitory and full of suffering. But there are other attitudes toward time. Often the glories of the past in Hitomaro's overtures or in Yakamochi's pride in the good name of the Ōtomo family are made to bear directly on the present and to fill it with meaning. A closely related theme, though far different in tone, is the lament for the glories of the past, a pity for those *qui ante nos fuerunt*. One of Hitomaro's most famous poems, "On Passing the Ruined Capital of Ōmi" (*MYS*, I: 29–31), created a genre which became more and more romantic and sentimental or else was altered into far different, neoclassical terms. Hitomaro does not say, as some later poets did, that the past is superior to the present; rather, he laments that the greatness of the past should suffer the ruin of time. Perhaps there are few things in Japanese poetry that call forth such a deep response as time, a confrontation of past and present, and a sense of change. The Japanese became fully aware of themselves only when they felt their past and the pressure of time upon them.

The private subjects and themes need only to be named to be understood, and many of them impinge upon the public themes. Death, love, children, personal possessions, and human affairs may be said to provide the major group. But there are also occasional subjects like departure and travel, and those of such informal genres as the *jeux d'esprit* and verse letters, which account for a large number of poems. The significant fact about these private subjects and themes is not their identity, however, but the way in which they come to dominate poetry toward the end of the period. It was now becoming easier to see the world in terms of one's self than as a wider realm of public affairs or universal human destiny. This increasing personalism was to lead to important developments in the next period of a now great literary tradition; but at the same time, it was for this age a diminution of its once various and versatile poetic creativity. The glories of the generation of Hitomaro were now more a memory than an actuality, and an age was in decline.

ATTENUATION AND DECLINE

"There is no stop to time," Okura had written. The major change in the course of the early literary period was not in the ability of poets to write moving poetry, but in the terms in which poetry came to be considered. Some of the new attitudes toward poetry were detrimental to the genius of the age; others strongly prefigured new poetic advances, even when, viewed in the context of the poetic practice of the age, they must often be deplored. If we did not have the poetry of Hitomaro, perhaps some of these developments would not seem to be as much of a decline as they do today. He had accomplished so much, had opened so wide a realm of poetic genres, styles, and techniques that the less grandly imaginative later poets often suffer by comparison. Much as there is to admire in their work, it is hard to avoid the conviction that they are lesser men as well as lesser artists.

The proper question, however, is what the changes were that led the world of Hitomaro to shrink into the world of Yakamochi's successors. As in all such historical changes, there are a number of complexly related developments. One of these may be characterized as limited and limiting refinement. Earlier poets had refined the materials they inherited, but they did so by redefinitions of materials postulated on a meaningful world view and by an art that expressed such a view with conviction. With the poets of Akahito's generation and following, there is not so much a cessation of experiment as an increasing tendency to experiment within narrower and less meaningful bounds. When gifted poets like Akahito spent their best energies in creating lovely melodic cadences, they were creating a style that well suited the tanka, which lent itself to a purer lyricism, but that took the vital strength and forward pressure from the chōka. And when we consider the contemporaneous trends toward description and private poetry which were also inimical to the sustained poetry of Hitomaro and Okura, we must wonder not so much that the chōka was becoming obsolescent as that it continued to be written at all and with any degree of success.

Of the poets whose chōka survive from the end of this and later periods, only Yakamochi seems to have been able to compose longer poems that were in any way comparable to those of the earlier masters of the form. So versatile was he, so skilled in older modes, and so much a precursor of the next poetic age, that we can say of him not only what Dr. Johnson said of Goldsmith, that he adorned everything he touched, but also that he touched nearly everything. Much of his success with the chōka may be attributed to his careful study of Hitomaro, Okura, and Akahito, but his styles remain particularly his own. His best chōka are reflective in mood, and often have the structure of association, as details and images rise to his mind and are shaped by his sensibility. His accomplishment was, therefore, a personal one, and after him the secret was lost.

The chōka of a contemporary and acquaintance of Yakamochi, Tanabe Sakimaro, show more clearly than Yakamochi's poems in this form what had happened to the style to render it unfit for poems like those of Hitomaro and Okura. Sakimaro's "Lament for the Old City of Nara" (*MYS*, VI: 1047) grows out of a public event—the temporary shifting of the capital from Nara to Kuni from 741 to 745—but the real intent of the poem seems almost to be imitation of Hitomaro's oft-imitated poem, "On Passing the Ruined Capital of Ōmi." By comparison, Sakimaro's chōka is prosaic and monotonous. The principal reason for the insipidness of the poem is that it lacks the internal tension that Hitomaro and Okura achieved by means of perturbations of syntax, irregular lines, complex contiguous and noncontiguous parallelisms, echoings, and larger but related divisions of thought. Without such stiffening and enrichment of the sustained syntactical flow, the liquid, polysyllabic nature of Japanese poetry inclines it toward either the attenuated sweetness of Akahito's style or the arrant prose of Sakimaro.

It seems fair to us to discuss the decline of the age in terms of the decline of the chōka, not because there is anything inherently sacrosanct about the form, but because almost everything that can be said about the excellence or deterioration of poetry in the period can be related to it. In the chōka, the age had found its most fruitful balance between personal interests and impersonal themes; or, to put it another way, the chōka was the vehicle of poetry of universal interest, while the tanka was still either an adjunct to the chōka or a form better suited to a narrower, personal lyricism.

Two attitudes lay behind the rise of the chōka—attitudes toward the poetic audience and the poetic materials. We can only speculate on what social changes may have taken place during this age to change the attitude of close relationship between the poet and his audience. Perhaps the Court failed to support the best poets; perhaps the inroads of Chinese poetry were too great. Whatever the causes, the effects of this breakdown between the poet and his public audience seem clear enough. The speakers of Hitomaro or Okura's poems—the poets' representations of themselves or other men—were persons engaged in the events and activities with which the poems deal. They are on the scene as participants with other actors, and as a result the poems achieve a dramatic intensity and carry the conviction both of actuality and universality—the words of the speaker seem to speak for all who were present at the scene or who would hear the poem. Even the elegies for private individuals include a wider world of families, fellow men, gods, and natural forces in which the speaker is as involved as the dead person. The dead body discovered by Hitomaro on the Island of Samine becomes a symbol both of experience shared by the poet and of man's position in the world. The chōka of Kasa Kanamura or Akahito, on the other hand, seem to have no special audience at all. The poems they wrote about imperial journeys contain little more than three elements—a statement of the fact of the journey, a lovely description of the place, and a personal exclamation over the imperial domain or the imperial succession. None of these elements suggests that the poet is talking to anyone besides himself; his role as an individual does not relate him to the people about him, to the scenery he observes, or even to the emperor himself in any meaningful artistic way. The poems give little sense of event— for all one can tell they might have been written in advance, composed miles away from the happenings, or much later from barely warmed-over notes taken at the time.

In conjunction with the increase of esthetic distance between poets and audiences, there was a change in the poet's relation to his materials. As these poets lost involvement with other men, they contemplated such subjects as nature in more detail. This did not mean, however, that nature was more significant to human life for them, but rather that they found it more simply beautiful than earlier poets had. Unlike Hitomaro, who found nature as much a part of his world as himself, these poets tended to description, with the result that they seem to have treated the world in which they lived more as pictures or recordings which they might contemplate at a distance. Nature changed from man's real environment to patterns which the poet might shape at his will, as in Akahito's poem on an imperial hunt (*MYS*, VI: 926–27). The scene of this lovely poem is perfectly realized, the style is assured, and the event emerges in great clarity. But everything in it is put into a pattern—the trackers are in the fields, bowmen in the hills; bears are hunted in the morning, and wild fowl in the afternoons. The poem has the imagistic richness of a chōka by Hitomaro, but it lacks movement, either in the verse or in the subject matter, and Akahito himself is not really on the scene. We may say that Akahito has written a fine poem, but its very excellences determine the nature of the disaster to come in the generation of Sakimaro. We must add in fairness to Akahito that his tanka is a masterpiece. The pattern of the hunters, arrows under their arms, spreading over the countryside is both kinetic and yet manipulated into a design of great loveliness. While description alone would in time destroy the chōka, it was one of the many possibilities that were now being glimpsed for the tanka form.

Even Yakamochi, who could write such public poems as one on "The Production of Gold in Michinoku" (MYS, XVIII: 4094–97) or an "Admonition to His Clansmen" (MYS, XX: 4465–67), tends toward description at times in his chōka, and as we have observed, they possess more the structure of miscellaneous private thoughts on a central subject than a development of poetic order through a theme in which all men's views can be assimilated. Moreover, it is particularly appropriate that many of his most deeply felt chōka should be on such private subjects as his hawk (MYS, XVII: 4011–15; XIX: 4154–55). No title seems more significant for what had happened to the balance between personal and impersonal interests during the age than Yakamochi's title for a chōka and two envoys, "Expressing My Own Thoughts" (MYS, XX: 4360–62). It would never have occurred to poets of the generation of Hitomaro that they might write a poem in which their thoughts were something apart from the thoughts of other men.

Perhaps no writer represented in the Man'yōshū shows as clearly how increasingly personal poetry had become as Yakamochi's aunt, Lady Ōtomo of Sakanoe. Almost without exception, those poems we have of hers are statements of private thought or discourse in verse sent by messenger to someone like her daughter, to Yakamochi, or to the various people with whom she kept up an elegant and often gallant correspondence. Moreover, her poetry also tends as a result to be cast either into short chōka or, more commonly, tanka. The short lyric is now the most expressive form for a poetry that has become increasingly private.

The decline in poetry at the end of this age is not just a matter of the loss of the public qualities it had once enjoyed. The Japanese distinction between formal and informal poems—between those composed with great care for many eyes and those more laxly written for but two or four—is also crucial. That strange poem of Lady Ōtomo's, "At a Religious Service for Her Ancestral God" (MYS, III: 379–80), in which she prays to meet her lover, would be in the worst taste if it were not an informal poem meant only for herself, perhaps the god, and the man she longs to see. Even if we exonerate her from bad taste in this poem, however, we must deplore it as a symptom of the growing tendency to write informal poetry toward the end of this age and the beginning of the next. If it were to become the dominant mode, such poetry would become a much more serious threat to the tradition than the private but formal beauty of the poetic art of Akahito and Yakamochi. And yet these greater poets must carry part of the blame, for their emphasis upon private, if formal, modes surely prepared the way for the unprepossessing informal poetry of the period, a poetry whose only public role seems to have been left to the servants of the great houses, who plied their way, day and night, back and forth, between the versifying correspondents. So strong did the tendency toward private, informal verse become that by the end of the eighth century it began to look as if the tanka would barely survive the chōka. Even the staple lyric form seemed to be relegated to a half-serious plaything for gallant communication.

To state the situation in these terms suggests that the nation had somehow become illiterate, but it seems rather that there were too many poets who were altogether too intent upon acquiring a fashionable literacy that did neither them nor, for a time, Japanese poetry much good. For what had happened was that the composition of Chinese poetry had attained such a feverish vogue among cultured men that Japanese poetry was left to care for itself. Only ladies were spared the pains of learning Chinese, so that the courtiers, who after all could not study Chinese both day and night, had to know how to write Japanese poems if they chose to win or keep a lady's heart. How seriously later Japanese have regarded the Chinese vogue as a poetic invasion can be understood by reading the Nō play, *Haku Rakuten,* by Zeami (1363–1443). Haku Rakuten is the Sinico-Japanese reading of one name for the great T'ang poet, Po Chü-i. In the play, quite out of the way of biographical fact, but all too appropriate to literary history, Haku Rakuten comes to Japan on a one-man invasion. He is sent sailing back to China by the divinity of native poetry, the god of Sumiyoshi. Po Chü-i had indeed invaded Japan, for he was almost the only Chinese poet who became popular in Japan during his own lifetime. In the early ninth century, he reigned as completely over the minds of China and Japan as Lord Byron was later to rule over the melting hearts of Europe.

The suddenness with which Po Chü-i and the earlier styles of Six Dynasties and early T'ang poetry overwhelmed Japanese poetry in this period should perhaps be attributed more to the exhaustion of Japanese poetry than to complete sympathy for Chinese modes or subjects. The first great cycle of Japanese poetry, not the Japanese desire to read and compose a great poetic literature, had ended. At the time, it was by no means clear that a god of Sumiyoshi would set things to rights and that a new poetic would emerge. How the new age came into being, how it absorbed the Chinese poetry it was now accepting unquestioningly, and how it achieved a new poetry of significance is the subject of the next chapter.

5

The Early Classical Period

784–1100

THE LAST DATABLE POEM in the *Man'yōshū* was written in 759; the next great collection of Court poetry was the first of the twenty-one imperial anthologies, which was compiled about 905. This was the *Kokinshū*, or "Collection of Ancient and Modern Times," whose poetry presents us with a world in which there is little in the way of familiar terrain. As its title implies, the *Kokinshū* contains poems written some years before the generation of the compilers, as well as contemporary works. But the century and a half between the *Man'yōshū* and the *Kokinshū* comprised a greater gulf in time than might be imagined. By the tenth century it had become extremely difficult to read the *Man'yōshū*, with its antiquated amalgam of Chinese and Japanese readings, and the literary development had led to very different poetic styles. The poems attributed to Hitomaro in the *Kokinshū* are suspect. In fact, the age of Hitomaro, which had made Japanese poetry literary and great, lay behind in a dim past. The changes in literature that coincided with the removal of the capital to Heiankyō (modern Kyoto) entailed a change to modernity, a change so fundamental that the tradition was not to see another such alteration for eleven centuries. Why we may call the new poetry modern, how the change came about, and what it entailed are all matters requiring some explanation.

The preceding age had achieved greatness by means of that universality which springs from a people newly conscious of its national culture and gifted for the first time with the means by which to express its awareness with richness and wonder, and in direct response to experience. The age retained a certain simplicity of attitude in spite of the sophistication of its art, in this respect reminding one of the Elizabethan Age. The new age was "modern" in its self-consciousness, in its refinement of what seemed to be certain crudities of the older tradition, and in its subjective complexities. Its modernity was that of the full adulthood of the race—of the seventeenth century in comparison with the Elizabethan Age. It is a world in which wonder, if not superstition, has dwindled, the kind of age to which we respond familiarly and appreciatively, if with some regret at the change. Perhaps its modernity can best be typified by its greatest single literary work, the *Genji Monogatari* of Murasaki Shikibu (?978–?1016), an anticipation of the modern psychological novel and one of the world's truly great books.

The modernity of the age is of course partial—it is relative to what had gone before. Certainly the period resembles in few particular ways our own day, and it must be characterized in other terms if the element of its modernity is to be cast into proper perspective. Choosing his words carefully, the distinguished historian of Japan Sir George Sansom has characterized the age by the terms "esthetic" and "unique." It is an esthetic age because the society of the Court placed an extraordinary emphasis upon achievements in such arts as calligraphy, music, dance, painting, and poetry. No other society of which we know has ever placed such importance upon poetry as a part of daily life—the minutest circumstances of social and private life required verse. This alone is enough to justify calling the age unique, but the society of the period was also courtly beyond anything we know in Western history. The Japanese Court, which was at its zenith in this period, was a regal, not a feudal, Court; its monarchy preceded rather than followed the period of feudalism. And it was a Court whose life was all but entirely civil—only later were military classes to rise to any position of ascendancy within it.

If to us the age seems now modern, now esthetic, now unique, to many modern Japanese it seems at once remote and bewildering, its poetry too much given to reasoning and wit. In more familiar terms we might create a representative poet of the age by combining qualities of certain English writers. We should imagine a poet who delighted in cleverness and metaphysical speculation like a Donne, who showed the negligent high spirits of a Suckling, and who possessed a greater "correctness" and refinement than a Pope. Within two centuries of the emergence of a literary tradition, more than a millennium before our day, a relatively small but homogeneous Court society had achieved a sophisticated civilization for which one can find no real parallel.

The achievement of the "unique" civilization was in part made possible by the natural development of native traditions and in part resulted from a new look at Chinese culture. The private, subjective turn of poetry at the end of the preceding period provided the basic native stock upon which might be grafted the Chinese elements that had become familiar to Japanese poets from their composition in Chinese. By the time conditions on the continent encouraged the Japanese to tend their own literary shop, they were ready to do so in a poetry no less their own for the help that the Chinese example had given them. The hostility of the Koreans made it necessary for them to visit China by passing across the China Sea, and survival of such trips was the exception. In China, the collapse of the T'ang dynasty meant that the hospitality extended earlier to such Japanese as Abe no Nakamaro (698–770) was impossible. Internal and external conditions alike urged the Japanese to proceed upon their own.

The *Kokinshū* and the next three imperial anthologies show the result. Tsurayuki's justly admired Preface to the *Kokinshū* is an "Apology for Japanese Poetry," giving critical expression to what had been for some generations a poetic fact—the Japanese literary tradition had taken on a new, independent life. As the creation of courtiers who had no doubt of their place in the world or of their own sophisticated codes, the poetry of the early classical period is often mannered, often frivolous. And when to such charges we add the fact that certain developments in the age may be thought inimical, as refinement led to debility and consolidation to uninspiring *bon ton* or solemnity, we have taxed the period with its sins. We have also neglected what is most significant in the age: its great poems, which arose from a milieu in which poetry was a living part of daily experience, in which beauty was the counterpart of refinement, in which *bon ton* also brought aristocratic liveliness, and in which solemnity was but one aspect of the importance of poetry to human life. Nothing indicates more clearly the vitality of literature in the period than the constancy of development; nothing indicates the strength of the tradition it was establishing more than the fact that the false starts of many writers were to define other periods of great poetry to follow. Poetry was never suffered to languish in indifference.

The poems of the period offer the best measure of its interests, explaining the kinds of experience that prompted the courtiers to write and the kinds of expression they employed. Kamutsuke Mineo (fl. ca. 890) is only one of a multitude of minor poets of the period, but for that very reason we may regard him as a typical writer. His poem on the death of the former Prime Minister, Fujiwara Mototsune (d. 891), is wholly representative in technique and quality (*KKS*, XVI: 832).

Fukakusa no	You cherry trees
Nobe no sakura shi	Growing along the moors of Fukakusa
Kokoro araba	Where our Lord now lies—
Kotoshi bakari wa	If you have any heart for man,
Sumizome ni sake.	At least this year put forth black flowers.

The conception of the poem lies somewhere between the far-fetched and the obvious, but it is nonetheless a very human cry. Grief-stricken men have always felt that the external world should show some reflection of the terrible events that seem to desolate their lives. There is another kind of logic in the poem with equal if less important psychological truth. Appreciation of the beauties of nature, in particular of cherry blossoms as the apex of vernal beauty, was expected of every man of taste. Now the cherry trees, in their turn, are being asked to show equal sensibility.

The poets of the early classical period sought again and again to discover the new, the unexpected, truth. Theirs is often a poetry of special cases. Discoveries of what is true in special instances must, however, have the final effect of confirming what we know to be true in important normative senses if they are to possess real significance for our lives. In such fashion one of the major poets of the age, Ki no Tsurayuki, makes a discovery whose novelty ultimately leads to a confirmation of what we know to be more typically true (*KKS,* V: 262).

Chihayaburu	Mighty they are,
Kami no igaki ni	The gods within this sacred shrine—
Hau kuzu mo	Yet even the laurel
Aki ni wa aezu	Creeping in their precincts could not hold
Utsuroinikeri.	Against the autumn's tingeing of its leaves.

The surprise is more wittily feigned than real, yet there is psychological justification for thinking that on holy grounds the usual effects of time and nature might be withstood. The result of the experience is not to lead us to question the power of the gods, nor even to make us wonder at the irresistible force of autumn. Rather we are meant to feel awe at the inexplicable but somehow benign comity of the gods and the great seasonal laws of nature.

Tsurayuki's poem takes us from one unexpected reality to a greater one, each denying certain superficial suppositions about the nature of things. Numerous poems of the age oppose appearance and reality in similar fashion, or play upon an inability to distinguish the one from the other when the world of appearance is, for some reason, suddenly truer or more forcibly felt than the world of reality. Such a thematic concern was perhaps inevitable to minds imbued with the Buddhist concept of the impermanence, even the illusory unreality, of what man commonly apprehends as the objective world outside himself. A common human reason for the reversal of what is and what seems to be is the absorption of the whole human being by a major experience like love, which often sheds so bright an illumination upon man's life that the mind is overpowered. One of the most remarkable examples of poems exemplifying such a bewildered heightening of normal experience is one in the genre of the "Next Morning Poem," verses exchanged by lovers after a secret tryst. One of the so-called Vestal Virgins of the Ise Shrine is said to have sent Ariwara Narihira such a poem the morning after having visited his sleeping quarters when he journeyed to the Shrine bearing an imperial message (*KKS,* XIII: 645; *Ise M.,* No. 141).

Kimi ya koshi	My mind is dazzled—
Ware ya yukiken	Did you come to visit me?
Omōezu	Or I to you?
Yume ka utsutsu ka	Was our night a dream? Reality?
Nete ka samete ka.	Was I sleeping? Was I awake?

Such extraordinary bewilderment is acceptable only for just cause. One can only say that, given the history of Japanese poetry and the legends about Narihira, he was cause enough.

He was also one of the greatest of all the Court poets. Quick-minded yet reflective, overwhelmingly attractive yet humanely considerate, many-sided yet profound, Narihira is remarkable for the way in which his personality and art have merged. Soon after his death, his life was rendered into art in the *Ise Monogatari* (*Tales of Ise*); and his art has become a part of Japanese life. His poems, however well-known, are unfortunately so much a part of their language that every translator seeks to take refuge in the lame excuse that they cannot be translated. His responsiveness to the problems of others, at least, may be demonstrated. When he heard that a certain lady of his household, who had been having an affair with Fujiwara Toshiyuki (d. 901), had received a letter from Toshiyuki, excusing his absence with a complaint about the heavy rains, Narihira composed a poem on her behalf (*KKS,* XIV: 705; for the situation, see the headnote).

> Kazu kazu ni
> Omoi omowazu
> Toigatami
> Mi o shiru ame wa
> Furi zo masareru.

> Wondering, wondering,
> "Does he love or love no more?"
> Yet I dare not ask—
> The rain that knows my destiny
> Ever more heavily weighs on my heavy
> heart.

The implicit analogy of tears to rain—of prophetic tears to a rain used transparently as an excuse not to do what was promised—and indeed the technique of the whole poem are typical of Narihira. His skill in expressing the woman's distress, and the humane prompting within him to use his skill, are alike tributes to the poet.

Each of the poems thus far examined shows the tendency of the poetry of the age to charge the phenomena of the natural world with a subjective human experience. In seeking for the larger significance of events, the poets often reverse normal expectations, as Tsurayuki's tinted laurel and Mineo's black cherry blossoms show. Such reversals are at once witty and serious, at least when the poet really has something to say. Narihira and Donne make wit an aspect of their ironic awareness of life; many of the followers of the Japanese poet as well as the English became merely tiresome with meaningless wit. With Narihira, wit seems a way of dropping everything not absolutely necessary from the expression of an intense experience. One scarcely knows whether the wit is the result of such harmonious economy or merely a symptom of it; but it is at all events not an end in itself. His poem refusing to admire the moon is not the most famous of his works treating the moon in relation to human experience, but it will serve to show how far the witty conception (who ever heard of not admiring the moon in Japanese poetry?) is made to incorporate the natural world into human life (*KKS*, XVII: 879).

Ōkata wa	Lovely as it is,
Tsuki o mo medeji	The moon will never win my praise—
Kore zo kono	No, not such a thing,
Tsumoreba hito no	Whose accumulated splendors heap
Oi to naru mono.	The burden of old age on man.

The radiance of the moon in all its phases and the many phases through which the speaker of the poem has seen it pass have not left him untouched. But he now speaks with a larger awareness. The moon is a natural symbol of change and of time, to the Japanese as to Western poets: however lovely it may be, each of its changes brings man nearer death. Its very beauty is a threat, because it tends to obscure the truth of man's great separation from the natural world that so attracts him. The moon and man are alike subject to change with the passage of time, but the less obvious change in man is final.

The difference between such poems and those of the early literary period is very striking. The balance between subject and object that gives the earlier poetry a classical repose has been altered so that the subject is now dominant. Man is the central figure even when he is conscious, as Narihira is, of his transience. Nature, clothes, buildings, utensils, indeed everything apart from man, is made to speak the language of man's mind and heart or be mute. By the same token, the expectation that every courtier and lady should be ready to produce a highly subjective poem, often on a moment's call, meant that there were many poetasters and fops. Yet only when poetry is a profound part of daily life can so small a society produce so many superior poets. It is a question of how its energy was directed. As Sir George Sansom well said of the age in his *Japan: A Short Cultural History* (p. 250), "though there must have been dilettantes without number, the standard of achievement was remarkably high." And what he has to say (p. 310) about the indigenous development of political institutions in the period must be our guide as we chart the development of a new native poetry by men who prized the Chinese heritage. He "recommends" such political developments (which might equally well be poetic)

to the attention of those who are inclined to think that the Japanese have excelled only as copyists of foreign institutions. That they had the courage and wisdom to copy in the first place is greatly to their credit, and their later history shows that they have never rested content with an uncritical acceptance of imported models.

With this principle and a few poems in mind, we may consider the developments that were to make the second great period of Japanese poetry the fountainhead of the classical Court tradition.

THE NEW POETIC

The hiatus in native poetry at the end of the early literary period, and the loss of the great bulk of the poetry of the *Man'yōshū* in the succeeding century, are historical facts requiring some adjustment. The so-called hiatus was neither long nor complete. It must not be imagined that Japanese poetry simply ceased to exist during the century and more between the compilation of the *Man'yōshū* and the completion of the *Kokinshū* in about 905. It would be more accurate to say that the tradition languished, that Japanese poetry lost status, and that the courtiers devoted their most serious efforts to versification in Chinese while at the same time continuing to exchange amorous if trifling lyrics in Japanese with their lady friends. But the rising prestige of native poetry was once again recognized officially when the Emperor Daigo (885–930) commanded Tsurayuki and others to compile the *Kokinshū*. The belated nature of this official recognition is clear from the fact that the oldest known poets of the post-*Man'yōshū* age represented in this collection—men such as Ono no Takamura (802–52) and Ariwara Yukihira (818–93)—were active during the third and fourth decades of the ninth century, and from the fact that the new poetry was already thriving in the age of the so-called Six Poetic Geniuses (Rokkasen) in the third quarter of the ninth century. (The Six Poetic Geniuses—so designated because they are mentioned by name in Tsurayuki's Preface to the *Kokinshū*—were the Bishop Henjō, Bunya Yasuhide, the priest Kisen, Ōtomo Kuronushi, Ono no Komachi, and Ariwara Narihira, the last two being the best known.) The hiatus, then, was of relatively short duration, and coincided only with the period of the greatest vogue of Chinese poetry (800–850). During these fifty years the Chinese fashion in poetry reigned supreme in prestige; indeed, three anthologies of Chinese verse by Japanese poets were compiled upon imperial command as the Emperors Saga (786–842) and Junna (786–840) and their courtiers zestfully labored in the techniques of the poetry of the late Six Dynasties (ca. 420–589). Nevertheless, we may suppose that even at the height of this rage for the Chinese mode, the most accomplished versifiers in the foreign tongue themselves had occasion to compose tanka in furthering their private affairs.

We may assume, therefore, that the native tradition endured, albeit diminished and attenuated, through this half-century of frenzied borrowing from China, and that the forms and many of the modes and techniques of Japanese poetry were handed down in a continuous tradition rather than suddenly "rediscovered," as it were, in the middle of the ninth century. Indeed, rediscovery was scarcely possible, for although the poets of the early classical revival had something in the way of a native tradition upon which to build, a precious part of their heritage was largely beyond their reach. As we have seen, the *Man'yōshū*, which Yakamochi and others had compiled with such care as a "Collection for Ten Thousand Generations," was well nigh unintelligible to the poets of the early Heian period—perhaps most of all to Tsurayuki and his generation in the first half of the tenth century.

But even if the poets of the early classical period had been able to read the *Man'yōshū* with ease, it is scarcely likely that they would have used it as a model. The social environment of the Court and the overwhelming prestige of the Chinese example had made it all but impossible, even for poets like Yakamochi, to write in the styles of Hitomaro and Okura. Each age, after all, must create for itself the kind of artistic expression that best suits its own needs. The half-dozen poems associated with Hitomaro in the *Kokinshū* are therefore more remarkable for what they show of altered literary tastes than as evidence of the compilers' ignorance of the older poetry. The following is a fair example (*KKS*, VI: 334):

Ume no hana	The blossoms of the plum
Sore to mo miezu	Do not appear to be themselves,
Hisakata no	For they are blanketed
Amagiru yuki no	With clouds of falling snow
Nabete furereba.	That swirl from the distant sky.

The ancient pillow-word, *hisakata no,* may seem at first glance to give the whole piece an old-fashioned flavor. In sound and rhythm, however, the poem is far different from Hitomaro's characteristic style: the first two lines constitute an independent syntactic unit that has a double logical function—to convey a conceit and to act as a topic statement. Given the normal Japanese word order, the syntax is inverted here, with the conclusion given first. Hitomaro not infrequently altered normal syntax, but it was for the purpose of stressing a word or a clause, not to stand syntax and logic on their heads. More than this, however, his world view was entirely different. This poem is private, as though its speaker were the only one to notice the scene. Hitomaro would have included all men with himself. The poet's attitude is one of a sophisticated elegance—he is confused because he cannot tell the plum blossoms from the snow, not sad because he has lost his wife or because his prince is dead. The elegant confusion between snow and plum blossoms in the present poem is characteristic of the poetry not of the age of Hitomaro, but of the generation of Tsurayuki himself. This is also true of the reasoning employed in the poem—the description of the scene is tied to an explanation for its particular appearance: the poet cannot see the plum blossoms because they are hidden by the swirling snow. The subject of reasoning in early classical poetry involves many other matters; here it is enough to remark that this technique, which is very nearly the backbone of the poetry of Tsurayuki's generation, was not used by Hitomaro, at least not as an end in itself.

Most of the poems of the earlier period that were actually known to the poets of the late ninth and the tenth centuries were probably known not because they had been recorded in written form for "ten thousand generations," but because they had been handed down orally through the years as songs and in versions that underwent significant changes in the process. We find in the *Kokinshū* a few poems (IV: 192, 247; XI: 551; XX: 1073, 1107, 1108) that are very like or even identical to poems in the *Man'yōshū*, while at the same time Tsurayuki states in his Preface to the *Kokinshū* that he and the other compilers were commanded to collect "old poems not included in the *Man'-yōshū*, adding our own to them." In several cases these duplicated poems are indicated as being on unknown "topics" or by anonymous poets, although both topics and poets are clearly recorded in the *Man'yōshū*. A variant of one poem, for example, which appears in the *Man'yōshū* together with seven others accompanied by the headnote "Eight travel poems by Takechi Kurohito" (*MYS*, III: 272), is found in the last volume of the *Kokinshū* as a song of unknown authorship to be sung to the "Shiwatsuyama Melody" (*KKS*, XX: 1073). Such poems were probably known to Tsurayuki and his contemporaries by way of the oral tradition, and their inclusion in the *Kokinshū* is one indication that the compilers were not familiar enough with the older collection to be aware of the duplication.

As we have noted, the poets of the tenth century were unable to read much of the poetry in the *Man'yōshū*, a loss that did not go unlamented. In the generation after Tsurayuki, the so-called Five Poets of the Pear-Jar Room, who compiled the second imperial anthology of Japanese poetry, the *Gosenshū* or *Later Collection,* were given the additional task of preparing glosses in the by then perfected and widely used *kana,* or syllabic alphabet, for the poems of the *Man'yōshū.* That they worked hard and long is beyond question—anecdotes about their prodigious labors even passed into the stream of literary folklore—but in all too many cases they were apparently able to reconstruct the originals only partially or in garbled versions. The manuscripts they prepared are no longer extant, but the general level of understanding of *Man'-yōshū* poetry among men who came after them and who no doubt benefited from their labors can be surmised from the corrupt versions of older poems that we find in such an "unofficial" but widely read collection as the *Kokin Waka Rokujō,* or *Six Volumes of Japanese Poems Ancient and Modern* of the late tenth century. (Compare, for example, *MYS*, XI: 2376 and the poem from the *Kokin Waka Rokujō* printed in *ZKT*: 32,642.)

The revival of Japanese poetry in the ninth and tenth centuries, then, in no sense involved a neoclassical turning to the past glories of Japanese poetry or an attempt to recapture the "spirit" of the earlier poetry. The revival was neoclassical, to be sure, but it was once again to China that poets turned for new materials, new themes, and most important of all, entirely new concepts of poetic technique. The experimentation in native poetry that followed this second long look at China produced a poetry whose greatness must be looked for in a poetic tradition more chastened by criticism and convention and less various in accomplishment than the poetry of the preceding age. The refinements accepted for Japanese poetry by Tsurayuki and his contemporaries, and thenceforth almost universally adopted by generations of Japanese poets, have been much lamented by those who would equate the true "Japanese spirit" with the traditional image of the "simple sincerity" and "folk cast" of the Man'yōshū. We have no consolation for these unhappy enthusiasts; the earlier poetry had been, in reality, a studied and brilliant artistic creation, and what decline there was was not in folk sincerity but in the narrowed realm of poetic forms and materials. If anything, the new age was more inclined to poetry than the old, and we must view its accomplishment as much in the light that literary history sheds upon its aims as with the pleasure that analysis gains from its lively practice. The other sections of this chapter are an attempt to describe what this accomplishment was, but first it is necessary to define the new ideals the poets set before themselves, the new relations between poets and their audiences, and the new critical attitude toward poetry that henceforth shaped and gave direction to the developing tradition.

For all of the frantic borrowing and assimilation of Chinese ideas and institutions during the late Nara period (750–84) and the early Heian period (794–866), Japanese society remained uncompromisingly aristocratic in nature. The efforts to adopt such Chinese institutions as the competitive examination system were largely abortive; hereditary privilege revived with new vigor as the dominant social force in the late ninth century. Other bureaucratic reforms imported from T'ang China were likewise rejected or modified as the Fujiwara clan succeeded in taking into its hands all the important offices of government and much of the wealth that went with them. The new temper of Heian society and its culture is not to be found, however, in the mere fact that it was aristocratic, since Japanese society and its poetry had been equally aristocratic—if not as distinctly and wholly courtly—in the preceding period. What is new is the character of the aristocracy and its conception of the nature and role of poetry. The earlier Court had been, if not insular, relatively isolated, small, and insecure. The new aristocracy moved in what was then one of the world's greatest cities, and as the Fujiwara clan grew in power, its courtiers settled into a comfort and assurance qualified only by nervous glances toward the vastly older and more powerful Chinese civilization across the sea. Once the new aristocracy could become confident that it had taken all that was needed from China, it could happily enjoy in its own language, as it were, the splendid life so beautifully depicted in the *Tale of Genji*. Such confidence came with time, as Chinese manners, institutions, and literary criteria were first imitated and then assimilated, and as the Court gained a power and wealth it had not known before. The rapidity with which this civilization became sophisticated is truly remarkable—by the late tenth century it was, after China, the most stable and cultured nation then flourishing.

The sophistication of the Court aristocracy is reflected in the numerous arts it cultivated and patronized. These courtiers demanded and produced a world of great buoyancy and elegance—whether they were engaged in shaky composition of Chinese verse or in a sophisticated *ars amatoria* that would have excited envy and admiration even in an Ovid. In such a society, breeding, cultivation, style, and aristocratic tone were the standards of admission, and those who lacked them by birth or training were excluded. Such standards in themselves are no guarantee of true culture, for without serious purpose, cultivation may become preciosity, style may degenerate into foppishness, and social tone may mean no more than aristocratic frivolity. Judging by many of the poems that survive from this period, no small number of the courtiers did pursue lives of just such superficiality. There were those who rode like froth on the tides of changing literary and social modes: many writers were stylishly modern or "Chinese" because to be so was the latest fashion, and they were as unconscious of the fact that their vaunted modernity was long since passé in China as they were of any important relevance of changing literary styles to the experience of their age. But so rich a society as this one cannot be made from the froth of frivolity, and there were certainly poets—and statesmen, scholars, and priests—whom history will always treat with respect. There were the poets like Narihira and Komachi to whom poetry was the expression of intensely personal experience that still lives in the universality of their work; and there were others like Tsurayuki and his fellow compilers of the *Kokinshū*, who found a technique and an esthetic for Japanese poetry that gave it a seriousness, stability, and dignity which enabled it to survive for centuries with their stamp.

When a society undergoes such changes as Japan did in the ninth and tenth centuries, the crucial relationship between the poet and his audience is also bound to change. In the early literary period, the relationship between a poet like Hitomaro and those who heard or read his poetry was based on a close social rapport. In his public poetry, Hitomaro took the position of spokesman for all men: his poems on the deaths of princes or the past glories of ruined capitals expressed the feelings of his whole society in the face of events common to all. Later in the period, this function of the poet as articulate spokesman for his fellows increasingly gave way to another, as poetry became more private and individualistic in its concerns. It would not be too great an exaggeration to say that during the fifty years from the end of the eighth century to the middle of the ninth, most Japanese poems were intended for only two people—a man and his mistress. Until something could be done to restore to Japanese poetry either its public character or some important social equivalent, it was fated to remain in limbo, neither poetry nor yet quite prose in its social function.

Fortunately, the "native poetry" (*waka*) was not relegated for all time to the function of the private love letter or greeting card while "Chinese" poetry held sway. No nation—whether Japan or Rome—can long be content with imitating foreign poetic styles, however worthy they are, when such poetry involves the frustration of inadequate expression in an alien language. It is often said that the Japanese began to feel a greater cultural independence and self-confidence during the course of the ninth century, and began increasingly to adapt and alter the things they had been borrowing from China. The vogue for Chinese poetry continued in this period almost unabated, but at the same time the difficulties of composing satisfactory verse in this stubbornly alien medium must have been enormous. Chinese-Japanese dictionaries did not exist, and even if they had, no poet called upon to produce an extemporaneous Chinese verse at a social gathering would have dared to pull a copy out of his sleeve and consult it. Aristocratic societies in general place a high premium upon the immediate, appropriate response to the stimulus of the moment, and these unfortunate courtiers with their sketchy knowledge of Chinese were put under a heavy strain. Verses produced under such adverse conditions were often but indifferent affairs—the patchwork of well-worn tags and clichés that make up the poems in Chinese preserved in such collections as the *Ryōunshū*, the *Bunka Shūreishū,* and the *Keikokushū* of the early ninth century.

The frustration of courtiers who wished to take advantage of Chinese styles but were unable really to write Chinese poetry found relief in the courtiers' adaptations to Japanese poetry of the techniques they had recently learned. As it became apparent that the Chinese techniques could be successfully adapted, and that the waka could be made to express the elegant tastes and subjective experience of the age, the re-emergence of the waka as a serious art form was practically assured. The possibilities for this change in attitude toward Japanese poetry already existed in the early literary period in Yaka-mochi's mellifluous verses, but Yakamochi and his contemporaries were experimenting in many different directions—not attempting to confine the waka to an elegant, subjective pattern, largely "Chinese" in origin. With the appearance of the Six Poetic Geniuses in the latter part of the ninth century, however, the waka began to re-emerge as the proper expression of the new Court society.

To the Western reader, one of the most interesting, most paradoxical features of the age is that its new poetry, so highly social and aristocratic in nature, is even more private and personal than that of the late eighth century. Although poetry was once again being composed and appreciated in the atmosphere of public gatherings and on social occasions, many poems appear to be addressed either to a private person or to no particular audience at all. Often the poet is, as it were, addressing himself or the empty air in his expression of a highly colored and subjective version of the natural scene or an emotional state. What makes these poems acceptable to the real audience before whom the poet seems to be thinking out loud is precisely this quality of subjective personalism in poetry whose techniques are adaptations of those the age admired in the style of the late Six Dynasties.

The highly ornate style characteristic of the late Six Dynasties period in China was called "oblique" (*i-p'ang*) by unsympathetic critics of the T'ang dynasty (618–907). The critics applied the epithet, which means literally "leaning to one side" or "going off on a tangent," to the congeries of techniques by which, in their view, the late Six Dynasties and early T'ang poets erected a barrier of rhetoric between the perceiving sensibility and the poetic materials. Elaborate metaphors, surprising conceits, subjective and sometimes apparently irrational analysis, elegant poses, and above all, a pervasive use of reasoning were distinctive elements of the style that aroused the ire of such T'ang critics as Wang Ch'ang-ling (fl. 726), but inspired the enthusiastic admiration of the Japanese Court. The following couplet by Hsieh Ling-yün (385–433) illustrates a technique that the late Six Dynasties poets frequently employed.

Niao ming chih yeh hsi   By the twittering of the birds I know that
Mu lo shih feng fa.   they are roosting for the night;
                                             By the falling of the leaves I perceive that
                                             the wind has risen.

The fact that these lines consist almost entirely of natural images makes the effect of the oblique treatment all the more noticeable. The natural scene is presented in terms of certain evidence—the twittering of the birds and the falling of the leaves—and the inferences to which the evidence leads: that the birds are roosting for the night and the wind has risen. The T'ang critics would have argued that these lines lead the reader off on a tangent, that they focus on the poet's mental processes rather than on the natural scene, and further, that such treatment has no purpose other than to call attention to itself. To the late Six Dynasties poets, however, this technique was fashionably sophisticated. The elegant subjectivity of these poets is often expressed in their treatment of such themes as the difference between appearance and reality, seen, for example, in the lines from Yü Hsin's (?513–?581) poem "Gazing at the Moon from a Boat."

Shan ming i yu hsieh
An po pu kuan sha.

So bright are the mountains one might
think there was snow,
But the whiteness of the shore is not due
to the sand.

It is not much of a mental leap from these lines to the Japanese poem by
Sakanoe Korenori (fl. ca. 910) in the *Kokinshū* (VI: 332).

Asaborake
Ariake no tsuki to
Miru made ni
Yoshino no sato ni
Fureru shirayuki.

In the early dawn
It looks like the brightness of the moon
Remaining in the sky—
The blanket of snow that through the
night
Has covered the village of Yoshino.

The impact of late Six Dynasties poetry was somewhat less direct than the
similarities between Korenori's poem and Yü Hsin's lines suggest. The Japanese poets first tried out in their own Chinese verse the techniques they
learned from the late Six Dynasties poems; the techniques were only gradually adapted to the native poetry. During the ninth century such Japanese
poets as Ono no Takamura (802–52), Fujiwara Sekio (d. 851), and Sugawara
Michizane (845–903) made their literary reputations with their imitations of
late Six Dynasties poetry rather than with their waka. At the same time, in
the Japanese poetry composed by these and other poets of their time, we can
see the native tradition being reshaped as a result of the borrowing, adaptation, and elaboration of the fashionable techniques of the oblique style. These
techniques, at once subjectively personal and considered socially elegant, gave
to the new poetry the necessary aristocratic, witty, and expressive qualities
sought by the age. While remaining lyrical and becoming even more personal, it was once more qualified to figure in a public context.

The social and elegant, yet highly personal and subjective, direction of the
new poetry seems to have been taken without the consciousness of an explicit
poetic by the Six Poetic Geniuses, as they and their contemporaries who composed alternatively in Chinese and Japanese naturally began to apply these
techniques to the native tradition. By the time of Tsurayuki and the other
compilers of the *Kokinshū*, however, a certain consolidation of ideas concerning poetic ideals and practice had taken place, and a new style of formal poetry
—what we shall call the Fujiwara style—had come into being. Very little in
the way of critical works was written, or at least survives, from this age, but
from the Preface to the *Kokinshū* and from such works as Mibu no Tadamine's (fl. ca. 910) *Ten Styles of Japanese Poetry (Wakatei Jusshu)*, we are
able to find parts of a picture of the contemporary poetic that can be further
pieced out by the evidence of poetic practice and the critical spirit reflected in

the arrangement of poems in the imperial anthologies compiled in this period.

The central value in Tsurayuki's poetic ideal, an ideal that was taken up and elaborated by his contemporaries and successors, was a strong sense of decorous elegance which involved an emphasis on style, a proper poetic diction, an accepted range of forms and themes, and virtuosity. A good poem was one that responded to given situations with purity of diction and in ways sanctioned by tradition, but one that also possessed a certain originality of treatment. There was a tendency to view materials, subjects, and decorum as aspects of diction, and attitude, technique, and theme as aspects of tone. Such a distinction, reflected in the Preface to the *Kokinshū* by the terms *kotoba,* "diction," and *kokoro,* "spirit," was to remain throughout the tradition as the central concept of the Japanese poetic; and although apprehended differently in successive ages, it may be said that the constant ideal was the achievement of balance between these two elements. Tsurayuki's famous comment on the style of Ariwara Narihira—that it has "too much spirit and too few words, like a drooping flower whose color is gone but whose fragrance remains"—is a criticism of Narihira's over-personalism, which leans too heavily on the side of the lyrical response and leaves too much unsaid. (See our analysis of Narihira's famous poem, *Tsuki ya aranu,* below, p. 193). Conversely, such a poet as the Bishop Henjō (816–90) seemed to Tsurayuki to run to the other extreme: "He has a grasp of poetic style, but his poems lack truth, as if one were to lose one's heart in vain to a woman painted in a picture."

In his comments on the style of Henjō, Narihira, and the other four Poetic Geniuses, Tsurayuki also uses the word *sama,* a term by which he appears to mean specifically the fashionable new techniques adapted from late Six Dynasties poetry. But this criterion was not applied universally to all poems of any kind and on any theme. The nature—that is, the decorum—of the particular occasion for which the poem was composed often countenanced the use of less elegance and less elaborate techniques. Here we find it necessary to recur to our distinction between formal poetry composed at public gatherings and intended for many eyes, and informal poetry composed in private and intended for a friend or lover. The two kinds often employ similar techniques, but it seems possible to say that while an informal poem might occasionally be as elaborate and full of striking metaphors and rhetorical techniques as a formal one, it might also be relatively "plain" and "simple" and still be considered decorous. It might have the complexity of allegory, but such a mode was usually fairly simple in technique, and an informal poem was often a simple declaration of the speaker's feelings.

Since they were often employed as sophisticated discourse, such informal poems frequently relied for effect upon what might be called "props" sent with the poems. Often unbearably trivial and evoked by a forgotten occasion, such poems disarm a purely literary criticism. They were usually delivered by a messenger and sent with a sprig of pine, a gift of clothes, or a letter; they were written on paper whose color was carefully chosen to harmonize with the season, with the sender's mood, or with the flower or other present to which the poem was attached. The quality of the calligraphy (written in faint strokes, perhaps, if the gentleman wished to signify that he was expiring with love) was examined by the recipient with as much care as the poem itself, and all the elements involved were expected to be in complete harmony. If the poet failed to make his meaning clear in his poem, he needed only to attach it to a sprig of withered cherry blossoms and his mistress could easily surmise the extent of his suffering. Such poems naturally often allude to the gift or to some secret shared by the poet and his audience of one.

Perhaps surprisingly, a number of such poems can stand alone as independent entities, and are meaningful to us as single expression, even when we are unaware that they are in fact allegorical in mode. But all too often the poem is so intimately related to these private allusions or "props" that it simply does not make sense to us without a prose context. For example, we might consider the following poem (*Katsura Series*, IX, 294) from the *Ise no Tayū Shū*, a private collection of poems by Ise no Tayū (?987–?1063), a lady-in-waiting in the service of the Empress Jōtō Mon'in (d. 1074):

Kiku wa aki   Although I thought
Ume wa haru to zo   The chrysanthemum was for autumn
Omoishi o   And the plum for spring,
Onaji ori ni mo   Now I see that they are flowers
Niou hana kana.   Which bloom together in a single season.

Taken at its face value, this poem seems completely irrational. We know perfectly well that the plum flower and the chrysanthemum could not possibly bloom at the same time, and we can only think that the poet must be suffering from some delusion. The prose context that accompanies the poem, however, makes the situation clear, for it explains that the poem was "composed when someone sent me a robe woven with a pattern of mingled plum blossoms and chrysanthemums." With this context to guide us, our attention is drawn to the pun on *ori* in the fourth line, which can mean "woven fabric" as well as "season," and we now realize that the last two lines also mean, "Now I can see that they are flowers / That bloom together in one woven pattern." Without the prose context, the poem would be illogical and baffling.

Informal poetry often uses such word play, sometimes in this trifling manner, and sometimes with rich poetic results. There was no feeling, however, that poems of this sort required the complex texture or the same kind of wit or ingenuity that was required of formal verse. Among the love poems included in the *Kokinshū*, for example, there are some that are quite simple:

they are complete in themselves, they are neither allegorically nor rhetorically complex, and they come close to the mode of simple declaration that had been traditional in informal love poetry from the primitive period. The following poem is representative of such simpler poems (*KKS*, XI: 517).

Koishiki ni	If such a life as mine
Inochi o kauru	Could only be exchanged for love,
Mono naraba	The agony of death
Shini wa yasuku zo	Would be the simplest thing
Aru bekarikeru.	Beside this secret agony I bear.

Like much of the love poetry in the *Kokinshū,* this poem is listed as "anonymous" and on an "unknown topic." But we must not take such statements too literally. No doubt the compilers' sense of social decorum made them hesitate to commit the indiscretion of recording the names of exalted living individuals whose informal love poetry they included, since this poetry presumably grew out of private affairs.

In the generation of Tsurayuki, the bulk of the love poetry was probably still mostly nonfictional in context; that is to say, although "Love" was already one of the formal topics included at poetry competitions, no small number of the poems on this subject in the *Kokinshū* may well have grown out of real affairs, or at least so the compilers believed. A feeling that these poems were not quite up to the mark because of their comparatively simple technique seems to be reflected in the place given to them in the *Kokinshū.* For although the poems in the category "Love" fill five of the twenty volumes of the anthology, they were still apparently considered secondary to the seasonal poems, and the poems on the topics "Congratulations," "Partings," "Travel," and "Names of Things." Informal poems were composed on these topics, too, but of course the topics are less intimately personal than love, and the volumes devoted to them in the *Kokinshū* contain a larger proportion of formal poetry than the books on love.

A consciousness of the distinction between formal and informal poetry is illustrated by the order in which the individual books of the anthology follow each other: the first major grouping, poems on the seasons, occupies six volumes (two on spring, one on summer, two on autumn, one on winter), and is followed by one volume on each of the topics of "Congratulations," "Partings," "Travel," and "Names of Things." The five books on "Love" come next; and they are in turn followed by one volume of "Laments," two of "Miscellaneous" poems (poems on topics other than those already mentioned, or poems that seem to concern both "Autumn" and "Love," for example), one volume of "Miscellaneous Forms" (chōka, sedōka, and *haikaiuta* or "unconventional poems"), and one volume of "Poems from the Bureau of Songs" and "Poems of the East" (poems that were sung to certain traditional melodies, and including some less courtly provincial poetry). It would seem more logical to the modern Western mind to place the large groups of seasonal and love poems together at the beginning of the anthology, and to follow them with the other, smaller categories. But in fact there appears to be a fairly clear break between the first and second groups of ten books of the *Kokinshū,* the first group containing the more formal and the second the more informal poetry, and the distinction seems to have determined the arrangement of the anthology.

The stricter requirements and higher standing of formal poetry led the Japanese critics and theorists from Tsurayuki on to give it their attention. The emphasis placed upon the ideals of elegance and decorum made them conspicuous qualities of the formal poetry of the whole Court tradition. In the tenth century, elegance was often synonymous with certain rhetorical techniques borrowed from Chinese poetry, especially the oblique style, in which, as we have seen, the paramount factor was the play of wit, ingenuity, and intellect upon the poetic materials.

In Japanese, such a style naturally exploits the use of conditionals, negatives, and other grammatical moods and aspects, and of other kinds of rhetorical indirection that enabled the poet to sidle up to his materials, as it were, rather than approach them directly. An example of such indirection is this Chinese couplet by the Emperor Chien Wen of the Liang Dynasty (502–57).

> Yü chih ch'uan tu so   If you wish to know where the boat is
> Tang k'an ho yeh k'ai   going,
> Observe the lotus pads spreading before its
> prow.

Here, instead of telling us that the boat is simply moving across the water— which would be prosaic and inelegant—the poet calls into play our intellectual faculties and invites us to solve a puzzle. We are told to observe the lotus pads as they give way before the prow of the boat and then to exercise our logical sense. It might be objected that all we need do is watch the boat itself, or even the wake that it leaves behind, and we could learn with very little trouble the direction in which it is moving. But this would be unpoetic. Our pleasure derives from the ingenuity with which the poet has presented his materials to us. The application of this technique to the waka may be seen in another poem by Sakanoe Korenori (*KKS,* V: 302).

> Momijiba no   Had one not seen
> Nagarezariseba   The scarlet maple leaves afloat
> Tatsutagawa   On the flowing stream,
> Mizu no aki oba   Who could say of the River of Tatsuta
> Tare ka shiramashi.   That there is autumn in the waves?

The pleasure to be gained from poems with conceits like these is one of surprise; but when, as in Korenori's poem, there is no real conviction of experience or insight into truth, the witty Heian courtiers seem to us to deserve those strictures which Dr. Johnson leveled at the English Metaphysical poets in his life of Cowley. "Their thoughts are often new, but seldom natural; they are not obvious, but neither are they just; and the reader, far from wondering that he missed them, wonders more frequently by what perverseness of industry they were ever found." Nothing more to the point could be said about the second-rate poets of this period; and yet, Dr. Johnson adds,

great labour, directed by great abilities, is never wholly lost: if the [Metaphysical poets] frequently threw away their wit upon false conceits, they likewise sometimes struck out unexpected truth; if their conceits were often far-fetched, they were often worth the carriage. To write on their plan, it was at least necessary to read and think.

Our strongest criticism of Donne and his followers is that they are smart-alecky and perverse. The classical bent of the Japanese poets saved them from such lapses in decorum, but at the same time, at their worst, their wit suffers from a bloodless monotony. We would not side with unsympathetic Japanese critics who say that the poetasters of this age are too given to reasoning, but we would say they are dull. Such a stigma is no doubt the worst a critic can apply, but in an age when every cultivated person was expected to perform as a poet, it is not surprising that when originality faltered, versifying might be a private folly and a social nuisance.

The increasingly social character of poetry from the ninth century on is best represented by the growing number of poetry contests (*utaawase*) that were held under the auspices first of members of the imperial family or the high nobility, and later of lesser nobles. At first the contests were largely ceremonial, and the competitive spirit was not very keen, but they provided an opportunity for the poet to display his skill in a public environment, and gave him perhaps the most ideal conditions for formal poetry. The topics for the poems produced on these occasions were of course prescribed, and often were the same as those upon which informal poetry was composed. However, Tsurayuki and his friends were so spectacularly successful in making formal waka conform to the technical requirements of the oblique style and other criteria for formal poetry that already in their generation the majority of poems composed on private subjects for such a public occasion as an uta-awase were in this formal style. We may take as typical the following poem by Ōshikōchi Mitsune (fl. ca. 900) from the fourth round on the topic "Love" at the poetry contest held at the Teiji Palace in the year 913. The poem is typically oblique in its play upon reality and dream, in its cause-and-effect reasoning, and in a preference for the night world over the day motivated by a passion so strong that it will settle for fulfillment in dreams over frustration in reality. (The poems composed for this contest are found in *K. Taikei*, XI, 829–46.)

Utsutsu ni mo	If in reality,
Yume ni mo hito ni	If even in my dreams, you and I
Yoru shi aeba	Could have a night alone,
Kureyuku bakari	Nothing would bring more joy
Ureshiki wa nashi.	Than the coming of the dark.

It would be much too great an over-simplification, however, to say that the use of the oblique technique was the only way to make poetry formally acceptable. Sufficient elevation, skill, and complexity, or an allusion to native or Chinese myths, legends, stories, or customs that possessed a satisfactory elegance could give a poem the necessary indirection. Similarly, the use of such traditionally Japanese rhetorical techniques as the makurakotoba and the jo, which by now had become valued traditional techniques requiring study for their mastery, could make the poem into the desired vehicle for the display of the poet's skill and erudition.

The use of such techniques in the formal poetry of the period may be illustrated by two examples. The first, by Minamoto Muneyuki (d. 939), is included in the *Kokinshū* (I: 24) with a headnote designating its formal occasion—"Composed at the Poetry Contest Held in the Palace of the Empress in the Kampyō Era [889–97]."

Tokiwa naru	Spring has come,
Matsu no midori mo	And even the pines, constant in their
Haru kureba	green
Ima hitoshio no	Through eternity,
Iro masarikeri.	Now turn, still more and more,
	To advancing depths of color.

On first reading, there is nothing very remarkable about this poem. We recognize a certain play of wit in the implied comparison between the evergreen pines and the other trees that are now putting forth new leaves, but this hardly seems sufficient to qualify the poem as one of special note. The point, however, is that the poet alludes to the treatment of the pine tree in Chinese poetry, where it is always said to remain the same shade of green through every season. We might paraphrase the poem, then, as follows: "The Chinese poems we read tell us that the green of the pines remains unchanged in any season, but I can see that this spring the pines have actually become more bright and fresh in color. This is truly a glorious, a Japanese spring."

The second example, by an unidentified poet, was pitted against Mitsune's poem in the fourth round on "Love" at the contest in the Teiji Palace.

Tamamo karu	Although no fisher
Ama to wa nashi ni	Reaping the gem-like seaweed,
Kimi kouru	I yearn for you
Wa ga koromode no	So deeply that the salt spray
Kawaku toki naki.	Never dries upon my sleeves.

The insistently logical syntax of this poem, with its use of the concessive ("although") is of course elegant and "Chinese" in itself, but probably the principal reason it won the victory over Mitsune's is that it employs the old pillow-word *tamamo ƙaru,* "Reaping the gem-like seaweed." One is strongly tempted to believe that this makurakotoba, which appears in the *Man'yōshū* and was therefore very old by the ninth century, represents a kind of primitivism—for to the Westerner the image of cutting the seaweed is a homely one, however beautiful the seaweed. To the Heian courtiers, however, the imagistic effect of this pillow-word was not nearly so vivid as it is to us, and at the same time it conveyed no vivid sense of rusticity. By using the pillow-word, the poet served notice to his audience that he knew his tradition, that he had mastered a technique both old and, by now, elevated in itself. The tone conveyed by *tamamo ƙaru* was really one of a distant beauty like Keats's "faery lands forlorn." Certain pillow-words used by the poets of remoter times were uncompromisingly homely in effect, but such a one as *mina no wata,* "the innards of the mud-snail," which was formerly used as a metaphor for glossy blackness, was avoided by the Heian courtiers, who considered such images unbearably coarse and distasteful. To the poet and his audience at the *utaawase* and other public gatherings in the Heian period, the pillow-word and the preface were now techniques for rhetorical elevation, but neither age nor tradition would sanction the inelegant image.

When Mibu no Tadamine (fl. ca. 910) rather arbitrarily designated his "Ten Styles" of Japanese poetry, it was almost unavoidable that his first should be the "archaic style." One of his illustrations is a poem by Tsurayuki that contains the pillow-word *shirotae no,* "of whitened hemp," and doubtless it was this elegant expression, with its connotations of purity and brightness, which gave the poem its aura of antiquity. Tadamine admits that this archaic style is less a style in itself than a synthesis of elements or techniques that are a part of other styles. Moreover, the archaic is not to be regarded as a survival of older modes in the conservative poetry of this period, or as an expression of a primitivistic impulse to return to the "simpler" and less elegant styles of the early literary age. It is rather a neoclassical style that was elegant precisely because of its quality of the special and esoteric—one of several alternative ways of satisfying the requirements for a formal, specifically aristocratic poetry.

The standard of elegance and refinement that was so important to the poets of the early classical period was applied to poetic diction as well as to imagery and technique. In this realm, too, the Heian courtiers appear to have drawn inspiration from the practice of late Six Dynasties poetry. The ingenuity and elegant conceits of which the late Six Dynasties poets were so fond were couched in language that was above all refined and "beautiful." Low, inelegant words were taboo to the Japanese poet, and at the same time poetic language had to have the prestige of long tradition and precedent. Ingenuity was sought and appreciated in the poet's handling (*kokoro*) of his materials, but the materials themselves (*kotoba*) had to be traditional. Moreover, the ingenuity exhibited in the handling was required to be subtle and unobtrusive —a kind of un-metaphysical ingenuity that could be adequately appreciated only by comparison with innumerable other poems that treated the same materials in similar but significantly different ways. In late Six Dynasties poetry, such an emphasis resulted in the standardization of the poetic vocabulary, the rejection of unconventional words that were thought to be inelegant and unpoetic, and a sense of stylistic decorum that kept the poet's technical ingenuity within traditional bounds. Whatever other qualities of depth or meaning were necessary for great poetry, there was little room for a poet who lacked virtuosity, style, and a knowledge of his tradition. A poet was free to pursue his individual way to greatness only after he had proved he knew the rules of the game.

Given the character of Heian society, it is not surprising that its courtiers should find such an attitude toward the nature and act of poetry congenial. For although the Japanese theory of poetry, not to mention its practice, often followed a course at variance with the Chinese, what might be called the basic and conservative attitude toward formal poetry throughout the life of the tradition was shaped by the Chinese example of this period. We need not take too seriously the "Six Genres" (*Rikugi*) of Japanese poetry mentioned by Tsurayuki in the Preface to the *Kokinshū,* nor his statement that "this is doubtless also the case with the poetry of China." Tsurayuki's six categories were an obvious attempt to produce equivalents for the six genres distinguished in China since the time of the *Classic of Songs* (*Shih Ching*), and they were not only meaningless in terms of Japanese poetic practice but also, like the pronouncements of our Renaissance critics, conveniently ignored by the poets. With certain reservations the same may be said of some of Tadamine's "ten styles," for although some of the distinctions he makes are significant from the point of view of lyric tone, the quality of the imagery, and the poet's attitude toward his subject, Tadamine's outlook and the sacred number ten come to him either from Chinese critical works or from Japanese imitations; they do not correspond to the realities of poetic practice. On the other hand, practice often follows ideals, if not theory, and the refinement of the Japanese poetic vocabulary stemmed from a deep impulse to produce a native tradition that could stand on a level of equality with that of China. Unlike the numerical categories, which remained largely theoretical, the refinement of poetic diction was carried out with great thoroughness.

Some consciousness of decorum in poetic diction is already evident in the *Man'yōshū,* in which, it will be recalled, humorous poems and poems using words of Sanskrit or Chinese origin tend to be grouped together in certain isolated volumes. The sense of decorum in diction was, however, much more marked in Tsurayuki and his generation, and they were largely responsible for the creation of a poetic vocabulary that remained relatively fixed for a thousand years. The standard here as elsewhere was elegance and refinement: only words and images felt to be courtly, traditional, and beautiful were acceptable; unconventional words and inelegant images were rejected as unpoetic, and poems that used them, whether seriously or for comic effect, either were not considered to be poetry at all, or else were labeled *haikaiuta,* "unconventional poems."

The second and third imperial anthologies, the *Gosenshū* and the *Shūishū,* contain a few words and expressions that are not found in the *Kokinshū,* but these are analogous to older expressions in imagery or tone, and the slight increment that they made to the poetic vocabulary did not represent the reversal of a trend or an effort to attain greater freedom of diction. In vocabulary as in technique, the standards were less rigid for informal than for formal poetry, but even here the diction tended to become subject to the formal standard, and we may still say that the vocabulary of the *Kokinshū* provided the basic materials for poetry throughout the early classical period. A gauge of the seriousness with which violations of this norm were regarded can be found in the scorn heaped on the occasional brash soul who ventured to stray from the true path. Such a person was Sone no Yoshitada (fl. ca. 985), whose eccentric personality and highly unconventional poetic style (in some experimental poems) led to his being virtually ostracized by the Fujiwara aristocrats of his day. The following poem by Yoshitada was particularly notorious (*Sotanshū* in *K. Taikei,* XIII, 41).

Nake ya nake	Cry on, cry on,
Yomogi ga soma no	You crickets underneath the mugwort
Kirigirisu	Corded into piles—
Kureyuku aki wa	The darkening vestiges of autumn
Ge ni zo kanashiki.	Are truly cause for sadness!

We may wonder what there is to cause offense in this innocent-looking poem, but we are told by Fujiwara Kiyosuke (1104–77) in his *Fukuro Sōshi* that when Fujiwara Nagatō (fl. ca. 980) read it, he exploded: "The fellow is mad! Whoever heard of such a thing as 'mugwort corded into piles'?" (*NKGT*, II, 93). There seem in fact to have been two reasons for Nagatō's violent reaction: first, the word *yomogi* ("mugwort") is the name of a common weed, which grows in desolate fields or ruined gardens, and therefore is an "ugly" image; second, the word *soma* actually means lumber—wood cut in the mountains and floated down to the towns and villages on rafts. What Yoshitada was apparently trying to do was to create the image of weeds cut and heaped up like wood for burning, and we would say that he was successful. To Nagatō and the great majority of poets of the late tenth century, however, the image was both ugly and unconventional, and Yoshitada was insane. A hundred years or so later, the same poet was accorded the honor of being included in the fourth imperial anthology, the *Goshūishū* (completed in 1086), and Yoshitada gradually came to be respected by certain later innovating poets, who saw a virtue in fresh diction and unconventional imagery. Such poets were in the minority, however, and experiments of this nature had no radical effect upon the tradition.

It is one of the ironic complexities of Japanese literary history that a Chinese example inspired not only the purism of conventional poets but also the seeming iconoclasm of poets like Yoshitada. Yoshitada's innovation was motivated by a neoclassical standard—the work of the great T'ang poet, Po Chü-i (772–846)—rather than by a primitivistic urge. Known to the Japanese as Haku Rakuten, Po Chü-i already enjoyed an enormous reputation in Japan even during his lifetime. In speaking of the Western tradition, C. S. Lewis has characterized the development of medieval and Renaissance courtly love as "Ovid misunderstood." It might be said similarly that no small part of the history of Japanese Court poetry can be summarized as "Po Chü-i half-understood." The differing, sometimes diametrically opposed, responses of Japanese poets to Po Chü-i can be partially explained by the fact that he was a poet of many styles and modes. Some of his poetry, including the famous "Song of Everlasting Grief" ("Ch'ang Hen Ko"; Japanese, "Chōgonka")—a long narrative poem describing the tragic love of the Emperor Hsüan Tsung (685–762) for his concubine Yang Kuei-fei, and extraordinarily popular in both China and Japan—is written in purely classical language and employs the beautiful, elegant imagery of the late Six Dynasties tradition. On the other hand, he often violated both tradition and prevailing contemporary practice by writing poems in which he used colloquial and otherwise unconventional diction.

The Japanese who visited China during this great poet's lifetime learned two things—that he was tremendously popular (even the taverns had his poetry on their walls) and that the Chinese thought his new poetry simpler in style than that of earlier poets. Simpler he was for the Chinese, since much of his most original poetry was written in a language close to the vernacular; but by virtue of this fact, he was all the more difficult for the Japanese, who had learned their Chinese from the classical, written style of older books. Since the Chinese Court was not in the habit of welcoming Japanese visitors into its midst, the Japanese had little inkling of the storm of aristocratic and academic criticism that Po Chü-i's poetry evoked owing to the very qualities that made it "easy" and popular. Instead, they returned home to begin generations of fruitful if confused imitation, selection, and finally adaptation to the native tradition.

At first, as one would expect, the Japanese imitated Po Chü-i in the poems they wrote in Chinese. In time, they began to adapt what they esteemed—and understood—to techniques of the tanka. The process of adaptation involved, in the first place, a rejection of what seemed alien—allusions to political events and poetic narrative—and a retention of lyrical qualities. Caught between the fame and the unintelligibility of the colloquial poems, the Japanese readily compromised, and extracted those passages they understood, including them in the popular poetic handbooks of the day. An aspiring Japanese poet had little difficulty in laying hands on such a widely admired collection as the *Wakan Rōeishū* of Fujiwara Kintō (966–1041), which is an anthology of some 215 Japanese poems and almost 600 short passages of Chinese verse and prose. Both this selection and its sequel, the *Shinsen Rōeishū* of Fujiwara Mototoshi (1056–1142), contained numerous passages from the poetry of Po Chü-i, and together they enjoyed a popularity attested to by the frequency with which their selections were echoed in Japanese poems. Gradually, certain techniques of imagery and ideals of tone and method began to emerge.

The paradoxes and ironies of the developing process can best be illustrated by the work of three men, Fujiwara Kintō, Sone no Yoshitada, and Minamoto Tsunenobu (1016–97), who may be characterized respectively as conservative, eccentric, and transitional poets. Kintō is the author of a very brief but influential guide called *The Essence of Poetry Newly Selected (Shinsen Zuinō)*. In it and in the example of his own poetry, he tried to adapt Po Chü-i to the formal poetic style without destroying the stylistic techniques adapted from late Six Dynasties poetry. Kintō perhaps rightly saw an elevated simplicity in the diction of Po's classical poetry. At the same time he had heard that his poetry was easy to understand. Faced with the dilemma presented by the prestige of the oblique style on the one hand and the simplicity of Po Chü-i's poetic method on the other, Kintō sought to harmonize the two. He came to the conclusion that Japanese poetry should continue to employ the techniques of late Six Dynasties poetry, but use them gently, as it were, with a diction smooth, pleasant, safe, and in a word, insipid. To enforce his ideal of a bland poetry, he turned to that criticism by late Six Dynasties writers that proscribed numerous "poetic ills" (*yamai*). If one wished to learn how to compose a poem that would offend nobody, one needed only to follow Kintō. But if one chose to write great poetry, one had need of a more venturesome guide.

Not all of the blame for this ideal of unerring mediocrity can be laid at the feet of Kintō, who was surely as much a child of his age as the greater poets who were his contemporaries. Moreover, it is a happy historical truth that although critics may legislate, poets write indifferent to the rule of law. Kintō served a constructive purpose in drawing attention to the importance of diction, and contributed to the development of a practical criticism that was gradually elaborated in this and the next period. His principal concerns, however, were taboos against the repetition within a poem of the same word or of words with very similar meanings, the repetition of a sound at the end of two or more lines, and other redundancies. Such rules were not invented by Kintō; they had been applied frequently in the poetry contests from the Teiji Palace contest of 913 on, and perhaps before, since this contest is the first which survives with the recorded criticisms of judge or judges. For example, the second round of the Teiji Palace contest was judged a draw, because one poet (Mitsune) had used the same auxiliary verb twice, and the other (Fujiwara Okikaze) had used the words *yama* ("mountain") and *mine* ("peak"), which were thought to be quasi-synonyms and therefore disqualifying.

The application of such rules to poetic composition is probably a good thing so long as they are intended to ensure variety and prevent monotony, but to Kintō they appear too often to have been quite otherwise—safeguards to guarantee, if not monotony, then so smooth and mellifluous a texture that the poem threatens to become almost all sound and very little sense. It is true that Kintō allowed exceptions in certain cases, such as the following anonymous poem preserved by the Bureau of Poetry (*KKS*, XX: 1077):

Mi*yama* ni wa	Within the mountains,
Arare furu rashi	The hail is doubtless falling now,
To*yama* naru	For in the foothills
Masaki no kazura	The creeping laurel vines are tinged
Irozukinikeri.	With their scarlet autumn hue.

Ordinarily the repetition of the word *yama* ("mountains") would disqualify this poem according to the theory of the "poetic ills," and the reason that Kintō lets it pass is because of what he calls its "greatness" (*Shinsen Zuinō* in *NKGT*, I, 115). The poem, which was apparently chanted at Shinto ceremonies and is found in the section of the *Kokinshū* devoted to such traditional songs, was probably composed toward the end of the early literary period. It does indeed create an effect of harmony and a pleasing rhythm despite the repetition, but perhaps a major reason for Kintō's fondness for it is its easy reasoning: "*Because* the laurel leaves have turned red here in the foothills, winter must be already there, deep in the mountains." There is nothing in the poem to shock the reader or to stir his being. It is pleasant, smooth, and very nearly commonplace. Kintō seems to flee before the robust rhythms and flaming passion of such poets as Ariwara Narihira and Ono no Komachi, who often made syntax, logic, and the very language cringe. In his eyes, one of the truly great poems is the following by Mibu no Tadamine, "Composed at a Poetry Contest at the House of Taira Sadabumi" (*SIS*, I: 1).

Haru tatsu to	Is it just because
Iu bakari ni ya	They say this is the day which marks
Mi-Yoshino no	The coming of the spring
Yama mo kasumite	That the mountains of fair Yoshino
Kesa wa miyu ran.	Are veiled this morning in a haze?

It is true that a hypersensitivity developed to such lengths as this almost inevitably leads either to over-conventionality or to inarticulateness, just as in the case of the ungifted, red-nosed Princess Suyetsumu in the *Tale of Genji* (Arthur Waley's translation, pp. 464–65). On the other hand, Kintō's emphasis upon limited virtuosity gave the better poets of the early classical period an almost unequaled control over their materials, a technical assurance with which they endowed their successors. Kintō, too, played his part in developing a consciousness of the decorum of alternative poetic styles. It was left to later poets to realize fully the potentialities that the descriptive mode held for Japanese poetry, but Kintō helped bring a growing recognition of the suitability for formal poetry of styles that derived ultimately from mid-T'ang rather than late Six Dynasties poetry, an awareness that was to have important later consequences.

The eccentric Yoshitada had a rather different view of what the poetry of Po Chü-i represented. His poetry and the general response to it make clear that he aimed at emulating what he regarded as the homely, "low" diction of Po Chü-i, partly we may suppose, to bring a new freshness to poetry, but in large measure simply because that was the way he assumed Po had written. Diction, especially in Japanese poetry, tends to involve imagery and, as in all languages, tone. Given the norms of diction and tone in his age, it is no wonder that Yoshitada was greeted with laughter and scorn when he wrote of hair soaked with sweat. Serious Japanese poetry was no more ready for that sort of image than English poetry was at the time of *Paradise Lost*. Usually, however, Yoshitada aimed at a somewhat Wordsworthian glorification of the commonplace, as we can see from his lovely poem about a raft of logs, a subject far removed from the splendor of the Heian Court (*SKS*, II: 74).

Somagawa no	The floating pillow
Ikada no toko no	Of a bed laid on a raft of logs

Ukimakura	Swaying down the river
Natsu wa suzushiki	Makes in summer a cool resting place
Fushido narikeri.	Through a night of drifting sleep.

A similarly unusual tone is conveyed by a poem on "The End of the Fourth Month" (*Sotanshū* in *K. Taikei*, XIII, 32).

Hi kurureba	The sun sets,
Shitaba koguraki	And the luminous underleaves
Ko no moto no	Low upon the trees
Mono osoroshiki	Are stifled in the shadowing
Natsu no yūgure.	Of the frightening summer dark.

Both poems emphasize description, and description of new subjects, in language differing from the canonical *Kokinshū*. The verbs alone are revealing. The only verb in the first poem is *narikeri,* the perfective (with durative and indicative) inflection of what we should call "to be." The second poem also has only one verb, and that not even finite—*kurureba* ("because" or "when" "the sun has set")—although the copula is again strongly implied at the end of the poem. This reliance upon few verbs, and those few largely copulas, marks an important departure from the elaborate inflections of verbs in the formal style, inflections used to convey degrees of questioning or doubt, or the formation of states of being or attitude. Along with the simpler diction and attention to new details, the verbs themselves or their absence do indeed create a novel effect.

For all of their freshness, however, the poems often have no larger significance than the emotions evoked by Yoshitada's observations. And the ones we have selected are, after all, among his best poems, and in their new qualities are rather the exception than the rule among his poems. He wrote hundreds of poems that tirelessly rehearse the techniques of the formal style. As a random example, one of the verses "From a Sequence of Three Hundred Sixty Poems" (*SIS,* XIII: 833) employs the pose of a woman who is betrayed and feels sad at neglect—but, alas, even sadder because the autumn wind rustles her door and reminds her that her lover is not there.

Wa ga seko ga	On such a night
Kimasanu yoi no	When my lover fails to come,
Akikaze wa	The autumn wind—
Konu hito yori mo	Even more than he who fails me—
Urameshiki kana.	Brings disappointment in its rustling
	sound.

Descriptive poetry has still not become a main current in the tradition. A poet like Yoshitada experiments, but gets his poems into contemporary anthologies only if they conform to the old standards. And yet the poetic currents began to flow in a new direction toward the middle of the early classical period, for descriptive poetry such as the poetry of the so-called Yamada priest (*Katsura Series*, II, 83–88) or the priest Nōin (998–1050) survives in sufficient quantity and quality in private collections or later anthologies to show us that the changes to the new age came step by step. Nōin's poem "Composed When I Went to a Mountain Village" (*SKKS*, II: 116), for example, has in spite of its plain diction a fineness and a purity of tone that give promise of greater things to come.

Yamazato no	As now I come
Haru no yūgure	And see the spring day grow to dusk
Kite mireba	In the mountain hamlet,
Iriai no kane ni	The cherry blossoms fall to earth
Hana zo chirikeru.	At the sounding of a temple's vesper bell.

In order for the descriptive poetry—inferred from Po Chü-i and developed along native lines—to become a vital part of the tradition, a more powerful advocacy was necessary than the bland conservatism of a Kintō, the eccentricities of a Yoshitada, or the uninfluential efforts of poets of low rank. At the end of the early classical period, the Great Counselor Minamoto Tsunenobu brought the power of prestige and the influence of his wealth to the new tendency in the face of strong conservative opposition. How strongly antipathetic the conservative partisans of the Fujiwara style were can be gauged by the fact that in spite of Tsunenobu's high rank and great poetic powers, only six of his poems were included in the collection of early- and mid-eleventh-century poetry, the *Goshūishū* (1086). More of his poems appeared in the *Kin'yōshū* (ca. 1125), but it remained for the next age to select his most descriptive poems for the *Shinkokinshū* (ca. 1210). Tsunenobu was not, indeed, a poet who found the Fujiwara style wholly uncongenial, and his "new" poems lack many of the qualities that were to characterize the best poetry of the next period. Nonetheless, he had considerable poetic powers and helped to give descriptive poetry a status as a formal style that could not be denied. Such poems as the one "Composed at a Poetry Contest at the Imperial Palace in 1049" (*SKKS*, IV: 411) are important both for their intrinsic value and for the evidence they give of the way in which a new element had entered into the formalities of imperial contests.

Tsukikage no	How bright the moon
Sumiwataru kana	That sheds its radiance over all—
Ama no hara	The plains of heaven
Kumo fukiharau	Have been scoured of their dark clouds
Yowa no arashi ni.	By the power of the midnight storm.

Both the imagery and the strength of the "k," "a," and "r" sounds create a grandeur that could be denied only by the bearish old-guard advocates of the Fujiwara style. With poems like this to choose from, the next age could address itself to the task of creating a new esthetic for a changing view of the nature of reality and of poetry. But no matter what direction poetry subsequently followed, the early classical period gave it a basic aristocratic character, a critical awareness, a strong consciousness of alternative styles, and what we hope in the remainder of this chapter to show—a large body of some of the finest poems in the language.

POETIC PRACTICE

The critical sense that emerged in the ninth century is all the more remarkable when one considers that after a false step or two it increasingly reflected and influenced poetic practice. One has only to think of the three centuries between Chaucer and Dryden, when literary criticism and poetic practice seemed to take little account of each other, to realize that the rapid emergence of criticism in the early classical age is remarkable in its parallel with the sudden flowering of the poetic tradition in the preceding period. To say that criticism paralleled practice and developed quickly is not to claim, however, that it was far ranging, or that the ideals of the age were always those which seem most worthy to the modern mind, or that theory covered every practical contingency. Nonetheless, criticism, ideal, and poetic practice meet harmoniously. The reasons for this are not hard to find. The poetic audience consisted of poets; the critics were themselves poets; audience, poet, and critic alike belonged to a closely knit group; and tradition, precedent, and established style became increasingly important. In such a social and literary atmosphere, poetic ideals might readily be translated into poetic practice.

THE SUBJECTIVE NATURE OF THE NEW POETRY

The practice of poetry in this period is in many ways so different from the practice in the last that it seems useful to take a general look at the basic character of the new poetry and the modes in which it was composed. Many factors—the private quality of poetry, the particular kind of Chinese verse adapted, and the lyrical nature of the tanka—combined to change the character of poetic literature. Essentially, the balance between the subject (the poet) and his object (nature, love, or whatever), so characteristic of the generation of Hitomaro, has disappeared, and in its place we find that the subject has become the poetic center. The external world gains a reality only by virtue of its effect upon the human sensibility or by its being ordered by the mind and heart. Truth is no longer so much a matter of what actually exists about the poet, as what his thought and emotion conceive the external world to be. This emphasis permeates the manners and arts of the age, for if there is any one term to designate what the courtiers sought as an ideal, it is *aware,* "sensibility." A man or woman who could not be sensitive and, what is equally important to the concept, could not respond sensitively in decorous ways, could play no role in the activities of life in the capital. Underlying the conception of sensibility were the latent artistic sense and love of beauty that have continued to mark the Japanese; and with such characteristic motives, there was a delight in the workings of one's own mind that sets this period apart from subsequent ages of Japanese literature. In some respects it is as though the writers of the age respond to the Buddhist idea of a world of impermanence and illusion, but do not wholly accept the religious implications. However bewildering or illusory the external world might be, the poets strive to shape it into meaningful and beautiful patterns by the exercise of the human sensibility. The poetry of the early classical period is, then, primarily an art that expresses subjective states—at least those subjective apprehensions of experience which interested the age.

There are perhaps half a dozen symptoms of this subjective genius: the importance of tone; psychological subtlety (whether searchingly new or conventional); elegance; philosophical speculation of a sort which might be called emotional reasoning; exploration of depths of consciousness; and increased interest in love as poetic subject matter. Tone is always of crucial importance to subjective poetry, since the bounds of taste must be set. The poet had to keep his subjectivity within bounds, lest, at worst, he met ostracism or, at best, had his poem put into the category of "unconventional poems." Fortunately, though the age was extremely conventional it was not prudish; though often superficial, not embarrassingly given to mawkish romantic confessions; and though it employed but one poetic form, that form possessed an extraordinary tonal range. A rather ordinary poem employing a highly conventional conceit will show how the poet has adjusted his tone successfully. Ono no Takamura chose to write "On Snow Falling on the Plum Blossoms" (*KKS*, VI: 335), which in this period means that the poet is about to show an elegant bewilderment—does he see snow or plum blossoms?

Hana no iro wa	Men cannot see
Yuki ni majirite	The color of the blossoms, a color
Miezu to mo	Mingled now with snow,
Ka o dani nioe	But only let them breathe the fragrance,
Hito no shiru beku.	And all must know the plum trees are in flower.

The conceit itself is so conventional that there is little to appreciate in it. As always, the tonal treatment is crucial. What is the attitude of the poet toward the scene? Toward other men? Toward himself? The scene is looked at with appreciation, because both the snow falling on the branches and the plum blossoms are lovely—so lovely as to be indistinguishable. But there is a way of finding out, not a pragmatic way of weighing masses, but a poetic way, by noticing the fragrance. Where before identity had been seen in color—the poet cleverly mingles only the *color* of the flowers with the snow as a whole—the appeal to beauty through another sense solves the problem. By implication, the poem praises the superior beauty of the plum. Not until the last line of the original, however, is there any clue about the relation of the poet to the scene and his audience. The crucial word is *hito*, "person," which refers both to the poet and to other men. He shares with the friend to whom the poem may have been sent and with all men an experience which shows that what is beautifully confused in the external world may be distinguished in such a way as to give a sense of still greater beauty. A poet of the preceding period would have *seen* the snow and the flowers; he would not have connected what might be called the metaphysical reality and unreality of the beauty of two beautiful objects, much less have distinguished between them on the basis of fragrance. But Takamura has praised beauty by discovering a means to perceive truth; and while doing so, he has unobtrusively placed himself in the midst of an esthetically-minded society. What the poem lacks is a perfected beauty of expression and that intensity which characterizes the best poets. Still, to be even a second-rate poet like Takamura was, in this period, to be a very subtle and assured craftsman.

The psychological subtlety of the poets of the age is not theoretically inspired, but rather based upon such common experience as love and death. On the record of her poetry at least, the famous beauty and great poetess Ono no Komachi, for example, seems to have been a woman who either never slept, or never lived freely in a world outside the dream-specters of her imagination. One of her love poems deals with an emotion commonly expressed by the Court ladies of the day—the fear that the love affair in which she is immersed will be revealed, exposing her to merciless gossip. Yet only Komachi could show such a fear in complete dominion over her personality, making the cadences of her verse bend under the strain of her agony (*KKS*, XIII: 656).

Utsutsu ni wa	In waking daylight,
Sa mo koso arame	Then, oh then it can be understood,
Yume ni sae	But when I see myself
Hitome o moru to	Shrinking from those hostile eyes
Miru ga wabishisa.	Even in my dreams: this is misery itself.

The poem is founded upon an opposition of ideas in lines one and three: *utsutsu, yume* ("waking daylight," "dreams"). Neither day nor night, sleeping nor waking, gives any respite to her anxiety. The two terms suggest other oppositions as well—reality and dream, the day-to-day actuality and the specter-haunted world of imagination. The nightmare world of her subconsciousness (as we would put it today) is only a reflection of her conscious, rational fears; but by a fine psychological truth, Komachi finds the obsessive, distorted reflection more terrifying than the mirrored reality. The fear is due to her awareness that she is directing at herself the same sort of scrutiny which she expects of the world and the day, but not of the night and herself. The complex awareness implied by self-consciousness is well conveyed by the last two lines (our last three). The world is given the "hostile eyes" (*hitome*), but it is she who sees (*miru*) herself. In contemporary terminology, her consciousness suffers in fear of the real world, her subconsciousness from fear in dreams. But the two are parts of the larger awareness which comprehends both and which, as conveyed in the last two lines, makes her misery complete.

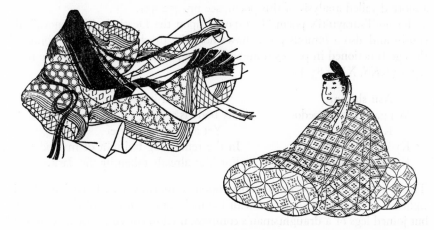

Drawings of Ono no Komachi (SEATED, BACK VIEW) *and Ariwara Narihira* (RIGHT) *by Reizei Tamechika*

Ariwara Narihira, like Komachi equally famous as a lover and a poet, could convey the subtle psychological shades of love with equal conviction. The headnote of one of his poems in the *Kokinshū* (XIII: 616) suggests that it was copied from a poetic diary: "From the first day of the third moon after I had been in secret contact with a certain lady, the spring rains began to fall softly and steadily, so I sent her this poem." It is an extraordinary love poem in that it conveys a mood in which neither love nor life seems to have much significance. The woman's response to this declaration of anesthetized love is not known, but it can hardly have been enthusiastic.

Oki mo sezu   I am at one with spring:
Ne mo sede yoru o   Neither sleeping, nor yet rising from
            my bed,

Akashite wa
Haru no mono tote
Nagamekurashitsu.

Till night turns into dawn,
And through the day my love for you continues
In listless looking at the ceaseless rains.

The warm, soft, long rains of spring and the woman alike hold him in abstracted inertia, not soft enough to allow him to sleep, nor yet powerful enough to rouse him to go about his business or visit the woman. The rains and the woman—and their muted effect on him—are conveyed by the element *nagame* in the last line. It means "listless looking," "long rains," and "thinking of you"—all three meanings of which are crucial. A single word describes the scene and his reaction to it, and renders the description of the poem as a whole into a metaphor for the woman he loves and his present reaction to her. (For a more detailed analysis of this poem, see pp. 452–53).

Ki no Tsurayuki's poem "Composed upon the Death of Tomonori," his cousin and also a famous poet, shows how the psychological self-probing of the age functioned in poems somewhat more public in nature than love messages (*KKS*, XVI: 838).

Asu shiranu
Wa ga mi to omoedo
Kurenu ma no
Kyō wa hito koso
Kanashikarikere.

Although I know
My body is a thing with no tomorrow,
Yet am I cast in grief
In the remaining twilight of my today
For him already taken by the dark.

This is a "conceited" poem in its play upon "tomorrow . . . today" and "twilight . . . the dark." Compared with Donne's famous image of the separable but joined legs of a draughtsman's compass, used to convince his wife he will return from a trip still faithful to her, Tsurayuki's images reveal greater universality and less wit. Tsurayuki's acknowledgment in the first two lines shows that he has given up hope for the future, the next two lines show that he has little time left for expectations in the present; and the last line of the original is a single exclamation of anguish in the here and now, anticipated rhetorically by the time imagery and verbally by the "k" sounds of the preceding two lines. The emotional and imagistic logic of the poem is complete in the terms of this poetic, and unless we expect an out-and-out Romantic cry, the imagery, however ingenious, gives us the artistic means to participate in the personal, subjective experience of the poet.

Few poetic ages make elegance a satisfactory vehicle of subjective states, probably in part because few ages are as sophisticated as the Heian society that produced a Tsurayuki, and in part because elegance may too easily lapse into artifice. The following poem by Bunya Yasuhide (fl. ca. 870) seems relatively simple, but it possesses a fashionable elegance of technique (*GSS*, XVII: 1246).

Shirakumo no	Do those little pines
Kiyadoru mine no	Growing upon the lofty peak
Komatsubara	Where white clouds dwell
Eda shigekere ya	Branch so thickly in their grove
Hi no hikari minu.	That they obscure the radiance of the sun?

The headnote makes clear what Yasuhide meant: "When I had shut myself up in my house out of pique at my failure to advance in the world." The poem is, then, an elegant allegory sent to the emperor asking if unsympathetic courtiers have come between Yasuhide and the light of imperial favor. The details of the poem are appropriate in every way, and the elegant allegory is wholly adequate, but we are left with some feeling of contrivance. Another poem by Tsurayuki shows, however, that elegance could be a skillful vehicle of subjective states (*SIS,* IV: 224).

Omoikane	As pressed by love,
Imogariyukeba	I go to hunt her in my yearning,
Fuyu no yo no	The wind blows cold
Kawakaze samumi	Through the winter darkness from the
Chidori naku nari.	river,
	Where on the banks the plovers cry.

It is somewhat difficult to explain why this fine poem should be called elegant as well as moving. One indication of the elegance can be found in the fashionable, although untranslatable, effect of *naku nari.* The *nari* is a copula and the *naku* an indicative: "it is that the plovers cry." The effect is to express doubt or hearsay, to speak of something not known at first hand: "the plovers seem to cry" or "I am told that the plovers cry." But this idiom clearly does not function in the poem to convey real doubt, since the point is that the birds accentuate the anguish felt by the speaker. In other words, Tsurayuki has employed a form of understatement that he appears, as much as anybody, to have made popular in poetry. Such understatement stresses the presence of the speaker in the poem and makes it clear that the cries of the plovers, the cold wind from the river, and the dark winter night are all tonal images and metaphors relating to the state of mind and feeling of the speaker of the poem. This subjective indirection in the treatment of the natural scene contrasts with the strong verbal quality of the first two lines (*omoi, kane, gari, yukeba*) and the vividness of *imogari,* "hunting my beloved." The two parts of the poem differ considerably in poetic effect and yet are integrated completely by the subjective cast of the whole.

Philosophical speculation or emotional reasoning is one of the hallmarks of the period. This technique, more than anything else, was what the late Six Dynasties style gave to the poets of the age. At times the techniques employed for such reasoning are tiresomely routine, but they are also at the heart of the best poetry of the period. Since nothing is more typical of the age at its best and its worst, the practice should be examined at length. Sometimes, as in Takamura's poem on the color of the plum blossoms mingled with snow, the speculation involves a confusion between two aspects of reality—a confusion which, it must be emphasized, is completely a product of the human sensibility, however firmly based on a logic of appearances. Sometimes the reasoning involves reality and dream, cause and effect, reason for being, or different aspects of time. In most poems, two or more of these elements make up the speculation, and the approach is one of inferring, questioning, suggesting, or exclaiming. A poem by Kiyowara Fukayabu deals with appearance and reality, cause and effect, in a statement of seeming (*SIS*, III: 202).

Kawagiri no	Because the mist
Fumoto o komete	Has risen from the river to conceal
Tachinureba	The lower slopes,
Sora ni zo aki no	The autumn-colored peaks appear
Yama wa miekeru.	Suspended floating in the sky.

Fukayabu's poem uses the technique as a means to a splendid imagistic end, but sometimes the technique itself was paramount, as we see in an anonymous poem that plays upon the differing nature of being at different times. The artifice is not made much more effective by the fact that the Asuka River (whose first two syllables mean "tomorrow") ran a particularly winding and inconstant course (*KKS*, XVIII: 933).

Yo no naka wa	This world's course—
Nani ka tsune naru	What is in it that is constant?
Asukagawa	Tomorrow River
Kinō no fuchi zo	Yesterday streamed in depths where
Kyō wa se ni naru.	Today its shallows flow.

Such punning speculation is little more than artifice, because the technique is an end in itself. Ki no Tomonori's poem "On the Falling Cherry Blossoms" (*KKS*, II: 84) is a very different matter.

Hisakata no	On this day in spring
Hikari nodokeki	When the lambent air suffuses
Haru no hi ni	Soft tranquillity,
Shizugokoro naku	Why should cherry petals flutter
Hana no chiru ran.	With unsettled heart to earth?

The lovely sounds and cadences of the Japanese are beyond the harsher voice of our English, but a glance at the transliteration will show that only the fourth line of the poem does not begin with an "h" sound. The exception to the alliteration is the phrase which shows that the cherry blossoms seem to be out of tune with the spring because of their "unsettled heart." And there are additional dimensions to the meaning as well as the technique, since the implied answer to the question is that the speaker himself is out of tune with the Buddhist natural laws that govern blossoms and man. He attributes to the flowers an unsettled heart that is a reflection of his own regret at the loss of beauty. Flowers and man must fall alike, but only man has the misdirected consciousness to regret the fate of either.

The even greater art of Narihira is reflected in Tsurayuki's observation in his Preface to the *Kokinshū* that this poet had too few words and too much spirit or meaning. Certainly there is no more elusive poem than Narihira's famous questioning of the world and himself (*KKS*, XV: 747). We begin with a transliteration and a prose rendering.

Tsuki ya aranu   Is there no moon? Is not this spring the
Haru ya mukashi no   spring of the past? My body the one thing
Haru naranu   remaining as it originally was . . . ?
Wa ga mi hitotsu wa
Moto no mi ni shite.

The poem develops in three waves of increasing length. The parallelism between line one and lines two and three shows that line one must mean, "Is not this moon the same moon as the one of the past?" The last two lines, however, show that the first three reverberate in three movements in the speaker's mind: the moon and the spring have violated natural laws by being different this year; but natural laws do not change, so they must really be the same; then I must be what has changed, since they do seem different. This succession of subjective states is immensely complicated by what implicitly follows. I alone remain the same; but I cannot remain the same, since time has elapsed; therefore nothing is what it seems, and all I know is that something extraordinary has happened to make every natural law seem so completely reversed. A further dimension of the poem explains how such a total disordering of the world could come about. The poem occurs in an episode of the *Tales of Ise* (*Ise M.*, No. 20, episode 4), in which the interruption of a love affair by outside interference is described. So intense is the poet's love and his present misery that all else seems unreal. We may now give a translation to join the host of others that have been made of this famous poem by Narihira.

What now is real?
This moon, this spring, are altered
    From their former being—
While this alone, my mortal body, remains
As ever changed by love beyond all change.

POETIC MODES

Such a highly subjective poetry led to the development of certain modes that are only faintly adumbrated in the preceding period, modes that may be divided into two groups, the technical and the conventional. The first group includes some poems in a quasi-public mode. These were collected in the *Kokinshū* under the rubric of "Poems of Congratulation" ("Ga no uta"); they were usually addressed to members of the imperial family or the higher aristocracy on such occasions as birthdays, and all were inferior to the great public poetry of the earlier age. The modes in which the genius of the age could express itself most wholly are the declarative (so pliable for private poetry, especially poems on the subject of love); the descriptive, in which the poet could explore his relation to the external world; the reflective, in which he could turn in upon himself; the philosophical, in which he could raise questions of a broader scope; and the allegorical, in which another mode might be given an added dimension. These modes are clear enough in the naming, but two cautions must be observed. So subjective is this age that the categories tend to fuse, with the result that a characterization of the main technique of the poem must often be supplemented with reference to auxiliary modes— descriptive poetry is usually allegorical. And we must say once again that all modes are colored by the social cast of the poetry. Our understanding of the poem often needs to be adjusted by considering that a poem of private reflection may be composed before a group on a social occasion. The simple light of description may take significance from its reflection on countless faces.

The social environment of this poetry had its effect in establishing certain modes that rise from new literary and social conventions. These conventional modes often combine with the technical ones in poetic practice, sometimes to help shape the meaning of the poem and sometimes merely to provide an occasion for composition or a critical category. From about the beginning of the tenth century, the practice of stating the *dai*, the topic or circumstances of composition, of the poem became standard. The *Kokinshū* states either the *dai* or the fact that it is "unknown" (*dai shirazu*); unknown to the compilers, that is, because the poem had never had a stated *dai*, because it had been lost, or because it was considered impolitic to state the circumstances of composition in the case of certain intimately private poems by exalted living persons. This critical procedure, modeled in part on a comparable Chinese practice, soon led to the conventional mode of composing poems on a specified topic—early spring, the nightingale, love, autumn at one's native home, and so on. Of course we cannot know to what extent poets set topics for their poems when they were not participating in some social occasion. But there were many such occasions. The social ritual that was by all odds the most important for developing conventional modes in this and the next two periods was the poetry contest (*utaawase*), and some further acquaintance with the nature of this social and literary institution is a prerequisite for understanding much about the age.

The three literary (as opposed to social) requirements for poetry contests were clearly poets who met in groups, the practice of "composition on a topic" (*daiei*), and a critical consciousness that would render distinctions and judgments possible. The fact that these prerequisites had been met in the preceding age without producing the poetry contest shows that there were also social requirements, chiefly the refined and leisured class so well exemplified by the Heian Court. The practice of comparison or contesting (*awase*) arose gradually, perhaps under the stimulus of Buddhist disputes in the palace (*dairongi*), and at first was largely confined to things (*monoawase*)—seashells, plants, and various specimens of art and craft. One of the oldest of such competitions was the root-comparing contest (*neawase*), held on the fifth day of the fifth month at the height of the iris season. Prizes were awarded for the longest and best iris roots submitted together with appropriate poems, and the day was given over to feasting, drinking, and flirting. The first dated poetry competitions extend back as far as the mid-ninth century, and the first contest to be transcribed was the one held at the Teiji Palace under the sponsorship of the retired emperor in 913. (It was customary for the emperor to "retire" from office, but he continued to direct affairs of state, the titular emperor usually exercising no real authority.) Poems were composed on the topics of the seasons and love, by two sides designated "left" and "right," although the famous poets who took part—Tsurayuki, Mitsune, and other luminaries of the time— appear to have shifted sides. Win, lose, or draw decisions were made by one or more judges, whose reasons for judgment were sometimes recorded. The reasons given at the Teiji Palace are important, both because they afforded critical precedents for later poetry contests, and, more important, because they show us that a social pastime is beginning to take on a spirit of serious literary competition.

Once decisions of this kind had been made, a man's reputation was at stake, and the Japanese fear of public humiliation led, we may suspect, to the composition of poems in advance on topics likely to come up. By 960, when one of the most famous poetry contests was held at the palace, we have more than suspicion to tell us that the serious business of competitive writing led to composition in advance. Both external and internal evidence show how seriously the contest was taken. Preparations were begun in the preceding year, and on the first day of the third month the topics were given out. The contest was held on the thirtieth day, and some notion of the vying of the two sides can be gained from what happened when one of the official readers, Hiromasa, started to read the wrong poem (which tells us conclusively that they were written in advance) to the dismay of his side and the elation of the other. "When he was told to go ahead and finish reading the poem, he was deathly pale; he did not respond for some time and finally recited it in a quavering voice amid laughter from the opposing side." Add to this the anecdote that Mibu no Tadami wagered his life on his poem in the last round of the contest, and it is clear that what was once a mere pastime was now a contest involving social and literary reputations.

The social environment that helped establish, and in turn was stimulated by, the poetry contests also served to encourage the development of conventional modes. On the one hand, poems were composed on fixed topics for social occasions—such as the new year, or certain seasonal activities of the aristocrats such as gathering young shoots in the spring—or to accompany and acknowledge gifts presented on formal occasions (visits and the like). On the other hand, the practice of exchanging poems on informal social occasions, such as love meetings or the casual exchange of gifts, gave rise to a second conventional mode of private, often allegorical poetry. Such poems are often so wholly private that their meaning is hidden from us, unless we have either the topic specified with the poem or the situation clarified by a headnote. Narihira's poem to a woman during the spring rains is an example of the great poetry such a practice might produce; a more typical example is this poem from a private anthology, the *Sanekata no Chūjō Shū* (*Katsura Series,* II, 108) with its elaborate headnote:

At the Horikawa Villa Lady Koma was seated behind a folding screen. Someone tossed a yellow rose to her over its top, and then, realizing from such an unusual act that the Emperor must be seated on the other side, she composed the following.

Yae nagara	The yellow rose
Iro mo kawaranu	Has blossomed in the unchanging color
Yamabuki no	Of its eightfold petals—
Kokonoe ni nado	Why can it have ceased to open
Sakazu narinishi.	And its petals not unfold to nine?

The punning play on eight and nine involves the connotations of *kokonoe* (ninefold) to mean the imperial court, so that there is another meaning just below the surface.

How did this yellow rose,
Though in full color still and petaled
In its eightfold form,
Cease to bloom in the imperial palace
And come suddenly to the Horikawa Villa?

Given the situation, this subsurface meaning has an allegorical significance— is it not the emperor before me, and why did Your Majesty throw the rose?

The emperor's fanciful reply is also preserved for the curious,* but the main point to be made is that this is a species of allegory growing out of apparent description and from the situation. The virtues of the poem are largely situational, springing as they do from Lady Koma's wit in replying to the gesture in a few seconds. For such a mode as this, the topic or headnote, which corresponds to our Western poetic titles, often carries no small amount of the meaning of the poem.

Two other conventional modes require our attention, one for its baroque eccentricity, and the other for what it reveals of the neoclassical impulses of this age. The first is the genre of the so-called Names of Things ("Mono no Na") with their "hidden topics" (*kakushidai*), a genre which might be termed "poems with topics hidden in word play." Such poems are not worth translating, even if translation were possible. The poets would take a topic, for example the *uguisu* ("warbler"), and weave the syllables (*u-gu-i-su*) into the poem so that it formed a different semantic and syntactical pattern that played off against the hidden word—or words, since as many as four words might be buried. To such patterns of ingenuity we must add the acrostics and similar devices roughly comparable in triviality and ingenuity to the Western baroque shaping of poems into altars and wings or to medieval acrostic poems. Perhaps Addison's definition of true wit as writing whose point survives in translation may be invoked to condemn, if condemnation is necessary, these verbal amusements of the age. The pleasure these verses gave their authors has not survived with the texts of the poems.

The practice of composing poems on Chinese topics at the university and the palace probably inspired the creation of another conventional mode for the tanka, a mode that might be called "poems on the topics of quotations from Chinese poems" (*kudai waka*). The object of this mode was to re-create the atmosphere of the original poem, by means of either "translation" or variation, and to fill out the emotional context of the passage by exploring hints in the text. If an English poet were to write a sonnet developing the feelings of Aeneas when he first saw Carthage, by using as his "topic" the famous line, "sunt lacrimae rerum et mentem mortalia tangunt," the effect would be very

---

* The emperor's poem, containing a play on *iro* ("color" and "love"), runs as follows:

Kokonoe ni	Although the yellow rose
Arade yae saku	Has blossomed in its eightfold petals
Yamabuki no	Outside the Ninefold Walls,
Iwanu iro oba	No person knows the fullness of its color
Shiru hito mo nashi.	Deepened by thoughts of which it dare not speak.

The meaning of the emperor's allegory may be summarized as "Although I came on purpose to the Horikawa Palace to make love to you, you do not seem to be aware of my undeclared feelings."

much the same. Many of these poems survive, sometimes in a series of tanka on different lines from the same Chinese poem, as in the *Daini Takatō Shū* (see *Katsura Series,* II, 253–311, *passim*). One of the poems (II, 294) develops the situation conveyed in a line from Po Chü-i's "Song of Everlasting Grief." The line chosen as topic is the fifteenth, "The spring night is painfully brief, and the sun too quickly rises" ("Ch'un hsia k'u tuan jih kao ch'i"), describing the feelings of the emperor as he spends his too brief nights with the beautiful Yang Kuei-fei.

Asahi sasu	Even the jeweled dais
Tama no utena mo	That sparkles in the light of morning
Kurenikeri	Yet contains the dark
Hito to nuru yo no	In pity for him whose passion still remains
Akanu nagori ni.	Unsatisfied by the pleasures of the night.

Although such a poem as this is in a conventional mode and embodies one of the fanciful conceits so typical of the period, the convention and the conceit alike become an excellent poetic vehicle. Literary tradition holds subjectivity in control, and the poet is allowed to express his personal emotions in developed art by placing his imagination, as it were, in the situation of a great event in the past. The neoclassical resonance of the poem is far different from the gaudy tinkle of the "poems on the names of things."

POETIC LANGUAGE AND IMAGERY

The different conventional modes illustrate the complex adjustment of personal response to social environment which is basic to the age. One will fail to understand either the good or the inferior poetry of the period unless one realizes that it produced poem after poem which was at once personal and conventional—or that the great poems of the age are not the songs of Romantic poets singing in the wilderness of their own originality but a personal lyricism in a social context. By comparison with Western poetry, this description is perhaps appropriate for the whole history of Japanese poetry down to modern times, but the particular combination was never more acutely a determinant than in the early classical period. Combined with the intensifying of technique within a narrowed range, the blend of personal lyricism and a social milieu makes it extremely difficult to isolate such aspects of poetic practice as diction, rhetoric, imagery, tone, theme, and styles. But in so far as they are separable, we shall deal with them in turn.

Some separate discussion of the diction of poetry in the early classical period is necessary, if only because the language of serious poetry for centuries afterward is almost wholly founded upon the precedent of the *Kokinshū* and the imperial anthologies that directly followed it. Like the *Man'yōshū*, the *Kokinshū* has a relatively limited vocabulary, something over 2,000 words, of which rather more than a hundred are not to be found in the *Man'yōshū*. While this lexicon is probably no larger than that of Anglo-Saxon poetry or Renaissance sonnets (*The Cid* has about 1,200 words), it must be remembered that it was developed for an almost restrictedly lyrical form, in a language whose agglutinative inflections often require extensive paraphrase in English, and whose words came to be a vehicle of connotations as much as denotation. And in order to maintain the native rhythms in a purity of style, it excluded all Chinese loan-words—words that were sometimes dormant, sometimes active in the minds of many writers as they composed Japanese poems, just as Latin lay in the minds of our poets till the end of the last century.

The poets were highly conscious of language as one of the determinants of their art. Often, indeed, a poem achieves its significance not by a strikingly new observation, but by the purity, the beauty, or the splendor of its diction, rendering translation even more difficult than usual. Although appropriate diction is but one of Narihira's many accomplishments, it is the language in cadences of Virgilian resonance more than anything else which makes his art so appealing. He and Komachi often fill the third and fifth lines with liquid, inflected adjectives or verbs that develop the sounds of preceding words with a perfected lyricism. The following poem by Narihira, for example, is one that will never have a wide appreciation among foreign readers, but its pure diction and lovely rhythms will always appeal to the Japanese. The major pause at the end of the third line anticipates the strong conclusion, in which the "o" and "k" sounds of the preceding line are given a new direction; the first and fourth lines have slightly longer pauses and their grammatical structure is similar, except that each of the two nouns in the fourth line has one more syllable than the corresponding noun in the first line (*KKS*, I: 53).

Yo no naka ni	If cherry flowers
Taete sakura no	Had never come into this world,
Nakariseba	The hearts of men
Haru no kokoro wa	Would have kept their tranquil freedom
Nodokekaramashi.	Even at the brilliant height of spring.

Such purity of language can only be achieved by poets with a strongly decorous concept of diction. If Chaucer is to our poets "the well of English undefiled," the poets of the *Kokinshū* are even more the source of pure poetic language to the rest of the Court tradition. Even the assured language of Narihira and Komachi was refined, especially by the choices exercised by compilers like Tsurayuki and by the judges at poetry contests, who often came to rule out diction that was not to be found in the first three imperial anthologies. No doubt there is something alien in this reverence for linguistic precedent from which the modern Western sensibility shrinks instinctively. We remember the glorious coinages and free-wheeling indifference to usual mean-ings and grammatical functions of a Rabelais or a Shakespeare, and feel there is something stultifying about a determined poetic diction. But surely it is a matter of degree. The example of refinement in diction from Ronsard or Dryden onward reminds us of similar tendencies in the West. And if we are to condemn the Japanese poets for restricting themselves to purity of aris-tocratic diction, what must we say of Wordsworth and his efforts to employ the speech of rural folk or of Burns and his Scots? As always, it is not the ideal that is so important, but the practice, and when a Pope, a Gray, a Wordsworth—or a Narihira, a Tsurayuki, or a Tomonori—achieves a dic-tion that is pure by whatever legitimate standard and able to express the im-portant interests of the age, it is folly to complain. Only in later centuries, when all experiment ceased, when the diction of the *Kokinshū* was no longer expressive of the interests of the age, ought we to condemn the standard of precedent in language.

Both the new words that appear in the *Kokinshū* and the words retained from the preceding age are those which do express the interests of the age. They are words that name the things the poets enjoyed seeing or experiencing, or their actions, or their attitudes toward their world. There were, it seems, three standards for admission of words to the poetic vocabulary. They had to be purely Japanese, since Chinese loan-words disrupt the sinuous fluidity of the verse and make poetry sound like prose. A "new" word had also to be one of common knowledge or sufficiently similar to other accepted words so as not to cause shock. And finally, a word had to have a degree of elegance about it—in sound, in connotation, and in propriety. Very good poems might be written in unusual diction, but although their quality was recognized, they were placed in the category of "unconventional poems" (*haikaiuta*). Ex-perimentation with diction which was inadmissible by such standards of ele-gant good taste was disastrous for a poet. When, for example, the official reader at the poetry contest at the Teiji Palace began to recite one of the poems on the *hototogisu*—

Kataoka no	Across the fields,
Ashita no hara o	The Morning Fields of Kataoka,
Toyomu made—	Reverberates—

the company roared so with laughter at "reverberate" for this bird's song that the reader was unable to finish his recitation.

The new words that appear in the *Kokinshū* naturally had their effect upon the imagery of the poetry. Some are images for natural phenomena that have now gained poetic attention. "Autumn mist" (*akigiri*), "spaces be-tween the rocks" (*iwama*), "robe of haze" (*kasumi no koromo*), "cricket" (*kirigirisu*), "moonlight" (*tsukikage*), "patches where the snow has melted" (*yukima*), and "the whole night" (*yomosugara*) are but a few. "Threads" (*itosuji*), "transferred scent" (*utsurika*), and "summer clothes" (*natsugoromo*) are among the new images that come from the daily life of the Court. Since such images as these are highly typical of the poetry of the age, we find it possible to draw several inferences that seem to us pertinent for the poetic practice and the underlying assumptions of the age. The new imagery from daily life is the imagery specifically of Court life, or, like the "jeweled seaweed," it has an elegance which precludes Okura's homely image of the destitute man's kettle filled only with a spider web. Poetry is, as in the preceding period, an art form developed and determined in style by the Court, but the Court poets no longer bother to project their feelings outside or "below" their own refined world.

The natural images that make their first appearance in the *Kokinshū* are even more significant. On the whole, they are finer or smaller and represent more detailed observation than is characteristic of the earlier age. They confirm the impression one has from the poetry as a whole that the poets stood, as it were, closer to the objects they describe and saw them in greater detail. It does not seem difficult to explain why the poets of this period drew into closer contact with their environment and observed it more intimately. The subjective cast of their art required that the observing sensibility deal with objects easily grasped as wholes, rather than sublime sights soaring above comprehension. When we come upon such a new image as "a robe of haze," we see the poet attributing a subjective quality of beauty and intimacy to natural phenomena; or again, the new words for night and the increased use of old images of night suggest the nocturnal activities of the courtiers in that most subjective of all normal human experience, love. A poem by Ariwara Yukihira (818–93) exemplifies this new subjectivizing of nature (*KKS*, I: 23).

Haru no kiru	The robe of haze
Kasumi no koromo	Now worn by Spring must indeed be
Nuki o usumi	woven
Yamakaze ni koso	Of threads of gossamer,
Midaru bera nare.	For the slightest breath of the mountain wind
	Seems to rend it into shreds.

Along with these developments, comparable new imagistic techniques appear that suggest the increased subjectivity of the age. The evidence available to the senses often is treated as if it were contradictory, as in Takamura's poem on the similarity of the appearance of snow and plum blossoms. Often, too, the senses are divided—hearing from sight or sight from smell—in highly subjective ways. Ariwara Motokata (888–953), for example, found no visible evidence that spring had come to the mountains, but his sense of smell declared it must be so (*KKS*, II: 103).

Kasumi tatsu	Far, far away,
Haru no yamabe wa	Those mountain slopes where the mist
Tōkeredo	Rises with the spring,
Fukikuru kaze wa	But the soft approaches of the breeze
Hana no ka zo suru.	Are laden with the fragrance of the flowers.

More often than in the earlier period, the imagery of the poetry of the age appeals to this less measurable, more subjective sense of smell. It is also characteristic that many of the images of sight represent visual confusions (of snow and plum blossoms, for example), or something only half seen or even beyond sight, as in the famous anonymous poem on dawn at Akashi Bay (*KKS*, IX: 409).

Honobono to	Dimly, dimly
Akashi no ura no	In the morning mist that lies
Asagiri ni	Over Akashi Bay,
Shimagakureyuku	My longings follow with the ship
Fune o shi zo omou.	That vanishes behind the distant isle.

Not only is the ship just faintly seen, but it is watched for subjective reasons—it carries away the person whom the speaker loves. Perhaps the ultimate in such indirect technique is the poem by Lady Ise (fl. ca. 935) on the cherry trees of her native village (*SIS*, I: 49).

Chiri chirazu	How I long to hear
Kikamahoshiki o	Whether the flowers have yet fallen—
Furusato no	If only there were someone
Hana mite kaeru	Come fresh from my native village
Hito mo awanan.	To tell me of the cherry blossoms there.

The cherry trees do have a real existence, but their reality is most important for its impingement upon the poetic sensibility, and there is no person at all to tell her of them. Yet this is only half the story. The headnote says that the poem was written on looking at "a scene of people going flower-viewing, painted on a folding screen at the palace." Lady Ise and other members of Court are assembled to see and appreciate the screen, and in this social context and from the stimulus of a work of art her memories and feelings are stirred for the distant, less elegant, quasi-pastoral scene of her province. One does not question the sincerity or the beauty of the poem, but it is a new thing for poets to be impelled to reverie by art.

There are other indications of the subjective handling of imagery. No small number of the new words in the *Kokinshū* are adjectives like "thin-hearted" or "lonely" (*kokorobososhi*), which often express attitudes and emotions, not imagistic qualities of objects. These new adjectives and pre-existing ones are, in addition, more often used to give the imagery a stronger coloring of human emotion than in the earlier period. Moreover, the imagery is often so directed toward generalization, though not abstraction, that it loses its imagistic concreteness. Narihira's lament "Composed When I Was Weak with Illness" (*KKS*, XVI: 861) does not have a single image that can be apprehended by the senses.

Tsui ni yuku	Though formerly I heard
Michi to wa kanete	About the road that all must travel
Kikishikado	At the inevitable end,
Kinō kyō to wa	I never thought, or felt, today
Omowazarishi o.	Would bring that far tomorrow.

"Road" may be visualized, but here it is of course a metaphor for death. The poem is a complete generalization, and as such carries the subjective tendencies of the age further than most poems. It is indeed one of the most perfect lyrics in Japanese and it is deservedly well known, but its techniques have the stamp of its age so markedly that such poems would not be written again for centuries, when the effect of unimagistic writing was to be far different. (See Chap. 7, below.) If it is an extraordinary example in quality as well as technique, it is nonetheless typical of an age in which reality exists not in the rapport of poet and nature, but in the significance of the external world to the consciousness of the poet.

RHETORIC AND SYNTAX

Poetic rhetoric is inextricably bound up with other aspects of poetry, since it involves the techniques for handling imagery and diction to express meaning. It is all the more important for an age like the early classical, in which aristocratic standards of decorous, elegant, and spirited writing make the manner of expression of paramount importance. One of the most striking and characteristic rhetorical techniques of the age is the pun and, with it, the closely related technique of the pivot-word (kakekotoba)—which we will remember is the use of a sequence of sounds in two senses, often through differing divisions and through the voicing or unvoicing of certain sounds. Poems employing this technique run the gamut in quality from the poems on the names of things with their topics buried in word-play, to some of the most consummate and moving poetry of the age. Ono no Komachi was by all odds pre-eminent among the poets of the age in her ability to use words and sounds meaningfully in different senses, with the result that her poems have a breathless intensity seldom equaled in Japanese poetry. Following is a prose rendering of one of her most famous poems (*KKS*, XV: 797).

Iro miede	A thing which fades without its color visible
Utsurou mono wa	is the flower of the heart of a man of the
Yo no naka no	middle of the world (i.e., of this world).
Hito no kokoro no	
Hana ni zo arikeru.	

About all the prose rendering shows is one aspect of the structure, although in reverse. The "of" phrases represent the four possessive particles (*no*) of lines three and four. With the particles functioning in Japanese order, Komachi orders her poetic materials by limiting the range of attention ever more narrowly and climactically as she ferrets out the changeful culprit—world, middle, man, heart, flower—and having found it exclaims, *ni zo,* "in it!" The climax of discovery is only partially a triumph for the speaker, since happiness is forestalled by the sense of misery she feels to be inflicted upon her by her lover's faithlessness. This is to say that the subject of the poem is love, which is treated with a generalization of its nature from the vantage point of the speaker's unhappy experience.

The subject of love emerges by implication from the diction (*hito,* "person," "lover"; *kokoro,* "heart," "mind," both with traditional connotations of love), but it is primarily the rhetoric that develops the implications into active meanings. The first, second, and fifth lines are made to begin with words bound together by the technique of association (engo). Color-fades-flower is clearly a cluster of similar concepts, even in English, and it functions in the poem to provide a strand of subdued imagery by the association of the concepts, even though their immediate contexts would, in English poetry, forestall any connection. The effect of the association and of the words connoting love in the fourth line is to show that neither *iro, utsurou,* nor *hana* ("color," "fades," "flower") is purely imagistic. The imagistic strand takes on a metaphorical character as vehicles whose tenor concerns love. The implied meaning of "fade" is therefore "grows untrue," "changes for the worse"; and "flower" becomes a symbol for the attractive yet transient nature of man's affection for women: the association shows that it is the flower of the heart of man which fades. Of the three associated words, however, it is the first whose function is the most significant. *Iro* is used in richly different senses. It refers most limitedly to the color that fades, the color of the symbolic flower of man's heart. Since the fading is metaphorical and the flower symbolic, it should be clear that color, too, must be taken in more complex senses. By perfectly normal usage in classical Japanese, *iro* may mean coloring in the sense of passion, so anticipating the fourth line in suggesting that the subject dealt with is love and, in particular, that the situation behind the outburst is a love affair now grown one-sided. *Iro* may also mean face or appearance, which is opposed in the poem to *kokoro,* the inner mind, the actual state of the man's feelings.

The complexity of Komachi's rhetoric can be appreciated by anyone who seeks to break the poem into divisions. Syntactically there are pauses at the ends of lines one and two, but they are bound together into a unit integrated by the association of words (*iro, utsurou*) in parallel positions and by the logic of the poem, since they tell what will be defined in the next three lines. Lines three to five are bound tightly together by the sequence of possessive particles leading to conceptually ever narrower elements. They are also joined less obviously to the first two lines. The crucial first word of the poem is played off against three words in the last three lines. It associates with *hana* ("flower"), as we have seen. In its secondary meaning of passion it combines by traditional connotation with *hito* ("person") to mean the man beloved by the speaker. And in its tertiary meaning it plays as appearance in contrast to the inner reality (*kokoro*).

Another rhetorical technique fuses the whole poem, a harmony and yet a reversal of states of mind for which the only English term is irony. The poem is ironic because what ought to change in a lover or any living thing, its appearance, remains constant; whereas that which should be so essentially the nature of the thing as its inner being has faithlessly altered. The irony is presented by a woman of intense passion, suffering from anger and fired by pride. Such motives lead her in her suffering to discover the cause—the faithless lover who protests a fidelity that he uses to mask his indifference—and lead her to a further ironic discovery that only appearances are real, that the vowed-for reality is only sham. Surely only Komachi would write a poem unifying all of these meanings into one outburst of passion:

> Find mutability
> In that being which alters without fading
> In its outward hue—
> In the color, looks, and the deceptive flower
> Of the heart of what this world calls man!

From such a building on the multiple meanings of one sound sequence (*iro*), it is not a far cry to Komachi's extraordinary dexterity in the use of pivot-words. The most complex of her poems employing the technique, which is to say the most complex of all poems employing it, is one in which she moves from emotional calm to frenzied passion within the compass of five lines (*KKS,* XIX: 1030). It might be read at first to mean:

Hito ni awan	On a moonless night when we have no
Tsuki no naki ni wa	chance to meet (because you cannot see
Omoiokite	the way to my house, I sleep, but) I awake
Mune hashiribi ni	longing for you so much that my breast
Kokoro yakeori.	excitedly heaves and my heart burns within me.

This reading conveys the play upon *tsuki,* "moon" and "chance," and something of the excitement of the poem. But the poem also has the most remarkably sustained and powerful imagery fused in its four word-plays in pivot-words. We must redefine the word clusters, for they have two simultaneously apprehended meanings, in order to understand the poem fully. (The italics indicate sounds with double meanings.)

1.	Hito ni awan	2.	Hito ni awan
	Tsuki no naki ni wa		*Tsuki* no naki ni wa
	Omoiokite		*Omo-hi okite*
	Mune *hashiribi* ni		Mune *hashiri-bi* ni
	Kokoro yakeori.		Kokoro yakeori.

On such a night as this
When the lack of moonlight shades your way to me,
I wake from sleep my passion blazing,
My breast a fire raging, exploding flame
While within me my heart chars.

We should also note in passing the superb emotional paradox that the darkness of the night is the cause of the searing flames. The technique of kakekotoba is here perfected art: not only does it enable Komachi to transcend the tanka form by creating, as it were, four new words, but the double meaning is also a tonal vehicle expressive of the most intense experience of the inner depths of the heart.

It will be recalled that in the preceding age the pivot-word was normally the technique of juncture in poems with prefaces (jo). We have been able to find very few unequivocal examples from the early classical period of this older rhetorical use of pivot-words. One of them is a poem very much in the older manner by Sone no Yoshitada, in which the juncture is a pivot-word in the fourth line (*GSIS,* I: 42).

Mishimae ni	Spring seems to have come
Tsunogumiwataru	Within the short space of a single night,
Ashi no ne no	Short as a single joint
Hitoyo no hodo ni	Of the roots of the reeds that sprout
Harumekinikeri.	Luxuriantly in the Inlet of Mishima.

Hitoyo no hodo ni means both "in the interval of a single joint" and "in the interval of a single night." The old-fashioned flavor of the poem lies in the weakness, the obviousness, of the metaphorical relation between the sprouting reeds and spring. There is a relation, but the last two lines of the Japanese (the first two of the translation) represent a single statement separable from the rest. In the characteristic poems of this period, the pivot-word functions not so much for juncture as to give increased complexity to what is already a poetic unit.

Another example of a poem employing a preface joined by a pivot-word to the statement will perhaps suggest why the technique was altered in this age. The poem (anonymous, *KKS*, V: 286) ought to be compared with Hitomaro's envoy to his poem on the death of Prince Takechi (*MYS*, II: 201), which it so much resembles. The italicized words are the pivot-words at the juncture. (Hitomaro's poem is first.)

Haniyasu no	Just as the waters
Ike no tsutsumi no	Pent-up by walls in Haniyasu Pool
Komorinu no	Do not know where to flow,
Yukue o shirani	So now the courtiers of the Prince
Toneri wa madou.	Are trapped with no direction to their lives.

Akikaze ni	Wretched my plight,
Aezu chirinuru	So like the drifting maple leaves
Momijiba no	Scattered in their fall
Yukue sadamenu	Before the gusts of autumn wind
Ware zo kanashiki.	And impotent to fix a course.

Hitomaro's world is the public world of city construction and Court business. The *Kokinshū* poet talks of himself and finds that the external world is relevant to the speaker only in terms of his personal response. Hitomaro's technique is therefore not unlike an epic simile that refers to what all men know, whereas the *Kokinshū* poet tends to assimilate the metaphorical vehicle into the emotional tenor. The result, for the poetry of this period, is that most of the metaphors are fused with other elements of the poem, not isolated by division into preface and statement. The typical poem of the age employs a simile, a metaphor, or an allegory in which the poem is not divided, in which the immediacy of subjective response to a stimulus is more instantaneous.

Two possibilities of the use of the old rhetorical techniques in fresh ways are shown by Tsurayuki. In a poem very greatly admired by later poets, he employs a jo in his first three and a half lines (*KKS*, VIII: 404).

Musubu te no	Like my cupped hands
Shizuku ni nigoru	Spilling drops back into the mountain pool

Yama no i no	And clouding its pure waters
Akade mo hito ni	Before the satisfaction of my thirst,
Wakarenuru kana.	So have I had to part from you too soon.

The preface extends through the word *akade* ("not satisfying"), which is employed as a pivot for what goes before and what follows. The old technique, the country setting, and the dipping hands to scoop up water all suggest an older, pastoral scene of somewhat rustic simplicity. If the parting is to be considered one from a woman loved, as some commentators have suggested, the element of pastoralism is considerably strengthened. Tsurayuki has employed a venerable technique which itself helps raise the image of a simpler past.

An even finer poem to our minds employs a pillow-word (makurakotoba) for somewhat similar effect. The quasi-pastoral element is made clear by comparison of the subject of the poem with its headnote: "Composed and Presented in Obedience to the Imperial Command" (*KKS*, I: 22).

Kasugano no	Do those girls set out
Wakana tsumi ni ya	On some excursion for young shoots,
Shirotae no	That they so gaily beckon,
Sode furihaete	Waving their white linen sleeves
Hito no yuku ran.	Toward the green fields of ancient
	Kasuga?

The italicized phrase represents a complex of techniques that distinguishes this poem from the two preceding poems. *Shirotae no* is a pillow-word for *sode,* "sleeves." But Tsurayuki uses the original meaning of the expression, "white hempen," in a literal way, while at the same time keeping the elegant amplification of the pillow-word associations. His phrase therefore means, "girls waving to each other their white-hempen sleeves." But the syllables *furihaete* also have a separate, pivotal significance: "deliberately," "on purpose." The effect of this, along with *hito* ("persons") in the last line, is to separate the poetic speaker from the girls. He wonders why they set out in just the way they do (a very male point of view toward the mysterious antics of young ladies), and wishes they would invite him to participate.

The first words of the poem help us to understand still more. Kasuga is just outside the ancient capital of Nara, not in the Heian capital at Kyoto where the poet is. The word perhaps carries something of the associations of its written characters meaning "spring day," but these overtones are minor compared to the fact that the place name tells us that the poet has created an entirely fictional situation. He represents himself as an observer of the old capital at Nara in its former days. The quasi-pillow-word function of *shirotae no* now appears in its full significance, to help convey the feeling of the past; and its literal meaning suggests (in a way that does not in the least destroy the poem's elegance) that the girls are perhaps of a lower social class. What we really have is a pastoral poem that creates an idyllic past.

One dimension of the poem remains. The poem was composed at imperial command and is therefore formal, although not precisely public in our sense. Tsurayuki's idyllic re-creation of the past is both a reminder to the emperor of the romantic beauty of the nation's past and, since the vehicle is pastoralism, a suggestion that today all are sophisticated and advanced enough to feel that slightest degree of condescension which lingers in our appreciation for the pastoral. The essential appeal of the poem lies in contrasts of speaker and girls, of past and present, and of two capitals, and in tone it has the charm of a painting by Watteau or Sir Joshua Reynolds. The gentle calm of the poem is accentuated by a quality of the distant and unknown which Tsurayuki's pillow-word has conveyed. How complex the art is can be gauged by its subjectivity. Tsurayuki is the man who presents the poem, the poet who composed it, and, by virtue of a fictional pose, the observer of the past.

Along with the pivot-word, there are some other techniques new to this period or redefinitions of old techniques which characterize the poetic interests of the age. As Tsurayuki's poem shows, pillow-words were still used, but to somewhat different effect. The technique itself suggested the traditional and elegant to the poets of the period. Sometimes the use of pillow-words seems to achieve no more than the appearance of elegance, but there usually appears to be an attempt to relate the literal meaning of the expression (and literal meanings were often made for old pillow-words by "folk etymology") to the poem by means of metaphor. This tendency can be seen most clearly in poems in which new pillow-words seem to be employed, as in the complaint of an anonymous woman to a faithless man whose higher rank enabled him to play a wide field in his amours (*KKS, XV*: 754).

Hanagatami	Have I been forgot
Me narabu hito no	Because I am one who does not count
Amata areba	To such a one as you,
Wasurarenu ran	Who may choose from women as countless
Kazu naranu mi wa.	As the gaps of weaving in a flower basket?

The first line of the original (and the last of the translation) is a pillow-word for *me*. It is typical of the age that *me*—which means both "eyes" and "interstices in the weaving"—functions (with *narabu hito*) by a word play to mean "women ranged before the eye." Perhaps the comparison of number develops into a metaphor—all these flowering beauties are in his basket, but the speaker has been left behind, no longer worth picking. In any case, the pillow-word has been given a personal significance, a role in a private poem that is more characteristic of this than of the preceding age.

Besides these redefinitions of old techniques, some more-or-less new techniques characterize much of the poetry of the period—association (engo), simile, and allegory. Association is a variety of word play which in some ways resembles the pivot-word, since it functions by giving two readings to a single sound sequence; but it differs in that a word later in the poem is given a meaning different from its immediate context by association with, or echo of, an earlier word. We shall render a poem by Tadamine, italicizing the associated phrases (*KKS,* VI: 328).

Shirayuki no	The *white snow* falls
Furite tsumoreru	Ever deeper on the mountain village—
Yamazato wa	To what loneliness
Sumu hito sae ya	Must even the *thoughts* of that man *fade*
Omoikiyu ran.	Who dwells amid the drifts that bury all.

Omoikiyu means "become nothing under the pressure of sad thoughts," but the element *kiyu* is a verb, meaning "fade" or "melt," which associates in both meanings with the "white snow" mentioned at the beginning of the poem: snow melts (*kiyu*), but only after it has buried everything under white drifts that cause the sharp outlines of the landscape to fade away (*kiyu*). Although this association acts as an ingenious method of binding the poem together, it represents more than ingenuity alone. The juxtaposition of *omoi* ("think") and *kiyu* shows both that the villager suffers a growing loss of identity and sense of isolation and that he knows the snow will melt and bring a desired springtime. The result is an irony of pathos: the snow will melt, but not until the villager has "faded away" because of loneliness. In this poem, in Komachi's poem on the faithless hearts of men, and in other fine poems, association is a characteristically Japanese means to a significant literary end.

The problem of the new technique of similes in the poetry of the period is an extremely intractable one. The agglutinative inflections, the fluid syntax, the attributive verbs, and the elusive particles—not to mention such techniques as that of the preface—often force the translator to use awkward similes where the Japanese poet is happily taking a more graceful path. There are some "signs" of similes resembling our "like" and "as": a verb or adjective with an attributive inflection followed by *gotoku* or *goto,* or a noun followed by the possessive particle *no* and *gotoku* or *goto,* or sometimes even by the particle alone, is an explicit comparison. Many other poems suggest comparisons by means of other constructions in which the technique of comparison is fairly obvious, but without a sign for the simile. If we may call these "implied similes" and add to them overt similes, we are ready to discuss this use of metaphor in the period.

Like the pillow-words, and like similes in Western rhetoric, the comparisons in this period are employed for amplification—by comparison something is made lovelier, dearer, and so on. The analogy with the pillow-word is useful, because the similes almost always observe the pillow-word order of preceding what they amplify, as if Burns had said, "Like a red, red rose is my luve." An anonymous bit of advice on love illustrates the technique (*KKS*, XIII: 652).

Koishikuba	If you choose to love,
Shita ni o omoe	Feel it only in deep reaches of the heart;
Murasaki no	Never let it show
Nezuri no koromo	Where its color will catch all people's eyes
Iro ni izu na yume.	*Like robes dyed purple with the violet*
	grass.

Lines three and four of the Japanese use the simile of clothes dyed a bright purple to convey the care that is necessary in matters of the heart. Another poem with an implied simile is Lady Ise's composed "At a Time When She Was Unhappy in Love." It is superior both in technique and in a convincing passion which finds expression only by her comparing herself to the fields she sees being burned over to increase the yield the next year (*KKS*, XV: 791).

Fuyugare no	If only the resemblance
Nobe to wa ga mi o	Of my fleshly body to the fields
Omoiseba	Withered dry by winter
Moete mo haru o	Meant that the way we both are seared by
Matamashi mono o.	fire
	Would bring me also the awaited spring.

Once the comparison is established by the particle *to*, the metaphor is extended throughout the poem, almost to the point of becoming allegory.

As we remarked in the preceding chapter, allegory worthy of the name is exceptional in the early literary period, but from the generation of Ōtomo Yakamochi on, the increasingly private nature of poetry led to allegory as an elegant and useful vehicle for poems of private discourse. The human mind takes as much pleasure in saying things indirectly as in saying things well, and we may suppose that this was one of the pleasures of allegory in private exchanges. In addition, the fear of exposure in the hazards of love affairs at the Heian Court led lovers to explore the benefits of ambiguous allegory—a fact that explains why some of the poems in the private anthologies are extremely difficult to understand. A further pleasure to be gained from allegory was one that comes from indirect reference to something intimately private—the sharing of knowledge about the significance of a certain place, for example, is a satisfaction all lovers know. Fortunately, the headnotes and various words often suggest allegory in poems whose hidden meanings might otherwise escape us. Such words as "person" (*hito*), the "heart" (*kokoro*) of something, "thought" (*omoi*), and various adjectives indicating sadness often give us the key to unlock a love allegory. This private allegory is often untranslatable, even when we possess its key, because the significance given objects is too wholly personal. But it may readily be found by leafing through the sections on love in such an anthology of the period as the *Kokinshū*, paying special attention to those poems with headnotes like "Sent to ———."

Private allegory may also be found in poems on other subjects. What appears on the surface to be description, for example, may turn out to be allegory. A postscript tells us that an anonymous poem is not purely descriptive, but a woman's lament for the loss of her husband (*KKS*, IX: 412).

Kita e yuku	How they cry
Kari zo naku naru	As they wing off to the north!
Tsurete koshi	It seems the geese
Kazu wa tarade zo	Have lost one from the number
Kaeru bera naru.	Which flew here with them in the fall.

The woman had taken a trip with her husband to the provinces, where he died, leaving her to return to the capital alone and to symbolize her grief in the crying of the geese.

Allegory is also to be found among the formal poems of the period, which, like informal poems, tend to be descriptive in appearance. The rarity of description employed as an end in itself shows that the complex minds of these poets tended to disdain poetry that only re-created a scene. For them, the external world held its prime significance only insofar as it was shaped by the human sensibility. Eight such apparently descriptive poems were "Written on a folding screen placed behind the seat of Lord Fujiwara Sadakuni, Colonel of the Right, when his sister The Lady of the Bedchamber gave a celebration in honor of his fortieth birthday." Two of the poems are on spring, one on summer, three on autumn, and two on winter—all by the most eminent poets of the day. The most famous is one by Mitsune (*KKS*, VII: 360):

Suminoe no	With the autumn wind
Matsu o akikaze	Blowing through the ageless pines
Fuku kara ni	Of auspicious Suminoe
Koe uchisouru	Are mingled the elated voices
Oki tsu shiranami.	Of the white waves out to sea.

The waves represent the guests; the inlet of Suminoe carries connotations of the shrine of the god of Sumiyoshi (literally, "auspicious" or "good life") there; pines are a symbol of longevity; and the autumn wind is a symbol of advancing but kindly age. So tonally apt are the images-become-metaphor that for centuries the poem was a model of its kind.

Rhetoric, imagery, and even the structure of Court poetry are closely related to the syntax employed. Narihira's poem on the seemingly changed moon (see above, p. 193) shows in its opening lines how similar syntactical forms might suggest parallelisms of thought and imagery, and Komachi's long series of possessives in her poem on the changeful heart of man (pp. 204-5) shows how the syntax orders the structure into progressive units. The crucial poetic role of syntax is of course not limited to this period of Japanese Court poetry, nor even to Japanese poetry as a whole, but the characteristic features of its syntax tell us a great deal about the special nature of the poetry of the early classical period. Japanese scholars have shown that whereas the tanka in the *Man'yōshū* normally employ a syntax demanding pauses after the second and fourth lines, the syntax of tanka poetry in the early classical period normally involves caesuras after the first and third lines. The fact is not to be disputed, but no one seems to know quite how to account for it. Whatever the explanation, the effect is certainly pleasing and the fact of importance to the practice of poetry. Such organization lends the tanka a structural pattern of three units of increasing length. The first line presents a short movement of five syllables; the next two a larger movement of twelve; and the last one a still longer movement of fourteen. The pattern is by no means inviolable, but it seems to provide a familiar structure, to arouse expectations that in English poetry are provided by the latent metrical pattern or by the division of sonnets into patterns determined by rhyme schemes.

The tripartite rhythm of lengthening units is usually played off against other syntactical qualities. Sometimes a poet calls attention to the division with a pivot-word—the effect is at once to intensify the sharpness of the caesura with increased attention and to smooth it over by double or overlapping syntax. (See the third line of Komachi's poem, p. 206.) More typically, the divisions are harmonized by making the poem consist of a single, complete, and naturally ordered sentence. By comparison with the frequently stiffened syntax of the early literary period with its recurrent parallelism, or with the fragmented syntax of mid-classical poetry, the poets of this age employed a purer, simpler, more lyrical syntax. Such purity combines with the tendency to use highly inflected verbs and adjectives, which often fill the entire third or fifth line, to produce poems whose sounds and cadences are of uncommon beauty. When such sounds and cadences are in addition made the vehicle of rich meaning, the result is a kind of perfection for which there is no comparison. In certain respects it is not so much Narihira's richness of meaning as his aural, syntactic perfection that makes him by far the most difficult of the Court poets to render without feeling one has the words right and everything else wrong.

It is just at this point—when syntax merges with sound, language, imagery, and rhetoric—that the true genius of the period seems to us to lie. In subsequent poetry, the unity of the poem is more intellectual, more artful, and often, to speak the truth, more significant. But except for some sporadic examples, Japanese Court poetry was never again to achieve the beauteous integrity of early classical poetry. It is such excellence of a craft of beauty which shows how positive the ideals of elegance, refinement, decorum, and courtliness truly were, for all of the somewhat negative connotations such terms have in our post-Romantic day. To give point to such generalizations, we may inspect in greater detail a poem long famous for its beauty of sound, imagery, and atmosphere (*KKS,* IX: 409).

Honobono to	Dimly, dimly
Akashi no ura no	In the morning mist that lies
Asagiri ni	Over Akashi Bay,
Shimagakureyuku	My longings follow with the ship
Fune o shi zo omou.	That vanishes behind the distant isle.

Part of the magic of the poem is attributable to its mystery—the pallor of dawn, the mists, the isle-hidden ship, and the relationship of the person on the ship to the speaker of the poem. But the poem's real beauty is so much a part of the language that it can more readily be declared than explained. Only in Japanese might one play upon a place name: Akashi is the name of the bay, but is also used to mean "dawned." The assonance of *Akashi/asagiri,* with *asagiri* picking up the *r* sound of *ura;* the rising excitement of the fourth line, with its combination of "island"–"hide"–"go" into a single verb modifying "ship" in the next line; and the perfect assonance of the last line, picking up and redefining the five *o* sounds of the first; all of this in a single lovely sentence with the usual caesuras is felt either deeply or not at all.

The pure lyricism of this anonymous poem is characteristic of the greater poetry of the age as well, although the great poets achieve their stature by adding thought and feeling of a higher order. In a technical sense, the higher order of poetic expression normally was achieved by means of the rhetorical devices, the wit, the complex tones, and the metaphysical interests of the age. But whether great or mediocre, the poetry of the early classical period possesses some quality that sets it off from all other periods. Against the repose of early literary poetry, the profundity of mid-classical poetry, and the intensity of late classical poetry, we would set the essential assurance of this age. During this period the Court was at its zenith. There was no need to look to the future with dread nor to the past with anything more than the slight nostalgia of Tsurayuki's dream of a rather simpler bygone day. The assurance might well have vanished had the courtiers been aware of their favored historical position. As it was, it would be the lot of later poets to look back with grief over their present to the earlier day as a norm of value, a day when, as Tsurayuki said in his Preface to the *Kokinshū,* all living beings seemed inclined to song, a day when the duties of military officers were to wait upon the emperor and to write poetry, not to cast the nation into civil strife.

The rhetoric of poetry—in the larger sense of its normative syntax and the disposition of elements—is the readiest indication of the poetic character of the age, whether we consider the pivot-word, the highly inflected verbs, the reasoning conceits, or syntactic integrity as particular signs. It was rhetoric in this sense that gave the age its means both of achieving aims of beauty and value and of exploring the subjective reaches of human experience. It is no accident that the greatest single Japanese literary work, the *Tale of Genji,* should have been written in this period, for it reflects the temper of the age by exploring—in a prose studded with poems and itself a marvel of lyric beauty —the same subjective complexities as the poetry, so creating a literary kind without comparison until the modern novel. The rhetoric of poetry in the first classical period is, therefore, the true vehicle of its thought and its greatness. It enabled poets to find a way to transcend the brevity of the tanka form and to convey subjective experience. The difference between this age and its predecessor can almost be represented in the older use of parallelism, a technique admirably suited for lyric narrative and public poetry, and the new use of the pivot-word, a technique ideal for short poems that explore the manifold richnesses of the human sensibility.

SUBJECTS, THEMES, AND TONES

In the early classical period, the important subjects, the predications about them (themes), and the attitudes toward them (tones) are, in general, of a narrower range than those of the early literary period, and of a greater complexity within the narrowed limits. As we have seen, poetry is almost entirely private, the triumph of lyricism is absolute, and the mind of the poet rules over reality, with the result that we can diagram the subjects of poetry in this age into a few divisions.

A. NATURE AND "THE WORLD"

B. HUMAN AFFAIRS

| 1. Parting and travel; Love; Death | 2. Beauty; Reality and Appearance; Truth | 3. Formal subjects (Congratulations, etc.) |

C. TIME

In B, we have three groups of subjects, treating different aspects of human experience. The first of these consists of personal experiences, the second of experience of the outer world and its significance, and the third of social or ritual experience. One of the surprises of this literary period is that poems with the single subject of nature are all but impossible to find. Time and again one comes upon poems that seem merely to describe, only to have closer examination show that they are allegories, or descriptions of screens, or intended to convey some metaphysical truth. And what is true of nature is true of "the world" (*yo no naka*); it, too, functions as a substantive means for a differing thematic end. We have, therefore, placed nature and "the world" above the three areas of experience that are usually the avenue to the expression of these themes. We have also separated time from other subjects, since it is the ground and being of almost all the literature of the age. The poets often wrote of time, but it is less a subject than a condition of reality that involves poet and subject matter, poet and other men, theme, and attitude.

The point upon which all these subjects converge is the subjective consciousness of the poet, and the proper mode of poetry was therefore lyricism. To say this is hardly to announce a discovery—but rather to make explicit in modern Western terms what is implicit in every sentence of Tsurayuki's Preface to the *Kokinshū*. In prose as lyrical—as marked by such contemporary techniques of comparisons, pivot-words, and even pillow-words—as the poetry he describes, Tsurayuki makes it clear that the response of Japanese poets to their subject matter is lyrical and subjective: "The poetry of Japan has its roots in the human heart."

The readiest way to show the force of generalizations about the subjects of poetry in the period is to examine poems with various subjects, themes, and tones, and of varying quality. The first, by Kiyowara Fukayabu, is one of the most purely descriptive poems we have been able to find. There is no surviving evidence to show that it contains an allegory or refers to some screen or picture. It is a poem about nature, specifically, "On Autumn" (*GSS*, VI: 322).

Aki no umi ni	On the autumn sea,
Utsureru tsuki o	The waves rise and fall, each in turn
Tachikaeri	Washing the reflection
Nami wa araedo	Of the floating moon—yet its appearance
Iro mo kawarazu.	Remains unaltered by the lapping waves.

The subject here is patently an event in autumn, and the imagery conveys it in lovely detail. The point, however, is one that the perceiving sensibility gives the scene: considering what is happening, the moon should change and does not. The poet chooses to focus upon the "color" (*iro*) of the moon, and as we have seen, *iro* means "appearance" and "form" as well as "color." The basic theme, then, is appearance and reality, with the "appearance" of such a flickering, altering thing as the reflection of the moon (itself inconstant) on waves in constant motion proving to be more steadfast than the "reality" of its being subjected to forces of change. The poem is more charming than profound, but we would mistake Fukayabu's intent and the character of the age if we failed to see the way in which his sensibility has shaped the subject into an intellectual theme.

The relation of nature to the perceiving sensibility is even clearer in Ono no Komachi's famous poem on growing old (*KKS*, II: 113).

Hana no iro wa	The color of these flowers
Utsurinikeri na	No longer has allure, and I am left
Itazura ni	To ponder unavailingly
Wa ga mi yo ni furu	The desire that my beauty once aroused
Nagame seshi ma ni.	Before it fell in this long rain of time.

The "color of flowers" (*hana no iro*) is clearly a symbol for "my physical being" (*wa ga mi*), and the natural imagery is sustained to the end by pivot-words. *Furu* means both to "grow old" and to "fall" as rain. *Nagame* means to "gaze" or to "think abstractedly," and "long rain." By establishing a symbol and developing it at length by means of pivot-words, Komachi has managed to suggest—in the very act of statement—the relation between nature and herself. Her view of nature and her attitude of what might be called passionately resigned despair are part of one brilliant poetic whole.

A poem by Narihira shows how "the world" might be brought into the subjective lyricism of the age (*KKS*, XIII: 646).

Kakikurasu	Through the blackest shadow
Kokoro no yami ni	Of the darkness of the heart I wander
Madoiniki	In bewilderment—
Yume utsutsu to wa	You people of this twilight world,
Yohito sadame yo.	Explain: is my love reality or dream?

It is extremely difficult to convey the force of *kokoro no yami* without destroying the imagery. The term, "darkness of the heart," anticipates the juxtaposition of *yume utsutsu,* "dream, reality," in the fourth line. A love affair seems to give rise to mixed emotions, while the experience is so intense that the speaker has lost his ability to distinguish appearance from truth. Such generalization of his experience into quasi-philosophical terms is appropriate to the appeal he makes to the people about him, asking them to help him resolve his confusion. The appeal is all the more subtle for Narihira's address, *yohito,* which means "you, I, everyone." Although he asks for advice, he points out that the people about him—who might very well censure him for the "darkness of his heart"—are as much in the psychological and moral dark as he. As a result, his bewilderment over appearance and reality is all the greater, and his love is shown to be even more intense than the imagery originally had suggested. The reference to the world about him is, then, only a means of conveying the depth of his subjective experience.

Death and love are perhaps the two most fertile subjects for lyric poetry. To take a poem with imagery somewhat like that in Narihira's poem, Izumi Shikibu's verses supposedly composed on her deathbed give us an idea of the handling of this subject (*SIS*, XX: 1342).

Kuraki yori	I now must set
Kuraki michi ni zo	"Out of darkness on yet a darker path"—
Irinu beki	O blest moon,
Haruka ni terase	Hovering upon the mountain rim,
Yama no ha no tsuki	Shine clearly on the way I take ahead.

This is clearly an allegory, and the personal relevance is unmistakable. It is interesting to notice the way in which natural imagery of darkness, mountain, and moon are applied to her situation. We have placed the second line of the translation in quotation marks because Izumi Shikibu echoes the *Lotus Sûtra* (VII): "Long night adds its curse to our lot: Out of darkness we enter into darkness" (Arthur Waley's translation). Since the poem was "Sent to His Eminence Shōkū," his priestly teaching is symbolized by the moon, and *michi* ("the way") also has religious overtones. The poem is both a prayer and a message, a literal statement of the need for light and an allegory for the need of enlightenment. And once more it is the mind of the poetic speaker which unifies the diverse elements into a whole.

Mitsune's poem "Composed While He Watched the Snow Falling" (*KKS*, VI: 329) is somewhat similar in imagery, but different in approach. He chooses to generalize about life and death by means of description.

Yuki furite	How sad this road
Hito mo kayowanu	Covered over with the obscuring snow,
Michi nare ya	Where not a person passes,
Atohaka mo naku	Where not a trace remains to mark the
Omoikiyu ran.	course
	Of travel through a world of fading hopes.

The last two lines of the Japanese grow increasingly subjective. *Atohaka mo naku* ("without an after-trace") must also be parsed *haka mo naku* ("unstable," "transitory"). *Omoikiyu* means "become nothing under the pressure of sad thoughts," and as we know *kiyu* ("fade" or "melt") is the familiar association for *yuki* ("snow") in the first line. What seems mere description is really an allegory for the speaker's life, and it would not violate the spirit of the poem to any great degree if the first line of the translation were extended to read, "How sad this road, my life."

One more poem seems to us worth quoting for what it shows of this creation of theme and tone by subjective handling of materials, not so much for the poem's quality as for the way it illustrates a variety of treatments characteristic of this age and foreshadows the direction poetry would take in the next period. The priest Sosei (fl. ca. 890) purports to convey a personal experience which shows how much the speaker appreciates the beauty of chrysanthemums (*KKS*, V: 273).

Nurete hosu	In what seemed a moment,
Yamaji no kiku no	As I gazed on the dew-laden chrysan-
Tsuyu no ma ni	themums
Itsu ka chitose o	By the mountain path,
Ware wa heniken.	How many ages passed by in that instant
	When my clothes were soaked and dried?

On face value the poem baldly presents a rhapsody over flowers, but Sosei had other business in mind than passing himself off as such a bewildered person. Behind this poem lies the Taoist legend of the woodcutter who saw some immortals playing chess in the mountains one day. He decided to watch the game a little while, and as at last he turned to depart, he discovered he had watched them so long that the shaft of his axe had rotted away. By echoing this legend, Sosei's hyperbole loses its extravagance. The headnote tells us still more: "On the appearance of a person making his way through the chrysanthemums to arrive at the palace of an immortal." In other words, the poem is written about a picture, and the words are represented as those of the man in the picture. This, too, has the effect of making hyperbole rather more acceptable. Sosei has managed to render a simple affirmation into art, but to leave behind the opinion that he, too, is a great lover of chrysanthemums—as well as a very clever man. This effect is pleasing, even if the play of an instant and several centuries is not a wholly moving treatment of the subject of time. The true center of the poem is an attitude rendered through complexly related allusions.

In our comments on these poems, we have not sought to convey the variety of tones in the poetry of the period, because the dominant attitude is the highly subjective response which we have seen expressed in different ways. Irony, humor, remorse, affirmation, regret—and a great range of other personal attitudes—are expressed in the poetry of the age, but all are part, as it were, of an overriding expression of personality, and the particular emotion is apt to be involved with the general subjective attitude. Such subjectivity in a social milieu helps determine the particular poetic cast of the age. The proliferation of these dual qualities makes the inferior poems of the age almost indistinguishable from each other. The best poets grew in the same environment and created highly individual poems in varying personal styles. But in addition to the style that marks the man, there is the vexing problem of general styles which now requires some consideration.

At one point in the *Tale of Genji,* Prince Genji scoffs at the poetic hand-books of the tenth century for the way in which they stressed the things to be avoided in writing poetry. But such primers as Tadamine's *Ten Styles of Japanese Poetry* also discussed alternative styles available to a poet. Without wishing to follow his somewhat forced categories or to speak of the entire stylistic range, we may still examine a few characteristic styles. The earliest poems that survive in any quantity from the ninth century are those from the period of the Six Poetic Geniuses (830–80). When one speaks of the style of the *Rokkasen,* he means complexity of a variety borrowed in part from late Six Dynasties poetry, developed with such native techniques as the pivot-word or association, and expressing a complex probing of personal thought and feeling.

The Poetic Geniuses lack the refinement and have rather too much passion for what we have called the Fujiwara style. The refinement, the grace, and the elegance of this style are best represented by Tsurayuki, Tomonori, Mi-tsune, and Lady Ise. Unfortunately, refinement sometimes led to debility and took much of the strength from the earlier manner of the *Rokkasen.* The Fuji-wara style reflected the assured elegance of Heian society as it developed under the powerful family of *de facto* rulers who bore this name, and it continued for many centuries as what might be called the official vehicle for formal po-etry. Centuries later, after the aristocracy had lost its cultural dominance and the style no longer expressed the needs of society, this official way of writing still retained its traditional prestige. At its worst, it is characterized by such conventional expressions as "Is it a cloud or cherry blossoms?" "What can I do to keep the nightingale here when spring passes?" "The maple leaves are like brocade" or by the queries Why? What? and How? Along with these characteristics borrowed from late Six Dynasties poetry, the Fujiwara style was characterized by elegance, refined diction, and graceful rhythms. It is easy to see why such a style should continue in popularity for so long. It was recog-nized at court; it was embodied in most of the poems of the *Kokinshū;* it was associated with the flowering of aristocratic society under the Fujiwara domi-nance; and it appealed to refinement and precedent—those lasting Japanese preferences.

In literary terms, the style also had much to recommend it. It had a fairly well articulated poetic—as a critical *apologia,* Tsurayuki's Preface to the *Ko-*

kinshū anticipates Sir Philip Sidney's *Defence* by seven centuries—and was therefore identifiable and an art that could be learned. It was also the perfect vehicle for aristocrats, since it could be now a plaything to lend some color to a pallid hour, now the very best way of winning a lady (or holding her off when you were interested in someone else), now a means of preferment if you were really a poet, now a vehicle for writing serious poems. Moreover, the Fujiwara style was a lyric style suited to the interests of the court and given to creating, comparing, or questioning states of being and of consciousness eminently suited to the language. It provided the basis of poetry—almost of prosody—and it was the central tradition from which flights of originality took their departure.

Another important style is what may be termed apparent description. Apparent, because it is almost always the vehicle of allegory, a form of compliment in social ritual, or of poetry based on a work of art. Few things are more characteristic of the age than the fact that pure description seemed to the poets so simple as not to qualify as poetry. And they were right to feel so, since for them reality lay in what the observer made of things, not in what seemed to strike the eye. At the same time, even if the descriptive style was used for other ends, it provided a native tradition that the next age might develop when it found a way to render description into meaningful art.

The Fujiwara style and the apparent descriptive style were, after the age of the Six Poetic Geniuses, the dominant formal styles. The difficult thing for us Westerners to comprehend is that although these two styles were for the most part styles for private poetry, the styles themselves and the poetic act had a degree of formality that made poetry and poetic practice (as opposed to the poem itself) into public, or, rather, "social" art, since the poems dealing with public subjects and occasions are relatively few. Mitsune's poem on the pines of Suminoe (see above, p. 212) illustrates the complexities of the matter. It is ostensibly a descriptive poem, but it has allegorical features (though to be sure, its allegory is only partial, metaphorical) that apply to the public occasion for which it was composed. A seemingly private poem has a seemingly public relevance. But this tide flows two ways, and if we look at the symbolic significance of the description we find, not public matters, but a compliment to Fujiwara Sadakuni more as a person than as a governmental official. This is not public poetry like Hitomaro's or Okura's *chōka,* but private, formal, and social poetry.

We have so far discussed style without mentioning tone, but of course it is very difficult to separate the two. Attitudes, intensity, decorum, esthetic distance—and many such elements manipulated by tone—are involved in what is most readily called style. It is in considering such elements that we are able to speak of a passionate style created by the period and bequeathed to later ages. Usually the style is associated with women—Ono no Komachi, Lady

Ise, Izumi Shikibu, Lady Sagami, and so on from generation to generation till the end of the Court period. The style presumes an attitude of self-aware-ness, often of pride mingled with self-pity. It is usually marked by burning intensity, although humor, archness, and reflective quiet may on occasion dominate. It is less decorous than the Fujiwara style—in fact, it is sometimes passionately erotic. And it is increasingly practiced by men who write love poetry representing the woman's point of view. The passionate style afforded one means of expressing a greater personalism than the more decorous styles permitted, although it would not be long before the passionate style itself would achieve its own decorum and lose something of its special character as it passed the bounds from informal to formal poetry.

Komachi shows the style at its informal beginnings. Replying to a joking invitation from her friend Bunya Yasuhide to accompany him to his post in the provinces, "to see the country scenery," she felt free to answer him as if he were seriously asking her to be his mistress. In some measure the poem is therefore reflective—it considers her advancing age and the earlier days when such an invitation might actually have been made—but the important thing is that the tone of mock concern inherent in the situation is transformed into genuine, passionate concern. The passion is controlled in expression by the differences between what is literally said, what appears to be said about a de-liberately misunderstood invitation, and what is meant (*KKS*, XVIII: 938).

Wabinureba	Misery holds me fixed,
Mi o ukigusa no	And I would eagerly cut loose these roots
Ne o taete	To become a floating plant—
Sasou mizu araba	I should yield myself up utterly
Inan to zo omou.	If the inviting stream might be relied upon.

It was not age, but an unfaithful lover which led Izumi Shikibu to bewail her plight (*GSIS*, XX: 1164).

Mono omoeba	As I fall in sadness
Sawa no hotaru mo	At his neglect, the firefly of the marsh
Wa ga mi yori	Seems to be my soul
Akugareizuru	Departing from my very flesh
Tama ka to zo miru.	And wandering in anguish off to him.

Such poems as these are informal; they convey intense feelings; and they grow from what we must presume to be real as opposed to obviously fictional situations. Like the other styles and their gradations, this is but one of the alternatives; and it is an important fact that the same poet composed both formal and informal poetry in all of the gradations of each. Tsurayuki is per-haps the exemplar of the formal Fujiwara style, demonstrating both its potentialities and its mannered limitations. He more than any writer had articulated and established the style, and yet his practice shows that even he could turn to a simpler, informal technique. In his *Tosa Diary* (*Tosa Nikki*), he wrote some formal poems but himself ridiculed their pretentiousness, and some simple poems that he evidently felt worth preserving, however much the world at large might laugh at their plainness. He did not live long enough to create superior poems in this simpler manner, but his efforts were a harbinger of developments later in the period and of new styles in the age to come.

CONSOLIDATION, NEW DEVELOPMENTS, AND DECLINE

The particular alternative styles available to a poet in the early classical period depended, to some extent, on when he was born. Most of the poetry we have discussed was composed between 850 and 950, a century marked by the period of the Six Poetic Geniuses; the generation of poets who took part in the compilation of the *Kokinshū* (Tsurayuki, Tomonori, Mitsune, and others); and the generation that followed them. So well was their work done and so appropriate to the society to which it was given, that the next century and a half largely contented itself with consolidating the gains, with adapting them to somewhat new purposes, and with handing down a coherent tradition. The influence of Tsurayuki—and when we name him, we do so to symbolize the accomplishment of the age through its most typical representative— was nowhere stronger than in the formal poetry of the Fujiwara style, which was really the only style deemed suitable for all important social occasions. Later poets might write in new ways, but they had to prove themselves poets first by composing works which conformed to the Fujiwara style. They often had no chance of being represented in an imperial anthology unless they did, and not a few poets who appear revolutionary in their best-known works composed the bulk of their poems in a manner that harked back to literary tastes developed long before their time.

It is to the informal poetry, then, that we must turn to find significant changes and developments. This is not to suggest that informal poetry was vastly different at every point from the formal Fujiwara style, and as we have seen, an informal style like the passionate might become formal; but informal poetry was at least less controlled by the pressures of social and literary decorum, and although the typical techniques of formal poetry usually exerted their claim, they did so less strongly. Often the informal poetry seems to express what the poets wished to say, often the formal poetry to express what they felt was expected of them. Often, but not always, since, as we shall see, informal poetry could become as conventional as the poetry written according to the official decorums, and since formal poetry might also express a poet's deepest concerns.

Some of the new developments in informal, and subsequently in formal, poetry are related to the social context in which such literature thrived. The informal poetry was pre-eminently a poetry of occasions. The expectation, always strong in Japanese minds, that a given poem grew from a situation that would lend interest to it seems to have grown progressively stronger. One symptom of the tendency is the increasing length and detail of headnotes in the imperial anthologies. When, where, and why was the poem written? Such are the questions that the lengthened headnotes of the *Gosenshū* (ordered in 951 by Emperor Murakami) seem to anticipate. Some of the headnotes are narrative in nature; many which appear with poems composed by the higher nobility employ honorific constructions, a fact that shows they were not written by the poet. Some poems run in series of four or five, usually as responses in gallant discourse. The tendency is toward a re-creation of the events that produced the poem, and where evidence was lacking, ingenuity might create a situation as fictional as the poems which the headnotes were meant to gloss. This fictionalizing of contexts or giving poems a significance outside themselves as autonomous artistic units could only have occurred if there was an expectation that a poem was composed upon a social or conventional occasion, and if there was a desire to have lyric units merge into larger quasi-dramatic or narrative wholes.

Nothing we know of in the history of Western poetry approximates this assumption that poetry is related to a real occasion, because our poetry has never been so closely and consistently inspired by actual situations. If a nobleman at the Heian Court chanced upon a lady-in-waiting and gave her a spray of blossoms he had just picked, she was expected to reply with an apposite poem then and there. Of course, since gifts were usually sent by messenger, and since love poems were often written after one was again alone, the need to respond with a poem was not usually so pressing; but the response to countless social occasions was poetry. Small wonder, then, that readers were interested in the occasion from which the poem grew, or that legends often grew up about poems.

This expectation and the practice of composing fictional situations is not new in this age. As we have noticed, many poems in the *Man'yōshū* are plainly written on occasions or have fictional, sometimes fanciful, headnotes (see above, pp. 90 and 91–92). These are little more than precursors, however, and a strong demand for the contexts of poems could only arise when poetry became private in nature and social in occasion—public poetry creates its own context. What the development of these prose contexts led to, or at any rate grew along with, was the genre of the *utamonogatari*. This form is often translated "lyrical tales," which is rather misleading. "Poems with prose contexts" probably means more to the Western reader, but a closer if awkward rendering of the Japanese describes their genesis and essential nature—"tales of poems." For example, some of the poems from Narihira's personal collection, often glossed by brief notations of his own, were set down with prose contexts in a loose sequence which was called *Ise Monogatari* (*Tales of Ise*). Later writers embellished the contexts, lengthened them, and often made them the setting for several poems. The poems themselves retained a central importance that is reflected by the fragmentary nature of the episodes, most of which begin afresh, "Once there was a man . . ." It was not until the *tsukurimonogatari* ("fictional tales") evolved as a genre that plot, character development, dialogue, and other such novelistic techniques were evolved, and the central importance of the poems was lost. Even so, the greatest exemplar of this form, the *Tale of Genji*, contains almost 800 poems, or roughly 4,000 lines of verse. One wonders what a Western reviewer would make of a psychological novel with a third as many lines of verse as *Paradise Lost*.

Poems, especially those composed on trips, also achieved prose contexts when they were written in diaries. Tsurayuki's *Tosa Diary*, written late in his life, is one of the most important. He tells in prose of the day's travels, gives the contexts of the poems, and sometimes comments on them. In terms of artistic unity, the diaries with poems tend to fall between the *utamonogatari* and the *tsukurimonogatari*. They have more unity than the former—a unity of voyage and personality—and less of a fictional, artistic being than the latter. In addition to such diaries as were composed with the intent of showing them to other people, there are those diaries which were set down for the interest of the writer himself. The poems composed for these "personal diaries," as they might be called, are often more purely descriptive or more wholly expressive of individual feeling, with little regard to the decorums of formal poetic technique. As such, they were hardly considered to be poems at all, and they seldom find their way into the anthologies, but they provided a continuing body of informal poetry which could later join with other forces to make possible a new poetic tradition.

The inference to be drawn from this composition of poetry upon so many occasions and the development of new genres in the ninth and tenth centuries is not that the poetry of the age grew steadily in greatness. For every Komachi or Tsurayuki, there were innumerable aristocrats who discoursed in verse without rising for a line into original poetry. If, like Pope, they "lisped in numbers, for the numbers came," the amorous murmurings of one aristocrat were often very much like those of another. We must not forget that the *Kokinshū*, whose title and Preface tell us that it is a "Collection of Ancient and Modern Times" (the best works of a century), contains only some 1,100 poems. On the other hand, we must also not underestimate the period. There were the usual number of great poets common to any age that esteems poetry, and an extraordinarily large group of poets of the second order. Moreover, if we realize that the population of Japan was still extremely small (perhaps between four and five million) and the poets were confined to a limited

Drawing of Izumi Shikibu by Reizei Tamechika

aristocratic group, the wonder grows that within two centuries after the establishment of a real literary tradition Japan had either a potential poet or poetaster in every cultivated member of its nation. These are historical facts which help give even the most private poetry a social function; and they also explain how the definition of poetry in the age of the Six Poetic Geniuses and the accomplishment of Tsurayuki's contemporaries could be so quickly spread throughout a country in which paper was extremely expensive and printing was used in only a few Buddhist monasteries. Unfortunately, it also explains why so much inferior verse might be written by aristocratic poseurs, and why what was fresh in the poetry of one generation might become conventional in the following. The historian of the culture of this age has indeed a heavy burden to sort out the good from the bad in literature. Good and bad grow so luxuriantly from the same soil that he needs discrimination to distinguish between the two and patience lest he either accept or reject all the poetry this most remarkable society has to offer.

The consolidation of the poetic of the early classical period undeniably had its good and bad points. The articulation of a literary criticism, the creation of styles meaningful to the age, the combination with prose for new genres, and the simple utility of poetry to the society which wrote it are all praiseworthy. But there is also room for adverse criticism of what is less a consolidation or proliferation than a petrifying within narrowed convention. In the second half of the period, even the better poets came to write poems very much like everybody else's. It began to look as though the styles that had been created to serve the society were making the poets serve them.

It must be admitted that if the formal style is symbolized by Tsurayuki, the informal style often seems to show a Tsurayuki in his shirtsleeves. The passionate style appears here and there in the period like a vein of rich ore upturned by a succession of women. It differs from the other styles in tone, but in at least one important respect it also differs in technique. It employs a direct declaration of feeling. Komachi's mode of expression is beyond doubt complex, but the complexity serves as the means to express her feelings in declarations of unequivocal intensity. Other poets lacked her particular genius, but the direct declaration—as opposed sometimes to direct expression—marks this style in the work of Izumi Shikibu in the tenth century, of Lady Sagami in the eleventh, of Princess Shokushi in the thirteenth, of ex-Empress Eifuku in the fourteenth, and of various men along the way. A glance at a poem or two by Izumi Shikibu and Lady Sagami will show how unlike Tsurayuki's characteristic styles their poetry is—and also how dimly they usually reflect Komachi's remarkable intensity.

The love affairs of Izumi Shikibu are recorded in somewhat greater detail than those of Komachi, but like her predecessor, she was given to strong expression of her feelings. She felt little compunction in complaining about faithless lovers or in declaring her passion for a man, as this poem shows (*GSIS,* XIII: 755).

Kurogami no	Lying down alone,
Midarete shirazu	My thoughts are fixed on you—so deeply
Uchifuseba	That I have forgot again
Mazu kakiyarishi	The tangles of my long black hair
Hito zo koishiki.	In yearning for the hand that stroked it
	clear.

Something of the strong physical suggestion of the image of the man straightening out the woman's body-length hair before sleeping with her is softened by Izumi Shikibu's casting the poem in terms of an echo of the Chinese romance entitled "Visit to the House of Beauties" (*Yu Hsien K'u*; Japanese, *Yusenkutsu*). While this echo does euphemize somewhat, and while we do not know whether the poetess's lover had indeed straightened her long hair, the sensuous vividness of the image remains and the implication of the poem is "I long to have you come to bed with me again." It is not hard to see why Murasaki Shikibu should regard Izumi Shikibu as an abandoned woman. Where Komachi's poetry derives its intensity from a complex and burning consciousness expressed in meaningful complex art, this poem reproduces the scene of love-making in almost photographic detail. In another poem, "Sent to Someone When She was Ill" (*GSIS,* XIII: 763), she exclaims—

Arazaran	This is a world
Kono yo no hoka no	Where I shall shortly be no more:
Omoide ni	If only you
Ima hitotabi no	Would come to visit me just once
Au koto mo ga na.	For a remembrance in the afterlife!

This is a surprising poem from one who should be thinking, according to Buddhist precepts, of renouncing this world and human affection. The fact that she could write not only poems like these but also the moving lyric beseeching the symbolic moon for religious enlightenment (see p. 218 above) shows that her consistency is not so much one of idea as the strong declaration of the feeling of the moment.

If Izumi Shikibu did not possess all of the genius of Komachi, neither were her talents much more than imitated in the eleventh century by Lady Sagami. Like her greater predecessors, Lady Sagami is best known for her poems on love and the pathos of being neglected by a faithless lover (*SKS*, VIII: 269):

Yūgure wa	In former days
Matareshi mono o	I waited for the dark to bring you here,
Ima wa tada	But now it falls
Yuku ran kata o	Only with the sadness of conjecture
Omoi koso yare.	About the new directions where you go.

The sounds and cadences of this poem are especially haunting, but it does not convey the force of Komachi or even of another poem of her own in which she asks her lover for one more visit, no matter how brief (*Sagami Shū* in *Katsura Series,* IX, 299).

Utatane ni	If but in a dream—
Hodo naku sameshi	Dreamt in the flicker of troubled sleep
Yume o dani	Of a moment's dozing—
Kono yo ni mata mo	If I can see you just once more,
Mite zo yaminan.	Then I shall be content our love should die.

The persistence of the passionate style in the poetry of women throughout the period is important because it kept alive the claim of the heart to a tradition in danger of over-intellectuality or artifice from the technique of the Fujiwara style. Too many women may have written poems that were only emotional—just as too many no doubt lapsed into artifice—but as the examples of Komachi, Izumi Shikibu, and Sagami show from three successive centuries, there were women who could convey the message of the heart in poems in which the mind furnished the techniques of expression.

Another stylistic possibility lay in the purely descriptive poetry that continued to be written in diaries, and other instances in which writers composed poems for themselves, with little thought of making them public. The importance of this continuing, half-submerged tradition can scarcely be exaggerated, since it explains why almost every major poet is known to have written poems that are not in the style of formal poetry. The strength of this underlying tradition also explains how it was possible for later ages to find in the canon of a Tsurayuki or an Izumi Shikibu poems sufficiently like their own to be esteemed and selected for imperial anthologies. Such poems appear side by side with poems contemporary with the compilers and do not seem out of place. If it is true that Tsurayuki and his generation created styles that outlasted the needs for which the styles were devised, it is also true that the age adumbrated new styles, whose possibilities were only gradually recognized. In most cases these foreshadowings of what was to be are found in private collections and are informal poems, but even in the poetry composed upon the most formal occasions, it will be recalled, there was a possibility of writing descriptive poetry—if it had an allegorical or symbolic significance. All in all, descriptive poetry was a distinct if dormant possibility throughout the early classical period.

Such dimly viewed alternative styles as the descriptive gradually emerged as marked possibilities for a new poetry. It is indeed a salient feature of the eleventh century—the end of the period—that convention is counterbalanced by innovation and decline by experimentation leading to new accomplishment. Such new developments belong more properly to the next chapter; but it is necessary to affirm in principle the vitality of the entire age from Narihira to Tsurayuki to such an eccentric innovator as Sone no Yoshitada and to such an important transitional poet as Minamoto Tsunenobu.

What is essentially at fault with the conservative poetry is its failure really to conserve the best—its over-conventionalism. If a word, a phrase, or the technique of a poem was unfamiliar, it was condemned out of hand. Whereas from the poetry written earlier in the period one had the task of selecting the poets from the countless poetasters, one must search in the poetry at the end of the period for a fresh nuance, a new version of an old image amid the ready-made sameness. If a poet were asked to participate in a poetry contest, he would receive the topics handed out and set to work, carefully eschewing any expression not in the early imperial anthologies, strenuously trying to find some new way of questioning whether what the eye sees are plum blossoms or snow, or trying to make unhappy love still unhappier—but without intruding anything shocking or novel or original. The conservative poets were too committed to tradition, too committed to keeping what the past had given, to value experimentation.

It is not so much that these conservative poets wrote bad poems, however, as that what they wrote had a cautious, safe homogeneity. What Sir George Sansom says of sculpture in this period might equally well be applied to poetry by a sympathetic critic (*Japan: A Short Cultural History,* p. 253): "During the second half of the 11th century, in the twilight of the Fujiwara, some lassitude is visible in the arts. In sculpture especially technique outstrips inspiration, and . . . sacred images achieve an elaborate nullity." The poetry of this twilight of the period has been aptly compared to the splendid gold and lacquer boxes produced in later centuries—attractive in the richness of stylized beauty, but containing nothing within. It may well be supposed that as much pleasure was gained in this "twilight of the Fujiwara" from the beauty of the calligraphy as from the poems themselves. One might look elsewhere in eleventh-century Japan and see similar deterioration—the increasing worldliness and bellicosity of the religious sects, the darkening fortunes of the Court class, the shifting of the powers of civil government in the capital from the Fujiwara clan to the rule of force among powerful military families. From such a look at changing conditions, one can see that the conservative poets adhered to the old, to the tried-and-true Fujiwara style almost as a symbol of a prestige and a splendor now passing from them to an upstart class.

However, the techniques of subjective, aristocratic poetry lost their meaning when they ceased to have relevance to human experience. Because it was an expression of what was deeply felt, the brilliant technique of poetry in the first half of the period answered to the world which a Narihira or a Tsurayuki knew. In a private poetry of a strongly Metaphysical and Cavalier cast, these and other poets found a proper poetic vehicle to express at once their personal thoughts and a world larger than themselves. That most crucial of all balances for Japanese Court poetry, the balance between the personal and the impersonal, is predicated upon expressive technique, upon a harmony of feeling and style, of conviction and convention. The old balance had been lost. The new poetic age about to come into being was perforce the child of the old, but it found new techniques, new ideals, and a new way of life to bring about the third of the four great periods of Japanese Court poetry.

6

The Mid-Classical Period

1100–1241

THE EARLY CLASSICAL PERIOD produced a wondrously large body of poetry, considering the relatively small circle of the Court. Not surprisingly, given the quantity, the quality of the poems varied from richness with a high-spirited, witty gusto to sloppiness and mannered indifference. Perhaps the best measure of the strength of the early classical period is not the number of poems written but the slowness with which the next age developed. The great writers of the mid-classical period appear not at its beginning but at its very end, and even the greatest of these poets write for the most part in the earlier Fujiwara style. Because of the slow, difficult transition to the new poetic age, any description of its poetry must begin with a historical account. Much of the effort of this journey to a new age is reflected in the emergence of literary criticism and its attendant disagreements. Tsurayuki's Preface to the *Kokin-shū* had been more an apology for Japanese poetry than true criticism, but the very eloquence of his statement made later poets search their art and their aims carefully before diverging from what they had inherited. To be a poet in this new period meant to be a critic and a scholar as well, and our historical sketch of poetic developments must include a discussion of the esthetics and poetics, and occasionally the Court politics, adhered to by the major poets—who were often at loggerheads with each other. Once the history of the development and the esthetic of the age are clear, poetic techniques and meanings are relatively easy to understand.

If there is any one word to characterize the poetry of the mid-classical period at its best, it is "depth." To some degree the depth derives from a complexity of technique, but the subjectivity lent poetry by the preceding period is absorbed by the new techniques, and charges them with a kind of resonance often belied by what on the surface is an easy intelligibility. When a poem seems to present us with description, we are apt to take the imagistic beauty of the poem at face value and to miss the deeper implications. A poem by Fujiwara Teika (1162–1241) on "The Moon" well illustrates this problem (*ShokuSIS*, VIII: 606).

Mukashi omou	I recollect the past:
Kusa ni yatsururu	Through my broken eaves now overgrown
Nokiba yori	With heavy grasses,
Arishi nagara no	The moon streams down as ever
Aki no yo no tsuki.	Radiant through the autumn night.

The speaker of this poem is clearly a lonely old man thinking of better days (the "broken eaves" being a synecdoche for a pitiable hut). If we took this at face value as the meaning of the poem, we would not be wrong; and yet there are two questions that should come to mind, leading us more deeply into the poetic experience. The first concerns the relation between the moon and the meditations of the speaker, the second the relation between the natural imagery of the last four lines and the longing for the past—does the imagery function only as setting? The second question ought to be answered at once, since it is essentially a more general version of the first. Teika echoes a poem by his father, Fujiwara Shunzei (1114–1204), a fact which would not have escaped the notice of his contemporaries (*SKKS*, III: 201).

Mukashi omou	I recollect the past
Kusa no iori no	While the summer rain falls through the
Yoru no ame ni	dark
Namida na soe so	About my grass-thatched hut,
Yamahototogisu.	But *hototogisu,* singing at last among the hills,
	Do not call out a freshening of my tears.

Teika has changed the season and much of the imagery (the treatment of "grass" in each poem shows both the similarity and the change), but his poem swallows up much of the experience dealt with in his father's. We can see that the natural beauty of the scene serves only to remind the speaker that his own life is miserable. The poems share a lonely old speaker, pitiful sur-roundings, and darkness, as well as a beauty apart from the speaker—the bird, the moon—which serves to heighten the prevailing sadness. The relation between the moon and the speaker is made even richer by an allusion to Narihira's famous poem on the seemingly changed spring and moon so much at variance with his own love-fixed self. (For discussion and translation, see p. 193.) The allusion to Narihira's very complex poem has both a general and a limiting effect. Generally, the allusion unifies Teika's poem at a second depth, as it were, by stressing the distinction between the speaker and the moon—it affirms the sad laws of human change and misery and the law of constancy in change that governs such a beautiful natural object as the moon. The allusion also acts to limit our associations; since Narihira's poem concerns the effects of love on man, the allusion implies that one of the major aspects of the past lost by Teika's speaker is love.

Nor is this all. Not only does the recollection of Narihira's poem suggest an emotionalism mingled with an acceptance of the natural laws by which man is bound, but Shunzei's poem too has an allusion that is carried over into Teika's. Po Chü-i had written: "In a grass hut on a rainy night at Mount Lu" ("Lu-shan yü yeh tsao an chung"). From this famous line, the custom grew of saying that the beauty of Mount Lu is best appreciated in the rain.

Shunzei takes the beauty of night, rain, and hills and the image of the hut and makes them sad by having them apprehended by an aged speaker, meanwhile transferring the beauty of the mountain to the Japanese bird whose song is so seldom heard. Teika accepts the basic alteration in Shunzei's poem, and chooses as his beauty the moon, thus recalling Narihira's poem as well as Shunzei's echo of Po Chü-i. The effect is depth, and depth achieved by specific detail charged with meaning as well as by general recollection. A single word in Teika's poem—*mukashi,* "the past"—takes on ever-widening dimensions of meaning: the speaker's personal past, the past of the speaker of Shunzei's poem, the past of the speaker of Narihira's poem, and the past of the Chinese poet.

Such allusive depth shows the extent to which a poem of this age is often neoclassical, since it may be fully appreciated and understood only through a knowledge of earlier portions of the Sino-Japanese literary tradition. In some respects, Teika's poem is richer and in some respects less satisfactory for us than other poems of this period, or of earlier or later periods. A Western reader may find it difficult to feel the force of allusions to Shunzei, Narihira, and Po Chü-i, and to the extent that the allusions fail to stir the reader, the allusive poetry of this age is the product of an alien culture. But at the same time, the more one learns of Japanese poetry, the more one is aware of the depths of such a poem as Teika's. True, such poetry runs the risk of seeming precious and detached from immediate human experience. These are the faults and the limitations of the age—the poetry, at its worst, is excessively refined and lacks the high spirits and vitality of the preceding period. But the virtues of each age are as much a part of its character as its faults. The flowers and weeds of poetry grow from the same soil.

The poetic depths of the mid-classical period are true human depths, but, as our illustration has shown, they must be plumbed by literary means. It is no accident that Shunzei and Teika were poets, critics, and scholars at the same time. They knew their tradition as Milton and Dryden knew the classical Roman and Greek authors, and, like these English poets, they found a way of ordering their experience through literary art. Fortunately, the great Japanese poets usually do not smell of books: their poems make sense in terms of the words themselves without recourse to the learned notes. Underneath their neoclassical temper of mind, moreover, lies an essential seriousness of attitude that can be contrasted, according to one's likes, favorably or unfavorably with the high-spirited wit of the preceding age. But a choice between the two is as unnecessary as one between Donne and Pope—both are part of one tradition and answer to different human and poetic needs.

The serious nature of this poetry grows out of the changed nature of human experience. The imperial Court had been at its zenith in the preceding age, and now was reduced to playing an increasingly impotent role in government. Yet, although superfluous in the society, the Court remained pre-eminent in culture and prestige. The change led courtiers to endeavor to sustain themselves and to reconcile their present position with their happier past by drawing upon the resources of their cultural tradition. Along with this cultural development, the influence of esoteric Buddhism helped lead to an idea of poetry as a "way of life" (*michi*). Theoretically at least, a farmer who pursued his way of life wholeheartedly, a shopkeeper who sold honest goods, and a poet who gave himself up to his art were all faithful adherents to their separate "ways." But poetry had a longer tradition, was more articulate, and was felt to be inherently superior to many other vocations. Such poets as Shunzei and Teika devoted themselves throughout their long lives to an art which was so important that even other, lesser poets would risk all they had for it. When Shunzei was selecting poems for the *Senzaishū* (completed ca. 1188) at the command of Emperor Shirakawa, he found that almost everybody who had written verse wanted to achieve poetic immortality in his anthology. A former student of his, Taira Tadanori (1144–84), risked his life to come to the capital, now full of Minamoto soldiers, with the request that Shunzei look over a hundred poems and choose one which would be suitable for the anthology. He promised to look them over, and Tadanori went gratefully off to his death in the great battle at Ichinotani. After this battle the Taira family was crushed, and, what with the Minamoto warriors hunting down the survivors, Shunzei's famed impartiality and catholicity of taste were put to the test—should he select one of Tadanori's poems? He was evidently a humane realist, for he selected one and listed it "Anonymous."

The inclusion of a poem in an anthology did not bring the poet money or even fame in the modern sense of wide recognition. But normal human vanity, adulation of imperial sponsorship, a desire to create something lasting for one's family, and an urge for poetic immortality led many people to the risks taken by Tadanori. One lady is said to have sacrificed her virtue and a man to have promised to the gods half his allotted life span, each merely to get a single poem into an imperial anthology. Such stories have an apocryphal sound to the modern ear, but even the ascetic, if robust, poet-priest Saigyō (1118–90) kept pressing Shunzei and Teika with poems for consideration. Poetry, calligraphy, and ceremonial music were clearly arts taken with the level of seriousness that human beings attach only to the things they deem most important in life. Poetry had truly become a way of life that transcended life, a serious business with religious overtones. The attitude of the poets was naturally reflected in the poetry itself and in the fervor of critical disputes over literary principles, techniques, and ideals. It should be no surprise to us, therefore, to discover that the poetry which survives from this period is almost without exception formal in nature, that it is poetry composed with profound earnestness and complete attention to the critical requirements of the style employed. The tanka is still the poetic norm, but there is a consciousness that the various styles inherited, altered, and created by the age have a decorum of technique which makes them suitable for differing occasions. Even the poets most given to innovation, originality, or divergence from the usual styles often compose poems in ordinary modes. A group of a hundred poems—a common unit in this age—by such original poets as Shunzei, Saigyō, or Teika exemplify widely varying styles for variety and, perhaps, for display of one's virtuosity as well as adherence to decorum.

The age, then, was not only serious and neoclassical, but full of experiment from beginning to end. In the first part of the period, the experimentation often entailed eccentric efforts to break through the circumscribed Fujiwara style by employing a new freedom of diction or treatment—at least in certain kinds of poems. Shunzei and Teika, the two great figures at the height of the period, lived to the unusually advanced ages of ninety and seventy-nine, steadily developing their poetic powers and seeking to create poems that realized their changing poetic ideals. And not infrequently, their tastes ran counter to the prevailing standards held by the more conservative writers and adhered to by the powerful emperors who had retired only to be free to exercise greater political and literary authority.

For if everyone accepted the view that the vocation of the poet was a way of life, not everyone would agree on the proper styles or techniques of poetry. Looking at the accomplishments of the age from the vantage point of time, we can, however, see two more or less common elements that help give the poetry its particular character. The descriptive mode assumes an importance it did not have in the preceding age, but only because techniques were found to harmonize the subjective observer and the objective materials he employed. The new balance of the personal and impersonal and the new means of integrating seeming poetic fragments are very complex, but it is clear enough that the subjectivity of the preceding age was retained in altered form, and that the external world was often rendered pertinent to the speaker by making natural details symbolic or otherwise reflective of human experience. The other common element in the poetry of the period is the consciousness of the past. The many little anthologies of selections from earlier poets and the study of the *Man'yōshū* that led to a fuller understanding of its accomplishment are but two symptoms of this tendency. There was no writing of any kind of poetry without a knowledge of the best writing of the past. The most important anthology of this period, the *Shinkokinshū*, shows in its title ("The New Kokinshū") the deliberate attempt to emulate and, to some extent, to improve upon the first imperial anthology. And as Teika's poem indicates, we cannot appreciate the poetry of this age without a knowledge of antecedent native and Chinese poetry. Such neoclassicism raises a problem which the writers of this age—like Dryden, Pope, and Dr. Johnson—were well aware of: namely, the proper balance between tradition and originality. After considerable experimentation and debate early in the period, the solution came to be the one iterated by Shunzei and Teika, "old diction, new treatment." But the Japanese—"kotoba furuku, kokoro atarashi"—implies much more than "diction" and "treatment." It may be said that the meaning, or rather the changing meanings, of these words and the transmutation of these ideals into poetry epitomize the history of the accomplishment of the age.

THE FORMATION OF A NEW ESTHETIC

By the beginning of the twelfth century nearly two hundred years had passed since the compiling of the *Kokinshū*. The first three imperial anthologies, the *Kokinshū*, the *Gosenshū*, and the *Shūishū*, had achieved the status of canonical works, with the result that the ideals of Tsurayuki and his contemporaries had been more than realized. Any deviation from the standard of poetic diction that they had established, any attempt to add more than a slight touch of novelty of detail within the framework of established modes and conventional treatment could be, and often was, decried as a revolt against orthodoxy. The robustness and uninhibited vigor of Komachi and Narihira were no longer possible to poets in an age when every new creation had to be measured against the accepted standards of two centuries.

This is not to say that poetry was now hopelessly fossilized, but only that change was slow, that new elements of diction, new modes, and new ideals of beauty had to undergo a period of probation before they were finally accepted as suitable for formal poetry. Further, most of the changes that resulted in the most original poetry of the age were neoclassical in inspiration. Every serious poet must now be a scholar as well as a poet, and it was largely to the great monuments of the past—the *Man'yōshū* and the first three imperial anthologies as well as the poetry of China—that the age turned for inspiration in creating its new ideals. Yet the conservative impulse was so strong during the mid-classical period that departure from accepted norms inevitably encountered stubborn opposition. A marked feature of the new age is the controversy and factionalism between innovators and traditionalists which replaced the poetic homogeneity of the early classical period.

The disputes between rival poets involved personal animosities, family pride, and worldly ambition fully as much, often more, than differences of opinion regarding poetry. The split between the reactionaries on the one hand and the innovators on the other first developed at the end of the preceding period, when Fujiwara Michitoshi (1047–99) and Minamoto Tsunenobu (1016–97) competed for official recognition as the poetic arbiters of their day and for the honor of compiling the fourth imperial anthology, the *Goshūishū* (1086); the reactionaries won, Tsunenobu, the innovator, losing out to Michitoshi. The competition was carried on with even greater animosity between the arch-conservative Fujiwara Mototoshi (1056–1142) and Tsunenobu's son Shunrai (or Toshiyori, ?1057–1129) at the beginning of the twelfth century. Shunrai made up for his father's failure to achieve the coveted honor of compiling an imperial anthology by being himself named compiler of the fifth imperial anthology, the *Kin'yōshū* (1124–27). (However, he was compelled to revise it twice before ex-Emperor Shirakawa would accept it.) Such poetic strife was continued into the late twelfth century and the early thirteenth. The principal competitors were members of two branches of the Fujiwara: the venerable and scholarly Rokujō family became the principal rivals of the great innovating poets Shunzei (or Toshinari) and his son Teika (or Sadaie), representatives of the Mikosa or Nijō family. A member of the Rokujō family, Akisuke (1090–1155), was the compiler of the sixth imperial anthology, the *Shikashū* (ca. 1151–54), whereas Shunzei compiled the seventh, the *Senzaishū* (ca. 1188). To compile the *Shinkokinshū,* the next anthology and the greatest of the age (compiled in 1206 and later revised), ex-Emperor Go-Toba (1180–1239) appointed a committee comprising members of both factions, including Teika, but retained the dominant role himself in the selection of poems. Teika, however, achieved recognition as the outstanding poet of his time when he alone was given the honor of compiling the ninth imperial anthology, the *Shinchokusenshū* (ca. 1234), thus becoming the first person ever to participate in the compilation of two imperial collections.

Although the age was one of many kinds of controversy, of competition for the honor of being appointed a compiler of an imperial anthology or a judge at a poetry contest, there were certain basic conceptions of poetry that were held by reactionaries and innovators alike. Poetry was now in fact a mature, even venerable art; it was assiduously studied as a way of life; it was a symbol of the cultural superiority of the aristocracy in a period when their political powers had been all but lost. The young Teika was expressing a semi-religious dedication to poetry typical of his age when in the year 1180, at the height of the epic struggles between the great warrior clans, the Taira and the Minamoto, he wrote in his diary a paraphrase of some lines of Po Chü-i: "My ears are full of tales about the current uprisings and the campaigns to quell them, but I pay no attention to them. 'The chastisement of the red banner of the insurgents is no concern of mine.'" The informal social role of poetry of course continued in this age, and it was still expected that any lady or gentleman should be able to toss off impromptu verses appropriate to the situation of the moment. But such informal verse lost status as the composition of poetry became an end in itself; the occasions that called for impromptu verse had in the course of the early classical period become thoroughly established as conventional topics (dai) for formal poetry as well, and in the new age it was the formal poetry composed on fixed topics that was taken seriously and considered most worthy of inclusion in the imperial anthologies.

In addition, all poets came to be concerned with subtle distinctions in the decorum and conventions of poetry for different occasions. Not only was poetry almost always a virtuoso performance on a given topic or theme, but there were now many levels of formality, alternative styles for the treatment of a given topic, and kinds of decorum depending upon the occasion for which the poem was composed. The occasions of formal poetry varied greatly—from relatively intimate exchanges with a friend or patron (who could be depended upon to view one's experiments with sympathy) to ritualized poetry contests sponsored by high Court nobles or members of the imperial family. The increasingly popular sequences of twenty, thirty, fifty, or, most often, a hundred poems were composed as practice exercises, for the inspection of friends, for poetry parties of varying degrees of formality, and sometimes at imperial command. Such sequences, which usually echoed the imperial anthologies in the choice of topics and the relative number of poems on each, had been assayed by two or three poets as far back as the tenth century. But their real vogue began with the *Horikawa-In Ontoki Hyakushu Waka,* or "Hundred-Poem Sequences Composed During the Reign of Ex-Emperor Horikawa," submitted on imperial command by sixteen prominent poets sometime between 1099 and 1104. The detailed specification of topics for these poems—a separate one for each of the hundred—was unprecedented and set the fashion for numerous later sequences composed on both formal and informal occasions.

The poetry contests were the most important formal social occasions for poetry in the period, with the result that the decisions made by the judges were most influential in shaping the generally accepted standards of the age. Approximately two hundred formal competitions, held at the imperial palace, in the mansions of the great, and at various shrines and temples, are recorded for the years between 1087 and 1199, and there may have been many more. The competitions differed considerably in their degree of formality and in such details as the number of participating poets, the number of judges, the number of "rounds," and the choice of topics. They even inspired such curious variants as the *jikaawase,* or "personal poetry competitions," for which a single poet would select his own topics, compose all the poems, and request some friend or authority to judge the winning poem for each round. The great formal competitions of the twelfth and thirteenth centuries took on a major importance in the eyes of every serious poet because they were the principal means, apart from having one or more poems chosen for an imperial anthology, of achieving poetic fame. The judges (of whom there might be one, two, or several, depending on the occasion) were chosen from among the most distinguished poets of the day. Not only was it an honor to be invited to participate: it was a matter of vital importance and keen competition, especially when, as occasionally happened, it was generally understood that one object in holding the contest was to assemble material for possible inclusion in an imperial anthology. The topics for such important contests as the *Roppyakuban Utaawase,* or "Poetry Contest in 600 Rounds," of 1193, and the great *Sengohyakuban Utaawase,* or "Poetry Contest in 1,500 Rounds," sponsored by ex-Emperor Go-Toba in 1201, were handed out months in advance. The participants were selected with much argument and discussion; the judges' decisions were sometimes appealed in formal letters of protest to the sponsors and occasionally changed. In general a desperate atmosphere prevailed. Shunzei, for example, was probably chosen as sole judge for the *Roppyakuban Utaawase* largely because he was the man most acceptable to all factions, but his decisions were nevertheless publicly attacked by the Rokujō poet Kenjō (fl. 1161–1207).

Although some of the poetry contests of the twelfth century produced lively disagreement between the judges, not to mention protests from the judged, the basis of criticism at these *utaawase* was almost entirely negative. However liberal he might be in less formal contexts, every poet tended to become a conservative when in the role of judge. The emphasis was on finding some technical flaw or violation of precedent that could serve to disqualify a poem, rather than on encouraging innovation. Such an attitude led in time to the development of a particularly rigid decorum, which gained wide acceptance for the *utaawase.* Shunzei, who was the first critic to bring positive standards into the formal context of the *utaawase,* fully supported the notion that such highly formal occasions called for a much greater adherence to precedent than occasions of a more informal kind. He even extended this rule to the personal poetry contest, presumably by reasoning that in such a case the very use of the *utaawase* form made it incumbent on the individual poet to observe the decorum of the public occasion.

Such was the import of Shunzei's detailed comment when, in 1189 or shortly before, his close friend the great poet-priest Saigyō sent him his famous *Poetry Contest at the Mimosuso River (Mimosusogawa Utaawase).* It consisted of thirty-six rounds in which Saigyō pitted his poems against each other under the fictional device of a contest between the "Visitor to the Mountain Hut" and the "Master of the Path Across the Moors." Saigyō's first poem in the eleventh round ran (Minegishi Yoshiaki, ed., *Utaawaseshū,* p. 346):

Tachikawaru	As if to say
Haru o shire to mo	By the expression on its face
Misegao ni	"Spring will return
Toshi o hedatsuru	When I rise again," the haze
Kasumi narikeri.	Has been absent for a year.

Shunzei commented: "The effect of this poem is in harmony with the conception, but the words 'by the expression on its face' (*misegao ni*) are questionable. I use these words in poems, and so does everyone else, but nevertheless I feel that they should still be avoided in the context of a poetry contest. Of course this also depends to some extent upon the requirements of the particular style chosen." In other words, Shunzei would have allowed Saigyō to use the faintly colloquial expression *misegao ni* in poetry written for other occasions, but he considered it indecorous for a real *utaawase,* and even if a poet chose to compete with himself, the conventions held. The degree of freedom with which a poet might treat a given topic was therefore not simply a matter of factional controversy: if he wished his poem to be acceptable even to his admirers, he must fit his style and diction to the formal level of the occasion.

By no means every poet would have agreed with Shunzei in the particular instance we have cited, and we have not done him justice in singling out this one pronouncement. He fulfilled the unique role of harmonizing, at the height of his career, the many different ideals and standards of his age, and developed from earlier poets a poetic that was inherited by the next two generations of poets (including his son Teika), whose practice frequently showed less disagreement than their theory. The gradual emergence of new styles marks the poetry of even the arch-conservatives, just as every innovator composed many highly conventional poems.

The adaptation to the native poetry of certain techniques and ideals of Chinese poetry appears in this age, no less than in the early classical period, to account for some important changes common to all schools. During most of the twelfth century, the poetry of the mid-T'ang dynasty, especially that of Po Chü-i, retained overwhelming popularity, although by the time of Teika late T'ang and perhaps even Sung (960-1279) poetry had begun to exert a growing influence upon the ideals and practice of the Japanese innovators. It was, however, a gradually increasing acceptance of mid-T'ang poetry on its own terms rather than of later Chinese poetry that resulted, together with a new understanding and appreciation of the *Man'yōshū,* in a growing acceptance of descriptive poetry as a kind worthy of respect, one having its own "elegance" to qualify it for formal occasions.

A major contributing role in creating the new descriptive poetry appears to have been played by the practice of *kudai waka,* or "poems on the topics of quotations from Chinese poems," described briefly in the preceding chapter (see pp. 197–98). Given the prestige of a line from Po Chü-i, and the obvious elegance in composing an allusive variation upon it, the *kudai waka,* however plain and devoid of elaborate rhetoric or involuted conceits, might be accorded a certain value which would not be allowed such plainness under other circumstances. The Chinese topic might of course be handled in various ways, and a line of descriptive Chinese verse frequently inspired a Japanese variation in typical Fujiwara style. Nevertheless, the poet might also choose to make his Japanese poem a reasonably accurate translation of the Chinese line, in which case the descriptive character of the model would inevitably be reflected in the Japanese poem. A tenth-century example is the following from the *Daini Takatō Shū*, based on the line, "The sun is warm and the men calmly fish" ("Jih nuan jen hsien t'iao") (*Katsura Series*, II, 280).

Yamakawa wa	The thin ice
Haru no usurai	Of early spring is melted
Tokenikeri	In the mountain brook,
Kokoro nodoka ni	Where, with their hearts composed,
Hito no tsuri suru.	The men now calmly fish.

The practice of composing *kudai waka* increased greatly in popularity during the eleventh century and helped the descriptive mode gain acceptance as suitable to formal poetry. By the time of the *Goshūishū*, the fourth imperial anthology completed in 1086, a few such relatively plain descriptive poems were beginning to find their way into the official collections. The fifth imperial anthology, the *Kin'yōshū*, compiled between 1124 and 1127, contains, in spite of its small size (ten scrolls and only 716 poems), a slightly higher percentage of descriptive poems; and the *Shikashū*, compiled about 1151–54, which is even smaller than the *Kin'yōshū* (ten scrolls but only 411 poems), contains more descriptive poetry than any of its predecessors. This does not mean, of course, that descriptive poetry was now all-popular, but it does indicate that it was gaining acceptance as one—if not necessarily the most esteemed —of the sanctioned modes.

The fact that the *Shikashū* was compiled by Fujiwara Akisuke, a member of the poetically conservative Rokujō family, is significant because it shows that the descriptive mode was promoted by conservatives as well as innovators. Indeed, to state the facts somewhat more fairly, the growing preference for descriptive poetry appears to have developed largely within, rather than in opposition to, the conservative group. Minamoto Shunrai, the leading innovator of the early twelfth century and the compiler of the *Kin'yōshū*, composed very successfully in the descriptive mode; but to judge from the nature of the majority of his innovating poems, he was far less enthusiastic about this new style than were his conservative opponents (or even his innovating father, Tsunenobu). In this respect he was resisting one of the major trends of his age. If the innovating poets in the following generation were able to compose their richest poetry in the descriptive mode, they may be fairly said to have built fully as much upon the heritage of the conservatives of the early twelfth century as upon the legacy of Shunrai.

The acceptance of descriptive poetry was, then, a development common to all schools. The most drastic points of controversy between conservatives and innovators in the first half of the twelfth century were largely matters of diction and of conventional versus unconventional treatment of accepted topics, and it is these problems that claim our attention.

The recognition of poetry as the highest of the arts and the growing seriousness with which it came to be regarded combined during the twelfth century with the deeply rooted aristocratic emphasis upon hereditary rights and privileges to produce for the first time what might be called true poetic families or houses. Or perhaps the term "school" would be more appropriate, because although the traditions of scholarship as well as of poetic ideals and practice were indeed handed down within a family, they were also communicated to outsiders who were received as pupils or disciples. Not every poet was a member of such a school: emperors, ex-emperors, courtiers of the highest rank, and certain other independent but influential poets like Saigyō remained aloof from such formal ties. At the same time schools were patronized by great lords and members of the imperial family, and helped to form the tastes of those whose prerogative it was to designate the poets who would be given the honor of compiling imperial anthologies or participating in the formal *uta-awase*. Competition between schools was therefore very keen, especially when family honor was at stake, and the arguments between schools should properly be set against a background of family antagonisms and political intrigue. Fortunately, such conditions did not lead in this period, as they did two and a half centuries later, to the monopoly of poetry by a single school and the stultification of the tradition. Nevertheless the trend toward the feudalization of poetry had already begun.

It is significant that the conservative, scholarly Rokujō school—the first real poetic "house," founded by Fujiwara Akisue (1055–1123)—was opposed by the innovator Minamoto Shunrai, a member of a different though noble clan. In other words, an attack upon the dominant Fujiwara style in poetry might very easily take on nuances of an attack upon the declining Fujiwara supremacy in the social and political spheres. Shunrai was able to attain the status of one of the most universally honored and respected poets of his day at least partly thanks to the influence and prestige of his father, Tsunenobu, who had held the position of Grand Counsellor and the second Court rank. Tsunenobu probably achieved such high estate owing to the favor of the determined and capable Emperor Go-Sanjō (1034–73) and his son, Emperor Shirakawa (1053–1129), whose policy it was to curb or, if possible, to break the power of the Fujiwara by governing their own courts as ex-emperors. To such ends they often included among their advisors representatives of other clans.

Shunrai did not prosper in a worldly way as his father had done: he apparently never rose above the minor and faintly ludicrous position of Director of the Bureau of Carpentry and Repairs for the Imperial Household. But although his personal poetry collection, the *Samboku Kikashū,* is full of lamentations on his low estate, he did attain late in life a public honor that had been denied his father. Tsunenobu, along with other "senior" poets, had been passed over by Emperor Shirakawa in favor of Fujiwara Michitoshi (1047–99), a much younger man, when, in 1075, the compiler of the fourth imperial anthology, the *Goshūishū*, was designated. Tsunenobu vented his rage and set a precedent for polemical criticism by writing a tract entitled *Errors in the Goshūishū* (*Nan Goshūi*), in which he attempted to discredit Michitoshi's judgment by pointing out as many defects as possible in the poems selected. Yet the same Shirakawa honored Shunrai in 1124 by appointing him the compiler of the fifth anthology, the *Kin'yōshū*. It has been traditionally held that this was due to an attack of bad conscience on Shirakawa's part for his neglect of Tsunenobu, and in fact Shunrai was under such constraint to please the ex-emperor and not unduly offend the conservatives that he had to consider personalities as well as poems in making his selection. As we have noted, he had to revise the collection twice before his royal patron would accept it, each time apparently deleting some of the newer, more unconventional poems and adding others by older, more conventional poets. Shirakawa, however, can scarcely have failed to foresee that his choice would be resented in any event by the conservative Fujiwara group, and one suspects that his decision was swayed by political considerations. Indeed, when the *Kinyōshū* was finally accepted by Shirakawa and made official, it evoked a storm of protest: according to tradition it was given various uncomplimentary nicknames, and the poet Fujiwara Akinaka (fl. ca. 1100–1125) is said to have put together a work in ten books (unfortunately not extant) called the *Collection of Genuine Jewels* (*Ryōgyokushū*), in which he heaped scorn on the anthology.

To the extent that Shunrai's unconventional ideals and practice may have been in part an expression of frustrated personal ambition and discontent, he reminds us of the eccentric Sone no Yoshitada, who had delighted in shocking Kintō and his circle with "vulgar" poems a century and a half before. The resemblance is not only one of social position and motivation: although Shunrai composed in various styles and modes, he seems to have had, like Yoshitada, a marked preference for poems whose chief effects were novelty and surprise. Most conspicuous among his techniques was the deliberate use of colloquial diction or even slang, "low" images, and startling metaphors. Indeed, it is quite probable that Shunrai admiringly imitated the practice of Yoshitada, as the following poem on the "Spirit of Love" (*Samboku Kikashū* in *K. Taikei*, XIII, 633) suggests.

Iisomeshi	Do those tender words
Kotoba to nochi no	You spoke to me when first we loved
Kokoro to wa	And your feelings now
Sore ka aranu ka	Agree as they did then, or not?—
Inu ka karasu ka.	Is a white dog a black crow?

Now dogs and crows were eventually admitted into the Japanese poetic vocabulary, partly because the work of people like Yoshitada and Shunrai tended to be gradually (though grudgingly) accepted with the passing of time, but more important because such images were used by Chinese poets of the mid- and late T'ang dynasty, and this gave them a certain attractiveness to later generations who read more widely in Chinese poetry. But the acceptance of such images was not to come until nearly a hundred years after Shunrai, and the Fujiwara esthetes of his day were just as horrified at this sort of thing as Fujiwara Nagatō had been at Yoshitada's image of "mugwort corded into piles." True, the wit and play on logic in this poem might have amused the conservatives, but no poet of the old school would have taken the verse seriously. If it had ever occurred to Tsurayuki to include such a composition in the *Kokinshū,* he would have consigned it summarily to the limbo of haikai. Shunrai, however, to judge from the large number of such poems he chose to include in his personal anthology, appears to have been sincere in the conviction that this was the best of all styles. That he was really earnest in his attempts to create serious art from "vulgar" or even comic materials is perhaps best shown by the fact that he dared to flaunt such compositions in the face of an emperor by including them among the poems which he submitted as one of the honored participants on the highly formal occasion of the "Hundred-Poem Sequences Composed During the Reign of Ex-Emperor Horikawa." His poem on the topic of "Love on a Journey," for example, runs as follows (*SZS*, XVIII: 1189).

Shitaikuru	Is it because
Koi no yatsuko no	To be love's coolie has become
Tabi nite mo	A habit I am stuck with,
Mi no kuse nare ya	That even on a journey it wells up,
Yūtodoroki wa.	This day's-end clatter banging in my breast?

Judged by the standards of Court poetry, the diction of the poem is inelegant to the point of vulgarity. The words *yatsuko, kuse,* and *yūtodoroki* are the offenders: the first is a low expression meaning "coolie" or "serf"; the second is a colloquialism for "habit"; and the third not only is a very strong colloquialism for the excitement of anticipation as the time approaches for the evening tryst with the beloved, but also implies the vulgar noises made at dusk by commoners or peasants, perhaps in a nearby country village, when they have come home from the day's work and are banging doors and windows, shouting back and forth in uncouth accents, and making a general commotion. Nevertheless, such images are found in Chinese poetry, and Shunrai must have had the inner conviction that such verses should be regarded as serious poetry, and the hope that some day they would be. As the citation indicates, this particular poem was actually included by Shunzei in the *Senzaishū*, the imperial anthology he compiled in 1187–88. But Shunrai would surely have been more chagrined than honored had he lived to know about it, for Shunzei placed the poem not where Shunrai would have wished it, in one of the books of love poetry, but among a group of haikai verses.

Another area in which poets of all persuasions were in general agreement but in which Shunrai displayed marked individuality was in their attitude toward the *Man'yōshū*. Most of the serious poets of his day, conservatives and innovators alike, studied the ancient collection with renewed enthusiasm and with somewhat more understanding than had been possible in the days of Tsurayuki and Kintō. It is doubtful whether more than three or four hundred Man'yō poems could actually be read with accuracy until the commentaries of the priest Senkaku (1203–?) laid the foundations of modern Man'yō scholarship, and in his poetical treatise Shunrai betrays his ignorance of what a sedōka is. Probably the 196 poems discussed by Shunzei in his *Korai Fūteishō*, or *Notes on Poetic Style Through the Ages*, approximate the number with which most poets were familiar. Nevertheless, no small part of the tradition of literary scholarship that grew up within the conservative Rokujō school and overshadowed poetic creativity as its main concern was based upon an esoteric knowledge of the *Man'yōshū*, and it became increasingly acceptable to cite precedents from the older collection as well as from the *Kokinshū* and other imperial anthologies as authority for unusual poetic materials or treatment. But if there was a general agreement that the *Man'yōshū* was a repository of great poetry worthy of the most serious study, there was considerable disagreement concerning the poetic uses to which such knowledge should be put. Shunrai's *Samboku Kikashū* contains a large number of poems that employ archaic words and phrases from the *Man'yōshū*, giving clear evidence that he recognized a positive value in employing this older diction for its effect of novelty, of solemnity, or of primitive simplicity. The conservatives, however, remained for the most part committed to the standard of the *Kokinshū* and followed the lead of Kintō, who had warned against the use, except in unusual circumstances, of such archaic phrases as the exclamatory particles *ka mo* and the adjective suffix *rashi* ("it seems"). (Cf. *Shinsen Zuinō* in *NKGT*, I, 116.) Occasional allusions to Man'yō poems were greatly appreciated, provided, of course, that they were easily recognizable, and the collection furnished a treasure-trove of recondite lore for the delight of pedants. As far as poetic practice was concerned, however, the conservative view was that while the *Man'yōshū* should be read and admired, its language was too old, too *mimitōshi* or "distant to the ear," for contemporary use.

The older conservative point of view was taken over by the innovators in the so-called age of the *Shinkokinshū*—the two generations represented by

Shunzei and Teika—so much so, in fact, that Shunzei was criticized by the traditionalists for his lukewarm attitude toward the collection. Against this background the celebrated Man'yō style affected by the young Minamoto shogun Sanetomo (1192–1219) stands out glaringly. (Sanetomo's style is discussed later in this chapter, pp. 329–37.) Sanetomo studied poetry under the tutelage of Teika, who delighted his young pupil with the present of a copy of part of the Man'yōshū. Further, Teika had a greater admiration for the Man'yōshū than had Shunzei, and some of his most famous compositions are allusive variations on Man'yō poems. It might therefore be imagined that Teika encouraged Sanetomo in his efforts to emulate the Man'yō style. The truth is quite otherwise, however. In what is perhaps the most important critical writing of the age—a letter written to one of his pupils (most probably Sanetomo, although the matter is in dispute) and known as the Maigetsushō, or Monthly Notes—Teika warned his young disciple emphatically against such experimentation. After an elegant introduction in which he praises extravagantly the most recent monthly batch of poems sent him for criticism by his pupil, Teika gets down to serious business (NKGT, III, 346–47):

Now then, as I have written to you numerous times, you should peruse at leisure the several imperial anthologies from the Man'yōshū down to the present and reach an understanding of the ways in which the various styles have changed with the passage of time. When you do this, however, it does not mean that you should necessarily take every single poem as a model simply because it is in an imperial anthology. Rise and decline can be observed in poetry depending on the quality of the poets and the vicissitudes of the times. As for the Man'yōshū, it represents a very ancient age when the hearts of men were unsophisticated, so that even if we try to emulate it, we cannot possibly succeed in this present generation. It is especially important for a novice that he not permit himself to become enamored of the archaic style. I do indeed feel that it is very bad for a poet not to be acquainted with the Man'yō style after many years of practice have enabled him to consolidate his own individual poetic manner. Yet even though you may compose in this style when your period of training is over, you should be careful, perhaps, for there are words and effects that you should not use in your poems under any circumstances. What I mean by words and effects that should not be used under any circumstances are those which are too close to the common and vulgar or those which are frightening. I need not settle this matter with you while you are still at your present stage of development. Please infer my reasons for this by reading between the lines. Since there are a great many poems in the archaic style in the hundred-poem sequence which you last sent me, I fear that you may be offended by what I say. Nevertheless, for the time being you should discipline yourself not to compose in this style. During the next year or two, at least, you should practice until you are able to compose without difficulty in the fundamental styles.

    Those styles I have called "fundamental" are the following four of the ten styles about which I have written to you previously: the "style of mystery and depth" [*yūgen'yō*], the "style of universally acceptable statement" [*koto shikarubeki yō*], the "style of elegant beauty" [*uruwashiki yō*], and the "style of intense feeling" [*ushintei*]. It is true that we occasionally find, even among these, poems which have archaic elements, but the over-all effect is such that their archaic style is not displeasing. After you have developed the ability to compose freely in these gentle and amiable styles, such others as the "lofty style" [*taketakaki yō*], the "style of describing things as one sees them" [*ken'yō*], the "style of interesting treatment" [*omoshiroki yō*], the "style of novel treatment" [*hitofushi aru yō*], and the "style of exquisite detail" [*komayaka naru yō*] are quite easy to master. The "style of demon-quelling force" [*onihishigitei*] is difficult to learn, but after you have attained the necessary proficiency I see no reason why you cannot master that also. By stating things in this way I do not mean to imply that the "style of demon-quelling force" is superior to all the others, but simply that you must not attempt to compose in it while you are still a novice. The waka is first and foremost an art peculiar to Japan, the "land of peace," which is one reason, perhaps, why we find in the documents written in such detail by the great poets of old that it should be composed with gentleness and sensitivity. Indeed, no matter how fearful a thing may be of itself, if it is treated in a poem, it is made to sound graceful and elegant. That being the case, what advantage is there in treating such things as cherry blossoms and the moon, which are by nature gentle, as if they were frightening?

Of the ten styles distinguished by Teika, two require special consideration here because of their connection with the *Man'yōshū*: the "style of demon-quelling force" and, more important, the "lofty style." Because Teika provides no examples of poems with his ten categories, it is practically impossible in some cases to ascertain exactly what he means. However, it may be assumed that the "style of demon-quelling force" refers to poems whose imagery or treatment conveys an impression of violence. Such poems are found in particular in Book XVI of the *Man'yōshū*—Naga Okimaro's tour-de-force on the kettle of boiling water, the fox, and the bridge (*MYS*, XVI:3824; see above, p. 111) is a good example—and several of the poems by Sanetomo most extravagantly admired by modern critics would also fit into the category. The *Sangoki*, a late-thirteenth-century or early-fourteenth-century poetical treatise spuriously attributed to Teika, contains three examples of the "style of demon-quelling force," including the following anonymous poem (*NKGT*, IV, 327):

Kamikaze ya	Breaking off the reeds
Ise no hamaogi	That grow along the beach at Ise
Orishikite	Of the Divine Wind,
Tabine ya su ran	Does he spread them for his traveler's
Araki hamabe ni.	bed
	There on the rough sea-strand?

While the use of this poem in the *Sangoki* is no proof that Teika would have considered the example appropriate, it does show how certain poets who were still close to Teika in time interpreted the category of "demon-quelling force." The adjective "rough" (*araki*), perhaps the pillow-word *kamikaze ya* ("of the Divine Wind"), and the imagery of breaking off and spreading out coarse reeds for bedding appear to be the "demon-quelling" elements in the poem. To classify such a tame example in this fashion no doubt exhibits a lamentable want of spirit, but it shows, together with Teika's own words of caution, how alien to the taste of the mid- and late classical periods was the powerful imagery of much Man'yō poetry.

Unlike the "style of demon-quelling force," which was more to be avoided than practiced, the *taketakaki yō*, or "lofty style" was of very real importance for the mid-classical period. The style, which was also sometimes called *tōjiroki*, or "noble," was classified by Teika next to the four "fundamental styles." It contributed to the new popularity of descriptive poetry, and it was in poems in this style that the influence of Man'yō diction and imagery exerted itself most directly upon the poetic practice of the twelfth and thirteenth centuries. The style was particularly identified with Minamoto Tsunenobu, Shunrai's father; Emperor Juntoku (1197–1242) stated in his encyclopedic treatise on poetry, the *Yakumo Mishō,* that "it was only Tsunenobu who preserved the ancient style single-handed . . . but although he was without peer in this, no one would accept it as good" (*NKGT*, III, 90). Owing to Tsunenobu's efforts, however, the style gradually gained acceptance, and Shunrai carried on his father's work in maintaining that poems in the "lofty and noble" (*kedakaku tōjiroki*) style should hold first place in the scale of values (*NKGT*, I, 189). Although Shunrai's practice evinces a marked preference for poems whose effect is more striking, among his experiments in the Man'yō style it was the "lofty and noble" poems which had the greatest appeal both to his contemporaries and later to Shunzei and Teika; the following poem, for example, was accorded the honor of inclusion among the summer poems in the *Shinkokinshū* (*SKKS*, III: 266).

Tōchi ni wa	It looks as if
Yūdachi su rashi	A cooling summer shower will fall
Hisakata no	At distant Tōchi,
Ama no Kaguyama	For the Heavenly Hill of Kagu
Kumogakureyuku.	Is hidden by the rolling clouds.

Although the poem is not particularly distinguished, it is nonetheless a good illustration of the combination of Man'yō language with the mode of elevated declaration characteristic of the lofty style. The very setting of the poem evokes the world and the age of the *Man'yōshū,* for the Hill of Kagu was situated near the ancient capital of Fujiwara, and the village of Tōchi, like the old capital, was located in the province of Yamato. The use at the end of the second line of *rashi,* forbidden by Kintō as too archaic, and of the pillow-word *hisakata no* in the third line intensifies the antique flavor of the poem. The archaic diction and rhetoric, like the place names associated with a distant, romantic past, are interwoven with the imagery of the summer storm and dark clouds moving rapidly across the sky into a panorama of pleasing but awe-inspiring beauty. The conception of the poem in terms of cause and effect is relatively unobtrusive, and the mode is really one of elevated declaration that comes very close to descriptive poetry.

Such poems, which present a vast landscape in terms of "large" images and convey a tone of openness, grandeur, auspiciousness, and superiority to petty human affairs, were characteristic of the "lofty style"; and while the use of archaic diction, rhetoric, and imagery associated with a romantic past was not essential, it was one sure way of conveying the desired tone. The "lofty style" was considered especially suited for those solemn social occasions for which public poetry was still composed at court, and its auspicious character recommended it for such special functions as the style appropriate to the first poem in an imperial anthology. It was therefore expected that every poet should be able to compose in the style, and the solid position which it gained as one of the fundamental styles helped raise the status of descriptive poetry and encourage a more than passive interest in the *Man'yōshū.*

Like other versatile poets of his age, Shunrai composed in a variety of styles, and although his personal preference appears to have run, like that of the late Metaphysical poets in England, to the bizarre and the baroque, the poems for which he was admired by the next generation were, like the summer poem just quoted, more sober and conventional. Further, Shunrai's comments on poetry, particularly in his judgments at *utaawase* and in his long treatise on poetics known as *Shunrai's Secret Notes (Shumpishō* or *Shunrai Zuinō),* reflect a traditional conservatism. Nowhere, perhaps, is the conservatism of Shunrai's comments on poetry more in contrast with his unconventional efforts to achieve a novelty of conception in actual practice than in his critical judgments at the poetry contest known as the *Naidaijinke Utaawase* (1118), in which he showed himself as much a reactionary as the other judge, Fujiwara Mototoshi, Shunrai's great rival and the outstanding representative of the ultra-conservative group. One suspects that the sponsor of this contest, the great lord Fujiwara Tadamichi (1097–1164) must have been laughing up his sleeve at the prospect of a public confrontation between these two literary foes, who were unlikely to observe for very long the decorum proper to *utaawase,* or even to pretend that the proceedings were being conducted in an auspicious and harmonious atmosphere.

Tadamichi must have been delighted with the results. The contest is famous in the annals of *utaawase* for the extent and vehemence of disagreement between the judges: Shunrai and Mototoshi awarded the decision to the same poem or agreed on a draw in only about a third of the thirty-six rounds, and even when they agreed it was sometimes for conflicting reasons. A greater amount of tension than usual was generated because the judges were at the same time participants, and were placed in the position of having to comment on their own poems on each of the three topics selected for the contest ("Autumn Drizzle," "Chrysanthemums in Late Autumn," and "Love"). And although Shunrai contented himself, as judges at *utaawase* until the time of Shunzei nearly always did, with finding some disqualifying "fault" in the poems instead of emphasizing their good points, the tone in which his comments are expressed conveys the impression that he was really most concerned on this occasion with beating Mototoshi at his own game—with showing that he, too, could be as much of a pedant as his more scholarly but poetically ungifted adversary.

This impression becomes stronger when we consider the poems that Shunrai submitted for the contest (a contest, it should be noted, in which the authorship of the individual poems was not revealed until after the proceedings were over, even though the names of the participants were known). He could not have expected any of his poems to win: each contains at least one obvious "fault" which he surely knew would disqualify it. Shunrai did in fact disqualify all of his poems, calling for a draw only in the case of the third—which, ironically, was pitted against a composition by his fellow judge—because of his insistence that the competing poem was also guilty of a violation of conventional treatment. In other words, Shunrai's aim must have been to win a moral victory rather than a technical one: to demonstrate the sterility of Mototoshi's approach by disqualifying unconventional poems on technical grounds while damning the "faultless" ones with faint praise.

This strategy vindicated Shunrai in the eyes of posterity, and a marvelous bit of luck—an unfortunate slip on Mototoshi's part—made Shunrai's rival look foolish to contemporaries. Moreover, the round which assured the moral victory for Shunrai was precisely the one in which the two judges' poems were pitted against each other. In this round, one of twelve on the topic of "Love," Shunrai's poem was the following complaint from a lover to his cruel mistress (*Shinkō Gunsho Ruijū*, VIII, 532).

Kuchioshi ya	How mean can you get?—
Kumoigakure ni	Even the dragon who dwells concealed
Sumu tatsu mo	In the region of the clouds
Omou hito ni wa	Revealed himself to him who truly yearned,
Miekeru mono o.	While you refuse to show yourself to me.

This was matched against Mototoshi's lament to a mistress not quite so cruel:

Katsu miredo	Although I sometimes see you,
Nao zo koishiki	Such is my longing that I wish
Wagimoko ga	Somehow to hold you close—
Yutsu no tsumagushi	To touch and wear you as you wear
Ikade sasamashi.	Your comb of closely wedded teeth.

As the translation shows, the first line of Shunrai's poem is colloquial and therefore possesses an obvious "fault" of unconventional diction. Further, the image of the dragon hidden in the clouds would probably have been considered almost unbearably overpowering, especially in view of the strict decorum of an *utaawase*. At any rate, Shunrai curtly dismissed his own poem with the comment, "The first poem is incomprehensible. It certainly seems to be in a strange and unconventional style." He continued, however, with an impressive display of erudition:

In the second poem, the "comb of closely wedded teeth" alludes to the first meeting of the god Susanoo with the Princess Inada, when the deity transformed the girl into a comb which he stuck into his hair. But while the line "although I sometimes see you" in this poem implies that the lovers are already intimate, the wish to "touch and wear" the beloved conveys the contrary idea that the man has not yet had access to the woman. There also seems to be some mistake here in the allusion. We should ask the poet about it. Certainly it is different from what I was taught in the old days, but then perhaps I have it wrong. There can be no question of awarding a victory in this round.

Mototoshi's shocked comment on Shunrai's poem was as follows:

I have never before seen an expression like "How mean can you get?" used on such an occasion as a poetry contest of this kind. I think it extremely vulgar. And the men of old also used to say that in both Japanese and Chinese poetry the words should be chosen with care—that "the fruit should follow after the blossoms." It is for this reason, no doubt, that I have never come across this expression in any of the collections of the poets, nor in the records of poetry contests, nor anywhere else for that matter. I need hardly add that in any case it would never have been used as a first line. Furthermore, I know of no precedent in Japanese poetry for treating a heron as "dwelling concealed in the region of the clouds," and I venture to doubt whether it can be found in the writings of China either, although one might think so. Could it be that the poet was trying to allude to the "crane crying at sundown" from the line in the *Shih Shuo?* But the following line in the Chinese has the white crane emerging into view as the blue clouds draw apart. Perhaps the poet is really trying to convey a picture of the bird flying off into the clouds. If he had said "crane" instead of "heron" he might conceivably be justified in treating it as dwelling among the clouds. It is written in the *Huai Nan Tze* that even a flightless barnyard fowl soared off into the clouds after tasting of the elixir of immortality, so that perhaps this could be said of a crane as well. But in that case, it is written . . . that the male and female crane do not meet and have intercourse until they reach the age of a hundred and eighty, so how could one possibly use the word in connection with people? Furthermore, since there is no statement that cranes dwell among the clouds, I do not think that such an idea can really be correct. In general, this poem is below standard in both language and conception. The second poem has no fault of diction, nor is the total effect of the treatment unpleasant. Can I be wrong to say it is the better of the two?

The question, of course, is why Mototoshi goes into such a frenzy on the subject of herons and cranes in connection with Shunrai's poem. The answer is in reality quite simple: the Japanese words for "dragon" and "heron" are respectively *tatsu* and *tazu*, and in the syllabic script both the syllable *tsu* and its voiced counterpart *zu* were written with the same symbol. In other words, it never occurred to Mototoshi when he read Shunrai's poem that the word might be "dragon" instead of "heron," and with all his display of outraged pedantry he has been demolishing a straw man. The sequel to this incident is recorded by the poet-priest Kamo no Chōmei (d. 1216) in his *Nameless Notes (Mumyōshō)*, a treatise on poetics and collection of miscellaneous anecdotes and lore. Chōmei, a contemporary of Teika, was a disciple of the priest Shun'e (fl. ca. 1160–80), who was Shunrai's son and poetic heir. Mototoshi, writes Chōmei (*NKGT*, III, 292), misunderstood *tatsu* as *tazu* in Shunrai's poem, and

disqualified it with the criticism that herons dwell in marshland and it was unheard-of that they should inhabit the sky. Shunrai, however, made no effort to explain at the time. It was only when Lord Tadamichi asked each of the judges to bring him a written record of the decisions and comments they had made during the evening's proceedings that Shunrai wrote, "This is not a heron; it is a dragon. I was referring to that old Chinese tale about the man who longed so fervently to see a dragon that the dragon revealed itself out of pity for him." Mototoshi was the more learned, but he had the bad habit of criticizing without judgment or forethought, thereby making himself ridiculous on numerous occasions.

Mototoshi's long-winded tirade about the heron and the crane may seem to be a tempest in a teapot, but it leads to a consideration of a poetic concept that was vitally important both in this generation and in the following generations of Shunzei and Teika. This is the concept expressed by the term *hon'i*, a word which, like most of the important critical terms of all languages, has such a wide range of meanings that we must resort to a number of English equivalents in discussing its various aspects. Perhaps the term as used by such poets as Shunzei and Teika might best be translated "essential nature," but in different contexts and to different poets it meant such things as "correct handling" (of a given topic), "decorum of feeling" (toward a subject), "conventional treatment" (of an image), and "real significance" (of an event or experience). The word *kokoro* was also often used by judges at *utaawase* and in the handbooks and critical writings of the age synonymously with *hon'i*, and it is frequently difficult to determine what meaning these ambiguous terms were intended to convey in a given situation. Throughout the history of Court poetry, the Japanese critical vocabulary consisted of a very small number of terms used in a variety of senses, and although we must not be impatient with the medieval poets for this (what, after all, have English critics meant by "wit," "nature," "form"?), it remains true that it is often impossible to arrive at precise definitions and single equivalents in our discussions of the principal concepts of Japanese literary criticism.

The term *hon'i* (Chinese, *pen-i*) was used frequently in China from the early T'ang dynasty onward, and it is obvious that the Japanese borrowed the word from Chinese sources. It appears originally to have meant something like "subjective will" or "personal desire," a meaning which it continued to carry in nontechnical contexts both in China and in Japan. Around the middle of the T'ang dynasty, however, the term came to be used by Chinese critics in the somewhat more limited sense of "poetic intent," or "what the poet really wants to say." For example, if a Chinese poet was supposed to compose a poem on the moon, and if in his poem he strayed from this "poetic intent" and emphasized imagery of blossoms or birds to the neglect of the moon, his poem might be said to have failed—to have missed the hon'i of the topic, the moon. It can readily be seen that such a concept already places severe restrictions on the poet: perhaps his real "poetic intent" is to use the moon as an excuse for a poem on blossoms and birds, or perhaps he really feels that devoting most of his poem to blossoms and birds is the best way to deal with the moon. But such personal freedom is not permitted: the poet must focus upon the topic and the imagery appropriate to it.

In this sense of the "correct handling" of a prescribed topic (dai), we find the term hon'i used in the critical judgments of Japanese *utaawase* from about the beginning of the eleventh century on; and as Japanese formal poetry tended increasingly to treat prescribed topics, the question naturally arose as to what really constituted such "correct handling." This became one of the major points of disagreement between the great poet Teika and other more conservative poets such as ex-Emperor Go-Toba in the age of the *Shinkokinshū*, and it may be illustrated by an example taken from a poetry contest held at the house of Taira Tsunemori (1125–?85) in 1167, a contest at which the influential Rokujō poet Fujiwara Kiyosuke (1104–77), Shunzei's great conservative rival, acted as judge. In the eighth round of the section devoted to the topic "Autumn Foliage," the following poems, composed respectively by one Fujiwara Koreyuki and a Court lady known as Kojijū, were matched (*Shinkō Gunsho Ruijū*, VIII, 615).

Momijiba wa   Although the scarlet
Kurenai fukaku   Of the maple leaves keeps growing
  Nariyukedo   Brighter in its hue,
Hitori sametaru   The color of the pine trees
Matsu no iro kana.   Alone becomes more faint.

Hahasobara   As the grove of oaks
Shigururu mama ni   Colors with the autumn drizzle,
  Tokiwagi no   It now appears
Sore narikeru mo   That the evergreens are truly so:
Ima zo miekeru.   Unchanging in their green.

Kiyosuke disqualified both of these poems and declared the match a draw on the grounds that "both poets have neglected the autumn foliage and treated the subject of evergreens, thus failing in the correct handling of the topic. The total effect of the second poem is more pleasing, but by some perversity it does not even use the words 'autumn foliage.' " In other words, to Kiyosuke, as to Go-Toba and other more "liberal" conservatives of the late twelfth century, the hon'i of a topic that happened at the same time to be an image required not merely that the image appear in the poem, but that it be the principal one: the topic must be the real "subject" of the poem and not simply mentioned or present, so to speak, by implication.

More abstract seasonal topics, such as "The Heat of Early Autumn," and topics involving human emotions or situations such as "First Love," "Love on a Journey," or "A Love Meeting that Is No Meeting" came to acquire along with imagistic topics a second kind of hon'i that might be called "decorum of feeling." No matter how a poet might personally feel as a private human being, the decorum of his topic or subject required that the speaker of his poem express feelings sanctioned by tradition. There may well have been misanthropes in the Japanese Court who hated both man and nature, but if they were poets, the "decorum of feeling" associated with cherry blossoms required that in poetry they express impatience in waiting for their blooming, delight in their beauty, and distress at their falling. To have treated such a subject in any other way would only have stamped the poet as an ignorant boor or at best a jokester. It is therefore easy to see why the poem we have quoted by Shunrai on the topic of "Love on a Journey"—a topic whose decorum of feeling required the expression of a wistful or somewhat more tearful yearning—would be regarded as indecorous for its violation of the proper decorum of feeling as well as for its use of colloquial diction.

In the hands of scholarly conservatives like Mototoshi the concept of hon'i came to be applied to the most minute details in the treatment of poetic materials. Mototoshi's comments on the first poem in the first round on the topic of "The Moon and the Hills" at a poetry contest sponsored by the Regent

Fujiwara Tadamichi in 1121 may serve as an illustration (*Shinkō Gunsho Ruijū*, VIII, 541). The poem, by a Court lady whose name is not preserved, ran as follows:

Ko no ma yori	In my delight to see
Izuru wa tsuki no	The moon come up between the trees,
Ureshiki ni	I wish only that
Nishi naru yama no	I might live west of those western hills
Nishi ni sumaba ya.	And watch its rising sooner still.

Insofar as the decorum of feeling is concerned, the poet has accredited herself well, for the rising of the moon ought to be impatiently awaited and greeted with joy. And since in this case the speaker expresses an unusually passionate desire to see the moon, the poem ought to rate as a reasonably successful one in the style of "intense feeling," later given the name *ushintei* or *kokoro aru tei* by Teika. But the hapless lady has made two fatal mistakes. In the words of Mototoshi—

It is well known that the moon conventionally comes up from behind the rim of the mountains, so how can it be treated as rising from between the trees? Although a number of old poems do indeed show that the *light* of the moon may be treated as filtering through the trees, this present treatment is unprecedented. Furthermore, the expression of the desire to dwell to the west of the western hills is quite incomprehensible: in expressing impatience to see the moon a poet must say that he wishes to dwell to the *east* of the *eastern* hills.

Insofar as such a concept as hon'i represents the consolidation of a now venerable poetic tradition and the imposition of severe limits upon the range of poetic subjects and expression, we may say that it was accepted by most of the major poets in this generally conservative age. Neither Shunzei nor Teika questioned the concept of hon'i as a standard to be applied to their own best poetry as well as to that of their contemporaries. Indeed, Shunzei accepted, as far as they went, the views of Mototoshi (under whom, it should be pointed out, he first studied poetry while still a young child), and a number of his comments as a judge at poetry contests reflect this conventional attitude toward the hon'i of topic, treatment, and response. On the other hand, Shunzei went far beyond his teacher in recognizing the need to maintain the vital balance between the personal response of the individual poet and the traditional, conventional character of his materials. Like other critics in his age, Shunzei frequently used such terms as *kokoro ari* (having decorum, intense feeling, or conviction of feeling) and *aware* (moving the sensibilities or evoking the proper response in a sensitive person) more or less synonymously with hon'i in its various meanings. But in his use of these critical terms he added a positive emphasis which gave a new direction and impetus to poetry within the limitations of a valued but restricted tradition.

Fujiwara Shunzei reciting his poem on the hototogisu *(see pp. 282–85). From a book, with commentary by Sōgi, of famous poems of the* SHINKO-KINSHŪ, *illustrated by Hishikawa Moronobu (d. 1694).*

Shunzei would probably have agreed with Mototoshi in criticizing the poem quoted above for its failure to treat the moon as rising from behind the hills rather than between the trees. But his reasons would have been significantly different. Mototoshi would no doubt have insisted upon the "proper" treatment simply because it was the conventional way and had the sanction of tradition and precedent. Shunzei, however, would have added that such treatment was the most beautiful, the most moving, the ideal way of conveying the nature, the essence, the real significance of the materials so as to evoke the most sympathetic response in the hearts and minds of all cultivated men. Poems that succeeded in doing this—in conveying the "real essence" of a natural phenomenon or human situation by treating it in a conventional way and at the same time with the conviction of personal lyricism—were moving (*aware*); they expressed the hon'i of the materials and "possessed *kokoro*." Shunzei's profound admiration for the *Tale of Genji*—he maintained that a familiarity with this great prose work was essential to the education of every poet—is quite understandable from the point of view of his esthetic ideals. To Shunzei, Murasaki's great novel was an ideal expression of the universal quality of *aware*: the individual episodes of the *Tale of Genji* conveyed each in its own sensitive way the essence or real significance of love in its various aspects, of man's response to the beauties of nature, and of such other human situations as suffering, old age, and death. In this sense the *Genji* could be considered indispensable to poets as a kind of handbook illustrating tone in all its subtle shadings.

To Shunzei, therefore, and especially to Teika, the most important of the several meanings of hon'i was its quasi-Platonic one of the "essence" suggested by a particular conventional poetic topic. To succeed in expressing the essential quality of a topic it was not enough merely to handle it according to the decorum of conventional treatment. It was necessary in their view that the poet undergo the most rigorous preparation—that he achieve a kind of mystical identification with the topic by means of intense concentration and meditation. Only then would he be able to transcend the restrictions of convention and infuse his creation with a feeling of conviction and artistic integrity. In his poetical treatise *Sasamegoto,* the poet Shinkei (1406–75) tells that Teika lectured his son, Tameie (1198–1275), on his cavalier attitude toward the art of poetry with the following touching description of Shunzei in the throes of composition (*NKGT,* V, 268).

Very late at night he would sit by his bed in front of an oil lamp so dim that it was difficult to tell whether it was burning or not, and with a tattered Court robe thrown over his shoulders and an old Court cap pulled down to his ears, he would lean on an arm-rest, hugging a wooden brazier for warmth, while he recited verse to himself in an undertone. Deep into the night when everyone else was asleep he would sit there bent over, weeping softly.

The insistence on a kind of mystical fusion of the poet and his materials achieved by intense concentration was influenced by the practice of *shikan,* or "concentration and insight," identified with the Tendai sect of esoteric Buddhism patronized by most of the Court. The religious exercise had as its purpose the achieving of a mystical insight into the nature of the Buddha by means of contemplating a painting or piece of sculpture. The individual would concentrate upon the icon with such intensity that his inner mind would become filled with a universal vision of the Buddha transcending the finite characteristics of the image before him. The similarity between the religious exercise and the esthetic ideal of grasping the "real significance" or "essence" of an experience by concentration upon a given topic is obvious. Shunzei's poetical treatise, the *Korai Fūteishō,* reflects his deep interest in the practice of *shikan* (*NKGT,* II, 359), and offers strong evidence that the kind of experience of poetic contemplation which he and Teika emphasized owed a good deal to the Tendai teachings. The adaptation of a religious ideal to poetic practice may seem remarkable, yet it is hardly surprising in this strongly religious age, when the art of poetry was regarded as a way of life and just as surely a means to ultimate truth as the sermons of the Buddha.

Among the ideals inherited from Shunzei, *ushin* became crucial for Teika, who further developed and elaborated upon it in ways important for theory and practice alike. In the *Maigetsushō*, the most important of his extant writings, Teika insists upon the supreme importance of what he calls the "style of intense feeling." He uses the term in both a narrow and a broad sense— as a separate category among the ten styles which he codifies ("the style of intense feeling") and as an element essential to all ten ("a conviction of feeling")—an overlapping system of classification which, together with the lack of specific examples of poems in the various styles named, has given rise to several different interpretations of what he actually meant by the terms. Teika's dual usage of the term *ushin* and the high estimation he gave the concept can best be illustrated by a crucial passage from the *Maigetsushō* (*NKGT*, III, 347–48).

Among the ten styles there is not one in which the true nature of poetry resides more wholly than in the style of intense feeling. It is extremely difficult to create, for it cannot by any means be put together at random in any of a variety of ways. Only when one has composed one's thoughts and entered into the unique realm of this style is it possible to compose in it, and even at that success is rare. It must be for this reason that great poetry has been said to be possible only when every poem is suffused with deep feeling. However, if one goes through excessive contortions in the effort to instill even greater feeling into it, the poem will be overdone and overcomplicated, and such defective, imperfect, and incomprehensible poems are even more distasteful and ugly than those which lack feeling. The borderline between success and failure is of supreme importance and must constantly be given the most careful thought. Those who are serious about this art must not even occasionally compose in an easygoing manner without concentrating their minds. To produce a faultily constructed poem not only becomes a source of embarrassment by inviting the adverse criticisms of one's detractors, but also leads to the debilitation of one's artistic powers. Thus one hears of people who, having brought criticism upon themselves, have pined away and died of chagrin, or who, having had a fine poem expropriated by someone else, have after death appeared in dreams weeping and lamenting and demanding the return of their poems, with the result that these have been expunged from the imperial anthologies. Instances of this kind are not limited to the ones I have cited, and I find them most affecting.

One must take pains, both on the days of preparation for a poetry meeting or competition, and on informal occasions, to compose one's poems with great care, reciting them over and over to oneself. Carelessness will inevitably give rise to adverse criticism later on. You, my lord, should continually have your mind fixed upon poems that are in the style of intense feeling. However, there are times when it is quite impossible to compose in this style. When one feels ill at ease and the depths of one's heart are in turmoil, no amount of effort will succeed in producing a poem in the style of intense feeling. If one persists in trying to produce such a poem under such conditions, one's artistic powers will weaken and the result will be a faultily constructed poem. At such times one should compose "lively" poems, that is, poems whose style and phrasing are light and easy, and whose over-all effect, though lacking in any deep emotion, is somehow pleasing to the ear. This advice should be especially borne in mind on informal occasions when the topics are not given out in advance, for even such trivial poems as these will, when one has composed four or five or as many as ten of them, disperse one's heavy spirits and quicken one's sensibilities so that one can compose with assurance. On the other hand, I feel that when one is assigned such topics as "Love" or "Expressing Personal Grievances," the style of intense feeling must be used exclusively. I do not mean to say that unless it is in this style a poem cannot possibly be good. Nevertheless, this style of intense feeling must extend over the other nine styles for the reason that the style of mystery and depth must possess conviction of feeling—so must the lofty style, and so must all of the others. It is indeed true that no matter what style it may be in, a poem which lacks conviction of feeling is bad. Among the examples of the ten styles which I have chosen and sent to you previously, those which were grouped under the heading the "style of intense feeling" were not poems in the other styles which also possessed conviction of feeling, but rather only those poems composed in the attempt to produce the single effect of intense feeling. Whatever the style may be, however, it must possess conviction of feeling.

Together with the insistence upon the philosophical ideal of ushin in the composition of poetry, Teika inherited from Shunzei and emphasized in his turn the prescriptive ideal of "old diction, new treatment" (*kotoba furuku, kokoro atarashi*). By "old diction," Shunzei and Teika meant primarily the language of the *Sandaishū* or *Three Collections* (the *Kokinshū*, the *Gosenshū*, and the *Shūishū*), and although they were willing to admit a few exceptions, they rejected as indecorous the two extremes of Man'yō archaism and new words from the colloquial language, used so freely by such innovators as Shunrai. In the face of opposition from the Rokujō school, Shunzei insisted upon the *Kokinshū* as the source of his neoclassical ideal of "old diction," for, as he wrote in his *Korai Fūteishō*, "From the time of this anthology the good and the bad in poetry were selected and fixed, so that for the basic elements of poetry one should look only to the *Kokinshū*" (*NKGT*, II, 367). Such terms as *iishiritari* and *iinaretari*, that is, "well-known" and "often expressed," were frequently used by Shunzei as terms of praise of poetic diction in his judgments at poetry competitions at the same time that these and similar terms were indicative of disapprobation when applied to the poetic treatment, or *kokoro*, which required originality rather than traditionalism. His critical comments and writings elsewhere as well reflect his esteem for a poetic language that long years of use had endowed with rich associations and overtones.

If Shunzei's preference for "old diction" shows the conservative side of his character, the second half of his prescriptive ideal, "new treatment," symbolizes his accomplishment as poetic innovator as well as consolidator and arbiter of poetic extremes. For both Shunzei and Teika played crucial roles in advocating as esthetic ideals and making significant in their practice new standards of beauty—the ideals of *sabi* or "loneliness," *yōen* or "ethereal charm," and *yūgen* or "mystery and depth." The ideals themselves were not new in the sense that Shunzei and Teika invented them or even introduced them into Japanese poetry, but they were given a new value, interpretation, and emphasis by the two poets, and their embodiment in a richly traditional poetic language produced the most significant poetry of the age—the new poetry of descriptive symbolism.

There is little in the Western tradition to prepare us for the concept of sabi as a poetic ideal. The reflective melancholy of the late Augustan poets with their elegies in country churchyards or the sadness of the Romantics contemplating vanished glories amid ruined piles furnish perhaps the closest parallels. The parallels are by no means exact, however, for the Japanese concept is more spontaneous than reflective, more intuitive than philosophical. Sabi resembles Wordsworth's "sweet mood when pleasant thoughts / Bring sad thoughts to the mind" in that the feeling of loneliness was regarded as something to be savored, but it was stimulated directly by certain aspects of life or nature rather than by meditation upon the relation of man to the universe. It is not surprising, given the neoclassical bent of the age, to find that the concept of sabi can be traced to the poetry of China, in particular the poetry of the mid- and late T'ang dynasty. In China we discover two different emotional reactions to loneliness. The first and most common reaction was that loneliness is unhappy, pitiful, and unpleasant; the second reaction (which harmonized with the Taoist ideal of the hermit living a life of primitive freedom in beneficent nature) was that loneliness is pleasant, imbued with unique qualities of beauty, and worthy of cultivation. In either case the poetry of loneliness tended to contain natural imagery of a somber, monochromatic, and even "ugly" character, which, depending on one's attitude, served either to heighten the pathos or to evoke with its crude, sad beauty the mood of sweet melancholy.

As we would expect, a similar ambivalent attitude toward loneliness is found in Japan. In the poetry of the late eleventh century, in which the concept and imagery of sabi first appear, loneliness is treated as a pathetic condition. The following example by the priest Ryōzen (fl. ca. 1040–70) is typical (*GSIS,* IV: 333).

Sabishisa ni	In my loneliness
Yado o tachiidete	I step outside my hut and gaze
Nagamureba	In quiet reverie,
Izuku mo onaji	But everywhere it is the same:
Aki no yūgure.	The melancholy autumn dusk.

The attitude expressed in Ryōzen's poem contrasts with the appreciation of loneliness that characterizes numerous poems of a century or so later, and it may be that the bitter experience of social, political, and economic decline made such a theme particularly congenial to the poets of the mid-classical period. Whether this is true, or whether the increase in poems that expatiate on the consolations of solitude is due to more specifically literary influences, a poem from the personal collection of the famous poet-priest Saigyō fairly represents the altered attitude (*Sankashū* in *K. Taikei*, XI, 255).

Tou hito mo	My mountain village,
Omoitaetaru	To which I have abandoned hope
Yamazato no	That any friend will come,
Sabishisa nakuba	Would be a wretched place to live
Sumiukaramashi.	Were it not for this sweet loneliness.

Although the number of poems on loneliness gradually increased from about the time of the *Goshūishū* (1086) onwards, the earliest instance of the use of sabi as a term of praise is to be found in one of Shunzei's critical comments as judge of a poetry competition held at the Hirota Shrine in the province of Settsu in 1172. Here he awarded the victory to an otherwise undistinguished poem for its melancholy imagery of frost-withered reeds on the tidal flats at Naniwa. So highly regarded was Shunzei as a critic that his taste for poems with an element of sabi gave a quasi-official stamp of approval to the concept of loneliness as an esthetic ideal, and to the imagery of a withered, monochromatic nature. The emotional content of sabi is close to that of Shunzei's other favorite concept of *aware* in that the sympathetic response of *aware* was usually, in poetic practice at least, one of wistful melancholy. But the consciousness of isolation and the astringent qualities of the imagery of sabi make it significantly different as well as more limited than the concept of *aware*. The beauty of sabi was especially to be found in the autumn dusk, in withered fields, or in the sight of drab brown birds winging across a marsh at twilight—sights which have none of the traditional bright loveliness of spring cherry blossoms or autumn foliage, but which are perhaps more profoundly moving in their somber, muted beauty. To quote a lovely poem by the priest Jakuren (d. 1202) (*SKKS*, IV: 361):

Sabishisa wa	Loneliness—
Sono iro to shi mo	The essential color of a beauty
Nakarikeri	Not to be defined:
Maki tatsu yama no	Over the dark evergreens, the dusk
Aki no yūgure.	That gathers on far autumn hills.

It so happens that the Japanese word for "rust" is also pronounced *sabi,* and although there was originally no etymological or other connection between the two words, "rust" was too apt a term to describe the imagery of sabi to be missed. Under the influence of Zen Buddhism, the haiku poets of the seventeenth century, especially the great Bashō, developed the concept of a corroded, moss-covered, "rusty" beauty into perhaps their most important esthetic ideal, and Bashō quite rightly acknowledged Saigyō and Shunzei as his masters.

If the esthetic of sabi represents a kind of sophisticated primitivism or pastoralism, its polar opposite is to be found in the ideal of yōen, or "ethereal charm." Like sabi, yōen was a concept borrowed from Chinese poetry, but of the late rather than the mid-T'ang dynasty. Its importance as a dominant ideal of the age of the *Shinkokinshū* is due to the remarkable genius of the youthful Teika who, evidently intrigued with the differences between the poetry of Po Chü-i and that of late T'ang with its ideal of yōen, was inspired to develop a new style for the waka. Thus although the ideal of "ethereal charm" had been officially recognized in the mid-twelfth century by Fujiwara Mototoshi as one kind of poetic beauty, it was left to Teika to advocate it against considerable opposition as a superior esthetic ideal.

Basically, yōen was the romantic idealization of a delicate, dreamlike beauty—the beauty of a peony or of an exquisite heavenly maiden descending to earth on a hazy spring night. Such beauty was elusive, ephemeral, the stuff that dreams are made on, and while the typical imagery of yōen had the delicate lightness of cherry petals, it was often used to convey a tone of sadness— of lovers parting or of nostalgia for the vision of a beauty not of this world. The following magnificent poem, composed in 1194 when Teika was thirty-two years old, shows his yōen style in all its rich complexity (*SKKS*, I: 38).

Haru no yo no	The bridge of dreams
Yume no ukihashi	Floating on the brief spring night
Todae shite	Soon breaks off:
Mine ni wakaruru	Now from the mountaintop a cloud
Yokogumo no sora.	Takes leave into the open sky.

The season of the poem is spring, the time of year most suited for love, but when the nights grow shorter and the dawn comes all too soon to interrupt the lovers' tryst. The rich traditional overtones of *haru no yo no yume*, a "dream on a spring night," imply that the speaker has been dreaming of love, but this love and this dream are of a very special kind, for the second line of the poem, *yume no ukihashi*, "the floating bridge of dreams," is an allusion to the title of the final chapter in the *Tale of Genji*, the last in a series of chapters that deal with the passionately romantic but ill-starred affair between the beautiful Ukifune and the dashing Prince Niou. The dream is therefore all the more rare, remote, and precious with its quality of idealized, fictional love rather than real experience. The speaker awakes reluctantly as the "floating bridge" breaks off before the dream is ended. It is not a rude awakening, however, because he awakes to the loveliness of a spring dawn, and as he glances up he sees the conclusion of his dream: a cloud trailing away into the open sky "takes leave" of the mountaintop just as the lover must take leave of his beloved. Thus the gulf between dream and reality, fiction and life, man and nature, time and timelessness, is bridged anew as the dream of lovers is fused into the symbolic personification of the cloud and the mountaintop, resolving into the harmony of a scene of surpassing loveliness. But this newly created beauty is as ephemeral as the dream, and the poem ends as it begins with a tone of regret—in the final event we are left with only the "open sky."

We have still not exhausted the tonal richness or possible implications of the poem, however, because it may also be interpreted as a religious allegory, as a symbolic depiction of the life of man. "The proud ones last but a little while; they are like a dream on a night in spring," says the *Heike Monogatari*, the great war tale which deals with the epic struggles between the Taira and the Minamoto clans that had ended only a few years before Teika wrote this poem. The "open sky" (*sora*) is the Buddhist "emptiness" (*kū*), to the realization of which we awaken when enlightenment ends the illusory dream of the reality of the phenomenal world.

It is not difficult to see why this beautiful poem has been traditionally regarded as the epitome of the style of ethereal charm, but the very richness of its tonal depth, its complexity of technique, and its ambiguity—the religious symbolism is implicit but perhaps unintentional—are qualities that brought cries of shocked indignation from many of the more conservative poets of Teika's day. The burning issue was the question of hon'i, the decorous response to the dai. Conservatives like the Rokujō poets and middle-of-the-roaders like ex-Emperor Go-Toba, the Tendai Abbot Jien, or Jichin (1155–1225), and others, who may be grouped together as the "rhetoricians," were baffled by poems such as this one, whose response to the topic of "Spring" or "A Spring Dawn" was to them an expressionistic potpourri of confusing symbols, overtones, unanticipated juxtapositions, and ungrammatical reversals of syntax. To such poets, as we have seen, a decorous poem was one that treated the topic in a conventional manner and used the words of the topic as the central imagery of the poem.

But Teika, as the retired sovereign wrote in his treatise, the *Go-Toba-In Kuden,* or *Oral Traditions of Ex-Emperor Go-Toba,* "pays no attention whatever to the topic. For this reason in recent times even beginners have all come to be like this. It is outrageous. Only when one concentrates very hard upon a compound topic and composes a poem which centers upon that topic is the result of any interest. This modern style is sheer carelessness" (*NKGT,* III, 2). Actually, as we have seen, Teika regarded the topic as of the utmost importance. But Go-Toba took offense at Teika's tendency to do what Go-Toba called "penetrating too far into the topic," that is, to place a greater emphasis upon the conventional overtones (*yojō*) of the words than upon the words themselves, or to distill the "essence" of a topic by treating it metaphorically or symbolically rather than as a realistic phenomenon. The following poem from Teika's personal collection illustrates his treatment of a topic—"An Imperial Banquet on the New Year"—whose public character practically demanded conventional handling (*Shūi Gusō* in *K. Taikei,* XI, 389).

Haru kureba	As spring comes
Hoshi no kurai ni	And the stars in the firmament
Kage miete	Shed their range of light,
Kumoi no hashi ni	At the edge of the cloud kingdom
Izuru taoyame.	Appear bright maidens of the stars.

The poem is of course an allegory, and not a very difficult one at that; the key can be found in the poem itself in the words *kurai,* which may mean "Court rank," and *kumoi,* "land of clouds," "cloud kingdom," a conventional metaphor for the Court. The "stars in the firmament" are the courtiers who, lined up in the palace courtyard, shed a "range of light" with their brilliant robes of different colors according to their rank, and the "bright maidens of the stars" are the Court ladies who appear walking up and down the stairs of the hall of state to wait upon the emperor. Nevertheless the poem is quite unconventional in that rather than treat the imagistic details of activities appropriate to the season, Teika has tried to convey by metaphorical means the tonal essence of the topic.

The originality of such treatment is more readily apparent when the poem is compared with another on the same topic composed for the same occasion, one from the personal collection of Fujiwara Ietaka, or Karyū (1158–1237), himself a major poet (*Minishū* in *K. Taikei,* XI, 721).

Morohito no	The brilliant sunlight
Tachiiru niwa no	Flashing in the winecups raised
Sakazuki ni	By the courtiers
Hikari wa shirushi	Attendant in the palace grounds
Chiyo no hatsuharu.	Augurs a thousand years of spring.

In contrast to this more conventional treatment, which uses imagery proper to the topic and leaves very little unsaid, Teika's method of handling the topic would have been severely criticized by Go-Toba and many others for its failure to handle the imagistic materials suggested by the dai. Such poems, which frequently made use of unusual rhetoric and syntax as well as unprecedented approaches to the topic (see pp. 276–77, below), were often called "Daruma-uta," or "Bodhidharma poems," from the name of the legendary founder of Zen Buddhism. The term "daruma" was equivalent to "nonsense" in Teika's time, because Zen was still very new and unpopular among the courtiers of the late twelfth century and the early thirteenth, its teachings being derided as so much incomprehensible gibberish. Teika, of course, would have held that he had conveyed the true essence of the topic with "conviction of feeling," and in fairness to him it must be said that the charge of obscurity which with some justice was brought against the new style was mainly due to the abuse of his techniques by lesser imitators. The significant albeit fleeting vogue of yōen in this period testifies both to Teika's individualism in espousing a novel, often criticized poetic style and to his qualities as the articulate and influential leader of a highly gifted coterie of poets. Under his leadership such talented poets, not to say important personages, as the Regent Fujiwara (or Kyōgoku) Yoshitsune (1169–1206), Princess Shokushi (d. 1201), the priest Jakuren, "Shunzei's daughter" (actually, granddaughter; fl. ca. 1200), Fujiwara Ietaka, and Fujiwara Masatsune (1170–1221) embraced the yōen style with enthusiasm and produced poems that are among the finest in the Shinkokinshū.

The style of ethereal charm cannot be considered as an isolated phenomenon, however; in particular it is related to the ideal of yūgen, or "mystery and depth." Indeed, so many varied impulses, influences, and innovations culminated in the style of yūgen that it must be regarded as the crowning poetic ideal in any discussion of the esthetic of the age. Perhaps no other Japanese critical term has been given such different emphases, interpretations, and applications over the centuries. Originally a Buddhist term, yūgen appears already in Ki no Yoshimochi's (d. 919) Chinese Preface to the Kokinshū, where it means little more than "difficult" or "obscure." Shunzei was the first to advocate yūgen as a major poetic ideal, and he employed the term in at least three different senses: meaning very much the same as sabi when speaking of the over-all effect or "configuration" of a poem ("sugata yūgen"); meaning technical complexity or tonal subtlety when speaking of the conception of a poem ("kokoro yūgen"); and meaning connotative richness when speaking of poetic diction ("kotoba yūgen"). Ultimately, but altered greatly to mean a kind of beauty very close to that of yōen, which it replaced as a critical term, yūgen became the dominant esthetic ideal of the Nō drama as perfected by Zeami, or Seami (1363–1443), and of the renga of Shōtetsu, Shinkei, and others in the fourteenth and fifteenth centuries. Learned treatises have been written about the processes by which yūgen developed as an esthetic ideal of Court poetry, flowed into the renga and the Nō, and changed in meaning over the years. Despite these historical, critical, and semantic vicissitudes, the core of yūgen remained the ideal of an artistic effect both mysterious and ineffable, of a subtle, complex tone achieved by emphasizing the unspoken connotations of words and the implications of a poetic situation. Like the ideals of sabi, yōen, and ushin, yūgen was made to harmonize with other poetic ideals to create complex effects. The principal vehicle for yūgen, however, was descriptive poetry (wit, elaborate conceits, and fancy rhetoric would distract attention from the effect of the overtones); its typical imagery was calm, quiet, and muted, though not necessarily "withered" like that of sabi; and its characteristic tone was one of sadness or wistful melancholy. Shunzei's favorite poem among his own work—surely one of the great poems of the Court tradition—displays these characteristics as well as other qualities of mystery and depth that will be treated more fully in our discussion of the poetic practice of the age (*SZS*, IV: 258).

Yū sareba	As evening falls,
Nobe no akikaze	From along the moors the autumn wind
Mi ni shimite	Blows chill into the heart,
Uzura naku nari	And the quails raise their plaintive cry
Fukakusa no sato.	In the deep grass of secluded Fukakusa.

So varied were Shunzei's tastes, and so reluctant was he to insist upon his personal preferences, that among the nearly 2,000 of his written *utaawase* decisions that survive, there is, paradoxically, nothing in the way of a detailed poetic of yūgen. In his *Korai Fūteishō*, however, he called attention to the difference between his own poetic ideal and the courtly elegance aimed at by the traditional Fujiwara style (*NKGT*, II, 360). "In order to express his standard of good poetry," he wrote,

Lord Kintō . . . made an anthology which he called the "Collection of Gold and Jewels," and Lord Michitoshi stated in his Preface to the *Goshūishū* that "the language of poetry should be like brocade and the feeling deeper than the ocean." For my part, however, I do not feel that a poem must necessarily be like a piece of brocade. It should, rather, whether recited aloud or read to oneself, strike the senses with an ineffable effect of charm and sensibility.

Again, in a postscript to a "personal poetry competition" submitted to him for judgment by the Abbot Jien, an outstanding rhetorician, Shunzei wrote in much the same manner:

It is not necessary that a poem always express some novel conception or treat an idea exhaustively, but . . . it should somehow . . . produce an effect both of charm and of mystery and depth. If it is a good poem, it will possess a kind of atmosphere that is distinct from its words and their configuration and yet accompanies them. The atmosphere hovers over the poem, as it were, like the haze that trails over the cherry blossoms in spring, like the cry of the deer heard against the autumn moon, like the fragrance of spring in the flowering plum by the garden fence, like the autumn drizzle that drifts down upon the crimson foliage on some mountain peak. As I have so often said before, there is an indefinable beauty in such lines as "What now is real? / This moon, this spring are altered / From their former being . . ." and "Like my cupped hands / Spilling drops back into the mountain pool / And clouding its pure waters." (*Jichin Oshō Jikaawase* in *NKGT*, II, 358.)

Shunzei's reference to the famous poems by Narihira (see p. 193) and Tsu-rayuki (see pp. 207–8) is especially significant because, despite his admiration for the Kokinshū, the anthology is not without its poems of poor quality (as he admitted in his comment on the first round of Saigyō's Mimosusogawa Utaawase), and it was pre-eminently in the highly compressed style of such poems as these, with their complex implications and overtones, that he found the historical precedent for his poetic ideal. Teika shared his father's preference, but his neoclassical ideal was historically narrower in that it was typically based almost entirely on the poetry of the late ninth century, when Narihira and Komachi were at their height. In his brief poetical essay known as the Kindai Shūka, or Great Poems of Modern Times, he even criticizes Tsurayuki for failing to exploit the possibilities of what he calls the "style of overtones and ethereal charm" (NKGT, III, 331). It will be remembered, however, that Tsurayuki had taken Narihira to task for his style of "too much spirit and too few words"; and although (their critics to the contrary) neither Shunzei nor Teika intended to make a fetish of obscurity, it must be granted that if the subtle qualities of atmosphere aimed at in both the yūgen and yōen styles required the utmost effort on the part of the poet, they also demanded much from the reader. The following poem by Shunzei illustrates the use of various techniques to create a complex atmosphere of yūgen within a highly subjective framework (SKKS, III: 238).

Tare ka mata	In a future age
Hanatachibana ni	Will the fragrance of these orange
Omoiiden	blossoms
Ware mo mukashi no	Move someone again
Hito to narinaba.	To think of me when in my turn
	I too shall be a person of the past?

The poem is typical of the age in its thematic concern with the passage of time and in its sad implication ("sugata yūgen") that the answer to the question posed by the speaker is in the negative. The speaker, stirred by the lovely fragrance of orange blossoms floating on the summer night, is moved to thoughts of some mysterious person (or persons, for the Japanese hito may be either singular or plural, male or female) who, for unspecified reasons, perhaps death, perhaps the end of a love affair, is now gone. His thoughts of the past lead him to ask whether at some future time anyone will be stirred in like fashion to think of him. It is to be assumed that the answer is "no," but again for unknown reasons—perhaps his insignificant social standing or some misfortune such as political disgrace or even unrequited love. We infer that the past about which the speaker is thinking must have been romantic and beautiful—why else would he be moved to think of it by the scent of orange blossoms?—but we know no more than that. The situation is full of mystery; the speaker's one question leaves us with several. Why is he lonely?

Of whom is he thinking? Why will he be forgotten in the future? All of this is left to the imagination. We must fill out in our minds the particularities of the human situation only hinted at by the poet.

In order to appreciate the tonal depths of the poem, however, we must also be aware that it is an allusive variation (honkadori) on an anonymous poem in the *Kokinshū* (*KKS*, III: 139):

Satsuki matsu	Now that I smell
Hanatachibana no	The fragrance of the flowering orange
Ka o kageba	trees
Mukashi no hito no	That wait for June to bloom,
Sode no ka zo suru.	I am reminded of the scented sleeves
	And wonder about that person of my past.

Shunzei knew that his contemporaries would recognize the allusion and re-call the phrasing and the situation of the older poem almost simultaneously with the new one. The older poem, though not so ambiguous as Shunzei's, also has its elements of mystery. In the first place, it is anonymous, and although the speaker is by implication a woman reminded of her lover, we do not know who she is, who her lover was, or what has become of him. The allusion deepens the atmosphere of mystery that already pervades Shunzei's poem, and qualifies the dominant tone of sadness with overtones of romantic love. We assume that Shunzei's speaker is reminded of the *Kokinshū* poem and wonders about its speaker, comparing his own situation with the more romantic one of the older poem ("I, *too*, shall be . . ."). The effect is a fusion of past, present, and future in a kaleidoscopic series of personal relationships that resolve into a subtle fineness of tone and create an atmosphere which is truly one of mystery and depth.

The emphasis upon overtones, the use of allusion, and the evocation of a romantic atmosphere of mysterious beauty were characteristic of the more ornate poetry of yōen as well as of yūgen. Indeed, these qualities constituted generalized ideals of poetic practice among the innovating poets of the age of the *Shinkokinshū*, and the term yūgen came to be used in a broad sense to designate the complex of ideals and techniques of the new poetry developed under Shunzei's leadership. A contemporary interpretation of this broad yūgen ideal can be found in a section of the *Mumyōshō* of Kamo no Chōmei under the heading of "The Modern Style" ("Kindai Katei"). Chōmei, him-self one of the most original poets among the contemporaries of Teika, was as we have seen a disciple of the priest Shun'e, and his anecdotal collection of notes reports the master's views, frequently in the form of answers to ques-tions posed by Chōmei. Concerning the "modern style," Chōmei wrote (*NKGT*, III, 312–13):

Question: I understand your explanations of the material under discussion thus far, but when it comes to the so-called style of mystery and depth, I find it very difficult to comprehend just how one should go about it. I wish you would be so kind as to teach it to me.

Answer: Every poetic style is difficult to master. Even the old collections of oral traditions and guides to composition only explain such difficulties as it is possible to resolve by taking someone by the hand and leading him along, as it were, and when it comes to poetic effects we find nothing at all precise. This is all the more true of the style of mystery and depth, whose very name is enough to confound one. Since I do not understand it at all well myself, I am at a loss as to how to describe it in any satisfactory manner, but according to the views of those who have developed the skill necessary to penetrate its mysteries, the qualities deemed essential to the style are overtones that do not appear in the words alone and an atmosphere that is not visible in the configuration of the poem. When both conception and diction are full of charm, these other virtues will be present of themselves. On an autumn evening, for example, there is no color in the sky nor any sound, yet although we cannot give any definite reason for it, we are somehow moved to tears. The average person lacking in sensibility finds nothing at all impressive in such a sight—he admires only the cherry blossoms and the scarlet autumn leaves that he can see with his own eyes. Or again, it is like the situation of a beautiful woman who, although she has cause for resentment, does not give vent to her feelings in words, but is only faintly discerned—at night, perhaps—to be in a profoundly distressed condition. The effect of such a discovery is far more painful and pathetic than if she had exhausted her vocabulary with jealous accusations or made a point of wringing out her tear-drenched sleeves to one's face. . . .

By these two analogies it should be evident that this is a matter impossible for people of little poetic sensibility and shallow feelings to understand. . . . How can such things be easily learned or expressed precisely in words? The individual can only comprehend them for himself. Again, when one gazes upon the autumn hills half-concealed by a curtain of mist, what one sees is veiled yet profoundly beautiful; such a shadowy scene, which permits free exercise of the imagination in picturing how lovely the whole panoply of scarlet leaves must be, is far better than to see them spread with dazzling clarity before our eyes. What is difficult about expressing one's personal feelings in so many words—in saying that the moon is bright or in praising the cherry blossoms simply by declaring that they are beautiful? What superiority do such poems have over mere ordinary prose? It is only when many meanings are compressed into a single word, when the depths of feeling are exhausted yet not expressed, when an unseen world hovers in the atmosphere of the poem, when the mean and common are used to express the elegant, when a poetic conception of rare beauty is developed to the fullest extent in a style of surface simplicity—only then, when the conception is exalted to the highest degree and "the words are too few," will the poem, by expressing one's feelings in this way, have the power of moving Heaven and Earth within the brief confines of a mere thirty-one syllables, and be capable of softening the hearts of gods and demons.

It would have shocked Tsurayuki to see his criticism of Narihira transformed into a poetic ideal, and even Shunzei might have balked at advocating "too few words" as a virtue. But Shun'e's (or Chōmei's) views represent a kind of logical conclusion to which the prescriptive ideals of the age could be pushed. To Shun'e, the ideal of yūgen called for a descriptive symbolism so complete that the subjective presence of the poetic speaker could be sensed only in the implicit tonal qualities of the imagery. It is consistent with such a view that he should have found fault with Shunzei's beautiful poem on autumn at Fukakusa, concerning which, according to Chōmei, he said (*NKGT*, III, 303):

In my opinion the third line of the poem, "penetrates the heart" [*mi ni shimite*], shows a serious lack of thought. In a poem of such superior quality, in which the description of the scene alone is quite sufficient to make us imagine that it must surely have "penetrated the heart," how distressing that he had to come out and say so! By blurting out what he should have revealed only gradually and with great restraint as the whole point of the poem, he has created an effect of vulgar superficiality.

Such a harsh judgment overlooks the fine balance in Shunzei's poem between the impersonalism of description and the personalism of the poet's lyrical response—Shun'e emerges as a fussy and carping critic. After all, it was Shunzei who succeeded, by virtue of his criticism and poetic practice, in harmonizing the conflicting impulses of his age in an ideal of descriptive symbolism that possessed at the same time a genuine lyricism. The innovating poets of the next period did indeed try their hand at "pure description," but to the degree that they actually succeeded in banishing the subjective presence of the poet from the scene, their descriptive poetry tended to suffer from a thinness of tone—a prosy flatness which their enemies were only too delighted to seize upon as evidence of poetic bankruptcy.

More than any other poet of his age, Teika was aware of the crucial importance of the continuing attempt to achieve a balance between personalism and impersonalism, originality and conventionality, directness of response and complexity of technique. Such an awareness is reflected in the artistic phases through which he passed during his long life. His development in terms of the poetic effect that he most preferred was from the ornate to the simple, from the highly contrived, fictional beauty of yōen, which he idealized in his youth, to the artful simplicity, directness, and passionate lyricism of his late style of "conviction of feeling." The change was most dramatic after the death of Shunzei in 1204. From about this time Teika gives every evidence of having gone through a period of intense inner struggle. He produced very little poetry during the next ten years, and in his *Kindai Shūka*, written in 1209 when he was forty-seven, he complained that he had "forgotten the color of the flowers of words; the well-springs of inspiration have run dry" (*NKGT*,

III, 327). By the time his poetic output began to increase, he had abandoned yōen as the supreme ideal and was moving in the direction of the ideal of ushin, or "conviction of feeling"—so much so that in his *Maigetsushō*, written probably in 1219, he did not even include yōen among the ten poetic styles that he distinguished. His new taste for poetry of an unpretentious, plain beauty (*heitambi*) is reflected in his choice of poems for the *Shinchokusenshū* (ca. 1234), the ninth imperial anthology, for which he was granted sole editorial responsibility; his fully developed "style of intense feeling" is to be found particularly in the passionate love poetry that he wrote in his late sixties and seventies.

Two reasons have been advanced for the alteration in Teika's poetic taste. The first explanation is that the change represents a decline in his artistic powers brought about by almost constant illness and advancing age; the second, that it represents a revulsion of feeling against the excessively artificial "chinoiserie" of the yōen and yūgen styles and a "return" to the peculiarly Japanese ideal of the simple, the direct, and the commonplace. The first theory will not survive even the most cursory examination of Teika's late poetry, the best of which is indeed relatively simple and direct, but with the simplicity that can only be produced by the most practiced art. The following poem on the topic of "Next Morning Love," from a sequence of one hundred poems composed in 1232, shows Teika at the age of seventy expressing the feelings of a young woman passionately in love (*Shūi Gusō* in *K. Taikei,* XI, 452).

Hajime yori	Although I heard
Au wa wakare to	From the outset that a meeting
Kikinagara	Can only mean to part,
Akatsuki shirade	I gave myself to love for you
Hito o koikeri.	Unconscious of the coming dawn.

The second explanation of Teika's late style—that it represents a reaction against excessive artificiality—has much to recommend it, but at the same time it must be pointed out that Teika continued to compose poems in every style. If his late poetry shows a new taste for simplicity, this does not by any means imply an outright rejection of the more elaborate styles of the age of the *Shinkokinshū.*

The death of Teika in 1241 marks the end of the great middle period of Japanese Court poetry. Much more bitter poetic controversy, intensified by personal animosities, family rivalries, and political competition, characterizes the following age. It is a tribute, albeit an ironic one, to Teika's position as the ultimate source of all subsequent authority in poetic matters that the history of poetry in the late classical period is to a large extent a history of the ways in which later generations espoused, interpreted, and misinterpreted the changing ideals and practice of this one great poet.

POETIC PRACTICE

A true union between literary ideals and literary practice is difficult to achieve: either the ideals are drawn from sources so foreign that any union is beyond realization, or what might be termed a marriage of convenience is brought about by the historian, at a later remove. In the mid-classical period, the Japanese poets continued to reveal a strong affection for Chinese poetry; but it remained an affection, not an infatuation. At the height of the age there is none of the foolish, wide-eyed adulation for Chinese poetry that led some earlier critics to try to impose a Chinese poetic on Japanese practice. What the god of Sumiyoshi put asunder let no man join. China retained a hold over the minds of Japanese poets, but the Japanese rejected more than they borrowed. In short, and happily for the poetry of the age, poetic practice was closely related to poetic ideals (in the conception of poetry as a way of life), and both were but distant cousins to the Chinese.

DICTION

Minamoto Shunrai's attempts to introduce new words into Japanese poetry were not crowned with either persistent literary success or general approbation. His worst poems often show a combination of wit of the by then old-fashioned *Kokinshū* variety and newfangled words taken from the slang of the day, from "low" scenes, or from the *Man'yōshū*. To his contemporaries, the effect was probably like that of an eccentric elderly gentleman baring his chest to show young people how lively he is. In his best poems he either sings the words that belong to the old tunes or, more rarely, blends the subjective techniques of the older poetry with description used partly for its own sake. All in all, he was most useful in showing the age what might best be avoided— apart from special cases in which new diction was absorbed into the context of the poem. Except for the amiable Shunzei, who could see the good in any style ("I dislike Shunrai as a person, but admire his poetry," he told those who complained about some selections in the *Senzaishū*), most of the important poets of the age felt that diction was not the realm in which to achieve originality.

The ideal of poetic language held by the best poets of the age may be expressed by an alteration of Pope's line: "Words often spoke, but ne'er so well express'd." They felt that the early classical age had bequeathed them a refined, elevated language for a poetry that was worthy of pursuit as a way of life. And no doubt as they saw their lives changing for the worse, and hard days coming with the rise of power of the military class, they held to traditional diction for moral as well as poetic support. The modern Western enthusiasm for the new or for brusque vernacular offered little appeal to men who were at once courtiers, scholars, and poets. They bent their efforts toward altering the sometimes brilliant and sometimes garish aristocratic elegance of earlier poetry into a more refined beauty, and sometimes in so doing created new faults and weaknesses. If the earlier age should have been more on its guard against the dangers of frivolity, this age was most prone to the sin of preciosity. Fortunately, in the decades just before and after the year 1200, a large number of excellent poets emerged to employ traditional diction in new ways.

Many of the new ways involve rhetoric and imagery, but there are some aspects of diction alone to claim attention. In negative terms, the poets avoided the two extremes of what they felt was the archaic language of the *Man'yōshū* and the too new, too inelegant language peculiar to their own time. They sought, as it were, a timelessly pure language that would be appreciated for generations to come. It was of course inevitable in a language like Japanese that the nature of imagery should also be affected, but to an ear used to the sounds and cadences of the *Man'yōshū* and of the early classical period, the language of this period has a character of its own. What this character is can be understood by comparing a poem in the *Man'yōshū* with its altered reincarnation in the *Shinkokinshū*. The old anthology had become increasingly familiar, but like the readers of any age, the compilers of the *Shinkokinshū* read earlier poems with a vision affected by the tastes of their time. Akahito's famous envoy on Mount Fuji (*MYS*, III: 318) undergoes a change when it appears in the later anthology (*SKKS*, VI: 675). (We have italicized the expressions that were altered.) Akahito had written:

Tago no ura *yu*	Emerging from behind
Uchiidete mireba	The barrier shadow cast by Tago's shore,
Mashiro ni zo	I am startled by
Fuji no takane ni	The lofty cone of Fuji whitely dazzling
Yuki wa furi*keru*.	Underneath its newly fallen snow.

And some later revisionist reordered it:

Tago no ura *ni*	When I emerge
Uchiidete mireba	Upon the shore of Tago I observe
Shirotae no	That white as hemp
Fuji no takane ni	The lofty cone of Fuji rises
Yuki wa furi*tsutsu*.	Half-hidden by the gently falling snow.

The sudden revelation of Fuji is retained, but the grandeur and the clarity of the surprise are changed to beauty and mystery. The archaic particle *yu* ("from") becomes *ni* ("to"), and the perfective, emphatic termination *keru* is changed to the continuative *tsutsu*. But what these changes represent can

be understood more clearly in the alteration of the exclamatory third line to
a makurakotoba, with its suggestions more of beauty and elegance than of delighted awe. These changes represent a poetic which, as we have said, aimed
at a comprehensive tonal integrity of beauty and depth. One cannot say that
the alteration of Akahito's poem is a translation, but it does fulfill Dryden's
standard of rendering the ancient poets in the manner of expression they
would have employed if they were the contemporaries of the translator.

It is not so much alterations of older poems, however, as new poems which
reveal the distinctive techniques of diction in this period. One of the first
things to impress the reader of such an anthology as the *Shinkokinshū* is the
way in which the complex, subjective effects gained by the manipulation of
verbs in the earlier poetry have been replaced by a greater reliance upon nouns.
A comparison between one of Komachi's less complex poems on love and
dreams and a poem by Shunzei's daughter on the same subject illustrates the
startling reversal of importance of these parts of speech (the nouns in each
poem are italicized). Komachi had written (*KKS*, XII: 552):

Omoitsutsu	Perhaps from longing,
Nureba ya *hito* no	From yearning for him I fell asleep
Mietsu ran	To see him by my side:
Yume to shiriseba	Had I been told it was a dream
Samezaramashi o.	Nothing would have torn me out of sleep.

And Shunzei's daughter (*SKKS*, XIV: 1326):

Tsuyu harau	Those mornings when
Nezame wa *aki* no	I awoke to brush away the mingled dew
Mukashi nite	and tears
Mihatenu *yume* ni	Have faded with the autumn
Nokoru *omokage*.	Of your satiety—now just your face
	remains,
	A vague image in an unfinished wintry
	dream.

As the italics show, Komachi uses only two nouns, whereas Shunzei's
daughter uses six; moreover, Komachi uses six verbs, including five highly
inflected ones, whereas the three verbs in Shunzei's daughter's poem have
little inflection. Again, Komachi's poem is a complete syntactical unit, while
the later poem is made inconclusive by its final noun. Such statistics mean
little in themselves, but they represent the differing effects of the poems.
Komachi's highly inflected verbs, and especially the long verb that all but fills
the last line, give a double effect of dramatic intensity and play of the subjective intellect upon states of being best conveyed by verbs. Shunzei's daughter, on the other hand, chooses to emphasize her theme of the bleakness of a

love affair grown cold by means of nouns that are largely imagistic in effect. The image of dew (which also signifies tears), the mention of autumn (and *aki* also means satiety), and the mention of times long past (*mukashi*) suggests a play on the seasons: spring and summer brought her a full happiness of joy in love; autumn her lover's rejection; and now winter a dreary blankness in which spring has all but passed from her mind, just as his image has. The incomplete syntax and its emphasis upon the fading image help stress the numbness she feels and the reflective nature of her experience.

Such an aura of private reflection or meditation is characteristic of most of the best poems of this age, and although there are many explanations behind this change from the drama and subjectivity of earlier poets, in terms of poetic technique the change in emphasis from verbs to nouns is of great importance. To employ nouns usually meant to use images; and to use images meant to explore their traditional tonal associations. As a result, the poems usually express an emotion-filled scene, and we find a descriptive poetry in which the associations of the images convey the significance of the scene for human experience. Such an analysis may indeed be translated into the retrospective historical explanation of an age slowly evolving meaningful descriptive poetry by gradually shifting from verbs and the vigorous exercise of the subjective mind to nouns, which suggest in their tone the less immediately perceived attitudes of the speaker and the poet.

The close tie between diction and tone is a characteristic of all poetry and especially of the Japanese, in which tone is the crucial vehicle of expression. In this age nouns achieve a new importance because of their imagistic role in description and their connotative richness in a traditional poetic language. Not only do verbs grow fewer in number, but they also tend to become less conspicuous. The copula is used more widely, and often a poem is reduced almost wholly to nouns with even the copula omitted. Only 52 poems in the *Kokinshū* terminate in nouns, whereas in the *Shinkokinshū* the number is 456. Many verbs are employed, of course, but these usually have simple inflections and are in the indicative mood. The ideal of hon'i or "essential nature" is more closely related to nouns and images than to verbs and actions, and it is significant that most of the topics (dai) of poems in this period are nouns referring to things and not verbs implying subjective states of mind. Such a development shows that the tanka had found renewed life and significance by means of a change in expression.

Two tendencies or complementary alternatives in the use of language function in the poetry of the period with the aim of creating a richly beautiful or exciting poetic texture. Many poems by Shunzei best represent the effort to refine the language to its peak of beauty. Such poems are usually very simple in their language, and their greatness lies in the total effect of lyric purity with each word seeming to have an inevitable place in the poetic whole. Such poetry has the lyric beauty of Ben Jonson's "Queen and Huntress Chaste and

Faire"—a beauty that the age preferred to consider in terms of its integrity of tone and technique—truly fulfilling the requirements of our paraphrase of Pope's line. Shunzei's poem on the quails crying in the village of Fukakusa perhaps marks the apogee of this style, but he employed it in simpler poems as well (*SKKS*, IV: 291).

Fushimiyama	Upon Fushimi Hill,
Matsu no kage yori	From this dark shelter of the pines
Miwataseba	I look across the plains,
Akuru tanomo ni	Where in the dawn the ripening fields
Akikaze zo fuku.	Bend in soft ripples to the autumn wind.

Perhaps a like smoothness and seeming simplicity of diction is what allows the priest Saigyō to remain a representative poet of this age despite all his divergent tastes. At his best he is a skilled lyricist, and at his worst he appears simple-minded and sentimental. His poem on spring and winter at Naniwa shows him at his best. Spring represents the conventionally beautiful and perhaps recalls the grandeur of the former capital there. But winter, for all its bleakness, has a sad beauty (sabi) without pretending to escape the Buddhist law of evanescence (*SKKS*, VI: 625).

Tsu no kuni no	Only a dream!
Naniwa no haru wa	The bygone glories of the spring
Yume nare ya	At Naniwa in Tsu—
Ashi no kareba ni	Everywhere the rough wind rustles over
Kaze wataru nari.	The frost-withered leaves of reeds.

The second stylistic tendency in diction was the one that Teika seems to exemplify best and one that his example made appealing to other poets of the age. Instead of attempting to make the conventional language achieve a reflective beauty of universal appeal, Teika often uses traditional diction in the most startling ways. The effect is one not of perfected simplicity but of rich surprise (*SKKS*, IV: 420).

Samushiro ya	For her straw-mat bedding,
Matsu yo no aki no	The Lady of the Bridge of Uji now
Kaze fukete	Spreads the moonlight out,
Tsuki o katashiku	And in the waiting autumn night
Uji no hashihime.	Still lies there in the darkening wind.

Word by word, the diction of this poem possesses the purity of Shunzei's style. But the words show up in the most unexpected combinations. The woman spreads out the moonlight and not her poor bedding, as we should expect.

The night is said to wait, not she for the man she loves and needs to protect her. And it is the wind, not the night, which grows dark. The effect is fresh in any language and not a little like Western poetry of the Symbolist school. One would underestimate Teika, however, if one thought he was trying to be bizarre. His sleight of hand with the diction is less mystifying than it seems, because he alludes to an anonymous poem in the *Kokinshū* (XIV: 689) in which the Lady of the Uji Bridge spreads out her gown in the usual fashion to cover her as she waits for her lover, the speaker of the poem. Teika presumes a knowledge of the older poem and so feels free to go on to greater depths. He also alludes to the mysterious beauty of the Uji chapters toward the end of the *Tale of Genji*. His unexpected rearrangement of nouns and verbs works with the allusions to create a world of imaginative, mysterious beauty out of the natural order of time and place.

RHETORIC AND SYNTAX

Such poems as those we have seen by Shunzei, Saigyō, and Teika show what traditional diction meant in the poetry of the age. But this is only part of the story. Teika wrote in his *Kindai Shūka* (*NKGT*, III, 332): "If in diction you admire the traditional; if in treatment you attempt the new; if you aim at an unobtainably lofty effect; and if you study the poetry from the Kampyō era* on—then how can you fail to succeed?" Originality was to build upon tradition, and to take the form of more serious aims and a new creativity in treatment. The "spirit of creativity" (*kokoro*) in any given age of Japanese poetry can be most readily understood by a Westerner not in terms of Japanese tonal ideals or the imagery, which might seem to have a sameness in all periods, but in terms of the poetic rhetoric of the age. The parallelisms, makurakotoba, and jo of the primitive songs and the poems of the early literary period give way to pivot-words, associations, and the handling of details for intellectual speculation in the early classical period. The mid-classical period also has its special rhetoric, although one salient fact of Japanese poetic history remains as true as ever: after the emergence of the tanka as a poetic norm in the ninth century, no major rhetorical or stylistic technique is discarded. Shunzei, Teika, and the other great poets of the period do not abandon the techniques and styles of their predecessors: quite the contrary—for every poem Shunzei wrote in the new style, he has a dozen in the old. Even Teika, one of the most individualistic and original of all Japanese poets, wrote poems that Tsurayuki, some two centuries before, would have thought *à la mode*. But although such poems in the older style may be more numerous in the mid-classical period as a whole, they do not represent the originality of the true

* Strictly speaking, the years 889–95, but used by Teika in a broader sense to mean the age of the Six Poetic Geniuses.

contribution of the age. The new creative spirit Teika spoke of is real, and we shall henceforth discuss only the poetry it produced, leaving out the continuing practice of old styles.

One of the striking rhetorical characteristics of the new poetry is what may be called the syntactical fragmentation of the poem. In addition to the incomplete syntax inherent in poems terminating in nouns, there is a sharp tendency to use full stops at the end of the first and third lines. If we postulate the *Kokinshū* and *Shinkokinshū* as hypothetical norms for the ages in which they appeared, we find that only 19 poems in the *Kokinshū* have full stops at the end of the first line and 160 at the end of the third, whereas the *Shinkokinshū* has 108 poems with full stops at the end of the first line and 476 at the end of the third. These figures require some adjustment and explanation. It is true that the *Shinkokinshū* has almost twice as many poems as the *Kokinshū* (1,981 as opposed to 1,111); but even when the proportions are adjusted to take this fact into account, we can still say with confidence that there are more than three times as many poems in the *Shinkokinshū* with full stops at the end of the first line, and nearly twice as many with full stops at the end of the third line. By full stops we mean not the light caesuras often employed at these points in the preceding age, but complete syntactical units or such fragments as apostrophes, exclamations, and disjunct clauses.

These statistics mean less in fact than in interpretation. Along with the omission of verbs and particles, with the elliptical statements, and with the reversed syntax, these full stops give a distinct impression of rhetorical fragmentation. Fujiwara Ariie's poem on "The Spirit of Travel" is wholly characteristic in its extreme fragmentation (*SKKS*, X: 961).

Fushiwabinu	I slept in suffering—
Shino no ozasa no	Cuttings from the small bamboos
Karimakura	Made an instant's pillow,
Hakana no tsuyu ya	Where the transitory dew and tears
Hitoyo bakari ni.	Elapsed with the anguish of a single night.

The translation conveys the implied sense; but a rendition that follows the Japanese phrasing more closely is necessary to show the fragmentation of the poem.

I slept in suffering.
An instant's pillow of cuttings
From the small bamboos:
The transience of dew and tears:
The anguish of a single night.

The only verb is the one that forms the first line, and it is a complete syntactical unit. At the same time the first line may be said to contain one noun because there is a play on *fushi* which means both "lie down" and "joint of bamboo." The next two lines contain three nouns (four, if one includes the play on *kari*—instant/ cuttings) joined by the possessive particle, *no*. The fourth line contains two nouns (three, if one includes the play on *tsuyu*—dew and its conventional metaphor of tears) similarly joined by particles, and is end-stopped with the particle, *ya*, used as exclamation. The last line has one noun, *hitoyo* (two, if one includes the play on *hitoyo*—single night/single joint of bamboo) and two particles. So intense is Ariie's desire to use nouns that instead of using the adjective "transitory" (*hakanaki*) in the fourth line, he chooses the noun and possessive particle (*hakana no*). The total result is a poem with six nouns, three of which involve word play or association, one verb with no syntactical relationship to the nouns but containing one additional noun closely associated with them, two full stops besides the one at the end of the poem, and a slightly less heavy caesura at the end of the third line.

Ariie's poem is an example of the extreme fragmentation—if not of syntactical involution—so typical of the period. Another poem, "Ice" by the Regent Fujiwara (Kujō) Yoshitsune (1169-1206), shows the same phenomenon to a somewhat lesser degree (*Akishino Gesseishū* in *K. Taikei*, XI, 11).

Naniwagata	The Bay of Naniwa:
Irihi no ashi wa	The water reeds touched with the sunset
Shimogarete	Are withered in the frost,
Kōri ni tayuru	And the choking ice has blocked
Fune no kayoiji.	The passageway of boats to open sea.

Once again, we ought to give a rendition closer to the original by dropping the words supplied from the poem's implications.

Naniwa Bay:
The water reeds of sunset
Frost-wither,
And choked by ice
The passageway of boats.

This version shows the full stop at the end of the first line, the lighter caesura at the end of the third, and that there are two verbs and six nouns. The last two lines of the Japanese can be parsed two ways. One could rewrite the Japanese by changing the cases of the nouns and the verb form, or, more easily, conclude the sentence with a copula or such another simple verb as "I see." But the point is that Yoshitsune has broken his syntax, interrupted the flow of the poem with pauses, and focused his poem on nouns. He, too, has fragmented the smooth, onward-pressing Japanese syntax.

It is possible to explain to some extent the motives behind such fragmentation. The last four lines of Ariie's poem, with their succession of nouns, give a quasi-Chinese effect that modifies somewhat the tone of the poem. The taste for descriptive poetry is also relevant, since it leads to a crowding together of as many noun images as possible, a technique well illustrated by Yoshitsune's poem. Another explanation is inherent in the formal nature of these poems. The typically informal, cavalier poetry of earlier poets put a premium on perspicacity, whereas the poets of this age tended to compose complex poems for audiences who were given to minute critical inspection and who therefore accepted complexity. But the explanation that seems to cover the most ground would relate the fragmentation to the poetic tradition. The poets of this age inherited a tradition of tanka lyricism which they prized, and they accepted the diction of their inheritance. Having started with a given mode and given materials, they needed to seek originality in the realm, as Teika put it, of creativity in treatment. By virtue of their acceptance of so much, they were also free to alter and leave out a great deal; consequently, although fragmentation was not logically the only possible result, in point of historical fact it is characteristic of much of the richest poetry of the age.

But to say this much and no more is to beg the most important esthetic question of how these poets managed to achieve artistic unity for poems whose syntax and grammar give such an impression of breakage and patching. The question is all the more acute when we remember that the poetic ideals of the age imply unity. *Sugata,* for example, may be glossed as "total effect" or "configuration"; hon'i means "essential nature"; ushin implies integrity of technique with conviction of feeling and tonal depth. The fragmentation is real and important, but the true genius of the age and the unique quality of the poetry in its tradition are revealed in the way in which the disparate parts are transcended, and unified poetic wholes achieved. Rhetorical techniques play an important, if not always the most important, part in putting the puzzle together, as one may see by referring to the poems by Ariie and Yoshitsune. To begin with, the reader is apprised of the direction the poems will take even before he reads them. Yoshitsune's poem is on "Ice," and he dutifully mentions his topic in the fourth line. Ariie's poem is more indirect, since it is "On the Spirit of Travel"—not so much a given trip as the states of awareness or experience evoked by this subject—and since he does not mention his topic explicitly. But at least we know the direction of the poems. To go further, we must look at the poems again.

> Naniwagata
> Irihi no ashi wa
> Shimogarete
> Kōri ni tayuru
> Fune no kayoiji.

In structural terms the rhetorical technique of Yoshitsune's poem involves, as it were, beginning with the pictorial frame in the first line. Then two sets of two lines follow, the first giving a close-up view, the second implying greater distance. Within each of these parallel pairs of lines there is a line (2, 5) with two nouns joined by the possessive particle and a line (3, 4) with verbs suggesting what happens to the nouns of the other lines. The effect of the lines with verbs is quite similar, since "withered by frost" and "blocked by ice" are parallel in sense as well as form, and frost and ice are closely related natural phenomena. By means of such rhetorical techniques, what is so disjunct in grammar and syntax is given unity by means of parallelism and development in the near–distant relationship of the imagery.

Ariie's poem is more complex.

> Fushiwabinu
> Shino no ozasa no
> Karimakura
> Hakana no tsuyu ya
> Hitoyo bakari ni.

The first line is a topic sentence which explains the succession of nouns which follows. *Fushi-* means "lie down" and *-wabinu* "have suffered," and everything in the poem grows in one way or another out of these two fused words. Lines two and three explain where the traveler has lain—on cuttings from small bamboo plants. But more than that, *fushi* also means "joint of bamboo," and so becomes an association with *ozasa,* "little bamboo," in the second line and with *hitoyo,* "a single joint of bamboo," in the last. Moreover, although *karimakura* means "pillow of an instant," *kari* also means "cut." The whole word is thus a pivot-word. The last two lines develop the idea of time and pain. Dew designates the season—autumn—and the "only for a single night" sets the time of day and period described. But as we have noted *tsuyu* ("dew") is also a conventional metaphor for tears, and so is an association with *wabinu* ("suffer") in the first line, and the play on *hitoyo* in the last line echoes both in technique and meaning the play on *fushi* in the first. The disjunctive effect of the full stop at the end of the fourth line is overcome by the alliterative "h" sounds at the beginning of lines four and five. The full stop at the end of the third line is also transcended by the related meanings of the initial words of each of the last three lines—"instant" (*kari*), "transience" (*hakana*), and "single night" (*hitoyo*).

The studied rhetorical techniques of the poets give their works what may be called a submerged unity. While going to such obvious pains to break up the normal unity of their language, the poets regroup the seemingly discrete parts into a new esthetic whole. Although the integration is often supplied in Ariie's manner by the rhetorical disposal of images and diction, syntax may be employed to the same end. A poem by Shunzei cited earlier (pp. 16, 232) is typical of the age in that its syntax is marked by noun termination, but in other crucial respects the syntax is representative of the entire tradition. The poem serves very well, therefore, to illustrate at once the syntactic practice of the period, and more general matters about Japanese Court poetry.

Mukashi omou	I recollect the past,
Kusa no iori no	While the summer rain falls through the
Yoru no ame ni	dark
Namida na soe so	About my grass-thatched hut,
Yamahototogisu.	But *hototogisu,* singing at last among the hills,
	Do not call out a freshening of my tears.

The poem consists of three syntactical units, the second of which may be divided into two:

Mukashi omou
Kusa no iori no yoru no ame ni / namida na soe so
Yamahototogisu.

The last unit is an address to the bird, calling it by its name and particularizing it by *yama* ("hills," "mountains"), a prefix which traditionally indicates that the bird has just sung its first, long-awaited, beautiful song. The second half of the second unit (*namida na soe so*) is a negative imperative— "Do not call out a freshening of my tears." The earlier portion of the second unit conveys, in the order of the images and words: "grasses' hut's night's rain in." The first unit is a two-word clause with no particle used to indicate the objective function of the noun: "past thinks," or in our translation, "I recollect the past."

There is nowhere in the Japanese a grammatical topic or subject, and no person is mentioned: the three personal pronouns we have used have no equivalents in the Japanese. As a result, the poem can be said to deal with processes, with objective images, and with an apostrophe to the bird. The objective world seems simply to exist in certain states and relationships, the overt process of most Japanese poems. The effect is to stress the importance of the related states, and accordingly to de-emphasize acts, actors, and the implication of responsibility so characteristic of Western poetry. To say this is not to suggest that the Japanese lacks subjective, human relevance, because it is obvious that only a human subject can shed tears in longing contemplation of the past; and similarly a hut implies a human occupant, just as an imperative construction implies a speaker to give a command. Furthermore, Shunzei suggests more specific details of the poetic situation by echoing an anonymous poem in the *Kokinshū* (III: 145).

Natsuyama ni	O *hototogisu*,
Naku hototogisu	Singing among the summer hills,
Kokoro araba	If you have heart for man,
Mono omou ware ni	Do not call out your song to me,
Koe na kikase so.	Whose longings even now can scarce be borne.

In the older poem the speaker is identified by the use of the first-person singular pronoun *ware* in the fourth line, and the expression *mono omou* (literally, "to think of things") in the same line conventionally implies the longings of love. Poetic tradition and certain conventions of expression thus enable us to justify using the first person for our translation rather than an impersonal rendering, such as "There is a hut in which someone recalls the past." Clear as these matters are, the fact remains that in this as in the majority of Japanese poems, the presence of human consciousness or agency is left to inference; and what is perhaps more important, the images and verbs function with a seeming independence. It is they which are emphasized, and not the agent or subject.

The first syntactical unit of Shunzei's poem (*Mukashi omou*) ends in an indicative inflection that is identical in form with the attributive. This ambiguity means that the verb can be parsed as one of those pauses or semi-stops so common in Japanese, or as an attributive to the long sequence of nouns joined by possessive particles that makes up the first part of the second syntactical unit. In this latter case, the sense would be: "In the grasses' hut's night's rain that recollects the past," since an attributive verb governs the last noun in a sequence like this. Such a construction is impossible, or at best Symbolistic, in English poetry; and it must be said that the principal sense of the Japanese is that of a pause at the end of the first line, rather than that of an attributive. However—and it is this point that bears emphasizing—the other reading as an attributive also functions, alogically perhaps, precisely because the human agency has not been stated. This second, attributive functioning—"rain that recollects the past"—provides a rich ambiguity because the noun following "rain" (*ame*) is "tears" (*namida*). These words are joined by their assonance and their conventional metaphorical association; as an idiom "rain of tears" (*namida no ame*); as related images of moisture; and in terms of the particular metaphor of this poem—the recluse in the hut has had his sleeves wetted by the rain and tears. Since such associations exist in a kind of metaphor of tradition made possible by syntactic structure here, the tears-rain are linked with the process of thinking longingly over the past. The metaphors of Western poetry are primarily imagistic vehicles of thought conveyed by way of assertions of likeness or identity. Our example shows that in Japanese there may often be metaphor wholly subdued and functioning by association, syntactical relationships, and tradition. And it must be added that here it is not agency that conveys the human, subjective meaning, but images functioning in a process that implicitly suggests the states of mind and feeling of the unspecified, first-person human subject who is the speaker of the poem.

How carefully the images and other constituents of the poem are related by the manipulation of syntax can be measured by certain other patterns in the poem. The sequence of words and possessive particles in lines two and three may seem strange and arbitrary—*Kusa no iori no / Yoru no ame ni*— whether we choose to render it as "grasses' hut's night's rain" or "rain of night of hut of grass." But the line break suggests the natural grouping: "grass-hut," "night-rain." Such a line division clarifies the relationship of the images and directs our response to the images: from the hut to the rain at night to, in what follows, the tears associated with the rain. As a result and since there is no agent specified, the poetic process of the images is precisely that of the experience of the poetic speaker. The imagistic succession is the one perceived by the old recluse in the hut, but the focus is upon the stimuli that provoke the affective and intellectual elements of his experience, upon the imagistic metaphors that yet retain the full sense of images. Inside his grass-thatched hut, he looks without into the dark, hears the rain, and sheds tears; but at the same time, he is not mentioned and we are deeply involved by the act of reading in a succession something like: inside, a very poor hut; outside, night and dark; rain—tears. The imperative follows this construction, and by now we should see the logic of his protesting command, even though the song of the *hototogisu* is so lovely and so seldom heard. The final image of the bird suggests great beauty, and although it may seem for a moment that the beauteous image conflicts with the sadder tone of the rest of the poem, it is not difficult to see either that sadness may harmonize with beauty or in particular that the transitory song of the bird has in it a quality of sadness that is well suited to a poem dealing with the emotions aroused by contemplation of the past. The image of the bird singing its first song is climactic in the poem, but it is governed by all that precedes, especially by the first line about recollecting the past. Time is an element in the experience treated by this poem, since the richer, superior past has fled and like the bird's song scarcely seems to have existed. Moreover, this image functions just as do the others in the poem, at once as an image like the other images of the scene, and as a metaphor to convey the sadness of the fleeting passage of time and to recall a past whose memory is so strong and precious in the speaker's thoughts that it may scarcely be recalled without anguish. This element in the poem is of course greatly strengthened by the way in which Shunzei's middle lines echo a Chinese poem (see p. 232 above), thereby suggesting an even larger past than that of the speaker himself.

(see p. 232 above)

IMAGERY

The poems of Ariie, Yoshitsune, and Shunzei have in common a descriptive mode. We have seen that although such poems existed in the preceding period, the description was scarcely ever an end in itself; allegory or attachment to a work of art—typically a painting or screen—was required to make them pass muster before the eyes of an age given to imposing its mind on every poetic subject. As description rose in critical estimation, the poetic center of the poem shifted from a unity gained by intellectual shaping of materials by the poet or poetic speaker to greater attention to the configuration (*sugata*) of closely related images. The change is reflected by the diction of poetry in the mid-classical period, specifically by the use of nouns instead of verbs to carry the chief poetic burden. Since most nouns employed in Japanese Court poetry convey images, the result is a poetry even more imagistic than that of earlier periods.

In terms of imagistic content, however, this development is not so much a change in the nature of imagery itself as in its handling. In English poetry, we may chart a course of emphasis from the imagery of personal and intellectual experience which the Metaphysical poets "yoked with violence together," to the imagery of literary and public experience in Augustan poetry, to the natural and medieval imagery of Romantic poets. But when ex-Emperor Go-Toba, Shunzei, and Teika argued for retaining the diction of the first three or four imperial anthologies, they committed themselves to using traditional images. Our earlier historical survey of these changes showed that individual images came to acquire a more or less traditional aura of association. To know these associations, one had to read the earlier poetry, and human nature being what it is, these poets argued the importance of what they found in their reading. Conservative and lesser poets tended to argue that an image or treatment of an image was acceptable only if it had a precedent. There were not a few times at poetry contests when judges blushed with the shame of having criticized an image or a treatment of an image on the grounds that it lacked precedent, only to have the poet triumphantly point his finger at an anonymous and perhaps trivial poem hidden in some forgotten nook of the *Gosenshū*. Such issues of another day are apt to be more amusing than important in historical retrospect, and we are interested rather in the attitudes and beliefs of the great poets of the age, who looked to the tradition more selectively and made it come to life by reinterpretation. It is no accident that just over half of the poems in the *Shinkokinshū* are by poets of preceding generations, some from a time as long ago as the *Man'yōshū*, for these are poems carefully selected, sometimes altered, and fully harmonious with the works of the generation of the compilers. This age is in fact an age of neoclassicism.

Neoclassicism is not a matter of citing obscure precedents. A great age of neoclassical poetry has several requisites. There must be, to begin with, a definable tradition, such as the Graeco-Roman and Biblical past for the English Augustan writers, or the first imperial anthologies and Chinese poetry for Shunzei and Teika. Further, certain aspects of this tradition must seem indispensable in terms of human need to the later generation. The past did indeed seem valuable to the poets we are speaking of, for when they looked about them in an age of wars and saw the splendor of their Court traditions darkening behind the emerging power of the warrior clans, they turned to poetry as a way of life, and just as T. S. Eliot and Ezra Pound have done in our time, they wove older poetry into their own in an attempt to give coherence to the confused spectacle of modern life. Neoclassicism also requires literary forms and conventions to make ideals translatable into practice. In the case of the Japanese neoclassicism, this meant the lyricism of the *tanka* and the several directions it might take in terms of alternate styles; and it meant a decorum for different occasions, along with certain meaningful poetic subjects. Finally, meaningful neoclassicism requires a sense of proportion, that is, of scope for originality and a distaste for cliché. Teika's insistence that "in treatment" one "attempt the new" shows a positive sense of proportion; his remarks in poetry contests, and Shunzei's before him, that certain expressions and conceptions are too familiar (*me naretari*) or too often heard (*kikinaretari*), and on the other hand that poems are new in conception (*kokoro atarashi*) or have a freshness (*hitofushi ari*), make clear that these poets did not take the past wholesale in order to retail it out in small parcels.

The important fact, however, is that neoclassicism grew from a theoretical ideal into actual poetic practice. In addition to forms, modes, themes, diction, and imagery supported by the foundation of tradition, there is a technique in Japanese as well as Western poetry that translates tradition into present poetic meaning. Allusive variation, as we have called the technique (the Japanese *honkadori* means "taking an original poem"), is a borrowing or echoing with a purpose, as we have explained in Chapter I. Such a technique assumes two things: a knowledge of the tradition on the part of the reader, and a responsibility on the part of the poet to refer to what is of central importance in the tradition. We can see Pope's discharge of his responsibility and test our own as readers when he describes Belinda at her toilette in *The Rape of the Lock*:

A heav'nly image in the Glass appears,
To that she bends, to that her Eyes she rears;
Th'inferior Priestess [the maid], at her Altar's side,
Trembling begins the sacred Rites of Pride.

We recognize with something of a shock ending in a condescending smile that Belinda begins her day with what looks like an epic sacrifice stolen from the pages of Homer or Virgil. There, battles and destinies hang in the balance; here, only female vanity and a lock of hair are involved. Moreover, when Belinda looks at the reflection of her face, she imitates the first act of feminine pride in the history of man as it is recorded in *Paradise Lost*: Eve's looking with great satisfaction at her image in the water, an act which foreshadows her giving in to Satan's flattery. To miss Pope's "allusive variations" is a loss comparable to what one misses in seeing a play performed in a language one does not know.

In English poetry, allusive variation is often satirical, although it can have the seriousness of Dryden's Biblical allusions in *Absalom and Achitophel* or of Dr. Johnson's Juvenalian patterns in *The Vanity of Human Wishes*. By contrast, it is typical of the Japanese poets of the mid-classical period that their allusions should always be employed for serious effect (although such a later writer as Ihara Saikaku [1642–93] might write a parody of the *Tale of Genji*). When the poets echoed familiar Japanese poems, it was with the intent of adding an extra dimension to their own creations. This is a Japanese technique easily appreciated in principle, but in practice it presents certain obstacles to the Western reader. He has the initial difficulty of recognizing allusions that were manifest to Japanese poets and audiences of the twelfth and thirteenth centuries. His cultural inheritance is not theirs, and it requires many years of reading and a considerable knowledge of the language to know when there is any allusion at all. Even after this obstacle is overcome another lies before him, because Japanese poetry tends to explore richness of tone rather than of idea, so that while the Western mind may quickly grasp the point of Pope's allusion to classical epics and *Paradise Lost*, it has some difficulty in apprehending the gradations of tone and feeling in which the particular genius of Japanese poetry lies. But to admit and to be conscious of such obstacles is to overcome them by half, and a Western reader with some poetic training and sensibility can quickly gain a lively appreciation of the Japanese practice, if not a mastery of its details.

We have already called attention to the use of the technique in several poems, and it is characteristic of the age that a great number of its finest poems achieve their rich complexity in this way. But one important distinction must be made, the distinction between borrowing and allusive variation. If a poet merely uses an old phrase that does not add to the dimension of the new poem, or if the phrasing has half a dozen precedents, the poet has borrowed from the tradition; he has not created an allusive variation. Moreover, the allusion must be specific and meaningful. Theoretically, a poet might allude to any earlier poem—from an unknown verse by his granduncle to a famous poem by Narihira. In practice, however, the reader must be considered, and if a Teika borrowed from an unknown poem by his granduncle, it was merely a choice of materials, not an allusion. Such considerations make it amply clear that the Western reader must not leap to his feet in the triumph of having recognized an allusion every time he hears a Japanese poet speak of the autumn wind blowing its melancholy way.

Such admonitory remarks serve at best to quicken appreciation of the poems themselves, but there is no one description for the effect of the technique of allusive variation. Often the technique helps to unify the seeming fragments of a poem. Inspired in part by the example of similar Chinese techniques, the poets of the age often divide their poems into two parts, one of statement and the other of description, and the relationship between the two is not always immediately clear. A poem by Minamoto Michimitsu (1187–1248) shows how symbolistic this technique may become (*SKKS,* XII: 1106).

Nagamewabi	Tired from aimless staring,
Sore to wa nashi ni	And unable to fix my mind on this or that,
Mono zo omou	My eyes are filled with longing:
Kumo no hatate no	The sky at twilight touches with its color
Yūgure no *sora.*	Only the utmost reaches of the clouds.

We can understand certain things: the diction of the first and third lines suggests love-longing, and, more important, these lines combine the abstract concepts of sight and thought in a somewhat vague way through the mood of the speaker. Still, the last two lines are elusive until we recall an anonymous poem from the *Kokinshū* (XI: 484).

Yūgure wa	Since the one I love
Kumo no hatate ni	Is a person inhabiting a realm
Mono zo omou	Lofty in the heavens,
Amatsu*sora* naru	I turn my longing in the evening
Hito o kou tote.	Toward the tips of the purple-tinted clouds.

The original shows that the color-lit edges of the clouds are a reminder of the woman the speaker loves. Because of a "classic" model that Michimitsu suggests by the phrases he borrows, his poem can move from the mood picture of the original to symbolism. The synthesis of sight and thought has little purpose for the unhappy man; he looks at a sky filled and darkened by clouds and sees nothing to satisfy his longing—except that beyond the clouds which hover over him there is a spot of brightness as attractive and unobtainable as the woman he loves. This sense of distance is expressed temporally as well, since his situation recalls the experience of the man in the earlier poem—just as his situation and Michimitsu's poem are clarified by the allusion.

This playing-off of the situation in one's own poem with the situation of the earlier poem alluded to is one of the most typical effects of the technique.

In other words, although a knowledge of the original is all but essential just to understand the unity of Michimitsu's poem, often the allusive technique serves to add a depth of atmosphere and mood. Such evocation of atmosphere often alters the tone of the original considerably, as we can see by comparing an "original," an anonymous poem in the *Kokinshū* (III: 139), with an allusive variation by Shunzei's daughter (*SKKS*, III: 245).

Satsuki matsu   Now that I smell
Hana*tachibana no*   The fragrance of the flowering orange
    Ka o kageba   trees
Mukashi no hito no   That wait for June to bloom,
Sode no ka zo suru.   I am reminded of the scented sleeves
                          And wonder about that person of my past.

In this earlier poem, the time and the action are clear, and the relation between cause and effect in the poem is perfectly natural. Not so for Shunzei's daughter.

Tachibana no   A moment's doze
Niou atari no   Within the circle of the scent
    Utatane wa   Of the orange flowers—
Yume mo *mukashi no*   Even in dreams that fragrance stirs my
Sode no ka zo suru.   heart
                          To recall his scented sleeves of long ago.

As the italicized words common to both poems show, thought and imagery are basically the same—orange blossoms remind the woman of the scent used by her lover of former days. But Shunzei's daughter has made a dream world out of the daylight of the original. The causal relationship is greatly intensified: the lovely fragrance of the orange flowers is so overpowering that it even suffuses the speaker's dreams. The aura of sensuous, mysterious beauty is not a little heightened by the last line and a half of the poem. Except for an ellipsis that is bridged by synecdoche, it is the same as that of the last two lines of the original; but in the later poem *mukashi* ("bygone times") means not only the lover of former days, but also the bygone times of the original poem. We are almost left wondering whether the speaker of the poem really had a lover or only dreamed she did when the scent of the flowers stirred her memory of the earlier poem. Whatever interpretation we give the poem, it must be in the realm of atmosphere or tone.

These examples show some of the technical forms that allusive variation might assume in poetic practice but do not make sufficiently explicit the relationship of allusion to neoclassic ideals. Although this relationship might be shown by reviewing the preceding examples, it probably can be best understood by examining yet another variety of allusive variation, one in which a few words and the general direction of thought and emotion bring to mind the memory of a famous older poem. Fujiwara Ietaka employs allusion in this way in a poem of soft, dim beauty (*SKKS,* I: 45).

Ume ga ka ni	Stirred by the fragrance
Mukashi o toeba	Of the flowering plum, I ask about the
Haru no tsuki	past,
Kotaenu kage zo	But the soft spring moon
Sode ni utsureru.	Beams unchanged with enigmatic radiance
	And glistens with a sadness on my sleeve.

The poetic logic of the poem leaps from the fragrance of plum blossoms to an inquiry of the past. The flowers bloom this spring as they always have, and he wonders what other men of former days have felt under such stimulus. The plum flowers raise the question, but, the poem argues, the equally cyclical and unchanged spring moon gives no answer. This cryptic poem attains its meaning by allusive variation, then, upon Narihira's great poem (*KKS,* XV: 747; cf. p. 193):

> What now is real?
> This moon, this spring, are altered
> From their former being—
> While this alone, my mortal body, remains
> As ever changed by love beyond all change.

Narihira's original makes it clear that Ietaka is asking the same question about man's identity in a world of change. Man, Narihira suggests, is the most changeable of all beings, and yet the most important human experience seems to alter this fundamental fact and give him an unchanging being that transcends the unchanging cycles of nature. But Narihira knew that such an impression was only illusion, that he, too, was subject to change, and even more so than the moon and spring. Ietaka raises the same question, and presumes the same answers in a day when his world was truly changing. Narihira's sense of experience transcending change seems even more illusory in these later times, and so Ietaka's poem ends in a greater sadness. In this period only the cultural strength of literature can overcome, and then for but a moment, the laws of change that Narihira's experience of love had transcended. The literary past, the cultural tradition, give meaning to the present and help sustain a man in the dignity of a civilized human being. Allusive variation is not just a technique—it is a way of finding significance in the disorder of incoherent contemporary experience.

What we have styled "allusive variation" to preserve some sense of the Japanese term honkadori has been called by one of Pope's best modern critics,

Maynard Mack, "the metaphor of tone." While appropriate for Pope, the term is even more apt for the effect of the Japanese use of this neoclassical technique in which the imagery of a "modern" poem metaphorically suggests the older poem, since Japanese poets characteristically work more in the realm of tone than theme. But since allusive variation is a metaphorical technique, discussion of it, as technique, does not explain the nature, the value, or the distinctive character of the images themselves. It is necessary to define the distinctive features of imagery in this period and to relate them to the neo-classical bent and intellectual suppositions of the age.

The place to begin is with the poetry contest. At the end of the last chapter, we remarked that the early classical period went into decline when the subjective play of mind characteristic of the age at its best degenerated into conventional conceits. Some writers, like Yoshitada and Shunrai, tried to escape the stifling effects of what had become an increasingly moribund convention by introducing new images whose traditional value was not fixed by custom, and especially by the custom of poetry contests. Gradually, however, it came to be realized that sterile convention might be made into live tradition, and that the more-or-less fixed values of images might be combined into new poetic wholes of description. Since the fixed values were subjective, a carefully composed poem, apparently of mere description, had connotations or symbolic meanings that were suggestive of human experience. This development from convention to tradition-supported and meaningful description can be traced in the poems and judgments of the poetry contests.

For our purposes, it is most useful to consider the poems on specific topics written by ex-Emperor Go-Toba, Shunzei, and Teika, since these writers represent what we may call the two extremes and the mean. Go-Toba held the most conservative position of the three, arguing that a poem should not depart from traditional handling of the imagery, and that the topic (dai) should be explored in ways which would evoke a common response from all educated men. When he was given the topic "A Spring View from a Village by the Water's Edge," he rendered it faithfully in a poem on a view from the village of Minase (SKKS, I: 36).

Miwataseba	As I gaze far out, I see
Yamamoto kasumu	The spring haze rise upon the lower slopes
Minasegawa	Along the River of Minase:
Yūbe wa aki to	Why had I always felt that evening
Nani omoiken.	Had beauty only in the autumn light?

The poem takes its origin in a hoary if polite controversy—whether spring or autumn held the most beauty—reflected for example in the differing tastes of Prince Genji's ladies who chose gardens lovely in one or the other season

(*Tale of Genji,* pp. 430–33). Autumn evenings were felt to be the apex of a melancholy beauty; Go-Toba grants this, but gives the palm to spring. His poem is justly famous, not so much for the freshness of its images, as for its perfect expression of the basic idea.

Teika, on the other hand, was accused by Go-Toba of violating the traditional values of imagery in poems that seemed to have little connection with the specified topic. Teika does indeed roam far from his topic, as we can see from one of his poems written at the age of sixty-nine. With no Go-Toba alive to complain, he wrote a passionate poem in the pose of a woman, on the topic of "A Love Meeting Which Is No Meeting" (*Shūi Gusō* in *K. Taikei,* XI, 452). Such a topic is one that our Restoration poets would have understood, and was conventionally treated in terms of the man's seeing the girl but not getting his desires. Not so Teika.

Haruka naru	That dim unknown,
Hito no kokoro no	That faraway Cathay which is your heart
Morokoshi wa	Lies estranged beyond the seas,
Sawagu minato ni	And no message of return arrives
Kotozute mo nashi.	To still the turbulent harbor of my breast.

The poet plays with the word *morokoshi,* which means "distant China," but whose etymological constituents signify "going and coming across the sea." The love-journey image is sustained throughout the whole poem, but the topic seems forgotten. Teika aims, however, at psychological not conventional truth, and creates for his speaker a woman who is so passionate that the meetings of the past seem to her present desires to have been no meeting at all. The only real meeting is the physical presence of her lover. Teika has dealt with the topic in terms of the essence of its meaning.

To speak of "the essence of its meaning" naturally brings us again to Shunzei, who felt, as we have seen, that in order to make the given topic meaningful for original literary compositions, the poet had to experience the topic so that he might, with integrity, truly explore and feel its meaning. In practice, he was less bound by convention than Go-Toba and less radical than Teika. He accepted, and indeed advocated, traditional imagery, but sought to render it with such fineness and depth that each image in the whole functions almost symbolically. In this attitude, as in so many others, Shunzei seems to be at the fine center of the developing tradition, Go-Toba to be just a bit stuffy, and Teika a most brilliant but eccentric offshoot. Shunzei's ability to give deep feeling to such conventional images as a stream half-frozen in a rocky channel, and to convey the traditional feeling that the winter pre-dawn brings the severest sensation of cold, are evident in such a poem as this one from the *Shinkokinshū* (VI: 631).

Katsu kōri	Now here frozen over,
Katsu wa kudakuru	Now there just fleeing from the grip of ice,
Yamagawa no	The stream between the hills
Iwama ni musebu	Is choked within its rocky channel
Akatsuki no koe.	And sobs its suffering in the winter dawn.

The "k" sounds of the first two lines help convey the anguished efforts of the stream and are delicately renewed in the last line. But these sound effects only stress Shunzei's skill with the images. The personification is a brilliant technique, both because of its fresh rendering of old images and its immediate effect on the reader, and because it makes nature symbolic of the human experience of winter cold.

The fact that such poems as these by Shunzei and Teika transcend description of the external world and create what might be called a symbolic landscape is most important to the Japanese poetic tradition. Not since such poets as Akahito and Yakamochi in the early literary period had description been regarded as a fit mode for poetry. The poets of the early classical period describe—but with some such ulterior motive as love allegory. The best poets of the mid-classical period combined the description with the ulterior motive to produce what sometimes resembles Akahito's pure description, but what is really emotionally symbolic of the human speaker. The subjective cast of poetry in the intervening period led to what may best be called descriptive symbolism.

The most obvious, and to the Western reader from another culture the least interesting, examples of descriptive symbolism in the period are the Shinto and Buddhist allegories that first appear in the *Goshūishū*, compiled in 1086, and that become a feature of the later anthologies. Except in the richer allegories of the late classical period, these poems do not represent true descriptive symbolism, because the allegorical significance of imagistic details is fixed and the emotional force is limited. An early poem by Shunzei shows the limitations of this mode (*Chōshū Eisō* in *K. Taikei,* X, 495).

Harusame wa	The soft spring rain
Konomo kanomo no	Descends upon all grasses and all trees
Kusa mo ki mo	Both near and far,
Wakezu midori ni	And avoiding favoritism dyes
Somuru nariken.	The world into a purer green.

The key to the allegory is the topic, which refers the reader to a chapter in the *Lotus Sûtra,* in which we are told that the Buddha offers salvation to all, high and low, sentient and non-sentient, without discrimination. Shunzei has put this gracious doctrine into allegory because most Buddhist terminology is taboo in Court poetry, and like the poets of the preceding age, he uses description as the vehicle of allegory. Unfortunately, sound doctrine does not of itself produce sound poetry, and it is almost always difficult in this period to find any depth of meaning between the two terms of such allegories.

The true poetic significance of these allegories lies in their influence upon the attitude toward poetry and the poetic act. Often religious diction or imagery adds richness to poems whose focus is on other subjects. Princess Shokushi employs religious materials in this way to give a sense of the conflict within her between love and the desire to follow Buddhist teaching (*SKKS,* XVIII: 1810).

Akatsuki no	The rooster calls,
Yūtsukedori zo	Announcing the coming daybreak,
Aware naru	And cries some hope
Nagaki neburi o	To a pillow sleepless in its longings
Omou makura ni.	Through the long dream of vain desires.

Daybreak, the usual time for lovers to part sadly, is altered into a symbol of hope that the speaker will be able to overcome her attachment to human love and endeavor. In such fashion, the poet has made a fine paradox out of the conventional figure of the woman pining in loneliness and unable to sleep, by focusing on her pillow and saying that she lies awake in a "long sleep," a Buddhist metaphor for lives of illusion. Significantly, this poem is among the unclassified miscellaneous poems (*zō no uta*); its religious suggestions prevent its inclusion among love poems, and its imagery is too close to that of love to permit classification with religious poems.

Such a poem may be regarded as an illustration of the greater seriousness attached to poetry in this period, a concomitant of the view of poetry as a way of life. In terms of poetic practice, however, the religious attitude more typically combines indirectly with neoclassical tendencies to help determine much of the imagery of the period, a consideration which takes us yet again to Shunzei, the seminal thinker of this poetic age. Without rehearsing the details of his theorizing, or the history of the practice of "concentration and insight" (*shikan*) in Tendai Buddhism, it is possible to discuss the effects of this ideal upon imagery. The conservative poets insisted that a given image should evoke a given response and, therefore, that the poet should handle the images in a set manner. Shunzei altered this rule, advocating that the poet contemplate the nature of the image and express that which was essentially and exclusively true of the image. In practice, this prescriptive ideal could develop in two directions. Either the imagery might be so carefully selected and arranged that the poem's total effect was one of rich, integrated depth, or a particular image might be so universal that the poem almost became an abstract expression of the "thingness of a thing." Often, perhaps characteristically, the alternatives are combined; either the poem is divided into two parts, one of generalization and the other of images intended as universal symbols, or the abstract and the concrete are interwoven. Saigyō is especially given to such two-part poems, but he is by no means unique. One of his poems shows the extent to which carefully chosen natural images become symbols of a generalization (*SKKS*, IV: 362).

Kokoro naki	While denying his heart,
Mi ni mo aware wa	Even a priest must feel his body know
Shirarekeri	The depths of a sad beauty:
Shigi tatsu sawa no	From a marsh at autumn twilight,
Aki no yūgure.	Snipe that rise to wing away.

Poem after poem reveals the extent to which such poetry was the result of an intent to depict what may almost be called Platonic ideas wedded to particular experience, but perhaps Shunzei's "On the Spirit of Searching from Afar for the Cherry Blossoms in the Mountains" (*SCSS*, I: 57) is the best possible illustration. This complicated topic exemplifies the fusion of neoclassicism (in the quasi-Chinese topic), images inherited from the early classical period, and the contemplation of essences. The poem does not deal with the search, but the "spirit" (*kokoro*) of the search.

Omokage ni	Sending on ahead
Hana no sugata o	My contemplated image of the form
Sakidatete	Of remembered cherry blossoms,
Ikue koekinu	How many ranges have I vainly crossed
Mine no shirakumo.	Taking for flowers the white clouds on the peaks?

One of the poets who carry such a contemplation of the semi-abstract essence of qualities farthest in this age is Ariie. His poems bring together a neoclassical searching of the past to give meaning to the present and an effort to express that meaning in terms of its most universal quality. In one poem he seems to have asked himself, "What is the essential meaning (*hon'i*) of 'Love at Daybreak' when the lover must depart from the woman he visits?" His reply to the challenge of such a topic is a poem that will match our most subtle moderns in its complexity (*SKKS*, XII: 1138).

Tsurenasa no	Is this not misery?
Tagui made ya wa	—Even to the extent of the very essence
Tsurakaranu	Of misery itself?
Tsuki o mo medeji	I refuse to admire even you, O Moon,
Ariake no sora.	Lingering coldly in the dawning sky.

The poem represents, almost to the point of critical distraction, a major style of the age. It has five nouns, including one as termination, and only two verbs. It is fragmented into four units, and divided into the generalization of the first three lines and the particularity of the last two. So much for its appearance. Its unity and meaning come, as we might expect, from allusive variation. Ariie's first and last lines allude to a love poem by Tadamine (*KKS,* XIII: 625).

Ariake no	Since that parting,
Tsurenaku mieshi	When your indifference was as cold
Wakare yori	As the fading moon at dawn,
Akatsuki bakari	I have known no kind of wretchedness
Uki mono wa nashi.	Like that brought by the break of day.

By recognizing this allusion, the reader of Ariie's poem would know the situation immediately. The misery he speaks of is not that of a lover who must part from a secret tryst with his mistress after a night of love, but one who has fruitlessly waited through the whole night without even getting near her. The moon is made a symbol of the coldness of the woman, and the speaker gives vent to his resentment of it, because although it would bring misery under the best of circumstances, now it only serves to remind him of humiliation and frustration.

Nor is this all. Ariie's fourth line alludes to a complex poem by Narihira (*KKS,* XVII: 879; see p. 162).

Ōkata wa	Lovely as it is,
Tsuki o mo medeji	The moon will never win my praise—
Kore zo kono	No, not such a thing,
Tsumoreba hito no	Whose accumulated splendors heap
Oi to naru mono.	The burden of old age on man.

By alluding to this poem, Ariie generalizes the experience he treats without losing the particularities gained by allusion to Tadamine. The moon remains a symbol of the woman's coldness, but it also becomes a symbol of time, and in a double sense. In the moon-woman's disdain, there is a waste of life for the speaker; and from the moon as a symbol in Narihira's poem centuries before, there is a suggestion that the specific experience of suffering rejection has taken place throughout time. If the allusion to Tadamine particularizes Ariie's poem, then the allusion to Narihira elevates the poem into universality. The "essence of misery itself" is made both immediate and general.

A few such poems as these—with Hitomaro's or Narihira's—lead one to wonder how the notion ever got abroad that Japanese poetry is simple. A reader might more properly ask if Japanese poetry is not too complex for lyricism; and the answer is surely, if not invariably, no. These poems, which analysis makes appear so highly wrought, are as much poetic wholes to a cultivated Japanese reader as *The Rape of the Lock* is to his Western counterpart. Analysis is proper and necessary, but it ought to be followed by re-readings of the poems for pleasure.

Not all such complex poems are wholly successful. Ariie's poetry un-doubtedly does possess less immediacy than the cavalier grace, sometimes superficial, of poetry in the preceding period. But one cannot have both re-flection and the sense of active participation. If the imagery of poetry in the mid-classical period has depth, it pays the price of all products of the human imagination—it loses the opposite virtue and so lacks the Cavalier spon-taneity and Metaphysical juggling of earlier poets. Still, readers are as human as poets, and we ask for poems which seem to transcend the limits of age and culture. The point of this digression, then, is to lead to a discussion of two poems that seem to us entirely different from each other, typical of their age in their imagery, easily understood at a careful first reading, and yet character-ized by the depth we require from all great poetry.

The first one is a poem of Teika's old age. It combines essences with richer particularities by fusing them as the Symbolists might have, and by heightening them with a strange glow of mystery. Teika's topic is "The Moon." The speaker of the poem is a young woman (*Shūi Gusō* in *K. Taikei,* XI, 450).

Shitaogi mo	Rising, falling, waiting
Okifushimachi no	Endlessly in the color of the moon,
Tsuki no iro ni	The lower reeds and I
Mi o fukishioru	Are drenched through to the lonely core
Toko no akikaze.	By the autumn wind that desolates my bed.

The diction implies that the woman is spending the night looking restlessly from her bed to the out-of-doors, waiting for a lover who does not come. The reeds are a symbol of herself—there is no pronoun in the poem referring to her—because they are withered, wet, and bent by the damp and dreary autumn wind, a symbol for her tearful grief, but also part of the "real" scene. Teika keeps the moon the center of the poem, however, both in the literal sense of its being in the third line, and more important, by his startling use of the "color" (*iro*) of the moon instead of its light. We have seen from Komachi's usage that *iro* is a very rich word in Japanese. In context here it means "light," "color," and "appearance," and it suggests "love." The startling richness of this word helps convey the distraught response of the woman, and her tense agony is conveyed by other verbal richnesses. The element *okifushi* in *okifu-shimachi* means "endlessly" or "repeatedly," but the whole word also means "rising, falling, waiting." *Oki* is therefore an association (*engo*) for "bed," as is *fushi* (literally "lying down"), and *machi* designates her "waiting." But these are richnesses we appreciate on reflection, and the poem expresses hu-man truth even on first reading.

For our tastes, the loneliness and mystery evoked by Teika is surpassed by what we regard as one of the truly great poems in the period, a poem by Shunzei that we have glanced at before. (pp. 17, 266). The poem is on Autumn," and in it the images of the description coalesce into a symbol of loneliness which any reader of any culture can feel immediately (SZS, IV: 258).

Yū sareba	As evening falls,
Nobe no akikaze	From along the moors the autumn wind
Mi ni shimite	Blows chill into the heart,
Uzura naku nari	And the quails raise their plaintive cry
Fukakusa no sato.	In the deep grass of secluded Fukakusa.

If the poem has an immediacy, it also attains depth ("Kokoro yūgen") by means of allusion. Shunzei alludes to a poetic exchange between Narihira and an anonymous woman. Narihira writes questioningly to the woman he must leave behind in the village of Fukakusa, (literally "deep grass"), wondering whether she will remain faithful (KKS, XVIII: 971). She replies (972) with an avowal of faithfulness and a plea for his fidelity. According to episode 123 (poems 221–22) in the Ise Monogatari, the woman's reply so moved Narihira that he resolved to stay on.

Toshi o hete	When I have left
Sumikoshi sato o	This village of Fukakusa where time
Idete inaba	Has drifted by,
Itodo Fukakusa	Will its "deep grass" grow ever taller
No to ya narinan.	And it become a barren moor?

No to naraba	Though it become a moor,
Uzura to nakite	With the quails I will raise my plaintive
Toshi wa hen	cry,
Kari ni dani ya wa	And pass the years, and wait,
Kimi wa kozaran.	For can it be you will not return
	If only briefly for the falconing?

These and similar poems had given Fukakusa a cultural significance, like Arcady or Cathay to our ears, and the hamlet, a secluded retreat in Shunzei's time, was a symbol of loneliness. Shunzei's speaker feels a double chill in his heart, both for the lonely autumn scene and for its associations of a love affair in the past so distant that not even the woman's name survives. Time has indeed passed, as the lovers of former days thought, but passed by their lives as well, leaving Fukakusa the moor they had feared, with only deep grasses and the cry of quails. Moreover, Narihira represented to Shunzei the height of the splendor of the imperial Court, which his age saw losing both power and grandeur. The desolation of Fukakusa was the desolation of a Court culture, the loss of a life of action and of splendor.

Shunzei's poem is one employing lyric description, but the images, so fine and rich in themselves, are also symbolic of the human state. His age found its finest expression in this descriptive symbolism in which the tone and situation are immediately understandable, but in which there were also depths of meaning leading to the heart of the experience of the age and backwards along the poetic tradition which they cherished. The emotional sublimity of this descriptive poetry made it an art for only the greatest poets, while lesser poets practiced a poetry that was more conventional, and handled images in time-worn ways. In a sense, the great poets did so too, for they practiced the old styles constantly, much as the painters of a later age were to practice conventional strokes to represent conventional images in order that, when the ripe moments came, they could turn out flawless original works, with a very few symbolic strokes. An art involving such reflection and practice leading to complete assurance in a formal poetry implies that the relation of the poet to his materials and audience had changed.

ESTHETIC DISTANCE

The quality of every literary work depends in part upon its successful solution of the dual problem of esthetic distance: the relation of the author to his audience and to his materials. Some of our remarks in passing, such as that the speaker in a certain poem by Teika at age sixty-nine is a young woman, show that the problem of the author's relationship to his audience in this period is crucial. Generally speaking, the more romantic one is about poetry, the more one wishes to look at a lyric poem as a "spontaneous overflow of powerful feeling." One expects an old man to write about age and a young man to burn with enthusiasm. Unfortunately, those who hold such a view know little about the history or practice of poetry. Many of the most delightful songs in Elizabethan plays were sung by young boys playing the parts of girls and were written by men who coldly calculated that a song would satisfy the popular fondness for music. All art is indeed a feigning of reality, and the question to be asked is not of its autobiographical "sincerity," but of its success in moving our minds and feelings. Our emotions should be roused at the sight of a moustachioed villain about to foreclose a mortgage, but we should not leap to the stage, pen and check in hand, to help the distressed heroine. In actuality, she may be happily married to the actor playing the villain and unable to abide the vanity of the blond hero.

Nonetheless, it is a historical fact differentiating the mid-classical period from the early classical that there is a greater distance between the poet and the speaker he creates for his poem. The poet may be an old man and write poems whose speaker is a young woman; he may be sitting at his desk in the capital and telling us of the hardships of travel; or he may be sweltering in the summer heat of central Japan while creating a speaker who tells us of the snow in his garden. At any event, he writes out of reflection and re-creates with a trained imagination. The same is not precisely true in the preceding period. The characteristically informal poetry of that age led to a decreased esthetic distance between poet and audience—but general esthetic propriety was maintained by the subjective alteration of the poetic materials. It is also true that since art is not life, the pose of speaking one's own thoughts or feelings is as much a convention as pretending to be someone else. There is a story about a priest in the preceding period who wrote a first-rate poem on travel. Because of the convention of informal poetry in his day, he could not show it around unless there was a proper occasion for the poem, that is, unless he made a trip. So he locked up his house, ordered his servants to tell visitors he was away, and spent a few weeks on the roof getting a fine suntan. Then, back from his "trip," he showed his poem to friends who enjoyed it only less than the joke of his supposed travels when he was found out. Such an effort would have seemed pointless in the mid-classical period, when it was expected that a pale poet could compose a poem whose speaker was sunburnt and tired with travel.

The historical explanation of this change is the practice of poetry contests and of writing a series of poems on stipulated topics. If a happily married poet was commanded by the retired emperor to compose ten poems on unrequited love, all of them might be written from the point of view of a woman. Poetry had become a highly conventional act, and even when the poet was free to write on any subject, in any way that seemed important to him, his literary conventions were such that he felt no obligation to speak autobiographical fact. Between the poet and the reader there stood a fictional creature, the imagined speaker of the poem; and the truth sought was that of the artistic whole, not of personal history.

Reading through the poetry, we find two partial exceptions to these generalizations. Saigyō often wrote poems whose esthetic distance is less than in the poems of his contemporaries. Unfortunately, many of these are unbearably sentimental or trivial, such as the one following (*Sankashū* in *K. Taikei*, XI, 233):

Yo no naka o	It is a fleeting thing—
Yume to miru miru	This world appears to be a dream
Hakanaku mo	Seen and seen again;
Nao odorokanu	Then why do you still refuse to be
Wa ga kokoro kana.	Startled into awakening, my heart?

In addition to poems like this one with its clichés and trivial sentiment, Saigyō often composed others in the pose of a woman in love or in the conventional Fujiwara style. His fine poems, and there are many of them, are excellent because of their imagistic technique; in them he characteristically adopts the pose, as conventional as any other, of a man pensively alone in nature. How little autobiographical this pose is can be realized from the fact that Saigyō was heartily welcomed everywhere he went, and in spite of the convincing melancholy of his best poems, he was robustly masculine and esteemed for his skill both in military matters and in the Japanese Court football of his day.

Drawings of the priest Saigyō and Princess Shokushi by Reizei Tamechika

The other notable partial exception is Princess Shokushi, most of whose poems convincingly express a fervent passion. We cannot say whether she was as indiscreet in reality as in her poetry. But such speculation is ultimately beside the point. Her poems are convincing expressions of feeling and are written in the conventional role of the passionate woman, a convention dating back to Ono no Komachi and continuing through Lady Ise and Izumi Shikibu. One of Princess Shokushi's finest poems is on the topic of "Hidden Love" (*SKKS*, XI: 1034). It plays upon the notion that while a person was still alive, his spirit might leave his body and go visit the object of his feeling—of love or hate—trailing an invisible, weightless cord that attached spirit and body. If this cord were broken, the person would die.

Tama no o yo	O cord of life!
Taenaba taene	Threading through the jewel of my soul,
Nagaraeba	If you will break, break now:
Shinoburu koto no	I shall weaken if this life continues,
Yowari mo zo suru.	Unable to bear such fearful strain.

Even in this poem, however, we have something less—and better—than "sincere" outpouring. The poetic speaker is the woman's body, the audience her soul. She addresses the invisible cord, calling it a "thread for jewels" ("tama no o"), but *tama* also means "soul" (*tamashii*), and the situation is one in which a woman's soul may go to her beloved but her body, roused with desire, must stay behind. Rather than love a person in secret after such a fashion, "she" would willingly die; and rather than autobiography, Princess Shokushi has created art.

Since it is the custom nowadays to call such vivid poetry "dramatic," a case might be made for so characterizing the poems of this whole period. Almost always, we have a clearly defined speaker and situation. But the term is really irresponsible, because in lyric poetry this particular kind of vividness is only the sign of an increased esthetic distance between the speaker and the reading audience. The combination of the particular and the general in the poetry of this period is in fact closely related to the two kinds of esthetic distance; the reflective character of poetry involves the second kind of esthetic distance, between the poet and his materials. To understand the problems involved here, we must consider further aspects of Japanese literary history, again in the light of critical common sense.

The practices of giving out specified topics (dai) for poetry contests and of commissioning poets to write poetic sequences gradually led to the fixing of the convention of the poet's formal relation to his materials. Often the poet did not himself choose the topic of his poem; he certainly had no choice at a competition, in which a judge would find it impossible to compare the merits, say, of a poem of felicitation addressed to the emperor and a lament on the death of one's wife. Sometimes the topic was simple (for example, "The Moon") and sometimes detailed "compound topics" (*musubidai*) were assigned (for example, "The Spirit of a Panoramic View of Boats upon the Water"). In either case, the poet's subject seems to have come first, either by commission or individual choice, and inspired creativity later.

The romantic reader—who seems to be our unhappy equivalent of Macaulay's schoolboy—is apt to protest that there was little room for the unfettered choice of subject for the poet in this period, and that poetry cannot be made at command. Such a view would certainly have surprised a Pindar or an Elizabethan dramatist who might receive a commission to praise an Olympic winner or to celebrate, as Shakespeare did in *The Tempest,* a noble marriage. In one sense, the area of poetic choice in any age is surprisingly small. There are countless Romantic poems on birds (preferably nightingales or skylarks), on medieval subjects, on great poets of the past who should be living at this hour, on injustice, and on the suffering poet. The Romantic poets, like all others, wrote on what their age considered important, and originality lay in the treatment. There is always room for a poem on the nightingale or the *hototogisu,* provided the poet knows his imaginative business. It is not fixed topics in themselves which might stifle Japanese poetry, but conventional treatment of fixed topics in order to elicit a stock response.

The poetic problem the poets faced was to achieve a balance between the impersonal force of their tradition and their own personal concerns. When they accepted the inheritance of a literary language, they accepted as well the limitations that the language imposed with respect to imagery and subject matter. They had to seek out new ways of treatment by which they could become deeply involved in their subjects. Their success in doing so entails something of a paradox, because they went the conservative poets one better in using conventional materials. First they learned all that a conservative critic could tell them about their tradition and its language, about decorum and proper response to certain images and conceptions. Then they asked the question, What is the real significance (hon'i) of, say, the moon? It was, perhaps, Shunzei's interest in the practice of concentration and insight that impelled him to ask such a question. When the answers came, they could take different forms. One was the creation of an imaginary situation, so that a moon might become a symbol of loneliness to a woman who suffered through an autumn night, waiting in vain for a faithless lover, as in Teika's poem. While Teika was not such a young woman, he of course knew the meaning of loneliness, and could, through such a fictional speaker and situation, create a poem whose totality was a symbol of loneliness that all men might understand.

Another form the answer might take was a presentation of the essential nature of the subject. In practicing concentration and insight, as we have seen, one was supposed to imbue himself so wholly with understanding of, say, an image of the Buddha that after a time the essence of the Buddha was fixed in the mind without the traces of any phenomenal embodiment in a statue. Such treatment of materials has obvious differences from the subjective wit of poets in the preceding period, or the ready acceptance of the world as it is by a Hitomaro; and it led to a poetry like Saigyō's, whose particular imagery is often combined with, for Japanese poets, a high degree of abstraction; or it led to a poetry like Shunzei's, Ariie's, and Teika's, in which the particular becomes symbolic of the essence. A third form the answer took was a reaching back in time to discover the meaning attached to the traditional materials by poets earlier in the tradition. When these older meanings were combined with newer experience through the practice of allusive variation, the poet achieved a sense of the timelessly true or universal.

These three chief answers to the question of the real significance of a subject were not disparate, as the discussion of the imagery of these poets has shown. The important fact is that answers were available in terms of poetic techniques that enabled these writers to achieve a meaningful harmony of their personal experience with the impersonal values of the tradition they followed with full seriousness as a way of life. If they answered the overriding question facing every poet—how to make poetry pleasurable and meaningful—in doing so they also solved the related but more technical problem of esthetic distance. In general, the pleasure their poems characteristically give is that of an imaginative neoclassicism, and specifically a descriptive symbolism harking back to the past in deep reflection.

POETIC SUBJECTS AND THEMES

The subjects of poetry in this period are the constant ones that we have referred to in the preceding two chapters. Nature is one principal subject; human affairs—travel, other kinds of human endeavor, love, celebrations— make up another. The subject which threatens these, and which is therefore often combined with them, is time. And then there are the transcending subjects—religion, mysticism, and the universal human truths. What gives any age its particular character are its themes, or predications, about these subjects. As in all Japanese poetry, the themes of poets in this age are apt to be more tonal, more a matter of attitudes, than intellectual matters of thought. This is of course a relative assessment, since attitudes and thoughts are closely allied, but the poetry of the mid-classical period resembles that of other ages in achieving its greatest victories by means of perfection of tone.

Perhaps the readiest way to understand the treatment of nature by these poets is to compare one of their descriptive poems with one by a poet of the preceding period. Comparison is difficult, if only because so few purely descriptive poems—those not the vehicle of allegory or subjective thought— remain from the early classical period. Those which do are usually found (selected with great effort from countless other poems in the private collections) among the poems in such later imperial anthologies as the *Shinkokinshū*. Fortunately for our purposes, there are some instances in which comparison is possible. A poem in the *Goshūishū* (VI: 419) by one Kaikaku, a priest, is descriptive and yet representative of its earlier age.

Sayo fukuru	As the darkening night
Mama ni migiwa ya	Advances in its cold, the strand
Kōru ran	Must surely freeze—
Tōzakariyuku	The waves in the Bay of Shiga
Shiga no uranami.	Departing from the shore.

The first three lines are wholly typical of the period in their offering a hypothesis—since the strand cannot be seen, the speaker can only speculate on the basis of cause and effect. The last two lines suggest the style of the next age in the incomplete syntax and the noun termination, but even here there is some suggestion of reasoning: if the waves depart, the strand must feel even colder in its loneliness.

Comparison is natural between this poem and one by Fujiwara Ietaka in the *Shinkokinshū* (VI: 639), because he alludes to the older poem, taking the idea of cold and departing waves to develop a description that becomes symbolic of essential cold.

Shiga no ura ya	The Bay of ancient Shiga—
Tōzakariyuku	From out the surges of the waves
Namima yori	Bound away from shore,
Kōrite izuru	It comes forward, frozen white,
Ariake no tsuki.	In the half-light of early dawn, the moon.

Ietaka organizes his poem so that each succeeding image narrows in scope and gives an increasing sense of cold. This basic structure is accompanied by the startling imagistic effect of the lake flowing in the opposite direction from the speaker, while the moon comes toward him in an undulant motion from the intervals between the waves. All the details add up to the final symbolic, if particular, representation of cold, and this in part explains the function of the allusive variation. The idea of cold in the present scene is immeasurably strengthened by allusion to Kaikaku's poem in which, in the darkness, he supposes it must be freezing cold on the strand. Ietaka begins where Kaikaku had stopped, by advancing the time some few hours to the half-light of the traditionally cold, sad pre-dawn in which the waves can be seen; but he adds the symbol of the frozen moon, which seems to have been splashed over and frozen by the waves like the strand in the earlier poem. Time has advanced in another sense, since generations separate the two poets. Now the cold is more directly apprehensible if symbolic—colder, as it were, and more universal—since it has lasted all these years. Such is the tonal logic of the poem.

Those descriptive poems of the mid-classical period that deal wholly with nature tend to select images carefully and then to bring them together in such a rich texture that the effect, even when not quite one of symbolism, is one of rich integrity. Nothing may be subtracted without ruining the tone, and we feel there is nothing that could possibly be added. One of Shunzei's poems aims not so much at an intellectual symbolism as at expressing a particularized but harmonious experience of summer. The images are so integrated that they seem, as the poet intended, inseparable, and so rich that each of our senses responds in turn, almost to satiety (*SKKS,* III: 202).

Ame sosogu	A stir of breeze
Hanatachibana ni	Touches the fragrant orange blossoms
Kaze sugite	Glistening with rain,
Yamahototogisu	And the first song of the *hototogisu*
Kumo ni naku nari.	Floats from clouds that hang upon the hills.

The close, even intimate, experience of beauty in Shunzei's poem expresses one aspect of the theme of nature's beauty—its vivid richness. Shunzei and other poets often widened the descriptive picture beyond the close observation of this poem to give a more sublime view of a lofty natural scene in which man seems small and nature's purpose beyond human affairs. Yoshitsune's "Cold of Early Spring" is such a poem (*SKKS*, I: 23).

Sora wa nao	The sky as yet
Kasumi mo yarazu	Gives no signs of a warming haze;
Kaze saete	The chill wind pierces,
Yukige ni kumoru	And clouding over with promises of snow,
Haru no yo no tsuki.	The moon drifts through a night of spring.

The speaker interprets what he sees, as we can see from the fusion of subjective and objective imagery, but the interpretation only conveys the grandeur and final inscrutability of nature.

The density of the imagistic texture of these poems often leads the poets to personification or synesthesia. But the poets are usually so careful to remain particular and accurate, that in such a poem as Saigyō's on the death of crickets in the late autumn cold (*SKKS*, V: 472), it is difficult to determine whether the metaphor of death presented in the image of voices traveling is personification, synesthesia, or both.

Kirigirisu	The crickets:
Yosamu ni aki no	With the quelling cold of night,
Naru mama ni	Autumn hastens on,
Yowaru ka koe no	And gradually they seem to falter,
Tōzakariyuku.	The voices traveling away.

The personification, or synesthesia, is appropriate for the theme of this priestly poet. Because although the *idea* that man, too, must die is not suggested, the tone, the image, and Buddhist thought make the *feeling* that this is so convincingly evident by means of a symbolic description.

The poems with natural themes discussed so far employ a poetic speaker who is an observer not present on the poetic scene. The human significance of such poems is inferred from the tone and images. There are also poems on nature in which man is part of the natural scene, as in Teika's travel poem in which the speaker comes alone upon a world covered everywhere by snow. He knows that there should be buildings and other men nearby, but the falling snow has obscured everything (*SKKS*, VI: 671).

Koma tomete	There is no shelter
Sode uchiharau	Where I can rest my weary horse
Kage mo nashi	And brush my laden sleeves:
Sano no watari no	The Sano ford and its adjoining fields
Yuki no yūgure.	Spread over with a twilight in the snow.

The sense of motion arrested at an artistic moment and yet continuing is important to the poem, since the beauty and infiniteness of the scene depend upon the speaker's finding himself in a place where there is at once no place to stop and no place to go. Human action has no scope in a scene so statically beautiful and yet changing with the continuing snowfall and increasing darkness of the scene. Man is caught between going and halting in a natural beauty that is universal and changing.

The age also produced poems in which some particular scene is infused with the subjective response of the speaker. Sometimes such poems seem almost to be in the tradition of the subjective poetry of the preceding period, but the tone usually reaches a conclusion which is different. One of Teika's early poems uses the old symbols of the beauty of spring and autumn, cherry blossoms and colored leaves, as negative comparisons for praising something else, a technique Milton would have understood (*SKKS*, IV: 363).

Miwataseba	I gaze afar
Hana mo momiji mo	And ask for neither cherry flowers
Nakarikeri	Nor crimson leaves:
Ura no tomaya no	The inlet with its grass-thatched huts
Aki no yūgure.	Clustered in the growing autumn dusk.

As in so many poems of the preceding period, the first three lines raise the question, Why? The last two lines suggest that the wide and distant scene, however pathetic and however emptied of human activity, has a human potentiality and a monochromatic, lonely beauty (sabi or sugata yūgen) that a more conventional beauty would only destroy.

Some of the poems on natural themes are so imbued with the subjective consciousness of the speaker that the images seem only half real in their ethereal, mysterious being. Such poems are characteristic of the mode of yōen or ethereal charm practiced, as we have seen, by Teika and his younger contemporaries. In these poems nature, no matter how keenly appreciated by the speaker, seems almost to be something other than reality. Princess Shokushi's poem on late spring, for example, startles us by its strange and rich use of "colorless" in the second line after the reference to the cherry trees formerly in bloom, and by the image of a spring shower falling from a vacant sky (*SKKS*, II: 149).

Hana wa chiri	The cherry petals gone,
Sono iro to naku	I gaze about in colorless reflection
Nagamureba	Of that beauty past,
Munashiki sora ni	And now the quiet rains of spring
Harusame zo furu.	Fall from out the vacant sky.

"The vacant sky" is a Buddhist metaphor that had been taken into poetry earlier in the tradition, and is especially common in poems with religious overtones. Here it refers less to a world of illusive nothingness than to the state of consciousness of the speaker. The sky is vacant to her, not necessarily because there are no clouds, but because there is nothing else to give substance to her thought. What she seeks in her musing is the embodiment of the ideal image held in her mind—cherry blossoms. And yet, so deep is her experience of the ideal image which she carries, that the image becomes more beautiful, more felt than the thing itself. Nature has become so much the landscape of the soul that reality is inferior. With such treatment of nature in terms of the esthetic equivalent of the concentration and insight of Buddhism, we have imperceptibly moved from natural themes to those on human affairs.

As a subject of Japanese poetry, human affairs are seldom separable from nature, both because man's response to nature is an important part of his life and because in this period poetic description is often symbolic of man's place in the world. Nonetheless, when we consider the themes, or the predications, about such subjects, we can usually say that the poem centers principally upon either nature or human affairs. Perhaps the human experience most frequently treated in lyric poetry is love; certainly even the most cursory glance at any imperial anthology will show how important this experience has been to the Japanese. Sometimes the subject is treated without reference to nature, as we can see in a poem by Saigyō in which the poetic speaker appears to be a priest who is willing to suffer the Buddhist "darkness of everlasting night" by rejecting the Law in favor of a fervent love (*SZS*, XIV: 874).

Au to mishi	We met in love,
Sono yo no yume no	And would that I should never wake
Samede are na	From such a night of dreams,
Nagaki neburi wa	In spite of the ignorant darkness
Ukaru bekeredo.	With its everlasting sleep of vain desire.

For all its Buddhist cast, Saigyō's expression of a love so strong that it makes the rejection of salvation worth while is sufficiently romantic to be universally understandable.

Japanese poetry, like Chinese, abounds with poems expressing various themes about the subject of travel. When Teika writes a poem on such a subject, we may be sure that his expression of the theme that travel is lonely and precarious will be fresh and rich (*SKKS*, X: 953).

Tabibito no	The traveler's sleeves
Sode fukikaesu	Blow back and forth on his solitary way
Akikaze ni	Through the autumn wind,
Yūhi sabishiki	And the sunset casts a lonely light beyond
Yama no kakehashi.	him
	On the bridge suspended over the vast
	gorge.

The scene is sad, because there is only one person taking his lonely way, but even sadder for Teika's focus on a small part of the traveler—his sleeves swaying in the chill autumn wind. As the man picks his way eastward from the capital, the sun sets behind him, lighting as it were the world he has left, and casting a few weak rays before him. The last line places him exactly on a bridge suspended on two mountains over a gulf, and the implication is that the bridge sways like his sleeves in the autumn wind. Caught almost in midair, in a fading light, the traveler becomes thematically a symbol of lonely isolation. The isolation is all the more profound, because the speaker of the poem is an observer but not part of the "painting." The effect is very like the vast panoramas of Chinese and Japanese ink-wash paintings, which catch man from a great distance and almost swallow him up in the vast scope of nature.

Poems on human affairs often take the form of a subjective, even symbolic treatment of other subjects. Ariie's poem on "Snow at the Village of Fushimi" (*SKKS*, VI: 673) transforms a winter landscape into symbols of a human experience that is related to nature, but ultimately goes beyond it. The poem is so elliptical that we must begin with a prose rendering.

Yume kayou
Michi sae taenu
Kuretake no
Fushimi no sato no
Yuki no shitaore.

Even the path to and fro in dreams is obliterated. The "Chinese bamboos" of Fushimi village break under the weight of snow.

The connection between the two sentences is hardly apparent from the English, or in the Japanese either, for that matter. The dream path suggests visits of love confined to dreams; and if even it is obliterated, then, from what follows, we must infer that the heavy snow has rendered the actual roads absolutely impassable. Taking another inferential step, we see that the real snow is so heavy that it breaks the bamboos, and as they crack loudly, they waken the dreamer; so that in effect, the snow that awakens the speaker has rendered passage as impossible in dreams as in actuality.

Beneath the piling snow
The nodding bamboos of Fushimi village
Crack loudly in the night—
Even the path to love in dreams collapses
Into waking from the sounding snow.

The poem is remarkable in its unity, for all the disparate appearance of the two syntactic units. *Kuretake no* ("of the Chinese bamboos") is a pillow-word for Fushimi village, because *fushi* may mean "joint of bamboo," and the village was famous for its exotic Chinese bamboos. But while enriching his verse texture with the traditional associations of the pillow-word, Ariie also extends its imagistic qualities. This fresh use of a traditional phrase has something of the startling effect of the poem as a whole. Even more unusual is his treatment of the topic, "Snow at the Village of Fushimi"; he incorporates the topic into his poem, but alters it completely from what might have been expected. Taking Fushimi in the literal sense of its characters, he relates their "lying down and seeing" by association to "dream" (*yume*) in the first line, thus drawing the two divisions of the poem together. Finally, the parallel construction of lines two and five with the parallel sense of *taenu* and *ore*, both of which may mean "break," the first in a subjective and the second in a literal sense, brings the poem completely together. The snowfall is doubly regrettable in that its effects are heard both in the real bamboo grove and in the world of dreams: the anguish caused by the snow echoes between what we today would call the conscious and subconscious realms of the human psyche.

The great enemy of nature and human affairs is time, perhaps the element that touches the Japanese sensibility most deeply and in the most various ways. So strongly are the poets affected by their consciousness of the passage of hours, days, or years, and so inexorable is the course of time for them, that in spite of the anguish and loss it provokes, no Japanese poet would think of denying its power. Protest is possible, but it is the protest of a suffering heart that knows no remedy for its pain. In his "Lament on the Instability of Human Life" (see pp. 804–5), Okura speaks for every Japanese when he concludes that in spite of his every wish to the contrary, "There is no stop to time."

The poets of the mid-classical period treat time again and again, but more obliquely than Okura. In Shunzei's poem on visiting the tomb of his wife, the abstract pressure of time is translated into suggestive images (*SKKS*, VIII: 796).

Mare ni kuru	So rare my visits,
Yowa mo kanashiki	And yet I too have heard the sadness
Matsukaze o	Of the midnight wind—
Taezu ya koke no	Must she forever lie beneath the mosses,
Shita ni kiku ran.	Listening to its moaning through the pines?

The italicized phrases, "rarely" and "without end" or "forever," are placed in key places at the beginnings of lines and suggest a contrast between the grieving husband, who has heard the lonely wind blow on a few occasions, and the dead wife, who is imagined to be so confined that she must listen to the wind forever. The treatment of the wife as one yet alive and sentient is particularly touching, since it suggests that she still lives as always in the lonely husband's mind and in a suffering existence of her own. The mosses function both as a realistic image and as a metaphor for the length of time that has passed since the woman's death. Similarly, the lonely sound of the pines rustling in the wind is part of the scene; but the pines are even more effective metaphorically in the ironic play upon their conventional symbolism of longevity and conjugal fidelity.

Like most of Shunzei's best poems, this one seems less a product of its age than a representative of the whole Japanese poetic tradition or of a universal tradition of lyric poetry in world literature. It might be taken as one of the most suitable examples of Japanese treatment of the theme of time. But the age was also one in which poets felt the past to be superior to the present. This was no sentimental idea that things were once better than now, but a consciousness that their courtly culture was falling from its central position in their national civilization. The civil wars between the great warrior clans involved a struggle for supremacy after which, whoever won, the Court class was doomed to decline. The capital and the splendid, civilized life it represented was in danger of destruction. Fujiwara Yoshitsune, who was Regent in name but not in fact, produced some of the most moving poems on the theme of the loss of grandeur in the course of time. His "Mist at the Site of a Former Capital" (*Akishino Gesseishū* in *K. Taikei*, XI, 98) treats the present as the last and worst of the three periods of Buddhist chronology, an idea similar to the Western notion of the Age of Iron.

Yamato ka mo	Once Yamato's glory,
Shikishima no miya	Our capital that stood at Shikishima
Shikishinobu	Fills me with yearning,
Mukashi o itodo	As with the grandeur of our past
Kiri ya hedaten.	It fades behind the deepening mist of time.

Two elements cannot be translated in this poem. The alliteration of the words *Shikishima* and *shikishinobu* is central in that it ties together the speaker's yearning with its object, the former capital, a symbol of the greater past. Also, the exclamatory particles, *ka mo,* in the first line comprise an expression which, although understandable to Yoshitsune's contemporaries, is not from the poetic language of this age, but from the *Man'yōshū*. This older diction of a former anthology is unobtrusive, but it adds to the theme and tone by recalling a better age.

Yoshitsune combined such subtle effects of style with more vivid imagery in a similar poem on the autumn wind at the ruins of the Barrier of Fuwa (*SKKS*, XVII: 1599). In former times, Fuwa had been one of three barriers at which internal customs were collected and soldiers were stationed as guards. The explanation why Yoshitsune chose Fuwa over the other barriers at Ōsaka and Shirakawa lies in the irony of the meaning of its characters—"The Indestructible."

Hito sumanu
Fuwa no sekiya no
Itabisashi
Arenishi nochi wa
Tada aki no kaze.

The plank-roofed halls
Of the barrier fort of Fuwa "The
Enduring"
Are emptied of their men,
And in the ruin of all that was before,
Only the rustle of the autumn wind.

Once more there are overtones that escape translation. The conception and arrangement of the images in the first four lines are unusual in the poetry of the age; the style of the poem suggests late T'ang poetry rather than a purely Japanese style. This subtle difference is important, because the later T'ang poets also felt that their culture was falling before barbarians. Yoshitsune's stylistic gradations distinguish an unhappy present from a better past, and universalize his theme of "the ruins of time" by echoing the poetry of another nation and age.

We also must not forget the image of the speaker in these two poems. In each case it is a courtier visiting a ruin. As he stands there alone, he either is separated from the past by the autumn mist or hears in the autumn wind only a sad echo of the splendid, busy life that was. The physical loneliness corresponds to the desolation of the scene, and both are symbolic of loss. This loss seems all the greater if we compare these poems with Hitomaro's "On Passing the Ruined Capital of Omi" (p. 101), which is public in nature. Unlike Yoshitsune, Hitomaro could speak for all men of his age and share his loss with them. By Yoshitsune's time, it was scarcely possible to speak in public terms. The fact that his poems, however universal in their appeal, have private speakers adds immeasurably to the tone of loss.

The conviction of loss and the relentless strength of time expressed by Shunzei and Yoshitsune make it seem impossible that there should be any means of transcending time available to the poets of the age. Such transcendent themes were found, however, by an effort to convey elements that are timeless. Not infrequently the timeless was discovered by entering deeply into the subject in order to convey its essential nature, a technique we have discussed in regard to the imagery growing out of the Tendai practice of concentration and insight. Other transcendent themes were achieved by creating a world superior to this world in its ethereal charm. Such secular mysticism, as it may be called, has its counterpart in poems of religious mysticism and both are often conveyed by the neoclassical technique of allusive variation.

The problem faced by the poets of the age in their attempt to transcend their personal world subject to time and reach a super-personal world of universality or beyond time can be understood by a glance at the congratulatory poems they wrote. Had theirs been an age of public poetry, they could have transcended their personal world in the way Hitomaro did; but it is one of the paradoxes of the age that although the act of presenting poetry was more social than it had ever been, the poetry remained wholly private. One of the best poems in a congratulatory vein is one Shunzei addressed to the god of the Hie Shrine (*SKKS*, I: 16).

Sazanami ya	At the beach of Shiga
Shiga no hamamatsu	Of the ceaseless waves, the ancient pines
Furinikeri	Have grown to glorious age—
Ta ga yo ni hikeru	How far past, the festivals of New
Nenobi naru ran.	Year's planting
	When these trees were set as saplings for
	the god?

Two matters attract our attention here. The speaker is alone; he is the private courtier and observer of so many poems in the period. The employment of such a poetic speaker is no doubt part of, or a cause of, the reflective mood of so much of the poetry of the age, but it seems possible to see an even greater poetic significance in the technique. Such a speaker seems to be as important to neoclassical as to reflective poetry, to Chinese and Western poetry of these kinds as to the Japanese. From Dryden to Dr. Johnson—and even Wordsworth and sometimes Byron, who share more with the Augustans in this respect than the other Romantic poets—poem after poem is presented through the consciousness of such an observer. It is such a point of view that colors *The Dunciad,* the *Elegy Written in a Country Churchyard,* and the *Intimations* ode. Such a speaker, and perhaps Addison and Steele's "Spectator" names him best, is reflective, given to comparing past to present, melancholy over the difference, and sometimes fortunate enough to find in contemplation a way to achieve a dignity in "the still, sad music of humanity" or the "glorious age" of the pines in Shunzei's poem. Such resemblances are more than fortuitous, since they show that certain kinds of poetry in different cultures share techniques that are meaningful for what they tell us of the assumptions—of the tone and meaning—underlying and infused in experiences that all men share. Important differences do indeed remain, but we may well remind ourselves from time to time of the basic similarities of certain kinds of poetic experience in different traditions.

Yoshitsune and Shunzei differ most from our Augustan poets, as from Hitomaro, in that their poems are not public but private. In Shunzei's poem, for example, there is none of the public sense of common interest or participation in a ritual that there had been when the courtiers first gathered to present the saplings. On the other hand, compared with the speakers of Yoshitsune's poems on the ruins of capital and barrier, Shunzei's speaker is positively well off. The ruinous effects of time have been transcended by means, as it were, of the very sense of time itself, as the poet imaginatively participates in a centuries-old Shinto ritual. In a sense, this poem is the arche-type of most of the transcending themes of the age: a lonely speaker achieves rapport with a world or ideal larger than himself and thereby transcends nature, human affairs, and time.

The act of transcendence often possesses a semi-mystical quality, but seldom if ever the rapture of a Keats or a St. Theresa. In fact melancholy (an attitude Keats would, however, have understood) is often the way to a wider world. Ariie, writing on "The Wind in the Pines," conveys a sense of the mystery of that quasi-romantic melancholy (sabi) close to the experience of the age (*SKKS*, XVII: 1636).

Ware nagara	So wet my sleeves
Omou ka mono o	From the wind that sweeps across the pines
To bakari ni	In my drizzling garden
Sode ni shigururu	That I might think them wet with tears
Niwa no matsukaze.	Caused by a grief not even I can know.

Even the elliptical and unusual syntax helps convey the sense of the unknown (the first two lines cannot be rendered in their order and effect by English, and one must be content with translating their prose order: "Ware nagara mono o omou ka," as we have in our translation). Does the speaker feel grief or not?

In addition to such avenues to the larger world beyond man, these poets also had Buddhist themes to explore. One of Shunzei's "Two Poems on Im-permanence," a concept basic to Buddhism of all sects, shows how the lonely observer might find his place in the universe by way of a poetry of religious overtones (*Chōshū Eisō* in *K. Taikei*, X, 447).

Yo no naka o	Gazing vacantly,
Omoitsuranete	And pondering without an answer
Nagamureba	The cares of this world—
Munashiki sora ni	No light flickers in the empty evening sky
Kiyuru shirakumo.	Where a white cloud fades away.

Munashiki sora means an evening sky without moon or stars, but Shunzei also uses it to convey the Buddhist idea of emptiness, the nothingness of the material world. The last line presents one of the descriptive symbols so com-mon in the poetry of the period, and presents it in terms of the concentration and insight of the Tendai Buddhism Shunzei favored. The white cloud fades from a sky already called empty, a paradox to be explained by the fact that its image lingers in the speaker's mind, even while the cloud becomes a symbol of impermanence, not only in the sky, but in the larger world that includes man's thought and feelings.

The poems we have used to illustrate transcending themes have all had a quietness and loneliness that does not answer to every experience of our lives. However, the strength of passion found in many of the poems of the period should warn us not to believe that a general silence descended on Japan at the close of the twelfth century. Teika, whose poetic strength in his old age has something of Yeats's "wild, old wicked man," wrote a passionate poem as a septuagenarian, posing as a lover sending a message in the genre of "Next Morning Poems." (Shūi Gusō in K. Taikei, XI, 452).

Asatsuyu no	To what can I compare
Oku o matsu ma no	The strength of my desire to extend forever
Hodo o dani	Our unfinished dream of love—
Mihatenu yume o	Or that failing, even for the little while the dew
Nani ni tatoen.	Takes to settle on our tear-stained world at dawn?

Love meetings were difficult to arrange in a Court society in which one's every move was subject to close scrutiny and gossip, and the happiness this lover feels is tempered by the fear that he and his beloved will not be able to meet again. He wishes their dream to last forever, but if that is impossible, he will make an eternity of the moment it takes the dew to fall. The dew is a symbol both of the tears they shed at parting and of evanescence. The effort to abolish time is of course tragically impossible, but time can in one sense be transcended. The phrase *mihatenu yume* is the title of the fourth chapter of the romantic *Tales of Glory and Splendor* (*Eiga Monogatari*), in which the newly appointed Regent, Fujiwara Michikane (961–95) is struck down by sudden death when at the peak of his youth and worldly power. This allusion suggests that if happiness itself may end abruptly in a world as evanescent as dew, its very brevity gives a greater quality of tragic beauty to such a life as Michikane's or to the situation of the youthful lovers in Teika's poem. The conflict, defeat, and yet partial victory in this poem clearly bear resemblances to the spirit of Western tragedy.

Another method of transcendence that the age discovered was the style of ethereal charm (yōen). As we have seen (p. 262), Teika's poem on the floating bridge of dreams is perhaps the grandest in this style, but Ariie, Princess Shokushi, the priest Jien, and, as the following poem shows, Shunzei's daughter also practiced the style with great success (*SKKS*, II: 112).

Kaze kayou	The wind breathes softly,
Nezame no sode no	Bringing the scent of flowers to my sleeve
Hana no ka ni	And calls me from my sleep;
Kaoru makura no	And, my pillow redolent with spring,
Haru no yo no yume.	I waken from a night of fragrant dreams.

The elusive character of Japanese is well demonstrated by this poem. The six possessive particles (*no*) are part of the untranslatable genius of the language: lines two and three mean more literally, but in reverse, "in the scent of the flowers of the sleeve of awakening"—suggestive but ultimately meaningless in English, in which the reversal destroys the carefully ordered progression. Moreover, "sleeve" is a synecdoche for "robe," since the Japanese of this period slept with their garments as covers, especially when lovers were abed together. There is a similar difficulty with the last two lines: "The dream of the night of spring of my pillow which smells fragrant," again to be taken in reverse—fragrant pillow, spring night's dream. The speaker awakens from a world of lovely dreams to a world equally dreamlike and lovely; she is, after all, called from sleep by the scent of cherry blossoms on her robe and pillow—and cherry blossoms have no fragrance!

The priest Jien, whom we have placed among the rhetoricians of the age, was also capable of one of the subtlest poems in the yōen style (*Shūgyokushū* in *K. Taikei*, X, 740). The complex conception of the poem is of a traveler on a ship who dreams of traveling on another ship; he awakes to find both ships gone, although in different ways.

Kajimakura	Pillowed above the oars
Nezame ni fukaki	And deep in sleep until dawn breaks,
Asaborake	I awake to find no ship:
Yume mo ato naki	The one which bears my longings in the
Fune o shi zo omou.	dream
	Has borne me in the daylight from this
	boat.

So intense was the dream experience that to the speaker all that really matters of himself still travels on the dream-boat; and now that he wakes, nothing of him remains on the real ship. The last line shows, moreover, that this poem is an allusive variation, one of the subtlest in this subtle period. The original is one of the most famous poems in Japanese, a lovely anonymous lyric in the *Kokinshū* (IX: 409).

Honobono to	Dimly, dimly
Akashi no ura no	In the morning mist that lies
Asagiri ni	Over Akashi Bay,
Shimagakureyuku	My longings follow with the ship
Fune o shi zo omou.	In vanishing behind the distant isle.

Jien alters the boat in the earlier poem into a distant, mysterious, and touching dream-ship. Not only has the human capacity to dream overcome actuality, but also the lovely past has fused with the present.

One final example of the yōen style must stand for the large number of such poems in the period. It is by Teika, who, after all, remains the greatest master of the style he devised. Two lovers are abed, covered by their two robes, but now are being forced to part in the light of early dawn (*SKKS*, XV: 1336).

Shirotae no	The white sleeves covering us
Sode no wakare ni	Glisten with the dew and, brightened by
Tsuyu ochite	our tears,
Mi ni shimu iro no	Are parted by the light of dawn;
Akikaze zo fuku.	And as we dress are shaken by the autumn wind,
	Which blows its color through our anguished hearts.

Two or three things strike our attention immediately—the treatment of the lovers in terms of their sleeves, the pillow-word *shirotae no* ("of whitened hemp"), and the attribution of piercing color to the autumn wind. The overtones of the pillow-word become clear when we realize that Teika has made an allusive variation of an anonymous poem in the *Man'yōshū* (XII: 3182).

Shirotae no	I dreaded it,
Sode no wakare wa	That parting of our sleeves of whitened
Oshikedo mo	hemp
Omoimidarete	Covering us abed,
Yurushitsuru ka mo.	But in the tangle of my thoughts I allowed your hand to slip away.

The situation in Teika's poem is considerably amplified and clarified by this allusion; he can afford to be elliptical, because he has alluded to a poem his age felt to be wholly in sympathy with its own experience. "The tangle of my thoughts," if not the free parting, comes over to Teika's poem by implication. As we shall see in a moment, however, Teika takes the pillow-word in a vividly imagistic sense it lacks in the earlier poem.

Teika's ascription of color to the autumn wind involves another, more complex allusive variation, this time on a poem by Tomonori (*Kokinwaka Rokujō* in *K. Taikei*, IX, 264).

Fukikureba	As it blows,
Mi ni mo shimikeru	The autumn wind comes penetrating
Akikaze o	Into one's very flesh—
Iro naki mono to	Why did I regard it as a thing
Omoikeru kana.	That lacks the color of our human love?

By means of his allusion and variation, Teika in effect affirms Tomonori's response but with an even greater sadness. The autumn wind does have a subjective color, and that is the anguishing thing about it. The effect of these

Drawing of Fujiwara Teika by Reizei Tamechika

two allusions is to universalize what seems not only a private but also a weirdly unique experience of love; and the autumn wind becomes a symbol of the forces inimical to this basic human experience.

The *color* of the autumn wind has, however, a more properly literary function in the poem. Teika plays on the conventional double meaning of dew in love poems—the dew at dawn when the lovers part and also the tears they shed. In context, the dew-tears glisten in the pale light of early dawn, and the images echo backward and forward in the poem. Their color brings to life the image of whiteness buried in the pillow-word, *shirotae,* and helps particularize the color which the autumn wind blows into the lovers' bodies. The color therefore becomes a symbol of the night of love, since it refers to their love under the cover of their robes; but this love is now past, and its very memory, with the reminder of its being past at dawn, leads to the whiteness of dew and tears, and so to a symbol of their anguish. The lovers part, penetrated to their utmost depths with the white of desolation. The agent is of course the autumn wind, a traditional symbol of sadness, and particularly appropriate here, where its chill contrasts so markedly with the warm intimacy the lovers had been enjoying. Finally, the poetic focus on the sleeves, the use of the part to represent the whole (the robe), and the object to represent those who use it, is a diminishing image, and in this diminution there is a further intensification of the pathos.

Such poems as this one or Teika's other on the floating bridge of dreams, and Shunzei's poem on the quails crying in the autumn dusk at Fukakusa are at the peak of greatness in the age. These poems retain the genius for particularity which is so much a part of the tradition, and yet move in many ways in ever widening circles of meaning to a universal significance. They are original poems in the highest sense of an art that creates new experience out of a keen awareness of tradition and its value. If the poetry of the age sometimes verges on preciosity, it is because its authors found in a world of art their only materials and means to express the experience of what was, for these Court poets, an unhappy age. And if the poetry lacks the immediacy and liveliness of poetry in earlier periods, it is because no human artist can have things both ways. These poets chose to sacrifice immediacy for a depth that their position of being turned in upon themselves made necessary, and a seriousness that expressed their conviction that poetry was a way of life. But by restricting our discussion to individual poems, we have not yet comprehended the full range of their poetic practice. There is also a technique of bringing poems together in larger units whose existence has been only recently rediscovered.

THE COMPOSITION OF POETIC SEQUENCES

The casual Western reader of Japanese poetry will hardly fail to be struck by the brevity of the major forms. As his acquaintance grows with the literary history of Japan, he observes that the forms become still shorter, and that within a given form there is usually a tendency toward still further division. This historical principle, for such it seems to be, may be termed fragmentation. But functioning alongside it in complementary fashion is another, equally important force that often goes unobserved by readers and that may be termed integration. Both of these motifs mark the mid-classical period, as other ages, although in a way that is particular to the interests of the period and expressive of its ideals. This age is not only one in which the tanka is often broken into three or even four sentences or sentence fragments but also one in which the composition of poetic sequences is at a height; and even within the tanka, fragmentation is only a step to a different kind of integration. Hundred-poem sequences, numerous private anthologies, and the imperial anthologies above all are arranged according to integrating principles at once more complex and unifying than Western methods of anthology-making along the lines of generic, chronological, or topical collection. The forms taken by integration varied over the centuries, but the result of this impulse was the creation of literary genres or structures that have no counterparts in Western literature. Some of these are familiar to Western readers, but one of the most exciting and interesting of the types of integration is not only unknown to the West, but also still unknown to most Japanese readers. This form may be called that of the poetic sequence ordered by association and progression.

The poetic sequences did not spring suddenly into being in the age of Shunzei and Teika. The genre is but one form of integration, and it had many predecessors, all of which seem to have developed out of two particularly Japanese ways of looking at poetry. The Japanese have perhaps had as highly developed a sense of poetic decorum as any nation, but yet have thought the same poetic materials suitable for a variety of purposes and uses. Natural images, for example, may be used for descriptive poetry, but also for love allegory, for public poetry, and for metaphor or symbolism. In short, the stuffs of Japanese poetry have appeared in many different products and guises. Along with this, the Japanese have from earliest times had a far greater interest than we in what might be called the possible contexts of a given poem—the social occasion, or relations to other poems or to prose. By looking upon poetry as something variable in nature and related to such "contexts," the Japanese have managed to integrate individual poems in ways unknown to our poets. These views explain why it was possible for the compilers of the chronicles to make wholesale re-use, sometimes through a kind of literary coercion, of primitive songs in their prose contexts without feeling that they had injured the integrity of the songs in any way. Similarly, in the early literary period poets used tanka as envoys to chōka in a fashion that tied two forms together, but without any sense of strain. And not infrequently they wrote or collected series of tanka like Tabito's on sake or Yakamochi's on his garden, series in which the poems are separate but yet related loosely in a whole.

These earlier periods show that the attitudes or the premises necessary for the poetic sequence had existed long before the sequence itself emerged as an artistically unified whole. It is with the early classical period, however, that literary developments ripened sufficiently to bear the sequence. Among the many symptoms of the maturation of this attitude are the long picture scrolls (emakimono) of disparate yet conventionally related parts and the imitation of such a Chinese genre as the formal essay, which alternated passages in simple prose with passages of rhymed prose. This period also produced certain narrative genres that typically combine prose and poetry. The tale (monogatari), of which the Tale of Genji is of course the greatest example, combines prose and poetry in a way that has no counterpart in Western fiction. The almost eight hundred poems in the Genji are more integrated, that is to say less discretely prominent, than in other earlier works like the Tales of Ise, in which the prose episodes into which the poems are fitted are little more than excuses to quote a few famous poems—but that little more is a unifying context for the poems, making their relation to each other plausible by supplying a context.

The tale, the formal essay, and the poetic diary are, however, casual forms in that each creates its own fictional prose contexts. Little could be learned from them about the art of poetic sequences alone. The poetry contests had developed another attitude that was to prove more immediately useful. As the poets gained experience with the problems of such contests, it became the practice to hand out the topics in advance, and although the topics were those of nearly the whole range of Japanese poetry, they were introduced in an order that had coherence. The seasonal topics, for example, were not given out in a haphazard fashion, but began with spring and followed in order. "Haze" (spring) might be followed by "The Warbler" (summer), then "Autumn Flowers," and finally "Snow." As time went on, the topics became more complicated; such compound topics (*musubidai*) as "Haze in the Hills," then "Haze in the Capital," or "Love in the Mountains," then "Love in the Foothills" might be introduced in order. As a result it was possible, and the possibility was quickly realized, to arrange a large number of topics and the poems written on them in a sequence of temporal or spatial progression according to logical stages. From there it was an easy step to the composition of poetic sequences employing progression or to making anthologies that employed progression as a principle of arrangement.

We have oversimplified the development of the sequences and have not followed a strictly historical order ourselves, because in a sense it is only necessary to consider the event that caused or confirmed this development (as it did so many others)—the compilation of the *Kokinshū*. This anthology differs from the *Man'yōshū* in that it was compiled as a unit, as a coherent whole. The division of poems into sections on the seasons, travel, love, and so on supplies a topical order that had been wholly lacking in the earlier collection. Moreover, in two groups of scrolls—those of seasonal and of love poems—the temporal progression implied by the order of the seasons or the progress of an affair is employed between one poem and the next within the group. Within the seasonal groups the order is that of the sequential appearance of natural events or of Court observances connected with nature, just as the order of the love poems is that of the course of an affair from its beginning, to its gradual development leading to union, and to its unhappy end. In each case there is a kind of narrative sequence or plot into which poems composed by poets of different times and on differing occasions are fitted to form an integrated whole that gives a pleasure of its own, above the pleasure to be gained from the individual poems themselves. No Western anthology we know of bears the remotest resemblance to this structure. The few topical anthologies that have appeared in the West have usually been met by the criticism that they obscure chronology or make the poems difficult to find. The West has not made the anthology itself a form for esthetic pleasure.

The imperial anthologies following the *Kokinshū* continued to employ this pattern of progression. From one collection to the next there is a steady tendency to employ progression in other books than those dealing with the seasons and love; and somewhat more slowly another technique of integration, one found only intermittently in the *Kokinshū*, is employed to make the integration more thoroughgoing. This technique is association, chiefly of the images of one poem with those of the poem it follows and the poem it precedes, but not infrequently of other techniques: association of rhetoric, of traditional connotations, and of ways of handling poetic materials.

It is not at all easy to say where this most subtle way of linking one poem to the next by association came from. Certain developments in the hundred-poem sequence may have played a part in the formation of a conscious esthetic of association. But perhaps the simplest and most convincing explanation is that the practice of association grew out of the practice of progression, whether in an anthology or in a hundred-poem sequence. When a compiler had several poems to fit into a progressive sequence—several poems whose chief constituent was imagery—the order he gave the poems would naturally take into account something of the force of the images so as to capitalize upon rather than to violate their associations. If he had, for example, three poems on the topics of "Love at Sea," "Love on the Coast," and "Love with a Distant View of the Sea," he would arrange them in this order, or in reverse; the order of the sea, the sea from a distance, and the sea from the shore would have been too abrupt in its near-far-near relation to the central image of the sea. Having concerned himself with the imagery this closely, a compiler might easily take the next step of ordering several poems on the same topic, say "Love on the Coast," on the basis of connections between the other images in the poems. A poem with such other images as clouds and waves might be followed by one with clouds and a ship, which might be followed by one with a ship and a person, and so on through yet other images. The techniques of progression seem gradually to have led to techniques of association.

The same integrating process leading from progression to progression with association can be observed in the hundred-poem sequences. Gradually and intermittently, the poets used association to give their groups of poems an even flow and development. Sone no Yoshitada was one of the first to use association thoroughly in some of his sequences, but in this, as in so many things, the eccentric Yoshitada foreshadowed subsequent events only to be ignored or laughed at by his contemporaries. The interest in association of ex-Emperor Go-Toba is another matter. His greater power and better opportunities enabled him to develop his taste for association to artistic heights previously undreamed of. Unlike Yoshitada and other poets who had sometimes used association in ordering their sequences, Go-Toba appears to have used the technique consistently in all of his sequences. The experience he gained from so ordering these sequences was put to startling use in the *Shinkokinshū*.

Go-Toba commissioned this anthology in 1201, appointing Teika and four other outstanding poets of the day as compilers. This committee, as we would call such a group today, chose poems on the basis of their merit and arranged them according to the practice of the *Kokinshū* and the six subsequent imperial anthologies. Go-Toba—a most remarkable combination of the littérateur, poet, and political storm-center—took a more than ordinary interest in his committee's work.* He rejected some of the poems they had chosen, inserted other choices of his own, and overruled even the strong-willed Teika, who objected to many of the ex-emperor's choices. What Go-Toba envisioned was a new kind of anthology in which the integration of poems through an associational progression was the prime consideration. No previous anthology had included poems that the compilers thought to be undistinguished in their kind. But the compilers of the *Shinkokinshū* broke from precedent, and following the practice (especially the practice of Go-Toba) first developed in the hundred-poem sequences, they used less distinguished poems to set off good ones and to provide a smooth associational progression from beginning to end. Go-Toba's obsession with the matter can be measured from the fact that after his abortive attempt to overthrow the shogunate and its *de facto* rulers, the Hōjō Regents, he took the text of the *Shinkokinshū* as we have it today with him into exile, and spent several years more in working on the anthology in an effort, we may suppose, to make the associational progession flow even more perfectly than our present text does through its almost two thousand poems.

Whether Go-Toba ever satisfied his fastidious tastes and how different his last draft was from those of the extant versions of the text that bear the marks of his revision are questions that cannot be answered, but even in its extant form the *Shinkokinshū* is a work for which we can find no adequate comparison in Western literary history. It has the extensive associations but not the erratic turns and sly humor of *Tristram Shandy,* and the subtlety but not the psychological analysis of *Ulysses.* Beside it, such Elizabethan collections as *Tottel's Miscellany* seem chaotic and almost ill-bred. It is simply a thing unto itself, the best-ordered of all the well-ordered imperial anthologies, a work that can be read as a unified whole from beginning to end, a succession of poems, one leading to the next in a flow of association, with a larger progression through various sequences and sub-sequences. In an unusual but real sense, the ex-emperor and the compilers under his direction made the anthology into one

---

* Perhaps the most gifted of Japan's many poetically-minded emperors, Go-Toba (1180–1239; r. 1185–98) was a highly accomplished poet, calligrapher, musician, painter, and football player as well as an ambitious ruler. More conservative than the innovators and more liberal than the Rokujō school, he was as poet and critic one of the "rhetoricians"; his passionate interest and coveted patronage did much to encourage the life-and-death seriousness with which poetry was regarded in his age. Upon abdicating in 1198, he assumed control of the "camera government," controlling a succession of emperors and ex-emperors with an iron hand; re-establishing the Bureau of Poetry (Wakadokoro) in 1201 for the express purpose of compiling the *Shinkokinshū*; and sponsoring numerous important poetry contests and sequences. But his political machinations brought about his downfall. Bitterly resentful of the new military dictatorship at Kamakura, in 1221 he attempted unsuccessfully to overthrow the regent Hōjō Yoshitoki, who forced him to take holy orders and banished him for the remainder of his life to the inhospitable island of Oki. There he spent nineteen wretched years consoled only by his unflagging devotion to poetry. A series of calamities that beset the nation after his death was attributed to his vengeful ghost, which the government went to great lengths to pacify.

of the largest poetic wholes in Japanese literature, and these almost ten thousand lines of nearly two thousand integrated poems make up a long, single lyric structure that has no comparison in world literature apart from the somewhat less perfectly integrated other Japanese anthologies, the shorter sequences, and the renga.

A close reading of the *Shinkokinshū* would give us almost innumerable examples to illustrate the techniques. A sequence of travel poems (X: 896-907) shows that the arrangement for progression alone is based in part on what might be called a plot (since there is a concatenation of situations), which takes us on a voyage from a forest, to the coast, to the sea, to China, back to Japan, and so on and on. But incredible as it seems, this book is at the same time also ordered as a kind of history of Japanese poetry. It opens with poems from the early literary period and moves by stages down to the poets of Go-Toba's own time. Or, to take another example, the first four poems on love in Book XI (990-93) show the techniques of associational development: the unity of the age of the poets who wrote the poems, in the distant past; a succession from mountains to hills to uplands to plains; an even subtler sequence of images from snow to waterfalls to grain; and all of these contained within a progression of geographical distance and further unified by the point of view of the speaker of the poems. The complexity of many of the poems themselves and of the integrating techniques precludes extensive illustration and analysis; we must be content to exemplify the techniques with seven winter poems from Book VI (667-73). This sequence has the advantage of containing only two very complex poems, both of which we have looked at before. The seven poems follow in order and with translation, their headnotes being omitted in order to convey something of the flow from one poem to the next.

667

Akeyaranu	Dawn has not broken,
Nezame no toko ni	But my bed is startled into waking
Kikoyu nari	As they sound—
Magaki no take no	The bamboo wattlings of the fence
Yuki no shitaore.	Crack beneath the piling snow.

FUJIWARA NORIKANE

668

Otowayama	The crowing cock
Sayaka ni misuru	Announces the arrival of the dawn—
Shirayuki o	But it is the snow
Akenu to tsuguru	Whose radiance displays the peak of
Tori no koe kana.	Otowa,
	The "Mount of Feathered Sound."

EX-EMPEROR TAKAKURA

669

Yamazato wa	In the mountains
Michi mo ya miezu	Even the single village path must lie
Narinu ran	Buried from the sight,
Momiji to tomo ni	For in the capital the snow has fallen
Yuki no furinuru.	Together with the crimson leaves.

FUJIWARA IETSUNE

670

Sabishisa o	Was it not enough
Ika ni seyo tote	To know loneliness without this?
Okabe naru	—Along the hillslopes
Nara no ha shidari	The oak trees droop their withered leaves
Yuki no furu ran.	And silently the snow still falls.

FUJIWARA KUNIFUSA

671

Koma tomete	There is no shelter
Sode uchiharau	Where I can rest my weary horse
Kage mo nashi	And brush my laden sleeves:
Sano no watari no	The Sano ford and its adjoining fields
Yuki no yūgure.	Spread over with a twilight in the snow.

FUJIWARA TEIKA

672

Matsu hito no	The path of him I long for
Fumoto no michi wa	Across the foothills to where I wait
Taenu ran	Must be wiped out:
Nokiba no sugi ni	The weight of snow has grown unbearable
Yuki omoru nari.	In the cedars standing at my eaves.

FUJIWARA TEIKA

673

Yume kayou	Beneath the piling snow
Michi sae taenu	The nodding bamboos of Fushimi village
Kuretake no	Crack loudly in the night—
Fushimi no sato no	Even the path to love in dreams collapses
Yuki no shitaore.	Into waking from the sounding snow.

FUJIWARA ARIIE

These seven poems make up a sequence within other, larger sequences.
The total sequence is of course the anthology, and within it Book VI containing poems on winter. In terms of sequences of still decreasing length, analysis
shows that these seven are part of a group of twenty-eight winter poems that
have snow as the central image (657–684) and are a sub-sequence of yet another

smaller sub-group of thirteen (661–73) emphasizing human emotions and human affairs. These seven poems themselves begin with four older and on the whole less distinguished compositions that alternate somewhat in quality between the rather good (667, 669) and the rather weak (668, 670)—an alternation of poetic quality which has the effect of setting off the brilliance of the good against the plainer background of the ordinary poems. They conclude with three by contemporary poets—two by Teika, one his splendid poem on snow at dusk at Sano, and finally one of Ariie's greatest poems. The transition between the old and the new is skillfully made, since Teika's first poem (671) echoes an old poem by Okimaro (*MYS,* III: 265). So that in general the rhythm of this short sequence is that of a movement from old to new in alternating but progressively rising waves of literary quality.

Although this qualitative and chronological rhythm provides the sequence with a kind of movement toward climax, the basic progression is to be found in the temporal succession employed. The temporal sequence is from pre-dawn (667) to dawn (668); from daylight (668 and 669) to dusk (671); and from evening (672) to late night (673)—stages covering a full twenty-four hour period. The other elements of progression are more subtle and more closely related to association. The spatial progression, for example, can best be understood by the location of the speakers of the poems and the scenery they observe. We begin with a speaker abed (667). The next poem (668) seems to take us abruptly to a mountain view, but because of the clear temporal progression we must assume that with the dawn the view of the speaker is now open as it was not before and that he has just risen from his bed and is looking out at the mountains. From these distant mountains we progress to a mountain village (669); from it to the lesser hillslopes (670); and thence to the plain (671). The next poem (672) implies that the speaker is in the mountains, but it is concerned with the lover whom the woman would like to have come to her along the road at the base of the hills, and is therefore a transition from the preceding poem in the play of outdoors and indoors in both poems, leading us back into the dwelling as night falls; and it is there that we once again find the speaker in the last poem (673). The sense of progression in this change is heightened by the intermittent use of place names, suggesting that we have indeed covered considerable ground—Mount Otowa (668), the ford at Sano (671), and the village of Fushimi (673).

The changing scope of the speakers' view provides a similar and perhaps still subtler progression. The darkness of the first poem (667) makes the view close, but the sounds outside suggest a widening view that is realized in the next poem (668) to a medium distance (the bird must be within earshot) and a larger view (the distant mountains). The third poem (669) contrasts the distance of the imagined mountain village with the medium view nearer at hand of the scenery in the capital, so preparing the way for the medium-wide view of the hillslopes in the fourth poem (670). Teika's first poem (671) provides a splendid transition in this as in other ways, since although the view is quite wide, it is limited by the falling snow and grows ever smaller as the darkness closes about. Something of the medium view of this poem is left in the imagination of the speaker of the next poem (672), who thinks of the road over which her lover must travel, but the scene itself is a closed one of night at the dwelling of the speaker. Ariie's poem (673) concludes the sequence by implying that actual journeys are impossible and dream journeys are broken, and by presenting a close "view" in the imagery of the breaking bamboos about the house.

Many of the steps in these less obvious kinds of progression involve association, but there are also patterns of association that have little to do with progression. This is to say that association links one poem with those before and after but does not give direction to the whole series. Such association is usually made through images other than the "ground" image, to borrow a musical term, of the snow. The first two poems (667 and 668) share imagery of sound—the breaking fence and the bird—and this link is made verbally specific by the *oto,* "sound," of *Otowayama* in the first line of the second poem. The image of mountains links this poem with the next (669), just as the imagery of leaves links that and the next (670). Teika's first poem (671) has no overt imagistic link with its predecessor, but the juxtaposition arouses certain associations. The plain on which the traveler has stopped seems to be below the hills of the preceding poem, since the loneliness (*sabishisa*) is heightened by Teika and given a quality of great beauty that is less stressed but present in the preceding poem. The relation between this and Teika's second poem (672) is once again one of an association of images. The "shelter" (*kage*) sought in vain by the speaker of the preceding poem suggests either trees or houses, both of which are present in the second. The last poem (673) is associated with the one before it by its images—of trees and bamboos, of the increasing heavy snow—and by implication. By implication, since in each poem the journeys for trysts are obstructed by snow, and the person waiting for her lover in Teika's poem is associated with the person to be visited in a dream in Ariie's poem.

Such are the main techniques of association and progression in this sequence of seven poems. Although these techniques alone are enough to show the astonishing degree of integration, the group reveals a further artistic dimension that must not be passed by. In this brief series, as in most of the sub-sequences of the *Shinkokinshū*, there is a beginning, middle, and end—a kind of ordering of musical themes and their resolution. The first poem is expository in that it presents the central images and implies the basic situation to be developed. The bed and the dwelling, the sense of interruption, the bamboos (or trees) near the dwelling, the imagery of sound, and snow as the agent deterring human affairs—all of these are developed in the sequence. The next three poems (668–70) develop various tonal aspects of these images

Drawing of Fujiwara Ariie by Hishikawa Moronobu

—isolation, beauty, sadness—which Teika's first poem (671) harmonizes so beautifully. Teika's second poem (672) develops from the very first poem of the series those two elements that prepare for the climax—sleeplessness and love. And Ariie's poem brings the group to its rich conclusion by heightening through diction and implication the chief images and tonal dimensions of all that has gone before. How far this is so can be gauged by the richness of meaning of his last line—a richness in part due of course to the superiority of his art but also due to its place in the sequence—in comparison with the identical last line of the first poem. These seven poems have been brought together in a way that calls forth their individual qualities and yet renders them into a new whole of transcendent beauty and subtlety. That the whole *Shinkokinshū,* and to somewhat lesser extent the earlier anthologies, are such transcendent lyric wholes is a marvel continuously heightened by repeated and closer scrutiny.

Such integration is clearly founded upon an exploration of tonal depths unknown to Western poetry. If our great poets achieve other, more intellectual or thematic victories, these should not blind us to the tonal or affective triumphs of the Japanese. Nor should our fascination with the associational progression of such large wholes as the anthologies or hundred-poem sequences blind us to the similarly integrated depths of the tanka itself. By eschewing extensive poetry, the Japanese poets were free to develop the intensive, and the wonder is not so much that the tanka is short as that it is so flexible and so rich, and that hundreds of them might be developed into such harmonious wholes as the *Shinkokinshū*.

The complementary impulses, as we have called them, of fragmentation and integration, continued to develop subsequently along new lines and produced new developments in tanka poetry, in the composition of poetic sequences, and in bringing about new literary genres. Many other and later factors are involved in such developments, as also in the answer to the question why the Japanese have themselves lost sight of the integrating techniques of association and progression in poetic sequences. There appear to be several answers. The chief historical consideration involved is the fact that from the mid-fifteenth century imperial anthologies were no longer compiled and tanka sequences fell out of fashion. With the loss of the practice came the loss of the ability to see the practice. Then, with the rise of scholarship in Edo and modern times, the poems have been separated in editions by lines or even pages of notes and commentary. The tanka is so complex that these editorial aids are essential for most students, but their presence has served to direct the attention of readers to individual poems in isolation, to discourage sequential reading. Another reason is that the modern Japanese have, like Western critics, tended to print selections or editions abridged, sometimes on the basis of quality and sometimes on other principles. Professor Kubota Utsubo, for example, compiled his splendid two-volume critical edition of the *Shinkokinshū* (*Shinkokinwakashū Hyōshaku*) on the principle of including only those poems which he feels belong to the generation of the compilers. A final reason is that the romantic revival of interest in the *Man'yōshū* in Edo and Meiji times—a revival that still blinds many Japanese scholars and readers to the merits of much of their own best poetry—stressed certain real and imaginary poetic qualities of the *Man'yōshū* so highly that the great virtues of the Court poetry of subsequent periods were either lost to sight or even termed defects. A similar romantic haze surrounds and distorts certain new directions in poetry at the end of this period. We must now try to tell, simply and fairly, the romanticized story of Minamoto Sanetomo—a pupil of Teika, an adulator of the *Man'yōshū*, and a shogun who might possibly have ruled Japan had he not been assassinated at the age of twenty-seven.

MINAMOTO SANETOMO AND ROMANTIC PRIMITIVISM

Minamoto Sanetomo (1192–1219) survives in history and legend. As a poet, he makes his first official appearance in the *Shinchokusenshū*, the imperial anthology compiled by Teika about 1234. There are some twenty-five of his more conventional poems here, but those in his private anthology, the *Kinkaishū,* are the ones that have brought him the attention and fame he has acquired today. His is truly a reputation that cannot be ignored. Nunami Mamoru, editor of the *Kinkaishū* in the *Great Compendium of Japanese Poetry (K. Taikei,* XIV, xxi), sets the issue squarely before us.

Considering the range of Sanetomo's poetic styles, Shunzei and Teika must be ranked far below him. It is not only in his poems in the Man'yō style, but also in those in the Kokin and Shinkokin styles—which is to say throughout the whole of the *Kinkaishū*—that we find the inexhaustible passion, the warrior of uncertain destiny, the poet of genius. Is it not true that the Spirit of Sanetomo calls out to our spirits through the *Kinkaishū?*

A poet so much greater than Shunzei and Teika must be a very great poet indeed, and to verify or disprove such an extraordinary judgment we can only examine the evidence of his poems, especially such poems as have been extolled by his admirers.

Saitō Mokichi, who admired Sanetomo greatly and was himself a poet, an editor of Sanetomo's works, and the author of the splendid multi-volume study of Hitomaro, praised highly the poem on "Geese Before the Moon" in the *Kinkaishū* (Saitō Mokichi, ed., *Kinkaiwakashū,* No. 217).

Ama no hara	As I look
Furisakemireba	Across the wide plains of heaven,
Masu kagami	In the moonlit sky,
Kiyoki tsukuyo ni	Pure as a shining mirror,
Kari nakiwataru.	The geese cry out in flight.

"This," Saitō remarks, "is a strong-lined, clear-cut, and direct poem, truly one that makes us feel good" (p. 119). But—by way of disagreement—this is a conventional, vague pastiche of old materials. The first two lines had been worn out through repetition even in the early literary period; the third line, "a shining mirror," is a pillow-word for "pure"; and what remains is a rather vague and conventional treatment of the topic on which Sanetomo had composed the poem. All is borrowed, nothing is repaid. Shunzei and Teika borrow as Milton borrows, in order to reshape into significant new wholes; they echo in order to deepen their own poetic creations. Sanetomo's verses have no depth because there is no real re-creation of experience. A Japanese school-boy could compose such a "poem" without really trying; and we wonder if such works of Sanetomo would have attracted the slightest attention if he had been, instead of a great lord, some anonymous young priest whose verses survived in the margin of a temple book.

Our skepticism about the Japanese estimation of this poem ought not to be taken as a denial that Sanetomo had any talent at all. Sometimes there are a few strong lines that stand out vividly, both from the remainder of the poem and from contemporary poetic styles, and more rarely a whole poem truly creates an esthetic experience. Sanetomo's most famous poem, "Expressing My Singleness of Heart" (Saitō ed., No. 663), begins with two powerful lines and then falls into insipid protestation. He wrote the poem for the ex-Emperor Go-Toba—the retired emperors held whatever power the Court still possessed in those years—who was resentful over the assumption of political power in Kamakura by Sanetomo's clan, the Minamoto.

Yama wa sake	Though the time come
Umi wa asenan	When the mountains split asunder
Yo nari to mo	And the seas drain dry,
Kimi ni futagokoro	I shall never show my lord
Wa ga arame ya mo.	A double-dealing heart.

The images of the mountain and the sea are powerful and have a freshness in spite of the fact that they are borrowed from Chinese poetry, but the last three lines of the Japanese (our first, fourth, and fifth) are about as fresh as "I plight my troth." Moreover, poor Sanetomo failed to see that the inauspicious nature of his powerful images, which suggest division and destruction, was singularly unfortunate if he wished to reassure Go-Toba of his loyalty. Such a faux pas makes it easy to understand why Teika was so insistent that a novice restrain his enthusiasm for the "demon-quelling style" until he had gained control of the more basic tools of the craft, including, one suspects, a greater familiarity with the niceties of decorum. We are once again led to ask whether the fame of this poem is not largely independent of its artistic interest, whether it is not more famous for the biography of the poet and the adulation it clumsily attempts to show for the imperial house.

A better realized, more wholly integrated poem is one Sanetomo wrote on the topic "Hail," in which he has managed to give a fresh treatment of an old subject (Saitō ed., No. 677).

Mononofu no	As the warrior
Yanami tsukurou	Straightens the arrows in his quiver,
Kote no ue ni	The hail pelts down
Arare tabashiru	Upon the wrist guard of his lifted hand,
Nasu no shinohara.	And beats before him in the bamboo plain
	of Nasu.

There is perhaps little depth to this poem, and its indelicate imagery of a warrior with quiver and arrows could scarcely have delighted the nervous Go-Toba. But the technique carries conviction, and there is an artistic unity that completely portrays the demanding life of the warrior who must face elements as hostile as his enemy. As Dr. Johnson said of a very different poet and a greater poem, "Had he written often thus, it would be vain to blame, and useless to praise him." The fact that the editor can adduce three earlier poems as sources means little in this instance. Sanetomo has not resorted to clichés and he has not merely borrowed; he has taken older elements and made them into a poem. The pity is that he wrote so few such poems and so many pieces of patchwork.

He may be termed a poet of two styles, the conventional and the simple—and not infrequently the two merge into a simple-minded conventionality. Insofar as these two styles differ, the conventional poems show his efforts to learn the craft of poetry through the practice any young poet must submit to with the styles of his day. The simple style—of declaration without reflection—usually shows him attempting to imitate the tanka poetry of the *Man'yōshū*. His simple declarative style, or the Man'yō style as it is usually called, makes up only the smaller part of his work, but it is taken by his admirers as his greatest accomplishment. This style is, then, founded upon the basic mode of declaration or exclamation; it is often laden with old diction, rhythms, or constructions; and its subject matter is vast, unusual, or full of morality and sentiment. Morality and sentiment in the poems of the young usually become idealistic sentimentality, and Sanetomo is no exception, as his verses on the topic "The Spirit of Pity" show (Saitō ed., No. 607).

Mono iwanu   Compassion!
Yomo no kedamono   For even among the speechless beasts
  Sura dani mo   Throughout the world
Aware naru *ƙana ya*   Each parent loves its child—
Oya no ko o omou.   ! ! ! ! ! ! !

Sanetomo meant that we human beings should be ashamed, that we who have the gift of speech ought to love our families even more than the beasts do. But the italicized exclamatory particles are symptoms of stridency and padding in a poetic form that can ill afford such extravagance. And the combination of *sura dani mo* itself is strange, ungrammatical, as if a young poet in English were to try to be archaistic and write, "Even forsooth, in faith." All these exclamations are, to recall Dr. Johnson once more, but standing upon tiptoe to be great.

A slightly better poem of the same moral and sentimental stripe has the following headnote (Saitō ed., No. 608).

Along the roadside was a child, weeping bitterly and calling for its mother. Inquiries were made of the people in the neighborhood, who replied that both of the child's parents were dead [probably at the hands of roving warriors in those unsettled times]. Whereupon I composed the following.

Itōshi ya	How pitiful!
Miru ni namida mo	I look and cannot stop my tears
Todomarazu	From streaming
Oya mo naki ko no	At the sight of the orphaned child
Haha o tazunuru.	Crying for its vanished mother.

For a young general of a powerful family to stop on a journey to take special note of such a regrettably common sight of those years is indeed a noble thing; and for a general to write a poem on such a subject, avoided for centuries by elegant courtiers, shows both originality and praiseworthy sentiment. Saitō Mokichi comments: "This poem of Sanetomo's is full of a feeling of reality; it is extremely good. There is a tone of pathos in the rhythms, too; and this tone is particularly moving in the lines, 'I look and cannot stop my tears / From streaming'" (p. 135).

But this goes too far. This is to say that because Sanetomo is a man of feeling he is, *ipso facto,* a great poet, as if all one had to do to write a poem is do something or feel something and then record the event in verse. Or to put the matter another way, many modern Japanese place such a high value on "sincerity" that they confuse it with poetic integrity; they confuse biography with art, the man with the speaker of the poem. And there is reason to believe that Sanetomo suffered the same kind of confusion. He begins with an explanation, with a request or demand that we open our hearts for what follows. And what does follow? Two lines in which he talks about himself, demonstrates fineness of feeling and ability to respond with streaming eyes. Only the last two lines offer any reason why we readers should respond—except of course to Sanetomo's tears. The poem is a dreadfully uncomfortable self-dramatization, and the fact that the self-praise is unconscious in no way puts us at our ease. Perhaps Sanetomo thought that he was only following his teacher's dictum to infuse every poem with "intense feeling," but there is a vast difference between the simple-mindedness of Sanetomo's poems and the effect of simplicity which Teika attempted to convey in his late ushin style. The following poem on "Snow," composed by Teika at the age of seventy, shows his use of simple declaration in an unconventional as well as highly personal treatment of a conventional topic (*Shūi Gusō* in *K. Taikei,* XI, 451).

Oiraku wa	To be old—
Yuki no naka ni zo	Now amid the swirling snow
Omoishiru	I understand:
Tou hito mo nashi	No one comes to visit me;
Yuku kata mo nashi.	There is no place to go.

In picturing the solitary speaker of Teika's poem standing in his garden as the snow falls about him, we should probably not be wrong to assume that he, like Sanetomo, cannot hold his tears in check. But the means Teika uses to convey the stark pathos of old age carry a conviction that Sanetomo's response to the plight of the orphaned child does not. The snow, conventionally treated as beautiful, welcome, a lovely sight to be shared with someone close, is transformed in Teika's poem into a symbol of the loneliness of the speaker and of the sad fact, old age, which condemns him to isolation. Unsullied by human footprints, the snow is indeed beautiful in its pure whiteness, but the whiteness is at the same time symbolic of the colorless monotony of the speaker's existence. Such a sophisticated treatment of the key image of the poem enables Teika to convey feeling without sentimentality; the declaration in the form of an intentionally choppy series of three short statements with parallelism between the last two reinforces the sense of finality in the situation. Sanetomo's poem is impulsive, unreflecting; Teika's is the result of a conscious choice of poetic techniques.

Further comparisons between two such disproportionately endowed poets would be invidious, but since Sanetomo and the Man'yō revival are something of a digression from Japanese literary history and the main tradition we are studying, it may be well to pause for a further digression and consider *Japanese* sentimentality. This is a subject of almost encylopedic scope and one capable of generating a good deal of misunderstanding. But the same might be said of every nation, for each has certain favorite subjects that it invests with an emotionalism that an outsider can only regard as excessive. It is wearying in the extreme to hear native authors extol Chinese filial piety, German efficiency, French clarity, English fair play, and American know-how. Similarly, one quickly tires of the Japanese esteem for saying in literature exactly what one feels, or rather, exactly what one believes others will appreciate one's saying one feels. In Japan as in the West, however, a persistent sentimentality in literature is a relatively late development in the history of taste, one that is associated with humanitarianism, moralizing, and romanticism. Apart from Sanetomo, the Japanese poets of the centuries we are dealing with are not sentimental. Tears are shed in abundance to moisten the sleeves and poems of countless courtiers and ladies. But at worst these tears are conventional and the expression of them trite or fantastic; they do not involve that self-concern and self-esteem which is sentimentality. One is, so to speak, baroque excess and the other well-intentioned lugubriousness. The attitude expressed by Saitō in commenting on another poem by Sanetomo is a modern Japanese attitude: "Lyric poetry is by nature something in which, from beginning to end, pretense is impossible and one's true feelings are unmistakable" (p. 179).

The modicum of truth in this theory is as relevant to the drama and the novel as to the lyric. Its limitation lies in its implication that tradition, convention, and imagination are suspect—a conception of poetry as an outpouring of the heart from diary to verse. Like those who feel that Shakespeare could not have written the great plays that bear his name, because he was never a member of the courtly class he so often describes, these Japanese feel that if a poet mentions a place or an event, he must infallibly have been there and have composed the poem on the spot. Surely Wordsworth put the matter justly when he said that the feeling expressed in poetry was "emotion recollected in tranquility"—when the poet's mind was free to create anew in a fashion that would make the reader feel the force of an experience, real or imaginary, in a poem that no longer was so full of its author that the reader was excluded from the experience. Sanetomo is useful in the history of Japanese Court poetry if only to show the difference between him and the great poets, between feeling and latter-day sentimentality.

It follows logically that Sanetomo, like other young poets in danger of lapsing into sentimentality, writes at his best in those poems which, like the one on hail, take him outside of himself, in those which create a scene and an action that enable the reader to feel without being told what to feel. In such works, and especially in those which have the vastness of scope and the affirmation that the age associated with the Man'yō style, he created a small body of poetry of lasting interest and considerable beauty. If he wrote only a few such poems, no one can deny their freshness and power—notable, for example, in "On Seeing the Waves Dashing Against a Rugged Beach" (Saitō ed., No. 641).

Ōumi no	From the vast sea
Iso mo todoro ni	The waves encroach in thunder
Yosuru nami	Upon the quaking shore—
Warete kudakete	Breaking, smashing, riving,
Sakete chiru ka mo.	Falling in great sheets of spray.

Sanetomo's reputation as the noble Chatterton of later Japanese romantic writers was in large measure created by the haiku poet Masaoka Shiki (1868–1902), who wrote such statements as the one in "An Open Letter to the Poets of Japan": "In recent years the art of Japanese poetry has not shown any signs of development. In fact, to speak forthrightly, it has shown no signs of development since the Man'yōshū and Sanetomo" (K. Taikei, XIV, xvii). In addition to revealing an exaggerated notion of the intrinsic worth of Sanetomo's poetry, this statement shows that Shiki lacked the historical knowledge which would have put the young shogun into the proper context of his age. (In fairness to Shiki it must be added that his statement was motivated by a desire to break with the reactionary conventionalism of the powerful schools of tanka poetry in his day.) Sanetomo was in fact but one of many poets who were studying the Man'yōshū and imitating its techniques and diction.

One must indeed be circumspect in speaking of the Manyō revival in this period. All the important poets of the age are conscious of the anthology; they all studied it and many experimented with its diction or techniques. Their revival was really a revival of interest that had certain poetic results. There is an unbroken line of study and interest from Tsunenobu to his son Shunrai; through Shunzei and Go-Toba; through Teika and his pupil Yoshitsune; and to that other pupil, Sanetomo. It seems inevitable that an age so given to considering and prizing the past should study the *Man'yōshū*, even if its dominant poetic was one largely defined by the poets represented in the *Kokinshū*. The most important result of their interest in the poetry of the more distant past was the style of affirmation and lofty tone (*taketakaki yō*) that Teika called one of the ten possible styles of poetry (and which might indeed be achieved in other ways than by imitation of the *Man'yōshū*); and the fact is that the most conservative as well as the most radical poets recognized and practiced this style. The difference is that these writers, and perhaps Yoshitsune most notably among them, merged the elements they saw in the *Man'yōshū* into a style which is recognizably of their age.

Sanetomo and a few other poets who like him lived away from the Court were both more radical and less successful. They failed time and again to create poetic wholes, because they lacked any consistent original styles of their own—which is to say that they could not shape the styles of their age into a vehicle of personal expression. Sanetomo appears to have been one of many provincial writers whom it is difficult to put into an organized group but who were apparently of the classes of warriors and priests. These writers were less obliged to the main literary tradition and perhaps even somewhat resented the Court tradition to which they could only with difficulty gain entrance. They were less students of the past than antiquarian revivalists as excited by their discovery of the *Man'yōshū* as the English poets of the late eighteenth century and Romantic movement were by their discovery of the ballads. With this excitement, with a desire to achieve poetic fame, and with a nervous eye cast at the Court, they wrote in styles that were either the safest sort of conventional expression or what they imagined to be characteristic of the *Man'yōshū*. Some of the private anthologies of these writers have recently been published (*Katsura Series,* VI) with titles that show their non-courtly background. There is "The Collection of the Priest Shinshō" (*Shinshō Hōshishū*), and the mouth-filling "Collection of Things Heard by the Rustic, Tokitomo, Former Governor of Nagato, on a Visit to the Capital" (*Saki no Nagato no Kami Tokitomo Nikkyō Inaka Uchigikishū*).

Like Sanetomo, these writers exhibit in their poetry two contradictory tendencies. They seem to have wished to write poems that were conventional enough not to disturb even a Kintō and at the same time to turn to the *Man'yōshū* for a style of their own. If their conventional poems fall short of originality, their more radical poems fall short of the main tradition that enabled them to set about to write. What such a writer as Sanetomo failed to see, or failed to live long enough to realize, was on the one hand that a poet learns his tradition only in order to adjust it, and on the other, that he can break successfully from it only by building upon it. Apart from a few good poems which hint to us what might have been, the collected works of Sanetomo are either the products of convention, pastiches of older poems in ways neither conventional nor poetic, or sentimental moralizing. At its freshest and most original best, his work is a cross ripple in the mainstream of Japanese poetry, but it was only a momentary disturbance of a force much greater than himself. The next age in poetry was not to follow such an antiquarian revivalism, but to develop its poetry by redefining the inheritance of the *Kokinshū* and *Shinkokinshū*—of the greatest writers of the Court tradition. The new poets were to write as if Sanetomo had never been, and their accomplishment was to create for the Japanese Court its last period of great poetry.

7

The Late Classical Period

1241–1350

SINCE THE LATE CLASSICAL period is the last great age of Japanese Court poetry, it possesses a certain historical as well as intrinsic interest. There are
two historical narratives to be told, one of the rivalry among the dissident
family groups descended from Teika, the other of the final and all but complete decline of the poetry of the Court in the middle of the fourteenth century.
As in earlier periods, but for somewhat different reasons, only part of the poetry
written between about 1242 and 1350 is sufficiently new and distinguished
to justify our setting it off from the work of earlier centuries and, more especially, from the poetry of those unhappy succeeding centuries of almost unre-
lieved monotony. This new poetry was written by the members and supporters
of two of the three family branches descended from Teika through his son, Tameie—the Kyōgoku and Reizei family groups. The third (and senior) family
branch, known as the Nijō group, was the strongest in every way except poetically; it and its adherents clung to a safe conventionalism that at once pre-
cluded originality and ensured the continuance of versifying in a society increasingly alien to the interests of the Court.

The Kyōgoku-Reizei branches and their supporters at the Court managed
to produce only two of the thirteen anthologies that followed the *Shinkokinshū*
But in these two, the *Gyokuyōshū* (ca. 1313) and the *Fūgashū* (ca. 1345), and
in the few private collections of these poets which have survived, we find a
practice and implicit poetic that are at once startlingly different from those of
earlier periods and yet grow naturally from them. At first glance, the differences seem so great that there appears to have been an almost complete break
with the past. The new love poetry of this period often employs no imagery
at all—an astonishing development in Japanese poetry. And what increases
one's astonishment is the fact that much of the characteristic seasonal poetry
consists of nothing but images. True, an occasional love poem from the early
classical period may be found which possesses no imagery, but such a poem is
very rare. And only very seldom in the descriptive poetry of the mid-classical
period does one find poems consisting entirely of images—poems, that is,
which lack the subjective overtones of personal pronouns or of generalized
language. Perhaps the most important problems posed by such an extreme

dualism of technique are those of discerning a single poetic impulse behind such divergent styles and of establishing a relationship between them and the tradition inherited by the new poets. A solution to the first problem suggests one for the second.

The seriousness with which Shunzei, Teika, and others had taken poetry as a way of life, and their redefinition of the subjectivity of the poetry of the early classical period, had led them to seek tonal complexity and depth in integrated poetic wholes. They therefore bequeathed to their successors an attitude that poetry expresses truth, not by setting down facts or describing what is seen, or by intellectual play with experience, but by an imaginative re-creation of reality. Now there is nothing radical or even particularly Japanese about such an attitude, but with it went many subordinate practices and ideals. Among these were Shunzei's insistence upon "entering into" the experience posed by the topic (dai) of the poem, and the ideal of old diction and new treatment ("kotoba furuku, kokoro atarashi"). By emphasizing a concentration upon the topic and original conception—at the same time being less concerned with traditional diction—the innovating poets of the Kyōgoku-Reizei school created a poetry which they felt to be true to the spirit of the preceding age and yet suitable for their own. They placed a greater emphasis, then, upon a continuity of literary values than upon preserving the techniques and detailed assumptions they had inherited; whereas the conservative Nijō poets contented themselves with the ceremony of poetry and hardly asked what the ritual meant. So simple a description is somewhat false in emphasis, since Japanese Court poets of whatever age were more apt to add to the techniques they had inherited than to discard them. The innovating poets of the late classical period were no exception, and often turned as conventional a poem as any Nijō poet could ask for. But insofar as the new poetry is new, its novelty is primarily one of technique and of the literary qualities that result from these changes in technique.

With such aims and ideals inherited from their predecessors and shaped in new ways, the Kyōgoku-Reizei poets were able to create for themselves the highly dissimilar styles they employed in their poems on love and nature. If, however, the ideals behind the two styles are the same, we ought also to be able to find that for all their real (as well as their merely apparent) differences, the two styles express common artistic aims. Both styles, the imagistic and the nonimagistic alike, are indeed serious; and whereas the preceding age had attempted to convey its serious purposes by achieving depth, the new age does so through intensity—an almost feverish observation and recording of detail, an obsession with minute differences, and certain extremities of technique. The differences and the resemblances alike can best be shown by illustration. A love poem by ex-Empress Eifuku (1271–1342) is a fair example of the subjective, non-imagistic style of many love poems (*GYS,* XII: 1665).

Hito ya kawaru   Is it that your feelings
Wa ga kokoro ni ya   Have begun to change into indifference,
Tanomimasaru   Or that now I need you more
Hakanaki koto mo   Which makes the most trivial occurrence
Tada tsune ni uki.   An unfailing omen of wretchedness to
                                  come?

And a poem by Kyōgoku Tamekane (1254–1332), "Spring Rain," illustrates
the completely imagistic style practiced in seasonal poems (*GYS*, I: 83).

Ume no hana   The plum in flower
Kurenai niou   Suffuses with a crimson glow
Yūgure ni   The early darkness—
Yanagi nabikite   The green willows bow to earth
Harusame zo furu.   And the spring rain softly falls.

Just as the love poem searches for the exact cause of misery, posing one
possibility against another, in order to convey the depth of the woman's agitation, so the seasonal poem sets the brilliant crimson of the plum flowers against
the bright green of the willows in order to bring together elements whose synthesis represents the essential experience of spring beauty. The tonal suggestions of the two poems differ greatly, but both aim to convey heightened experience with styles given a rich texture by the very careful posings of exact
elements. The elements are appropriate in either case to the realm of life considered—whether the subjective experience of love conveyed without images
or the world of nature for which images seem the inevitable means of expression.

If such common ideals and aims underlie these seemingly disparate styles,
they are surely not as wholly dissimilar as they at first seem to be. Such a
supposition receives considerable support from those poems of the age which,
although retaining the chief characteristics of the divergent styles, nonetheless employ some imagery if they are love poems or some subjective diction or
reference to human concerns if they are seasonal poems. Moreover, the carefully alternated pattern of light and dark images in Tamekane's poem (plum,
dusk; willow, rain) shows that even the imagistic style implies a strong element of subjective control; and although ex-Empress Eifuku's poem employs
scarcely any imagery, the dramatic particulars of love at a certain stage of the
traditional course of a love affair have a conversely imagistic implication. The
very richness of the tradition, whose age was now counted in centuries, enabled
the new poets to suggest a great deal more than would have been possible in
earlier times. The two styles are less different than they seem. But this is not
to deny that a considerable degree of difference remains, both between the
imagistic and generalized styles and between the poetry of this and preceding

ages. A common rationale and basic identity of approach does not alter the dissimilar literary effects.

Both the love poems and the seasonal poems are extremely difficult to understand, so much so in fact that even Japanese scholars have been reluctant to approach the love poems, which are by all odds the most difficult, at times the most obscure, of all the poetry in the Court tradition. At the same time, it is a curious fact that once the grammatical niceties, the fineness of distinctions, and the subtlety of emphasis have been understood, the poems are easier to translate than those of earlier periods. In many poems, the intensity of expression and the completeness with which a subject is explored leave little in the way of overtones or suggestions of depth once the complex expression has been understood. As a result, the less successful poems of this period have a flatness or prosiness that seems to be the less happy counterpart to the complex verse texture and the apperceptive awareness reflected in the poems. These qualities, both good and bad, are enough to set this period apart from the periods that preceded it; and they might have led to still further developments in the tradition, if those historical events, which sooner or later must claim the attention of the student of the period, had allowed the Kyō-goku-Reizei poetry to gain ascendency.

HISTORICAL DEVELOPMENTS AND LITERARY ISSUES

The increasingly restless state of Japanese society in the later years of rule by the military government at Kamakura, and the national chaos in the period that followed, do not provide a very tranquil background for the new age of poetry. Most Japanese literary historians tend to look upon the late classical period as little more than a time of steady decline from the accomplishment represented by the *Shinkokinshū,* however interesting certain seasonal poems in the *Gyokuyōshū* and *Fūgashū* may be in this or that minor way. But we agree with the minority view, with those Japanese writers who believe a close examination of the poetry in these two anthologies shows that if the age did not achieve the greatness of the preceding one, its achievement is still distinctively rich enough to call for special consideration. Moreover, without an understanding of the new character of the poetry in the late classical period, the continuity of Japanese poetry between the tradition of the Court and the characteristic new forms of feudal Japan is either lost or misunderstood.

It is cause for wonder that a nation suffering the breakdown of its institutions, falling into the chaos of civil war, and undergoing the traumatic effects of political, social and economic upheaval could have found the cultural resources to create a new age of poetry. The wonder grows with the consideration that the new poetry was produced by a Court society that had long since ceased to wield the real power of government or to enjoy the wealth that had made it what it was. And though in decline, the Court managed, thanks to some inner vitality or authority, to withstand the pressures forcing it toward the day when one emperor would be too poor for his survivors to give him a decent burial, and another would attempt to raise money by selling autographs. It might be argued that the Court was sustained by the richness of its past; and certainly the fact that it survived its own corruption and intrigue, that it maintained an authority long after it had ceased to exercise real power, political or economic, and that it could produce a fresh and original poetry as late as the mid-fourteenth century indicates that it possessed a strength which the usual modern criteria for judging societies are scarcely able to explain.

Such a wise historian as Sir George Sansom is amply aware of the anomaly of the survival of the Court, and he finds that the almost mystic veneration accorded the office of the emperor—as opposed to any individual holding the office—enabled the Court to survive. The explanation is no doubt correct, and it may even be extended. Again and again one cannot help but observe that the Japanese, who are so highly social in their literature as well as their behavior in intimate groups, are also extraordinarily anarchistic in public behavior. It was not only the throne as an office, but the homogeneous cultural tradition which it had represented that gave some continuity to a society in such seeming danger of collapse into anarchy. If the ranks and dignities of courtiers in, say, the year 1300 meant little in terms of power, it was still the courtiers who provided the nation with its cultural tradition, with its learning, and even with such members of professional groups as specialists in law and ceremony to advise the military autocracy. The comparison is hardly exact, but in a sense the Court continued to exercise some governmental power for the same reason that the medieval European Church did—namely, that there was no other cultural alternative.

The Court had, after all, the significant advantages of tradition and homogeneity, and since poetry had reflected the social patterns of the Court, any new poetry had perforce to grow from the same social forms. The late classical poetry did just that, for the major poetic factions harked back in literary as well as other ways to Teika. It may indeed be argued that the more tenuous their social position became, the more important it was for the poets of the age to be able to claim that they and their family were the true heirs to Shunzei and Teika. In an earlier day such a claim would probably have seemed rather beside the point, and the courtiers would merely have intrigued for political power. Now, however, the literary heritage was the source of eminence and therefore the focus of the disputes. Any dispute must be settled by an appeal to authority or force; without recourse to the latter, the descendants of Teika appealed to the former, and so became enmeshed in a tangle of affairs whose literary, legal, and political threads are all but impossible to unravel.

POLITICAL AND POETIC DISPUTES

The dispute over Teika's heritage can be regarded in different ways. The grandchildren of Teika fell out over such familiar human issues as who should inherit the estates of his son, Tameie (1198-1275), and over such more properly literary issues as what were the best styles of Japanese poetry. These were in reality aspects of one issue; and the resolution took place against an extremely confused historical background of a Japan whose security was threatened by Mongol invasion, rival imperial lines, the collapse of the military government at Kamakura, and other alarums and excursions.

The mid-classical period had invested poetry with a seriousness of purpose that made literary issues of prime human importance. When poetry is considered a way of life in which one's personal or family fame and even religious salvation are at stake, much of one's life naturally becomes directed toward defining literary excellence and trying to achieve it. The position achieved by Shunzei as the arbiter of literary taste in his long lifetime and Teika's honor in being the first to participate in the compilation of two anthologies (the *Shinkokinshū* and the *Shinchokusenshū*) lent their family line a unique prestige. Further Court honors followed for the literary dynasty. Teika was made Acting Middle Counselor (*Gon Chūnagon*), the second highest office in the Supreme Council of State; and his son, Tameie, achieved the even higher rank of Acting Great Counselor (*Gon Dainagon*). It is of course true that with the center of real authority in the military government at Kamakura, such Court titles carried more rank than power; and the military authorities usually found it convenient and profitable to let the emperors dub their courtiers what they wished and even to let noblemen "own" large manors as they had in the past, while commonly awarding loyal military retainers the much more profitable steward's rights to the same lands. Still, even Kamakura knew of the Acting Middle Counselor Teika, made him teacher of poetry to the young shogun Sanetomo, granted him rights of stewardship, and sought his assistance in certain building enterprises at the capital. Teika's worldly success grew at once from poetic ability, the prestige of his father, a long if not always healthy life, and a strength of ambition which the Japanese have seldom lacked.

The two generations of literary excellence had accumulated many rewards that were inherited by the third, although Tameie fell far short of his father and grandfather as a poet. The inheritance of the grandson of Shunzei included much that was tangible along with much that was only prestigious. The scholarly inclinations of the preceding two generations had led them to investigate earlier manuscripts, to copy them, to comment on them, and to preserve them among the family holdings. In addition to these family treasures, for such they were to a poetic dynasty, Tameie inherited the critical writings of his forebears. Given the eminence of their authors and their intrinsic worth, such documents established their possessor as the inheritor of authority, and even seemed to invest him with the authority itself. Other families might once have had literary prestige, but the intangible quality was now Tameie's by claim of blood, by title to estates, and by possession of the writings of two of the greatest Japanese poets. What had happened so gradually that it must have been scarcely noticed at first was that poetry had become one kind of family property, a property inextricably bound up with the prestige, the lands, and the manuscripts of the Mikosa (Nijō) house. It will quickly be realized that, human nature being what it is, the family should come to make unfortunate equations between what had been and what was, between inheriting poetic eminence and possessing it.

Like his father and grandfather, Tameie lived to an unusually advanced age. Some fifteen years before his death, he began to will his property to his children, showing preference for his eldest son, Tameuji (1222–86), progenitor of the Nijō branch of the family. His affairs thus settled, Tameie and Japanese Court poetry might have passed serenely into extinction had he not shortly before this time taken to wife a most remarkable woman, commonly known by the religious name she took after his death, the Nun Abutsu (d. ca. 1283). Abutsu was a poet of some stature, a fertile wife, and an ambitious mother. She bore Tameie two sons and persuaded him to change his will, awarding an estate near the capital to the elder of his sons by her, Tamesuke (b. 1263). When Tameie died in 1275, his eldest and now partially disinherited son, Tameuji, sought to lay claim to the whole inheritance, no doubt feeling that a half-brother more than forty years his junior and an ambitious stepmother had to be dealt with firmly, lest their flimsy pretensions to the inheritance threaten the stability of the family and his own perquisites.

Abutsu, however, was not easily discouraged. She recognized that the intangible poetic prestige of the house was closely linked to its material possessions, and she also had important differences in poetic opinion with Tameuji. Accordingly, she decided to take legal action to secure her sons' share in the family inheritance. Since there were two legal systems in the country, she had to calculate which would be more likely to render her a favorable decision. The law of the imperial Court allowed a parent to will his property as he wished (primogeniture was not established as an exclusive principle and women often held large properties), but once willed to one person, property might not be designated for another. The law of the military government at Kamakura permitted any number of revisions of a will. Abutsu had also to consider that the law of the Court was applicable to owner's rights, whereas military law dealt with steward's rights, for in this instance both were involved. She calculated her chances carefully and decided to make the arduous journey to Kamakura, knowing that she stood a far better chance of gaining the steward's rights from an altered will there than the owner's rights at the

Court; and she must have hoped that once the stewardship had been awarded, the prestige of the Kamakura government would enable her to get the owner's rights at the Court, so giving her sons a share in the property and poetic inheritance of Teika.

Although Abutsu stayed in Kamakura some four years or so, she died before a favorable decision was granted. (The steward's rights were granted Tamesuke by the Kamakura authorities in 1291, and the owner's rights were given to his descendants about a century later.) When she arrived, the Kamakura government was mustering the nation's resources against a second Mongol invasion. She had come between the first invasion of 1274 and the second of 1281, and the military government can hardly have been deeply concerned over so small a dispute as hers. Yet her efforts had the effect of intensifying family differences over what was to be done with the poetic as well as the more tangible inheritance. Although not a great poet herself, Abutsu was a writer of some talent. She celebrated her visit to Kamakura in her *Diary of the Waning Moon (Izayoi Nikki)*, a record which shows that she had close relations with the Kyōgoku branch of Tameie's family, the line descended from his son Tamenori (1226–79). This line and that of her own sons, who came to bear the name Reizei, argued for much greater freedom, originality, and experimentalism than was espoused by the conventional Tameuji or, indeed, by the father of them all, Tameie. The Kyōgoku-Reizei alliance was to produce the most important poetry of the age, and had it not been for Abutsu's disputes over property it is doubtful that the poetic differences would have been drawn so clearly.

During the period of such bitter dispute within the foremost literary family Japan had known and of the national crisis caused by the Mongol invasions and the subsequent unrest, the emperors and retired emperors intrigued against each other and the feudal government. Only a few things stand out clearly from such a confused state of political and poetic affairs. The Kyōgoku-Reizei rivalry with the Nijō line became involved with the political rivalry of disputant imperial factions; or to put it differently, the rival imperial lines supported one or the other of the poetic schools. Imperial support was crucial to a poet, since the "publication" of poetry meant imperial commissions to compile the anthologies, to submit poetic sequences, and to participate in important poetry contests. The political background of Court poetry had a way of becoming the literary foreground in a manner for which Western literary history has no real parallel. This fact is demonstrated by the political triumph of the Nijō family, which managed to support, and to gain the support of, the imperial line that was the more consistently in power. Consequently, as we have seen, it was commissioned to compile all of the imperial anthologies of the period except the *Gyokuyōshū* and the *Fūgashū,* which alone reflect the preferences of the Kyōgoku-Reizei families and their adherents. Behind all of the developments and intrigue there is the new concept of the social role of poetry: it is family property. The succession of eminence is conceived of in almost feudal terms as if it were property itself, for legal and literary differences came to seem no more than aspects of the same thing.

THE HERITAGE OF TEIKA

The new concept of poetry characterizes the age and sets it off from earlier periods, when a Kintō might write a handbook of poetry which any courtier could study in order to polish his verse. Reflecting these new social attitudes, the more purely literary aspects of the disputes of the day can best be understood in the terms they were thought of by the disputants—by reference to Teika. He had left an inheritance that the whole family valued. The problem involved just who was to receive it and what it meant. The first aspect of the problem implied legal as well as literary issues and was partly settled in the law courts. The second led to opposing interpretations of Teika's critical pronouncements, conflicting emphases upon one or another of the poetic styles which he had espoused, and consequent differences of opinion over the ideals and practice of poetry.

The ultra-conservatism of the Nijō poets becomes more understandable when we consider their assumptions. Basing their poetic practice upon the blandly conventional style of Tameie, they looked back upon Shunzei and Teika with the kind of awe and veneration due great poets whose genius was considered unique to an earlier age. They seem also to have been pessimistically passive in certain social and religious matters. With the nation in a turmoil, with the Court periodically near collapse, and with the members of their own family quarreling with them over their inheritance, it must have seemed to them that their age was truly that of the Last Period of the Law (*Mappō*). It followed that in such unhappy days lesser men than Teika might well consider it their obligation to preserve the heritage without misguided efforts to improve it in any way. By eschewing experimentation or futile efforts toward greatness, they might still write poetry of a mellifluous and satisfactory kind. Radicalism was at once foolish and dangerous.

The Kyōgoku-Reizei poets, on the other hand, had everything to gain by setting themselves off from their Nijō contemporaries. They looked to Teika with veneration but looked elsewhere as well for possible ways of developing a poetic as appropriate to their own age as Shunzei's and Teika's new styles had been for theirs. In Chinese poetry and criticism of the Sung dynasty and in the Zen priests with whom they had contact, they found encouragement for their own interests. With such optimism, and with their desire to show that they were the proper inheritors, their reading of Teika differed from that of the Nijō poets. If Teika had been an experimentalist to his last years, so should they; and it was more in his spirit to regard him, as he had regarded his predecessors, as an ideal example rather than as a pattern whose details must be followed even at the cost of the design as a whole.

The dispute can be most conveniently represented by the differing interpretations of the phrase iterated by Shunzei and Teika: "kotoba furuku, kokoro atarashi." We have rendered the dictum as "old diction, new treatment," but as we know, *kotoba* and *kokoro* are terms charged with a wealth of meaning. *Kotoba* means words, a tradition of decorous diction, purity of language, imagery, poetic materials, and more. *Kokoro* means heart, feeling, spirit, tone, technique, harmony of poetic elements, decorous treatment of materials, integrity, creativity, and more. No English terms can possibly render these rich and much employed Japanese words, but it is perfectly clear that Shunzei and Teika had designated two general aspects of poetry, arguing for traditionalism or conservatism with the one and for originality with the other. Following in the footsteps of Tameie, the Nijō poets dwelt upon the conservative side of the dictum, seeing in it the proper emphasis for the lesser generations who succeeded Teika. The Kyōgoku-Reizei poets justified themselves by emphasizing the original side, properly believing that it represented what was most vital in the poetry of Teika.

Such a basic disagreement led to innumerable disputes over details. Many of these can be inferred from differences in poetic practice, but neither side was content to rest its case on example alone. The age is not nearly so rich in significant critical writings as the mid-classical period, partly because of the nature of the disputes, partly because the innovating poets were seldom if ever called upon to preside at poetry competitions or other public functions, and partly because a great many documents either have been irrevocably lost or remain among the secret family treasures of the present-day descendants of Tameie and Abutsu. However, the views of Tamekane were presented in *Lord Tamekane's Poetic Notes* (*Tamekane-Kyō Wakashō*) and those of his Nijō opponents in a number of polemic writings and forged poetic documents that they claimed to have inherited from Teika through Tameie. Several of the Nijō documents and Tamekane's *Notes* survive and are reprinted in the *Compendium of Japanese Poetic Writings* (*NKGT,* IV; the page references below refer to this volume). The Nijō controversialists often heaped criticism upon their rivals for what seem to be the most trivial offenses or matters of least moment. In one of their most brilliantly conceived polemics, the *Particulars of Protest Jointly Submitted by Several Inhabitants of the Poetic Garden* (*Kaen Rensho Kotogaki*), they objected to new words (p. 101); to untraditional handling of imagery (pp. 98, 102); to the repetition of sounds in poems they quote and criticize very much in the manner of some pronouncements at poetry contests (p. 98); to too strong caesuras between lines (p. 98); to what they considered rough, careless, vulgar, or prosaic writing (pp. 99, 100, 101), and even to the title and arrangement of poems in the anthology compiled by Tamekane, the *Gyokuyōshū* (pp. 97–98). Even if their criticism descends at times to trivialities or abuse, is is very much to the point, since it accurately distinguishes the Kyōgoku-Reizei styles from their own in clear if technical fashion, and since it shows how the innovating poets were departing from the conservative norm of the tradition. Lively and pointed as the criticism is, however, it is only criticism and is not supported by the proper justification—embodiment of principles in a living poetic practice. The "inhabitants of the poetic garden" failed to see the garden for the weeds they sought to uproot. It is as though they adhered rigorously to the letter of the law of *kotoba*, while the Kyōgoku-Reizei poets created a new poetry by observing the spirit of the law of *kokoro*.

The quarrels of another day, whether literary or political, seldom seem as crucial in their details as they once did to their disputants. Certainly such an issue as the proper sounds for ending one line and beginning the next seems incredibly foolish, almost as if the quarreling parties had chosen as small a question as possible to disagree over. So it seems, and so in itself it was; yet it was symptomatic of far greater issues. It was of course related to the fundamental difference between originality and conventionalism, but as we shall see, it came more specifically to have important effects upon techniques of integrating poetic sequences, it influenced other poetic genres, and it was related to other, more significant changes in the rhetoric of poetry.

Such changes in poetic technique as the Kyōgoku-Reizei poets brought about were, then, in the spirit of Teika, if not in direct imitation of his own styles. In fact neither school copied Teika's characteristic personal styles to any great extent, apart from the plainer style of "intense feeling" or "conviction of feeling" (ushin) of Teika's late years, which served as inspiration for the Kyōgoku-Reizei poets. The Nijō poets, feeling it impossible for the men of their degenerate age to approximate the greatness of Teika, or even to imitate his styles successfully, modeled their poetry more directly upon the example of Tameie, whose ideal had been the style of "describing things as one sees them" (*ken'yō*). One of the less important of the ten categories distinguished by Teika in his *Maigetsushō*, this style bore certain superficial resemblances to his late style of artful simplicity but placed far less strain upon Tameie's limited resources. In practice, most of the Nijō poets slipped back into something like the old Fujiwara style, now grown more descriptive and less witty, although no less smooth, harmless, and empty.

FORGERIES, POLEMIC, AND COMPETITION

It is no wonder that in such a struggle for survival the issues should be at times unliterary or that they should often seem trivial. The triumph of the Nijō faction was indeed almost restrictedly political, and it was not gained without some very strange turns—some of which made the faction look very silly indeed—nor without a considerable amount of polemic. As the Nijō family sought to consolidate its power at court, its chief opponent was Kyōgoku Tamekane (1254–1332), who turned out to be even more formidable than Abutsu. Like the more important Nijō adherents, he played a very dangerous game of politics along with his poetry, supporting the senior (Jimyōin) line of emperors against the junior (Daikakuji) line supported by the Nijō, and even seeking to help overthrow the military government at Kamakura. So deeply committed to politics was he that he was twice exiled, and each political setback was also regarded as a defeat for his kind of poetry.

The Kyōgoku position was immeasurably strengthened, however, by the support of the Reizei family. As a coalition closely bound by similarity of poetic ideals and by hatred of the Nijō, the two houses were able to offer strong collective opposition to their more powerful rivals. Further, although they were the weakest of the three families economically and politically, the Reizei turned out to hold the highest poetic credentials in the form of valuable documents hoarded by Abutsu and passed on to Reizei Tamesuke, the elder of her two sons by Tameie. When in 1286 the court of ex-Emperor Kameyama awarded the owner's rights to the disputed Hosokawa estate to Tameie's eldest son Nijō Tameuji, it also ordered the loser, Tamesuke, to turn over to the Nijō line the corpus of manuscripts he had aquired from Tameie through Abutsu. The most important documents were some of the manuscripts of Teika. As long as they rested in Kyōgoku-Reizei hands, the manuscripts could only embarrass the Nijō poets. They were priding themselves on conserving Teika's tradition without possessing all of the tangible literary evidence for it. Both sides appear to have been greedy for property, but it must have been a source of perpetual embarrassment to the Nijō and of special pleasure to their opponents that the conservatives did not have the best documents to conserve. As long as the Kyōgoku-Reizei faction had some of the most precious of Teika's writings safely in their possession, they could challenge Nijō doctrine on the basis of documents they refused to show their opposition.

When the Reizei family were ordered to turn over the manuscripts, they did something which is without parallel in the history of Western or Japanese literature. They forged a number of manuscripts, taking care to distort what Teika had really written and to fill the manuscripts with commonplaces, trivial "secret traditions" such as the "proper" way to pronounce a certain name, the number of grand ministers represented in the Kokinshū but not so identified, and other meaningless statements calculated to appeal to the pedantic interests of the Nijō poets. These they handed over, together with a few genuine documents with which their rivals were already familiar, quietly putting the most valuable manuscripts aside. The famous warrior,

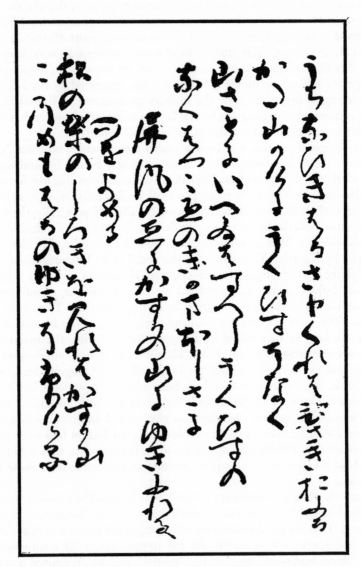

Teika's holograph: three poems from the poet's own copy of the personal collection of his pupil Minamoto Sanetomo (see pp. 329–34).

historian, and literary scholar, Kitabatake (or Minamoto) Chikafusa (1292–1354), gives an account of these remarkable events in his *Commentary on the Prefaces to the Kokinshū* (*Kokinshūjo Chū*). In a passage concerned with the "Six Genres" of Japanese poetry (*Rikugi*) mentioned in the Japanese and Chinese Prefaces to the *Kokinshū* (see above, p. 178), Chikafusa wrote (*NKGT*, IV, xlix):

Down to the time of their lordships Teika and Tameie, it seems that a great deal of importance was attached to the Six Genres. Furthermore, in modern times there have been in the possession of the family two sets of documents recording Teika's pronouncements on these and other matters. One set was kept in a box with the figure of a cormorant inlaid on the cover and the other in a box inlaid with a heron. Thus the two sets were called "The Cormorant and the Heron." They were so precious that even Lord Tameie would not let them out of his sight. When Lord Tameie died, his wife, Lady Abutsu the Nun, took the poetic documents with her to Kamakura. Later, Tameie's heir, Lord Tameuji, brought suit, and in consequence, during the time of the ex-Emperor Kameyama, a command was issued from the court of the ex-Emperor to the authorities in Kamakura ordering the documents to be handed over. At that time they surrendered all the writings that had been catalogued long ago and were well known to various people, but apparently because not even Lord Tameuji had any clear idea of the contents of the Cormorant and Heron boxes, they retained the secret writings, filled the boxes with forgeries, and handed those over instead. This perhaps accounts for the fact that since the time of Lord Tameuji very little attention has come to be paid to such matters as the Six Genres. On Tamesuke's side they have boasted in private about their possession of these oral traditions of Teika, but since both the court of the ex-Emperor and the military authorities have been involved in the affair, they do not mention it openly for fear of being punished if it were publicly admitted that they retained possession of the contents of the Cormorant and Heron boxes at the time the documents were handed over.

According to the priest Genshō (fl. ca. 1300), younger brother of Tameuji and outspoken partisan of the Nijō, the crafty Abutsu had taken additional measures to ensure that the most precious items in Tameie's collection of poetic documents should pass to Tamesuke rather than to Tameuji. Genshō records in his *Oral Traditions of Poetry* (*Waka Kuden,* also *Gukanshō,* in *NKGT*, IV, 46) that "The Nun Abutsu and the Great Counselor [Tameuji] quarreled over the poetic documents. . . . Abutsu hid the catalog of poetic writings written in the former Middle Counselor's [Tameie's] own hand, and held back a number of important documents which she proceeded to display to all and sundry. She was twice warned in a dream and then she and her two sisters died in rapid succession."

The Nijō poets were thus placed in a very awkward position. They knew that the Reizei family, who had aligned themselves with the Kyōgoku, possessed certain crucial documents, but they had no idea of their contents, and they could not be certain to what extent the writings which had been foisted upon them had been altered or forged. There was little they could do but brazen it out, and they busily set to work forging documents of their own which they claimed to have obtained from Tameie and to have had in their possession all along.

The location of some of the genuine manuscripts in Teika's holograph is known. He had copied out earlier literary works and had written critical essays for such highly placed poetic aspirants as the shogun Sanetomo, and some of his manuscripts were in the Nijō possession already. The real mystery is of course the survival and present location of the remaining genuine manuscripts. It is believed—strange but poetically just as it may seem—that they have survived through six centuries in the hands of the Reizei family line. In the years since World War II, the present descendants of Abutsu and Tameie —and of Teika, Shunzei, and Fujiwara Michinaga—have from time to time raised money by selling small portions of what are reputed to be extraordinary holdings. Of course, the Japanese are as fond as any people of a romantic story, but if some of the papers of Teika are still jealously guarded, it is for an economic reason Abutsu would have little difficulty in appreciating—to avoid taxation. The most remarkable thing about this extraordinary woman is that in the centuries following her death her efforts have achieved the kind of triumph dearest to her: the retention of crucial poetic documents in her family and the achievement of a body of poetry far greater than the largely atrophied and conventional verse of her Nijō opponents.

The Nijō writers did, however, excel their clever rivals in one literary realm. One can only admire the energy and skill of their polemical criticism and appreciate the way in which their specific attacks help us to define the poetic issues of the day. Some of the criticism is heavy-handed, but at other times the polemicists achieve what is perhaps the first extant literary satire in Japanese. For when we read in the *Particulars of Protest Jointly Submitted by Several Inhabitants of the Poetic Garden* of the misdeeds of "this lord," i.e., Tamekane, and discover that the criticism is "signed" by such worthy, although long since dead, priest-poets as Saigyō, we clearly have before us a very workable satiric device, the *persona* or mask. The conservative cause can well be argued by raising up the great of the past to criticize the erring writers of the present. The device no doubt made yet another, more oblique point. The Kyōgoku-Reizei poets were known to be on close terms with many Zen priests, so that such figures as the priest-poet Saigyō of two generations before were the very best persons to tell them of the error of their ways.

The details of the Nijō criticism often involve the kind of specific points at issue that we have mentioned earlier and shall examine at greater length in the discussion of poetic practice: new diction, sharply marked caesuras, prosiness, an altered rhetoric, and new handling of imagery. A poem by ex-

Empress Eifuku will, however, demonstrate the kind of "fault" criticized by the Nijō writers (*FGS*, XI: 1036).

Kurenikeri	It has grown dark.
Ama tobu *kumo no*	How I wish that even by the clouds
Yukiki ni mo	That come and go
Koyoi ika ni to	Across the sky I might send on
Tsutaeteshi ga na.	The question whether you will come
	tonight.

The poem is indeed not a very distinguished work. It might justifiably have been criticized for being insipid, but this was not a quality to offend the Nijō critics. One feature of the poem would have disqualified it not only in their minds but even at poetry contests in previous generations—the use of three successive rhymes, the terminal "o" sounds of lines two, three, and four. Such skirting of the traditional offenses, the "sicknesses" (*yamai*) of poetry, is typical of ex-Empress Eifuku, who often offends by repeating the same word or particle as well as similar sounds. However, the italicized phrase would probably have been regarded as the most willful and serious offense in the poem. It is an example of what the Nijō critics called reversed diction (*kotoba no irihoga* or *tōgo*). Normal Japanese syntax demands *yukiki no kumo ni*, "by the clouds of going and coming," rather than *kumo no yukiki ni*, "by the going and coming of the clouds," as ex-Empress Eifuku has it.

Most of the Nijō criticisms have their point. They deal with specific matters, and quite justly assume that Shunzei and perhaps even Teika would have criticized such a technique as reversed diction if the poem that employed it had been presented in the formal situation of a poetry contest. Indeed, Kamo no Chōmei had written in his *Mumyōshō* (*NKGT*, III, 311–12) that his teacher Shun'e regarded the use of reversed diction as deliberate obscurantism perpetrated by ignorant young poets who thought they were imitating the yūgen style of Shunzei and Teika but were actually producing only *Daruma-uta* or "nonsense verse." Yet the Kyōgoku-Reizei poets could, with equal justice, argue that such experimentation as theirs had ample precedent in the writings of those radicals long since become classics, Sone no Yoshitada and Minamoto Shunrai. Nor would it have taken much time to discover in Teika's canon such a poem as the one on the Lady of the Uji Bridge (see p. 276), with even more startling use of language. Almost all of the issues were specific in themselves and represented fundamentally opposed concepts of poetry. The real problem was which view was to survive.

The courting of rival imperial lines was therefore, as we have noted, a contest with very practical and important literary stakes. The events that lay behind the compilation of the two Kyōgoku-Reizei anthologies, the *Gyokuyō-shū* and the *Fūgashū*, reflect the almost incredible degree of jealousy, hostility, and intrigue that characterized the struggles between the dissident factions. The story properly begins with the compilation of the *Shingosenshū*, the thirteenth imperial anthology completed some ten years before the *Gyokuyōshū*. Kyōgoku Tamekane had been exiled to the island of Sado in 1298 in punishment for his political machinations. He was pardoned in 1303 and returned to the capital to find that his arch-rival Nijō Tameyo (1250–1338) had been appointed by ex-Emperor Go-Uda as compiler of the *Shingosenshū*. Both Go-Uda and the reigning emperor, Go-Nijō, belonged to the junior imperial line, the faction which had the support of the Nijō family, so that Go-Uda's choice of Tameyo was hardly surprising. Tamekane was much disgruntled nonetheless, and began to criticize the anthology publicly even before it had been completed.

Tamekane's opportunity came with the accession in 1308 of Hanazono (1297–1348) of the senior line. Hanazono, a very gifted poet in his own right, was a pupil of Tamekane and planned to appoint him compiler of a new imperial anthology very soon after he came to the throne. No sooner did Tameyo get wind of this, however, than he lodged a formal written protest, insisting that Tamekane's "criminal" record and "illegitimacy," among other things, disqualified him from performing such an honorable function. Tamekane was not slow in submitting a rejoinder to the effect that Tameyo was mentally incompetent. This prompted another petition from Tameyo, a second rejoinder from Tamekane, and so on, until to what must have been the utter bewilderment of the young Hanazono a total of eleven such exchanges had taken place. Meanwhile, Reizei Tamesuke had been intriguing at Court to get himself appointed compiler, and even wrote to the military authorities at Kamakura in an attempt to persuade them to exert pressure upon the Court. Rather than have Tameyo win out, Tamekane lent temporary support to Tamesuke, but Kamakura remained aloof and Tamekane resumed his own fight. This time he enlisted the aid of the politically powerful Saionji Sanekane (1249–1322), who was the go-between in dealings of the military government and the Court, and finally, with the added support of ex-Emperor Fushimi (1265–1317) of the Senior line, who had taken over control of the "camera government" from Go-Uda, he triumphed: in 1311 the coveted appointment was made in the form of a commission from ex-Emperor Fushimi to Tamekane. Tameyo, who had never left off protesting, was so incensed that he resigned his post at Court and went into retirement.

It is scarcely to be wondered at that when, some thirty years later, the second and last opportunity came for the Kyōgoku-Reizei poets to compile an imperial anthology, Hanazono (then the retired emperor) decided to break precedent and assume responsibility for the new collection himself. No matter how outraged the Nijō poets might feel, they would hardly dare to make a public attack upon an ex-Emperor. Hanazono was suffering from constant illness at the time, and it is doubtful that he compiled the *Fūgashū* single-handed or even exerted the kind of over-all editorial supervision that Go-Toba had done in the case of the *Shinkokinshū*. Indeed, there is evidence that most of the work was done by the young ex-Emperor Kōgon (1313–64), assisted by Reizei Tamehide (d. 1372) and others. Nevertheless, with Hanazono as the official compiler, the *Fūgashū* was safely completed in 1346.

The anthologies compiled by the rival poets illustrate in other ways than by their contents alone the significance of the issues involved and the nature of the poetic differences. The very titles of the anthologies are revealing. (For a full listing of the imperial collections and information about them, see the Appendix.) The Nijō compilers chose titles that reflected their conservative thought and even their pessimism, for the names are usually versions of earlier titles, and significantly of the most conventional, least distinguished collections. About a decade before the first Kyōgoku-Reizei collection was completed, the Nijō poets had compiled the *Shingosenshū* or "New *Gosenshū*"; and about two decades before the second Kyōgoku-Reizei collection, they completed the *Shokugoshūishū*, "The *Goshūishū* Continued," or, in full translation, "The Later Collection of Gleanings Continued." The Kyōgoku-Reizei poets appropriately chose more original titles, and titles moreover whose associations were radical. The *Gyokuyōshū*, compiled by Tamekane, is not a "continuation" of some earlier collection. Insofar as its name, "Collection of Jeweled Leaves," carries any associations, it recalls Shunrai's *Kin'yōshū* or "Collection of Golden Leaves." The echo served Tamekane well, since Shunrai was known as an innovating poet; "*Gyokuyōshū*" was therefore a manifest declaration of radical intentions. Tamekane must have expected that he would be criticized as Shunrai had been for such a pretentious title, and he was, but his point was clear. Ex-Emperor Hanazono, in compiling the *Fūgashū*, also chose a fresh name, "The Collection of Elegance." The title represented a partial compromise, an effort to pick up some of the poetic pieces scattered by Tameyo and Tamekane. It recalled no earlier anthology, but it suggested what was one of the persistent stylistic ideals of Court poetry of all schools from the *Man'yōshū* on.

To his defiance, Tamekane added pride and incurred additional criticism by compiling the largest of the imperial collections: the *Gyokuyōshū* contains 2,796 poems compared to the *Kokinshū*'s 1,111 and the *Shingosenshū*'s 1,606. Hanazono followed Tamekane's lead by including 2,210 poems in the *Fūgashū*. The size of the Kyōgoku-Reizei collections probably reflects more than the compilers' pride in their styles; no doubt they feared that each might be their last chance to "publish" their work.

The Kyōgoku-Reizei poets, and the Nijō poets as well, made some point of including in their anthologies poems written by the opposition. The Nijō compilers selected the most conventional compositions of the Kyōgoku-Reizei school, while the Kyōgoku-Reizei compilers exasperated their opponents by selecting those poems which were closest to their own styles. Other tendencies in the *Gyokuyōshū* and *Fūgashū* imply the interests of the innovating poets. The poems they selected to represent such conventional and by now hackneyed topics as the coming of spring are commonly either by poets of earlier days or by their opponents. Their own poems are usually composed on more flexible topics. Further, the large numbers of poems they classified as *zō*, or "miscellaneous" poems, reflect criteria never before applied in an imperial anthology. Traditionally, "miscellaneous" poems were either those in which elements of such categories as "Spring" and "Love" were so blended that neither category clearly predominated, or those composed on topics not included in other books of the anthology. While continuing to employ the traditional criteria, the compilers of the *Gyokuyōshū* and *Fūgashū* also placed in the miscellaneous books poems that were quite unmixed with respect to category but that seemed to them for one reason or another not sufficiently descriptive. The effect was to narrow the acceptable limits of treatment for seasonal topics and greatly increase the number and size of the books of *zō* poems. Thus, the *Gyokuyōshū* has five books of miscellaneous poems (788 poems in all), while its predecessor, the *Shingosenshū,* has but three such books (353 poems). Had the Court continued to enjoy its cultural supremacy and had the Kyōgoku-Reizei poets achieved the dominance they sought, Japanese literary history might have recorded that later imperial anthologies were based on a pattern radically different from the lines established by the *Kokinshū* and followed more or less faithfully by all subsequent collections.

KYŌGOKU-REIZEI IDEALS: THE CHINESE EXAMPLE

The issues between the Kyōgoku-Reizei poets and their Nijō opponents varied as greatly in significance as the disputes over particularities of diction and the proper construction of an anthology suggest. They reflected no less than a controversy over the nature of poetry. Both sides of course held many of the same assumptions, both were conscious of the long poetic tradition behind them, and both shared concepts that distinguish them from other poetic traditions, Western and earlier Japanese as well. But to say this is to say no more than that both sides belonged to the same poetic tradition, for within it they differed over the beauty and truth to be expected from poetry, and their differences are, for our present purposes, far more significant than their resemblances. As in other periods, the particular standards of what was valuable in poetry held by the Kyōgoku-Reizei poets had their classical, Chinese example. The Sung poets had reacted against the rich, voluptuous style of such late T'ang poets as Wen T'ing-yün (812–?70), Li Shang-yin (813–58), and Han Wu (844–923), whose lushness they called *hsiang-lien t'i,* or "vanity-case style." Wen T'ing-yün and other late T'ang poets were represented in such Japanese anthologies as the *Wakan Rōeishū* and the *Shinsen Rōeishū* as well as in individual collections, and their works had been one source of inspiration to the youthful Teika in creating his style of ethereal charm (yōen). But the Sung poets and critics had also been known to Teika; his late style of artful simplicity may owe something to their example. Whatever the source of the new interest in the Sung poets, certain qualities appealed to the innovating Japanese poets. Stated most simply, the new Sung poets held to an ideal of outward plainness and inward beauty, a modest exterior with suggestions of inner richness. Such an ideal was advanced most notably by Su Tung-p'o (1036–1101). The following quotations from *Tung-p'o's Comments on Poetry* (*Tung-p'o Shih-hua*), a posthumous collection of Su Tung-p'o's scattered critical comments, and from *Tsang-hai's Comments on Poetry* (*Tsang-hai Shih-hua*), attributed to Wu K'o (fl. ca. 1126), are representative.

We make the most of simplicity; simplicity, I mean, should be mellow within though it may appear dreary; it should be beautiful though it appear plain. Yüan-ming and Tsu-hou are poets of this kind. But if a poem is simple *both* in core and in skin, it is not poetry (*Tung-p'o Shih-hua*).

Literary works should first be gorgeous and later plain, just like the order of the seasons: gorgeous like the flowers in spring, richly fruitful in summer, and withered in autumn and winter. "Mellow on the inside though dreary in appearance" means the same thing. The gorgeous and the fruitful are both hidden within the plain (*Tsang-hai Shih-hua*).

The Sung poets were also ink-wash painters and students of Zen Buddhism. The relation between Su Tung-p'o's poetic ideals and the apparent simplicity of ink-wash painting will be clear enough: the painting was the visual representation of the same ideals that he exemplified in poetry. And the austere refinement of Zen esthetic ideals, even in the Japan of later centuries, is also clearly related to Sung poetry and painting. The Kyōgoku-Reizei poets shared such an ideal of beauty, and sought to embody it in poetic practice by the use of certain new, "lower" images or by scenes of monochromatic or softly colored beauty reminiscent of Shunzei's poetry of sabi or loneliness. The Chinese example was of course of most use to them in their nature poetry —the tendency to nonimagistic love poetry made the ideals of only limited practical appeal there. Lady Eifuku Mon'in, by no means the most ingenuous writer of the age, nonetheless exemplifies well the ideal of plainness in an autumn poem (*FGS,* VII: 664).

Someyaranu	The sun at dusk
Kozue no hikage	Is not strong enough to tint the tops
Utsurisamete	Of the maple trees with red,
Yaya karewataru	And growing weaker, gives in its setting
Yama no shitakusa.	The mountain plants a slightly withered look.

The emphasis of the poem is upon the subdued plainness of the scene, and yet there is a mellow inner beauty to the "withered" exterior that meets the ideal taken from the Sung poets. In the very statement of the beauty the scene does not have, and in the metaphor implied (and which we have rendered as an image) of the colored rays of sunset for colored autumn leaves, the richer beauties are suggested as latent possibilities.

Lady Eifuku Mon'in's poem illustrates other important characteristics of the Kyōgoku-Reizei poets. As any number of other similar poems would show, their poetry is often rather prosaic in its tone and presentation. By comparison with the metaphysical probings and wit to be found in the *Kokinshū* or with the depths possessed by the poems in the *Shinkokinshū,* there is an undeniable flatness in a statement that one thing is not so and another is. Although the same imagery might well have been used by Shunzei or Saigyō to express the lyric melancholy of sabi, Lady Eifuku Mon'in's poem conveys no such tone. The prosiness may be partly accounted for by the desire for exterior plainness, but it is also true that the ideal entailed in practice a rejection of some of the typical means of attaining poetic richness in earlier periods. The best poets of the age seem to have been aware of the difficulty, if not the danger, inherent in plainness, and to have sought for new means to give excitement to their styles without forfeiting their ideals of beauty. Often, although not in the poem we have quoted, new rhetorical techniques or patterns of images are employed to lend poems a richness of texture they would otherwise lack. It may also be the case that the tendency to fill the seasonal poems with images to the exclusion of generalized language reflected a sense that the dangers of flatness might be avoided by employing as much figurative language as possible. Unquestionably the best works overcome the dangers, but just as certainly their peculiar richness is not that of poetry in earlier periods.

Lady Eifuku Mon'in's poem illustrates a second important ideal of the Kyōgoku-Reizei school—the ideal of truth (*makoto*) or verisimilitude. The seriousness with which poetry was regarded as a way of life in the preceding period was accentuated by the new poets to what seems an advocacy of Realism. The use of less dazzling imagery, of "low" diction, and the like are but symptoms of a larger ideal of truth. Significantly, the modern Japanese Realists in haiku poetry have found the plainness and "truthfulness" of the nature poetry of this age more appealing than the dazzling art of a Komachi or a Teika. Such latter-day enthusiasts have failed to see, however, both that the plainness grows from a conscious and studied esthetic—that it is as conventional as the "reasoning" of early classical poets—and that the expression of truth often led the poets into examination of the unexpectedly true or to the expression of truths that are far from ordinary.

The effort to find expression for the true things, conditions, and feelings has always led in art to unusual techniques and at times to very unreal or unordinary expression. Impressionism, Naturalism, and Expressionism are more realistic in theory than in effect, and it might well be argued that the most unaffectedly realistic art is often the product of those ages we call classical, neoclassical, or even Romantic. The statues of Periclean Greece, the novels of Fielding, or Wordsworth's *Michael* have an effect of reality all the more convincing for their making no claim to a special realism. It is the difference between presenting what is and what is true on the one hand, and presenting on the other hand what the sensitive observer is proud (or outraged) to find "real," as in Naturalism, or asserts to be real in spite of a seeming distortion, as in Impressionism. The Kyōgoku-Reizei poets were more like our Impressionists in that they endeavored to represent as real what they subjectively apprehended after close, even minute, scrutiny. Often the poetic results of the search are somewhat prosaic statements like that of Lady Eifuku Mon'in; often they are unexpectedly strange, as when Kyōgoku Tamekane writes that the voice of the *hototogisu* is pure and cool (*FGS*, IV: 312; see below, p. 384). The exact words to describe what has been so closely observed often turn out to be unusual, since the "real truth" is presumed not to have been observed before or because ordinary descriptions do not truly express the reality. In this sense, the diction of the Kyōgoku-Reizei poets is often new—the words have been heard before, but they turn up in unexpected ways; and what is realistic may be either flat statement of fact or startling observation of experience.

Such Impressionism appears to have come about, then, partly because of the Chinese-inspired ideal of simplicity and partly because of the minuteness of the poets' observations. The minute observation would not have been possible without the rise of descriptive poetry in the preceding period: the poets had to be taught to look before they could learn to look carefully. But when they sought to give interesting expression to what they had observed—especially in the experience of love treated in nonimagistic styles, they could only look farther back in their tradition to the early classical poets, where they found close observation in the service of subjective wit. Discarding the wit for the most part, they were left with subjectivity as the only means of making the detailed, the minute, or the brief seem significant. And when they sought for the most usable modes of expression, they found them in the more direct styles of the *Man'yōshū* and in certain later, simpler styles. Such modes were essentially declarative; for apart from any other stylistic brilliance they might seek, their aim of outward simplicity was most often realized in declaration.

From each of the periods of their now ancient tradition these poets took what they desired and shaped what they took according to their own interests. From the *Man'yōshū*, for example, they took more than eighty poems for the

Gyokuyōshū—the largest number of *Man'yōshū* poems in any of the imperial anthologies—and the declarative style which they extolled for its directness and plainness, even at the cost of repetition. Or in the words of *Lord Tamekane's Poetic Notes* (*NKGT*, IV, 110): "At the time of the *Man'yōshū*, poets gave direct expression to what they felt in their hearts, not hesitating to say the same thing twice . . . making no distinction between poetic diction and ordinary speech, they simply followed the dictates of their heart and said things just as they wished." A careless critic might indeed make more of this passage than Tamekane intended. He meant to justify the "low" diction and the plain style of Kyōgoku-Reizei poets, not to advocate an artless lyricism, as some later writers have supposed. His view of the *Man'yōshū* was qualified by the aspects of poetic practice which he admired in early and mid-classical poetry (he repeatedly cites Teika and concludes with a quotation from Murasaki Shikibu), and his apparently simple concept of speaking what is in the heart is every bit as complex as Sir Philip Sidney's art in the sonnet concluding "look in thy heart and write." He sought a diction that was liberal but not radical, and a naturalness of expression of true emotions that has its roots in the ideals of the Sung poets, in Shunzei's ideal of concentration and insight taken from Tendai Buddhism, and in Teika's ideal of conviction of feeling (ushin).

  With such eclectic interests, it is only natural that the poetry of the Kyōgoku-Reizei poets at their best should be less exalted than intense, less commonplace than idiosyncratic, less profound than acute. Some of their natural scenes are panoramic, but typically the breadth of vision is very restricted. Repeatedly the poets use, as Lady Eifuku Mon'in does, not the simpler word for branches, *eda*, but *kozue*, the "ends of trees." Lightning does not cut across the heavens or illuminate mountains: it shows exactly how many drops of rain there are, and not in masses upon a plain but in beads upon the leaves of plants (*FGS*, VI: 563; see p. 384). The exactness and the reduction of physical scope are accompanied by a corresponding precision and shortening of temporal scope. In the natural sphere, the scene is usually narrowed to the moment, as in Lady Eifuku Mon'in's poem, to the fraction of a second just before the scene changes into something different, or during which the lightning illuminates the plants near the speaker. By describing such moments—moments that are either fleeting or changeful—the poets chose a kind of realistic subject matter that might be explored completely, and that had to be explored subjectively. For in order to render such greatly reduced materials significant, the poets had to attribute to them a value and a meaning that do not invariably enter into ordinary experience, or that may not be common to our observation and that therefore require unusual expression.

  The effort to arrive at truth which we have described largely in terms of careful observation and subjective expression was thought of by the poets themselves in terms of an almost mystic contemplation, a oneness with the truth or the spirit (*makoto* or *kokoro*) of the objects of nature which is reminiscent of the Tendai Buddhist concentration and insight but which doubtless reflects more directly their contemporary experience of Zen. What is essential to their description as to ours is an intensity of observation and a subjectivity of attitude toward poetry. It is difficult to render such crucial words as *kokoro*, *makoto*, and *kokorozashi*, but another sentence or two from *Lord Tamekane's Poetic Notes* will demonstrate the kind of ideals underlying the poetry of the age (*NKGT*, IV, 109).

In order to express the true nature of the natural scene, one must focus one's attention and concentrate deeply upon it. It has been said, "Do not fail to treat what is most appropriate to each of the four seasons. Make your feelings accord with the season, with the scenes of spring, summer, autumn, or winter." Therefore, if you try to harmonize your feelings with the sight of cherry blossoms in spring or with the autumnal scene, and if you express them in words without allowing anything to intervene between your feelings and the scene, then your work will become at one with the very spirit of heaven and earth.

Such dedication, such intense contemplation, presumes an almost mystical state of rapport with the natural world which obviously has elements in common with the meditation of Zen Buddhism. However, as we have already suggested, such meditative scrutiny of nature with the accompanying search for a close rapport with it continues the tradition of contemplation that Shunzei had extolled in an effort to make poetry an almost religious "way of life." Shunzei's idea of contemplation was absorbed, re-directed, and modified in more specifically literary terms in Teika's *Maigetsushō*, which is one of Tamekane's major sources for his *Notes*. The truly significant thing about his borrowing of theory is that it produced a greatly different poetic practice, as the Nijō poets knew only too well. For the goal of Tamekane and his like-minded contemporaries was less the quasi-mysticism and religious commitment to a poetic way of life than the discovery and embodiment of truth. This goal, with the ideals of exterior simplicity or plainness, of inner richness, and of withered beauty—which had been borrowed from the earlier poetry of sabi and from the Sung critics—led to the new poetry. The new style was distinguished by intense observation and a plainness of statement that can best be described as subjective realism. The prosaic surface is important, and yet the quasi-mystic statement of poetic ideals well serves to remind us that these poets were no more content than great poets anywhere with the drab exterior appearance which has sometimes passed for realism. They sought to express truth, to become at one with their subject, and in so doing could only give the natural world a human truth, a subjectivity at first belied by the wholly imagistic styles characteristic of the seasonal poems.

We have chosen to emphasize the subjective realism of the seasonal poems because it is not apparent at first glance, owing to the highly imagistic texture of such poems. Certainly what can be discovered after close study of the seasonal poems can be seen at once in the nonimagistic and thus obviously subjective love poems. In searching back along their now lengthy poetic tradition for inspiration in the kind of love poetry they sought to write, they found their masters not in the preceding age, but in the early classical period. It cannot be said that the early classical poets typically or even often wrote nonimagistic poems, but it is true that some of the finest poems of that high-spirited age either lack images, or bury them within pivot-words, or use them with such open metaphorical intent that they offered the Kyōgoku-Reizei poets what they needed—a precedent, an example to clarify their own intentions. It is typical of them that unlike their Nijō opponents, they did not justify themselves by arguing that their work was traditional; yet they were after all Japanese courtiers and it is to be expected that they would feel the need to find justification for their poetic practice.

We can see their search, or the results of it, in the two anthologies they compiled. Among the love poems of the *Gyokuyōshū* and *Fūgashū,* there are many poems taken from the still unexhausted canon of the early classical period. Like other compilers before them, they found poems to suit their own standard, works that had been passed over by their predecessors to whose tastes they had little appeal. Such poems, found in private collections and hitherto not chosen for imperial anthologies, are often love poems without imagery or with few and weak images. As they appear beside Kyōgoku-Reizei poems, the older ones seem rather unlike themselves—less witty, less metaphysical, more prosy: they resemble the productions of the later age. (It must be admitted, however, that the earlier works are seldom striking, and one suspects that their authors might well have regarded them as less distinguished verses.) Thus, the new poets had their precedent, although in their avoidance of the conceits, the wit, and the constant questioning of the early classical models, they clearly did not intend to follow the example of their ancestors in any thoroughgoing fashion.

The love poetry of the age is extraordinarily difficult. And the difficulty is not the familiar modern one of obscurity, although the love poetry somewhat resembles the poetry of Yeats and Rilke in that the words may be perfectly clear in themselves while their integrated meanings are elusive. Nor is the difficulty that of Narihira's style, in which there is "too much spirit and too few words," or of Shunzei's, in which images and ideas acquire a great resonance through allusion or the tonal depths of yūgen. Stated most simply, it is rather that the reader is hard put to seize upon the simplest, paraphrastic meaning of a poem. If the difficulty grows from an inability to relate the words to each other or to understand the function of crucial particles, or because the sum of meaning seems to be different from the total of the units, the reasons are not, however, far to seek. For all of its stylistic differences, the love poetry is the seasonal poetry without the garment of imagery. The scrutiny of the moment, the analytical discrimination of seemingly identical states, the choice of moments in which one thing or feeling is about to become another, and the basic subjectivity are the same as in the seasonal poems, but here wrought to a higher pitch. Sometimes the extremity seems little more than a frenzy that is not worth the effort of explication, but in the love poems at their best, the real does become the true, the agitated plainness the rich, and the exacerbated traditionalism of courtly love turns out to be extraordinarily well perceived.

A love poem by Lady Jūsammi Chikako on "Love Promises Broken" (*GYS*, XII: 1702) is fairly representative of the style.

Higoro yori	In recent days
Uki o mo ushi to	I can no longer say of wretchedness
E zo iwanu	That it is wretched,
Ge ni omowazu mo	Because my hopeless love has reached
Naru ka to omoeba.	A state I find impossible to understand.

The poem begins by limiting the time, goes on to deny the essential quality of the suffering the speaker feels, and justifies her rejection of the wretched nature of wretchedness by offering a rational, sufficient cause and so suggesting, as exactly as language can, the even greater degree of the betrayed woman's misery. The fineness of the discriminations of her state requires lengthier analysis than is appropriate here, but it should be possible to see that the esthetic ideals of outward plainness possessing inner truth may indeed be realized in a richly subjective poetic style.

Other elements of a less determinate nature appear to have entered into the formation of the esthetic of the age. We know, for example, that, like the Sung poets whom they so greatly admired, the Kyōgoku-Reizei poets were interested in Zen Buddhism and had close contact with Zen priests. It has therefore sometimes been assumed that the Zen esthetic ideal of a simplicity embodying refinement or of plainness embracing all richness influenced the formation of the similar esthetic ideal of the poets. But evidence justifying the assumption is hard to discover; indeed, it may well have been the poets and artists who influenced Zen thought. Whatever the source of influence, and there is evidence for both sides, it seems most likely to us that the development of the similar ideals was concurrent. It is no new thing to see men of different occupations in the same age exhibiting similar tendencies of thought, and the friendly relations between the poets and priests may have come about simply because they shared similar tastes and outlooks.

Without wishing to exaggerate the importance of such associations, we may fairly say that the friendships and shared ideals had the effect of heightening the esthetic awareness of the priests, drawing them into poetry at times, and of lending conviction to the poets' aim of discovering truth at those moments when close attention might provide an insight denied to less meditative minds. Another result was that the religious poems in the *Gyokuyōshū* and *Fūgashū* are of a higher quality than comparable poems in earlier anthologies. The contact with Zen priests clearly had some important poetic results for priests and courtiers alike, although the exact nature of Zen influence is difficult to determine.

Another uncertain factor in determining the esthetic of the Kyōgoku-Reizei poets is the matter of contemporary secular ways of thought. The political as well as the religious writings of the time tend to use more abstract terms than had been common earlier. And there appears to have been increased speculation over psychological processes. Such changes in emphasis might be supposed to have influenced the esthetic of the love poetry in particular, with its avoidance of imagery and close concern with the workings of the mind and heart. Again, however, other explanations are equally plausible—or insufficient. Given the conservative nature of all Japanese Court poetry, however innovating or radical, the example of the nonimagistic poetry of the early classical period might be considered sufficient impetus. Or perhaps the changes in ways of thought led the poets to examine the tradition and to seek out poems that exemplified their own new interests. It must be admitted that all of the explanations are partial: they explain each other a good deal better than they explain the fact that the age saw the birth of two styles, one imagistic, the other nonimagistic. Given the fact, much that is meaningful may be said about the literary history and esthetic ideals of the age; but stemming from the fact of divergent styles as they do, such observations cannot in turn be expected to explain their major assumption.

We have referred to the high quality of the religious poems of this period, which show not only a greater interest in the subject but also a vastly improved skill with allegory. Many of them are totally imagistic and would pass for seasonal poems if their headnotes specifying religious topics had been lost. The meanings of the symbols in the allegory are, on the other hand, sufficiently subjective and abstract to make it seem as if the religious allegories are a perfect fusion of the imagistic seasonal poems and the nonimagistic love poems. Abstractions of a religious nature especially were often conveyed through imagistic symbols by the Zen priests. If someone asked, "What is the Law?"—a question not unlike one asking about the nature of the Christian Trinity—a standard answer was, "The willows are green; the blossoms are red." It almost seems that, like Europe on the threshold of feudal times, Japan and its poets were about to evolve a tradition of allegorical poetry. Such an event, if indeed it really was in the offing, did not occur apart from the short religious poems surviving in the two Kyōgoku-Reizei collections. Intriguing as it is to speculate over what might have been had the Kyōgoku-Reizei poets achieved power, we may happily content ourselves with the satisfaction given by the new styles of the last flowering of Court poetry.

POETIC PRACTICE

THE NEW STYLES

It is almost an axiom of Japanese Court poetry that once styles and techniques have been invented, they are not dropped in favor of new ones, but are maintained for certain kinds of practice. Shunzei himself, who had perhaps the largest hand in shaping the poetry of the preceding period, was one of that age's most prolific practitioners of the facile Fujiwara style, which his own efforts were replacing. Similarly, the experimenting poets of this period continue to write in the Fujiwara style or in the descriptive style when decorum seems to call for one or the other. These styles survive, much as if Wordsworth had written poems in the manner of Elizabethan aureate "copy," Metaphysical wit, and Augustan harmony in addition to his own Romantic purity. There are perhaps many elements in Wordsworth's style that he owes to earlier poets, but we would feel justified in rejecting stylistic imitativeness if we sought to consider what is essentially Wordsworthian. Similarly, while recognizing the fact that the Kyōgoku-Reizei poets as well as their Nijō rivals practiced the Fujiwara style and other styles as well, we feel justified in devoting all but exclusive attention to those styles of the age that are particularly its own.

It will be clear by now that these styles are chiefly those represented by the love poems and the seasonal poems. So extreme at times do the differences between the two become that even the scattered examples of love poems in the early classical period by, say, Komachi (see *KKS*, XIII: 656, and above, p. 188), or from the mid-classical period by Teika, which consist entirely of images (see *SKKS*, VI: 671, and above, p. 306), provide us with no real anticipation—any more than an occasional robin in late winter would be comparable to flocks in February. The difference is one between an occasional exception to a rule and a wholly new rule. We have quoted enough poems in these extreme styles to make their differences evident. The problems that remain concerning these new styles are to show how modified versions of them—a love poem with only few images, for example—preserve the important characteristics of the styles at their extremes; and perhaps paradoxically to show, beyond what has already been said, how the divergent styles share the same stylistic intentions.

The facts of poetic composition often made it impossible for a poet to write purely imagistic or nonimagistic verse. Many of the compound topics (musubidai) employed by the poets meant that they had, perforce, to use imagery in love poems or overtly subjective elements in seasonal poems. Ex-Emperor Fushimi's poem on the compound topic of "Love and the Evening" (*GYS,* XII: 1719) is an example. It could not avoid employing imagery when treating "evening," but the kind of treatment is typical of the age.

Taezu naran	It is evening now,
Mi o sae kakete	And with the sadness of my fruitless waiting
Kanashiki wa	It marks the day from night,
Tsurasa o kagiru	Bounding the limits of a wretchedness
Ima no yūgure.	And this love-wager of my life.

The woman who is the speaker of this poem is deeply conscious of evening, and Fushimi has stressed the image by placing it in his last line. But the phrasing and the handling of the image are such that it is treated less as an image than as an agent. *Ima no yūgure* literally means "evening of now," with the dusk but a part of the larger whole—the present moment of suffering. Moreover, the stress on "evening" is so strong that it is treated more as a metaphor than an image. This is the time of day when a woman waits for her lover to visit her, as the speaker's lover no longer does, so that the moment is filled more with deep feeling than with tinted clouds. But most importantly, *yūgure* is governed by the verb *kagiru* ("to bound," "set limits to"), making it in English the subject of the verb. The dusk, and not the speaker or her lover, is therefore the active agent of the poem, for it ends the day and also the speaker's life. This metaphor of agency, almost of personification, is indeed one of the most striking features of the poem, and its effect is at once to heighten the importance of evening as a concept and to diminish its imagistic qualities.

In such fashion, the nonimagistic quality of this style is preserved, even when imagery is employed. Something of the reverse is also true of those imagistic poems which employ generalized, nonimagistic language. Tamekane's poem describing the chiaroscuro effects of sunlight on a bamboo grove has two clear abstractions, which would be surprising in Japanese Court poetry of any period, but the total effect is to lend them an imagistic quality (*GYS,* III: 419).

Eda ni moru	In their rareness,
Asahi no kage no	The rays of the morning sun
Sukunasa ni	Filter brightly through
Suzushisa fukaki	The branches where the coolness
Take no oku kana.	Is deep within the bamboo grove.

As perhaps our translation shows, the abstractions—*sukunasa* ("fewness," "rareness") and *suzushisa* ("coolness")—do not have the effect of abstraction in this poem. The first of them functions imagistically to limit the amount of light that can penetrate into the thick stand of bamboo; and the second, which perhaps inherently retains some imagistic quality despite its abstraction, is rendered even more imagistic by its combination with specific and detailed images. In addition, the word *fukaki* ("deep") is so employed as to modify both "coolness" and "grove" (*oku*), a kind of rhetorical "yoking" or zeugma that for once can be conveyed quite naturally in English.

As these examples indicate, the new styles retain for the most part their dissimilar effects, even when images or abstractions appear unexpectedly. Although there are not infrequent exceptions to this rule, it holds in the main, so that the chief critical problem is one of accounting for or reconciling the differences between the styles. If after all the two styles have common literary as well as philosophical ideals about desirable poetic ends, then we may say that the stylistic schizophrenia is more apparent than real. And it does seem possible to say this, for the explanation is to be found in a basic subjectivity that as we have noted underlies both styles, a motive and mode of apprehension which rises from the search for truth in a moment of intense experience that can be apprehended only by a human subject—the speaker of the poem and the poet. Such a subjectivity can be demonstrated in various ways. Historically we can see that in the thirty-odd years between the compilation of the *Gyokuyōshū* (1313 or 1314) and of the *Fūgashū* (ca. 1345) literary taste became increasingly subjective, as if this latent quality was more and more highly esteemed. For in the *Fūgashū* the seasonal poems more often use such images as eaves, bedroom, and pillow (to specify but one kind of evidence) that suggest more strongly the presence of the human observer and his relation to the natural scene. Such words are crucial in the elliptical style of Japanese poetry, because not only do they help establish esthetic distance, but they also indicate whether the natural scene is to be overtly appreciated for itself or whether a strong human element is to be inferred. The change in taste seems to show that the latent subjectivity of the poetry in the *Gyokuyōshū* was more highly esteemed and stressed by the next generation of poets and compilers. Many of the same poets are represented in both anthologies, but the selections differ most on precisely this score; and the poets new to the *Fūgashū* show the same tendency.

There is evidence of other kinds. One kind, exemplified by a poem of ex-Emperor Hanazono, is perhaps somewhat fortuitous but nonetheless very striking (*FGS,* XVIII: 2046).

Tsubame naku	The sun at dusk
Nokiba no yūhi	Fades in brightness from the eaves
Kage kiete	Where swallows twitter;
Yanagi ni aoki	And among the willows in the garden
Niwa no harukaze.	Blows the green breeze of the spring.

The subjective element of this poem, which is made up entirely of images, is implicit throughout and obvious in the last image. Not even the Impressionist painters have created a green breeze, and of course we know that its greenness here is the purely subjective one of its association with the willows, the garden, and spring. Such Impressionism, if we may call it that, is governed by the premise that what the subject beholds in the object is true. The same technique is to be found in other seasonal poems of the age, as we shall see.

And yet this Impressionism by no means comprehends the poem's meaning. The poem is to be found in the book or scroll of Buddhist poems (Shakkyō) in the *Fūgashū,* and carries the headnote: "On the topic, 'This is the true preparation; this is the true Dharma-offering to the Buddha,' in the chapter on the Medicine King [*Lotus Sûtra,* XXIII]." In other words, what appears to be a wholly imagistic poem of the period, subjective in its handling of imagery, turns out to have the further subjective dimension of complete allegory. The chapter referred to tells how Kiken Bosatsu, or the Bodhisattva Beautiful, was so grateful for having heard the Buddha preach that he wished to immolate himself as an offering. This he does, after spending eons beautifying his body so that it will be a suitable offering. After the immolation, the body disappears but the Buddha-spirit of the Bodhisattva remains. In terms of the allegory, the sun stands for the Bodhisattva's body, the swallows for human beings, the willows for existence, and the spring breeze for the Buddha-spirit. Just as the poem suggests that the evening scene is more beautiful after the light fades, so, too, allegorically it means that the spirit of the Bodhisattva Beautiful is even more beautiful after his body is gone.

There are other religious and secular allegories in the poetry of this period, not always as perfect or precise as this one; but the main point is not so much that the poems may occasionally be allegorical as that they are, even when fashioned entirely from images, the products of a basic subjectivity. Sometimes this quality emerges from a suggestion of human concerns in an image such as a pillow; sometimes by the use of such words of generalized comment as "in tranquility," which implies a human estimation and attribution of emotion; but chiefly through the poetic treatment, the shaping of the materials. This is largely a matter of the rhetoric of this age, but one green breeze is perhaps sufficient to show that the most imagistic seasonal poem is the product of a highly considered and deliberate art. And one allegory is enough to show that the images are less crucial in themselves than expressive of the overriding subjective concern of these poets.

The love poems present the problem in reverse, since we wish to show that in spite of their generalized language, something akin to imagery is implied. Our best evidence must be found in a poem with few or no images of any force, such a poem as Lady Jūsammi Tameko's "Love Poem" (*GYS,* XI: 1527).

Mono omoeba	Filled with longing,
Hakanaki fude no	I turned for distraction to my brush
Susabi ni mo	And idle scribbling—
Kokoro ni nitaru	The casual play brings fervent words
Koto zo kakaruru.	That write themselves in miming of my heart.

The writing brush is an image, but a very weak one, and the poem's real force emerges from the implication that the woman's longing for her lover expresses itself in the most trivial matters. If she had tried to write down a description of her sufferings, it would be different, but in spite of her unconscious, undeliberate self, the words expressing her suffering write themselves just as they are written in her heart. To say this much is to show that, for all its general language and its single weak image, the more one ponders the poem the more vivid its effect seems. Perhaps because of the intensity of the experience presented by the poem, but without specification of detail, it leads us to fill in the details of the speaker's appearance, her room, her writing box, just as we tend to do in reading the climactic portions of a novel, even when there is no description.

More particularly, the position of the poem, toward the beginning of the third of the five books of love poems in the *Gyokuyōshū,* tells us in terms of the specific progression of a love affair that the woman has entered upon an affair, has enjoyed her period of happiness, and is now in the throes of suffering over her lover's unfaithfulness. In such manner, the quasi-narrative circumstances are even clearer than her surroundings, and the almost entirely imageless poem takes on a quality, not precisely imagistic, but particular enough in details of situation and the progression of the affair to be anything but abstract. To a degree unknown even in Western medieval courtly love, the stages of an affair represented in Japanese poetry were worked out in such definite detail that, with the weight of centuries of tradition behind such a poem as this, a poem without imagery yet takes on the vividness of a specific situation. Consequently, just as the seasonal poems are highly subjective in spite of their imagistic nature and so resemble the love poems, from which they differ in effect, so the love poems, for all their startling lack of imagery, are yet so particular and vivid in their implications that they resemble the seasonal poems.

There is, then, no denying the very different literary effects of the two styles; but what is equally important is that behind the apparently generalized façade of the love poems, as behind the imagistic façade of the seasonal poems, lies essentially the same creative spirit, the same assumptions about the nature and ends of poetry. The common elements of each style are a subjectivity most reminiscent of the early classical period and a particularity suggestive of the mid-classical period. These poets drew upon differing parts of their heritage to create two discrete styles that nonetheless represent the same basic stylistic principles, two differing methods for expressing the same interests in the dissimilar subject matter of love and nature. Further resemblances, as well as further differences, are revealed in more particular aspects of poetic practice.

DICTION

For the most part, the language of poetry in this period is the same as that of the two preceding ages and any discussion of differences must be founded upon the postulate of basic similarity. Once the largely traditional character of the poetic language has been acknowledged, however, one may speak of some significant alterations and, what is more important, some new emphases. Certainly the diction employed by the Kyōgoku-Reizei poets exacerbated the hostility of the conventional Nijō poets. This new exploration of the diction inherited by tradition seems to be in part a natural concomitant of the divergent styles and more basically a symptom of the poetic interests of the age: the desire of these poets to make distinctions and discriminations, to emphasize particularity, and above all to convey the actuality of a moment of intense experience, whether of nature or in the course of a love affair.

To begin with the two styles, it is obvious that even if these poets had never departed from traditional language, the diction of the love poems would be unusual in its extremely high proportion of generalized words and even abstractions, while that of the seasonal poems might be regarded as equally unusual in the large number of images drawn from the great storehouse of traditional imagery. But as a matter of fact, the diction of both styles is often new; poets both introduce new words and, more typically, use the generalized diction of an earlier period, but very precisely, discriminating between two words used virtually as synonyms, in order to reveal the dissimilarities in things apparently alike. And in this difference, so small and yet so crucial in defining the essential nature of an intense experience, lies the character of much of the poetry of the age.

We have all felt that at times our emotions elude expression, because such words as joy, happiness, or elation do not sufficiently discriminate the nature of what we feel. The Kyōgoku-Reizei poets dwelt upon experiences in which such distinctions of feeling or between the phenomena of nature were crucial. In this as in certain other respects, the poets of the age reveal their debt to the early classical period, whose love poetry often employs—although intermittently and to a lesser degree—the same generalized diction, and whose seasonal poetry often discriminates between this and that phenomenon of nature. And for their seasonal poetry, they developed further the tendency of the descriptive poetry of the mid-classical period to use noun images as the primary basis of poetic expression. The Shunzeis and the Teikas also instilled an essential seriousness into the minds of subsequent poets; and this attitude, which amounts at times to solemnity among the Tamekanes and Tamekos, led the new poets to reject the wit and high spirits that accompanied the subjectivity of a Komachi or a Tsurayuki. Since the love poems of the early classical period had used their wit in allegories and conceits, the new poets—in their rejection of the wit in favor of gravity—also seem to have been led to eschew imagery in love poems. Similarly, by focusing upon the experience of a natural scene and by avoiding comments about it, the age tended to develop from the descriptive poetry of a Saigyō a diction that was almost wholly imagistic in the seasonal poems. A Saigyō might well begin a poem with such a generalized expression as, "Loneliness . . . " (*sabishisa wa*), but the new poets tended to avoid such overt predications and to arrange the details so that the images carried the whole poetic burden.

Although such a historical explanation of the styles and their diction gives us a useful perspective from which to judge the continuity of the tradition, it does not say very much about the distinctive features of the poetic language of this period. Most frequently, the novelty in diction is too slight to be rendered with much success into modern English, in which there is little left of the decorous character of the poetic diction to be found in our eighteenth-century poetry. Slight as these changes often are, they are important in effect. Ex-Empress Eifuku's phrase *kumo no yukiki ni,* "by the going and coming of the clouds" (see above, p. 353) turns out about the same in translation as would the more natural *yukiki no kumo ni,* although, as we have seen, the effect in the original would have differed considerably. The unconventional *kumo no yukiki ni* suggests greater activity, and this very quality of movement is one of the prime differences between the seasonal poetry of the late classical period and that of the preceding ages. For without introducing new words, this poetry often gives a very different effect, as we can see in ex-Emperor Go-Fushimi's poem "On a Winter Garden" (*FGS,* VIII: 739).

Shiguru to mo	The leaves are moist
Shirarenu niwa wa	In the garden where the silent drizzle
Ko no ha nurete	Leaves little trace;
Samuki yūhi wa	And the cold sun of evening
Kage ochinikeri.	Has dropped beneath the hills.

To say the evening sunlight is cold is not to use new language, but to use language differently; and to say the light has dropped is to use a verb of action where earlier poets would have been content with "fade" (*kienikeri*).

Such a substitution as that of *kumo no yukiki ni* for *yukiki no kumo ni* is more properly a rhetorical figure (hypallage) than a matter of diction, but we shall follow the Nijō critics of these poets and consider it for the moment as a matter of diction. The Kyōgoku-Reizei poets were roundly berated for such a practice of reversed diction, and to an extent justly so, since the technique seems at times to be little more than a mannerism. What they aimed at, however, was to present a scene with psychological truth, and such reversals were often used with calculation in order to give a fresh view of a familiar scene.

Differences in poetic language such as these are symptomatic of changed poetic aims. Where Shunzei had led the poets of his age to seek a purity of diction that conveyed rich tonal depths, these poets sought to convey an intense experience. The effect is often that of a freshness of language or expression, a novelty in the language that is scarcely diminished by the fact that there is often a Chinese precedent. At other times, "fresh" language is often colloquial language newly used in poetry, and it must be admitted that such effects are easier to specify than to translate. In a poem of Tamekane's, for example, there is one word that is colloquial and another that is Chinese in its imagistic overtones (*GYS*, VI: 1011).

Neya no ue wa	It makes no sound
Tsumoreru yuki ni	On the snow piled deeply on the roof
Oto mo sede	Of my bed chamber,
Yokogiru arare	But instead the hail *slants down*
Mado tataku nari.	And taps in visit on my *window*.

To say the hail "slants" is to use the diction of everyday speech, not the traditional poetic word hoard; and windows were not part of the architecture of Japanese Court dwellings, but at most of houses of the poor or of country villas. Ultimately the image was Chinese, and the image here of the hail tapping like a visitor on the shuttered window suggests an isolated retreat that was probably closer to Tamekane's experience of Chinese poetry than of visits to the country.

The age was, after all, most successful in its use of fresh diction when such usage lay closest to its poetic interests. The repetition of words, which had so long been considered a fault in the tanka, and the discrimination between—almost the redefinition of—very similar words, reflect, as we have noticed, the poets' desire to discriminate the exact nature of a moment of rich experience. Of all the innovating poets, ex-Empress Eifuku seems most given to repetitions. As her poem "Waiting in Vain for Her Lover" demonstrates, the repetitions might be used as meaningfully in love poems as in seasonal poems, when they serve to distinguish the seemingly similar but really different elements of experience (*FGS*, XI: 1066).

Iishi mama no	If this evening
Koyoi tagawanu	Were truly the "this evening"
Koyoi nite	Of your promises,
Mata asu naraba	And if you would only come again
Ureshikaramashi.	tomorrow,
	Then would I know true happiness.

Sometimes the results were trivial and the effect is one of a redundancy that the tanka can ill afford. Ex-Empress Eifuku is one of the best poets of the age and also one who frequently took such risks. It is often difficult to decide whether or not she has been wholly successful (*FGS*, XIII: 1223).

Kyō wa moshi	Is it the case
Hito mo ya ware o	That you today have given me
Omoiizuru	Some passing thought,
Ware mo tsune yori	That I, even more than usual,
Hito no koishiki.	Long for you with such intensity?

The repetition of "I" (*ware*) and "you" (*hito*, literally "person") is particularly obtrusive, especially since it is enforced by parallelism and accompanied by other near repetitions and contrasts (such as "to give passing thought" / "long for"; "today" / "more than usual"), expressions which are more nearly alike in the Japanese than the English. These techniques so nearly fill the poem that it is hard to know whether they are in the best taste; but it is also difficult to say that the poem is a failure. The ironic contrast between the accidental way in which the lover's fickle mind has happened to think of the woman and her uninterrupted longing for him is a fine touch that would not have gone unnoticed by a male recipient of such a message. And the superstitious wondering about the illogical increase of longing is true to the psychology of love. One's judgment of the poem must depend upon one's own taste and the tastes of one's age. An Elizabethan poet probably would have felt that this is brave language indeed; today we have our doubts.

A poem by ex-Emperor Fushimi on lightning does not give us such qualms. It is remarkable for its effective use of different words for light (*FGS*, VI: 566).

Nioi shirami	The sudden *brightness*
Tsuki no chikazuku	Of the lightning fades in the white
Yama no ha no	*radiance*
Hikari ni yowaru	At the mountain's edge,
Inazuma no *kage*.	Where the not yet risen moon
	Casts its *foreglowing* on the sky.

The italicized words have differing meanings and functions, for all of their essential similarity. The distinctions are those of the degree of intensity and differing kinds of beauty.

RHETORIC

The repetitions and distinctions we have discussed are as much a part of the rhetoric of poetry as of the diction. They are formal techniques, literary means employed to gain certain poetic ends. Ex-Empress Eifuku's repetitions have every justification (except perhaps the final one of complete success), given the desire of these poets to create a rich poetic texture that would convey the truth of a perception or the intensity of an experience at a given moment. Such artistic motives tend to make the poems of the age appear "busy" in their functioning; the repetitions, the parallelisms, the discriminations, the reversals of diction, the frequent use of supernumerary syllables—these and other techniques give the poems a rich and somewhat nervous style. They also contribute to the great difficulty, sometimes the obscurity, of these poems, for instead of clarifying and arresting the fluid sweetness of the language, the rhetorical stiffening frequently makes comprehension all the more difficult. The effect is often one of armor under velvet, of rigidity under a rippling style.

Like the preceding ages, the late classical period also needed to establish a rhetoric that suited its particular purposes. The unchanged fluidity of the language still needed direction to make it flow where one wished it to, and the change in aim required certain changes in technique. It is a simplification of course, but each age seems to have one typical rhetorical characteristic: simple declaration typifies the rhetoric of primitive song; complex parallelism the age of Hitomaro; the pivot-word the poetry of Komachi, Tsurayuki, and their fellows; and allusive variation the poetry of Shunzei and Teika. In the late classical period, however, there is no such single technique by which one may characterize the rhetoric of its poetry; rather, there is a general rhetorical impulse toward what may be called rearrangement of the materials into an order that best conveys the experience in which the poet is interested. Ex-Emperor Hanazono's green spring breeze blowing allegorically is a characteristic example.

Although this impulse to rearrange usually took different forms from those the tradition had known before, it cannot be claimed that the old rhetorical resources were completely ignored. Although used but infrequently, the pillow-word is occasionally employed when stylistic decorum seems to call for it. The first poem in even such a relatively radical anthology as the *Fūga-shū* was thought to be one which required a solemnity that observed the old forms in announcing spring with its trailing haze. Accordingly, Tamekane's poem, the first in the anthology, begins with the old pillow-word, *ashihiki no,* most commonly used as here for mountains or hills (*yama*). It is not certain what this expression originally meant, but by the time of the *Kokinshū* it was generally glossed by folk etymology to mean "the foot-dragging"—or steep. By Tamekane's time, however, such a familiar pillow-word was less imagistic than tonal, and almost ritualistic or incantatory, as if one should begin, "Verily, verily I say unto you, the hills . . ." Except for the decorum of such instances as this, the age seemed content to leave the pillow-words where they found them in the older poetry and seek new techniques or altered versions of the old.

The pivot-word is similarly hard to find in the poetry of this age, but a somewhat analogous technique is used repeatedly. While the pivot-word involved the use of two or more parsings of a single series of sounds that took on simultaneous but different meanings according to the parsings, the new technique involves the use of a single word, usually an adjective, with two different words or clauses. The technique in English poetry that most resembles this has been called zeugma, or "yoking," and perhaps the most famous examples are to be found in *The Rape of the Lock,* where Pope worries over Belinda at tea, fearing lest she "stain her Honour or her new Brocade." "Stain" of course governs both "Honour" and "Brocade," but the meanings of the two kinds of blemish are startlingly different. Ex-Emperor Go-Fushimi employs a similar yoking in a poem on spring (*FGS,* I: 44).

Hana tori no	This is a scene
Nasake made koso	So rich in the beauty of flowers and birds
Omoikomuru	That it colors me:
Yūyama *fukaki*	In the dusk the distant hills
Haru no kasumi ni.	*Deep* within the haze of spring.

As we have tried to show in our translation, the depth refers both to the mountains and the haze, harmonizing them as the speaker's thoughts have also been filled both with the intrinsic beauty of the scene and with the associations of elegance—the "beauty of flowers and birds"—with which it has been invested by centuries of tradition.

It is difficult to say why the poets of this age preferred such yokings to pivot-words. Perhaps the preference was simply for new techniques, or more probably it was based upon a changed poetic taste. The pivot-word was a technique esteemed for its wit and perhaps for its economy. The new poets were not drawn to the wit of the early classical period, in this as in other respects; but at the same time they sought a comparable rhetorical richness that yet retained an essential clarity. Go-Fushimi's poem therefore uses the word "deep" with applications to two different nouns, but in each case it possesses nearly the same meaning. It may seem a paradox that we should attribute both clarity and difficulty to this poetry, and yet the paradox is easily resolved. The poetry is not so much rich in ambiguity or depth as extremely nice in its discriminations. This tendency can be observed in poem after poem in which similar natural phenomena are so finely discriminated that the distinction to be made is often difficult to perceive, or in love poems in which the minute distinction between misery and wretchedness may convey the essential experience of the poem.

Of the major rhetorical techniques inherited from earlier periods, allusive variation (honkadori) is perhaps the most often employed and the least changed. If it is not a technique that seems to be most expressive of the major interests of the age—which lay not with depth but with exploration of the moment—it is nonetheless used with considerable frequency and occasionally in new ways. One of these novelties, well calculated to arouse the ire of the Nijō critics, can be found in ex-Emperor Fushimi's lovely poem, "On Stopping Overnight on a Journey" (*GYS*, VIII: 1239).

Kajimakura	Pillowed above the oars—
Hitoyo naraburu	Will these ships now lying side by side
Tomobune mo	For a night's companionship
Asu no tomari ya	Anchor in loneliness for tomorrow's sleep,
Ono ga uraura.	Each in the harbor of its separate bay?

This is an allusive variation upon what is perhaps an even finer poem, by the priest Jien (*K. Taikei*, X, 740; see p. 316 above).

Kajimakura	Pillowed above the oars
Nezame ni fukaki	And deep in sleep until dawn breaks,
Asaborake	I wake to find no ship:
Yume mo ato naki	The one that bears my longings in the
Fune o shi zo omou.	dream
	Has borne me in the daylight from this
	boat.

The function of the allusion is of course to increase the tonal intensity of Fushimi's poem. In addition it serves to clarify the relation between his speaker, the first line, and the rest of the poem. The allusion shows that the speaker is lonely enough on a journey from the capital when there are other ships tied up alongside his, but that the next evening he will be even more isolated and sad when he must anchor apart from the rest. In effect, Fushimi has taken the experience in Jien's poem another step in order to heighten the loneliness. The allusion has another dimension, since the poem alluded to is itself an allusive variation upon the famous anonymous poem on dawn at Akashi Bay (*KKS*, IX: 409). This double allusion was not entirely new to Japanese poetry with the practice of the Kyōgoku-Reizei poets, but to allude, as Fushimi has done, to such a recent poem as Jien's rather than to a well-known poem from one of the first three imperial anthologies was to assign to the poetry of the recent past a significance that the conservative Nijō poets would never allow.

These several rhetorical techniques were not innovations; they had been practiced, although sometimes differently, in earlier periods. As employed by these poets, they function primarily to shape details, to clarify, and to show the poets' competence with the poetic practice they had inherited. Besides these there are what may be called the major rhetorical characteristics of the new poetry, major both because of their frequency and importance as well as because of their marked difference from the rhetoric of earlier ages. One of these is the expression of logic or reasoning, a kind of dialectic. This dialectic is clearly descended from the reasoning wit of the early classical period with its determination of causes and effects or its distinctions between appearance and reality, and from the less obtrusive intellectuality of the rhetoricians of the preceding age. The older reasoning was different, however, in its wit, which so often found expression in conceits, and in its philosophical basis. The new reasoning is less mannered, simpler, more factual, and often closer to the ordinary logic of prose. There is not so much a questioning about the nature of what appears before the speaker as a strong sense of cause and effect and a subtle discrimination of detail.

Such reasoning marks the seasonal and the love poems alike. Its resemblances to the earlier techniques and its differences from them can be understood by examination of a rather simple poem on spring by Saionji Sanekane (*GYS*, II: 225).

Shirakumo no	On the mountain peaks
Tanabiku iro mo	Even the whiteness of trailing clouds
Katsu kienu	Slowly fades away
Hana chiru yama no	In the wake of the spring breeze
Mine no harukaze.	That blows the blossoms in a colored whirl.

A poet of the earlier period would probably have concerned himself with the apparent resemblance of the white clouds and the "clouds" of cherry blossoms. Sanekane emphasizes both as elements that suffer the same effect from the same cause, the wind; the colors of the two may be intermingled, but there is never any doubt about the component colors and where they come from. In addition to such clear causal reasoning, the age delighted in observing phenomena and events that either happen without quite seeming to or should be expected to do something but do not. Another spring poem, ex-Empress Eifuku's on "Cherry Blossoms in the Evening" (*FGS*, II: 189), is a typical example of such rhetorical interests.

Hana no ue ni	The evening sun
Shibashi utsurou	Flickers upon the cherry blossoms
Yūzukuhi	With a moment's light,
Iru to mo nashi ni	And though it does not seem to set,
Kage kienikeri.	Its glowing softly melts away.

Such a poem is really one employing a dialectic, since we are meant to understand first the brevity of the scene ("a moment's light"), then its timelessness ("does not seem to set"), and once again its change ("melts away").

The poem argues, although in an altogether pleasant fashion, in order to convince us that this one moment, so brief in time and yet so slowed in the consciousness of the speaker, is very special. Here the beauty is emphasized; in comparable love poems, the dialectic may stress such an altogether different tone as misery.

Another kind of reasoning dialectic builds upon the two already mentioned. If the cause is of overwhelming power and the moment of experience very intense, then the effect may be different in kind from what is expected. Extremities often lead to change in this poetry, just as if heat were applied to ice to such a degree that the result was not melting but vaporizing; and sometimes the result is so unexpected that, to follow our analogy, the ice becomes colder. A love poem by Tamekane employs such a dialectic; the woman who is the speaker of the poem has experienced the suffering of betrayal so intensely that her attitude undergoes an unexpected change (*GYS*, XIII: 1768).

Tsuraki amari	So great my misery
Ushi to mo iwade	That I have passed my days reluctant
Sugosu hi o	To speak aloud of suffering,
Uraminu ni koso	Till now my exhaustion is complete
Omoihatenure.	And my bitterness toward you disappears.

In spite of our surprise at the metamorphosis in her feelings, we are convinced by its psychological truth. The poem reduces the woman's life to such essentials of suffering that the moment of change—which a Proust would have spent pages in recounting and explaining—seems one of life's major experiences. Such a persuasive dialectic is, however, a kind of rhetoric, and its success depends upon the skill of its employment, the skill with which conviction is instilled within us. It must be admitted that the relation of cause to effect is often obvious, and sometimes the extremities seem so forced that they are hardly worth bothering about. On such occasions the technique appears baldly before us, and we wish for either the less mannered presentation of prose or the wit of earlier poets. But these poets at their best achieve a kind of psychological truth through their dialectic that seems extremely modern in its searching analysis.

Another characteristic new aspect of the rhetoric of the Kyōgoku-Reizei poets is the one most easily described by the complementary terms division and synthesis. If such poets as Shunzei, Saigyō, and Teika had tended to fragment their poems into several syntactical units that were integrated by tonal harmony, the poets who succeeded them tended to divide a poem into two units, or sometimes more, whose integration was less one of common tonal elements than of an intensity of feeling reflected in a rich verse texture. Poem after poem is divided at the end of the third line with either an infinitive or a participial continuative (*-i, -te*) that seems in this period to have almost the effect of a full stop, or perhaps a degree of coordination comparable to those cases in English in which we employ a semicolon. Tamekane's poem on hail is typical (*FGS*, VIII: 794).

Furiharuru	Outside, the running hail
Niwa no arare wa	Falls, then stops, and falls again
Katayorite	In patches on the garden;
Iro naru kumo zo	Above, the beauteously colored clouds
Sora ni kureyuku.	Grow dark in passage through the sky.

There seems at first to be little connection between the first three and the last two lines. To Tamekane, the chief logical connection was no doubt the fact that the clouds are part of the same moment of experience as the hail, and may even be its source. More important in one's experience of the poem, however, is the degree of unobtrusive parallelism that unites the two parts. Our "outside" and "above" are more obtrusive but necessary to show a Western reader the position of the speaker. In the Japanese, the hail and the clouds are the two points of focus; each is followed by a particle functioning to stress the noun; each is preceded by an attributive verb giving it an action or state; each is followed by the main verb of the clause; and each has its sphere of influence, the garden or the sky. The two parts have been fused into a single experience.

Often the synthesis is effected by a logic of cause and effect, by pairings, or by contrast. Of all these poets ex-Empress Eifuku is the fondest of the various balances, contrasts, and parallelisms possible in Japanese, as another divided and integrated poem, "On Waiting for the Lover Nights on End," shows in extreme fashion (*FGS*, XI: 1052).

Ware mo hito mo	For me, for you,
Aware tsurenaki	How fantastic our indifference
Yonayona yo	Night after night!
Tanome mo yamazu	You do not care how frequent your
Machi mo yowarazu.	deception
	And I refuse to weaken with your lies.

The rhetorical techniques we have been discussing have mainly concerned forms of expression and types of structure, but the rhetoric of poetry in a given period is also significant for its characteristic approach to the experience the age deems most suitable for poetry. This rhetoric is one of selection and arrangement, of what is chosen or rejected, and of presentation of the material selected. The age sought to arrange the details of poetic experience in an order that conveyed the most "truth" or reality to the poet and the reader, and often at the expense of normal syntax or traditional expression. This is as true of the seemingly objective, but often Impressionistic, seasonal poems as of the love poems. Such a description of the poetry emphasizes the deliberate, conscious artistry of these poets, for if the order in a given case is Impressionistic, it is not vague; and if it follows the subjective apprehension of reality by an individual speaker who sees the world in new ways, it is meant to convey a hitherto unnoticed but still valid truth.

This rhetoric of arrangement or ordering is often almost pictorial in nature, since it involves a composition of the materials in relation to the geographical or psychological position of the speaker of the poem. Tamekane's "composition" in his poem on a late summer scene, for example, begins in the distant mountains, descends to the nearer foothills, and ends near at hand (*FGS*, IV: 398).

Matsu o harau	Ruffling down the pines,
Kaze wa susono no	The wind at dusk tumbles upon the grasses
Kusa ni ochite	Of the foothill plains below;
Yūdatsu kumo ni	The rain vies with the racing summer
Ame kiou nari.	clouds
	To be the first to bring the shower.

Lady Jūsammi Chikako's poem on "A Moor in Late Autumn" (*GYS*, V: 819) is arranged in reverse. The line of vision sweeps away from the speaker, across the moor to the sunset beyond, and, as in so many of these poems, into another dimension, that of time. Distance changes to the close of day visible on the horizon and beyond that, as it were, the autumn also drawing to its close.

Nobe tōki	Wide across the moors
Obana ni kaze wa	Bend the tassels of the pampas grass
Fukimichite	In the swelling breeze;
Samuki yūhi ni	And in the cold of the evening sun
Aki zo kureyuku.	Autumn darkens to its close.

Without such a careful organizing principle, the poem no doubt would fall into the two disparate parts that the scandalized Nijō critics saw in these poems.

Such principles of composition are more readily discernible in the seasonal poems, in which the many images related to each other by reference to the position of the speaker are more concrete than the materials of the more generalized love poems. The same techniques are used in these all but non-imagistic poems nonetheless, as a love poem by Saionji Sanekane shows. In a sense, the composition here is the reverse of that in Chikako's poem, both because it moves from near to far and because subjectivity ends in a natural image, whereas Chikako's images had ended in the more generalized concept of time (*GYS*, XI: 1569).

Koishisa wa	In my suffering,
Nagame no sue ni	Longing takes on a shape far off
Katachi shite	At my reverie's end—
Namida ni ukabu	Floating in a blur of tears,
Tōyama no matsu.	The green pines on the distant hills.

In her reverie, the speaker looks out beyond her on a world she scarcely sees, and at the end of her distracted thoughts her feelings assume a physical form. To have an abstraction ("longing") "take shape" is very unusual diction; and the "end" is even more remarkable, since it is used spatially for the scene before her, temporally for her reverie, and symbolically also—the shape is only a distant blur in her tears, but the green of the pine trees suggests the man she longs for, since to the Japanese there is a suggestion of masculinity in this color. The composition of a poem in which longing leads us beyond to the symbolic tear-blurred greenness is subtle enough, and yet it may be easier to grasp than similar compositions in love poems that are entirely without imagery. A complicated poem by ex-Empress Eifuku has the same basic composition (*FGS*, XIV: 1355).

Itoioshimi	Though I alone am anxious
Ware nomi mi oba	And do not wish to hate myself so much
Ureuredo	That I lose hold of life,
Kou naru hate o	This misery called love and its far limits
Shiru hito mo nashi.	Are things that no one knows about or
	cares.

The poem begins with the speaker herself and her attitudes toward herself; it goes on to the abstraction—love—and its limits; and it ends with the attitudes of others, especially of course those of the unfaithful lover. It might at first seem, at least to a Westerner, that the natural order would be that of speaker, other human beings, and abstraction; but the point of the poem depends upon the arrangement it employs. The speaker knows, and has concern for, herself. And what gives her concern, what is the cause of her suffering and even self-loathing, is a bitter experience of love. Only when we know she suffers from "this misery called love" and hates herself for it, does the true pathos of the indifference of others to her and their lack of understanding of the real nature of love emerge in its full force.

We have dwelt at such length on the rhetoric employed by the poets in this period for a number of reasons. It is new to the tradition, at least in its particular emphases, and except for such obvious techniques as parallelism, it is a kind of rhetoric that may be too easily overlooked. More important, however, an understanding of the rhetoric is necessary for an understanding of the poetry, with respect to both proper appreciation and simple comprehension. And finally, the rhetoric shows the extent to which the divergent styles of the love and the seasonal poems are fundamentally the same in technique, except for the one startling difference of imagery. In many important respects, the rhetoric is more significant than the imagery, something that can be said about no previous age; because the imagery, or for that matter the generalized vocabulary of the love poems, is not as rich as in other periods. The richness of tonal depth in imagery gives way to a richness of verse texture in rhetoric—although this must of course be understood as a relative judgment. For these poets would not be Japanese if imagery were not for them a crucial aspect of their poetry.

IMAGERY AND THE PROBLEM OF GENERALIZATION

We have anticipated our discussion of imagery and generalization in three important respects. An examination of the rhetoric has shown how images are fitted into patterns of a composition, into arrangements that determine the order and therefore the effect of the images. A study of the diction has shown that both images and generalized words are used characteristically for their particular meanings and for distinctions that carry the exact nature of an experience. And a consideration of the generalized style of the love poems in contrast to the imagistic style of the seasonal poems has shown that the love poems imply a specific, vivid situation rich in particulars and the seasonal poems reveal subjective elements that make the divergent styles more alike than they seem at first to be. These three points are important enough to require some elaboration.

The images employed by the poets of preceding periods carry a weight of tonal richness—even when they are not metaphorical—that gives them an emotional resonance. The poets of the late classical period do not indeed entirely forgo these tonal riches of their language, but by comparison they use images in the same way they use generalized words—that is, as units to be arranged into a total composition. Sometimes this tendency reaches the point of treating as quite ordinary words those images which traditionally had evoked the richest associations. The suggestiveness of *iro,* "color," to earlier poets who used it to mean complexion, love, or appearance is reduced to its simple English meaning. And "dream" (*yume*) is similarly reduced, although it had been one of the central images for poets of the early classical period, who employed it to explore states of reality and feeling; and to poets of the mid-classical period, who imbued it with a richness of apprehension and sense of time. But to Lady Ensei Mon'in Shindainagon, a dream is only something that happens at night (*GYS*, IX: 1266).

Mishi yume o	How I would forget
Wa ga kokoro ni mo	Even in my own mind the dream
Wasureba ya	I had of love,
Towazugatari ni	Lest in some casual conversation
Iware mo zo suru.	I might reveal it unawares.

Instead of a richness of tonal depth, these poets seem to have prided themselves on an "accuracy" of imagistic detail that sometimes is flatly photographic and other times is rich in an Impressionistic revelation. Usually the vividness is heightened by a shortening of the interval of time in which the images function or by such techniques as synesthesia. A poem by ex-Empress Kōgi, "Waterfowl on a Pond" (*GYS*, VI: 943), is a representative example of the synesthetic imagery of the period.

Asaake no	On the pond the birds
Kōru namima ni	Flutter upwards and return to sitting—
Tachii suru	Even the beating
Haoto mo samuki	Of their wings is cold within the ripples
Ike no muratori.	Of those waves frozen in the early dawn.

A sound may not be cold unless the details of the poem prepare us for such a transfer of the senses, as in this instance they do, in the image of the birds stirring and fluttering their wings like human beings arousing circulation in the cold. Still, when we ask what are the tonal implications of the images, we can say little more than what the poem overtly implies—the scene is very cold and has a monochromatic beauty.

The tendency to use detailed imagery and especially images with very narrow focus is a feature of the poems in the *Fūgashū,* and somewhat less markedly of the poetry of the period as a whole. Instead of using an image of the moon to create a vast panorama, these poets reduce its scope by filtering its light through the eaves of a hut or shining it upon the dew-laden grass. And their repeated use of the image of tree-tops (*kozue*) does not give the sense of lofty view, but of one specified, small part of a tree—the "end of the tree" as the Japanese word says. This tendency seems to grow from a desire to treat the moment with complete accuracy, whether of observation or impression, as if the closeness of their observation drew the poets ever nearer to what they chose to describe. Both the temporal and the spatial dimensions of the natural scene are often reduced in order both that observation may be as accurate as possible and that perception may be comparably intense, as Reizei Tamehide's poem "On Lightning" (*FGS*, VI: 563) shows to perfection.

Inazuma no	Even in the flashing
Shibashi mo tomenu	Of the lightning that does not linger
Hikari ni mo	Even for a moment,
Kusaba no tsuyu no	The very number of the drops of rain
Kazu wa miekeri.	Could be counted on the leaves of plants.

A subject such as lightning might have been treated for its grandeur, but Tamehide has reduced its temporal scope to an almost imperceptible instant and its geographical sweep to its illumination of drops of rain on leaves so close at hand that they may be counted. And to stress such fineness, he has put his final verb (*miekeri*) into a perfective rather than into a simple indicative. The lightning has flashed in one brilliant moment and the drops have been counted. The event is over almost before it has begun.

Such minuteness of observation runs the risk of preciosity—of treating the world in such microscopic detail that, no matter how accurate the description, it hardly seems to matter. The poets seem to have been conscious of this danger (of course not all their poems are of such limited scope) and to have sought to avoid it by varying kinds of freshness in their imagery. One of these, as we have seen, is synesthesia; another is unusual combinations of imagery; and a third is the use of images that are new to Japanese poetry. Synesthesia may reach the point of a Tamekane's saying that the color of the voice of the *hototogisu* is pure and cool (*FGS*, IV: 312), a telescoping of images that is almost surrealistic. And a poem by ex-Emperor Fushimi, "The Wind" (*GYS*, XV: 2172), shows how images may, by combination, fuse into metaphor and personification.

Hibikikuru	The mountain wind
Matsu no ure yori	Rushes down upon the pine trees,
Fukiochite	Falling from their tops,
Kusa ni koe yamu	Swishing downward in its roaring
Yama no shitakaze.	Till its voice grows silent in the grass.

The scene is far larger here than in Tamehide's poem on lightning, but the poem is more remarkable for its handling of the imagery than for its scope. To say the wind falls or tumbles from the trees is an unusual image, and the diminuendo achieved by the voice growing silent at last in the grass shows how the wind, so strong in the mountains, gradually loses its force in moving toward the plain. The treatment is at once detailed, accurate, and fresh; moreover, the individual images function together to animate the wind as if it were some great beast expending its energies.

There are many pitfalls in a discussion of the new imagery in the poetry of this period. Yoshitada and Shunrai may have been laughed at or scorned by their contemporaries for their use of unusual images; but in the soothing passage of time these innovators had achieved, for the most part, the status of reputable worthies whose precedents might be invoked to justify still newer departures and experiments with imagery. In addition to such native precedents for the principle of using new images, there was always the great unused capital of Chinese images that had been left untouched by earlier Japanese poets or introduced from Chinese poetry of a later generation. These images might safely be drawn upon by Japanese poets, if they showed a care in handling them decorously or in introducing them in ways analagous to comparable traditional images. To say, therefore, that a given image is new is not necessarily to say either that the use of previously unemployed images is wholly radical or that the images were always novel to the literary experience of educated men. Nonetheless, the principle comes to life only when applied: an image may be a cliché in Chinese or Latin and yet fresh in Japanese or English. And by comparison with the conventional Nijō poets, the members of the Kyōgoku-Reizei school certainly used images that were fresh, sometimes startlingly so.

Some of these images were new in themselves; others were new by virtue of their being made to do things they had not been made to do before. To say the wind falls from the trees is new, not in the separate images of the wind or of falling but in the combined image of the wind's being made to fall. An even better illustration of this kind of novelty is a poem on sparrows (*FGS*, XVI: 1728) by the little-known poet Fujiwara Tsunehira (fl. ca. 1310).

Kurenuru ka	Has night now come?
Magaki no take no	Outside by the wattled brushwood fence
Murasuzume	A flock of sparrows
Negura arasou	Seems to raise excited voices
Koe sawagu nari.	In quarrels for a place to sleep.

Such a quarreling group of sparrows could only have seemed unpoetic to the Nijō poets, although the sparrows themselves were not entirely new to Japanese poetry. Ex-Emperor Hanazono's poem on a dog barking in a dilapidated village is, on the other hand, new in its basic images—new to formal Japanese poetry, that is, for the images had long since been common in the Chinese, and Shunrai, it will be recalled (see pp. 243–44), had used such images as that of a dog for their startling effect in informal poems (*FGS*, XVI: 1764).

Ato mo naki	No trace remains
Shizu ga iei no	Among all the crumbling hovels
Take no kaki	Of their bamboo fences,
Inu no koe nomi	And only a dog breaks the silence,
Oku fukaku shite.	Barking from the hindmost shack.

Such novel images usually do not appear in the love poems, partly, of course, because the style is prevailingly generalized. The love poems that do employ imagery—and perhaps a majority have at least one image—normally employ traditional images, although not necessarily in traditional ways. Often a love poem will have a single image, of evening for example, that serves less to evoke the dusk than adverbially, as it were, to set the time of day. Such an image also suggests the particulars of the love affair. If a woman is miserable and it is evening, we know that her affair has run its course and she is now waiting in vain for a lover she knows will not come. Such a subjective treatment of imagery often reaches a point at which the images become synecdoches, metaphors, symbols, and other tropes. As a result, a traditional image in a love poem is often least interesting as an image and most significant for what it represents. Ex-Empress Eifuku's poem on "Waiting for the Lover" (*GYS*, X: 1383), for example, uses evening to show at once the day and the love affair advancing to their close; she extends the image into an ironic symbol of hope doomed to despair.

Oto senu ga
Ureshiki ori mo
Arikeru yo
Tanomisadamete
Nochi no yūgure.

It is evening,
But this time the lack of word from you
Brings happiness,
For now that I have given you my trust
Surely your silence means that you will
    come.

Metaphor is also employed in some love poems that have no imagery at all. In a poem by Lady Jūnii Tameko, the speaker addresses her heart in much the same fashion employed in Western dialogues between the Body and the Soul. The heart here personifies the woman's feelings, and the speaker is her mind, which knows what the end of love will be (*FGS*, XIII: 1297).

Wa ga kokoro
Urami ni mukite
Uramihate yo
Aware ni nareba
Shinobigataki o.

O my heart,
If you are turning to resentment,
Do so to the limit,
For if you turn to weaker sorrow,
It will be impossible to bear.

The metaphor is very striking, for all its nonimagistic nature, and in combination with the distinction between resentment and sorrow, it enables us to understand the total woman, the exact nature of the affair, and the behavior of her lover, even though none of these has been mentioned. She has fallen in love, enjoyed her happiness, gone through the agonies of betrayal thinking that there is yet hope, and now in her despair has begun to turn bitter with resentment. Later she will probably be left sad and lonely, but at this moment she finds the active satisfaction of bitterness easier to bear than the passive desolation of sorrow.

The image-laden seasonal poems are, as one would expect, more often metaphorical in nature than the love poems. Many of these metaphors are of the more traditional kind, rising as they do tonally from images, even when the images are novel. We have seen that two common images—of a wind and of falling—may combine into a new image of a falling wind, and may suggest animation, if not quite personification. Such a technique is typical of the age at its best—the unusual treatment of familiar poetic elements. Sometimes the imagery seems truly unusual, however, as in a poem by Lady Jūsammi Tameko (*GYS*, VIII: 1203).

Ame no ashi mo	In the wind
Yokosama ni naru	That blows aslant the running legs
Yūkaze ni	Of the rain at dusk,
Mino fukaseyuku	The traveler also strides across the moor,
Nobe no tabibito.	Letting his straw raincoat flap behind.

The metaphorical image of the legs of the rain moving across the countryside is very startling in English. But in Chinese poetry the comparison had been worn to a cliché, and as such had long been current in the Japanese colloquial language. Its use in Japanese poetry is, however, daring and fresh. Tameko has, moreover, imbued the expression with new imagistic life. The two elements moving over the moor at dusk are the rain and the traveler, each moved by the force of the wind. And just as the man's raincoat rather than the man himself is said to be blown along, so too the "legs" of the rain are affected. Such a transference is very subtle and satisfying.

The seasonal poems do not normally employ imagery for the purpose of allegory. In Japanese, as in Western poetry, allegory is usually confined to poems on love and religious subjects. Love allegories are, however, rarer than in the early or mid-classical periods, no doubt because the popularity of the generalized vocabulary discouraged such "darke conceits." What love allegories there are show that the poets of the period did not avoid allegory because of an inability to convey two meanings at once. Their allegories are almost always interesting, although one hesitates to compliment them with higher praise. Such interest is often difficult to convey in translation, since one almost has to choose between rendering the surface meaning and explaining the implied, or rendering both in somewhat awkward postures. We have tried the second alternative for a poem by Lady Jūsammi Chikako (*FGS*, X: 958), whose interest lies in the almost distasteful but very apt vividness of the images used to shadow forth a lover's troubled emotions.

Fukaki e no	Sunken my love,
Ashi no shitane yo	Like reed roots deep within a tidal pool—
Yoshi saraba	So be it if it must;
Tada kuchihatene	But then let it rot away completely,
Migomori ni shite.	Hidden within those secret depths.

Sometimes the allegory is "perfect" or complete: the metaphor is unbroken throughout the poem, and one must have the "key" to unlock the secret meaning. Lady Jūnii Tameko employs such a technique in a poem whose key may be found in a free translation of its headnote: "Sent anonymously with a spray of cherry blossoms to a lady who, too soon after her lover's death, became involved with another man" (*FGS*, XIV: 1334).

Hodo naku zo	How your whole heart
Nokoru katae ni	Was given to the blossoms that have gone!
Utsushikeru	But in no time at all
Chirinishi hana ni	You turn from those so freshly fallen
Someshi kokoro o.	To the one branch whose flowers yet remain.

The vivid picture given by this poem, one of the rare informal poems of the age to be preserved, of the Court life of the day with its affairs and of feminine severity with imprudent sisters is no doubt far more interesting than the allegorical mode itself. And at the same time as we are amused to think of the timeless femininity of such a reproach—and of the bearing of the woman who received it—we are led to wonder how frequently such informal poems were composed. Perhaps more of the high spirit and wit of the early classical period survived than the anthologies and collections of this very serious period seem to indicate.

Like this clever reproof, many of the religious allegories of the period are perfect allegories, and the chief difference between them and the love allegories is their greater complexity. Some of the most abstruse points of Buddhist dogma are rendered into poems whose allegorical "keys" seem themselves to need explanation. Ex-Emperor Fushimi, for example, wrote what one must admit is a fine poem (*FGS*, XVIII: 2057), although its headnote hardly prepares us for it. His subject is a Buddhist mystery comparable to that of the Holy Trinity of Christianity: "On the topic, 'The Three Dogmas Are Not One Dogma, Nor Are They Three Separate Dogmas.'"

Mado no to ni	As I listen
Shitataru ame o	To the rain outside my window
Kiku nabe ni	Fall in gentle drops,
Kabe ni somukuru	I turn my midnight lamp around,
Yowa no tomoshibi.	Dimming its light against the wall.

Of all the poem's complexities, only one emerges readily, the strange implication that by dimming the light one can hear the rain better. Now although the three dogmas are those of the Void, the Phenomenal, and the Mean; although the separation of the senses shows the dogmas are not one; and although the synesthesia shows they are not three, yet basically the poem is too symbolic, too fraught with the niceties of another religion, and too allusive (the last two lines echo a poem by Po Chü-i) to gloss without a tiresomely long explanation. The remarkable thing is that such a complex symbolism has been rendered so gracefully into a poem which, if it lacked a headnote and were in another book of the *Fūgashū,* would not seem to have the slightest religious significance.

Such symbolism has its counterparts in other poems, in which a given image may be filled with such meaning that it suggests other values, emotions, or images. Such a poem is one by Sanekane discussed earlier (p. 381), in which the woman's longing takes shape in the tear-blurred green of distant pines. Most of the symbolism of the period is to be found in love poems like this one, which fills a single image with the subjective meaning of the rest of the poem, and in poems that either are Buddhist allegories or suggest the techniques of the religious poems. Poems on other subjects dwell too much on the "actual" details of a scene or shape them too wholly into impressions for the images to acquire that depth of meaning which can be termed symbolic. In rejecting the descriptive styles of the preceding period, these poets also rejected their tonal depths. They sought to achieve other effects with imagery, and although they succeeded, one cannot but feel that their devotion to accuracy and to individual perception deprives their poetry of a desirable depth, even as a like devotion has affected the work of many modern Western poets or the Impressionist painters.

Such a judgment is, however, an ultimate judgment, and it must be added in fairness that theirs is a new poetry, fresh to the tradition and yet organically evolved from it; and that it is in any case a far happier alternative than the insipid conventionalism of their Nijō contemporaries. Not every age has poets who can write like a Chaucer or a Wordsworth—or a Narihira or a Teika. Moreover, the poetry of the period has at its best an integrity that is all the more gratifying in view of the preponderance of its imagistic and subjective detail. This integrity sometimes makes a poem seem to have the weight and the inevitability of the whole tradition behind it, as is the case with Tamekane's poem on travel (*FGS,* IX: 948).

Musubisutete	Rolled up every night,
Yonayona kawaru	And changed with every changing night,
Tabimakura	The pillow-grass of travel—
Karine no yume no	And the sleep cut short brings dreams
Ato mo hakanashi.	Whose traces also wither in the dawn.

Other poems are equally integrated in their total effect but have qualities that make them seem more characteristic of the age. A poem by Sanekane has that monochromatic, withered beauty the age esteemed, and yet manages to suggest a richer beauty within the very plainness, as the Sung critics had urged (*GYS*, II: 283).

Haru o shitō	A last reminder
Nagori no hana mo	Of a spring loved for its beauty,
Iro kurenu	The remaining cherry blossoms
Toyora no tera no	At the ancient temple of Toyora
Iriai no sora.	Now also darken with the vesper sky.

Each of the images is governed by the temporal context in such a way that it is led to disappearance, darkness, and loss. Yet the poem's deeper suggestions are affirmative, and not just because of the somber beauty of the scene. No matter how far gone the flowers, they are made into a reminder of their beauty at their height—indeed of the whole spring season. And although the light fades in the sky over the temple, it leaves all in peace behind. There has not really been a loss—only a fading away from the beauty in actuality to the beauty prized in the memory of the observer. And the creation of an observer who can remember implies more than imagistic technique; it involves the problem of esthetic distance—the relation of the poet to his speaker, to his poetic materials, and to his audience.

ESTHETIC DISTANCE

In our brief discussion of the late classical period in Chapter 2, we called attention not only to the desire of the poets of the age to explore the particular, but also to the results of this desire in a decreased esthetic distance between them and their materials and the corresponding increase in distance between them and their audience. The shortening of the esthetic distance between the poets and their materials is easily demonstrated. Such a poem as Reizei Tamehide's—in which lightning is made to illuminate a specifiable number of raindrops—shows how close these poets could come to the scene they so absorbingly described. The love poems are cut from the same cloth, because the distinctions made in poem after poem—between various words for suffering or for different states of longing that had been treated by earlier poets as if they were largely synonymous—suggest a similar attention to detail, a turning over of feelings in the private mind. This interior exploration substitutes the world of thought and feeling for the world of nature, but in each case the poet contemplates his world as closely and as finely as possible. The increased esthetic distance between the poet and his audience follows logically from the decreased distance between the poet and his materials. Dr. Johnson, who as an Augustan poet believed in public poetry or in poetry that expressed universal truth, esteemed therefore a poetry in which all men might share, in which the distance between the poet and his audience was not great. And when he advocated a greater distance between the poet and his materials by declaring that the poet should not paint the stripes of the tulip but try to give the sense of "tulipness," he was being as consistent as the Japanese poets of this period, or our Romantic poets, were in taking the opposite stands on the desirable kinds of esthetic distance.

Confusion over such technical aspects of poetry often leads to misunderstanding: we must not expect of a poet what he never set out to provide us with. Dr. Johnson never for a moment wished "To see a World in a Grain of Sand, / And a Heaven in a Wild Flower," any more than Blake chose to "Let observation with extensive view, / Survey mankind, from China to Peru." Sensible readers, those with catholic tastes, have enough literary experience to seek in a writer what he may provide and withhold their ultimate judgment for later reflection. It is therefore desirable that we read late classical poetry with the realization that its authors do indeed choose to paint the stripes of the tulip and to see a world of interest and truth, if not in a grain of sand, then in the light cast on treetops at sunset. We must not expect them to convey universals in the techniques of descriptive symbolism, as Shunzei and Teika had in the preceding period.

All poetry, the most sophisticated and the most naïve alike, may quickly be reduced to its conventions; and often such an effort illuminates the writings of an age, if one does not take the reduction for the whole. The stylistic divergence in this period makes such a discussion of convention especially convenient, since a knowledge of the conventions provides us with a simplified means of treating the rather technical question of esthetic distance. The two major conventions, which might be termed "Japanese courtly love" and "the descriptive fallacy," are not the sole property of this age, nor even of Japanese poetry, but they are especially marked in the separation of poetic styles.

The code of love represented in Japanese love poetry from about the ninth century onwards bears certain resemblances to the Western courtly love we know of in medieval literature. It is based upon passion, has recognized stages of development and a code of personal behavior and manners, and is for aristocrats and not commoners (Andreas Capellanus and the men in the *Tale of Genji* are at one in thinking that a nobleman's behavior toward women of the lower classes is determined only by the *droit de seigneur*); moreover, both codes have a gloss of idealism. In other respects, the two codes differ as widely as the societies, religions, and histories of the two cultures in which they originated. The course of Japanese courtly love can best be understood by reading through in order the books of love poems in any of the imperial anthologies. Love begins at first sight of the beloved, or even before—with a glance at her handwriting, perhaps. The next stage is that of secret, unrequited love, which is followed by negotiation in which the man fears he will not gain the woman, and the woman both that the man is insincere and that she will lose her reputation. With the consummation of love, more poems are exchanged, especially on the mornings after secret nocturnal

A scene illustrating an early stage in a courtly love affair: A lovesick courtier (RIGHT) has a friend slip his letter into the women's apartments on a snowy morning. From EHON YAMATO HIJI, *an illustrated book of anecdotes (Edo, 1735).*

trysts. Then, given a polygamous society, the man's visits grow less frequent, the woman becomes apprehensive, the man grows cold, and finally the affair ends, leaving the woman to sorrow, resentment, or despair.

The pattern is susceptible to many variations and each stage to minute explorations, and the fact must be stressed that although this literary treatment grew from the actualities of love at Court, it is as conventional as our courtly love; and that with the passage of time, as society changed, the code grew further and further out of touch with actuality, just as Spenser's presentation of love in *The Faerie Queene* gives an outmoded reflection of love in an earlier period. Some readers may be upset by the undoubted degree of artifice in such conventions, but while it is true that conventions such as these enable a writer to treat his subjects with either banality or originality, it is also true that they enable him to write at all. And for the Japanese poets, convention enabled them to suggest with a word or phrase the whole pattern of courtly love, to raise the image of the larger whole by treating a part of the affair, and to establish a situation with the merest of hints. To mention dusk was to suggest that the time for the lover's visit was at hand, and to speak of sadness was enough to tell that the woman had been betrayed.

By the late classical period both the general outlines and the specific steps of a love affair had been treated so often that there was little freshness to be found in a simple rehearsing of the old themes. Consequently, the poets of the period contented themselves with raising the image of courtly love with a word or phrase that would both show that the poem was a love poem and identify the particular stage of the affair which it was intended to treat. They could allow the conventions to supply a wealth of background if they could give the subject freshness of another sort. The freshness chosen by the age lay in the minute examination of a moment in the progress of love. Such attention to a single moment made it seem to be of extreme importance, and of course such importance could exist vividly only in the minds of the persons undergoing the experience of love according to the general rules.

As a result, we find the subjective treatment of love that so marks the age, and with it a decreased esthetic distance between the poet and his materials; for the only way to examine the richness of the moment is to strive, like Proust, to approach it as nearly as possible and even to seem to enter into it, as Tamekane had urged (see above, p. 361). This attention to the minutiae of experience and to the fineness of apprehension of a moment can be shared by the poet's audience, but the reader shares the experience out of detached interest more than from any sense that he is involved in it equally with the man and the woman in love. Moreover, the act of poetic composition and "publication" in the period tended to increase this esthetic distance between the poet and the audience. The formalities of a poetry contest or the composition of a sequence of poems call for a different literary response from the audience than, say, the sonnets addressed by an Elizabethan poet to the lady of his choice. This kind of esthetic distance had been increasing steadily since the composition of the Kokinshū in the early tenth century, when most love poetry was informal and when a poem, however conventional, was usually addressed directly to the man or woman who constituted its primary audience. That audience became more and more fictional, and the poet's real audience consisted of men and women who knew that the characters who suffered the agonies of love in a sequence were creations whose sex and circumstances had no necessary correspondence with those of the writer. The point of interest in love poetry had shifted, and with it esthetic distance. Readers' expectations had changed, as ours must when we read love poetry composed in different periods. No doubt the great love poems of any period transcend the style of the age, but the true nature of their greatness is founded upon different assumptions of the relation between the poet, his speaker, his materials, and his audience.

The second convention, the descriptive fallacy, takes many forms in Japanese as well as in Western poetry. Basically it is a contradiction of the premise that things external to us are unknowable in themselves, whether that premise be founded on common sense or Kant's idea of the *Ding an sich*. To make such a contradiction meaningful, techniques and conventions are necessary to invest the natural world with human significance. The difficulty in creating such artistic means helps explain why poetry that describes nature is such a late development in the West, which lacks the premise of Buddhist monism. But the descriptive fallacy itself depends upon one more assumption—not only must nature be treated as knowable in itself and as significant for man, but also one must presume that the external world can be presented as it actually is. The poets of the early classical period and before had not properly created a descriptive poetry at all, since they made little pretense of picturing nature as it is. Either nature was made a condition of the scene in poems that focused on human affairs (Hitomaro uses nature in this way when he tells about the leaves falling as he parts from his wife) or it was treated as showing an emotion, though in fact the poets were interested in the workings of their own minds and not the natural scene (thus Tomonori attributes to the cherry blossoms falling on a lovely day an unsettled heart that is really his own). The poets of the mid-classical period slowly created a true descriptive poetry that portrays nature "as it is," and by virtue of a Buddhist monism made natural laws symbolic of human affairs.

In the late classical period, the poets strengthened the descriptive fallacy still more by treating nature with particular imagistic details that seem to declare the accuracy of presentation. To do this, they had perforce to treat smaller scenes, use more minute observation, and reduce the esthetic distance between themselves and their materials. But we have also observed how subjectively the materials are shaped. It could not be otherwise, for whether or not Kant's concept is correct, artistic experience requires form, order, and convention; moreover, the greater the amount of detail, the greater the amount of formal shaping that is necessary.

Paradoxically, then, the more realistic description tends to be, the more artificial its premises grow. A poem like ex-Emperor Fushimi's on the wind that is loud in the peaks, falls on the pines, then moves rapidly down the slopes and grows silent in the grass is realistically accurate in its description of the progress of the wind; but at the same time, this accuracy is conventional, as we have seen. Many such descriptions are based upon a common structure of having the phenomena of nature grow ever closer to, or farther away from, the speaker who is fixed at a specified point of observation. So that such a "realistic" poem is no less conventional—and subjectively shaped—than this one by Lady Eifuku Mon'in (*FGS*, II: 115).

Neya made mo	Before the dawn
Hana no ka fukaki	The moon is hazy at the window
Haru no yo no	On a soft spring night,
Mado ni kasumeru	When the deep scent of cherry blossoms
Irigata no tsuki.	Presses even to where I sleep.

Now cherry blossoms have no odor at all, and such an attribution of fragrance is a kind of synesthetic hyperbole for the great visual beauty of the flowers. And yet this poem is hardly more ordered than Fushimi's on the mountain wind. Both imply a human sensibility close to the details—close in the sense of intent observation and also in the sense of so handling the details of nature that they are shaped into intelligible experience. In either case, to become poetry nature must be transformed by the imagination—and never more than when the art is concealed under a pretense of artlessness.

To say this is to emphasize once more the underlying subjectivity of the age, to stress the fact that the human subject who is normally not mentioned in this poetry is more important than the objective world, whether the poetic materials are those of the purely subjective experience of love or of the seemingly objective details of nature. Such a nineteenth-century Japanese poet as Masaoka Shiki might choose to see true objectivity and realism in the seasonal poems of this age in order to promote his own style of haiku, but the disinterested reader can only feel that the poets of the period would have been surprised and even angered to hear works they esteemed for their artistic skill extolled for an artless "realism." One may say that Shiki properly saw the decreased esthetic distance between poets and their materials, but was so taken in by the realistic façade of such poems that he failed to see the way in which subjectivity and distance from the audience had shaped the poems into art. At the same time, it must be admitted that when the poems of this age are most prosy, least poetic and successful, they are often matter-of-fact pretenses to objectivity, just as the Impressionists at their worst lose their magic in what amount to paintings like tinted photographs. Only perversity would extol the virtues of such an artlessness that, rather than concealing a true art, has no art, no richness at all.

The conventions of courtly love and the descriptive fallacy had the effect, as we have noted, of drawing the poet closer to his materials and farther from his audience. But as in all periods of Court poetry, the poets sought a careful balance in the relationship between themselves and their materials on the one hand and the relationship between themselves and their audience on the other. The ways in which the poets attempted to deal with the problems of esthetic distance posed by these two relationships cannot be understood without taking into account a third—the relationship between the poet and the speaker of his poem.

In most of the poems of the age the speakers are fictional embodiments of the poet's own personality (the observer of the natural scene) or are clearly identifiable characters in the drama of courtly love (the eager lover, the woman betrayed). And although the convention of the poetic speaker serves to increase the distance between the poet and his audience, since the speaker stands between poet and reader, at the same time it helps establish a necessary degree of distance between the poet and his materials, since the speaker intervenes in this relationship as well. To the modern reader the poets of this age may seem to be so completely involved in their materials that balance is impossible.

Paradoxically, however, given a poetic tradition in which conventional norms of lyrical response (hon'i) were prescribed, the poets of the late classical period were much more deeply concerned with overcoming what seemed to them the far greater distance between the personal response of the poet and the conventional response prescribed by his materials. Tamekane, like Shunzei and Teika before him, insisted that a good poem must convey a conviction of feeling that was only possible when the poet so identified himself with his materials and with the emotions appropriate to his poetic speaker that he was able to imbue his restatement of a conventional response with a deep personal lyricism. It was taken for granted that there was a close rapport between poet and audience, since the audience, themselves poets, knew the conventions thoroughly and were extremely sensitive to those variations of treatment or tone, however slight, by which the poet communicated through his speaker a vivid sense of his own individual personality and poetic vision. To these poets, then, the fictional poetic speaker was of as much importance in maintaining the bond between themselves and their audience as in creating esthetic distance between them. It will be remembered that some of Teika's most impassioned and individualistic poems had been those in which he presents the feelings of a woman in love; similarly among the liveliest and most original poems by ex-Empress Eifuku is one in which she creates a male speaker in deep if somewhat comic distress upon discovering that he has slept so late with his mistress that he will probably be detected as he leaves her room (*FGS*, XI: 1109).

Kinuginu o	I put on my clothes
Isogu wakare wa	To hasten unobserved in parting
Yo fukakute	In the depths of night;
Mata ne hisashiki	But yielding to her, I lay down again
Akatsuki no toko.	And now the dawn reveals our bed.

The seasonal poems have speakers too, although their voices are more disembodied (and almost invariably unspecified) than the dramatic speakers of the love poems. The speaker of a seasonal poem is really the sensibility which perceives the natural scene in detail and which, as it approaches the scene, observes, shapes, and grows progressively distant from us, the audience. If such a speaker turned his back on the scene for a moment to tell us that his vision is lovely or true, that distance would immediately shrink. But close as he is to the scene, such a sudden change would be startling; it would break the illusion as awkwardly as if an actor were to stop his wooing of the heroine, turn to the audience, and ask for a light for his cigarette. So that instead of doing as Saigyō often did and beginning a poem with two or three lines of comment that showed the speaker's distance from the scene and nearness to us, the audience, these speakers are so close to nature that their subjective viewpoint is attributed to the scene itself. Thus we read of such unrealistic "realism" as the wind's tumbling, scented cherry blossoms, or the cool, pure voice of the *hototogisu*. To maintain some distance from the materials and at the same time bridge the apparent gulf between himself and his audience, the poet needed to infuse his description of the objective world with subjective qualities transferred from himself to an observing sensibility that we call the speaker. The result is a kind of impressionism in which accuracy mingles with a pleasing distortion that passes itself off as objectivity. Consequently, the "truth" of these poets is one founded upon a careful balance of the relationship between the poet, the speaker or observer of the poem, the poetic materials, and the audience.

SUBJECTS, THEMES, AND TONES

Considered broadly, the subjects of the poetry of this period are the same as those of earlier times. There are no major additions to such basic concerns of Court poetry as nature, love, or travel, and the originality of the period is rather to be found in its emphases and alterations. Time continues to be a subject, or at least a force that affects these fundamental concerns of Japanese poetry, and there are religious and other interests that transcend the basic subjects. Shifts in emphasis may of course be important; certainly the higher quality of the religious poetry reflects a change from a ceremonial concept of religious poetry to a deeply felt poetic concept, if not to more earnest devotion.

We have tried to demonstrate that the same impulses and interests underlie all the poetry of the age, but the divergence in the poetic styles makes it convenient to speak of poems on love apart from the others—the nature and travel poems (congratulatory poems and the like are not very exciting in this period), and the poems on related subjects to be found in the unusually large number of "Miscellaneous Poems" (*zō no uta*). (It is of some interest to note that one often finds such "miscellaneous" or "unspecified" topics assigned as formal topics in the poetry contests or acting as divisions in the poetic sequences of the period. If it seems illogical that an unspecified topic might be specified, one should recall that the term primarily refers to a poem in which no single element—love, a season, travel—predominates sufficiently to allow classification in a single category. Is it too speculative to suggest that the abundance of such poems may imply an impending breakdown of the particular categories, or at least a feeling that they need some sort of alteration to be fruitful subjects of poetry?) All these topics are treated with an unusual emphasis upon the particular, the small, and the delimited. We read over and over again of treetops, of underleaves, of lower plants; similarly, the moon is caught at the very moment of rising, the sun sets at a particular moment of dusk rather than throughout an evening, and sun and moon alike cast their light on small objects or parts of large ones. The extent to which these poets avoided large scenes and the lofty style can also be appreciated by reading the first books of spring poems in the *Gyokuyōshū* and *Fūgashū*. Imperial anthologies traditionally began with lofty poems or broad scenes, and although these anthologies do follow the pattern, such poems are usually not by the poets of the period but were selected from earlier times. The interests of the Kyōgoku-Reizei poets are clearly different. They choose to study intensely that which is limited in time and scope.

The same generalization is true of the love poetry in its way, although here, too, one may of course find exceptions. The subject is usually limited to the experience of an intense moment, and to further such a practice the poets are more careful even than earlier poets in making clear the particular step in the progress of courtly love with which the poem is concerned. It is easy to understand that such specificity was necessary for poems employing the generalized vocabulary the age esteemed for this subject. Had the moment been left as vague as the language of the poetry is general, the poems would themselves be vague, which no Court poet would consider acceptable. Earlier poets had achieved their vividness in love poetry by employing imagery, so that to the extent these poets eschewed images, they had to rely upon clear "dramatic" circumstances. A Western and even a Japanese reader is often at a loss with these love poems, for he may not know who is speaking to whom about what—unless and until he decides when, at precisely what stage in the affair, the events are taking place. Within such a specific context, the poets distinguish emotional states with the same particularity and discrimination that characterize the poems on the seasonal topics and the like.

Time is less often a separate subject or explicit threat in this period than in earlier times. It is more an auxiliary subject, the condition of human and natural events. There are indeed a few poems that celebrate the past and long periods of time, as, for example, Tamekane's "On Longing for the Past While the Moon Shines Overhead" (*GYS*, V: 690).

Ika narishi	What was he like,
Hito no nasake ka	The man whose feelings were so fine
Omoiizuru	As to summon you to rise?
Koshi kata katare	Tell me of the past from which you come,
Aki no yo no tsuki.	O moon of the clear autumn night.

But such poems are rare and usually, like this one, are composed in the style of the preceding age. Normally time is the brief period of the moment in which events take place and the experience is intensely felt.

Those subjects such as religion which transcend the basic subjects and the threat of time in earlier periods are partly the same in this period, in that there are poems on what might be called the orthodox religious subjects of Buddhism and Shinto. But these subjects are different in two important respects. To begin with, there are in addition to the general, constant religious subjects some subjects that owe their conception to that overly extolled and much misunderstood branch of Buddhism, Zen. Zen varies as much in its history as Calvinism (and if the Far East were to become as ignorantly excited about Calvinism as the West has over Zen the situation would be equally foolish), but its central ethical code is the simple imperative to live a better life tomorrow than one has lived today; and its central philosophical doctrines are that the world exists in flux and that contemplation may lead to an individual's enlightenment with respect to his place in such a world.

It is this simple code, and not either a mysterious symbolism or an anticipation of the democratic spirit, that led ex-Emperor Fushimi to compose the following poem on "Personal Grievances" (*GYS*, XVIII: 2519).

Itazura ni	When I consider
Yasuki wa ga mi zo	The sufferings of the mass of people,
Hazukashiki	I am filled with shame—
Kurushimu tami no	At myself, who am all too prone to live
Kokoro omoeba.	In the languor of my easy days.

This insight, with its premise that one should strive to do better, is one kind of Zen enlightenment. The other kind, the one that has for so long fired Western sensibilities, grows out of this very pragmatism of Zen. The more practical one is (as, say, the English pride themselves on their lack of "nonsense" or Americans on their "know-how"), the more one is beleaguered by those mysteries of life that the Chinese and the French had been analyzing, or the Indians and Germans theorizing about, for centuries. As a result, the pragmatic mind can only make Mysteries of mysteries and approach them symbolically, whether with poetic metaphors or with such emblems as Commonwealth, Establishment, Fair Play, Free Enterprise, and the New Model. So the Zen priests approached the mysteries of Buddhism with symbols, when it was necessary to approach them at all; for in the fourteenth century at least, priests did not go out of their way to symbolize unless pressed by ardent disciples. If someone had the temerity to ask, "What is the ultimate principle of Buddhism?" the only reply was something like, "The cypress tree in the courtyard." And perhaps a sharp rap on the questioner's tonsured head. The poets who associated with these priests naturally found such symbols useful in their poetry for rendering moments of insight or mysteries of faith and dogma. Consequently, the age produced such poems as ex-Emperor Hanazono's on the green spring breeze; although as a matter of fact, allegory apart, the technique of this poem is no different from Tamekane's observation that the color of the voice of the *hototogisu* is pure and cool—a technique to be found in poems that have nothing to do with Zen.

Zen Buddhism seems to have had one other effect on the poets of the period. In advocating contemplation, it confirmed their intense preoccupation with the details of experience. Too much must not be made of this, however, for it was only a confirmation of an inclination that had been brought about by much stronger historical forces. It must indeed be said that these poets were first of all poets, then Buddhists, and only finally and partially Zen Buddhists. One can, indeed, with persistent diligence, find a rare poem that is founded upon a familiarity with Zen notions about contemplation and enlightenment—for example, Lady Jūsammi Chikako's "On the Full Moon of the Eighth Month" (*GYS*, V: 684).

Onozukara	This heart of mine
Sumanu kokoro mo	Long since clouded over, now has cleared
Sumarekeri	Spontaneously—
Tsuki wa narete zo	It is good to gaze continuously
Miru bekarikeru.	Until one has absorbed the moon.

The influence of Zen is indisputable here, but the poem is hardly typical of the age. It is unusual both in the sense that one would be hard put to find another like it, and by virtue of the fact that its associations (engo) between "cleared" (*sumarekeri*) and "moon" (*tsuki*) are those of an earlier poetic style.

The second difference between the transcending subjects of this and earlier periods involves something of a paradox that takes us to the themes expressed in the poetry. By prizing the moment and its detail, the poets invested both with an importance that transcends both. Whether the event is one that takes place in nature or in the affairs of life, it is so intensely real to these poets that it constitutes an overriding "truth." In this the poets may be compared—if the analogy is not taken too far—to Western literary Naturalists of this and the last century. Both groups of writers treated a "slice of life," a moment, a detail, because it seemed to them to possess more essential truth than larger subjects. Why such moments should be prized calls for some explanation, and the poetry seems to show two contradictory reasons. Either the moment offers an intense experience within a parenthesis of change or, contrariwise, it is intense as a phenomenon of change in a parenthesis of constancy. If one delighted in the more abstruse paradoxes of Buddhism, he might see in such a dual treatment of time and nature the doctrine that all is evanescent but all exists forever, that constancy changes and change is constant. Some such philosophy may well underlie the apparent paradox, but it seems more likely that the poets dealt intently with the particular, now at a moment of change and now apparently constant, believing only that what is intensely felt is important, no matter whether it was constant or in change.

The poets esteemed the real; but by the real they meant not so much the thing or state in itself as the thing or state infused with the observer's apprehension of it. The results were certain to vary, both in their nature and in poetic quality. Sometimes we find a great to-do about next to nothing; sometimes we discover an interest in an intense expression of the commonplace; and sometimes we see that the subjective element is so great that perfectly ordinary things appear under the most unusual coloring. In each case, there are similar predications about the subject: it is "true" or interesting or valuable precisely because it strikes the perceiving sensibility with such force. Another theme grows out of this preoccupation with the moment, and high valuation of it. Under the pressure of the poets' gaze, the reality they contemplated often undergoes a change into something else. Bitterness becomes languor, or a cloud of haze gradually intensifies along its length to the point of falling as rain at its extreme end. In such poems, and there are many of them, constancy and change somehow seem to merge, and at the point of change it is difficult to say whether it is time or timelessness that predominates.

The tonal range of the poetry of this age is, as we have implied, more limited than that of the poetry of earlier periods. The poets' intense, even solemn, preoccupation with their materials allows them only occasional scope for wit, irony, and humor. In this they followed the preceding age, whose seriousness seems to have been punished with solemnity in the third and fourth generations. But there is another, more truly literary reason for this, which concerns their technique. A concentration on details and a complete exploration of a limited subject leaves little to be inferred emotionally by the reader. The feverish interest in the subject of the poem is typically communicated to the reader only while he is reading the poem. It is used up by the poem itself. And the fever is sometimes followed by a sense of flatness. This relative absence of implication and overtones in poems that are intense in themselves is a remarkable, if at times distressing, poetic phenomenon. Like the Sung poets they admired, these Japanese writers have a "withered" quality of prosiness or flatness, in spite of their sophistication, their technical ability, and their freshening of the poetic tradition.

It is useful to contrast this flatness with that of the primitive songs. The songs seem limited because of their narrow outlook, their lack of awareness, and our inability to share the experience they present. In the poems at the end of the tradition, the awareness is far greater, but it is used up, so to speak, by its absorption into the poem. To compare this poetry once again to Impressionist painting or Imagist poetry, we recall that these styles have suffered adverse criticism in the West for the same reason—the intense individual observations and detailed presentation of a scene is often intellectually poor. Translated into the terms of Japanese poetry, this means a tonal rather than a thematic poverty.

Such limitations are the natural concomitants of the particular excellences of this poetry, and we do not wish to stress them to the point of obscuring their accompanying virtues. The poets of the period inherited a rich tradition and seem to have assumed its importance as their major premise and originality as their minor. By such logic, they produced many poems that are at once wholly Japanese and particularly their own. A love poem by ex-Empress Eifuku is typical of this unique poetry at its best; the dramatic situation is one in which a woman is at the extremities of suffering from her lover's betrayal—the affair has reached its end (*GYS*, XII: 1707).

> Yowarihatsuru   In my heart,
> Ima wa no kiwa no   Weakened now by your betrayal
>   Omoi ni wa   To the point of death,
> Usa mo aware ni   Even misery takes on pathetic beauty
> Naru ni zo arikeru.   And my bitterness is gone.

By assuming so much in the way of the tradition of Japanese courtly love, ex-Empress Eifuku has been able to suggest the whole course of an affair by writing its surprising conclusion—that suffering at its worst point yields to beauty and release, if only in death. This has clearly been no ordinary affair whose end is so remarkably close to the experience of tragedy: the writer feels an exhilaration in suffering to the point of death.

The poem is one of those in the age which deal with a metamorphosis, the change in an intense moment of one quality or thing into what is very nearly its opposite. Such a poem could not have been written in any other period of Japanese Court poetry, and in its technique at least it differs from similar statements in Western literature. In *Cities of the Plain,* Proust's narrator decides to give up Albertine, but is suddenly shocked by the realization that she is an all too intimate friend of Mlle. Vinteuil and her "older sister." The effect of the shock is not to make him give up Albertine the more readily or to hate her, as one might expect, but to make him feel that he cannot do without her. A scene of a few pages is followed by a generalization that is in turn succeeded by some twenty pages of introspection and reflection over what action he should take. The generalization is thematically very like what we see in ex-Empress Eifuku's poem:

It is often simply from want of the creative spirit that we do not go to the full extent of suffering. And the most terrible reality brings us, with our suffering, the joy of a great discovery, because it merely gives a new and clear form to what we have long been ruminating without suspecting it. (Mod. Lib. ed., II, 363).

Proust's theme is almost the same as that of the Japanese poem, but is presented in a highly abstract language that separates it not only from the Japanese, but even from the preceding and following narration. These Japanese poets may use generalized language, but their thought and writing are not abstract. The general is wedded to the particular, and the particular is part of a series of concatenated situations comprising a whole inherited with the poetic tradition. The short poem employs the general in a context of the particular to suggest the abstract; the intensity comes from the treatment, and extensiveness comes from the tradition, which suggests the whole preceding course of the love affair and which places this poem in a book of others in which it is modified and deepened by the effect of the others in the sequence. How far tradition may aid in effecting such distillation and in creating larger wholes can be appreciated from new developments in the integration, not now of individual poems, but of sequences of poems.

NEW DEVELOPMENTS IN THE COMPOSITION OF POETIC SEQUENCES

In our discussion of the integration of poetic sequences in the last chapter, we treated it as a complement to fragmentation and traced the development of two kinds of integrating techniques, progressions (temporal, spatial, and the like) and associations, which link one poem to the next. The *Shinkokinshū* is of pivotal importance in this historical development, because it employs both forms of integration to a most remarkable degree. In the thirteen anthologies that follow the *Shinkokinshū,* there is a gradual slackening of interest in progression and a development of the techniques of association. Temporal progression is of course inherent to a considerable extent in the successive seasonal order of the poems on nature or in the arrangement of love poems into the progress of a courtly affair. But the other, more particular progressions—from, say, mountains, to hills, to plains, to villages, to the capital— are no longer used with any consistency.

The two anthologies compiled by the Kyōgoku-Reizei poets stand out from the rest, however, because the associations often seem very tenuous and sometimes seem to break down altogether. The fact that a dozen poems may move along in the *Gyokuyōshū* or *Fūgashū* with clear, if also studied and subtle, association naturally leads one to suspect that there are perhaps new techniques of integration to be discovered in these two anthologies when the associational sequence appears to break down. And such techniques there are, although to understand them we must first reconsider certain aspects of poetic practice already touched upon. Many of the poems we have translated from this period fall into a natural division between what the Japanese call their "upper verses" (*kami no ku*) or first three lines and the "lower verses" (*shimo no ku*) or last two lines. The division is one of grammar and syntax and often overtly one of sense as well. Poems so divided by a caesura and on the surface divided into two logical parts were said to be "distantly related verses" (*soku*), while those not so divided were termed "closely related verses" (*shin-ku*). The opposing poetic factions recognized both kinds of verses but differed in the degree of relative importance which they ascribed to them. The innovating poets preferred the technique of distantly related verses, while the Nijō poets, holding to an ideal of poems that flowed smoothly from beginning to end, followed Tameie in proclaiming the superiority of closely related verses. They were also severely critical of what they considered to be the excessive fragmentation of the distantly related verses produced by the Kyōgoku-Reizei poets.

In fact, as we have seen, the distantly related verses of the Kyōgoku-Reizei poets are integrated satisfactorily by the ordering of materials into a meaningful sequence of development, say from far to near. It is not surprising, therefore, that when the Kyōgoku-Reizei poets came to integrate poetic sequences for an anthology, the associational linkings between some poems should be comparably distant. The compilers alternated groups of poems whose associations were often very distant with poems whose images and other qualities were closely related. It must be emphasized that the techniques of distant association are specific and clear, even if it does sometimes require a considerable knowledge of Japanese poetry to discover the associations at all. The effect sought seems to have been very much like that achieved in the *Shinkokinshū* by rhythmical alterations of good and weak poems to build up to a climax. These rhythms of distant and close associations also help give something of an effect of the movement, if not precisely of the progression, to be found in the *Shinkokinshū* and earlier anthologies. In order to illustrate such movements, rhythms, and associations, we shall analyze a sequence of thirteen poems from the first book of love poems in the *Fūgashū* (X: 950–62).

950

Chigiri arite	Was it a previous life
Kakaru omoi ya	Which binds our fates, decrees that now
Tsukubane no	My feelings must be stirred—
Minedo mo hito no	Rushing into love with you, so hidden
Yagate koishiki.	Like the peak of Mount Tsukuba from
	my sight?

FUJIWARA KIMIKAGE (fl. ca. 1350)

951

Shirareji na	It must not be known:
Osauru sode no	That stirring under the river of these tears
Namidagawa	Flowing on the sleeve
Shita ni wa hayaki	With which I blot my eyes, there is a heart
Mizu no kokoro o.	Now turbid like an agitated stream.

NIJŌ YOSHIMOTO (1320–88)

952
Shibashi koso	For a slight moment
Sode ni mo tsutsume	I may enfold within my sleeve
Namidagawa	The river of my tears,
Tagitsu kokoro o	But how can I dam up my heart
Ikade sekamashi.	So overbrimming with its love?

FUJIWARA NORINAGA (fl. ca. 1145–60)

953
Wa ga koi wa	Despite my efforts,
Hatsumotoyui no	My love betrays itself in the color
Komurasaki	Of this recent passion,
Itsushika fukaki	Deep as the purple of the ribbon used
Iro ni mietsutsu.	For the First Binding of the Hair.

EMPEROR GO-DAIGO (1288–1339)

954
Kinō kyō	Yesterday, today—
Kumo no hatate ni	No matter how I gaze in vacant reverie
Nagamu tote	Toward the cloud-tips
Mi mo senu hito no	Tinted in the evening, how can I know
Omoi ya wa shiru.	The feelings of her I cannot see?

FUJIWARA TEIKA

955
Mono omou to	How strange it is:
Ware dani shiranu	I keep falling into a vacant reverie
Kono goro no	Of vague awareness
Ayashiku tsune wa	These days when in my mind itself
Nagamegachi naru.	I do not really know I love.

EMPEROR KŌMYŌ (1321–80)

956
Hito shirenu	Because of feelings
Kokoro no uchi no	Now agitated in the reaches of my heart
Omoi yue	Unknown to her and all,
Tsune wa nagame no	My state is no longer quite like that
Higoro ni mo ninu.	Of days spent in a vacant reverie of love.

LADY REIZEI

957
Iwa ga ne no	Although her heart
Korishiku yama ni	Is no mountain of thick-set boulders
Aranaku ni	Rooted in their place,
Imo ga kokoro no	My beloved's feelings toward me
Ware ni ugokanu.	Stay adamantly unmoved.

FUJIWARA KIMIKAGE

958

Fukaki e no
Ashi no shitane yo
Yoshi saraba
Tada kuchihatene
Migomori ni shite.

Sunken my love,
Like reed roots deep within a tidal pool—
So be it if it must;
But then let it rot away completely,
Hidden within those secret depths.

LADY JŪSAMMI CHIKAKO

959

Uzumoruru
Yuki no shitakusa
Ika ni shite
Tsuma komoreri to
Hito ni shirasen.

Since this love of mine
Is like the grass all buried by the snow,
What means have I to say
That I would hide within those fields
With you there by my side?

LADY DAINI SAMMI (fl. ca. 1100)

960

Yoso nite wa
Hana no tayori to
Mienagara
Kokoro no uchi ni
Kokoro aru mono o.

To us remote observers
This couple seems absorbed in speaking
Of the cherry flowers,
But deep within their heart of hearts
Still other feelings lie concealed.

KI NO TSURAYUKI

961

Aoyagi no
Kazurakiyama no
Yoso nagara
Kimi ni kokoro o
Kakenu hi wa nashi.

You are as remote
As Mount Kazuraki with its slopes
Covered by green willows,
Yet no day passes but my heart
Turns toward you in its longing.

FUJIWARA IETAKA

962

Hatsushigure
Omoisomete mo
Itazura ni
Maki no shitaba no
Iro zo tsurenaki.

Though now I love,
Wishing to change the color of your
feelings
As the drizzle tints the leaves,
You remain as obstinately indifferent
As black pines whose color nothing dyes.

KYŌGOKU TAMEKANE

The poems are all on the subject of the beginning of love, and at this stage in the affair love is very much a one-sided thing. The person for whom an attachment is being formed—the state of feeling has not yet developed into a mutual confirmation of passion—is unaware of the effect he or she has had on someone else. Consequently, the concerns of the speakers of these poems are those of their own feelings (is this agitation really love?), those of communicating their feelings to a person perhaps only glimpsed or heard, and those of trying to arouse a corresponding passion in the person who has been the cause of the attraction. Within the sequence there is some progression, although intermittent and irregular, from uncertainty about oneself to efforts, as yet unsuccessful, to gain the love of the person with whom the speaker has fallen in love.

This subject is a constant element, and this progression is the "dramatic" one of Japanese courtly love. It is difficult, however, to find a coherent progression of images such as those we found in the sequence of winter poems in the *Shinkokinshū*, in which the images progress in a kind of subplot or motif from mountains, to hills, to plains, and finally to a house. Some such progression can be found from the second poem by Kimikage on—from mountains (957), to a bay (958), to a plain (959), to (implied) hills (960), to a mountain (961), and to (implied) mountain slopes (962). But the two poems that precede this sub-sequence (955–56) are so much in the style of the period that they have no imagery at all; and given such generalized language, it is clear that no consistent imagistic progression is possible. Moreover, such progressions of imagery are apt to be sporadic even in the seasonal books of the *Gyokuyōshū* and the *Fūgashū*, except of course for the larger and simpler progression of the seasons.

We must search for integration in the techniques of association, rather than those of progression. It is indeed something of a search, since the absence of imagery from many of these poems often makes association seem impossible. To a much more marked degree here than in the *Shinkokinshū*, integration is often effected by associations of rhetorical techniques, shared or related nonimagistic diction, common ideas, and similar ways of treating a subject. Sometimes these associations seem rather creakingly mechanical, and on other occasions they are most subtle. Whatever the form of association, however, there are some instances in which two poems are juxtaposed with no apparent connection. The first two poems, for example (950–51), both have images, but no images in common, and the same thing is true for the most part of the fourth and fifth (953–54). These are truly "distantly related verses," and to explain how they are related at whatever distance, we may as well study in order these thirteen poems selected by the compilers from the compositions of their own and earlier ages.

The first two poems (950–51) share no associations, but by the particular juxtaposition they are made to allude to a poem by the ex-Emperor Yōzei (868–949) which joins the apparently unrelated images. This technique clearly resembles allusive variation (honkadori), in which a poet raises the image of an earlier poem to heighten his own creation. The difference lies in the fact that in this anthology the authors of the two poems themselves made no such allusion, and that the allusion exists only by the compiler's putting the two poems side by side. Such a technique, for want of a better name, may be called editorial allusion, and may be distinguished from authorial allusion. Such editorial allusion was not without precedent. Two poems in the first book of the *Shinkokinshū* (54 and 55), for example, depend for their association upon a recollection of Narihira's famous poem on the seemingly changed moon and spring (*KKS*, XV: 747). And two love poems from the same anthology (*SKKS*, XI: 1021 and 1022) likewise depend for association on an editorial allusion to Komachi's poem (*KKS*, XVIII: 938) to Bunya Yasuhide, playfully suggesting that she would be happy to enter into an affair with him if she thought she could depend upon him. Such precedents are rare, however, and it was left to the Kyōgoku-Reizei poets with a taste formed for distant associations to develop the technique of editorial allusion to any consistent practice and to start off the books of love poems in an anthology with such an apparently broken association.

The first two poems of our sequence are, then, related by associations, although the single strong image of the first poem is that of the peak of Mount Tsukuba, and the images in the second are those of the sleeve pressed to the face, the "river of tears," and the rapidly flowing water—between which there is no apparent connection. The association becomes clear when we take cognizance of Yōzei's poem (*GSS*, XI: 777).

Tsukubane no	Like the Minano River
Mine yori otsuru	That splashes in its coursing from the peak
Minanogawa	Of Mount Tsukuba,
Koi zo tsumorite	My love has flowed increasingly
Fuchi to narikeru.	And collected deeply in a pool.

The river of tears of the second poem becomes the Minano flowing rapidly down Mount Tsukuba, the mountain mentioned in the first poem. The two poems are therefore skillfully joined in association, albeit at a considerable remove.

The second and the third poems (951–52) are closely related. The relationship is chiefly one of the most obvious kind, since they share such words as "sleeve" (*sode*), "river of tears" (*namidagawa*), and "heart" (*kokoro*). Besides these rather mechanical associations, there is the subtler one between the effort to blot tears with one's sleeve (951) and to dam up an overbrimming heart (952)—neither act meets with any success and both have common imagistic elements. The relation between the third and the fourth poems (952–53) is once again very distant and to be found only by discerning the editorial allusion, this time to a poem by Tsurayuki in the *Kokinshū* (XII: 572).

Kimi kouru	But for the tears
Namida shi nakuba	I shed in my unhappy love for you,
Karagoromo	The feverish breast
Mune no atari wa	Within the cover of my Chinese robe
Iro moenamashi.	Would be bursting with red flames.

This allusion is a very subtle means of association, since it is employed to relate the tears of the one poem (952) with the passion of the other; moreover, although the color of love is not specified in Go-Daigo's poem, the traditional redness of passion is implicitly contrasted with the purple of the ribbon, and this implicit image of red is strengthened by the image of flames in Tsurayuki's poem. Finally, the Chinese robe of Tsurayuki's poem is also traditionally red, so that it both reinforces the implicit image of a red passion and suggests an association between this red color and the sleeve in the preceding poem. But even with the editorial allusion established, the association remains very distant indeed.

The relation between the fourth and fifth poems (953, 954) is also distant, although the poems share the use of forms of the verb "to see" toward their conclusions. This is hardly enough to relate the poems, however, and the imagistic association depends upon a wholly implied relationship between "purple" (*komurasaki*) and the clouds in Teika's poem. Now, our translation sets the time of day in Teika's poem and so makes such an imagistic association possible, although there is nothing in his poem itself about the evening. Once again the association depends upon an allusion, this time by the author himself, but also recognized by the compiler and used for an editorial allusion. Teika has alluded to an anonymous poem in which the time of day, and consequently the color of the clouds, is made clear (*KKS*, XI: 484).

Yūgure wa	Since the one I love
Kumo no hatate ni	Is a person inhabiting a realm
Mono zo omou	Lofty in the heavens,
Amatsu sora naru	I turn my longing in the evening
Hito o kou tote.	Toward the tips of the purple-tinted
	clouds.

The subtleties of such an association are clear from the fact that the compilers of the *Fūgashū*, ex-Emperor Hanazono and his assistants, have recognized the allusion in Teika's poem, used it as the basis for amplifying details of images in Teika's poem, and associated these amplifications with images in the preceding poem. They would have failed to appreciate Teika's art if they had not recognized the allusion; and we readers would fail to recognize the complex art of compiling an anthology if we did not see their adaptation of Teika's allusion. Such an original departure in methods of associating images is clearly dependent upon a high regard for a tradition that is thoroughly studied and known.

The more or less distant associations of these first few poems give way to close associations between Teika's poem (954) and the next (955)—a pattern followed through the four succeeding poems (956–59). In this subgroup, the associations are clear and closely related. The "Yesterday, today" (*kinō kyō*) of Teika's poem has a corresponding "These days" (*kono goro*) in the next (955); both poems speak of reveries (*nagamu*, 954; *nagame*, 955), and both employ some form of the verb *omou*—"think," "feel," or "love." Poem 955 is related to the next one, by Lady Reizei, in similar fashion, sharing with it such words as "reverie," "love," and words used to show time (*tsune, higoro*). Lady Reizei's poem is related to the one following through their common use of "heart" (*kokoro*) and through the common rhetorical form of negative inflections of their concluding verbs. And more subtle than such rather mechanical connections, the very similar amorous implications of *hito* ("person," "her") in Lady Reizei's poem and *imo* (literally, "younger sister") in the next provide a link—because each expression is a periphrasis for "the one I love" or "you," although of course either word might be used denotatively as well.

Poem 957 is followed by one we have seen before, Lady Jūsammi Chikako's allegorical play on the roots of reeds. They are related overtly by the shared word *ne* ("root"), and more interestingly by the traditional association of "mountain" (957) with "deep" (958). Moreover, these poems show, for the first time in this sequence, the technique of association through contrast. With imagery as traditional as it is and with the sensibilities of poets and readers developed to such a point, in juxtaposing "mountain" in one poem (957) and "tidal pool" in the next (958), the compilers of the anthology felt free to assume a degree of contrast comparable but opposed to the degree of association in the traditional imagistic epithet, "deep" for mountains. Chikako's poem and the next (959) are related overtly through the imagery of hiding and burial and rhetorically through the common syntactical pattern of *ashi no shitane* ("reed roots deep") and *yuki no shitakusa* ("grass all buried"), an effect only imperfectly rendered in our translation. And the "deep" of Chikako's poem is a traditional association for "buried" in the next. So that for six poems the associations have been close; the associational linking moves smoothly from one poem to the next, with techniques varying widely from such obvious ones as shared words to such more subtle ones as imagistic contrast.

It is difficult to know whether to term close or distant the relation between the last poem of this closely related series (959) and the next, by Tsurayuki. There are so many associations that the poems are tightly linked, and yet all the associations are so subtle that the relation seems distant. Perhaps the clearest association is that between "buried" (*uzumoruru*) and "heart of hearts" (more literally, "heart within a heart," *kokoro no uchi ni kokoro*). This is an association, because of the common element of the hidden or enclosed. As a motif of enclosure, the association joins not only these two, but also the preceding poem (958) into a little sequence, as very close inspection would show. Tsurayuki's poem is further associated with the one that precedes it by another imagistic technique new to this series, that of images belonging to the same category of phenomena. The shared category is that of growing phenomena, represented by grass (959) and cherry flowers (960). Other such categories whose imagistic phenomena might be used associationally are rising phenomena (smoke or haze), falling phenomena (precipitation), and so on. Such names for the categories were not coined until later poets of the renga, or linked verses, set out to codify their imagery. As so often happens in literary history, the practice of one age—association through such classes of images by the Kyōgoku-Reizei poets—becomes part of the critical apparatus and convention of writers in a later period—the poets of the renga.

Tsurayuki's poem has yet another kind of association with the one before it, although this technique is difficult to name. It is a species of editorial rhetoric not unlike editorial allusion. For the preceding poem asks, in effect, how could the speaker possibly get his message of love through to the woman who attracts him, with the implication that communication is impossible. The compiler responds to this rhetorical question by juxtaposing Tsurayuki's poem, which offers some hope to the frustrated lover—it brings the lovers together, and also suggests that perhaps in her inmost heart the woman unconsciously senses his passion and feels similarly toward him without his being aware of it.

The relation between Tsurayuki's poem and the next (961) is once again indisputably close, just as is the relation between poems 961 and 962. Poem 961 shares with Tsurayuki's poem such words as "heart" and "remote," and both have images belonging to the category of growing things—cherry blossoms in Tsurayuki's and green willows in the next. The last two poems in our sequence of thirteen are similarly associated, with green willows (961) and black pines (962) related as growing phenomena. Moreover, there is a traditional association between "mountain" (Mount Kazuraki) and the "black pines" that grow only on the mountainsides.

The preceding analysis has hardly done justice to the poems themselves. Our translation does not make clear, for example, that Tsurayuki's poem concerns two figures painted on a screen. Moreover, the intricacies of the sixth poem (955), as perhaps of others, call for explanation. This poem by Emperor Kōmyō typifies the subtle psychological analysis of the love poetry of the late classical period in its discussion of varying kinds, or as a Freudian would have it, various levels, of consciousness or awareness.

Mono omou to   How strange it is:
Ware dani shiranu   I keep falling into a vacant reverie
Kono goro no   Of vague awareness
Ayashiku tsune wa   These days when in my mind itself
Nagamegachi naru.   I do not really know I love.

The poem is extremely difficult in the Japanese and perhaps the translation has not clarified matters much. The speaker, who is addressing himself ("himself"—but the speaker could as easily be a woman), feels a certain agitation. One part of his sensibility represents a state that may possibly be love. Another part of him does not know it with any certainty. And a third, rather shadowy or intuitive awareness apprehends the other two to tell him that he is probably falling in love without really perceiving it. To put it this way is somewhat to distort the Japanese, which conveys the experience itself by verbs and contrasts between states that seem nearly alike but that are finely distinguished. Such difficulties are numerous in the poetry of the period and have their counterparts in other periods. Fortunately, the reader can obtain help for understanding and analysis by examining a poem in its context with other poems in a sequence. This fact—that the poems in a sequence illuminate one another—is really but one dimension and affirmation of the degree of integration achieved in the imperial collections and the sequences of thirty, a hundred, or five hundred poems. The particular quality of integration in the *Gyokuyōshū* and *Fūgashū* lies in the changing distance of the integrating associations and of poems that are often different in nature from those in earlier anthologies. Both follow, and both develop afresh, traditional techniques of integration of single poems into new lyric structures.

Such apparent breaks in continuity, spanned as they are by new or newly redefined techniques of integration, give these two anthologies their individual quality, a quality one might almost say of a new musical harmony. Where the *Shinkokinshū* had developed rhythms and progressions to climaxes by using alternations of mediocre, good, and excellent poems in ways that set off and culminated certain "movements," the *Gyokuyōshū* and *Fūgashū* characteristically achieve their rhythms and climaxes by alternating closely with distantly related poems. Reinforced by lesser rhythms of poems of varying quality, of poems by contemporary and older poets or in contemporary and older styles, and of sporadic progressions in "subplots" and motifs, this larger rhythm provides a fundamentally different form of integration from those in earlier anthologies, or from those in the contemporary and later collections brought together by representatives of the Nijō family. The Nijō and Kyōgoku-Reizei collections share an emphasis upon association rather than progression as a means of integration, but the Nijō poets and compilers employ more closely related associations. Their movement is smoother and tends to be monotonous. The importance of this distinction, which may seem so slight in itself, can be appreciated differently. Distant associations reflect the underlying subjectivity of the age and its preoccupation with fine particularities. So slight a change in emphasis with the methods of integration therefore reflects the fundamental poetic ideals and practice of the Kyōgoku-Reizei poets. The importance of this distinction may be understood in still another way when one realizes that the characteristic new techniques of association employed in the *Gyokuyōshū* and *Fūgashū* were to have important influence in later times, on poets outside the Court, and on new poetic genres.

THE DECLINE OF COURT POETRY AND THE RISE OF NEW FORMS

"The period of the *Fūgashū* brings the last splendors to the tradition of Court poetry which, from the fifteenth century, sinks steadily into an age of darkness." With these melancholy words from a modern Japanese critical study, we mark the final decline of the Court tradition. There is little we can add to the comment, apart from some brief explanation for the cause of the decline and a general reminder that literary history is seldom marked by unqualified conclusions: the burial ground of one tradition is commonly the garden site of others. Before assessing the intrinsic achievement of Japanese Court poetry, we wish therefore to relate its devolution to other matters, and to trace the main lines of its influence upon the form that superseded it in importance—the linked verses or renga.

THE ECLIPSE OF THE COURT

As all historians of Japanese literature are at pains to show, the Court had been in decline for many generations before the fourteenth century. The final breakdown of the Court government had many causes, primarily political, economic, and social in nature. We shall speak briefly here of the course of this breakdown, because in order for the new literary forms to come into being, the old social order had to change.

In 1300 there was as always a reigning emperor, however powerless, and the organs of real power went to considerable pains to justify the exercise of rule in the name of the Throne. The office of the shogun (general-governor) had developed as the most powerful office in the land and had subsequently declined into impotence, as behind it grew up the shogunal regents drawn from the Hōjō family and directed by the office of high commissioner. The emperor reigned in Kyoto, the regency ruled in Kamakura (near the site of what was to become Tokyo), and for years the system worked remarkably well.

By 1304, however, the dispersal of authority had reached lengths extraordinary even in Japan, and the situation had become more complex. The

Court was altered in tone by the presence in the capital of retainers of the military regents and of such courtiers as Sanekane, whose interests were served by serving the regents in Kamakura; while Kamakura had undergone a similar change with the choosing of shoguns from among princes of the blood, bringing to Kamakura a train of courtiers with their sophisticated tastes. The system itself was in confusion. There were five retired emperors ranging in age from sixteen to sixty-one, while the reigning emperor was only nineteen. Hōjō Sadatoki, the former high commissioner, had emulated the practice of emperors and had retired to religious life, disburdening himself of the ceremony of office, which he left to a new commissioner, while he himself retained the actual power. But the Court system might have survived such confusion had it not produced on the one hand a succession of emperors and courtiers (Go-Daigo and Tamekane, for example) who were able and ambitious, and who wished to regain the lost power of their offices, and on the other hand a regency weakened from without by the tremendous outlays required to repel two foreign invasions and from within by a dearth of ability in the Hōjō family.

There were other complexities as well. Such disputes as the one that developed between rival imperial lines caught the regency at a loss, and it is a nice irony that problems of the dynastic succession of emperors with no real power should finally have brought down a system long since dominated by hard-headed warriors. In the bloody anarchy that marked the fourteenth century, Japan was thrown into a strife between rival barons, who replaced the indigent emperor and courtiers as the patrons of arts and letters.

Characteristically, the Throne survived the organs of power that had grown up about it. The *Fūgashū* was completed by ex-Emperor Hanazono about 1345, over a decade after the Hōjō family had fallen; and four subsequent collections were made, the last in 1439—the *Shinzokukokinshū*—echoing in its title the first anthology, the *Kokinshū*, which had been compiled almost five and a half centuries before. The four last collections were of course undistinguished, but that they were compiled at all is a tribute to the strength of the Court tradition. One need not be mystically inclined to agree with the Japanese that monarchy and art, especially poetry, were in an unusual sense the dual testament left by the Court to subsequent generations.

COURT POETRY AND RENGA

It is easier to say that the serious linked verses, or renga, succeeded the tanka as the most significant poetic form than it is to describe the nature or genesis of this extraordinarily complex form. In formal terms, the renga which was codified and practiced by such important poets as Nijō Yoshimoto (1320–88), the priest Shinkei (1406–75), and the priest Sōgi (1421–1502) consisted of a hundred parts. The parts were stanzas of three and two lines in alternation, and the whole might be viewed as fifty tanka merged together into one loosely flowing whole, if it were not that the parts were composed in alternation by a small number of poets gathered together and that each part had a function of its own. The extraordinarily complex conventions of the genre kept the form from degenerating into a pastiche of improvisations and are of so high a degree of sophistication as well that they could not have sprung fully devised from any single human mind. In searching for their origins, historians usually go back as far as the dialogue poems of the *Kojiki* or to the *Man'yōshū,* in which as we might expect, Yakamochi among others had had a hand in verses, also called renga, which were composed by two people. (See, for example, *MYS,* VIII: 1635.) Yet there is no need to trace each act of human frailty back to Adam and, without doubt, the real origins of the linked poetic forms—whether considered historically or technically—are to be found within Court poetry.

The forms of linked poetry go under several names, of which renga is the most common. *Tanrenga* is sometimes used to refer to tanka whose first three lines by one poet are capped with the couplet by another—the kind of short poem of two links to be found in the *Man'yōshū* and the *Kin'yōshū.* True linked verse with alternating three- and two-line stanzas begins to appear from about the thirteenth century. Even in this late period, when the traditional forms of Court poetry were taken with utter seriousness, the renga is considered as something apart, a pastime, "for the most part a breather after the rigors of composing *waka,*" as a modern critic puts it. Quite naturally under such relaxed circumstances, the renga composed in this period were often playful and even comic; such sportive linked verses naturally came to be known as *haikai,* or "comic," renga. As one might expect, what began in jest soon turned to earnest, and a distinction came to be made between two kinds of renga: the serious (*ushin*) and the playful (*mushin*). The important serious renga of the fourteenth, fifteenth, and sixteenth centuries of course developed from the former, but it would be a mistake to dismiss the playful, or *haikai,* renga of the thirteenth century and the early fourteenth as merely frivolous exercises of wit. They may not have been profound in tone and theme, but they encouraged the development of technical skill which was admirable in itself and which was an important discipline for such a haiku poet as Bashō or such a writer of prose fiction as Saikaku (1642–93). Indeed it might even be argued that the less elevated *haikai* provides the mainstream of development over the centuries and that the serious renga (or *renku,* as it was often called after the seventeenth century) developed as a parallel when the form's potentialities for serious elevation were recognized. We shall in any case take renga as the generic term and concern ourselves chiefly with the more serious kind.

Renga is surely *sui generis* as a literary form. The idea that a single poem might be composed by three or more poets at a sitting runs counter to Western assumptions of the nature of poetic composition, even of artistic integrity.

Sōgi and friends composing renga at the grave of Teika on the night of the full moon in the eighth month. From EHON YAMATO HIJI

It is as difficult to admit further that great poems might be so written as to imagine an age in which the genre was the most important poetic form. Western prejudices are still further aroused by the conventions of the genre, by the fact that, for example, the fourth stanza (a 7-syllable couplet) not only must be taken as an expansion or fulfillment of the third (5, 7, 5), but is also in turn modified in tone and meaning by the fifth (5, 7, 5) and so on to the end of the poem. In short, the different poets move at once separately and in concert with units of ever-shifting sets of two stanzas. By Western standards at least, there may be a beginning and end, of sorts, but there is no middle, no climax, no sense of inevitable direction apart from its rigid conventions. In order to become a true literary form, the renga clearly required such a set of formal conventions; these it rapidly acquired from the Court poetry during the thirteenth and fourteenth centuries, to such a complex extent that, as the Japanese say, it takes twenty years to acquire ease in handling them. Far from being the artless or anarchic composition it at first appears to be, the renga is in fact one of the most intricate, not to say contrived, poetic forms ever devised.

The most cursory examination of renga should suggest the resemblances between it and important esthetic tendencies or impulses already observed in Court poetry. In each case there are numerous conventions regarding the handling of diction and imagery, the so-called rules of renga often making explicit what had been silently practiced in the earlier poetry. For example, the rule that "travel" (*tabi*) must always refer to movement away from the capital and never to it or between other points is implicit in Court poetry, explicit in the rules of renga. Moreover, the very range of language, the body of imagery and diction itself, is that of Court poetry, although *haikai* renga provides exceptions. More fundamentally, the concept of the poetic act underlying renga is like that of Court poetry in two basic respects. The opposed yet complementary Japanese poetic impulses toward fragmentation and integration are represented in renga by multiple authorship on the one hand and on the other by the complicated conventions governing the relations of one stanza to the next and the place of each in the whole. In method of composition nothing could be more fragmented, in result nothing more carefully integrated. Moreover, the impulse to fragmentation–integration had already found almost identical expression in the integration of poetic sequences of Court poems. When ex-Emperor Go-Toba spent years integrating the poems by diverse authors in the *Shinkokinshū,* he was fulfilling, as a single compiler, the function exercised as a group by renga poets. In addition, the most common unit of poetic sequences by single authors, the hundred-poem sequence (*hyaku-shuuta*) became the standard number of stanzas for renga practiced by the masters of the form.

Other technical as well as historical considerations show the extent to which the renga represents an unbroken literary development from Court poetry.

Just as descriptive nature poetry in English develops out of late-seventeenth-century and early-eighteenth-century pastorals and poems on places and "graveyard" scenes, finally flowering in the genius of the Romantic poets, so does renga develop in both its serious and playful styles out of the pastimes of Court poets. More fundamental than such a historical pattern of development, however, is the fact that the poetic subjects and the techniques of integration in renga are in most respects those of Court poetry. A famous renga like the "Three Poets at Minase" (*Minase Sangin Hyakuin*) can serve as an example. The location of composition, appropriately enough the site of the Minase Palace of ex-Emperor Go-Toba, was itself a reminder of the courtly past, and the first stanza by Sōgi alludes to one of Go-Toba's most famous poems (*SKKS*, I: 36; see above, p. 291). As the renga unfolds, the subjects are those which even Tsurayuki would have found comfortably familiar: the natural scene presented in terms of specific seasons and with familiar images; love; travel; Buddhism; the topic *jukkai* (personal distress or grievance); and even that seemingly uncategorical category, *zō*. In short, the "Three Poets at Minase" is a poem which moves, however subtly and flickeringly, through the usual topics (dai) of the hundred-poem sequence, itself a microcosm of the imperial anthology.

The true significance of the renga lies not in the subjects through which it moves, however, but in the movement itself. Some of the conventions of movement are translations of techniques of the tanka into terms peculiar to the new form. The idea that the opening stanza, *hokku,* should end with a full stop, or that the third stanza should end with a verb in the participial (*–te*), has its counterpart in the fragmentation of the tanka itself, even though such possibilities did not exist in sequences of tanka. At the same time, the earlier sequences were expected to begin, as imperial anthologies began, with a poem especially lofty and auspicious in tone, and the same requirement held for the *hokku* in renga. Such requirements are at best either obvious choices or mechanical, and we learn of the real debt of renga to Court poetry—as also of the true genius of linked verse—only by comparing the techniques of relating stanzas to the techniques of relating poems in a sequence. As we have seen, these techniques were progression and association. The same is true of renga. The *Kokinshū* had employed chiefly progression in the seasonal and love poems; progression and other practices had led to association; and after the *Shinkokinshū,* association had become the dominant technique. The renga picks up at this point, using minor and usually short progressive movements such as from far to near ("Three Poets at Minase," stanzas three and four) or temporal progressions within a day or season. The primary technique is association.

We have noted that the compilers of the *Gyokuyōshū* and *Fūgashū* evolved a rhythm of associational technique in their alternation of closely related verses (*shinku*) and distantly related verses (*soku*). Both kinds of association are employed in the renga, although the first impression of Japanese and Western readers alike is apt to be that the stanzas are very distantly related indeed. What the renga masters did was in effect to codify, specify, and refine the associational techniques of tanka. Whereas the Court poets had used such categories of images as rising phenomena (*sobikimono*) without naming them, the renga critics named them and set conventions for their use. Whereas the Court poets had tended to form rather large groups of poems with certain central or "ground" images or with certain clear progressions, the renga poets made shorter units and set more rigorous patterns for images. Two examples will suffice: in renga the image of the moon ideally appeared eight times and at more or less specified points in the sequence; "dream" (*yume*) was considered so precious a verbal concept that it was to be used only once in a sequence of a hundred stanzas.

Since the renga owes so much to Court poetry, it might be expected that literary histories would give an account of its growth from the Court tradition in the terms of our brief description. The case is otherwise. The techniques of association and progression—the most important connection between renga and Court poetry—have been rediscovered only so recently that historians have not yet had time to adjust their accounts. Yet the fact that renga is a descendant of Court poetry is less startling than the mistaken idea that it is not, given what everyone knows to be true of literary developments— changes come slowly and one new element grows from several of the old. The real question is why the great Court poets of the twelfth, thirteenth, and fourteenth centuries, who had most of the elements at hand, failed to shape them into the perfected form of renga. Answers to questions of what might have been are no doubt futile and usually explain a situation many times over; but in this case the answers can tell us a good deal about the differences between the poetry of the Court period and of subsequent periods.

The most obvious explanation is that although the Court poets had devised the renga, they had also inherited forms for poems and sequences that were quite satisfactory for their purposes and, the force of Japanese tradition being what it was, felt no need to go afield for new forms. The same explanation may be phrased in very different, rather more meaningful terms. In order for the renga to develop as the outstanding poetic form, the Court society had to lose its literary pre-eminence—as it did with the events we have recounted. A real break was necessary if the continuity of tradition was to yield a new dominant form. It is one of the paradoxes with which history endows us that the change to a new form came from the line of Court poets who most resisted change in the older tradition, the Nijō family and its adherents. Not long after the *Fūgashū* was completed (ca. 1345), Nijō Yoshimoto* had codified the

* It should be noted that although Yoshimoto was both an adherent and a politically influential patron of the Nijō faction, he was not related by blood to the poetic dynasty. His family, despite the identical name, represented a separate branch of the Fujiwara.

fundamental concepts and laid the basis for renga up to the nineteenth century. Like many Nijō poets, Yoshimoto was a critic of great powers, if not a poet of the first or second magnitude. If it seems strange that the conservatives should sponsor the new, the fact is hardly unprecedented in human events. Moreover, the renga, which is so anarchic a thing viewed one way, requires tradition, convention, and rules that are downright arbitrary, if it is to possess any form at all. In this respect the renga was well suited to the Nijō sensibility, and it required only a change in the manner of poetic composition in order to come into being.

Such a change became possible, even inevitable, with the break-up of Court society. The poetry contests and submissions of sequences could not be norms when there were no longer emperors or nobles with sufficient wealth, leisure, and taste to commission them. In consequence, poets found that they could meet most easily in the small groups that came to compose renga. But the renga poets turned back to the Court tradition for renewed inspiration. Shōtetsu (1381–1459) and his disciple Shinkei returned to Teika's ideal of ethereal charm (yōen) to help form and confirm the ideals they called coolness (hie) and slenderness (yase). Sōgi sought for techniques in the works of the Kyōgoku-Reizei poets.

With Shinkei and Sōgi, however, we have come to the end of the fifteenth century; we have moved from the world of the courtiers to the tea rooms of the feudal barons, the patrons of Zen and of the Nō drama. Like all artistic forms, the renga in its remarkable beauties as well as in its extraordinary restrictions is the product of an age. That age was no longer one in which the Court society was dominant, but neither was it a static age. It produced other literary forms that bear the imprint of the Court tradition. The history of the Nō drama or of the haiku lies outside the scope of this book, but it is no exaggeration to say that the study of these forms, like that of the renga, must ultimately begin with Court poetry. While no one will deny that the most diverse elements were combined in the development of the Nō and even of the haiku, some of which had no connection with the Court, it remains true that the process by which these forms were refined, elevated, and developed into great literature was to a large extent a process of borrowing, adapting, and re-defining the ideals, and to a lesser extent the techniques, of Court poetry. One cannot pursue one's study of the esthetic ideals of Zeami or Bashō very far without returning to Shunzei's ideal of yūgen or Saigyō's poetry of sabi, any more than one can approach the renga of Shōtetsu, Shinkei, and Sōgi except through the ideals of Teika and the practice of the Kyōgoku-Reizei poets.

If such later developments lie outside the scope of this study, it may still be added that in one particular, the self-sustaining power of the Court tradition of poetry has been remarkable. It can be said of the typical Court form, the tanka, as it cannot be said, for example, of the sonnet, that in every period of the long literary tradition after primitive song the tanka has continued to be written in large numbers and with sufficient distinction to merit attention. The Nijō poets and their lesser successors were, after all, not completely without merit, and certainly not without skill. The vitality of the form, however diminished during the late feudal period, is attested to both by the number of poems which continued to be written in the form and also by the fact that the form had retained enough potentiality to be revived and practiced widely in modern times. Even today the Imperial Poetry Contest held each New Year's season reflects the brilliance of the courtly past, and amid the movements of free verse with mixed Japanese and "Chinese" diction there have been sporadic attempts to establish something like the old prosody and imagery. The persistence is remarkable and seems particularly Japanese, for it reflects the natural love of continuity, the desire to preserve what has been gained. Such motives are of fundamental importance to the human enterprise of civilization, and the crucial role of the Court poets in establishing the motives may not be denied. The literature that follows the period of the Court demonstrates the importance of the earlier poets in yet another way: they defined to the Japanese in terms which have never been seriously challenged the concept of beauty, the values to be sought in poetry, and the nature of poetry itself. Perhaps this in a sense extrinsic importance of Court poetry can be felt most readily by readers grounded in other poetic traditions. It is now necessary to make a different assessment—of the intrinsic achievement of the Court. In such an enterprise, cultural differences are in some ways a handicap, but perhaps the fact of difference itself may be used as an aid in translating the achievement into Western terms.

PART THREE

The Tradition of Japanese
Court Poetry

8

The Tradition of Japanese Court Poetry

THE EIGHT CENTURIES of Japanese poetry discussed in the preceding chapters make up a literary tradition that is easier to analyze in terms of a given poet, a given genre, or a given age than to sum up as a whole. Moreover, since it is always more interesting to consider the poems in themselves, we turn now almost with reluctance to a more general discussion of the nature of the poetic tradition developed by the Japanese over this long period. After a review of the distinguishing features of the tradition, we shall assume the role of the devil's advocate to discuss its limitations (offering perhaps a few rejoinders) and close by comparing the achievement of the tradition with that of Western poetry.

THE COURTLY NATURE OF THE TRADITION

Although the period spanned by the Court tradition is roughly comparable to the period from the Norman Conquest to the present, and although many significant changes took place in this period, one significant and constant fact gives this poetry a homogeneity, a special character, that enables us to regard the eight hundred or so years as a single literary tradition. The poetry is the product of a Court society and reveals the values as well as the limitations of an aristocratic culture. Noblemen are of course human beings whose interests are basically those of other men, but one has only to compare Pope's *Rape of the Lock* or *Moral Essays* with Defoe's *Robinson Crusoe* or Richardson's *Pamela*—all works of the same period—to realize that the tastes of the modified court tradition which Pope represents are very different from the interests of those middle classes who so tirelessly rise in the pages of our histories. The interests of the Japanese nobility changed with the growth of their culture, and of course reflected many events of the sort that only indirectly affect literature. But these interests can consistently be characterized by the Japanese word *miyabi*, or "courtliness"—a certain aristocratic elegance and accomplishment.

In his *Tsurezuregusa*, Yoshida Kenkō (1283–1350) jotted down his ideals for human behavior and his tastes in mundane as well as spiritual matters; and although he died in the year that we have fixed as our terminal date, his statements express the ideals of social accomplishment held by the majority of the aristocracy from early times (quoted in Sir George Sansom's translation, pp. 10–11).

It is desirable to have a knowledge of true literature, of composition and versifying, of wind and string instruments; and it is well, moreover, to be learned in precedent and Court ceremonies, so as to be a model for others. One should write not unskillfully in the running hand, be able to sing in a pleasing voice and keep good time to music; and lastly, a man should not refuse a little wine when it is pressed upon him. . . . However gifted and accomplished a young man may be, if he has no fondness for women, one has a feeling of something lacking, as of a precious wine cup without a bottom . . . But it is well that a man do not become addicted to lewdness, a constant and familiar companion of women.

These preferences are aristocratic preferences — varied accomplishments without impossible notions that any man can achieve perfection in them all— and they are those which are fundamentally social and esthetic, not philosophical or ethical. Such tastes produce a homogeneous, well-knit aristocratic society, a milieu in which the arts flourish. To say the arts flourish in such an atmosphere is not, however, to say they necessarily flower into greatness, for greatness requires more than accomplishment. Perception, feeling, thought, ethics, faith, and—for poetry—mastery of conventions, as well as that freshness, that personal contribution we call originality, these are also necessary. Japanese "courtliness" created a milieu for poetry of a certain kind, then, but the great poets appeared at moments decreed by the same obscure laws that have brought our great writers into the world at their proper moments. And these great Japanese poets had to rise above a mass of dilettantism and facility that engulfed lesser men.

Pope's famous description of the Cavalier poets—"the mob of gentlemen that wrote with ease"—seems even more appropriate for the courtier-poets of Japan. Significantly, Pope does not speak of a mob of noblemen, but of gentlemen, and this difference is important for Japan as well as England. For while nearly everybody who was a nobleman seems to have versified, the important writers in Japan, as in England, were usually not from the very top of the aristocracy. The great nobles were usually too involved with affairs of state or the ceremonies of court to write poetry of surpassing quality; they were patrons of the arts rather than serious artists. The great poets of Japan, like their counterparts in Western aristocratic societies, were usually courtiers of lesser rank and of a scholarly turn of mind. Perhaps to this group we should add some nobles of higher rank and even a few emperors (for example, Go-Toba and Hanazono) who turned to poetry after retiring or when the actual powers of government were no longer theirs to enjoy.

Even after allowances have been made for would-be rulers who turned to poetry partly out of frustration, one must admit that the Japanese nobility set a higher value upon poetry than, say, the English kings and queens. James I is the only English king who was really a poet, for none of the flattery of Elizabeth I can gild the leaden mediocrity of her verses. Certainly the later Stuarts, the Hanoverians, and the Windsors produced no poetry. And yet, although Rochester wrote with witty malice of Charles II that "He never said a foolish thing / And never did a wise one," it is also true that Charles supported the Drydens and Purcells even while feeling it beneath the royal dignity to be an artist himself. And this is after all the great difference between a Prince Genji and a Duke of York. The Japanese nobleman composes poetry and would not be considered to have the accomplishments of his class if he failed to perform as a literary amateur. The British nobleman who writes poetry is regarded by his peers with wonder, if not suspicion.

If the aristocratic character of the Japanese artistic tradition is of undeniable and continuous importance, something must be said about what in particular the aristocratic tradition entailed. Insofar as the interests of the Court involve such other arts as calligraphy, painting, and music, they present too large a subject for treatment here; but one who has studied the eight centuries or so of Court poetry cannot fail to be struck by the persistency of certain concerns and certain views of experience. One of these is the classical Chinese past, which some Japanese of some periods have been at pains to deny and others to overstress. Study of Japan's literary debt to China is truly fraught with perils of exaggeration and underestimation, but two matters seem to be incontrovertible truths. The first is that the poetic example of China was translated, so to speak, into two Japanese forms—Chinese poetry written by Japanese and native verse (the waka). Chinese poetry composed by the Japanese shows direct Chinese influence and rather little originality, and often it seems to have been a kind of testing-ground for what the Japanese might use in their native forms. The effect of Chinese poetry on the native Japanese poetry is more difficult to characterize, but in the main the relationship is more one of example, the Chinese providing sources for allusion and technique, than one of imitation. And this leads us to our second truth. China is the classical "past" for Japan even when, in a given age, the "past" might be nearly contemporaneous with the Japanese poet who looked westward to the continent. It is the past in the sense of a time and a place that are valued for qualities of endurance and for reference points of value and beauty. The process of acceptance and use is therefore one of selection, at most allusion, not of the direct imitation which may mark a vogue but is not sufficiently absorbed to create lasting poetry. China is to Japan, as many people have recognized, as Greece and Rome are to modern Western literatures—the classical past.

Japanese poets looked to their own environment as well as to the riches of Chinese culture. And so important was the particular experience of the Japanese Court in terms of its customs, its history, and the very landscape on which its buildings rose, that the Chinese discoveries of the poets were colored by native experience to the point that what seemed to the Japanese to have been particularly Chinese in their writings would often have seemed incontrovertibly Japanese to a Chinese reader. This can be seen if we compare treatments of two Japanese poetic subjects which are closest to the Chinese—praise of the emperor and partings. As a whole, the Chinese songs of praise show an abstract political quality, the Japanese a tendency toward natural imagery or allegory. The Japanese poems typically exhibit a stronger sense of the decorum of the auspicious, so that one senses a greater emphasis upon the ritualistic as opposed to specific praise.

But it is not only a difference in decorum and a distaste for the political that marks the Japanese poems. The natural scene is different in itself and is felt differently. Li Po's (701–62) splendid poem on "Sending Off a Friend" (translated by Soame Jenyns) illustrates such differences.

> Looking north of the city you see a line of blue hills,
> Sparkling water flows past the eastern gate.
> Here we part once for all;
> A solitary waterweed drifts off into the distance.
> When I think of the wandering clouds you will
>   come back into my thoughts;
> Sunset will bring with it memories of you.
> We part now with a wave of the hand; as we turn
>   our horses they neigh farewell.

The last three lines are peculiarly Chinese: the images of clouds and sunset have different tonal associations in Japan, and would be used in a Japanese poem of farewell for the present scene, not for some imaginings about the future; and the vivid last line is particularly un-Japanese, not because Japanese poetry is not vivid, but because the act of parting is not treated in Japanese poetry. The first four lines, on the other hand, could illustrate the typical method of Japanese poems—excepting the third with its indecorously ominous suggestion of no return. The method is the one which we have called descriptive symbolism, but again there is a difference, since the images of blue hills, sparkling water, eastern gate, and a drifting water weed either are un-Japanese or would not be thought appropriate for poems of parting.

These differences involve a concept of nature with important dissimilarities. The Japanese view of nature is of course conditioned by the topography, climate, beliefs, and poetic customs of Japan. Japan's scenery is smaller in scale than China's and more varied within a short distance, so that an image of a mountain or a river is apt to be very different—smaller, tidier, lovelier— in Japanese poetry than Chinese, just as the scenery of *Tom Jones* is implicitly different from that of *Dead Souls*. It is more difficult to say just what other elements in Japanese experience contribute to the view of nature in poetry, or at least what proportion of significance is to be attributed to each. However, with Japanese scenery one must take note of native animism, the ritual purity of Shinto, the Buddhist doctrine of the sanctity of all living things, the outdoor activities of Court life, and poetic tradition. These different aspects of the Japanese experience of nature led poets to write of picking young shoots in the spring but not of dead animals, and of storms but not of the destruction caused by earthquakes.

As a consideration of Western poetry should tell us, we must also take into account certain historical changes. Until near the end of the early classical period, nature is not described but used for setting the scene—which might also be drawn by reference to boats or buildings—and for metaphorical purposes. The earliest "descriptive" poems are descriptive at a remove, since they portray not what the poet sees outside but what has been portrayed on a screen, or what may be so described as to convey an allegorical meaning. Only after nature had been made to seem literary in this way, and only after it could be made significant for human affairs without overt metaphor, could descriptive poetry emerge. The same thing is true of English poetry, for only with descriptions of gardens and places like Cooper's Hill or Windsor Forest—with intrusions of classical deities, abstractions, and borrowings from the graphic arts—did poetic "nature" come gradually to mean the external world rather than human nature or various abstract conceptions of *natura*. Moreover, only after science had shown an interest in what we call the natural world could a Thomson write his *Seasons,* and only when civilization had tamed the wilds with roads and towns could a Thomas Gray delight in the rugged Alps. In order for nature to become a fit subject for poetry, the external world must somehow become significant and beautiful.

This "somehow" which renders nature literary is of course poetic convention as well as a changed attitude toward the external world. Such conventions are not meaningless, for to call a cave gloomy or a skylark blithe is to draw upon our typical experience; but they are arbitrary, since caves are not necessarily gloomy and a skylark silent on the ground before us may look more drab and frightened than blithe. Meaningful and arbitrary, then, the conventions are selected, from among various possibilities, as the most typically useful for the practice of poetry. It need hardly be said that the task of the poet is to give life to a convention either by proving its truth once more under new circumstances or by an alteration whose significance is clear only to those who know the convention.

Aristocratic societies are governed by social conventions which the poets must render in terms of literary decorum—the appropriateness of certain subjects, certain tones, and certain styles for differing audiences and occasions. Just as poetic conventions enable a writer to treat experience, so decorum suggests the nature of the treatment in a given instance. It is clear that Japanese Court poetry grew from a society that put a higher value on both convention and decorum than any modern Western society, and probably more than English society of any period. This emphasis may be due in part to the strong Japanese regard for the ceremonial, but it is different in degree rather than in kind from classical Western notions of the styles appropriate for different kinds of orations, or Renaissance distinctions between appropriate subjects, rhetorical figures, and tones for different genres.

Convention and decorum in Japanese poetry are, then, partly inevitable elements in the literary tradition and partly the result of the courtly nature of the society that produced this poetry. And we must try to understand Japanese convention and decorum as thoroughly and as sympathetically as possible, because it is only through a grasp of such matters that we can read the poetry in anything like the same spirit in which it was written. We need hardly be surprised to discover that according to poetic convention, each of the seasons has its appropriate, if not invariable, tones. Spring is marked by a joyousness and a beauty that are tempered only by melancholy during the rainy season and regret over the passing of that which is conventionally the season's most beautiful emblem, cherry blossoms. Summer is perhaps the most neutral of the seasons, and with winter, usually gets the shortest treatment in the anthologies. The natural scenery of summer is usually treated for its beauty, but no other tone is considered especially appropriate; winter's characteristic scenery is either dreary or beautiful. Autumn is perhaps tonally the richest of all the seasons: beauty vies with melancholy, the two usually harmonizing. Although spring suggests renewal and is probably the happier season, autumn with its end of joy suggests more forcibly the Buddhist truth of impermanence. What should be noted in the Japanese treatment of nature in all seasons is that the special tones of each are felt to be harmonious with beauty. There is a certain estheticism in the tradition which either omits the ugly or finds a way of rendering it in such guises that it may be appreciated. As Teika wrote, "No matter how fearful a thing may be of itself, if it is treated in a poem, it is made to sound graceful and elegant."

The second great subject of Japanese poetry is human affairs—the experience of death, unhappiness, parting, and good fortune, social and private activities, and (above all) love. Of all these, love shows the courtly nature of the tradition most clearly. But to call love courtly necessitates some qualifications. First, changes in marriage customs and the gradual rise and decline of the Court made relations between the sexes rather different in 950 from what they had been in 550 or were to be in 1350. The settled code of courtly love dates probably from the ninth century, when it had fairly close ties to contemporary experience, but lasts into feudal times, when the code was as much a fiction as a reality.

Second, it is important to remember that Japanese courtly love is quite unlike Western courtly love. Two points of difference are suggested by the Western word, "chivalry." The wooer in Japanese courtly love is not expected to throw himself at his lady's feet and to make those vows of eternal service which may one day be rewarded by her acquiescence. He might woo his lady without ever having seen her. Tastefully arranged colors in sleeves that a gust of wind revealed behind curtains of state, skilled calligraphy, poetic talent, and hearsay attracted him. Once he was allowed behind the curtains, wooing at once gave way to loving. Chivalry suggests another kind of service to the lady—defending her honor with feats of arms. This is never an element in Japanese love poetry, because the courtiers, though perhaps they were captains of the palace guards, were never warriors.

Another difference in these two codes of courtly love lies in the different status of women and marriage. Until Kamakura times property could be owned and inherited by women, and many Court ladies possessed large personal fortunes. Women had therefore a degree of independence as well as isolation that made them, in a certain limited sense, equal partners in the love affair. Finally, we have only to compare the roster of love poets in Japan and in medieval England to note one outstanding difference: Japanese women write love poetry as often as men. Western courtly love poetry extols the lady so far beyond her actual position in society that some historians have seen in courtly love a reflection of the worship of the Blessed Virgin. In Japan, where the points of view of both man and woman were represented, this particular kind of exaggeration could hardly occur.

This is not to suggest that the plight of the woman in Japanese love poetry is a happy one. Her position is, in its way, as ambiguous as that of her counterpart in Western courtly love. For the society was a polygamous one, with lawful consorts often losing out, except legally, to concubines, who in turn might be left lonely in a house while the man pursued a secret affair elsewhere. A man had the mobility of a bee; a woman was rooted like a flower in her house. This situation accounts for the sad tone of so much Japanese love poetry, since a woman's joy was apt to be short-lived and complicated by the birth of children in the bewildering fashion so well depicted in the *Tale of Genji*. Moreover, as courtly love became increasingly codified, it grew fixed in forms that did not always reflect current relations between the sexes. It became, in short, a fiction like our courtly love, and with two important results. In composing love poems for such a conventional code, men might write poems whose speakers were women, and women poems whose speakers were men. And so certain was the outcome to be unhappy that gradually even poems celebrating a momentary happiness in love came to be tinged with a degree of foreboding or melancholy.

There are two other subtraditions in Japanese courtly love poetry that must be taken into account to modify these generalizations. As we have seen, that most remarkable woman Ono no Komachi established a stylistic tradition of the passionate woman that continued through Lady Ise, Izumi Shikibu, Lady Sagami, and Princess Shokushi, to ex-Empress Eifuku at the end of the poetic tradition—and not without help along the way from men like Teika. These poems of passion are not so much sad as such strong expressions of attachment or desire that sadness seems irrelevant. A second subtradition is one that can only loosely be called reflective love poetry. This style was in a sense created by Narihira, and almost, one might say, by his one poem on the apparently changed moon (p. 193). In many poems, as in Narihira's, this reflection takes on a philosophical character, although in others it is more simply esthetic. The style of ethereal charm (yōen) practiced for a time by Teika's circle, and those poems by poets of the late classical period in which analysis or metamorphosis is stressed, are later variants of the reflective mode. For if courtly love was to a considerable degree a fiction, it was a fiction that might represent some of the most important aspects of human experience.

In our remarks on the subjects of poetry in each of the periods, we have repeatedly stressed the importance of time to Japanese poets. Donald Keene has made the same point in speaking of the *Tale of Genji* and its "obsession with the idea of time similar to that observable in much of Japanese poetry." And he speaks again of "the inexorable motion of time" in Japanese literature. This latter phrase suggests one reason for, or one realization of, the preoccupation with time—it seemed to the Japanese in part to be a great, slow, irresistible wave that engulfs all men. Buddhism taught that happiness yields to sorrow in a world of transience, but it also taught that sorrow yields to happiness. If the Japanese Court poets paid more heed to the sadder of these lessons, it is no doubt partly because the forms of Buddhism most of them believed in are fundamentally counsels of resignation rather than hope. Such other causes as the esthetic beauty of loneliness (sabi) and the gradual decline of the Court itself only strengthened this melancholy attitude.

"The inexorable motion" is, however, only one aspect of this theme of time. Time is also the primary condition of reality to Hitomaro and Okura. The subject involves differences between the appearance of the moment and enduring reality for the poets of the early classical period, it is a valid past to be evoked for strength in the mid-classical period, and a source of rich moments that seem to transcend time itself in the late classical period. These different reflections of the "obsession with time" presume different treatments of the subject, and differing manipulations of it in poems that seem at first not to be aware of it at all. Time is, therefore, as much a matter of technique as it is of subject matter; and Western readers who wish to explore Japanese poetry in depth and who are yet put off by other considerations would do well to investigate this theme. It is one, we feel, more subtly handled in Japanese than in Western poetry.

The practice of poetry throughout the tradition reveals its courtly emphasis in other ways. The language, or diction, of poetry is as much determined by decorum as the style practiced on varying occasions. No bourgeois society would assign the same value as these poets did to purity of diction and traditional language. Perhaps at first the language was kept free from Chinese loan-words because the Chinese ideas could be expressed in Chinese poems written by the same poets, and free from "low" or ugly expressions because inauspicious words were feared at the turn of the millennium by a Court much concerned with taboos and ritual pollutions. But there are also other, less obvious, reasons, one of the chief of which is the relative stability of the Court society of A.D. 1000. When a language and a society are undergoing the exciting if bewildering changes of the English Renaissance, brave new words are necessary to describe brave new worlds; but the Japanese in the eleventh century, like the French in the seventeenth, were not exhilarated by linguistic change. A somewhat different motivation may lead other men to resist linguistic changes, or at least unbridled experimentation with language. Toward the end of the tradition, when the Court was losing its power to the military, traditional diction was one way of preserving other poetic values. The truly remarkable fact about the poetic language of the Court is its long continuance, the survival of its imagery and phrasing if not wholly of its grammar; for it has lived not only in the tanka from ancient to modern times, but also to a considerable degree in the renga, the haiku, and some modern poetry.

Another aspect of poetic practice which seems particularly related to the Court society is the kind of occasion which involved composition. With the rise of informal poetry—when public poetry declined after Hitomaro's generation—it is not a great exaggeration to say that every occasion except the most inauspicious was one on which the composition of a poem was pleasing, and that there were few occasions on which poetry was unwelcome. This attitude reflects the high value set by a Court on poetry, for if we do not expect the Secretary of Defense to compose poetry today, his Japanese counterpart in the middle ages felt the obligation. Strong as this social duty is and as much as it reflects a courtier's training, there are two accidental reasons that made it easier for him to fulfill such an obligation than it would be for a Western minister of state or a president of a great corporation. The tanka is, after all, a short form and one that may be composed and recited after a few moments' thought much more readily than a sonnet. Moreover, allegory as a technique and the allegorical turn of mind made it possible to employ imagery far more flexibly and with greater appropriateness than a poet today could readily manage. A given poem might therefore be quickly composed by a person with training: it would reaffirm the social bond by its appropriateness for the occasion, and would carry private significance for this special occasion to an audience perhaps as limited as a single person.

We in the West find it difficult to understand this kind of Japanese poetry; at one moment we think it to be wholly a social gesture, and at the next it seems as private as a message, whereas in fact it is truly both social and personal at once. The same problem confronts us in poems written in the study. One poem will seem personal in its treatment of love, but is meant to be judged at a poetry contest; another seems to be an impersonal observation of nature sent to a high Court official when actually the poet is expressing his disappointment in being passed over in the promotions list. Once again the conventions and decorum of a Court society give us our bearings, and we can only repeat by way of generalization that Japanese poetry is best characterized as poetry with varieties of personal lyricism in varieties of social contexts.

Such general remarks as these about the courtly nature of the Japanese poetic tradition ought to be read with the theoretical and analytical chapters that open this study. A true description of the poetry demands theory, analysis, and conclusion, for only from a combination of these three can a picture be drawn of the Court tradition without exaggerations or distortions. It is, after all, like all other integrated literary traditions, a continuous whole that undergoes change and is full of survivals, cross-currents, and false steps as well as seemingly sudden achievements. It is necessary to talk about periods because one cannot talk about the whole, and also because no matter how steady certain constant elements are, change gradually shapes them into new forms. This poetry is governed, like that of all other traditions, by change within constancy; but the particular nature of the conjunction of the two distinguishes Japanese poetry from our own and Court poetry from that of later times. The underlying law seems to be one of development, because development is meaningful change or growth; and when it ceases, as Japanese Court poetry seems to have ceased to develop in the mid-fourteenth century, no amount of change in society or constancy of poetic practice can produce poetry of interest. But before such an end came to the long tradition of Court poetry, the poets of this aristocratic society had produced forms, conventions, and techniques that reflected their experience with an interest, a pleasure, a conviction, and a truth that can be felt deeply today, and even by Westerners with another culture to shape their responses. And so true to human experience was this poetry that it in turn could shape, and still can shape, the understanding man may bring to bear upon his life, his world, and his destiny.

JAPANESE POETRY AND THE WESTERN READER: THE PROBLEM OF LIMITATIONS

A Chinese, a Japanese, and an Englishman would no doubt be equally startled and resentful if a foreigner were to ask them what they considered the major limitations of the poetry of their respective nations to be. And yet each would find the literature of the others lacking in qualities that seem meaningful and important. "Where is your epic?" the Englishman might ask both. And the Japanese would reply, "Where is your *Man'yōshū*?" While the Chinese would feel he had silenced both his friends by posing, "Where is your Po Chü-i?" And the busy recording angel, not to mention an eavesdropping Frenchman or German, might think all three were a trifle mad. So perhaps it is folly as well as temerity to attempt to outline the limitations of Japanese Court poetry. We doubt that any Western reader will accuse us of lacking enthusiasm for our subject, and to a Japanese we can only say that the poetry of any nation lacks the characteristic strengths of others, and that a study of limitations is a first step to the study of accomplishment.

A Western reader may ask such questions as why the Japanese Court produced no *Faerie Queene,* no *Paradise Lost,* no *Dunciad,* no *Idylls of the King.* So put, the questions are no doubt partly foolish and partly irrelevant, but the impulse to raise them is serious. We shall try to pose the basic problem or accusation of limitations in terms of four different but related strictures and, while qualifying their force somewhat, make the general point that the questions suggest four aspects of Japanese Court poetry which seem to be important limitations to readers who have been educated primarily in Anglo-American literature.

1. *Japanese Court poetry is confined to lyric modes.* This first charge seems to us to be true, and its truth entails two limitations—in variety and in dimension. No one would deny the beauty or importance of lyric poetry, but it is difficult for a Westerner to feel that a tradition is fully developed if it lacks narrative and epic, or, at any rate, at least one other poetic mode.

Someone might object that the *Man'yōshū* has some longish narrative poems, such as Hitomaro's on parting from his wife and on her death, and poems of a social import, such as Okura's "Dialogue on Poverty" and Yakamochi's on "The Discovery of Gold in Michinoku." Another might point out that this poem or that by Narihira or Teika or Tamekane is philosophical. The objections have some force, but a close examination of these poems would reveal that the narrative is not really extended or complex enough *as narrative* to deserve the term, that the social poetry is couched in a style that is lyric, and that the philosophical works are closer to song than to such philosophical poetry as we remember from Lucretius, Dante, and Pope.

The issue of whether there is really narrative poetry in the Japanese tradition may be taken as the crucial one and examined in detail. Hitomaro's great poem "On Seeing the Body of a Man" begins with a typical overture setting the divine and the human scene. The second section relates the voyage through the storm and the landing on Samine, where the body is discovered. The last part of the chōka addresses the dead man in terms of gentle irony. Of these three sections, only the second can be called narrative, and if this relatively short passage is compared to Spenser's *Epithalamion,* it is evident that the longer English poem is far more narrative in nature than the Japanese, but is nonetheless a lyric. Despite the narrative elements, Hitomaro's poem is lyrical in conception. And if this is true of perhaps the most narrative of Hitomaro's poems, it is certainly true of the poems by Okura, Yakamochi, and any other Japanese poet between earliest times and 1350, or until this very day for that matter.

We do not see how any Westerner can fail to believe that such prevailing lyricism lacks the variety of English—or of Italian—poetry, or how he can fail to find the variety preferable. Moreover, most of us feel that the question is also one of dimension, for what lyric poem do we include among those we regard as works of the truly first order? *The Inferno* and *Paradise Lost* are not lyric poems; rather, they incorporate lyricism into other modes as a part of the beauty of what we consider larger wholes. It would be a very unusual Englishman or American indeed whose sensibility did not respond to the dramatic force and epic sweep of these great poems by Dante and Milton with more enthusiasm than to any Japanese or Chinese poem. And it is an easy step from such a fact to the judgment that Western poetry is not only different in kind and more various, but also superior in absolute terms.

Such a judgment is, however, one which makes us pause and consider that we are Westerners looking upon another culture from the outside. Over the centuries, Japanese and Chinese poems have clearly satisfied and moved their readers in ways that our poetry never will. We can of course say that Japanese and Chinese lyricism has varieties of expression and appeal beyond our lyric poetry—but, the Westerner will add, it is lyric poetry all the same, no matter to what extent it absorbs narrative and other modes. One wishes to know how these two great cultures have satisfied their people without producing poetry of other kinds. But one looks only into the darkness and cannot say really what he sees. Such a question is not to be answered by the explanations of history or anthropology. One wishes to know rather what it is that one has failed to see, or to have some Japanese or Chinese tell us what he finds wanting in our poetry. Until that time, we must seek to understand and appreciate Japanese poetry, but we must also be forgiven if we turn first to our own poets.

2. *Japanese poetry consists of forms too short to be taken seriously by the Western reader.* We do not for a minute hold to the notion that Japanese poems are little gems with some magical power of irradiation. Such answers to this second stricture are basically as frivolous as they are vague, and even ultimately are condescending. The issue must be met squarely, and to pose the problem honestly we must consider the tanka as the norm of the Court tradition. The longer primitive songs and the chōka disappear early in the Court's history, at least as living poetry, leaving us as the poetic norm this form of thirty-one syllables. That five short lines could be considered the unit of poetry for centuries is a fact that leaves a Westerner almost breathless with amazement. And following hard upon surprise are such questions as whether or not the form can be considered to be a poem.

It seems self-evident to us that the tanka is a species of poetry, and that no pettifogging play with definitions can alter the fact. To read or hear a tanka carries complete conviction: "If the tanka be not poetry, where is poetry to be found?" we may ask, paraphrasing Dr. Johnson. But this fact does not really answer the charge of brevity. Is not a tanka so short that degree becomes almost a matter of kind; that we must look upon it as an inferior species of poetry? Our answer is that it is not inferior in the sense of quality within the limited dimensions. For these poems are undoubtedly executed with a skill, a virtuosity, and a perfectionism that no Western poet we know of has expended on his lines. Moreover, the strength and the background of tradition and the use of such techniques as allusive variation truly do enlarge the dimensions of the poem, if not its length.

The tanka also has quasi-poetic dimensions unknown to Western poetry by virtue of its social and conventional contexts. A Japanese reader who learns from a headnote that such-and-such a poem was composed when a certain person bade farewell to a friend who took a trip in the autumn immediately sees in this image or that phrase a far greater wealth of situation, circumstance, and tone than any Westerner does in his poetry. Similarly, a love poem suggests the whole order of courtly love, and the speaker need only be a woman—a fact left wholly to inference—and mention the evening, and the scene is drawn. We see not only her sitting in finery behind curtains of state as the sunlight fades, but also the whole history of an unhappy affair and the knowledge that the lover will fail to come. If the poem is also an allusive variation, the situation of the poem alluded to arises as well and harmonizes with the present. Almost before one knows it, the experience of reading the tanka has led one to forget questions of length.

To acknowledge that the tanka has an effect far greater than its size, or at any rate far greater than any English poem of comparable length could have, does not prove that the effect of a tanka is in any sensible way comparable to that of an English poem of any length. The accusation that Japanese poems are too short may have been answered in part, but not in absolute terms. As we have suggested, the problem does not arise while one is reading, understanding, and appreciating; then the artistic experience carries conviction. Rather, after one has returned to one's Spenser or Wordsworth, one recalls how short the tanka is. This brings the accusation back to mind, and it can be answered only by the integrated sequences of tanka.

We have discussed such integration before, with respect to the sequences of thirty, fifty, or a hundred poems and the imperial collections, and in enough detail to show that the integration is real and as much or more complex than the development of any Western poem of comparable length. Certainly the Japanese conception of poetic form is different from our own, as these integrated sequences show to perfection. Our idea of structure presumes a principle or idea which interrelates everything, or nearly everything: a work of art in which many elements are related to each other and to some over-all thematic idea or related ideas. The emphasis is upon unity arrived at through the exercise of intellectual processes, as Dante shows perhaps better than any other Western poet, but as Spenser also shows by his allegory and abstractions, for all of the apparent casualness of events in *The Faerie Queene*. The Japanese appear either to be very weak in what might be called structural intellect or not to have chosen to exercise these powers; but this is not to say they lack structural imagination. They do not organize or give structural unity to a work so much as develop it around focal points of feeling which pass one to the next in waves or rhythmical advances. If we may resort to symbols, it is possible to postulate a Western and a Japanese work, each of five parts—A, B, C, D, E. The Western work might be organized logically: A and B and C and D and therefore E; or it might have subparts that lead to a climactic final whole—Ax, By, Cxz, Dxy, Exyz. These subparts would probably be intellectual aspects of the main parts, or strands of images and characterization which buttress the main ideas.

The Japanese work in five parts, on the other hand, would probably move in the following fashion: A, ABC, BCD, CDE, DE, E—with one part linked to, or rather merging into, the next. Rather than direct itself toward a brilliant dénouement or stunning climax, the Japanese work would aim to control the experience of the reader at each point in the work by changes in pace, including stops and rapid movements over large portions of ground, and in moves of development. This Japanese structural scheme is that of the poetic sequences, the renga, the *Tale of Genji*, and much of the best modern fiction. So much are the writers concerned with the quality of the experience between A and E, that it makes little difference if, when we reach the conclusion of E, we do not learn whether the hero died. To put it crudely, the Japanese is interested in how the hero lived, what kind of life, not in whether he lived happily ever after.

3. *Japanese poetry is limited in scope.* There is no doubt that in some sense Japanese Court poetry is restricted in its range. The problem is to decide where the limitation lies. Partly it is a limitation of subject matter, or at least one often feels that a given theme has had as many variations and changes rung upon it as the mind can conceive. And so after reading countless fine poems on the beauties of nature or trials of love, we ask for a poem on something ugly or referring openly to some political event; but neither is forthcoming. Another limitation in scope is an apparent lack of energy. Tsurayuki's criticism of Narihira—that there was too much meaning and too few words in his poems—seems just. But it is impossible to imagine any Japanese poet's characterizing the style of another as Pope did Dryden's:

The varying verse, the full-resounding line;
The long majestic march, and energy divine.

"Varying" and "full," yes, but never "resounding," "long march," and "energy" as descriptive terms. Why this is so must be discussed later, but at present this lack of energy, movement, and force must be counted a limitation.

Another limitation in scope that seems particularly Japanese is the lack of grandeur, of the high flight. It was said of Milton that the sonnet was a trumpet in his hands; this is hardly a description for any Japanese poem we know. The instruments are rather the flute, the zither, and the human voice; and at least a representative effect of such instrumentation can be gauged from this passage in the *Tale of Genji*:

The sound of [Genji's] zithern reached the house on the hillside nearby, mingled with the sighing of pine woods and the rustling of summer waves. . . . Even gnarled old peasants, whom one would not have expected to make head or tail of this Chinese music, poked their noses out of their cottage-doors and presently came to take an airing along the shore. . . . the notes sped across the bay. Nor indeed could any flowering groves of spring nor russet winter woods have made a better setting for his music than this huge space of open sea. Somewhere in the region of soft, vague shadows along the shore, shrike were making that strange tapping sound with their bills (Arthur Waley's translation, pp. 264–65).

It does not seem unjust or exaggerated, although it may seem paradoxical, to say that the effect is one of greatness without grandeur. Milton is, however, grand. His God the Father and God the Son speak as if they are beings of an order greater than ourselves, and his Satan sheds "tears such as angels weep." But the Japanese divinities of the chronicles, for all their mouth-filling names, speak not like gods but like the men which perhaps they truly are. Japanese Court poetry does not really deal with the celestial, and consequently it fails to raise us above ourselves in the usual Western sense. The poems in the so-called lofty style are apt to be rather simple and vague, rather like those ink-wash paintings in which the towering mountain consists largely of mist or cloud, requiring us to take the solidity on faith.

The lack of grandeur may be partially explained by the natural scenery in the areas of the old capitals (Nara and Kyoto) in central Japan. There is no Grand Canyon, no Yangtze gorge, but a smaller scale of hills, mountains, and valleys. Sesshū (1420–1506), perhaps the greatest and grandest of Japanese painters, said that the scenery of China was his best teacher, and the remark seems to tell us a good deal about Japanese poetry as well. Living close to the natural scene they so admired, the Japanese poets appreciated natural scenery of limited size, rather than grand. This explanation can only be accepted as a partial one, however, for the Japanese still had the sky to people with celestial beings. But they did not choose to do so, and the single legend of the sky to find its way into Japanese poetry is the Chinese one of the Herd Boy and Weaver Maiden, the Celestial Lovers who meet once each year by fording the River of Heaven, the Milky Way. Without wishing to be unjust or to overlook poems that do show a certain vastness of celestial effect, we think it fair to say that the Japanese poetic treatment of the heavenly can be typified in a poem from the "Hitomaro Collection" (*MYS*, VII: 1068; see above, p. 88). (We have chosen this poem, and indeed all the Japanese poems in this chapter, from among those discussed in earlier chapters, in order not to trouble the reader with preliminary details of explication, and also, by supplying a larger context, to demonstrate through representative poems that there are further reaches of meaning beyond those suggested by analysis in the historical chapters above.)

Ame no umi ni	In the ocean of the sky
Kumo no nami tachi	Course the undulating waves of clouds,
Tsuki no fune	Rising by the moon-boat
Hoshi ni hayashi ni	As it seems to disappear in rowing
Kogikakuru miyu.	Through the forest of the stars.

This is a lovely poem, but its metaphors are reductive. Whereas the vast panorama of heaven might have suggested vast reaches of time and space, it is instead reduced to more familiar earthly images—waves, a boat. Apart from a few exceptions, the canon of Japanese poetry contains no poems that treat grand subjects in the grand manner. The poets looked to earth, as it were, and nature stays for the most part in proportion to man.

The absence of energy seems to be best explained by a taste for the beautiful rather than the strong and quick. Those subjects which are painful or "low" are either avoided or rendered into beauty. The same generalization is partly true of the poetic treatment of suffering or desolation, although this is a complicated matter. All art must treat suffering in terms of significance or beauty, lest it become intolerable and awkward. In seeing a play, we need to know that the suffering is feigned or we would be outraged; but more than that, the agonies of a Desdemona must be rendered so that we appreciate as well as understand them. An actress who can only shed tears when directed to will not move us. Shakespeare's portrayal of the plucking out of Gloucester's eyes on stage succeeds gloriously, but at a very narrow remove from wanton melodrama. We naturally expect the Japanese to treat suffering in poetry with an element of artistic distortion and beauty, and this they do more successfully than our poets. What is virtually lacking, however, is the significance of suffering. No Japanese poet would think of asking with Shakespeare of the Gonerils and Regans, "Is there any cause in nature that makes these hard hearts?" The Japanese interest themselves in cause and effect, but not in abstract philosophical causes. They treat what happens either in terms of the efficient causes or in terms of the happening itself. The world of flux, the resignation to it, and the attempt to detach oneself from such a world—these Buddhist concepts do not put a value upon energy or on grandeur, but upon the quality of experience.

These limitations of scope are explainable, then, on the basis of Japanese experience, a world view different from our own, and differing poetic tastes. But to explain them is not to explain them away, and the Westerner in a different culture may well feel that after all is said they remain limitations still. Fortunately, if the grandeur of our Miltons or the energy of our Drydens is not to be found in Japanese poetry, beauty is. We can appreciate this beauty and return to Milton, perhaps not having seen Japanese poetry as a Japanese sees it, but having seen it appreciatively. And this will be enough for most of us. But there is another kind of limitation, which is perhaps also one of scope, that we must consider before coming to more positive conclusions about the Court tradition.

4. *Japanese poetry has no poems of didactic, tragic, or epic greatness.* This charge is clearly one that combines the other three, although perhaps from a somewhat different point of view. Phrased in this fashion, the charge concedes that Japanese poetry may be great in one or more ways, but it alleges that its greatness is ultimately inferior to that of Western poetry.

Didactic poetry has been in bad odor for so long that some people may find Japanese poetry well off without it. We cannot agree, for after one has excluded the poems of Juvenal, Lucretius, and Milton, many of the best poems of Dryden and Pope, and a good deal of French poetry, the Western world is considerably impoverished of many of its characteristic works. Moreover, many Western works not primarily didactic—and by now it should be clear that we do not consider didactic poetry to be filled with tedious sententiousness, but to be poetry in which the poet informs or "teaches"—are characteristically Western in that they have didactic elements unknown, or at least unused, by Japanese poets. If one takes the "teaching" or serious moral purpose out of Dante, Milton, and Wordsworth, hell loses its terrors and Tintern Abbey its significance. According to medieval legend, Virgil was gifted with magical powers because he knew so much; and the Renaissance thought that one of Homer's greatest merits was that he taught the art of warfare. The legends surrounding the Japanese poets of over a millennium ago do not portray them as teachers. The two most famous of the Six Poetic Geniuses, Narihira and Komachi, were personally renowned for their physical attractiveness, their busy practice of love, and their ready wit. It may be said with some justice that our poets delight and teach while the Japanese delight and portray living.

There can be no doubt that the Japanese scholars and poets of the Court were learned men when much of Europe was shadowed in feudal darkness, but this learning is, in its relation to poetry, of a special kind. It is the literary learning of a Chaucer, that knowledge gained by poring over old manuscripts and collections of poems, both native and foreign. It is not the learning of history or science which will be useful for poetry, as on the other hand Chaucer's astrological studies were. When a Japanese poet was praised for what he knew, his knowledge was not abstract but of earlier poems. Poetry was not looked upon as an art that could teach useful facts, but as an art that could make men (and gods) feel. "It is poetry which, without exertion, moves heaven and earth, stirs the feelings of gods and spirits invisible to the eye, softens the relations between men and women, calms the hearts of fierce warriors," Tsurayuki wrote in his Preface to the *Kokinshū*; and however many meanings *kokoro* ("spirit" or "heart") may have in Japanese poetic criticism, it does not mean the disembodied intellect. By comparison to the Japanese, almost all our Western poetry, at least all poetry we consider great, is didactic. Occasionally, a Japanese poet like Okura, Yakamochi, or Sanetomo essays didactic poetry, but the ideas are not complex and the result is usually either tedious moralizing or sententious sentimentality. Perhaps some may argue that Japanese poetry is somehow "purer" for its avoidance of didactic elements, but when our impurities are those of Milton or Pope, it seems foolish to wish them away.

The absence of tragic or epic qualities in Japanese poetry can scarcely be denied: if we consider grandeur, conflict, and suffering to be the chief elements in tragedy and epic, we search for them in Japanese Court literature in vain. Even such a masterpiece as the *Heike Monogatari* shows no true tragic or epic qualities. Those it possesses are simply not developed or carried to the point of what we vaguely term the tragic or epic spirit. An example or two will illustrate what we mean. A climax occurs in the *Heike Monogatari* when, as they are defeated at the battle of Dannoura, the Taira heroes—Tomomori, Ienaga, and others—rush to their death in the sea (A. L. Sadler's translation, XI, xi):

And now the whole sea was red with the banners and insignia that they tore off and cut away, so that it looked like the waters of the Tatsuta [River] when it is flecked with the maple leaves that the wind brings down in autumn, while the white breakers that rolled up on the beach were dyed a scarlet colour. The deserted empty ships rocked mournfully on the waves, driven aimlessly hither and thither by the wind and tide.

This is a fine translation, for although of course it cannot convey the rhythms of the Japanese, the three images of leaves, dyed waves, and empty ships are carefully set forth. Yet the last sentence has been stiffened by demoting the final word of the Japanese, "How mournful it was!" (*kanashi-*

kere), to an adverb. And the waves are perhaps pink (*usukurenai*) rather than scarlet. These liberties are justifiable, but we wish to make the point that the effect in Japanese is more muted and there is greater stress upon the feelings. More than this, the metaphor of the leaves for the torn red banners of the Taira seems particularly Japanese. The colored maple leaves in the Tatsuta River had often been celebrated by the Court poets, and the image is here both appropriate and beautiful. It is this beauty—of the red leaves on the river, the waves, and even the ships—that is the dominant quality, and one that overrides pathos, suffering and the carnage of battle. Moreover, it is just this beauty which seems to us to soften the shock of conflict and, at least to the Western eye, diminish the grandeur of a story of epic proportions by employing something less than what we expect as epic treatment.

A comparable passage from Milton will show the difference. In Book I of *Paradise Lost,* Satan first awakes upon the burning lake; he stands and calls

> His Legions, Angel Forms, who lay intrans't
> Thick as Autumnal Leaves that strow the Brooks
> In *Vallombrosa* where th' *Etrurian* shades
> High overarch't imbow'r; or scattered sedge
> Afloat, when with fierce winds *Orion* arm'd
> Hath vext the Red-Sea Coast, whose waves o'erthrew
> *Busiris* and his *Memphian* Chivalry,
> While with perfidious hatred they pursu'd
> The Sojourners of *Goshen,* who beheld
> From the safe shore their floating Carcasses
> And broken chariot wheels, so thick bestrown
> Abject and lost lay these, covering the Flood,
> Under amazement of thir hideous change.

Like the banners of the Taira, the fallen angels lie upon the waves like fallen leaves, and like sedge, like the Egyptians, men and chariots, in the Red Sea. But there is little color here; instead, we see violent or agitated motion, floating bodies and broken chariot wheels instead of aimlessly wandering empty ships, waves filled with sedge instead of bright color, and most important of all, fallen leaves. The leaves in the *Heike* were bright and the allusive force to older poetry made them still more beautiful in their associations. Milton's leaves are "autumnal," but not bright (the next image of the sedge helps modify our impressions), and his point is intellectual. His leaves have fallen, just as Satan's legions have fallen, and both have left their source of life, God and the living tree. And his imagery echoes an equally active passage from the *Inferno,* itself an echo of the *Aeneid.* Both passages have qualities of the epic and of beauty, but where Milton's is the beauty of the epic, we may turn the words about for the *Heike*: it is an epic of the beautiful.

Very much the same holds true for the Japanese works that might have been tragic in English. In the *Tale of Genji,* Murasaki's death takes place, as it were, on stage, but the stage is really the mind and heart of Genji, not the platform before the reader's eyes. We do not so much experience her death as Genji's experience of it. This is fair enough, and Henry James would have felt no doubt that Genji is an admirably handled "center of consciousness." But what of the death of Genji? He dies between two volumes, and in between them, as between two pictures in the *Genji* scroll, trails a mist that symbolizes time, change, impermanence, and beauty. Like the characters in a Websterian tragedy, Japanese heroes often die in such a mist; the tragedy occurs, but in a periphrasis. Tsurayuki's poem on the death of Tomonori is an illustration (*KKS,* XVI: 838).

Asu shiranu
Wa ga mi to omoedo
  Kurenu ma no
Kyō wa hito koso
Kanashikarikere.

Although I know
My body is a thing with no tomorrow,
  Yet am I cast in grief
In the remaining twilight of my today
For him already taken by the dark.

Tomonori has died, but we do not know how, whether peacefully or in agony, violently or in sickness. Instead, the poem deals with the experience of an interplay of time, feeling, and images of darkness. The poem is a fine one, but the possibility of a tragic effect has been disregarded.

Other poems on such themes as death and time might be quoted, but all would show the same tendencies. The tragic experience is replaced by something else. Whatever this other experience is, it does not preclude the experience of suffering or a certain kind of greatness for which our critical vocabulary is deficient. We think, however, that if a distinction is made between the epic or the tragic on the one hand and the pathetic on the other, the difference is described about as well as it can be—if in the term pathetic we may include beauty and misery, delight and irony, and countless gradations of feeling unknown to, and unharmonized by, Western poetry. In this sense, pathos implies not self-indulgence in feeling or piteousness, but richnesses of feeling and tone, and—in a very broad sense—acceptance rather than struggle. Protest is indeed possible, but it itself implies acceptance; for it is the experience that is prized, not some notion that Heaven will repay the effort of reaching for more than may be grasped. We Westerners prefer the exhilaration of tragedy or the active sweep of epic to the fineness or depth of "pathos" preferred by the Japanese and Chinese. This difference no doubt helps explain why their literatures are basically lyric—or at least seem so to the Western reader. Such a qualification is clearly necessary, because this difference in taste and literary effect is clearly founded upon a more fundamental cultural difference. For if tragedy and epic are not to be found in these literatures, it is not because the poets were less ambitious than our own; it is because the attitudes that produce these genres are not those of the East Asian civilizations.

Violent as the theater and the military romances of feudal Japan were at times to become, there is nothing in the Court tradition like the extrusion of Gloucester's eyes in *King Lear* or like this passage taken at random from Richmond Lattimore's translation of the *Iliad* (XVII, ll. 616–18).

> [Koiranos] lost his life at the hands of manslaughtering
> Hektor,
> who hit him under the jaw by the ear, and the spearshaft
> pushed out
> his teeth by the roots from the base, and split the tongue
> through the middle.

The taboos—of certain words, things, and ugly sights like violent death—which survive from primitive times make it necessary to treat events such as this with indirection, lest one become ritually defiled. The primitive war songs are, therefore, rather pale beside the boasts of the Germanic heroes. Even Hitomaro addresses the body of the dead man on Samine in terms of polite address, using honorific verbs and pronouns, and it has been suggested that one purpose of the poem may have been to remove the possibility of ritual defilement. Such an attitude seems gradually to disappear from Japanese thought, although traces of it may still be seen today in Shinto ceremonies of ritual purification and even in the Japanese love of personal cleanliness.

If this early attitude was altered by any force other than the historical process of an advancing civilization, that force was Buddhism. But as the literature of the other great Buddhist cultures of India and China also shows, Buddhism is no more conducive to the tragic attitude than Shinto. The fatalism implicit in the concept of karma and the concept of this world as a place of change, impermanence, and illusion made the world a stage and man an actor in a drama that could not be tragic. And an even more crucial element in Buddhist thought is probably its concept of morality. With good and evil considered as complementary to each other, as the male and female principles or as light and darkness, and with morality considered not a matter of absolutes but one of relativism to possible varieties of situations, there is no possibility for a tragic issue to be drawn or a tragic choice to be made. Suffering is not so much a matter of choice or the result of a specific anterior action as a condition of life determined by one's forgotten behavior in a previous existence. When ultimate distinctions between good and evil are considered to be illusory, there is no metaphysic for tragedy. Stoicism has been called a confused philosophy, but the stoic attitude of participation in a world in which there is much to be endured and little to be enjoyed seems common to most Western tragedy. This attitude is surprisingly like and yet at bottom utterly different from the one inspired by Buddhism, for which asceticism is the better word. Resignation, detachment from a world of sinful illusion, and search for enlightenment make up the ascetic attitude. These ways of thought have produced literature in three great cultures, but they have not produced tragedy, and it seems perverse to expect that they should.

The difficulty in assessing Japanese poetry is one of steering between perversity and the equally repugnant notions of some anthropologists that every society has a "culture," and that the culture of one is as good as that of another because it serves the uses of the society which produced it. We at least do not choose to carry relativism to such an extreme. The few American Indian songs for rain and West Indies laments that we have heard seem to us far inferior to the Asian literatures as well as to our own. Such comparison between the literatures of the world's great cultures or—to use a less tainted word—of the great civilizations is more difficult. While acknowledging that to ask for a tragic attitude from a Buddhist-inspired civilization like the Japanese would be perverse, surely only the most enthusiastic Japanophile would say that the lack of tragedy makes no difference to him. It is bound to make a difference. And so, ultimately and as a whole, we do prefer our own poetry to the Japanese. But this is an ultimate choice and one which really need not be made. There is no reason why we cannot possess both, inheriting our own, and borrowing the Japanese. So that the task we face is less to define the limitations of Japanese poetry than to describe its achievements. This is not an easy task, since the Western critical vocabulary has been developed to describe its own literature. At this point the difficulties of critical analysis become heightened by what can only be called the difficulties of translation.

THE ACHIEVEMENTS OF JAPANESE COURT POETRY

Translation is a highly irregular, even questionable, occupation that has few unabashed supporters; for as Lord Chesterfield remarked, the only thing that does not suffer by it is a bishop. The difficulties as well as the irregularities of translation have led many to attempt to justify their occupation with the support of ingenious theories that might be quite dangerous if they were more to the point. Theorists to the contrary, there is this advantage in translating a poem: it is a practical act involving the solution of, or more often compromise with, specific problems and alternatives.

The kind of translation we must now attempt is not of particular poems, but of rendering the achievements of one literature clear by using terms invented to describe another. Yet this task has its own special excitement, and like all translation is performed no less earnestly because the difficulties may at times seem insurmountable. The real problem is clearly to find a workable manner of approach. There is no one key to the understanding of any poetry, whether Japanese or our own; but among the various alternative bases for analysis and comparison, it seems to us that the study of the Japanese poetic language is the most informative. Our analysis will be largely founded upon the premises we stated in the first chapter, and our comparisons will be chiefly with the language of English poetry. What we have to say will often be couched in terms of absolute differences, when in fact the differences are usually those of degree; but in these differences of degree and in gradations of importance attached to various elements common to poetry the world over lie the distinguishing features between two poets, two ages, two literatures. Without some cognizance of these gradations, a given literature seems monolithic and unvaried—so that a Japanese considering the disdainful ladies of Renaissance sonnets or the skylarks of Romantic poems would find it difficult to see any difference until he saw the significance of this variation and that alteration from familiar norms. The same is of course true of Japanese poetry to the untutored Westerner, and perhaps of all poetry to the Philistine.

Compared with Japanese, English is an abstract poetic language. Even those Japanese love poems of the late classical period that most nearly approach English in their generalization are still not vehicles of abstract thought in the sense that a typical English poem is. Our abstraction leads to the treatment of ideas, and our chief poetic predications are those of theme. The Japanese particularities and even generalizations primarily lead to the exploration of feeling and the discrimination of states of awareness; consequently, the important predications are those of tone and atmosphere. This distinction can best be understood by the use of examples, with the proviso that the only undistorted comparison which can be drawn is between Japanese poems in Japanese and English poems in English. Translate the English into Japanese and the very qualities one seeks to elucidate have for the most part disappeared; and the same is true of translations from the Japanese. The only possible alternative to this confusion is to quote the English poem in English, the Japanese in both transliteration and translation, and hope that commentary will remedy the distortions.

One of Shakespeare's "Dark Lady" sonnets (cxlvii) and a love poem or two of the late classical period ought to be reasonably comparable as poems on the misery of love. We shall choose two Japanese poems, one without imagery and one with some imagery to make the comparison more exact, and we shall begin with the sonnet.

> My love is as a fever, longing still
> For that which longer nurseth the disease,
> Feeding on that which doth preserve the ill,
> Th' uncertain sickly appetite to please.

My reason, the physician to my love,
Angry that his prescriptions are not kept,
Hath left me, and I desperate now approve
Desire is death, which physic did except.
Past cure I am, now reason is past care,
And frantic-mad with ever more unrest;
My thoughts and my discourse as madmen's are,
At random from the truth vainly express'd;
    For I have sworn thee fair and thought thee bright,
    Who art as black as hell, as dark as night.

A reductive paraphrase of the sonnet might run: "My love is a sickness so anxious to feed on its cause that my reason has left me to a passion apparent in my thinking you fair and good when you are dark and evil." Each step of the poem is based upon logic: the last two lines give the cause for the situation in the first twelve, where cause and effect are explored on the basis of ideas. Reason does the reasonable thing and love the passionate—the actors in this interior drama are distinct and their motivation clear.

Our first Japanese poem is one by ex-Empress Eifuku (*FGS*, XIV: 1355).

Itoioshimi	Though I alone am anxious,
Ware nomi mi oba	And do not wish to hate myself so much
Ureuredo	That I lose hold of life,
Kou naru hate o	Love and its extremities are things
Shiru hito mo nashi.	No other person knows about or cares.

One of the first things to be noted about this poem, as in other Japanese poems, is that paraphrase is extremely difficult. A reductive paraphrase would only specify the emotion: "I am miserable in the extreme." But this might equally serve for dozens of other Japanese love poems, Shakespeare's sonnet, and countless Renaissance complaints. Another sort of paraphrase would be, in effect, a second translation: "I am the only one who cares about me, and the only one who, loathing my emotions, yet is concerned enough to hope I do not die; but no one apart from me, least of all my faithless lover, really knows what my love is or what its sufferings entail, and no one even wishes to care." This paraphrase has at least the virtue of being specific, but it says nothing that has not already been conveyed, or should have been conveyed, by our translation. One feels no closer to the center of the poem. The third kind of paraphrase is not properly paraphrase at all, but a clarification of the situation: "A woman in love has seen her lover's visits grow less frequent and then stop; his vague protests have neither deceived her nor lessened her dependence on him; now that she suffers in isolation, he not visiting her and she unable to bare her shame to others, she hates herself and would almost wish to die, except that she feels a great wrong in her suffering for something others do not care about and cannot possibly understand." This is perhaps the most useful sort of statement about the poem, but it is less a paraphrase than a kind of headnote. It is not very different from those prose contexts used to introduce the poems in the *Tales of Ise*.

Why should paraphrase be so difficult for the Japanese poem when it is easy enough for Shakespeare's sonnet? It is not because Shakespeare is simpler or clearer. The answer is surely that paraphrase in English suits the English poem as it does not the Japanese. Our language permits us to reduce the sonnet to the play of its ideas, while the play of ideas is not central to ex-Empress Eifuku's poem. Perhaps one would accomplish more with the Japanese by specifying emotions: anxiety and self-hatred poised against a desire to live; love and limits of endurance; frustration and isolation. Such a succession as this is really closer to the experience of the poem, but one would have the same difficulty in applying this method to Shakespeare's sonnet that one has in paraphrasing the Japanese. These contrary methods work for contrary kinds of poetry to a point, because both poems deal with ideas and emotions. Yet the fact that one is centered on ideas and logic and the other on tone and feeling requires a different critical approach if one wishes to understand the poem.

Shakespeare's sonnet employs metaphors as well as abstraction, since Reason is the physician who gives prescriptions to Passion, who ignores them. Another poem from the late classical period will distinguish the effects of imagery in the two languages. This one is a love poem by Sanekane, and the speaker is a woman in somewhat less desperate straits than the woman in ex-Empress Eifuku's poem (*GYS*, XI: 1569).

Koishisa wa	In my suffering,
Nagame no sue ni	Longing takes on a shape far off
Katachi shite	At my reverie's end—
Namida ni ukabu	Floating in a blur of tears,
Tōyama no matsu.	The green pines on the distant hills.

In both poems, an abstraction is rendered vivid by virtue of metaphor. Having become a physician, Reason is entitled to write prescriptions and give over the patient when he refuses to follow medical advice. The personification works splendidly, because Reason was to Shakespeare the highest faculty, one that should guide, control, and correct the others, although in this instance Passion has usurped his role and made the whole body sick. In the Japanese poem, Longing takes shape. The question is what this longing is for and what shape it takes. The word we have rendered "longing" (*koishisa*) means something like "longingness" or "lovingness." It is the longing of love, of a woman in love who yearns for the man to come and keep his promises, to give her a return for her feeling. The shape assumed by such longing is a metaphor, or rather, a symbol. The shape is that of the pine trees she sees at a distance as she gazes blankly out in a reverie at dusk. (We know the time of day because of this poem's association with others in the immediate sequence, just as a good many more associations and feelings fill this poem by virtue of its place in a context of other poems in the anthology. We have disregarded these for the most part in order to simplify the discussion.) She hopes her lover will come, since it is the time of day when he should, but of course he does not. So longing takes the shape of the far-off stand of pines, which she sees at the end of a blank reverie. At the end geographically, since they are in the distance; and at the end temporally, since she has just seen them now, her vacant pensiveness over, when their green appears, blurred by her tears. As we have noted, for the Japanese, this color (a traditional association of pine trees as distinguished from certain other green trees) has a quality of masculinity, which here reinforces her misery. In contrast to Shakespeare's use of metaphorical abstractions to present the actors conflicting within the human psyche, Sanekane, like all Japanese poets, chooses primarily to convey the states comprising the experience. The quality of the experience interests him more than the forces in it, and the experience more than commentary upon it. English poetry employs a poetic language well suited to analysis, and the Japanese to a presentation of the experience itself. English poetry seems far more alert but mechanical, Japanese poetry passive but much more subtle in its awareness.

In discussing the apparent limitations of Japanese poetry, we remarked that it seemed deficient in energy and grandeur in comparison with the writings of our Drydens and Miltons. And this lack of spiritedness and elevation seemed to be one of the reasons Japanese poetry can lay claim to no epics or tragedies—at least as we know these genres. We wish now to attempt to say what it is that Japanse poetry does instead, what realm of human experience it takes as its province and how it explores and gives expression to this realm. It is at this point that we must put the greatest strain upon our Western critical vocabulary, but we feel that this attempt is essentially fairer to the Japanese and more useful to Western readers than the less fruitful search in Japanese poetry for things the Western mind would like to find or, failing to find, assumes cannot possibly be replaced by any other interest worthy of poetry. If our attempt succeeds, it will avoid that faulty logic attributed by C. S. Lewis to a certain Scot, who, upon learning that the Roman soldiers wore kilts, assumed they were Presbyterians; but more especially, it should prevent our assuming that because the Romans were not Presbyterians, they therefore had no religion at all.

Once again, our approach will be through the language. We have seen that the Japanese poetic language stresses particularities, emotions, and tone, while English is more concerned with abstraction, ideas, and theme. But that is only part of the difference. English poetry also stresses agents or actors, and therefore actions and responsibility for them. These are the staples of tragedy and epic. Macbeth does what is abstractly wrong and suffers as a responsible being. Aeneas is given the burden of carrying Trojan civilization to the Lavinian shore, and carry it he must, although he longs to stay with Dido in Carthage. Japanese poetry—not to mention prose—is different because the language is different. The problem has been put amusingly by one of the best Western translators from the Japanese.

"He showed his aunt to her room." A sentence that would not strike one as particularly good or particularly bad English. Hardly anyone would notice that it is half pronoun. But Japanese pronouns . . . are more obtrusive than English pronouns, and the same sentence in Japanese becomes: *"Kare wa kare no* oba wo *kanojo no* heya e" and so on. (Edward G. Seidensticker, "On Trying to Translate from the Japanese," *Encounter,* XI.)

The italicized words and particles make the Japanese something like, *"He his* aunt *her* room to . . ." And it is certainly proper to suggest that the Japanese pronouns clutter the sentence and simply would not be used in Japanese unless perhaps one were dictating to a lawyer. But the author's "and so on" omits something of over-riding importance, namely, the verb. And the omission of Japanese verbs and adjectives, for the poetry we are considering at least, is tantamount to the omission of the nouns in Shakespeare's sonnet or in the opening lines of *Paradise Lost.*

The matter is put more fairly in the same essay in an earlier passage, which begins with an imaginary conversation.

"You didn't!"
"Oh, yes, I did."
"But why?"
"Can't you guess?"

If this is a conversation in English between Maude and George, the properly introduced reader has no trouble in following it. But let us imagine that the speakers are respectively Maude, George, Aunt Margaret and Uncle John. An English writer must come right out and say so. In Japanese, however, a skillful use of verbs, plus an occasional pronoun, can make the conversation quite clear as it stands. It could go on for pages, as even Ivy Compton-Burnett could not, without overt reference to a speaker.

This description eminently suits Japanese fiction, and to a degree Japanese poetry, but it does not suggest what the classical Japanese novelist set before him as his aim, much less a poet centuries ago with a complex system of highly inflected verbs and adjectives.

Such a poet used nouns and, less frequently, pronouns, but the verbs and adjectives seem to us to show most convincingly the nature of his aims. His poetry deals not with actors and actions but states of mind and stimuli, and these convey perception and awareness rather than responsibility. In a typical love poem we are not told who is speaking to whom, not because this is unimportant, but because that much can usually be inferred and because the poet is more interested in the experience than in the person who is undergoing the experience. Surely Japanese poetry, if it is not unique in this respect, belongs to one of the few literary traditions in which the love poetry is not concerned with either the identification of the people in love or a description of them. One cannot imagine a medieval European romance without its interminable descriptions of the woman from top to toe. If an edition were published omitting the description and set pieces of characterization from *Antony and Cleopatra, Paradise Lost,* or the latest sentimental novel, not only would these works be far shorter than they are, but also the public would be scandalized. Perhaps the works would be unreadable. In a sense, our mystery stories are the typical product of our literature, and they are called "Whodunits" with good reason. We wish to know who is responsible for what act. And to follow the same terminology, Japanese poems are rather "Happens" and "Perceives."

To convey in English these qualities of states of mind and feeling, of awareness, and of perception is extremely difficult. The translator must indicate the who and whom, which immediately focuses the lens for the English reader and blurs the Japanese. A poem by Narihira serves as a good example of this difficulty (*KKS,* XIII: 616).

Oki mo sezu	I am at one with spring:
Ne mo sede yoru o	Neither sleeping, nor yet rising from my
Akashite wa	bed,
Haru no mono tote	Till night turns into dawn,
Nagamekurashitsu.	And through the day my love for you
	continues
	In listless looking at the ceaseless rains.

We should be somewhat more faithful to the words in the Japanese if we rendered the poem in another way.

As a thing of spring:
Neither sleeping nor rising up from bed
Till night dawns,
And through the day kept living
In listless looking at the ceaseless rains.

Such a translation means almost nothing as poetry—who, for example, is speaking? and about what? The languages are fundamentally such different vehicles of expression that the poetic aims and effects must perforce also differ. The problem is to elucidate Narihira's aim. Something of the poem's intention might be revealed by manufacturing a title that involves some statement of feelings or perceptions and some connection between them and the imagery. "Fascination and Apathy: Love in Springtime" might do as well as any. We must imagine that the speaker, a man, has sent this poem to a woman with whom he has been having an affair. He has not been visiting her lately, and the poem gives his excuse. He is fascinated by her and yet apathetic. Spring, a time of beauty and love, has not simply motivated him; it has permeated him completely. Night falls, and with its coming, the time to visit her is at hand. He stays sleepless in bed, but at home; dawn comes and he does not set about his business but gazes vacantly outside. He is living in *nagame*, the poem tells us. *Nagame* has three possible meanings, and all of them function simultaneously here. It means "thinking of love," as he is thinking of the woman—but from a distance. It means "a vacant reverie" such as spring has inspired in him. And by word play it means "long rains," the slow, close, continuous drizzle of late spring which is at once symbolically like the woman in the feeling it inspires, and at the same time—certainly from the woman's point of view!—utterly different. The poem is witty, for never was an eager woman more slyly turned down with a reason good but not quite good enough; and it is seriously ironic. For Narihira's Buddhism as for Wordsworth's transcendentalism, it is an admirable thing to understand Nature and to be in tune with it. But Narihira has not detached himself from the attractions of this world; the final ironic joke is one on himself—he really does love the woman and life more than ever, and yet the stimulus to this greater attachment has been so great that he is fixed by it and unable to do what it has inspired him to do. The poem is not easy in Japanese, but no such long periphrasis as this is necessary to make its point, as it is in a Western language.

Such exploration of states of mind and feeling, the stimuli that provoke them, and the awareness and perceptions to which they lead, are most readily available to a Western reader in the love poems. Perhaps this is because love is a subject of universal significance and appeal, while attitudes toward nature and human affairs may change from age to age and differ from culture to culture. At the same time, Japanese poems on natural subjects and on human affairs apart from love are of particular interest because they evoke states of mind, as even our love poems must to some extent, at an additional remove. This interposed realm is of course the natural scene, and the task of a Japanese poet, like that of a Western poet with different aims in mind, is to make nature seem significant for human experience. That the Japanese Court poets regarded this to be an important subject of poetry can be realized at once by the large number of poems they composed on seasonal topics. That they succeeded in their way is, we think, equally clear. To show the nature of their treatment, it will therefore be useful to re-examine several seasonal poems

454   THE TRADITION OF JAPANESE COURT POETRY

and poems on human affairs in which the element of love plays little or no part.

One of the poems on an autumnal topic in the *Shinkokinshū* (IV: 420) is Teika's on the legendary Lady of the Bridge of Uji.

Samushiro ya	For her straw-mat bedding
Matsu yo no aki no	The Lady of the Bridge of Uji now
Kaze fukete	Spreads the moonlight out,
Tsuki o katashiku	And in the waiting autumn night
Uji no hashihime.	Still lies there in the darkening wind.

Teika's poem is not strictly a seasonal poem, for there is a strong element of love in it; he has alluded to an anonymous poem in the *Kokinshū* (XIV: 689), in which the speaker is the lover, imagining how the Lady is even now spreading out her robe to cover herself as she waits for his impending visit. The earlier poem has that tender satisfaction one feels in knowing what the person one loves is doing at a given moment—something the lover shares with only his mistress. But another background is provided for the poem as well. Teika has alluded to the closing chapters of the *Tale of Genji,* chapters permeated by a sadness, a sense of an inability to achieve one's aims, even to make them clear to others. Teika combines this sadness with the tenderness of the earlier poem by treating them both with an ethereal beauty appropriate to a situation from the romantic past.

His Lady has only straw-mat bedding, or rather no bedding at all, to spread out. But perhaps what she does have is, if extremely sad, even more beautiful after all. She spreads out the moonlight for her bedding, and in such a wondrous atmosphere it is not she who waits, but the autumn night; and it is not the night that grows dark and late as the vain waiting continues, but the wind. Every natural image takes on a state that is different from our usual expectations—the moonlight and the night are given qualities of human emotion that of course they do not have. The effect of such treatment is freshness and a certain unearthliness of atmosphere. More important, the poem involves three persons (not to mention the characters in the works alluded to)—the lover who does not come and whose role is slight, the waiting Lady, and the speaker of the poem. For the Lady, the images combine in such a way as to express the integration of her experience of love and isolation with the beauty of the autumn moonlight upon which her body will rest, the night that waits with her, and the wind that darkens with the night and her own feelings.

We know of no existing critical term to describe the technique (perhaps the poem employs transferred and integrated metaphors or symbols in a context of allusion) or to describe the effect of the integration of the Lady's experience. The inclusion of the speaker in the poem creates more complex states of mind and feeling, for the handling of transferred metaphors is appropriate for him as well. He feels the Lady's experience, expressed so complexly, and for him the metaphorical fusion is further appropriate because all the elements of the particular situation merge with the reminiscences of the earlier poem and the *Tale of Genji*. Moreover, the poem is in one of the books of autumn poems in the *Shinkokinshū,* and we must take its topic, "The Moon," as the central subject of the poem. "What is most moon-like?" Teika seems to have asked, and to have given this as his answer. An autumn night with a beautiful moon and a wind are staples of the tradition, but in order to achieve meaning they must be made fresh and meaningful, as Teika succeeds in doing by adding a person who experiences the night most deeply and, one might almost say, is in turn experienced or absorbed by the autumn moon, and by creating a whole that is experienced in turn by the poetic speaker. To ask for a "meaning" in our moral or philosophical sense of theme is impertinent, since the poem has created a complex of emotions and perceptions in the experience of love, of times past and present, and of three different Ladies merging into one, and the whole complex illuminating what is essentially a conception of the autumn moon.

And yet it is instructive to compare this poem to similar English poems— to Keats's ode "To Autumn" with its similar subject but different technique, or to Dryden's "To the Memory of Mr. Oldham" with its similar techniques of allusion and a different subject. Neither comparison takes us very far, and it is this fact which is most instructive. Keats and Dryden are far more like each other than either is like Teika. As English writers they share poetic qualities which are so basic that we take them for granted and therefore overlook them. Such a line as Dryden's "Thy generous fruits, tho' gather'd ere their prime" might have been written by Keats. Other lines—"Where are the songs of Spring? Ay, where are they?" or "But fate and gloomy night encompass thee around"—have, one feels, the mark of their author on them. Yet all three lines are alike in being basically thematic, however filled with emotion they may be in context. Teika's *tsuki o katashiku* ("spreads the moonlight out"), on the other hand, functions to give us the feeling, quality, and very state of the experience without becoming emotional—in the sense of becoming intellectually stirred about emotions as Dryden, Keats, and our other poets do. Our poetry is apperceptive and self-conscious, the Japanese perceptive, conscious, and in a certain sense classical in its desire to portray experience as it is. The differences between Japanese poetry and our own are of course more easily felt than specified, and better specified than labeled. If labeling is necessary, then Schiller's *naif* and *sentimentalisch* may be applied respectively, in the light of his conception and of what has been said, to Japanese and Western poetry.

Our literary experience tells us that Dryden and Keats are very different poets, and it is only when we enlarge our field of reference that their likenesses emerge. Similarly, within Japanese Court poetry itself, Teika possesses a very marked and idiosyncratic range of styles; his father, Shunzei, is more conventional when treating the same general topics as that of the Lady of the Uji Bridge. Indeed, Shunzei seems to us to represent in his use of language and in his poetic aims what is essentially characteristic of the tradition. His best poems, the following poem on autumn among them, have the luster of rich perfection and an ease that seems to sound the very richest notes of his medium (*SKKS,* IV: 291).

Fushimiyama	Upon Fushimi Hill,
Matsu no kage yori	From this dark shelter of the pines,
Miwataseba	I look across the plains,
Akuru tanomo ni	Where in the dawn the ripening fields
Akikaze zo fuku.	Bend in soft ripples to the autumn wind.

What a lovely scene, we say, and wonder if it "means" anything. To understand it, we might first consider Wordsworth's splendid appreciation of a similar scene in "Lines Written Above Tintern Abbey."

> Once again
> Do I behold these steep and lofty cliffs,
> That on a wild secluded scene impress
> Thoughts of more deep seclusion; and connect
> The landscape with the quiet of the sky.
> The day is come when I again repose
> Here, under this dark sycamore, and view
> These plots of cottage-ground, these orchard-tufts,
> Which at this season, with their unripe fruits,
> Are clad in one green hue, and lose themselves
> 'Mid groves and copses . . .

The situation is remarkably like the one in Shunzei's poem, and again we may ask, "What do these lovely images mean?" In this case the poet himself tells us later that "these beauteous forms" have been ever present in his mind from a former visit, and have given him a "tranquil restoration"; they have helped him learn, he trusts, "the burthen of the mystery," to "see into the life of things." Perhaps he is wrong, but he thinks that this is the meaning of the scene; he recalls his unphilosophical pleasures as a boy in the same area and now believes he hears in nature "the still, sad music of humanity" and finds in the scene something to share with his beloved sister. We see of course that the re-experience of nature as an adult has led Wordsworth to an idea of the human condition and greater love for his fellow men. The poem is very moving—its changing cadences alone carry the play of the speaker's mind—but the attempt is one to give intellectual substance to an emotional experience, to get at the idea of Nature and to learn "the burthen" of man's mystery. It is a poem which searches for the secret idea that will explain our lives.

Shunzei's poem has no such meaning, if by "meaning" we imply an idea or the search for an idea. But when the poem is analyzed into its elements, we see that it attempts to create an illusion of the experience itself, and to convey predications about that experience. The objective images that make it up are presented in such a way that they are symbolic of the states of human response. The most obvious aspect of the poem is its series of parallel contrasts: near/far; pines/grain; shade/light. The speaker looks out from his vantage point over a wide, peaceful scene, and he is the one element that gives the contrasts unity, just as the contrasts are the elements of his experience. At this point our progress becomes more difficult, because we must move with the Japanese from these to us understandable abstractions—near and far—to tones and states. The time is dawn, and the scene Fushimi Hill. If it seems strange that the speaker should be there at that time, the place name should help us out. Its associations apart, the verbal constituents of *fushi-mi* mean "lying, seeing." These words imply that the speaker has slept through the night, or part of it, on the mountain, and is awake at dawn to view the scene described. He is lonely, even isolated, away from the capital, but these emotions are tempered by the pleasantness of the place where he has stopped and the beauty of the broad view lying before him.

The last two lines are still more difficult. The fourth line means something like "over the dawning surfaces of the fields." Like the speaker who watches, these fields dawn or awaken as part of an all-inclusive natural scene. By reddening in the dawn, the fields also contrast in color with the shadowed greens of the pines above. Only the last line sets the season; it tells us that the autumn wind is blowing, and we infer that the fields are of ripened grain. The image of the autumn wind is stressed by the emphatic particle, *zo,* as well as by its climactic position. The result of this stress is to make it the single unifying image, or at least the most important image, of the poem. This wind, an autumn wind, tells us that the grain now touched so lightly will soon be cut away, and since the pines above are an image of traditional association with wind, they and the speaker among them must also feel the effects of the autumn wind, even while on this specific occasion they represent a secure vantage point from which to behold the scene below. He, too, shares the end of all things natural. But to say this is to carry things too far, or to upset the poem's fine balance; for the scene remains beautiful, the speaker remains to appreciate it, and the moment lasts. It lasts, but with the reminder of the discomfort and loneliness of the preceding night and the threat implied by the stress upon the autumn wind. These states harmonize into a quiet balance that is as integrated as the images of the poem. Such a poem can, therefore, show us what is inferior by Japanese standards in Wordsworth's fine lines. Our poetry seems crudely lacking in feeling, unrelated or unharmonized, bald and didactic, and less a medium of representing experience than a busy bother to say what it means. The critical coin clearly has two sides.

Shunzei's poem harmonizes descriptive images and uses the natural scene in such a way that it achieves a significance for human affairs as well. Contrariwise, almost all of the poems dealing with human affairs show some concern with nature. The poem by the priest Jien on ship travel shows both this concern and the subtle play of states of mind and feeling we have come to expect (*Shūgyokushū* in *K. Taikei,* X, 740).

> Kajimakura   Pillowed above the oars
> Nezame ni fukaki   And deep in sleep until dawn breaks,
> Asaborake   I wake to find no ship:
> Yume mo ato naki   The one which bears my longings in the
> Fune o shi zo omou.   dream
>   Has borne me in the daylight from this
>   boat.

One of the striking characteristics of this poem is its combination of some of the techniques and interests of both the early classical and the mid-classical periods. The poising of states of awareness represented by sleep and waking, dreams and reality, suggests the earlier period, while the harmonious depth of tone suggests the later age. Such a backward look over parts of the tradition is helpful, because the poem typifies two ways of attaining a complex of states of awareness which is to Japanese poetry what forcefulness of thought— "meaning"—is to ours.

Jien's first line sets the situation. The speaker is on a sea journey, and the ship has no doubt anchored for the night in some inlet. Travel was hard for a courtier, both physically and, more important for poetry at least, emotionally, because it meant leaving the capital, and one's friends, family, and habitual interests for the uncertainties of voyaging to a wild provincial destination. These feelings are postulated by almost every travel poem. So that the question is what a poet can make of the materials, much as we wonder what Western artists will achieve with the subject of the Madonna and Child. The rest of the poem contrasts sleeping and waking: in waking the speaker is on a certain boat headed for a real place; in his dreams he sees still another ship which is bound for another destination. The dream-ship is invested with an attraction the real one does not have; the realm of appearance, the imagined world (perhaps we would call it the world of subconscious desire), is by far

Drawing of the priest Jien by Hishikawa Moronobu

preferable to the real world. So strong is this attachment that when the speaker awakes and finds that the dream-ship has disappeared, it seems that the real one has also. This is of course merely a way of stating the greater attractiveness of the ship he has dreamed of, the imaginary world. He still "travels" on the dream-ship insofar as his own desires are concerned, and his real travel on the boat on which he awakens is no longer real to him; the experience of the dream has been so intense that all of him that matters has disappeared with the vanishing of the dream.

Such a re-creation of experience is essentially a kind of psychological analysis, or if "analysis" is too Western in its overtones, a presentation of related psychological states. And as such it is not unlike much of our own medieval literature, which makes extremely subtle observations of the human psyche, even though the poets lacked our modern psychoanalytic terminology and advanced understanding of the workings of the mind. The Japanese poets differ from our medieval romancers in several ways, but the important poetic difference is one of technique. The great psychological studies of medieval poetry consist of either fine discussions of love and honor or allegorical analyses of the abstractly conceived elements that make up the human psyche. The poem of the priest Jien shows that the Japanese, on the other hand, work within the particulars of a realized situation. The states of mind and feeling conveyed by the poem are not abstracted or analyzed, but aroused by the stimuli of a specific situation. *The Romance of the Rose* gives the appearance of having happened nowhere—or to be something which may happen anywhere—while the Japanese poet begins with a specific situation founded in a more real world. This seems to us one of the most significant facts about Japanese Court poetry—in it the objective world is set forth in vivid detail, and the detail harmonizes in such a fashion that it conveys the states of mind and feeling that make up the human experience and awareness of it. Those readers who see in this poetry only a sensuous richness see but a small part. And those who look upon the images as being only vehicles of states of mind and feeling distort the poetry. For both are harmonized, and ultimately the poetic experience is such that subject and object are parts of one whole.

In this poem Jien has begun with the specific real world of ship travel, but the developing states of feeling soon take us into an imagined world of greater beauty. Such a better realm of experience does not represent a place to which one would escape if only one could, because the world of "dreams" is as real as this actual world which, at moments of intense experience, melts away as readily as the ship upon which the speaker of the poem travels. Another dimension reveals a second reason why the poem is not merely a pleasant piece of escapism. As we noted earlier, Jien's last line shows the reader that his poem is an allusive variation on one of the loveliest poems in the *Kokinshū* (IX: 409).

Honobono to	Dimly, dimly
Akashi no ura no	In the morning mist that lies
Asagiri ni	Over Akashi Bay,
Shimagakureyuku	My longings follow with the ship
Fune o shi zo omou.	That vanishes behind the distant isle.

The ship of the dream merges with the ship of this earlier poem, and the dream-world of our imaginations with the world of the past. The speaker of Jien's poem participates in the experience of the earlier poem, in which a ship has also disappeared into a dreamlike mist. The allusion deepens the tone in another way, since it brings a suggestion of love. The ship that disappears carries the longings of the speaker, because on it is a person he loves. Jien has intensified the loss by allusion, by making it happen in a dream, and by offering a parallel loss in reality. The various states exist at once: appearance and reality, both vying for the claim of greater truth; waking and dreaming; past and present; travel and love. The balance is so delicate and the harmony so complete that one can only speak of interrelated states of feeling and thought, presented as a perfect and unified whole.

We have analyzed a few poems at such length in an effort to show as best we can the functioning of Japanese Court poetry. If these poems do not convey the kinds of meanings typical of our poetry, this is not a sign of failure, but because it is the poets' aim to do something rather different. The difference can be understood by examining the various means by which Japanese Court poetry makes its predications and generalizations. The true significance of any literary work resides of course in the way it imposes order upon our experience. By providing us with an illusion of our world and by giving this imaginative world an order that true experience lacks, poetry helps our lives take on an order, a beauty, and a significance they did not have. Consequently, the predications made by poetry are those which invest experience with order and significance in the telling. Art is imperious in keeping us to the esthetic detail—to technique and the formal means of achieving order and beauty. Our aim must be to suggest formal means that create significance and beauty which lead to a fuller appreciation of a given poem or a given tradition of poetry.

English poetry (and Western poetry in general) possesses a splendid quality of openness even when it is most indirect. Burns's line "O my luve's like a red, red rose" suggests this openness at its simplest. Edmund Waller's song "Go, Lovely Rose" is somewhat less direct, but still involves open statement. Thomas Carew's "Ask me no more" treats the rose even more indirectly, but we still recognize the play of ideas. *The Romance of the Rose* renders experience almost wholly in terms of complexly related ideas, and this is even more true of Dante's multifoliate rose. In each case, the rose is a metaphor governing an idea; and no matter how difficult the poem, we feel that we need only find the significance of the rose—need only discover what it *represents*—and all lies directly clear before us. Because Japanese Court poetry utilizes the imagistic content of metaphors more fully, its predications are based upon what the images *imply*. This relative difference between the use of images for representation and for implication is the ordering principle behind the remarks that follow. Both representation and implication are essentially metaphorical, since both are ways of giving significance to a particular image, situation, character, or course of events.

The implications of Japanese poetry vary widely in importance and quality, just as there is a great distinction between the simple freshness of Burns's simile and the complex symbolic import of Dante's rose. The simplest form of Japanese implication may be called the particular or private, and is especially characteristic of the informal poetry written by the Court poets. We may imagine a hypothetical poem that says, in effect, "The moonlight is beautiful on the colored maple leaves in my garden tonight." In the absence of any complicating significance, we seize upon the word, "tonight." The particular or the private implication is clearly "Will you not come for a visit tonight?" And the nature of the visit depends upon the sexes, ages, and circumstances of the people involved. There is nothing about such a poem to make us feel that it deserves very much of our time, for the very privacy of the implication resents, as it were, our being concerned with the meaning of the poem. But such a poem does underline the basic technique of the poetry of the Court: it does not state, it implies. None of the poem's images represents an idea, but together they provide a suggestion. Thousands of such poems must have been composed every month during the heyday of the Court, and hundreds have survived. Each of them has its private implication that we understand today with the help of a headnote, by its position in a poetic sequence, by some hint it carries, or wholly by inference based upon experience in reading similar verse. Such poems were the staple of social intercourse, private as they were, and often give us a better notion of the sophisticated milieu of this society than of their author's literary talents.

Some of these poems of private implication stand out above the rest because they possess a richness that raises them above the level of a private message. The most common degrees of complexity are those of wit and allegory, often combined. Such a poem is Jūnii Tameko's ironic allegory that we have noticed before, with its explanatory headnote which we have paraphrased: "Sent anonymously to a lady who, too soon after her lover's death, became involved with another man" (*FGS*, XIV: 1334).

Hodo naku zo	How your whole heart
Nokoru katae ni	Was given to the blossoms that have gone!
Utsushikeru	But in no time at all
Chirinishi hana ni	You turn from those so freshly fallen
Someshi kokoro o.	To the one branch whose flowers yet
	remain.

This poem's appeal rests on witty malice put to good use. The fickle lady has got what she deserves, and the malice is all the more effective for the indirectness of the poem.

The poems of private implication that have this greater interest usually gain it by employing other forms of implication as well. Tameko's poem is a case in point, since her allegory is significant—it carries a charge of wrongdoing—only because it also makes use of what we must call traditional implications, the fixed associations or tenors of imagery. If there were no tradition that a person of sensibility regretted the cherry blossoms as they fall, even though in fact there might be some flowers still left on the tree, the poem would have no tone apart from that produced by the situation which led to its writing. But as it is, the fickle lady has violated the decorum of the traditional implications of certain imagery as well as the canons of good form in her private behavior. Such a piece of reproof could not be written in English, which has a different poetic method. One searches in vain in the language of modern English poetry for more than a few images that have any but the simplest traditional associations. A rose is a conventional image for a woman's beauty, but of so little use today that Gertrude Stein had to shout that it is a rose. One of the few images in English poetry that still suggests anything like the possible Japanese range between banality and richness is that of the nightingale. It possesses a range of association extending from the loveliness of its song to the legend of Philomela. This image has remained useful, although often with ironic alteration, up to the present time, and whatever its treatment, it carries a wealth of both classical and modern association. A poor poet tries to mumble the spell and fails; a Keats, an Arnold, or an Eliot uses the image to enrich his poetry.

The same is true of the Japanese Court poets, except that the greater amount of their imagery has such associations. These riches could be thoughtlessly squandered or put to meaningful use; and it is the nature of this use that is significant. If a young Western poet were to treat the nightingale for the beauty of its appearance, call its song happy, or personify the bird as a man, we would feel ill at ease. Our dismay would not really be factual but associational. Nightingales in fact are not lovely, but the poetic point is that their literary interest resides solely in their singing hidden at night. A person in a certain mood might find their song happy, but tradition holds otherwise. And while the song is the mating-call of the male bird, the Philomela legend will not allow us to personify the bird as a man. Such negative associations are the necessary complements to the positive ones, and as a result a Japanese Court poet needed to know a vast amount of poetry before he could possibly make use of the traditional imagery in a way not calculated to embarrass him and upset his reader.

Having learned his tradition, the Japanese courtier was free at last to show whether he had any originality as a poet, whether he could treat the traditional in a meaningful way. The line between the meaningless recitation of convention and the significant reshaping of it is not easy for an untrained outsider to draw. He is apt to make one of two contrary mistakes, either by assuming that the conventional is very fresh because it is new to him (as one unfamiliar with the literature of the American West might assume when he reads that an Indian "bit the dust"), or by failing to see significant differences in treatment of similar subjects (as an American tourist in Italy might foolishly insist that one Madonna and Child looks just like every other). A very good ear or eye and considerable experience are required to avoid these two mistakes. In reading the work of our hypothetical Japanese poet, we should look for three possible reshapings of the traditional. One is slight but meaningful alteration. Another is such skillful use of a body of traditional material that it comes to life with affirmation of the inevitability of its truth. The third can only be felt as a kind of supererogation, a rising above the tradition.

As a group, the innovating poets of the late classical period were perhaps most inclined to refresh tradition by means of alteration, as we can see from Tamekane's poem on the wind (*FGS*, IV: 398).

Matsu o harau	Ruffling down the pines,
Kaze wa susono no	The wind at dusk tumbles upon the grasses
Kusa ni ochite	Of the foothill plains below;
Yūdatsu kumo ni	The rain vies with the racing summer
Ame kiou nari.	clouds
	To be the first to bring the shower.

Tamekane makes use of the traditional associations of wind in that he has chosen for a powerful wind one that blows from the mountains. Because of the attribution of particular force to this wind, he need only mention the foot-hill plains to arouse these associations in a poem in which the moving air strikes everything with such force. But with this economy goes an alteration of diction in the three verbs that lends the poem its particular freshness. The image of a "ruffling wind" (*harau*: to touch violently and put into motion) is a Chinese idiom which lends a newness to a poem with traditional imagery. To say the wind "tumbles" (*otsu*: drop, fall) is to use an accepted verb, but unexpectedly, for the reader would expect "blow." And to have the rain vying (*kiou*: compete) with clouds is also a new expression. As a result, although every separate word and image is traditional, the effect of the combination is original.

Shunzei's summer poem shows how traditional images might be so inte-grated that they seem inevitably involved with each other in a rich experience (*SKKS*, III: 202).

Ame sosogu	A stir of breeze
Hanatachibana ni	Touches the fragrant orange blossoms
Kaze sugite	Glistening with rain,
Yamahototogisu	And the first song of the *hototogisu*
Kumo ni naku nari.	Floats from clouds that hang upon the
	hills.

Shunzei uses each traditional image in order to take advantage of its associ-ations. An early summer breeze is light and refreshing but not constant; and we are meant to sense its effect, blowing, bringing with it—and thus appealing to another sense—the fragrance of the orange blossoms. These glisten in a visual-tactile image, and Shunzei needs only a climactic final image of sound. His image of the *hototogisu* provides the climax, since it is a "mountain *hoto-togisu*," that is, the bird just come from the mountains and singing its long-awaited first song. The effect is almost to fill our senses to overflowing with rich images, an effect which Shunzei avoids by his presentation of the scene as a whole. Such threats as those of more rain, of the wind's blowing too hard or stopping altogether, and of the bird's not singing soon again make us value this moment in summer when nature has conspired, almost miraculously, to make its beauty perfect.

The really great poems of the tradition have freshness, inevitability, and something more. Shunzei's poem on the quails at Fukakusa or Narihira's poem on the seemingly changed moon and spring, to name but two, move the reader for reasons ultimately beyond the powers of analysis. They seem to prove for the first time the deepest truths about the images they employ and to become the tradition rather than parts of it. To follow this logic, the tradition itself is made up of somewhat lesser poems that vary from the quite ordinary to the extremely good; and of course, it is not fashioned in a day. The age of primitive song and even the age of Hitomaro were times of preparation, of experimentation leading to the later periods when the tradition became wholly mature. The experimentation continued, with frequent attention to China, throughout the eighth and ninth centuries, and when Tsurayuki wrote his Preface to the *Kokinshū* it was the sign that the tradition had come of age. Subsequent interest in the *Man'yōshū,* like our post-medieval interest in the ballads, could neither obscure the fact of difference nor change the traditional implications of diction and imagery reflected in the later poetry of the *Kokinshū*. To ignore the inheritance would have meant not only to deny history— an impossible attempt—but also to make a desert where once the Muses' springs had flowed.

In addition to the private and traditional implications of Court poetry, there are what may be called contextual implications. These are the associations and tenors that arise from the particular poem and its treatment rather than from tradition, and which have more universal significance than the implications of a private "message." We often find that the poet's particular vision goes beyond what might be suggested by the tradition alone. Such contextual implications are closest to the use of imagery and metaphor in Western poetry. W. B. Yeats's "Sailing to Byzantium," for example, employs the capital of the Eastern Empire only partly for its historical associations of art; we should hardly conceive of it as a country for "old men" or a place where poets might be metamorphosed into golden birds without the context which this poem as a whole provides us. But Yeats's images are again those of representation, as we have typified Western poetry, while the Japanese are those of implication.

Since most of the images in the poetry of the Court have traditional overtones or function as metaphors with traditional tenors, the implications rising from a particular context and distinguishable from this traditional weight of meaning must grow from images that are relatively neutral in tone, or that have a variety of possible tonal range, or that are combined in new ways. A completely neutral image is hard to find, and of course will yield little meaning. Such simple images as those of common acts like writing and speaking are neutral, but in implication as well as tone. Consequently we must study those images which are but relatively neutral. Yoshitsune's poem on the autumn wind at the ruins of the Barrier of Fuwa (SKKS, XVII: 1599) is a good example.

Hito sumanu	The plank-roofed halls
Fuwa no sekiya no	Of the barrier fort of Fuwa "The
Itabisashi	Enduring"
Arenishi nochi wa	Are emptied of their men,
Tada aki no kaze.	And in the ruin of all that was before,
	Only the rustle of the autumn wind.

The "plank-roofed halls" are relatively neutral; although they might have some associations of sturdiness and life at the frontier, the poet can use them here to represent in ruin the glories of an earlier age. Similarly, Fuwa, one of the three great barriers in the Nara period, has certain historical associations, but Yoshitsune has ignored these and played instead upon the meaning of the place and name—"The Indestructible," "The Enduring"—stressing the irony which grows from the discrepancy between the haughty name and the present ruin. These contextual implications are governed and given direction by the last line, for the men are no longer in those halls where only the autumn wind stirs. The word tada ("only") emphasizes the traditional sadness of the autumn wind, since if it is all that moves through the once busy fort, the place must truly be very desolate.

Certain other images have rather general traditional implications of beauty, but with no further designation of tone. These might be shaped in different ways, much as a poet today might write a poem on Byzantium whose particular associations differed from Yeats's. An image such as "white linen sleeves" (shirotae no sode, which is really a pillow-word usually followed by the image of "sleeves"), is capable of various associations and tenors. Tsurayuki's poem envisioning the girls of an earlier age setting out from Nara into the countryside treats the image as a beautiful one of the past which arouses the speaker's admiration and nostalgia (KKS, I: 22).

Kasugano no	Do those girls set out
Wakana tsumi ni ya	On some excursion for young shoots,
Shirotae no	That they so gaily beckon,
Sode furihaete	Waving their white linen sleeves
Hito no yuku ran.	Toward the green fields of ancient
	Kasuga?

In a typically complex poem, Teika uses the same image, treating it as one of beauty, but beauty mingled with sadness. The sleeves are white with dew and tears as the lovers part in the morning, and this whiteness is carried into their very bodies by an autumn wind symbolic of the death of beauty, love, and happiness (*SKKS*, XV: 1336).

Shirotae no	The white sleeves covering us
Sode no wakare ni	Glisten with the dew and, brightened by
Tsuyu ochite	our tears,
Mi ni shimu iro no	Are parted by the light of dawn;
Akikaze zo fuku.	And as we dress are shaken by the autumn wind,
	Which blows its color through our anguished hearts.

Both Teika's poem and Tsurayuki's have wider dimensions than may be immediately apparent; but at least they show how a single image may achieve a very different implication in context. The difference can be accounted for in large measure by the presence in the poem of other images with strong traditional implications—the fields of Kasuga or the autumn wind. At the same time, these traditional associations are themselves affected, in that they come to life in a context of images of less conventional association, just as having tired of hearing of Philomela's singing in sylvan shades, we feel that when Matthew Arnold has her sing in a particular place by the Thames, both the neutral image of the Thames and the traditional one of the nightingale have gained poetic life.

In Teika's poem about snow at dusk by the Sano ford (*SKKS*, VI: 671), neutral images, images of varied association, and a recombination of imagery are given life by their contextual associations.

Koma tomete	There is no shelter
Sode uchiharau	Where I can rest my weary horse
Kage mo nashi	And brush my laden sleeves:
Sano no watari no	The Sano ford and its adjoining fields
Yuki no yūgure.	Spread over with a twilight in the snow.

The image of the horse is neutral and those of the sleeves and the Sano ford are capable of varied association. Sleeves, for example, may recall the beauty of Tsurayuki's poem on the girls going to pick young shoots or the sadness of the lovers in Teika's poem on parting at dawn. The associations of the Sano ford are, however, the crucial ones for an understanding of Teika's technique. His poem alludes to an earlier treatment of the same scene by Naga Okimaro (*MYS*, III: 265), in which the rain (Teika's snow) falls so heavily that the traveler experiences extreme discomfort in not finding a single house (Teika's lack of shelter) in which to escape the downpour.

Teika's alteration of the original imagery changes the tonal implication from one of physical discomfort to one of a deep sense of isolation (the allusion reminds us that the area near the ford has been desolate of habitation and human beings for centuries); and it fuses with this sense of isolation the sense of beauty, for the snow on the ground and still falling is lovely in the fading twilight. The sense of time and motion is also crucial. The traveler is in motion and yet arrested for this brief artistic moment as he contemplates himself in his world. The snow has been falling and continues to fall, but his chief thoughts are of his horse and himself caught at a certain moment in a certain place, and he seems to be contemplating what has happened up to the moment rather than what will happen next. There is still some light left to show the beauty of the scene, and the threat of the coming dark remains, as it were, only at a distance.

And finally, the past of Okimaro's poem enters the poem in the same fashion that the horse and the traveler do, to be arrested by the movement, now one of beauty changed into lonely beauty, in a moment of stasis and impending change. In comparison with Western poetry, the poem is almost niggardly in its refusal to state or hint these relations of images, and time, and motion. In fact at face value the poem might seem to deny all we have said about the tonal richness of Japanese poetry. But if there are no statements, there are implications in abundance: residing in the allusion, in crucial images with traditional implications (such as that of twilight over snow), and in the integrated composition of the poem. The images are metaphorical, but they "mean" by implication rather than representation, and their meanings are tonal rather than thematic.

The private, traditional, and contextual implications that constitute the most immediate kinds of predication in Japanese poetry are conveyed primarily by means of diction and imagery, that is, by individual words and phrases. A less immediate but equally important kind of predication is accomplished by rhetoric and syntax, that is by the manner in which the individual elements of imagery and diction are integrated in a given poetic statement. It is no easy matter to generalize about rhetoric and syntax in Japanese poetry. For one thing, syntactical analysis is as yet a largely untried tool of literary criticism. For another, there is the problem of change within the tradition; the syntax of any century is different from the syntax of several centuries later. And finally, it is not easy to separate rhetoric from syntax: simple rhetoric is usually found with simple syntax, complex rhetoric with complex syntax, so that when a simple poem is judged to have certain special qualities of beauty or sincerity, one can scarcely say whether it is so judged for its rhetoric or its syntax.

Viewed from the standpoint of syntax, the relation of rhetoric and syntax to the larger implications of Japanese poetry is a question of the essential character—what may be called the genius—of the language. All the varieties of syntax in the successive periods we have delineated should not discourage our attempt to discover the essential character of the language: rather they are tributes to its flexibility, to the range of possibilities from which different generations chose. In every period, even at times when the borrowing of images, rhetoric, and subjects from China was most feverish, Japanese poetry remained irrevocably Japanese, largely because its syntax was so categorically different from the Chinese. Japanese Court poets might have admitted Chinese diction, but the introduction of Chinese syntax in any direct fashion was unthinkable. There was never any equivalent to Milton's Latinate syntax in Japanese Court poetry.

This is not to suggest that Japanese poetic syntax is inflexible, but that Chinese and Japanese are too unlike. In fact, the syntax of Japanese poetry seems basically more flexible than either Chinese or English. It is true that the syntactic patterns admissible were often circumscribed by convention, but then to compensate for this there was a large number of patterns. The number of long sentences built up from smaller units in a chōka is proportionately higher than in a comparable English form; and what is more striking, breaks in syntax or incomplete syntax are admitted far beyond English practice. Perhaps this is no more than to say that, unlike Chinese and English, Japanese is an agglutinative language whose potential variety falls somewhere between English and Latin.

A second point leads us to the kinds of larger predications the poets sought to make. The syntax of every language is complex enough to allow for choices; the choices actually made reveal a great deal about the nature of the poetry created. When Hitomaro chose to avoid almost entirely the use of grammatical topics and subjects in his poem "On Discovering the Body of a Man" (see pp. 97–98 and 143–46), he exercised a choice available to Japanese but not to English poets; and his choice was consistently followed by the generations of poets that succeeded him. To put the matter affirmatively, the relative lack of concern with grammatical subjects (and therefore with actors, acts, and issues of responsibility) was but the obverse side of an exploration of the experience itself by the more extensive use of verbs, adjectives, and impersonal noun-images. The result is a greater sense of immediacy; human actors do not intrude between the experience (whether in nature or in love poetry) and its perception to the extent that they do in English.

The business of Japanese poetry is, therefore, in certain major respects radically different from our own. The presentation of experience, rather than attention to those who are undergoing it, does not exclude human concerns: these enter at one remove, by implication, just as in Western poetry the experience is secondary to the actors' awareness of it. To a degree, therefore, the descriptive symbolism practiced by mid-classical poets is representative of the entire tradition of Court poetry. The experience presented is evocative (it would be too much to say it is always symbolic) of states of mind and feeling, and the meaning of the poem grows from the poising, the setting in conflict, or the resolving of such states. When the states are poised, as they so often are in Narihira's poems or in the poems of the mid-classical period that break into two halves, one imagistic and the other of generalization, the result is a poetry for which there is no real counterpart in English. When the states are in conflict, as in the poems of Ono no Komachi and many other early classical writers, the result is a poetry somewhat like the so-called dramatic lyrics of Donne and other seventeenth-century English poets, except that our poets usually employ clear successions of feelings, turnings-about upon the speaker's part, whereas the Japanese merely imply conflict by juxtaposing states of mind and feeling. When the poised states are resolved, as in the late-classical poems suggesting a metamorphosis of event or feeling or in the larger integrations provided by Hitomaro's irony and by allusive variation, the poetry is perhaps closest in nature to that of Dryden and Pope, in which such an inclusive controlling metaphor as the heroic is used to resolve the tensions created in the use of diverse subject matter. In none of the three cases, however, is the poetry of the two traditions altogether comparable on the basis of technical functioning.

If the syntactic medium given to the Japanese poets by their language allowed a choice between poetry with or without grammatical subjects and topics, they chose to explore the less overtly personal sides of poetry. Partly because of the choice, and partly because of the nature of the syntax from which the choice was made, a final point of contrast with the syntactic practice of Western poetry emerges. Poets writing in an agglutinative language and choosing to explore the grammatically nonsubjective realm of their language possessed a working syntax whose unusual fluidity was heightened by the highly vocalic, lightly stressed nature of the language. To direct such fluidity, they sought out a range of rhetorical and structural techniques—frequent caesuras, broken syntax, a degree of parallelism unthinkable in English, subordination, climaxes indicated by particles and inflections, and many other devices; but the devices must be viewed for what they are, means to restrain the natural fluidity of the language, not to render the poems stiff. The most "broken" poetry of the mid-classical period retains a surprising degree of liquidity within the scope of five lines. There is seldom the air of finality, of absolute beginning, of unquestioned ending that so marks our poetry; for the syntactic stops seem no more than pauses between glimpses of unfolding experience. The flow of events and the corresponding fluidity of syntax help explain why tanka by different authors could be integrated so naturally into the larger wholes of poetic sequences.

Far more than in Western poetry, Japanese poems end with an apparent or real syntactic incompleteness, with the suggestion that all has not been said, and more important, with a posing of two or more states in such a way that resolution is left to inference—or to further and yet further development in a continuing sequence of poems. Western ideas of the discrete nature of human experience demand conclusion: the hero must die, be married, or return to his Penelope. But Japanese conceptions of the continual flux of events insist upon the process of moments in larger wholes. The degree to which this is conveyed by syntax is clear, and it is noteworthy that one finds the same mirroring of the concept of human experience in the forms and prosody of Japanese poetry. There is no form that has the finality of the weighty Alexandrine with which Spenser concludes his stanzas or of the couplet that ties up a Shakespearean sonnet. And the chanting delivery which was practiced lent to any given poem the quality of being only a stanza that by virtue of its fluid syntax might readily overflow into another.

It can be seen that the means of expressing implications—diction, imagery, rhetoric, syntax, and individual structures—are the same expressive means as those employed by Western poetry. The difference is not in the kinds of means, but in their nature. Such differences help reveal larger as well as lesser kinds of implication; for the predications made by Japanese poetry also include those which we may call, in terms of our own civilization, the universals of human experience. The "universals" of Japanese poetry are not necessarily any more truly universal than such a persistent Western concern as the tragic struggle of man against his fate. But neither are they so exotic that a Westerner is excluded from an understanding of them. What those universals are can best be understood by beginning with general considerations and following them to particular poems.

The imperial anthologies seem to us to provide some hints of the more generalized implications of Japanese poetry. Both these collections and, in most respects, the smaller sequences ordered on their pattern, have a structure based upon two important groups of poems, the seasonal poems with which the anthologies begin and the love poems that may be said to begin the second half of the anthology. Doubtless no such implication was ever deliberately intended by the compilers, but it seems revealing that it is the seasonal and not the love poems which introduce an anthology. We know that in the *Kokinshū,* the first of these collections, the seasonal poems were considered to be the prime example of formal poetry and the love poems of informal poetry; and no doubt this fact accounts in large measure for their relative positions. But why should the seasonal poems achieve formal status first? A Western compiler who sought to make a topical anthology would surely begin first with human affairs, and probably in the order of birth, love, and death. Poems on natural objects would follow, with occasional poems perhaps ending the collection. This is not to suggest that the Japanese treat nature as something quite divorced from human affairs. Quite the contrary, but why should man be seen through the images of his environment before he is considered in terms of his most characteristically human roles?

No doubt various answers might be given. One might say that in Japanese poetry there is a greater tendency to study man in terms of the natural surroundings that set his place in the world; or one might say that man looms smaller in the Japanese view than ours. Both seem to be true, and it takes very little acquaintance with such Buddhist concepts as the unity of all natural life and the subjection of man to laws true of all nature to understand why. But to say only this would grievously distort the matter by over-simplification; the natural world is also affirmed for its beauty and its hospitality to man. The dominant tone of the seasonal poems is, after all, prevailingly much more optimistic than that of poems on such human affairs as love and travel. All in all, one may best say that the Japanese Court poets felt themselves far closer to nature in its beauty, in its changes, and in its constant laws than Western poets ever have. Wordsworth's sense of "the burthen of the mystery" is very vague, and he only hopes that it will be revealed to him. When he declares that a single impulse from the vernal wood will teach man more than all the sages have, we mark the abstract vagueness of his "impulse" and sense an agonized dualism of man the receiver and nature the sender that is far greater than any dualism in the Japanese. At the same time, however monistic Buddhism may be in theory, the practice of the Court poets shows a perhaps inevitably human sense of man's separate identity; for although man is involved in all natural life, only he has the capacity to observe the rest and experience it as a self-conscious being.

The results of such a relationship are certain discrepancies between the monism of theory and the dualism of experience too fine to be called conflicts and perhaps best termed ironies. Ki no Tomonori's poem "On the Falling Cherry Blossoms" (KKS, II: 84) can help clarify these.

Hisakata no   On this day in spring
Hikari nodokeki   When the lambent air suffuses
    Haru no hi ni   Soft tranquility,
Shizugokoro naku   Why should the cherry petals flutter
Hana no chiru ran.   With unsettled heart to earth?

To begin with, Tomonori affirms the beauty of the natural world. The cherry blossoms are so beautiful that he is distressed that they must fall. His distress is quite understandable because, to put the matter in Western terms, their fall seems unjust, seems to lack correspondence with the rest of nature on this day. All is perfect, or would be if only the blossoms might stay on the bough.

But Tomonori is well aware of the true nature of the problem, for when he speaks of the "unsettled heart" of the flowers, he is really speaking of the human observer, of himself. It is he who is out of touch with the natural laws of constancy in change. That his consciousness and desires are misdirected is an irony possible only if one holds at once a monistic concept of nature that includes man, and a dualistic sense of the separation between man and nature which may give rise to such failures to understand one's place. One further point must be made. There are three, not one, states of consciousness or awareness here. There is the consciousness of the lover of nature, of the person who regrets its change, and of the person or state of mind that encompasses both. For both are true: it is sad that the flowers should fall, and it is true that man should know they must.

Such a poem should show that the repeated celebration of a particular natural image—in this instance cherry blossoms—is not a quaint pastime of the Mysterious East. For the cherry blossoms are symbols of the greatest beauty of spring (a Japanese would say merely that they are the most beautiful thing in this season), and this is why their passing marks the loss of more than pink petals. And if their beauty passes, other things of less attraction and value, and even man himself, will also pass, according to the rhythm of nature's laws. This irony is only implicit and distant, but its distance indicates how deeply felt it is. Lest this last statement seem to be begging the question, we may again recall Hitomaro's poem, "On Seeing the Body of a Man" (see above, pp. 97–98). The poem begins with an overture in praise of the divinity and beauty of nature, especially of the Island of Samine, "The isle so beautiful in name." In name and also in actuality, but this does not prevent the dead man from having been thrown upon it to his death. Man is clearly helpless before a force like the storm. The narrator would gladly tell the wife and family of the dead man what has happened, but he does not know them. If the wife were there, she would pick for food what greens she could from the hillslopes in order to cook them for her husband. But, Hitomaro asks in his gentle irony, has not the season for such greens passed? Perhaps it has; but the season that has irrevocably passed is the season of a man's life. Nature is indeed beautiful, and the purposes that shape it are divine. But such beauty and such purpose include the death of man as well as the fall of cherry blossoms.

This ironic concept of nature and man's place in it helps explain why the beauty of evening, when day dies, and the beauty of autumn, when the year dies, are kinds of beauty that express states of mind and feeling tinged with melancholy. And yet "melancholy" or "pathos" (which we said Japanese poetry possesses instead of tragic and epic tones) are unsatisfactory words. We simply lack terms in English to describe such a poise of states of mind or to convey adequately what Japanese poems imply. Affirmation and acceptance tinged with ironic awareness, which do not exclude the possibility of wit, mark these tones. If classical Japanese was a very imperfect medium to express abstract ideas, modern English is not much better equipped, at least in its traditional literary vocabulary, for dealing with the poetry of the Japanese Court.

The love poems seem more complex than the seasonal poems, chiefly because Japanese courtly love is different from that of our own medieval past, but also because the seasonal elements are harmonized with them. To speak once more of irony, the love poems show an understanding that love, the most exalted state of human emotion and awareness, is also the least apt to endure. Again and again, happiness in love, or rather the experience of happiness, is called a dream, because it is but a moment in a continuous reality which is prevailingly inimical to such happiness. That this is so is due, once again ironically, to the very actors themselves. Man, who most needs love, is least capable of sustaining it. Moreover, the Buddhist suspicion of earthly attachments that interfere with salvation casts a shadow over such deep attachments as love. Desire is selfish, and Buddhahood requires renunciation of passion. This is the shadow cast by theory and theology, but the Japanese in practice sought less to renounce the world (as our Christianity would also bid us do) than to seek happiness in it. The play between the ideal and the natural impulse produced such a poem as Narihira's address to those about him (*KKS*, XIII: 646).

Kakikurasu	Through the blackest shadow
Kokoro no yami ni	Of the darkness of the heart I wander
Madoiniki	In bewilderment—
Yume utsutsu to wa	You people of this twilight world,
Yohito sadame yo.	Explain: is my love reality or dream?

The "darkness of the heart" is human passion, and the speaker admits that he is unillumined by religious light. But so real and intense is the experience of love that it cannot be an illusory dream. So he feels, and with an irony of his own, he turns on those in his world who would criticize him; of course they cannot answer his question—they are as much the creatures of darkness as he.

Japanese predications about time are so varied and so complex that no simple explanation of the generalizations made about them is possible. It is far easier to specify the orders of time that are treated, for of course it is not a matter simply of past, present, and future any more than in our poetry. The moment in itself, the moment in an eternal flux, the moment that transcends the flux; the past in itself, in comparison with the present, in fusion with the present; and other simple and complex orders of time are developed. It is easy enough to enumerate these variations, but the fact that Japanese verbs focus upon aspect rather than tense makes it much harder to explain how time is treated. The aspectual inflections of verbs may mean that in a poem one verb may be simply perfective, and another both durative and perfective. In English both verbs might emerge in past tenses, while one in Japanese emphasizes the perfection of an action and the other stresses a state now over. Most difficult of all are those poems in which the verbs are few or couched in simple indicatives and non-finite inflections. Shunzei's great poem on the quails at Fukakusa is an example (*SZS*, IV: 258).

Yū sareba	As evening falls,
Nobe no akikaze	From along the moors the autumn wind
Mi ni shimite	Blows chill into the heart,
Uzura naku nari	And the quails raise their plaintive cry
Fukakusa no sato.	In the deep grass of secluded Fukakusa.

The first line contains a conditional (*sareba*) that cannot be rendered so in English; the third line a participial continuative (*shimite*) which cannot be so rendered; and the fourth line a verb phrase consisting of *naku,* a non-finite indicative, and the poem's single finite verb, a simple indicative (*nari*), the copula used with the implication that "it is, but not right at hand where I can see it." Moreover, the last line has no grammatical, verbal relation to the rest of the poem. The copula is crucial, for it suggests a removal in space, and in time, of the natural scene from the speaker, and of course this removal is vital to a poem alluding to two older poems in a prose context of love. (See Chapter 6, pp. 298–99). The different orders of time are thus inseparable from the states of mind and feeling that accompany them; and although they often cast light on each other, the illumination is such that there is reflection with an increment of meaning back upon the light itself.

Man's involvement in time is rather different from his involvement in nature, although both evoke interrelated states of mind and awareness. Nature and man are inseparable, since man is part of nature; and yet man stands apart from nature. Time, on the other hand, is a force over which man has no control at all. He is its subject, and unlike nature, it is not subject to the same laws as he. As a result of this relationship, the consciousness of time produces a state of awareness and poetic tones that fall somewhere between melancholy and tragedy, an area comparable to that of the acceptance of our tragic heroes, if for their tragic struggle one substitutes degrees of awareness and acceptance. It is, moreover, extremely revealing that those Japanese poems which attempt to treat the subject of time most abstractly and thematically are the least successful. Okura's "Lament on the Instability of Human Life" (*MYS*, V: 804–5; pp. 133–35), concludes with a rather ponderous envoy.

Tokiwa nasu   How I yearn to be
Kaku shi mo ga mo to   Unalterably what once I was,
Omoedo mo   Immovable as a rock,
Yo no koto nareba   But because I belong to this world,
Todomikanetsu mo.   There is no stop to time.

The Japanese may be more graceful than our translation, but it is no more searching. Okura simply has not made the best use of his language and the potentialities of the Japanese literary sensibility. Narihira's most famous poem (*KKS*, XV: 747) is another matter.

Tsuki ya aranu   What now is real?
Haru ya mukashi no   This moon, this spring, are altered
Haru naranu   From their former being—
Wa ga mi hitotsu wa   While this alone, my mortal body, remains
Moto no mi ni shite.   As ever changed by love beyond all change.

Time is not specifically mentioned in the poem, nor is the theme of appearance and reality—or love for that matter. The first two verbs are non-finite indicatives (*aranu, naranu*) and the final one (*shite*) a participle. The speaker seems to remain unaffected by time, while the constantly recurring aspects of nature seem altered. But this is impossible, and it is the experience of love which has reversed what must be true: that man is subject to the changes of time while the moon and spring, which change more rapidly than he, are natural things that alone may be forever the same amid cyclic change. And yet both the seeming and the real are true, one subjectively, the other objectively; and time may have various kinds of reality, depending upon the experience of man which, however fleeting, may at certain moments of religious experience, or of love, or of other kinds of intense awareness, transcend it.

Such generalized implication is like the more technical implications of private messages, traditional associations, and contextual meanings in that it is not overt; and naturally the general predications grow from the technical ones. That Japanese Court poetry could achieve such indirection and complexity without falling into a gulf of obscurity—which is not to argue that a poem like Narihira's is for a moment easy—is due not to an inherently superior ability granted by fate to Japanese poets, but to a poetic method different in its functioning from our own. It seems to us that this difference can be best explained by repeating that the Japanese poets with their treatment of states and awareness explore the realm of tone, while our poets concern themselves with theme. This explanation holds, if to it we add that our poets also explore tonal depths on their way to expression of theme, and the Japanese use tone for thematic purposes. Comparison is, after all, most valuable not so much for the differences it reveals as for the way in which these differences enlarge our sensibilities. For the experience of reading Japanese Court poetry should bring us to a greater understanding of our own; and it should also strike us with an increased appreciation of the richness of the human mind and the possibilities of new and important experiences open to us by study of a literature different from our own. It seems wisest to us to conclude that Japanese Court poetry is at once different from our own and yet sufficiently similar that we may appreciate it and find that it illuminates our lives in ways that Western poetry does not. Such difference in similarity makes this poetry as valuable, as unique an element and illumination of our personal experience, and indeed of our culture, as it is also one of the world's great poetic traditions.

If the "discoveries" of poetry are different from those of science in that one does not replace another, this is reason enough to read the poetry written by Japanese poets over a period of some eight centuries. An American or European who does not understand his own English and Western tradition will not go far in understanding the Japanese. But by the same token, one who is aware of the possibilities of both will have greater resources and a richer formulation of experience than one who can lay claim to only one literature. And if one great literary work or cultural tradition does not replace but exists side by side with another, this is also true, although perhaps in another sense, of such literary studies as this.

Some people may raise the theoretical objection to our study of Japanese literature that Westerners may not really understand the works of another culture. The theory may be ultimately correct, but it is perniciously out of contact with the human enterprise. The only alternative to serious study, no matter how imperfect, is total ignorance, or the kinds of ignorance—rhapsodic exoticism and condescending disdain—which only contribute to the perverse survival of a distorted image of Japan. The gulf between the Japanese Court and us is certainly insuperable in absolute terms. But Matthew Arnold's dictum that it is the business of criticism to see the work as what in itself it really is clearly lies beyond human achievement. The day will never come when the West will have exhausted what it can know of Japanese poetry, even if every effort is made to do so. For our understanding of literature is unceasingly cumulative, and the changing experience of each generation will lead it to discover new meaning in all the great literary traditions. Just as the historical search is not a recovery of the past but an attempt to understand the past in terms of ourselves and in the light of what we can discern it to have been, so the literary search brings, not a recovery of the exact experience created centuries ago, but a re-experiencing of the creations of the Court poets in terms of our own awareness and also an extension of our awareness.

There is one thing more. It is futile to deny the existence of cultural differences: the quotation from Tsurayuki's Preface to the *Kokinshū* with which this book opens could not have been written by a Westerner. But the enterprise of civilization is, if not everywhere the same, alike in such means as society, religion, and the arts. It is the special province of literature and the other arts to enable the individual to transcend his time and place and to give him pleasure, to affirm the worth of human experience. For this reason we read—and for similar reasons men create—poems that others will not willingly forget. The most convincing explanation we know of why men write was given nine and a half centuries ago by the author of the *Tale of Genji* (pp. 501–2). Prince Genji is speaking of the art of prose fiction in eleventh-century Japan, but what he says applies to literature universally. He admits of change and difference:

> The outward forms of this art will not of course be everywhere the same. At the Court of China and in other foreign lands both the genius of the writers and their actual methods of composition are necessarily very different from ours; and even here in Japan the art of storytelling has in course of time undergone great changes.

But developing the thesis of Tsurayuki a century before—that men create poetry simply because their sensibility requires them to—Genji advances a "theory" about the impulse to literature which is universally valid:

> I have a theory of my own about what this art of the novel is, and how it came into being. To begin with, it does not simply consist in the author's telling a story about the adventures of some other person. On the contrary, it happens because the storyteller's own experience of men and things, whether for good or for ill—not only what he has passed through himself, but even events which he has only witnessed or been told of—has moved him to an emotion so passionate that he can no longer keep it shut up in his heart. Again and again something in his own life or in that around him will seem to the writer so important that he cannot bear to let it pass into oblivion. There must never come a time, he feels, when men do not know about it.

In such words, a half-century before the Norman Conquest, Japanese writers received their classic *apologia*. For the reasons voiced by Prince Genji, and in spite of the differences in literature "at the Court of China and in other foreign lands," we may share in the experience of the Japanese Court poets, finding in their works not a replacement or an inferior version of our own experience, but an artistic definition of the nature of all human experience by one of the world's great literary civilizations.

APPENDIX

Imperial Anthologies

AND OTHER COLLECTIONS OF JAPANESE COURT POETRY

The purpose of this Appendix is to give an account of the nature of the principal collections referred to in the study—the titles, compilers, numbers of poems, and similar information. Much of the information about the imperial anthologies is taken from Appendix E to the translation of the *Izayoi Nikki* in Edwin O. Reischauer and Joseph K. Yamagiwa, *Translations from Early Japanese Literature* (Cambridge, Mass.: Harvard University Press, 1951), pp. 131–35. The total number of poems in a given collection often varies with the manuscript chosen as the copy text. With the exception of the *Shinkokinshū*, the *Gyokuyōshū*, and the *Fūgashū*, our numbers are the same as those given in *Kokka Taikan*, or *The Great Canon of Japanese Poetry* (the numbers 1351 and 1748 of the *Shinkokinshū*, 1463 through 1471 of the *Gyokuyōshū*, and 36 through 45 of the *Fūgashū* are repeated in *Kokka Taikan*).

I

Man'yōshū. MYS. Collection for Ten Thousand Generations.

Twenty books (i.e., manuscript scrolls); 4,516 poems (the tanka envoys of the chōka are numbered as separate poems). The identity of the compilers and the date of compilation are uncertain. However, Ōtomo Yakamochi, generally considered the last to have edited the whole collection, died in 785.

There is no consistent system of organization. Sometimes a single author dominates a book, sometimes a single type of poetry. Some series are chronologically organized, some topically, and some on the basis of occasion. Poems or groups of poems are usually introduced by a headnote and sometimes are followed by footnotes. The notes supply such information as the author's name, the occasion, the form or genre, the source, and the manner of transmission, as well as stories about the poems and comments by the compilers.

The system of writing, the so-called *Man'yōgana* or "Syllabary of the *Man'yōshū*," commonly employs the Japanese version of the Chinese monosyllabic pronunciation for Chinese characters, using them as syllabic phonological symbols. Very often, however, the characters are used for their semantic value, and a given poem is likely to be written in a mixture of the two methods.

II. THE IMPERIAL ANTHOLOGIES

The Japanese names for the twenty-one imperial anthologies are: (1) *Chokusenwakashū* (or simply *Chokusenshū*), *The Anthologies of Japanese Poetry Compiled by Imperial Command*, and thus distinguished from "unofficial" collections and collections of Chinese poetry written by Japanese; and (2) *Nijūichidaishū, The Collections of Twenty-one Eras*. The Japanese often distinguish subgroups: the *Sandaishū, Collections of Three Eras*, made up of the first three anthologies; the *Hachidaishū, Collections of Eight Eras*, made up of the first eight anthologies; and the *Jūsandaishū, Collections of Thirteen Eras*, made up of the last thirteen anthologies. In the full title of all the imperial anthologies the word *waka* (i.e., "Japanese" poetry rather than Chinese) precedes the element *–shū*. Hence *Kokinshū* is in fact an abbreviation of *Kokinwakashū*. The period covered by our study ends with the seventeenth collection, the *Fūgashū*, but for the reader's convenience the other four are also listed.

1. *Kokinshū. KKS. Collection of Ancient and Modern Times.*

Twenty books; 1,111 poems. Ordered by Emperor Daigo (885–930; r. 897–930); completed ca. 905. Compiled by Ki no Tsurayuki, Ki no Tomonori, Ōshikōchi Mitsune, and Mibu no Tadamine.

Japanese Preface by Ki no Tsurayuki; Chinese Preface by Ki no Yoshimochi.

The first imperial anthology, the *Kokinshū* sets the general pattern for those which follow. Two groups of Books—seasonal and love poems—dominate the collection, dividing it in two. The pattern is: I–VI seasonal poems (I–II Spring, III Summer, IV–V Autumn, VI Winter); VII–X formal and ingenious poems (Congratulations, Partings, Travel, Acrostics); XI–XV Love; XVI–XX miscellaneous and traditional poems (Laments, Miscellaneous, in which no one subject predominates, Miscellaneous Forms, and Traditional Poems from the Bureau of Song). Later collections are also divided into two parts by the seasonal and love poems, although apart from this there are many variations.

2. *Gosenshū. GSS. Later Collection.*

Twenty books; 1,426 poems. Ordered in 951 by Emperor Murakami (926–67; r. 946–67). Compiled by the so-called Five Poets of the Pear-Jar Room: Ōnakatomi Yoshinobu, Kiyowara Motosuke, Minamoto Shitagō, Ki no Tokibumi, and Sakanoe Mochiki.

As its name suggests, this anthology presents the leftovers of the *Kokinshū*. As such, it is inferior in quality, and its interest lies in its lengthy headnotes, often composed by the compilers rather than the poets, and often providing fictional, narrative introductions to the poems.

3. *Shūishū. SIS. Collection of Gleanings.*

Twenty books; 1,351 poems. Ordered by ex-Emperor Kazan (968–1008; r. 984–86). Compiled by Fujiwara Kintō, whose manuscript was circulated with the unofficial title *Draft of the Shūishū (Shūishō)*. Present official collection believed to be a revision and enlargement by Kazan of Kintō's manuscript.

The collection is dominated by Kintō's preference for smooth, inoffensive styles, by attenuation, and by a conservative emphasis on poems and poets of the early tenth century.

4. *Goshūishū. GSIS. Later Collection of Gleanings.*

Twenty books; 1,220 poems. Ordered in 1075 by Emperor Shirakawa (1053–1129; r. 1072–86); completed in 1086. Compiled by Fujiwara Michitoshi, who also contributed the Japanese Preface.

In general the collection reflects the compiler's conservative tastes, its novelty lying in the large representation of women poets and in the re-emergence of descriptive poetry.

5. *Kin'yōshū. KYS. Collection of Golden Leaves.*

Ten books; 716 poems. Ordered by ex-Emperor Shirakawa; drafts completed 1124–27. Compiled by Minamoto Shunrai (Toshiyori).

One of the shortest collections, the *Kin'yōshū* was beset with many difficulties. Shunrai's radical tastes led the conservative Shirakawa to reject at least two drafts. The result is in general less advanced than Shunrai's own preferences, but the emphasis is upon contemporary and innovating poets; and if few radical poems are included, many are more descriptive than are the selections for earlier anthologies.

6. *Shikashū. SKS. Collection of Verbal Flowers.*

Ten books; 411 poems. Ordered in 1144 by ex-Emperor Sutoku (1119–64; r. 1123–41); completed ca. 1151–54. Compiled by Fujiwara Akisuke.

The *Shikashū* is the shortest of the anthologies; but although Akisuke was a member of the conservative Rokujō school, his tastes were eclectic, so that such innovating poets as Sone no Yoshitada and Minamoto Shunrai are well represented along with older and conservative poets.

7. *Senzaishū. SZS. Collection of a Thousand Years.*

Twenty books; 1,285 poems. Ordered in 1183 by ex-Emperor Go-Shirakawa (1127–92; r. 1155–58); probably completed in 1188. Compiled by Fujiwara Shunzei (Toshinari), who contributed the Japanese Preface.

The selections reflect Shunzei's catholic tastes for poems by conservative as well as innovating poets, by women (even a prostitute) as well as men. His standard—a poem must be the best of its kind—makes the anthology very representative, although contemporary poets are given greater prominence.

8. *Shinkokinshū. SKKS. New Collection of Ancient and Modern Times.*

Twenty books; 1,981 poems. Ordered in 1201 by ex-Emperor Go-Toba (1180–1239; r. 1183–98); first completed in 1206, various later revisions. Compiled by Fujiwara Teika (Sadaie), Fujiwara Ariie, Fujiwara Ietaka (Karyū), the priest Jakuren, Minamoto Michitomo, and Asukai Masatsune; but Go-Toba also took an unusual interest in the collection. Japanese Preface by Fujiwara Yoshitsune; Chinese Preface by Hino Chikatsune.

Like its model, the *Kokinshū,* the collection contains both old and contemporary poems; here they are mingled with consummate art. The best poems by contemporary poets display great subtlety of feeling and atmosphere, and show the slowly formed style of descriptive symbolism in its highest state. The *Shinkokinshū* is traditionally held to be the greatest of the imperial anthologies after the *Kokinshū.*

9. *Shinchokusenshū. SCSS. New Imperial Collection.*

Twenty books; 1,376 poems. Ordered by ex-Emperor Go-Horikawa (1212–34; r. 1221–32); probably completed in 1234 with later revisions. Compiled by Fujiwara Teika (Sadaie), who contributed the Japanese Preface.

The collection reflects Teika's late preference for poetry of a relatively plain, simple style.

10. *Shokugosenshū. ShokuGSS. Later Collection Continued.*

Twenty books; 1,368 poems. Ordered in 1248 by ex-Emperor Go-Saga (1220–72; r. 1242–46); completed in 1251. Compiled by Fujiwara Tameie.

This collection and the three that followed it were compiled by the conservative Nijō branch of Teika's descendants. Reflecting Tameie's conservative tastes, the selections in the *Shokugosenshū* are in general even but mediocre.

11. *Shokukokinshū. ShokuKKS. Collection of Ancient and Modern Times Continued.*

Twenty books; 1,925 poems. Ordered in 1259 by ex-Emperor Go-Saga; completed in 1265. Compiled by Fujiwara Tameie with Fujiwara Motoie,

Fujiwara Ieyoshi, Fujiwara Yukiie, and Fujiwara Mitsutoshi. The contributors of the Japanese and Chinese Prefaces are of uncertain identity.

12. *Shokushūishū. ShokuSIS. Collection of Gleanings Continued.*

Twenty books; 1,461 poems. Ordered, probably in 1276, by ex-Emperor Kameyama (1249–1305; r. 1259–74); probably completed in 1278. Compiled by Fujiwara Tameuji.

13. *Shingosenshū. SGSS. New Later Collection.*

Twenty books; 1,606 poems. Ordered in 1301 by ex-Emperor Go-Uda (1267–1324; r. 1274–87); completed in 1303. Compiled by Fujiwara Tameyo.

14. *Gyokuyōshū. GYS. Collection of Jeweled Leaves.*

Twenty books; 2,796 poems. Ordered in 1311 by ex-Emperor Fushimi (1265–1317; r. 1287–98); completed in 1313 or 1314. Compiled by Kyōgoku Tamekane.

This anthology and the *Fūgashū* (no. 17) are the two imperial anthologies compiled by the innovating Kyōgoku-Reizei branches of Teika's descendants. The *Gyokuyōshū* has more poems than any other imperial collection, perhaps because the compiler feared this would be the only chance to make an anthology reflecting the tastes of the Kyōgoku-Reizei poets.

15. *Shokusenzaishū. ShokuSZS. Collection of a Thousand Years Continued.*

Twenty books; 2,159 poems. Ordered in 1318 by ex-Emperor Go-Uda; probably completed in 1320. Compiled by Fujiwara Tameyo (compiler of the *Shingosenshū,* and a member of the Nijō line descended from Teika).

16. *Shokugoshūishū. ShokuGSIS. Later Collection of Gleanings Continued.*

Twenty books; 1,347 poems. Ordered in 1323 by Emperor Go-Daigo (1288–1339; r. 1318–39); completed in 1325 or 1326. Compilation begun by Fujiwara Tamefuji and completed by Fujiwara Tamesada, both members of the conservative Nijō line.

17. *Fūgashū. FGS. Collection of Elegance.*

Twenty books; 2,210 poems. Compiled between 1344 and 1346 by ex-Emperor Hanazono (1297–1348; r. 1308–18) and others. Chinese and Japanese Prefaces by Hanazono.

This anthology and the *Gyokuyōshū* (no. 14) are the two collections compiled by partisans of the innovating Kyōgoku-Reizei family lines descended from Teika. Both anthologies emphasize the styles of these poets, and this anthology may be considered the last of the great collections of Court poetry.

18. *Shinsenzaishū. SSZS. New Collection of a Thousand Years.*

Twenty books; 2,364 poems. Ordered in 1356 by Emperor Go-Kōgon (1338–74; r. 1352–71) at the request of the shogun, Ashikaga Takauji; completed in 1359. Compiled by Fujiwara Tamesada.

This collection and the three that followed it were compiled by members or partisans of the conservative Nijō line and show Court poetry in steady decline. The political eclipse of the Court is well shown by the part played in these last four anthologies by the feudal government.

19. *Shinshūishū. SSIS. New Collection of Gleanings.*

Twenty books; 1,920 poems. Ordered in 1363 by Emperor Go-Kōgon at the request of the shogun, Ashikaga Yoshiakira; completed in 1364. Compilation begun by Fujiwara Tameaki of the Nijō line and completed by the priest Ton'a.

20. *Shingoshūishū. SGSIS. New Later Collection of Gleanings.*

Twenty books; 1,554 poems. Ordered in 1375 by Emperor Go-Enyū (1358–93; r. 1371–82) at the request of the shogun, Ashikaga Yoshimitsu; first completed in 1383; revised in 1384. Compilation begun by Fujiwara Tametō and completed by Fujiwara Tameshige, both of the Nijō line. Japanese Preface by Nijō Yoshimoto, an important conservative critic and poet of the renga, or linked verses.

21. *Shinzokukokinshū. SZKKS. New Collection of Ancient and Modern Times Continued.*

Twenty books; 2,144 poems. Ordered in 1433 by Emperor Go-Hanazono (1419–70; r. 1429–65) at the request of the shogun, Ashikaga Yoshinori; completed in 1439. Compiled by Asukai Masayo, member of a family hereditarily allied with the Nijō line. Japanese and Chinese Prefaces by Ichijō Kanera.

III. OTHER SOURCES AND COLLECTIONS

As the Bibliographical Note indicates, there are many other sources and collections of Court poetry besides the *Man'yōshū* and the imperial anthologies. To a considerable degree these greatest collections are anthologies of anthologies, although none of the collections mentioned as sources in the *Man'yōshū* have survived. From the end of the early literary period, materials survive in increasing number and variety. The following are typical.

Ki no Tsurayuki, *Tosa Nikki. Diary of a Journey from Tosa.* A travel diary studded with poems.

Ariwara Narihira (attrib. author). *Ise Monogatari. Tales of Ise.* A collection of poems with fictionalized prose contexts.

Izumi Shikibu, *Izumi Shikibu Shū. The Collection of Izumi Shikibu.* A private collection.

To these must be added the records of poetry contests and poetic sequences, which survive in increasing numbers from the tenth century onward. Many of the private collections, sequences, and records of poetry contests can be found in *Kōchū Kokka Taikei* (*The Great Compendium of Japanese Poetry*), *Zoku Kokka Taikan* (*The Great Canon of Japanese Poetry, Continued*), *Gunsho Ruijū* (*Classified Series of Collected Texts*), and *Zoku Gunsho Ruijū* (*Classified Series of Collected Texts, Continued*), although good modern editions exist for only the most famous. The Imperial Household is currently sponsoring the publication of manuscripts that have been in its possession but unexamined for centuries, and as our references to the published volumes (*Katsura Series*) show, such lesser collections often illuminate developments in poetic taste and history.

Bibliographical Note

N<small>O SERIOUS STUDY</small> of any aspect of Japanese literature can be undertaken without reliance upon the many excellent standard editions of texts, literary histories, and critical writings of Japanese scholars. We wish to list here with a few words of comment the principal Japanese works we have drawn upon, together with certain translations and other works in Western languages from which we have quoted or which we believe to be of special interest to our readers. We have not attempted to give a bibliography *in extenso* of works on Japanese Court poetry. Representative bibliographies of important editions, compilations, monographs, and periodical articles may be found in such works as Asō Isoji, ed., *Kokubungaku Shomoku Kaidai* (Tokyo: Shibundō, 1957), a useful annotated bibliography of works on Japanese literature; and at the end of the chapters on waka in Hisamatsu Sen'ichi, ed., *Nihon Bungakushi* (6 vols. Tokyo: Shibundō, 1955–60), which is the most recent and up-to-date of several important histories of Japanese literature. New and important editions, textual and historical studies, and essays on many aspects of our subject continue to appear in great numbers. The Western student will find that among these abundant studies, some are more useful for his particular purposes than others, and perhaps a brief account of the history and concerns of Japanese literary scholarship relating to Court poetry is in order.

If scholarship is the effort to preserve literature and to render it intelligible to successive ages, then Japanese scholarship may be said to have an ancient and all but continuous history. The first collections of poetry were made some thirteen centuries ago; prose glosses and commentaries are but slightly younger. If by criticism we mean theories of poetry, canons of style, and literary judgments, Japanese criticism has a history dating back to the oldest extant anthologies. To a degree unknown in the West, the creators, readers, and critics of Court poetry were the same men and women. With the decline of the Court and of Court poetry in the late fourteenth century, there was for a time a parallel falling-off in scholarship and criticism as well. Rigid orthodoxy, haughty claims to poetic prestige by certain families, and futile conceptions of poetry as family property led the latter-day descendants of the great Court poets to preserve the great achievements of the past as secret—and lifeless—family treasures rather than to make them live anew. Consequently, in the later centuries of the feudal period the creative work of scholarship and

criticism was carried on largely outside the Court, among the classes of warriors, priests, and commoners—the classes that produced the important poets
of the renga and the greatest of the *Kokugakusha* or National Scholars of the
seventeenth, eighteenth, and nineteenth centuries. The National Scholars began the monumental task of reconstructing, re-evaluating, and re-interpreting
the literary heritage of the Court, beginning with the earliest chronicles of the
eighth century; if it is true that their nationalistic and sometimes naïve predi-
lections led them to some strange conclusions, it is also true that the best modern editions and detailed commentaries of such great collections of Court
poetry as the *Man'yōshū,* the *Kokinshū,* and the *Shinkokinshū* are based sol-
idly upon their accomplishment.

At the same time, many of the National Scholars, and certain influential
poets and critics of the early years of this century, have been hostile to the
reactionary schools of Court poets surviving in their day, criticizing them
sharply for clinging to their secret traditions without showing any signs of
poetic creativity. As the Court nobility gradually lost prestige and power,
most scholars assigned the sophisticated decadence they saw in their own day
to what had in reality been a vital culture centuries before: looking at the
corpse, they could not imagine the life it had once possessed. Such a prejudice
on the part of many National Scholars combined with their nationalistic, anti-
Chinese views to encourage them in their efforts to glorify the remote past before the great age of the Court and the New Learning from China—to seek
in the age of primitive song and a naïvely construed *Man'yōshū* the true, un-
adulterated products of Japanese literary and moral greatness. Their attitudes
have survived in different forms and among various groups down to the present day; they were particularly widespread during the years of this century
prior to World War II, partly owing to the Japanese experience of modern
nationalism and partly because confirmation for these views was easily found
in certain Western Romantic and post-Romantic ideals of primitivism, simple
directness, and artless realism.

This is not to suggest that the Japanese have failed to appreciate their own
best poetry. Such historical considerations help explain, however, why only
the three greatest anthologies—the *Man'yōshū,* the *Kokinshū,* and the *Shinkokinshū*—have been studied in detail by any appreciable number of Japanese
scholars, why it is that there are as yet scarcely any reliable exegetical commentaries on the other imperial anthologies or on most of the private collections of the poets. Moreover, the historic concern of Japanese literary scholars
with certain limited aspects and segments of the Court tradition helps explain
why such an important literary phenomenon as the integration of anthologies
and sequences by the principles of association and progression has only recently been rediscovered and remains as yet almost wholly unknown to students of literature.

But if the coverage of the whole range of Court poetry by modern Japanese literary scholarship has varied in range and depth, its volume has been immense and its achievements impressive. The greatest accomplishments—apart from the exegesis of texts—have been in the related fields of philological, textual, and historical studies, concerns that stem directly from the interests of the National Scholars. Virtually all of the major works of the "classical" past have been subjected to intense scrutiny: their authenticity, age, and authorship have been sharply questioned and vigorously debated; their original form, relation to other works, and growth as texts have been established with increasing precision; their linguistic and orthographic peculiarities have been isolated and explained. The increased technical skill shown in these studies derives in part from the influence of Western methods of textual criticism, in part from the experience of generations of Japanese scholars.

In addition to these concerns there is an admirable tradition of what might be called intuitive or taste criticism that derives from the diaries, miscellanies, and critical writings of the Court. Finally, there is a line of theoretical inquiry pursued by some of the most distinguished modern scholars—an effort to establish the meaning and essential character of such esthetic concepts as beauty and form, or to determine what is characteristically medieval about medieval literature—which owes a great deal of its nature and method to German conceptualist scholarship of the last century.

As for our own use of Japanese materials, since our overriding concern has been with the poetry itself, we have used secondary materials (apart from reference works) to a far lesser extent than editions of the great anthologies, private collections, records of poetry contests, and the critical writings of the Court poets, although we have of course been careful to consult the best literary histories and summaries of recent scholarship, drawing from them much valuable historical and factual information. Owing to the nature of our study, we have had least occasion to use the more theoretical writings of Japanese scholars. We do not question the value of such studies, but we have usually found them too remote from the problems of practical criticism that have claimed our attention. To say this is only to emphasize that we have used a modified form of Western literary criticism in our study—a method which has been largely untried as yet by scholars of Japanese literature in Japan. In a sense, then, we have relied continuously upon Japanese scholarship, without following it in some of its most characteristic methods and emphases. Our results have been closer to evaluations by Japanese of their poetry than might have been expected, although we have often appreciated the great writers for rather different reasons, even as some poems seem more or less significant to us than to the Japanese.

THE INTEGRATION OF ANTHOLOGIES AND SEQUENCES

The sections of Chapters 6 and 7 of this study dealing with the integration of anthologies and sequences of Court poetry and with the importance of the integrating techniques to the development of the renga present information which is so new and, we believe, important, that a special note seems in order.

We were first informed by Professor Konishi that techniques of association and progression were used to integrate poems in the imperial anthologies during the summer of 1957, when we were intensively studying the *Gyokuyōshū* and *Fūgashū* with him. He related to us how he had gained his first insight into the existence of such techniques from his renga teacher, the distinguished scholar Yamada Yoshio, who once casually observed to him that the poems throughout the *Shinkokinshū* are arranged for calculated artistic effect. Professor Konishi then set out to explore the practice historically and critically, planning to incorporate his discoveries in a lengthy study he is now completing on the development of Japanese literature, intrinsically and in relation to Chinese ideas and practice. Upon hearing of his findings, we urged him to write an essay on the subject that we might translate into English. He consented, developed in the course of frequent discussions with us those aspects of the practice that we felt would most interest Western students of literature, and graciously allowed us to adapt his essay with the same freedom that characterized our discussions of Japanese poetry with him. The results were published as follows: Konishi Jin'ichi. "Association and Progression: Principles of Integration in Anthologies and Sequences of Japanese Court Poetry, A.D. 900–1350," *Harvard Journal of Asiatic Studies*, XXI (1958).

As is stated in notes 2 and 26 of that article, Professor Konishi has been partially anticipated by two other Japanese scholars. Kazamaki Keijirō remarked in his *Shinkokin Jidai* (p. 79) on the similarity between certain techniques of association in the *Shinkokinshū* and in the renga. This brief observation was perhaps the first published insight into the use of association in anthologies and sequences of Court poetry and specifically into the integrated nature of the *Shinkokinshū*. Matsuda Takeo, in his *Kin'yōshū no Kenkyū* (pp. 13–48), noted the use of the techniques of association and progression and the consciousness of the imperial anthology as an integrated structure. He did not discuss the origins of the techniques, analyze them in detail, or relate the practice to that found in other sequences and to the renga. Professor Matsuda has since published another book, *Shikashū no Kenkyū* (Shibundō, 1960), which is a detailed study of the arrangement of poems in the shortest of the imperial anthologies, the *Shikashū*. At the time of writing he was still unaware of Professor Konishi's article, and he does not attempt in this book to relate his study of the *Shikashū* to the larger history of the imperial anthologies and the renga. Therefore, although it seems fair to say that the first published study of the origins, history, and practice of the techniques of integration and their relation to the renga is, as far as we know, Professor Konishi's essay, at least one other scholar has been working for some time independently on aspects of the subject. It is to be hoped that as the findings of Professors

Konishi and Matsuda become better known in Japan, other Japanese scholars will interest themselves in tracing in detail the history and practice of these important techniques.

PRINCIPLES AND FORMS OF CITATION USED IN THIS BOOK

Our general method of citation is set forth in the note on p. 5, but certain refinements and exceptions may be noted here.

1. References to such collections as *Kōchū Kokka Taikei* (*K. Taikei*), *Nihon Kagaku Taikei* (*NKGT*), and *Katsuranomiyabon Sōsho* (*Katsura Series*) include the title of the particular work quoted from, unless it is clear from the context. Thus "*Samboku Kikashū* in *K. Taikei*, XIII, 633" means that the poem in question is in the *Samboku Kikashū* (the personal collection of Minamoto Shunrai) and is printed in *Kōchū Kokka Taikei*, Vol. XIII, p. 633. "*Shinsen Zuinō* in *NKGT*, I, 116" means that the prose passage quoted or referred to is in the *Shinsen Zuinō* (a poetic treatise by Fujiwara Kintō), and is printed in *Nihon Kagaku Taikei*, Vol. I, p. 116.

2. References to *Zoku Kokka Taikan* (*ZKT*) give the number of the poem as indexed in that work. Thus: *ZKT*: 15,364.

3. The poems and songs quoted from works other than the *Man'yōshū* in Chapter 3 are numbered as in Tsuchihashi and Konishi, *Kodai Kayōshū* (*Anthology of Ancient Song*), not as indexed in *Kokka Taikan*. Poems from the *Ise Monogatari* are numbered as indexed in *Kokka Taikan*.

4. A list of all abbreviations used in the text is given below; imperial anthologies that are described in the Appendix, but from which we have not chosen poems, are not included.

Before listing the primary and secondary sources that we found especially useful or from which we have quoted, we should describe a few principles of bibliographical citation that we have adopted.

1. A work is published in Tokyo unless another place of publication is given.

2. Both Japanese and Western surnames precede given names.

3. Articles, reference works, and non-literary histories are not listed unless they are of unusual importance or we have quoted from them.

4. Translations from Japanese into Western languages are not given unless we have quoted from them, or they possess special historical or literary significance for Court poetry.

ABBREVIATIONS

MYS	*Man'yōshū*	*GSIS*	*Goshūishū*
KKS	*Kokinshū*	*SKS*	*Shikashū*
GSS	*Gosenshū*	*SZS*	*Senzaishū*
SIS	*Shūishū*	*SKKS*	*Shinkokinshū*

SCSS	Shinchokusenshū	K. Taikei	Kōchū Kokka Taikei
ShokuSIS	Shokushūishū	ZKT	Zoku Kokka Taikan
Ise M.	Ise Monogatari	Katsura	
GYS	Gyokuyōshū	Series	Katsuranomiyabon Sōsho
FGS	Fūgashū	NKGT	Nihon Kagaku Taikei

Bibliographical information for these works is supplied under the appropriate categories below.

SOURCES

One work is of such importance as an index for the *Man'yōshū* and the twenty-one imperial anthologies that it must be given special notice here: Matsushita Daizaburō and Watanabe Fumio, *Kokka Taikan* (*The Great Canon of Japanese Poetry*). 2 vols. Kyōbunsha, 1903, and often reprinted.

The reader should note that descriptions of the *Man'yōshū* and the twenty-one imperial anthologies can be found in the Appendix, pp. 481-87.

PRIMARY SOURCES

1. Collections and Indexes

A few major collections and indexes constitute the materials we have used most intensively. As we have noted, the two volumes of *Kokka Taikan* are indispensable as an index for the *Man'yōshū* and the imperial anthologies, but they contain other materials as well. Vol. I prints texts not only of these collections, but also of the poems in the *Kojiki,* the *Nihongi,* and the other chronicles and belletristic historical writings of the Court period, and of the poems in the principal diaries, miscellanies, travel accounts, and novels of the Heian period. The poems are printed and numbered in the order in which they appear in the original works. Vol. II consists of an index by lines, arranged in the order of the Japanese syllabary, to the poems in Vol. I. At the time the work was first compiled (1903), some of the materials indexed were not available in the best texts, and we have therefore in some instances (as with the *Kojiki* and the *Nihongi*) referred to better editions, provided we knew them to be easily available to specialists.

As a working text, Vol. I of *Kokka Taikan* is useful. Although the poems are printed in triple columns in rather fine print, this very feature is an advantage for sequential reading of the poems in the imperial collections and for the study of their techniques of integration; and although individual poems must be checked against more recent and reliable editions, the student will in general find that the more he studies Court poetry the more he will use this convenient work.

A second index also deserves special comment: Matsushita Daizaburō, *Zoku Kokka Taikan* (*The Great Canon of Japanese Poetry Continued*). 2 vols. Kigensha, 1925-26. Intended as a supplement to *Kokka Taikan,* this work collects the poems from the personal collections of more than one hundred important Court poets as well as poems found in certain unofficial anthologies and records of poetry contests. Unfortunately, the numbering system differs from the one in *Kokka Taikan*: the poems are numbered sequentially from the beginning to the end of the index rather than in separate series for each work. Since a total of 41,076 poems are printed, and the manner in which the numbers are indicated is somewhat confusing, the index is extremely cumbersome to use. It is not commonly cited by Japanese scholars, and although we have used it as a working text, we have for the most part not cited it.

Of the special collections devoted to the waka, the most important is: *Kōchū Kokka Taikei* (*The Great Compendium of Japanese Poetry, Collated and Annotated*). 28 vols. Kokumin Tosho Kabushiki Kaisha, 1927–31. In this work, Vols. I–XIV are devoted to the period covered by our study. A brief summary of their contents is as follows:

Vol. I: collection of ancient songs and poems, including the songs in the *Kojiki* and the *Nihongi, kagura, saibara, Azumaasobiuta,* and *rōei.*
Vol. II: the *Man'yōshū.*
Vols. III–VIII: the twenty-one imperial anthologies.
Vol. IX: unofficial anthologies and records of *utaawase.*
Vols. X–XIV: personal collections of important poets of the early and midclassical periods.

In addition, Vol. XXIII contains a rather sketchy and incomplete index of poets, which nonetheless provides some useful biographical information; and Vols. XXIV–XXVIII are a complete index to the poems. Although "collated and annotated," the texts are not wholly reliable, and the annotations are skimpy and occasionally inaccurate. We have, however, used the work constantly; not only does its format make it convenient to use, but more important, apart from the *Kokinshū* and *Shinkokinshū,* it contains the best available annotated texts of the imperial anthologies. In citing poems from personal collections and the like, we have used *Kokka Taikei* in preference to *Zoku Kokka Taikan.*

In the *Shinkō Gunsho Ruijū,* or *Classified Series of Collected Texts, Newly Collated* (24 vols.; Naigai Shoseki Kabushiki Kaisha, 1928–37), a modern edition of the older *Gunsho Ruijū,* Vols. VII–XIII are devoted to the waka. These volumes contain more than 400 separate items: private anthologies, personal collections of the poets, texts of utaawase, critical and polemical writings, and the like. Originally compiled by the great National Scholar Hanawa Hokiichi (1745–1822), a number of the items were copied from poor texts, and some are of doubtful authenticity, but as our citations in the text show, the collection is very valuable and we have used it extensively. The same may be said of the continuation, *Zoku Gunsho Ruijū* (19 vols.; Keizai Zasshisha, 1902–12), of which Vols. XIV–XVII contain some 200 items.

Representative of the exciting new materials currently appearing in Japan is the *Katsuranomiyabon Sōsho* (18 vols. to date; Yōtokusha, 1949–60). These materials were formerly in the library of the now defunct Katsura family of Princes of the Blood descended from Emperor Ōgimachi (1517–93), and are in the possession of the Imperial Household. When complete, the series will comprise more than a hundred items, largely waka, renga, and fiction. The manuscripts are mostly seventeenth and eighteenth century copies of much older works, but they are said to be unusually reliable, and many of them are unique copies of materials formerly treasured in the Imperial Family and noble houses and since destroyed or lost. We have found such personal collections as that of the "Yamada Priest" (II, 83–88) and the *Daini Takatō Shū* (II, 253–311) of extraordinary value for the evidence they give of survivals, cross-currents, and pre-figurings within the great periods of Japanese Court poetry.

The most important collection of critical and polemical writings and guides to composition by the Court poets is: Sasaki Nobutsuna, ed. *Nihon Kagaku Taikei*, or *Great Compendium of Japanese Poetic Writings* (6 vols.; Bummei-sha, 1935; recently reprinted; supplement by the Kazama Shobō). Vols. I–V cover the period of our study; they contain more than eighty items, of which a few are variants of the same texts. Valuable introductions to the individual works are provided in the prefaces to each volume, but there are no exegetical notes, and many of the texts are extremely difficult. We have, however, studied the most important of these works with the help of Professor Konishi, and have cited them extensively in Chapters 5–7.

Some of the other large series of classical texts contain good annotated editions of the most important anthologies and private collections, although different collections tend to duplicate the same items. The older *Kōchū Nihon Bungaku Taikei* (25 vols.; Kokumin Tosho Kabushiki Kaisha, 1925–28) contains in Vols. II and III texts of the principal diaries and *utamonogatari* of the Court period, and in Vol. XXV a useful index to all the Japanese poems that appear in the various prose works in the series. The more recent *Nihon Koten Zensho* (83 vols. to date; Asahi Shimbunsha, 1946–60) and the monumental *Nihon Koten Bungaku Taikei* (51 vols. to date; Iwanami Shoten, 1957–61) are collections of poetry and prose from earliest times to the mid-nineteenth century. They contain a number of items important to the study of Court poetry—editions of the *Man'yōshū, Kokinshū,* and *Shinkokinshū,* personal collections of certain major poets, diaries, *utamonogatari,* and records of utaawase. The separate volumes of these and similar series are edited by different people, and their quality tends to vary; but with respect to the *Man'yōshū,* for example, the *Nihon Koten Bungaku Taikei* edition (as yet incomplete, edited by the eminent scholar Takagi Ichinosuke and others) offers unquestionably the best text of the *Man'yōshū* produced to date, and also has excellent exegetical notes embodying the results of the latest scholarship. We have used the published volumes of this edition intensively in our study, and have listed it separately below along with additional works of this and other similar series that have been particularly helpful to us.

2. Single Works

(a) Primitive Period

We have used as our basic text for this period: Tsuchihashi Yutaka and Konishi Jin'ichi, eds. *Kodai Kayōshū*. Iwanami Shoten, 1957. In *Nihon Koten Bungaku Taikei*. This is the most recent and authoritative edition and is provided with excellent notes and commentary.

(b) Early Literary Period

The following excellent annotated editions of the *Man'yōshū* have been used:

Kubota Utsubo, ed. *Man'yōshū Hyōshaku*. 12 vols. Tōkyōdō, 1950–52.
Takagi Ichinosuke, Gomi Tomohide, and Ōno Susumu, eds. *Man'yōshū*. 3 vols. to date. Iwanami Shoten, 1957–60. In *Nihon Koten Bungaku Taikei*.
Takeda Yukichi, ed. *Man'yōshū Zenchūshaku*. 16 vols. Kaizōsha, 1948–51.
Tsuchiya Fumiaki, ed. *Man'yōshū Shichū*. 20 vols. Chikuma Shobō, 1956.

We are also indebted to the monumental study and exegesis of the poems of Hitomaro: Saitō Mokichi. *Kakinomoto Hitomaro*. 5 vols. Iwanami Shoten, 1934–40.

(c) Early Classical Period

Four annotated editions of the *Kokinshū*, particularly the detailed exegeses of Kaneko and Kubota, have been especially helpful:

Kaneko Genshin, ed. *Kokinwakashū Hyōshaku*. Meiji Shoin, 1927.
Konishi Jin'ichi, ed. *Kokinwakashū*. Dai Nihon Yūbenkai Kōdansha, 1949. In *Shinchū Kokubungaku Sōsho*.
Kubota Utsubo, ed. *Kokinwakashū Hyōshaku*. 2 vols. 11th printing. Tōkyōdō, 1957. Rev. ed. 3 vols. Tōkyōdō, 1960.
Saeki Umetomo, ed. *Kokinwakashū*. Iwanami Shoten, 1958. In *Nihon Koten Bungaku Taikei*.

*

Hagitani Boku, ed. *Tosa Nikki*. Asahi Shimbunsha, 1950. In *Nihon Koten Zensho*. An excellent exegetical edition of Tsurayuki's travel diary.
Minegishi Yoshiaki, ed. *Utaawaseshū*. Asahi Shimbunsha, 1947. In *Nihon Koten Zensho*. A valuable collection of the records of important poetry competitions with helpful notes.

Miyoshi Eiji, ed. *Kōhon Shūishō to Sono Kenkyū.* Sanseidō, 1944. A detailed study of the text of Kintō's *Draft of the Shūishū.*
Yamagishi Tokuhei, ed. *Hachidaishūshō.* 3 vols. Yūseidō, 1960. A modern edition, with biographical and other indexes, of Kitamura Kigin's (1624–1705) *Notes on the Collections of Eight Eras.* Kigin's annotations on the poems of the first eight imperial anthologies are so brief and sometimes misleading that the text is of limited value to the novice, but the indexes are very useful.

(d) Mid-Classical Period

We are indebted to the exegeses in three annotated editions of the *Shinkokinshū,* particularly to the detailed commentaries of Kubota and of Shionoi and Ōmachi.

Hisamatsu Sen'ichi, Yamazaki Toshio, and Gotō Shigeo, eds. *Shinkokinwakashū.* Iwanami Shoten, 1958. In *Nihon Koten Bungaku Taikei.*
Kubota Utsubo, ed. *Shinkokinwakashū Hyōshaku.* 2 vols. 9th printing. Tōkyōdō, 1946–47. The student should take special note that only the poems the editor attributes to the generation of the compilers are included in this edition.
Shionoi Masao and Ōmachi Yoshie, eds. *Shinkokinwakashū Shōkai.* Meiji Shoin, 1925.

*

Itō Yoshio, ed. *Sankashū.* Asahi Shimbunsha, 1947. In *Nihon Koten Zensho.* An annotated edition of the priest Saigyō's personal collection.
——. *Saigyō Hōshi Zenkashū.* Ōokayama Shoten, 1935. The complete poems of Saigyō.
Matsuda Takeo. *Kin'yōshū no Kenkyū.* Yamada Shoten, 1956. An important detailed study of the history and structure of the *Kin'yōshū.* (See the note on the principles of association and progression in the integration of anthologies and sequences above.)
Nose Asaji. *Roppyakuban Utaawase, Kenjō Chinjō.* Bungakusha, 1935. A good edition of the records of an important poetry competition, together with the official protest against the decisions of the judge, Fujiwara Shunzei, by the Rokujō poet, the priest Kenjō.
Sasaki Nobutsuna, ed. *Chūko Sanjo Kajinshū.* Asahi Shimbunsha, 1948. In *Nihon Koten Zensho.* An edition of the personal collections of some important women poets.
Saitō Mokichi, ed. *Kinkaiwakashū.* Asahi Shimbunsha, 1950. An annotated edition of Minamoto Sanetomo's personal collection.
Sekine Yoshiko, ed. *Samboku Kikashū no Kenkyū to Kōhon.* Meiji Tosho Shuppan Kabushiki Kaisha, 1952. A detailed textual study of Minamoto Shunrai's personal collection.

(e) Late Classical Period

Apart from the texts in the series and collections cited above, there are no important modern editions of materials from this period.

SECONDARY SOURCES

1. General

Hisamatsu Sen'ichi. *Nihon Bungaku Hyōronshi.* 5 vols. Shibundō, 1936–50. The standard history of Japanese critical concepts.

———, ed. *Nihon Bungakushi.* 6 vols. Shibundō, 1955–59. The most up-to-date detailed history of Japanese literature. Compiled from the work of many contributors, the individual chapters vary greatly in quality. Contains useful summaries of recent historical scholarship and bibliographies.

Konishi Jin'ichi. *Nihon Bungakushi.* Kōbundō, 1953. A highly stimulating essay on Japanese literature that contains much new information.

Minegishi Yoshiaki. *Karonshi Gaisetsu.* Shun'yōdō, 1933. A useful short history of Japanese poetic theory and criticism.

Ōta Mizuho. *Nihon Wakashi Ron.* 2 vols. Iwanami Shoten, 1949–54. A history of Japanese poetry from the theoretical point of view.

Takano Tatsuyuki. *Nihon Kayōshi.* Rev. ed. Shunjusha, 1938. A detailed history of Japanese song and its performance by a distinguished authority.

Tsugita Jun. *Kokubungakushi Shinkō.* 2 vols. Meiji Shoin, 1932–36. The most useful of the older, shorter histories of Japanese literature.

2. Special Studies

Doki Zemmaro. *Kyōgoku Tamekane.* Seikō Shobō, 1947. A short biography of the important late classical poet.

Fujioka Sakutarō. *Kamakura-Muromachi Jidai Bungakushi.* Kunimoto Shuppansha, 1935. A history of Japanese literature in the Kamakura and Muromachi periods.

———. *Kokubungaku Zenshi: Heianchōhen.* Iwanami Shoten, 1923. A history of Japanese literature in the Heian period.

Igarashi Tsutomu. *Heianchō Bungakushi.* 2 vols. Tōkyōdō, 1937, 1939. A detailed history of Heian literature.

Inoue Toyoshi. *Gyokuyō to Fūga.* Kōbundō, 1955. A very brief study of late classical poetry, but one of the few works on the subject.

Ishida Yoshisada. *Fujiwara Teika no Kenkyū.* Bungadō, 1957. A detailed biography of the great mid-classical poet Fujiwara Teika.

———. *Tonna, Keiun.* Sanseidō, 1943. Short biographies of two conservative late classical poets.

Kaneko Hikojirō. *Heian Jidai Bungaku to Hakushi Monjū.* Baifūkan, 1943. An important, detailed study of the influence of the Chinese poet Po Chü-i on Japanese literature in the Heian period.

Kazamaki Keijirō. *Shinkokin Jidai.* Hanawa Shobō, 1955. A valuable compilation of articles on the poetry, poets, and ethos of the age of the *Shinkokinshū* previously published elsewhere.

Kojima Yoshio. *Shinkokinwakashū no Kenkyū.* 2 vols. Hoshino Shoten, 1944, 1946. A detailed study of the history of the text of the *Shinkokinshū* and the circumstances of its compilation.

Konishi Jin'ichi. "Chūsei ni okeru Hyōgensha to Kyōjusha," *Bungaku,* XXI (1953). An important article on the relation between poet and audience in the classical periods.

———. "Chūseibi no Hi-Nihonteki Seikaku," *Bungaku,* XXI (1953). On the importance of Chinese concepts to the formation of the medieval esthetic.

———. *"Gyokuyōshū* Jidai to Sōshi," in Jōkō Kan'ichi, ed., *Chūsei Bungaku no Sekai.* Iwanami Shoten, 1960. On the influence of Sung poetry in the late classical period.

———. " 'Hie' to 'Yase,' " *Bungaku Gogaku,* No. 10 (1958). On the concepts of "coolness" and "slenderness" in the poetic of the renga and their relation to the ideals of mid-classical poetry.

———. "Kokinshūteki Hyōgen no Seiritsu," *Nihon Gakushiin Kiyō*, VII, No. 3 (1949). A valuable article on the importance of Chinese poetry of the late Six Dynasties in the formation of the esthetic of the early classical period.

———. "Michi no Keisei to Kairitsuteki Sekai," *Kokugakuin Zasshi*, LVII (1954). On the development of the concept of poetry and the other arts as a "way of life" in the medieval period.

———. "New Approaches to the Study of the *Nō* Drama," *Tōkyō Kyōiku Daigaku Bungakubu Kiyō*, V (1960). An article (in English) showing, among other things, the influence of the poetic ideals of Fujiwara Teika on the theories of the *Nō* dramatist Zeami.

———. "Shunzei no Yūgentei to Shikan," *Bungaku*, XX (1952).

———. "Ushintei Shiken," *Nihon Gakushiin Kiyō*, IX (1951).

———. "Yōembi," *Kokugo Kokubun*, XXII (1953). These last three articles are important studies of the major esthetic ideals of the mid-classical poets Shunzei and Teika.

Kyūsōjin Noboru. *Kenjō, Jakuren.* Sanseidō, 1942. Short biographies of two important mid-classical poets.

Man'yōshū Taisei. 22 vols. Heibonsha, 1953–56. A valuable compilation of articles by many scholars on various aspects of the poetry and life of the age of the *Man'yōshū.* Includes a reprint of the important index to the *Man'yōshū* originally published in 4 vols. by Masamune Atsuo, *Man'yōshū Sōsakuin* (Hakusuisha, 1929–31).

Minegishi Yoshiaki. *Utaawase no Kenkyū.* Sanseidō, 1954. A convenient survey of the history and extant texts of the poetry competitions.

Minemura Fumito. "Yūgembi no Keisei Katei," *Tōkyō Kyōiku Daigaku Bungakubu Kiyō*, I (1955). A study of the development of the ideal of mystery and depth in mid-classical poetry.

Murayama Shūichi. *Fujiwara Teika.* Sekishoin, 1956. A biography of Teika.

Nose Asaji. *Yūgen Ron.* Kawade Shobō, 1944. An important monograph on the history of the concept of yūgen.

Omodaka Hisataka. *Man'yō Kajin no Tanjō.* Heibonsha, 1956. Essays on the poets of the *Man'yōshū.*

Ōnishi Yoshinori. *Yūgen to Aware.* Iwanami Shoten, 1939. A study of two important esthetic ideals of classical literature.

Orikuchi Shinobu. *Kodai Kenkyū,* II: *Kokubungakuhen.* Ōokayama Shoten, 1929. A study of the origins of Japanese literature in folk custom and religion by a controversial scholar and poet.

Sasaki Harutsuna. *Eifuku Mon'in.* Seikatsusha, 1943. A brief sketch of the life of ex-Empress Eifuku together with her collected poems.

Sasaki Nobutsuna. *Jōdai Bungakushi.* 2 vols. Tōkyōdō, 1936. A detailed history of the literature of the primitive and early literary periods.

Takagi Ichinosuke. *Yoshino no Ayu.* Iwanami Shoten, 1941. Valuable essays on the social origins and literary characteristics of poetry in the primitive and early literary periods.

Takeda Yukichi. *Jōdai Kokubungaku no Kenkyū.* Hakubunkan, 1921. A short but distinguished study of early Japanese literature.

Taniyama Shigeru. *Yūgen no Kenkyū.* Kyōiku Tosho Kabushiki Kaisha, 1943. A monograph on the esthetic of *yūgen,* most notable for its chronology of the life of Fujiwara Shunzei.

Yamada Yoshio. *Renga Gaisetsu.* Iwanami Shoten, 1937. The most important single work on the renga.

Yoshizawa Yoshinori. *Kamakura Bungakushi.* Tōkyōdō, 1935. A useful history of Kamakura literature.

TRANSLATIONS, WORKS QUOTED,
AND OTHER WORKS IN WESTERN LANGUAGES

For detailed bibliographies of translations from Japanese literature into Western languages see:

Borton, Hugh, *et al. A Selected List of Books and Articles on Japan in English, French and German.* Rev. ed. Cambridge, Mass.: Harvard University Press, 1954.
Japan P.E.N. Club. *Japanese Literature in European Languages.* No pub., ?1957.

*

Aston, W. G. *Japanese Literature.* 2d ed. London: William Heinemann, 1899. A typical "Victorian" treatment of Japanese literature.
———. *Nihongi, Chronicles of Japan from Earliest Times to A.D. 697.* 2 vols. *Transactions and Proceedings of the Japan Society, London,* Supplement I, 1896. A pioneer translation, still a standard work.
Benl, Oscar. *Die Entwicklung der japanischen Poetik bis zum 16. Jahrhundert. Universität Hamburg, Abhandlungen,* LVI, No. 31 (1951). A study of Japanese critical and esthetic concepts based on the work of Hisamatsu and other Japanese scholars.
Bonneau, Georges. *Le Monument poétique de Heian: le Kokinshū.* 3 vols. Paris: Librairie Orientaliste Paul Guenther, 1933–35. Translations, of high quality, of the prefaces and famous poems of the *Kokinshū,* together with a romanized text of the complete collection.
Chamberlain, B. H. *Japanese Poetry.* London: John Murray, 1910. A typical "Victorian" treatment of Japanese poetry, but a pioneer work.
———. *Translation of "Ko-Ji-Ki" or "Records of Ancient Matters."* 2d ed., with annotations by W. G. Aston. Kobe: J. L. Thompson, 1932. Still a standard work.
Jenyns, Soame. *A Further Selection from the Three Hundred Poems of the T'ang Dynasty.* London: John Murray, 1944.
Keene, Donald, ed. *Anthology of Japanese Literature.* New York: Grove Press, 1955. The best anthology in English of older Japanese literature; contains fine translations of waka and of the first 50 stanzas of the renga "Three Poets at Minase."
———. *Japanese Literature: An Introduction for Western Readers.* London: John Murray, 1953. Stimulating essays on important aspects of Japanese literature, including poetry, by a recognized Western authority.
Lattimore, Richmond. *The Iliad of Homer.* Chicago: University of Chicago Press, 1951.
———. *The Odes of Pindar.* Chicago: University of Chicago Press, 1947.
MacCauley, Clay, trans. *Hyakunin-Isshu and Nori no Hatsune.* Yokohama: Kelly and Walsh, 1917. Perhaps the best of several translations of the popular short anthology, *Single Poems by One Hundred Poets,* attributed to Fujiwara Teika.
Miyamori, Asataro. *Masterpieces of Japanese Poetry, Ancient and Modern.* Maruzen Co. Ltd., 1936. Contains many poems by Court poets, often with helpful notes.
Nippon Gakujutsu Shinkōkai. *The Man'yōshū: One Thousand Poems.* Iwanami

Shoten, 1940. Good translations of a generous selection of poems.

Philippi, D. L. "Four Song Dramas from the *Kojiki*," *Orient/West*, Vol. V, No. 1 (1960).

———. "Ancient Japanese Tales of Supernatural Marriage," *Orient/West*, Vol. V, No. 3 (1960).

Pierson, E. J. *The Manyôsû.* 10 vols. to date. Leyden: E. J. Brill, 1929–58. The published portion of a projected complete translation of the *Man'yōshū* "from the linguistic point of view" and with some strange characteristics.

Reischauer, Edwin O., and Joseph K. Yamagiwa. *Translations from Early Japanese Literature.* Cambridge, Mass.: Harvard University Press, 1951. Translations of important works of the Court period with many helpful notes and appendixes.

Sadler, A. L. *The Heike Monogatari.* 2 vols. *Transactions of the Asiatic Society of Japan,* XLVI, 2 (1918) and XLIX, 1 (1921).

Sansom, George. *A History of Japan to 1334.* Stanford: Stanford University Press, 1958. This and the author's other distinguished historical writings that deal with the period covered by our study have been indispensable to us. Our terminal date (1350) practically coincides with that of this volume.

———. *A History of Japan, 1334–1615.* Stanford: Stanford University Press, 1961.

———. *An Historical Grammar of Japanese.* Oxford: Clarendon Press, 1928. A valuable study, particularly helpful to the student.

———. *Japan: A Short Cultural History.* Rev. ed. New York: D. Appleton-Century, 1943.

Seidensticker, Edward G. "On Trying to Translate Japanese," *Encounter,* XI (1958).

Tsunoda, Ryusaku, Wm. Theodore de Bary, and Donald Keene, eds. *Sources of the Japanese Tradition.* New York: Columbia University Press, 1958. A valuable compilation of translations, with excellent introductions, from important source materials in religion, philosophy, esthetics, and political and social thought.

Waley, Arthur. *Japanese Poetry: The "Uta."* Oxford: Clarendon Press, 1919. Line-by-line translations from the *Man'yōshū* and early imperial anthologies with notes on grammar.

———. *The Tale of Genji.* One vol. ed. Boston and New York: Houghton Mifflin, 1935. A beautiful translation of Japan's greatest novel by the distinguished translator from the Chinese and Japanese.

Yasuda, Kenneth. *Minase Sangin Hyakuin: A Poem of One Hundred Links Composed by Three Poets at Minase.* Kogakusha, 1956. A complete translation, with an introduction, of the best known of the renga.

Yokoyama, Masako. "The Inflections of 8th Century Japanese," *Language,* XXVI (1950), Supplement. A valuable descriptive study.

Yoshida Kaneyoshi [Kenkō]. "The *Tsuredzuregusa* of Yoshida no Kaneyoshi." Trans. George Sansom. *Transactions of the Asiatic Society of Japan,* XXXIX (1911). A complete translation of an important classic.

Glossary of Literary Terms

Many of the following terms are discussed in greater detail in the text; for references, see the Index. Cross-references within the glossary are indicated by words printed in SMALL CAPITALS.

AWARE: also MONO NO AWARE. Touching, pathetic, beautiful, moving the sensibilities, evoking the proper emotional response. Applied to those aspects of life and nature or their embodiment in art which stir the sympathies of the sensitive person of cultivation and breeding, impressing him with a deep awareness of the ephemeral beauty of a world in which only change is constant. Also applied to the person's response itself, which is usually one of bittersweet melancholy, although often combined with joy, delight, or awe. See also KOKORO, SABI, USHIN, YŪGEN.

AZUMAASOBIUTA. Songs for the Eastern Dances. Group of thirteen extant songs of varied ages and forms (including TANKA) sung at Shinto festivals as accompaniment to the so-called Eastern Dances. Although one or two songs are obviously late compositions by Court poets substituted for earlier primitive verses, most are primitive songs of eastern provincial origin containing some nonstandard dialect words. More primitive in form than the Poems of the East (AZUMAUTA), from which they should be distinguished.

AZUMAUTA. Poems of the East. Group of 238 tanka collected under this heading in Vol. XIV of the *Man'yōshū,* where they are arranged in subgroups by province. Contain many eastern dialect words and have a strong "folk" flavor, but their consistently regular tanka form is evidence either of revision by Court poets or of the spread of Court influence to the provinces. Takahashi Mushimaro (fl. ca. 730) and other Court poets who served as officials in the eastern provinces are believed to have had a hand in collecting and perhaps revising these poems. Group includes some Poems of the Frontier Guards (SAKIMORI NO UTA). To be distinguished from AZUMAASO-BIUTA.

BUSSOKUSEKIKA: also BUSSOKUSEKI NO UTA. Buddha's foot-stone poems. Poems in praise of the Buddha, in the form of tanka plus an extra line, i.e., six lines of 5, 7, 5, 7, 7, 7 syllables. Name derives from stele with a carving of Buddha's footprint, on the back of which these poems have been etched. The twenty-one poems on this stone are the only known examples of the form.

CHŌKA: also NAGAUTA. Long poem. Poetic form alternating 5 and 7 syllable lines, concluding with extra 7 syllable line. Although "long," extant poems are as short as 7 lines, and never longer than 149 lines. Often followed by one or more envoys (HANKA). Flourished during first half of 8th century.

DAI. Topic of a poem. Meaning of this term varies somewhat; in earlier times meant something close to "circumstances of poem," and later referred to the "fixed topic" assigned to participants in poetry competition or set by poet or others for poetic sequence or used in manner of title. "Composing on a topic" (*daiei*) came to be accepted practice for formal, elevated poetry, in which the dai functions as topic title, analogous to "On the Nightingale." Earlier, more situational dai are often like "When I visited . . ." and are more or less synonymous with KOTOBAGAKI or headnotes; the statement *dai shirazu* ("topic unknown") preceding a poem in the earlier imperial anthologies usually refers to the circumstances of composition. Critical disputes arose over dai: how conventional it was, how much it should represent the poet's own imaginative experience, and how far the poet might depart from the associations or imagery suggested by it. Dai cover the normal topics of Japanese poetry—elements of nature, travel, and the like. They are often compounded of two topics (MUSUBIDAI); may consist of fragments of Chinese verse (KUDAI WAKA); and even include such a category as "miscellaneous" (ZŌ).

DARUMAUTA. Nonsense poems (literally, "Bodhidharma poems" or "Zen poems"). Term of contempt used by conservative contemporaries of Fujiwara Teika for the more extreme attempts to express the quasi-Platonic "essences" (HON'I) of conventional topics (DAI) in startlingly unconventional ways. Reflects the hostility of the courtiers of the late 12th century and the early 13th century to the new Zen Buddhism. Carried to an extreme by lesser imitators of Teika, certain techniques such as reversed diction (TŌGO) as well as excessively ingenious approaches to the topic became conventional mannerisms (*irihoga*) associated with such poems.

ENGO. Word association. Relation of disparate elements in a poem by the use of a word that has or creates an "association" with a preceding word or situation, often bringing out an additional dimension of meaning and giving two expressions a secondary richness. For example, the association of *omoikiyu* ("fade away in grief") with *yuki* ("snow"), in which -*kiyu* ("fade," "melt") is brought to life by the image of snow, which in turn is made more specific, made to suggest both snow obscuring familiar objects in the landscape and snow about to melt.

HAIKAI. Unconventional verses, humorous verses. Found as a category in imperial anthologies as early as the *Kokinshū*, the term was applied generally to poems whose use of colloquial, foreign, or other unconventional diction, farfetched conceits, or overly ingenious word play created an effect of humorous unconventionality. Although the best haikai poems (*haikai-uta*) were considered suitable for inclusion in imperial anthologies, the genre was nevertheless regarded as an inferior species of poetry. Any poem, however serious in intent, containing indecorous diction was classified as haikai. The term was inherited by the renga poets, who applied it to RENGA containing humorous elements or unconventional diction, including Chinese loan-words, as contrasted with the serious (*ushin*) renga; such haikai renga were also known as MUSHIN ("careless," "not serious") RENGA. In the late feudal period, the term haikai was also used synonymously with HAIKU.

HAIKU. Seventeen syllable poem of three lines of 5, 7, 5 syllables. Derived from the first stanza (*hokku*) of the *renga*, and thus ultimately from the first three lines (KAMI NO KU) of the tanka. It emerged as an independent form in the late feudal period and was identified as such with the great 17th-century poet Matsuo Bashō, many of whose haiku were, however, composed as first stanzas for haikai renga. The term is a compound of the first element in *haikai* and the second element in *hokku,* both of which terms were used interchangeably with it until modern times. The most popular poetic form in Japan from the late 17th century to the present.

HANKA: also KAESHIUTA. Envoy. Envoys in the TANKA form to the body of a long poem (CHŌKA). Some chōka are accompanied by no envoys, others by one or more; the practice of adding envoys to chōka became standard during the early 8th century. Envoys usually function to complete the development of the poem, occasionally to demarcate another speaker or a change in tone.

HOKKU. First stanza. The first "stanza" of a linked poem (RENGA) in three lines of 5, 7, 5 syllables. Derived from the "upper verses" (KAMI NO KU) of the tanka. Often used as a synonym for HAIKU.

HON'I. Essential nature. Term used in widely different senses and contexts by critics of various periods and persuasions, but basically applied to the tone, atmosphere, and treatment considered most effective in conveying the essence or real significance of a phenomenon or experience. Thus, depending on context, it meant such things as the correct handling of a fixed topic (*dai*), the proper attitude to express toward a given subject, the decorous treatment of materials, and the quasi-Platonic "thingness" of an event or experience. Often used interchangeably with KOKORO, and sometimes with AWARE.

HONKADORI. Allusive variation. Echoing of the words, sometimes only the situation or conception, of a well-known earlier poem in such a way that recognizable elements are incorporated into a new meaning, but one in which the meaning of the earlier poem also enters, in a manner distinguished from mere borrowing and use of similar materials and expressions.

HYAKUSHUUTA. Hundred-poem sequence. The most common length of the poetic sequences; widely practiced by individual poets in the 12th and 13th centuries. The poems in such sequences were formal compositions whose fixed topics (DAI) often echoed in kind and arrangement the classifications of the imperial anthologies; the poems were sometimes integrated into a single lyrical structure by the techniques of progression and association. The integrated structure of one hundred units was adapted to the RENGA, whose standard length was one hundred stanzas. The sequences of twenty, thirty, fifty, and sometimes five hundred poems may be considered variants of the *hyakushuuta*. See also JI NO UTA.

I-P'ANG. Oblique style. Term applied by critics of the T'ang dynasty (618–907) to the style and techniques of elegant subjectivity and intellectuality characteristic of the poetry of the late Six Dynasties (ca. 420–589) in China. Adapted in modified form to Japanese poetry in the early classical period as the standard decorum for formal poetry in the Fujiwara style. See also SAMA.

JI NO UTA. Background poems. Poems in a smoothly conventional style used in HYAKUSHUUTA and other poetic sequences and in the imperial anthologies from the *Shinkokinshū* on as background against which were contrasted the more striking and elaborate "design poems" (*mon no uta*). The background poems were sometimes of inferior quality as well as merely conventional, but were nevertheless deliberately chosen for their faults, the better to enhance the effect of the design poems. The alternating waves of quality, interest, and complexity of technique provided by skillful alternations of background and design poems combined with the techniques of association and progression to create from the disparate poems in a sequence or anthology an integrated lyrical structure with artfully controlled rhythms, tensions, and changes of pace.

JIKAAWASE. Personal poetry competition. A variety of poetic sequence developed in the 12th century on the model of the formal poetry competitions (UTAAWASE). The poet selected his own topics, composed one or more "rounds" of poems on each, and pitted them against each other, sometimes ascribing the poems to fictitious characters. The finished sequence was often sent to a friend or patron for judging. A famous example is the *Mimosusogawa Utaawase* of Saigyō (1118–90).

JO: also JOKOTOBA, JOSHI. Preface, anticipation. A section of no fixed length preceding the main statement in the poem and related to it by connotative or metaphorical means in such a way as frequently to resemble a simile. Juncture of the two parts is usually made by implicit comparison and often by word play. Used mostly in the primitive and early literary periods.

JUKKAI. Expressing personal grievances. A topic (DAI) introduced into the poetry competitions and imperial anthologies in the 12th century. The topic is usually treated in terms of a lament by the speaker on his low estate or failure to advance in the world.

KAESHIUTA. See HANKA.

KAKEKOTOBA. Pivot-word. Rhetorical scheme of word play in which a series of sounds is so employed as to mean two or more things at once by different parsings. For example, *nagame* used to mean reverie (*nagame*) and long rains (*naga-ame*).

KAMI NO KU. Upper verses. The first three lines (5, 7, 5 syllables) of a TANKA, as distinguished from the *shimo no ku,* or last two lines (7, 7 syllables). The terms *kami no ku* and *shimo no ku* reflect the important concept of the tanka as a unit composed of two parts, and came into wide use during the mid-classical period, when there was a marked tendency to fragment the tanka into two rhetorically and syntactically distinct units marked by a strong caesura at the end of the third line. See also HAIKU, SHINKU.

KATAUTA. Half-poem. A fragmentary form of three lines of 5, 7, 7 syllables. Sometimes used in pairs for dialogue; suggests incompleteness when alone. Disappears after early times. See also SEDŌKA.

KOKORO. Spirit, feeling, conception. Together with KOTOBA, one of the two basic critical terms of Japanese Court poetics. Kokoro has wide range of meanings depending on the context, but may be translated "spirit" as opposed to *kotoba,* "materials." Thus kokoro embraces all aspects of tone and treatment, including theme, conception, atmosphere, emotion, meaning, personalism, technique, decorum, and originality or conventionality of treatment. Often used in the phrases *kokoro ari* or USHIN ("possessing *kokoro*") and *kokoro nashi* or *mushin* ("lacking *kokoro*"). See also HON'I.

KOTOBA. Materials, diction. With KOKORO, one of the two most important critical terms used by Japanese Court poets. Used in many senses depending on context, but may be translated "materials" in contrast to *kokoro,* "spirit." "Materials" included poetic diction, imagery, prosody, rhetoric, syntax, and beauty and elegance of phrasing and sound.

KOTOBA NO IRIHOGA. See TŌGO.

KOTOBAGAKI. Headnote. A note accompanying a poem and giving details of the circumstances, real or fictional, in which the poem was composed. Sometimes in Chinese, sometimes very elaborate and so providing a prose context, sometimes merely a statement of the topic (DAI), sometimes giving clues suggesting allegory. Headnotes precede poems. See also UTAMONO-GATARI.

KUDAI WAKA. Poems with Chinese verses as topics. Expansion or translation of a verse in a well-known Chinese poem by taking it as the topic (DAI).

MAKOTO. Truth. An important ideal of Court poetry, primarily in the late classical period. Represented to the innovating Kyōgoku-Reizei poets the ideal of penetrating to the "truth" of things, of treating nature and human experience with such careful observation of detail as to capture the essential reality of the subject. A development of the ideals of USHIN and HON'I of the mid-classical age. The ideal and its pursuit account for much of the quality of intensity characteristic of late classical poetry. The term is commonly used by modern critics in a very different sense to express the romantic-primitive ideals of naïveté, sincerity, and artlessness attributed to the poetry of the primitive and early literary periods.

MAKURAKOTOBA. Pillow-word. A conventional epithet or attribute for a word; it usually occupies a short, 5-syllable line and modifies a word, usually the first, in the next line. Some pillow-words are unclear in meaning; those whose meanings are known function rhetorically to raise the tone and to some degree also function as images. For example, shirotae no ("white hempen," "white linen") is the conventional attribute for sode ("sleeves").

MON NO UTA. See under JI NO UTA.

MONO NO NA. Names of things. A genre of acrostic poem in which the successive syllables of a "hidden topic" (kakushidai) were woven into the poem either as the first syllables of successive lines or extending over two or more words in a given line. Appears as a separate category of poems in the Kokinshū.

MIYABI. Courtliness, elegance. The dominant ideal of life and art throughout the Court tradition, but most particularly in the early classical period. In life the ideal implied the acquisition of courtly graces and accomplishments, sensibility, and good taste; in poetry, a strong tradition of decorous diction, avoidance of the ugly, and the basic congeries of subjective techniques inherited by generations of Court poets from the early classical age. See also SAMA.

MUSHIN. Careless, not serious, comic. The unconventional RENGA or HAIKAI as opposed to the serious (USHIN) renga. The presence or absence of humor was one important difference between the two genres, but the primary distinction was one of unconventional versus conventional diction: *mushin renga* used with relative freedom such unconventional language as Chinese loan-words, slang, and "ugly" images—all taboo in the serious waka and renga. Term also used as the negative of *kokoro ari* or *ushin* in the waka.

MUSUBIDAI. Compound topic. A poetic topic (DAI) employing two or more substantive elements: e.g., Love in the Mountains; A Temple Bell at a Village in Autumn. Often given in Chinese characters and syntax, so resembling KUDAI WAKA.

NAGAUTA. See CHŌKA.

NŌ. Aristocratic drama which developed during the 14th century, reaching its highest achievement in the work of Zeami (Seami) Motokiyo (1363–1443). Although largely patronized by the feudal nobility, its language and esthetic ideals, and many of its themes, materials, and techniques were derived from Court poetry.

ONIHISHIGITEI. Style of demon-quelling force. One of the ten styles or TEI enumerated by Fujiwara Teika (1162–1241) in his essay on poetics, the *Maigetsushō*. Apparently referred to the treatment of natural subjects with what Teika regarded as overly powerful or violent imagery, as in some poems in the *Man'yōshū* and in some of the most celebrated poems in the Man'yō style by Teika's pupil Minamoto Sanetomo. Recognized by Teika as an acceptable style, but not one of the best and not for amateurs.

RENGA. Linked verses. Historically two different forms, both involving more than one author. The earlier form, called *tanrenga*, or "short *renga*," is a TANKA whose first three lines were composed by one poet, and last two lines by another; examples are found in the *Man'yōshū* and included under the rubric "renga" in the *Kin'yōshū*. In the later form, dating from the 14th century, several authors would compose a sequence of usually a hundred sections or stanzas, alternately of 5, 7, 5 and 7, 7 syllables. The practice of composing renga was governed by extremely numerous and complex rules involving the proper techniques of progression and association, the use of certain images and grammatical forms at certain points, and the like. Most of the rules were codified by the *renga* poets from the implicit practice of Court poetry, to whose conventions the serious renga closely adhered, whereas the distinctive character of the haikai renga lay in its divergence from the conventions. See also HAIKAI, HYAKUSHUUTA, KAMI NO KU.

RŌEI. Originally a method of reciting Chinese poems. Verses so recited gradually came to be sung to fixed melodies, and grew steadily in number during the 9th, 10th, and 11th centuries. Came to include famous Japanese poems as well as fragments (usually couplets) of Chinese verse. Collections were made by Fujiwara Kintō (966–1041) and Fujiwara Mototoshi (1056–1142). One of the principal means by which a knowledge of selected verses of Po Chü-i and other popular Chinese poets was spread through the Court.

SABI. Loneliness. The tone of lyric melancholy prized by the mid-classical poets Shunzei and Saigyō, and others. Though primarily used to describe the tone or atmosphere of a poem, sabi was also associated with certain kinds of imagery of a withered, monochromatic nature, to which unique qualities of beauty were attributed. The ideal was inherited by the later poets of the renga and haiku, particularly Bashō. See also YŪGEN.

SAIBARA. Horse-readying music. Group of 60 extant primitive folk songs of irregular form and prosody; fitted, during late 8th century and the 9th century, to Court music from China, but considerably older in origin. Name believed derived from Chinese melodies and rhythms originally used for songs sung to send off horses carrying tribute from provinces to capital.

SAKIMORI NO UTA. Poems of the Frontier Guards. Group of TANKA in Vols. XIV and XX of the Man'yōshū ostensibly composed by men of the eastern provinces who went on military duty to the southern island of Kyushu. Those in Vol. XX were probably collected, edited, and arranged by Ōtomo Yakamochi in 755 when he was an official of the Board of War; other scattered examples, including some CHŌKA and some poems by Yakamochi himself, were avowedly fictional, being composed by Court poets in the pose of frontier guards on analogy with a similar and very common Chinese practice. See also AZUMAUTA.

SAMA. Term used by Ki no Tsurayuki in his Preface to the Kokinshū in the sense of "elegant style," i.e., the new subjectivity of the early classical period and the techniques employed to express it. See also I-P'ANG, MIYABI.

SEDŌKA. Head-repeated poem. A poetic form owing its name to its repeated tercet forms in 6 lines of 5, 7, 7, 5, 7, 7 syllables, thus in effect consisting of two KATAUTA; and often used for dialogue. A rare form, and only a few examples of literary interest survive.

SHAKKYŌ. Explaining the Buddhist teachings. Term used of WAKA on Buddhist subjects; first appears as a category in imperial anthologies with the Goshūishū; later became one of the topical categories of the RENGA.

SHIMO NO KU. See under KAMI NO KU.

SHINKU. Closely related verses. TANKA in which the upper verses (KAMI NO KU) and lower verses (shimo no ku) were tightly integrated by common or related imagery, word associations and other rhetorical means, and often also by smooth syntax which made of the poem a single flowing move-ment. Contrasted to *soku,* or distantly related verses, in which the syntactic fragmentation of the poem into upper and lower verses was reinforced by rhetorical means and by the use in the two parts of the poem of categories of imagery whose associations were sometimes so distant as not to be im-mediately apparent. Although both kinds of verses were generally recog-nized to have a distinct value, the conservative poets of the late classical period preferred the shinku, the innovating poets the soku. These differ-ences in critical preference and poetic practice were reflected in the tech-niques of integrating imperial anthologies and were passed on to the poets of the RENGA.

SOKU. See SHINKU.

SUGATA. Total effect, configuration (literally, "form": cf. German, *Gestalt*). The composition of a poem as a single whole made up of various elements, and the effect of the poem as a whole upon the reader or hearer. Some-times used with other critical terms to designate specific tonal effects, such as *sugata yūgen* (usually synonymous with SABI), the tone of loneliness or lyric melancholy. See also YŪGEN.

TAKETAKASHI. Lofty style. Alternative style for formal poetry; increasingly popular from the 11th century on. Considered particularly appropriate for solemn occasions calling for a decorum of the auspicious. Tended to treat large subjects from nature with simple description or direct declaration and often used archaic diction to enhance the effect of noble forthrightness and superiority to mundane concerns. Also called *taketakaki yō, tōjiroshi,* and *kedakaku tōjiroshi.* See also TEI.

TANKA: also UTA, WAKA. Short poem. Poetic form of 31 syllables in 5 lines: 5, 7, 5, 7, 7. Used both as HANKA and as an integral, separate form. The première form of Japanese Court poetry.

TANRENGA. See RENGA.

TEI. Poetic style. Also alternatively *yō* and often pronounced *tai.* A given "style" of poetry as distinguished by Court poets in their poetic treatises and critical pronouncements. The principal difference between one style and another was most often one of tone (thus, the "lofty style," the "style of intense feeling"), but also sometimes primarily one of diction (the "archaic style"), of technique (the "style of describing things as one sees them"), or of a combination of different elements (the "style of mystery and depth"). By analogy with Chinese poetics, the number of styles dis-tinguished in any given critical writing from the *Kakyō Hyōshiki* of 772 on was usually ten, but their names and characteristics varied considerably.

During the classical periods, critical differences arose as to the importance of one or other of the accepted styles in relation to the others, but this was offset by general agreement on the suitability of certain styles for particular occasions and the expectation that an accomplished poet should be able to compose in all styles.

TŌGO: also KOTOBA NO IRIHOGA. Reversed diction. Reversal of the usual word order in noun phrases. For example: *kaze no yūgure* (evening of wind) instead of *yūgure no kaze* (wind of evening), *kumo no yukiki* (coming and going of the clouds) instead of *yukiki no kumo* (clouds of coming and going). Technique used by Fujiwara Teika in some of his best poems and also used for vivid effect by innovating poets of late classical period. Severely criticized in work by Teika's imitators, who employed it as a mere artificial mannerism, and identified by conservative critics with DARU-MAUTA; attacked by conservative Nijō critics of the late classical period in the work of Kyōgoku-Reizei poets.

TSUKURIMONOGATARI. Fictional tales. Stories ranging in length and subject matter from short Chinese-inspired tales of the marvelous to the long, analytical, social novel of which the *Tale of Genji* is the great masterpiece. Although such stories often contained many poems (there are nearly 800 in the *Genji*), the prose narrative was of greater importance. Transparently fictional, in contrast to the UTAMONOGATARI, the diaries (*nikki*), and travel accounts (*kikō*), which purport to be factual accounts.

USHIN: also KOKORO ARI. Intense feeling, conviction of feeling (literally, "possessing *kokoro*"). Used in two important ways: as the name of a poetic style (the "style of intense feeling"); and as a quality deemed essential to all poetry ("conviction of feeling"). The style of intense feeling was one in which the element of passion predominated; as such the style was distinguished by critics of the early classical period, inherited as one of the usual ten styles by later poets and critics, and preferred by Fujiwara Teika in his late period. In the broader sense of the poetic ideal of conviction of feeling, the term was used by mid-classical poets, particularly Shunzei and Teika, for an integrity and conviction of personal lyric response to conventional materials. This latter interpretation of ushin is questioned by many scholars, who hold the term to be synonymous with YŌEN. See also AWARE, HON'I, KOKORO, MUSHIN, TEI.

UTA. See TANKA, for which a synonym. Sometimes used in looser sense of "poem" or "song" (Cf. German, *Lied*).

UTAAWASE. Poetry competition. A matching of poems composed on stated topics (DAI). At first, topics seem not to have been announced in advance, but soon the practice of giving them out was established. Poets were divided into two sides, left and right; the contest consisted of a stated number of rounds (*ban*), in which two poems were read; one or more judges made decisions of win, lose, and draw. Originally a kind of ceremonial game related to other types of ritualized contests such as root-matching (*ne-awase*) and picture competitions (*eawase*), the *utaawase* soon became the principal means by which poets might publicly display their skill, and were carried on in an atmosphere of deadly earnest. The formal nature of the contests demanded a higher decorum and stricter practice than for certain other kinds of composition. Similar competitions were held for poetry in Chinese (*shiawase*), and numerous variations were elaborated, such as competitions between Chinese and Japanese poems (*shiikaawase*) and the personal poetry competitions (JIKAAWASE).

UTAMONOGATARI. Tales of poems. Collections of poems with prose contexts, usually fictionalized, purporting to give the true circumstances of the occasions on which the poems were composed. Developed from the headnotes to poems (KOTOBAGAKI), in the *Man'yōshū* and later collections, the uta-monogatari represent an important stage in the development of the Court novel. The most famous example is the *Ise Monogatari,* a collection of 125 short episodes intended as a kind of chronicle of the life and loves of Ari-wara Narihira (825–80) and traditionally attributed to him.

WAKA. See TANKA, for which a synonym. Also signifies Court poetry in all forms, including CHŌKA, SEDŌKA, and the like, in contrast to popular songs, religious hymns, and such later forms derivative from Court poetry as the RENGA, HAIKAI, and HAIKU. Also used in a general sense for poetry of all kinds in Japanese, as opposed to poetry written by Japanese in Chinese or poetry of other nations.

YŌ. See TEI.

YŌEN. Ethereal charm. The esthetic ideal of a romantic, unworldly beauty, like that of "a heavenly maiden descending to earth on a hazy moonlit night in spring." Advocated by the mid-classical poet Fujiwara Teika during his early manhood. Characterized by complexity of technique and tending to express subtle shades of pathos, the poetry of yōen typically combined elements of more sombre styles with "beautiful" imagery and an ethereal atmosphere. See also SABI, YŪGEN.

YOJŌ. Overtones. The implications or associations evoked by a poem. As used by modern scholars, the term covers a wide range from the very simple "implied meaning" (often called *yoi*) of a message-poem to the rich tonal complexity of the mid-classical poetry of descriptive symbolism. The overtones often depended upon allusion to older poetry or the conventional associations of poetic diction. Sometimes used synonymously with YŪGEN.

YŪGEN. Mystery and depth. The mid-classical ideal of tonal complexity conveyed by the overtones, or YOJŌ, of poems typically in the mode of descriptive symbolism. Associated with the poet-critic Fujiwara Shunzei, the style was made to harmonize with other ideals of the age, particularly SABI and YŌEN, and was normally characterized by sadness, imagery of a veiled, monochromatic nature, and an atmosphere of rich, mysterious beauty. Inherited by renga poets and the Nō dramatists, who tended to apply the term to an ideal of beauty more closely resembling yōen.

ZŌ. Miscellaneous. Rubric under which certain poems (called *zōka, zō no uta,* or *kusagusa no uta*) were grouped in the *Man'yōshū* and the imperial anthologies. In the *Man'yōshū,* the category includes loosely all poems not classified as "love poems" (*sōmon*) or "elegies" (*banka*); in the *Kokinshū* and later imperial anthologies, it normally comprises poems that either are "mixed" as to category (e.g., a poem containing elements of "love" and "spring" but a preponderance of neither), or are on subjects not classifiable among the other headings in these collections (e.g., a poem on the mountain wind, which, in the absence of qualifying imagery or implications, is neutral as to season). The imperial anthologies compiled by the innovating poets of the late classical period show a tendency to classify as "miscellaneous" seasonal poems which are regular as to category but are in modes other than the descriptive. The category was also used in the poetic sequences and was taken over into the RENGA and HAIKU.

Finding List for Japanese Poems Translated in the Text

The poems are arranged according to the sources from which they are taken. The *Man'yoshu* and the imperial anthologies are listed first, in chronological order; the *Kokka Taikan* index numbers are given for poems from these sources, with envoys to chōka numbered separately. Poems from the *Kojiki* and the *Nihongi, Kagura,* and *Azumaasobiuta* are identified by the numbers assigned to them in Tsuchihashi and Konishi, *Kodai Kayōshū.* Page references to *Kokka Taikei* or other standard editions are given for the poems taken from private collections and records of *utaawase,* which are listed alphabetically by title within their respective groups. In each entry, the first line of the poem is given (although in some instances only a part of the poem is translated), followed by the page or pages on which it appears. For further discussion of the sources, see p. 5n, the Appendix (pp. 481–87), and the Index.

MYS

I. 1. Ko mo yo, 48–49
   15. Watatsumi no, 85
   16. Fuyugomori, 85
   30. Sasanami no, 101
II. 135. Tsuno sahau, 115–17
   136. Aogoma no, 116
   137. Akiyama ni, 117
   148. Aohata no, 27
   152. Yasumishishi, 101
   169. Akane sasu, 132
   201. Haniyasu no, 138, 207
   219. Sora kazou, 150
   220. Tamamo yoshi, 28, 97–98
   221. Tsuma mo araba, 98
   222. Oki tsu nami, 98
III. 250. Tamamo karu, 136–37
   318. Tago no ura yu, 150, 273
   379. Hisakata no, 102
V. 800. Chichi haha o, 111
   804. Yo no naka no, 133–35
   805. Tokiwa nasu, 28, 135, 151, 476
   892. Kaze majiri, 111, 121–23
   893. Yo no naka o, 123

905. Wakakereba, 151
VI. 923. Yasumishishi, 126–27
   924. Mi-Yoshino no, 127
   925. Nubatama no, 127
   1001. Masurao wa, 112
VII. 1068. Ame no umi ni, 88, 440
   1294. Asazukuhi, 5
VIII. 1463. Wagimoko ga, 132
IX. 1800. Okakitsu no, 124–25
X. 2033. Ama no gawa, 89
XI. 2440. Ōmi no umi, 14
   2643. Tamahoko no, 138
XII. 3182. Shirotae no, 317
XIV. 3373. Tamagawa ni, 106
   3570. Ashi no ha ni, 150
XVI. 3824. Sashinabe ni, 111–12
XIX. 4139. Haru no sono, 103
   4140. Wa ga sono no, 113
   4214. Ame tsuchi no, 129–31
   4215. Tōto ni mo, 130–31
   4216. Yo no naka no, 131
   4290. Haru no no ni, 103
   4291. Wa ga yado no, 103
   4292. Uraura ni, 103
XX. 4360. Ōkimi no, 113

CHRONICLES, AZUMAASOBI, AND KAGURA

RECORDS OF UTAAWASE

PRIVATE COLLECTIONS AND POETIC DOCUMENTS

Index

Page numbers in parentheses indicate repetitions of poems.

Abutsu, nun (d. ca. 1283), 344–45
Adjectives. *See* Language
Akahito (d. ?736), 126–28, 140, 146–47, 154–55; poems, 112–13, 126–27, 150 (273–74)
Akashi Bay, dawn at, 202 (214, 316, 460)
Akisuke (1090–1155), 237, 483
Allegory, 16–17, 433, 462–63; in prim. song, 71–72; in early lit. pd., 132–37; in early c. pd., 207, 211–12, 218; in mid-c. pd., 293–95; in late c. pd., 364–65, 368, 387–89
—: POEMS AND SONGS, 45 (46), 65 (71), 191; Buddhist, 31 (276), 218, 293f, 307, 314, 367, 388; formal, 132, 212, 264; informal, 172, 196f, 212, 388; love, 132, 387f
Allusive variation. *See* Honkadori
Ariie (1155–1216), 303, 484; drawing of, 328; poems, 278–82, 295–96, 314; "Bamboos of Fushimi," 309–10, 325–28 *passim*
Ariwara Motokata (883–953), poem by, 202
Ariwara Narihira. *See* Narihira
Ariwara Yukihira. *See* Yukihira
Arnold, Matthew, 467, 477
Ashikaga shoguns, and Imperial Anthologies, 486
Association, principle of: in sequences, 319–29, 403–13; in hundred-poem sequence, 322, 506; editorial allusion, 407–9; editorial rhetoric, 411; in renga, 418–19. *See also* Sequences
Asukai Masatsune (1170–1221), 484
Autumn, poems on. *See under* Nature
Aware (sensibility), 187, 255, 261, 503
Azumaasobiuta (Songs for the Eastern Dances), 44, 56, 503
Azumauta (Poems of the East), 95, 105–6, 173–74, 503

Bashō (1644–94), 34, 261–62, 505, 510; quoted, 11
Berenson, Bernard, quoted, 39
Blake, William, quoted, 391
Blossoms, poems on. *See under* Nature
Buddha, Way of the, 91, 93, 148
Buddhism: symbolic natural scene, 30, 307–8, 314, 472; concept of impermanence, 148, 160, 430, 432; *shikan*, 257; Zen, 261–62, 360–61, 363–64, 399–400, 504; allegories, 31 (276), 218, 293–95, 307, 314; importance

of, in Japanese poetry, 445–46, 510; mentioned, 428, 474
Bunya Yasuhide (fl. ca. 870), 163, 222; poem, 191. *See also* Rokkasen
Burns, Robert, quoted, 461
Bussokusekika (Buddha's foot-stone poems), 47, 503

Chamberlain, Basil Hall, 44
Chesterfield, Lord, 446
Chien Wen, Emperor (502–57), 174
China and Chinese poetry: example of, in prim. songs, 55f, 58; example of, in early lit. pd., 79, 85–95; example of, in early c. pd., 29; example of, in mid-c. pd., 240–41, 272; example of, in late c. pd. (Kyōgoku-Reizei poets), 346, 356–65; language, 6, 15, 469; borrowing of themes from, 23–26, 166; Six Dynasties, 23, 83; Six Dynasties, late, 24–25, 163, 169–70, 171, 174, 178, 180f, 191–92, 220; example of, in Japanese chronicles, 81, 83–84; and *Tanabata*, 89, 107, 440; Po Chü-i, 156, 180–81, 182f, 198, 232; and *hon'i*, 253; and sabi, 260; and *yōen*, 262; as Japan's classical past, 99, 427–28; *rōei*, 509–10
Chōka (long poem), 11, 49, 85–87, 115–21; defined, 4, 503–4; hanka of, 85, 505; Hitomaro's, 97–98, 115–17; Okura's, 121–24, 133–35; decline of, 153–56
Chokusenshū (The Imperial Anthologies), 471–72, 481–86. *See also by name*
Chōmei (d. 1216), 268, 353; quoted, 269f
Congratulation, poems of. *See under* Human affairs
Consort of the Emperor Tenchi (626–71), poem by, 27
Court, the, 413–14, 419f, 425–27; in early lit. pd., 87ff; in early c. pd., 158, 166–67; in mid-c. pd., 233–34; in late c. pd., 34, 341–42. *See also* Love, Japanese courtly

Dai (topic of a poem), 504, 506; in early lit. pd., 96, 104; in early c. pd., 194–95; in mid-c. pd., 237, 275, 291–93; correct handling of, (*hon'i*), 253–54, 263; and esthetic distance, 302–3; and Shunzei, 339; and Teika, 263–65
Daiei (composing on a topic), 504